249

THE PSYCHOLOGY OF LEARNING AND INSTRUCTION: EDUCATIONAL PSYCHOLOGY

THE PSYCHOLOGY OF LEARNING AND INSTRUCTION:

EDUCATIONAL PSYCHOLOGY

JOHN P. De CECCO SAN FRANCISCO STATE COLLEGE

PRENTICE-HALL, INC. Englewood Cliffs, New Jersey

THE PSYCHOLOGY OF LEARNING AND INSTRUCTION:
EDUCATIONAL PSYCHOLOGY

John P. De Cecco

Library of Congress Catalog Card No.: 68-13127

Current printing (last digit):
10 9 8 7 6 5 4 3 2 1

Printed in the United States of America

PRENTICE-HALL INTERNATIONAL, INC. *London*
PRENTICE-HALL OF AUSTRALIA, PTY. LTD. *Sydney*
PRENTICE-HALL OF CANADA, LTD. *Toronto*
PRENTICE-HALL OF INDIA PRIVATE LTD. *New Delhi*
PRENTICE-HALL OF JAPAN, INC. *Tokyo*

A Special Note to the Student

ON BECOMING A VERY GOOD TEACHER

There is a time for speculation and a time for teaching, but equally important for you as a prospective teacher there must be a time for acquiring basic knowledge about the conditions of learning which your teaching must always provide. The purpose of this book is to introduce you to our present knowledge about learning and teaching. If the book fulfills this purpose you should be a better teacher after you read it than you were before.

This general purpose suggests four ways in which this book can be useful to you. (1) It provides you with a general conception, or model, of teaching which is useful in describing and analyzing the instruction you read about and observe and in organizing and executing your own teaching. (2) It provides you with a body of knowledge which is useful to you throughout your teaching career as you engage in the description of instructional objectives, in the accommodation of the entering behavior of individual students, in the selection of instructional materials and procedures, and in the assessment of the performances of your students. (3) It provides you with a theoretical and factual basis for making teaching decisions which are apart from but not necessarily inconsistent with or opposed to your own preferences, intuitions, and impressions about teaching. (4) It provides you with some fairly specific guidelines for important teaching functions, such as stating your objectives, analyzing student entering behavior, providing the necessary conditions for various types of learning, programing instructional materials, constructing tests and interpreting test scores, and evaluating research reports. If you learn or only begin to learn to perform the teaching functions described in this book, you may indeed become a very good teacher.

There are three ways in which this book is *not* useful. First, you will find that it does not always concur with many of your present opinions about teaching. Instead it gives you knowledge you do not have and, in this way, changes and develops your behavior. When you argue with the book, which at times will seem almost unavoidable, you should observe one rule. In settling debates on the best procedures for teaching we must make the final appeal to the evidence we gather in our research and classrooms and to the theories which organize this evidence into general teaching procedures. The final arbiter, that is, must be what actually works in the classroom. To engage in debates which ignore the concrete evidence of student success and failure is a training activity of dubious merit.

Second, you will find that the book is *not* a list of do's and don't's. Although suggestions for performing some teaching functions (e.g., programing and constructing tests) are more specific than are those for other teaching functions (e.g., teaching concepts and problem solving), the level of discourse is somewhat more general than you may expect. The book teaches a basic core of knowledge which has general applicability throughout your teaching career. Lists of do's and don't's are usually very specific and pertain to particular instructional objectives, students, procedures, and tests. You should acquire most of this specific knowledge in other professional courses and in your teaching experience in the classroom.

Third, you will find that the book is *not* based on a conception of teaching which places the personalities of the teacher and of the student at the center of the stage. In a refrain I hope you do not find tedious, I reiterate that the important focus of all classroom effort, the teacher's and the student's, is the student's achievement of the instructional objectives. The teacher should subordinate his personality to a professional role that requires him to provide those conditions of learning which guarantee the student's full achievement of the instructional objectives. The student should subordinate his personality to an educational role that requires responses which lead to the full achievement of these objectives. Subordination should not imply obliteration. In a lengthy chapter on motivation you will see how personality factors can facilitate as well as impede the achievement of instructional objectives.

ON GETTING THE MOST FROM THIS BOOK

We have designed both the textbook and the *Student Guide* to help you learn and remember as much as you can. Consider the textbook first. A perusal of the Contents (which you can do after reading this paragraph) shows that the book has five parts. Later you will see that each part has an introduction, which describes its general purposes and the contents of its chapters. The Contents also lists the major headings in each chapter.

The following suggestions should be helpful to you in achieving the instructional objectives of each chapter:

1. Read the introduction to the chapter. It briefly describes the general purpose and the contents of the three or four sections of the chapter.
2. Read the list of instructional objectives which follows the chapter introduction. These statements tell you in advance what you should be able to do upon completing the chapter. At the conclusion of each chapter section you are asked to return to the list of objectives for that section. By checking your own performances you can determine what you have learned well and what requires further study. You should make generous use of these lists.
3. Read the headings within the chapter. There are three types of headings, distinguished by type size and location on the page. The section headings (in green) are the largest and begin in the margin of the page. The subsection headings (also in green) are somewhat smaller and also begin in the margin. The smaller headings, in black capital letters, are paragraph indentations. Some students find it useful to turn headings into questions and to return to the questions upon completing the material to which the headings refer.
4. Read the contents of the chapter, which I present in an expository style. Very often the definition of a technical term occurs at the beginning of the paragraph. The Index will tell you where to find an explanation of each technical term. Make full use of the tables, charts, and figures. They have been chosen carefully and will significantly increase your understanding of the text.
5. Read the summaries which follow each chapter section. Written in paragraph form, they list the major points of each section.
6. Read and answer the embedded questions. At the conclusion of each chapter section, a question, usually in multiple-choice form, assesses your achievement of the major objectives of that section.

In selecting your answer, explain to yourself the basis for your choice and for your rejection of the alternatives. *After* this self-explanation, turn to the answer section at the back of the book and read the correct answer and its defense. If you miss a question, return to the pertinent portion of the chapter and review it.

7. Read the summary which concludes the chapter. It draws together the major points and enables you to review important conceptual relationships.
8. Use the two sources of suggested readings. First, the annotated list of suggested readings following the chapter summary usually contains references to both elementary and advanced treatments of the chapter topics. Second, the Cross-Reference Chart (in the *Instructor's Manual*) correlates readings in various books of readings with each of the chapters in this textbook.

The *Student Guide* has been designed to help you achieve the instructional objectives of the textbook. It has a corresponding chapter for each chapter of the textbook. Each chapter of the *Guide* contains (1) a detailed outline of each textbook chapter, (2) a list of readings to improve your entering behavior, (3) multiple-choice questions which serve as a self-test, (4) discussion questions, and (5) descriptions of projects. You may find the following suggestions helpful in using the *Student Guide:*

1. Read the detailed outline of each textbook chapter *before* you begin the chapter so that you have an overview of the chapter contents; read it again *after* you finish the chapter for a review of the major topics and their relationships.
2. Choose an appropriate selection from the list of suggested readings if you lack the prerequisite knowledge for the chapter.
3. Answer the self-test questions after you have completed the chapter. For those questions you miss, refer to the pertinent section in the text and review it.
4. Answer the discussion questions as a means of exploring the broader implications of the chapter contents and relate new concepts you learn to concepts you have previously acquired.
5. Carry out one or both projects described in the *Guide*. Some projects are broader than others and can be used as quarter or semester projects. The projects provide some of the best evidence of your achievement of the instructional objectives.

The Bibliography at the end of the book fully describes all the references mentioned in the text. It is an excellent source for suggested readings, especially for research articles in educational psychology.

A Note to the Instructor

This textbook is the major part of an instructional package which also includes the *Instructor's Manual* and the *Student Guide*. This package provides the student with the essential materials for independent study and the instructor with the materials for periodically assessing what the student has learned. The careful organization of the textbook, with its systematic interrelationship of topics, lists of instructional objectives for each chapter, and embedded questions with accompanying answers and explanations, makes this book a maximally effective teaching instrument in its own right. Although you will find ample opportunity to amplify, omit, and add topics of your own choice, the careful presentation of material here relieves you of much of the burden of explaining the text as well.

The book allows considerable flexibility in the assignment of material because each chapter divides clearly into three or four sections and thus it is possible to assign particular sections only. The Contents indicates these section divisions and facilitates your choice of assignments.

The following chapters, although of considerable concern and relevance on the contemporary educational scene, are perhaps less basic than those that remain: Chapter 6—The Education of the Disadvantaged Child; Chapter 12—Programed Instruction and Educational Technology; Chapter 13—The New Science and Mathematics; Chapter 15—How to Use Standardized Test Scores; Chapter 16—How to Evaluate Research in Educational Psychology. If you want to include part or all of this material, you can assign one or more chapters to individuals and groups of students, particularly in connection with term projects and reports. In a full semester course you may be able to assign all the chapters.

The textbook and the *Student Guide* provide several sources of supplementary reading. The list of suggested readings at the end of each chapter contains references which treat the related subject matter at different levels of complexity and allow the student to pursue a topic in a way consonant with his objectives, interests, and abilities. The extensive Bibliography at the end of the book lists innumerable research reports. The Cross-Reference Chart in the *Instructor's Manual* correlates textbook chapters with articles in current books of readings in educational psychology. Lists of readings in the *Student Guide* provide background material for students who lack the entering behavior necessary for achieving chapter objectives.

The instructional package suggests several classroom uses, some of which are listed here:

1. For any given class session the instructor may select particular instructional objectives from the list for each chapter and require the student to demonstrate his achievement of that objective. The instructor, of course, must provide the student with the necessary conditions and materials for performance.
2. The instructor may select discussion questions from the *Student Guide* and direct discussion in a way which elucidates concepts and principles the student has learned in reading the text and which enables the student to achieve the chapter objectives.
3. The instructor may use one or both of the projects described for each chapter in the *Student Guide*. Some projects can be completed within one classroom period, while others require more extended periods of time.
4. The instructor may review the keyed answers to the questions in the self-tests in the *Student Guide* and clarify any inconsistencies which the student finds between the text and the keyed responses.
5. The instructor may require the student to teach a concept or principle explained in the text and to demonstrate in his teaching the knowledge he has gained in reading the text. The student may also administer a test to determine the effectiveness of his teaching.
6. The instructor may ask the student to make reports on those chapters which are not required reading for all the class and to apply these materials to teaching situations with which he is familiar.
7. The instructor may administer quizzes based on questions in the

Instructor's Manual and use the scoring of the tests as a basis of classroom discussion.

8. The instructor may assign particular projects for which the text offers considerable guidance. Among these are the following: (a) the explicit description of instructional objectives; (b) the analysis of student entering behavior; (c) the arrangement of teaching conditions for a particular type of learning; (d) the programing of instructional materials; (e) the construction of a classroom test; (f) the administration of a standardized test and the interpretation of the test scores using particular statistical concepts; and (g) the evaluation of research reports.

Many other classroom and term projects are possible.

Acknowledgments

It is impossible to name all the individuals who have contributed to the writing of this book and whose help I deeply appreciate. Among the educational psychologists whose research and articles I have found exceedingly fruitful are the following: Professor Robert M. Gagné of the University of California, Berkeley, whose *Conditions of Learning* provided a firm bridge between experimental learning psychology and the psychology of school learning; Professor Robert Glaser of the University of Pittsburgh, whose teaching model enabled me to organize and present the vast amount of information this book contains; and Professor Arthur R. Jensen of the University of California, Berkeley, whose studies of individual differences and verbal learning have opened research vistas we have only begun to explore.

For reviews and critiques of the manuscript at various times in its development I express my deep appreciation to Professor Donald Ross Green of the California Test Bureau, to Professor John R. Feldhusen of Purdue University, and to Professor Ronald W. Mayer of San Francisco State College.

I also want to thank my many colleagues in the faculties of education and psychology at Michigan State University and San Francisco State College for their initial and continued help and encouragement. I especially thank Professor Bernard R. Corman of the University of Alberta, Professors Richard Fresco and Alfred C. Jensen of San Francisco State College, and Professor John D. Krumboltz of Stanford University. For their help with the chapter on educational technology I wish especially to thank Professors A. Daniel Peck and Francis X. Moakley of San Francisco State College.

For their invaluable help in shepherding the manuscript through its various stages I wish to express my deep appreciation to Professor Ann Paterson of San Francisco State College, especially for her reading of the page proofs, and to Miss Patricia Quance, whose typing competence and saintly forbearance are unmatched.

Table of Contents

To my father
and the memory of my mother

PART ONE

INSTRUCTIONAL MODELS AND OBJECTIVES

The first of the two chapters in Part 1 of this book describes a basic teaching model. This model, you will see, consists of four components, each of which corresponds to a major part of the book. The model, therefore, provides a general conception of teaching and a means for organizing the subject matter introduced here. The second chapter describes the first component of the basic teaching model by explaining how you can state and analyze your instructional objectives in ways which are practical for your teaching.

Part 1 has two general purposes. First, by describing several psychological and historical conceptions of teaching, it should help you develop a general conception of teaching which raises these questions: what is taught, who is taught, how is it taught, and with what degree of success. Although varying in the degree of priority and consideration it gives these questions, each conception of teaching raises each question. Second, by describing a basic teaching model and methods for making explicit statements of instructional objectives, Part 1 provides a conception of teaching and learning which is objective in character and useful for the actual practice of teaching.

A list of instructional objectives at the beginning of each chapter tells you before you read the chapter what you should be able to do after you have read it. At various points in the chapter you are asked to return to the list to determine whether you have achieved particular objectives. The lists of instructional objectives will be useful to you in several ways: (1) they help you determine how much you are learning and have learned as you study the book; (2) they focus your attention on the major points in each chapter; (3) they help you summarize and rehearse what you have learned when you have completed each chapter; and (4) to the extent that they are the bases for constructing examination questions, they help you review for course examinations. In studying this book you should make generous use of the lists of instructional objectives.

A Basic Teaching Model

1

This chapter has three major sections. The first explains what a theory of teaching is and points out how theories of teaching relate to theories of learning and philosophies of education. The second and third sections describe the basic teaching model and three psychological and three historical teaching models.

The chapter has three general purposes: to help you understand what a theory of teaching must comprise; to provide a model of teaching general enough to cover a wide range of instructional behavior, concrete enough to have practical utility, and simple enough for you to retain and use throughout this book; and to describe the psychological and historical teaching models so that you may understand the general applicability and limitations of the basic teaching model.

Upon reading the first section of this chapter (on a theory of teaching), you should be able to meet these objectives:

1. Indicate the three questions about teaching behavior which a theory of teaching answers and provide an illustration of a theory of teaching which raises and answers these questions.

2. Point out characteristics (in terms of questions raised and answered) which distinguish a theory of teaching from a theory of learning; describe the relationship between a theory of teaching and a theory of

learning; and provide illustrations of a theory of teaching and of a theory of learning which indicate these distinctions and relationships.

3. Point out characteristics (in terms of questions raised and answered) which distinguish a theory of teaching from a philosophy of education; illustrate these distinctions by comparing a teaching theory and a philosophy of education.

Upon reading the second and third sections of this chapter (on models of teaching), you should be able to meet these objectives:

4. List the four components of the basic teaching model and illustrate how a feedback loop from performance assessment (the fourth component) results in adjustments in the three remaining components.

5. Describe the psychological teaching models of (a) Stolurow, (b) Carroll, and (c) Flanders in terms of the components of the basic teaching model.

6. Describe the historical teaching models of (a) Socrates, (b) the Jesuits, and (c) Combs and Snygg in terms of the components of the basic teaching model.

A THEORY OF TEACHING

Although we are all students for many years, we develop no systematic conception of teaching because we are inclined to believe that teaching is something one does, not something one studies. Yet we need a general conception of teaching for organizing our present knowledge about teaching, proposing research which will advance our knowledge, and guiding our teaching practice. In asserting the need for a theory of teaching, however, we should sound two precautionary notes. First, with proper veneration of the past, we should remind ourselves that teaching has been with us a long time, and that, to the extent that human beings (and teachers) learn from experience, teaching has not been carried on in total ignorance of its conditions and effects. Thus, experience and tradition have been sources of knowledge. Second, we should appreciate that there is no single conception of teaching. Perhaps every teacher has at least a primitive notion of teaching which may very well fail to stand the test of research and time. At this early point in the development of our knowledge about teaching you should be willing to consider alternative conceptions of teaching for whatever light they may shed on its nature and practice. The time is hardly ripe for doctrine and dogma.

What Is a Theory of Teaching?

A theory of teaching should answer three questions (Gage, 1963, p. 133): how teachers behave, why they behave as they do, and with what effects. It should be a general concept which applies to all teachers, to all students, to all subject matter, and to all situations, both in and out of school, in which teaching may occur. It should consider the behavior of teachers, the cause and the learning of students, the effect (Gage, 1964, p. 272). And, it should explain, predict, and control the ways in which the behavior of the teacher affects the learning of the students. You must remember that we do not presently have theories of teaching which embody these characteristics. We can indicate which questions theories of teaching must answer—that is, we can describe the form or shape theories must take—but we cannot describe the theories themselves. The fact that our knowledge is in such a primitive state may increase your skepticism about educational psychology and teacher training and confirm your fears that they are rather prosaic rituals and incantations based more on myth than on fact. If you will bear with me, however, you will discover that, even though we have no well-developed theories of teaching, we do have a firm base of knowledge upon which to build them.

Professor I. Noall has a theory of teaching. He states that students learn more in noisy than in quiet surroundings. To put his theory into practice, he has developed a noise machine with "thermostatic" noise control; when the noise level of the classroom falls below a level conducive to efficient learning, the machine emits a cacophony which would put the worst high school band to shame. So that the students do not become bored with hearing the same noises, Professor Noall has displayed inventive genius in developing new noisemakers, which he blows, squeezes, and beats in the interest of increased academic achievement. In a recent article, "Schools of Tomorrow," Professor Noall states that increased noise reduces the amount of static electricity in the air and thereby speeds vital brain processes. In a hypothetical situation, if the teacher did not want the students to learn anything, he would raise the amounts of static electricity to intolerable limits by keeping a soundproof room very quiet. In such a situation, Professor Noall has observed certain eyelid-drooping and head-nodding responses which he believes are the result of the assault of silence on the brain cells. Although he concludes that he is not sure what practical implications his theory has for a large neighborhood school with a hundred or more noisy classrooms, his theory does answer all the questions posed by a theory of teaching. How should the teacher behave? He should provide more or at least always enough noise. With what effect? Sufficient noise increases student learning (as indicated by test scores). Why? Noise reduces the amount of static electricity, and this reduction stimulates brain-cell activity.

We will probably never have a single theory of teaching. Nathan Gage (1964, p. 274) points out that teaching embraces "far too many kinds of process, of behavior, of activity, to be the proper subject of a single theory. We must not be misled by one word, 'teaching', into searching for one theory to explain it." Gage uses the analogy of getting rich. We can get rich by inheriting, gambling, stealing, making profits, or earning wages—no single theory covers all the possible ways.

Theories of Learning

Theories of learning describe and explain the conditions under which learning does and does not occur. A theory of learning is a general concept which applies to all organisms, to all learning tasks, and to all situations, both in and out of school, in which learning may occur. It considers the conditions which give rise to learning the cause and the learning itself the effect. And, it explains, predicts, and controls the way in which environmental conditions affect the learning of the organism. For example, Edward Thorndike (1913) developed a theory of learning to explain how animals and humans learn to make particular responses to particular stimuli in their environments. According to this theory, two conditions provide for the gradual "stamping in" of stimulus-response connections: The stimulus and the response must occur together, and the response must be followed by a satisfier, or reward. In a typical experiment, Thorndike placed a hungry cat in a cage and an irresistible piece of fish outside. To obtain the fish, the cat had to learn to pull a string which opened the cage door. Through trial and error, the cat gradually learned to pull the string, escape from the cage, and devour the fish. In this simple experiment, the key stimulus was the string which opened the cage, the key response was pulling the string, and the satisfier was the fish. An annoyer (punishment) could substitute for the satisfier. For example, a mild electric shock given to the cat each time it pulled the string would prevent it from learning a particular mode of escape. Thorndike's theory (described more fully in Chapter 7) fulfills the requirements of our original definition of a theory of learning: It describes and explains the conditions under which learning does and does not occur.

This brief explanation and illustration of learning theory show that a theory of learning is much broader and more basic than a theory of teaching. In fact, theories of teaching must be based on theories of learning. You will recall that a theory of teaching considers the behavior of teachers the cause and the learning of students the effect. But, the behavior of teachers is only one special category of environmental conditions under which learning occurs. Similarly, the learning of students is only one special category of effects produced by these conditions.

For example, learning occurs in animal as well as in human organisms. It also occurs without teachers. Children learn before they enter school, and adults who do not entirely surrender their intellectual prerogatives upon graduation, continue to learn all their lives. Learning then is a more ubiquitous experience than teaching.

Theories of learning are much more highly developed than theories of teaching. Yet learning theory is itself a young and growing field in much need of further development (Hill, 1963). We have no single theory of learning, and the prospects for one are dim. Considerable controversy takes place even over the form learning theory should take. Winfred Hill (1963, p. 204) distinguishes between narrow theories, which are developed in the laboratory and are more precise than the broad ones, and the broad theories, which deal with everyday situations and are less precise than the narrow ones. The narrow theories have the greater rigor, the broad theories the greater relevance. Hill uses this illustration:

> For a person who deals with a great variety of people in different situations, it may be both useful and more satisfying to have such a broad generalization as, "Learning is most effective when the learner is 'motivated' but not 'threatened.' " As a scientific law, this generalization is not very meaningful since it leaves unspecified what we mean by "motivated" and by "threatened." It does, however, have a valuable use in telling us what to look for in a learning situation. Another person, dealing with one particular learning situation, might find it both more useful and more satisfying to know that "Infantrymen learn to use this weapon most effectively if they are trained three hours after breakfast, given knowledge of results after every shot, and told their scores will go on their service record." This generalization permits more precise predictions than the previous one and hence can be more easily and accurately used, but its range of application is too narrow to give it any general significance. Ideally we would like to be able to combine the precision of the second generalization with the breadth of the first. This goal keeps many theorists working.

In the further development of learning theory we need not eschew either rigor or relevance. In fact, evidence increasingly shows that basic research on teaching and training may contribute to as well as borrow from theories of learning (Gagné, 1962).

Philosophies of Education

We should also distinguish theories of teaching from philosophies of education. Philosophies of education deal with the goals and values educational systems embrace and propagate. They include not only Western philosophy and political theory from that of Socrates to the latest brand of existentialism but also the ideas of those schools of psychology like psychoanalysis and phenomenology which are broad value orientations to modern life. Their primary concern is with ends rather than with means, and their importance lies in keeping us aware of the alternative goals of all our educational efforts. When educators caution parents and teachers about the tender psyches of children and the need to foster Athenian democracy in the classroom, their primary attention is not on teaching or on educational method but on the ultimate welfare of the child and the survival of the community. In a democratic society the electorate determines the values of the schools and the goals toward which they work.

Philosophies of education influence theories of teaching. Philosophers of science have made scientists aware of how subjectivity enters their work. And even though the psychologists may cherish the belief that theories of learning and teaching can develop in a climate of philosophical and ethical neutrality, we know now that such absolute neutrality is not possible, especially since we have the dual and overlapping roles of educators and citizens. As teachers we can aspire only to relative neutrality. Our teaching expertise must consist of knowledge of means—of how we should behave to produce effective learning in our students. There may be considerable folly in professional educators' fiercely pursuing goals and values which are seriously at odds with those of the lay public, which provides both the children and the money we need to run the schools.

You should now return to objectives 1–3 (pp. 5–6) and determine how well you have achieved them.

QUESTION 1-1

> The speaker raised his arms, fixed his eyes, and, with deep conviction, uttered these words: "What we need are teaching methods which free the mind of the child. Teachers who make all the classroom decisions, materials which are remote from the child's interests, and procedures which make the child an automaton reduce the child to slavery and increase his feelings of frustration and guilt."
>
> Is the above quotation chiefly (a) a theory of teaching, (b) a theory of learning, or (c) a philosophy of education?
>
> After you have selected your answer, list the characteristics the quotation lacks which justify your rejection of the remaining two choices.

PSYCHOLOGICAL TEACHING MODELS

The best substitute for a theory of teaching is a model of teaching. Teaching models merely suggest how various teaching and learning conditions are interrelated. In many fields, models are prototypes of theories because they make possible our early conceptualization and study of phenomena. Unlike theories, in their early state of development models lack factual support. Eventually useful models give way to empirically supported theories. In this section of the chapter we shall examine and relate several models of teaching.

A Basic Teaching Model

Robert Glaser (1962) has developed a stripped-down teaching model which, with modifications, is the basic teaching model of this book. The basic teaching model divides the teaching process into four components or parts. You will find it useful in several ways. It provides an uncomplicated, yet fairly adequate, conceptualization of the teaching process. It helps you organize the great body of facts, concepts, and principles which makes up the field of educational psychology. And it helps you understand other, more complicated, teaching models. In this book, we use the basic teaching model for all three purposes.

Figure 1-1 is a diagram of the basic teaching model. The four parts of the model correspond to the basic divisions of this book. Box A, instructional objectives, includes the material in Part 1 (Chapter 2). Box B, entering behavior, includes the material in Part 2 (Chapters 3–6). Box C, instructional procedures, makes up the material in Part 3 on the teaching of skills, language, concepts, principles, and problem solving and the material in Part 4 dealing with educational innovations. Finally, box D, performance assessment, covers the material in Part 5 on the construction and use of tests. A final chapter, Chapter 16, on research in educational psychology, applies to the four components of the basic teaching model. Figure 1-1, with its connecting arrows, shows only the major sequence of events in the instructional process; you could add many more connecting lines. Lines which connect components later in

Fig. 1-1. *A Basic Teaching Model (after Glaser, 1962, p. 6).*

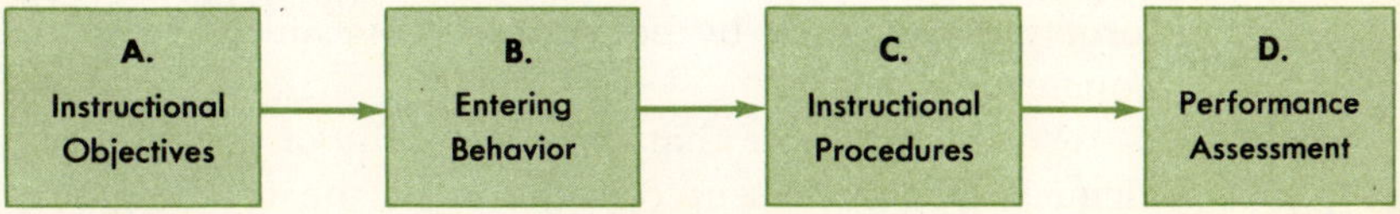

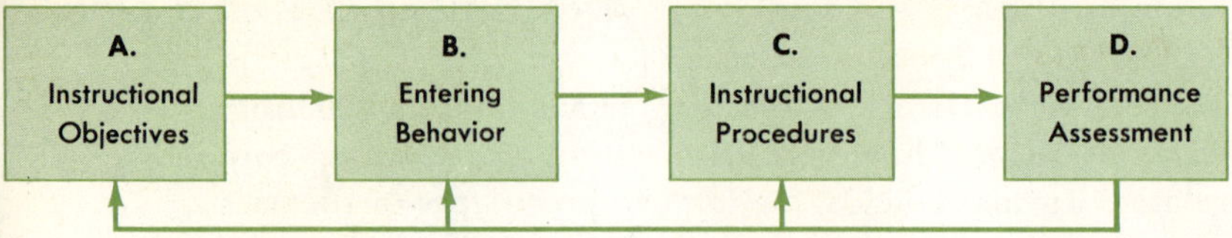

Fig. 1-2. *Feedback loops for performance assessments.*

the sequence with earlier ones are called *feedback loops.* The three feedback loops in Fig. 1-2, for example, connect performance assessment with each of the earlier components of the model. In ensuing chapters, discussions of the model components will refer to several feedback loops.

I will briefly define here the components of the basic teaching model. Later chapters will give detailed consideration to each component. *Instructional objectives* (box A) are those the student should attain upon completion of a segment of instruction. In theory, objectives can vary in scope and character from the mastery of a spelling list to the acquisition of Greek virtue. Chapter 2 tells you how to make useful statements of your instructional objectives. *Entering behavior* (box B) describes the student's level before instruction begins. It refers to what he has previously learned, his intellectual ability and development, his motivational state, and certain social and cultural determinants of his learning ability. Entering behavior is a more precise term than its usual alternatives—human ability, individual differences, and readiness. Although the model gives priority to the selection of instructional objectives over the assessment of entering behavior, in practice these two components must interact. *Instructional procedures* (box C) describe the teaching process; most decisions a teacher makes are on these procedures. Proper management of this component results in those changes in student behavior which we call learning or achievement. Procedures must vary with the instructional objectives. Later chapters describe procedures for teaching skills, language, concepts, principles, and problem solving. Finally, *performance assessment* (box D) consists of the tests and observations used to determine how well the student has achieved the instructional objectives. If performance assessment indicates that the student has fallen short of mastery or some lesser standard of achievement, one or all of the preceding components of the basic teaching model may require adjustment. The feedback loops in Fig. 1-2 show how the information provided by performance assessment feeds back to each component.

You should note that the personality of the teacher is not the central element in the present conception of the teaching process. The model indicates that teaching includes a broad range of decision and practice—

much of which requires little or no personal contact between teacher and student. The widespread use of technological devices, team teaching, and nongraded instruction (see Chapter 12) will undoubtedly modify the traditional nature of the personal contact between teacher and student. Depending on the requirements of the instructional situation, particularly on the entering behavior of the student, the classroom of the future will provide for more or less personal contact than the conventional classroom does now. Accordingly, the model implies a greater emphasis on teacher competence than on personal charisma without, of course, objecting to a useful combination of the two.

To illustrate the possible interrelationships among the four components of the basic teaching model and the varying emphasis we can give each component, I will describe three additional psychological models of teaching. These models are more complex than the basic teaching model, but they include each of its components.

A Computer-Based Teaching Model

By far the most complex teaching model you will study is one developed by Lawrence Stolurow and Daniel Davis (1965). In this model the computer replaces the teacher in making decisions and providing the actual instruction. Stolurow and Davis divide the teaching process into two phases. The *pretutorial phase* has a single purpose: to select for a particular student a teaching program that will achieve particular instructional objectives. The *tutorial phase* has two purposes: to put the program which has been selected into use, and to monitor the student's performance to discover whether a new program may be more suitable than the original one.

Figure 1-3 diagrams the pretutorial phase; it indicates the decisions the computer must make before instruction actually begins. This phase includes decisions on instructional objectives and entering behavior (see boxes under Input in Fig. 1-3). For instructional objectives, three factors must be considered: (1) the final level of performance P_f (2) to be achieved in a given topic or subject matter T (3) within a given time t. For entering behavior, the decisions are somewhat more difficult. Figure 1-3 shows the two aspects considered: the student's achievement level P_e, or what he has already learned that is relevant to the instructional objectives and his aptitude level Ap, or set of skills, which is not necessarily tied to a particular subject.

Given particular instructional objectives and entering behavior, the computer must now search for a suitable program of instruction. This search can have one of three results: More than one program may be located; only one program may be located; or no program may be located. When more than one program is available, economic factors select

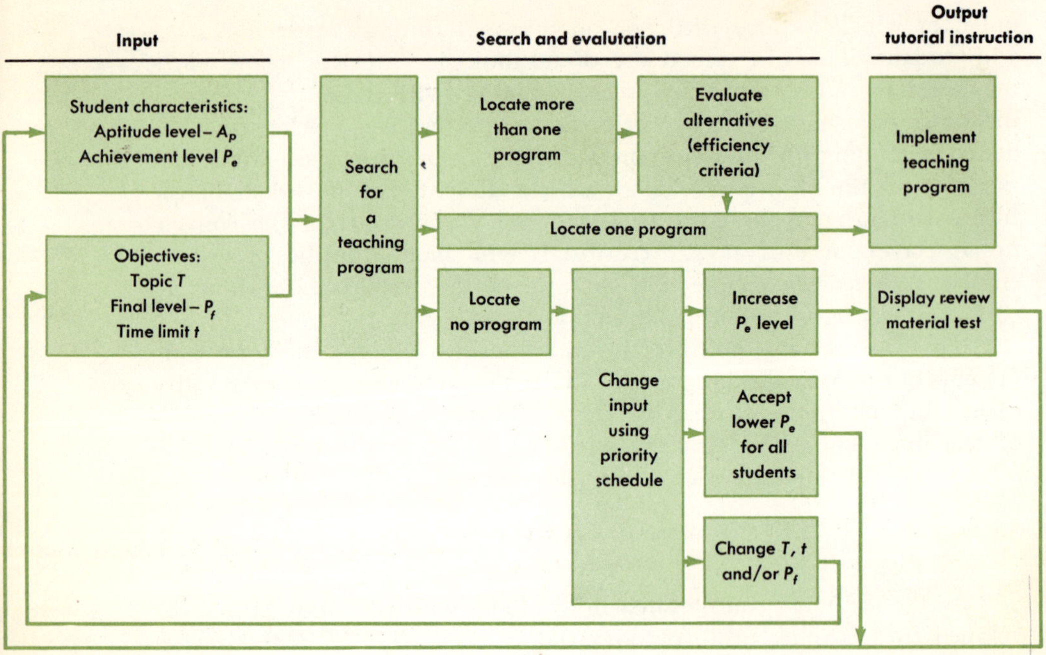

Fig. 1-3. *The pretutorial decision process (after Stolurow and Davis, 1965, p. 176).*

the program which costs the least or requires the least amount of time. The real problem arises when no program is located. In this case the computer either rejects the student or changes the instructional objectives *or* the *required* entering behavior. Figure 1-3 suggests three such changes: raise the students' entering behavior by a review exercise (increase P_e level); accept high-aptitude students whose entering behavior is above the minimum; give students more time for practice (increase t), change the topics (change T), or raise or lower the acceptable level of final performance (P_f).

The tutorial phase consists of two functions: The teacher function puts the program selected in the pretutorial phase to work. The professor function is more complex. It decides which changes to make in the program if the program is not effective. It also monitors the responses of the students as they proceed through a program. If, for example, the teaching strategy or content is too demanding, the professor function decides on the basis of the performance records of a large number of students to provide a new strategy or content.

We can now compare this computer-based teaching model with the basic teaching model and with conventional instruction. The pretutorial phase of the computer-based model embraces the first three components of the basic teaching model: instructional objectives, entering behavior, and instructional procedures. The *teaching program,* as Stolurow and Davis call it, corresponds to instructional procedures. Their model ingeniously demonstrates how adjustments must be made in all three components so they can function together smoothly. The tutorial phase includes chiefly the third and fourth components of the basic teaching model. The teacher function actually uses the procedures previously selected. The professor function is an on-going performance assessment used to make adjustments in both instructional objectives and procedures. You may view the computer-based model as a detailed analysis of the possible interrelationships of the components of the basic teaching model.

In conventional instruction, the classroom teacher must make the decisions made by the computer. He must decide what to teach (objectives), to whom (entering behavior), and how (procedures). And he must determine the extent of the student's success (performance assessment). All decisions are interrelated and interdependent. Failure of the teacher to make good decisions in the pretutorial phase condemns much instruction to the fate of the characters in a Greek tragedy. Frequently the teacher has only one program available for students of widely varying entering behavior. As a result he tries to teach students subject matter which they already have mastered or for which they are not adequately prepared. Since the professor function in the computer model has access to a store of knowledge and alternative programs which the teacher cannot have, Stolurow and Davis believe (although it is now mostly an act of faith) that only computers have the capacity to make all the decisions and accommodations an enlightened pedagogy requires.

A Model for School Learning

We shall now examine a second psychological model of teaching. John Carroll (1962, 1963, 1965) describes most of the components of his teaching model in terms of time. He assumes that the student will attain a particular instructional objective to the extent that he spends the time he needs to learn the task. (Time here is not elapsed time but time actually spent on learning.)

The model has five major components. Three of these pertain to entering behavior, two to instructional procedures. For entering behavior, Carroll describes the first component, *aptitude,* in terms of the amount of learning time the student will require to reach a particular instructional objective under optimal learning conditions. He assumes that students with high aptitude require less learning time than those with low aptitude. The second component, *perseverance,* is the amount of time the student is willing to spend in attaining the instructional objective. Laboring beyond the required time, withstanding discomfort, and facing failure are examples of perseverance. The third component, the *ability to comprehend instruction,* refers to the general or verbal intelligence of the student. (Aptitude, on the other hand, refers to specific learning ability—the ability to reach particular instructional objectives.) Because of their greater ability to comprehend instruction, the achievement of the more able students is less affected by poor instruction than the achievement of the less able students.

Two components of Carroll's model refer to instructional procedures. The first of these, the *opportunity to learn,* is the amount of time actually allowed for learning in a particular teaching situation. In Carroll's opinion, inattention to this variable usually results in too little time being allotted to learning various tasks and in too much material being presented too fast. Insufficient opportunity to learn one task before another is taken up is particularly frustrating to the student who has high perseverance. The second component, the *quality of instruction,* is the degree to which the instruction is organized so that it is easily acquired by the student. Quality often depends on the clarity of the teacher's language and on his adaptation to the special needs and characteristics of the students. One can find instruction of high quality in textbooks, films, workbooks, and teaching-machine programs as well as in live performance. As the quality of instruction deteriorates, the student must rely more on his own resources.

How does Carroll's model compare with the basic teaching model? Carroll does not deal directly with instructional objectives, although the implication is that these objectives must be determined and stated before instruction begins. Most components of his model concern entering behavior: aptitude (or special ability), perseverance (or motivation), and ability to comprehend instruction (or general intelligence). Two components pertain to instructional procedures: opportunity to learn and quality of instruction. Three components can be precisely measured in time: aptitude, perseverance, and opportunity to learn. In applying his model, Carroll (1965, p. 256) hopes to fill in the blanks in such statements as this: A student of age *a* and aptitude *w* requires *x* hours of training to attain level *y* proficiency in (foreign) language *l*. Carroll's model does not provide for systematic performance assessment, but it does assume that the student must achieve mastery of a given task or assignment.

An Interaction Model

Our third psychological model is called a *social-interaction model.* Ned Flanders (1960) has developed one of the best known of these. Flanders classifies the statements of students and teachers into ten categories. At the end of each three-second period, the observer decides which category best represents the communication behavior of that period. Table 1-1 lists the ten categories; they include seven assigned to teacher talk, two to student talk, and one to silence or confusion. For example, when the teacher is talking, the observer can classify the statements as "criticizing or justifying authority" or he can put them into one of the

TABLE 1-1

SUMMARY OF CATEGORIES OF INTERACTION ANALYSIS (after Amidon and Flanders, 1963, p. 12).

Teacher Talk	Indirect Influence	1. *Accepts feeling:* accepts and clarifies the feeling of the students in a nonthreatening manner. Feelings may be positive or negative. Predicting and recalling feelings are included.
		2. *Praises or encourages:* praises or encourages student action or behavior. Jokes that release tension, not at the expense of another individual, nodding head, and saying, "um hm?" or "go on" are included.
		3. *Accepts or uses ideas of student:* clarifying, building, or developing ideas suggested by a student. As teacher brings more of his own ideas into play, shift to category 5.
		4. *Asks questions:* asking a question about content or procedure with the intent that a student answer.
	Direct Influence	5. *Lectures:* giving facts or opinions about content or procedure; expressing his own ideas, asking rhetorical questions.
		6. *Gives directions:* directions, commands, or orders to which a student is expected to comply.
		7. *Criticizes or justifies authority:* statements intended to change student behavior from nonacceptable to acceptable pattern; bawling someone out; stating why the teacher is doing what he is doing; extreme self-reference.
Student Talk		8. *Student talk—response:* talk by students in response to teacher. Teacher initiates the contact or solicits student statement.
		9. *Student talk—initiation:* talk by students which they initiate. If "calling on" student is only to indicate who may talk next, observer must decide whether student wanted to talk. If he did, use this category.
		10. *Silence or confusion:* pauses, short periods of silence, and periods of confusion in which communication cannot be understood by the observer.

six other categories. He can classify the statements of the students as response or initiation. In one study (Flanders, 1964) the observer also kept a record of the six different types of classroom activity. During one hour he collected data separately for all periods of routine administration (settling down to work, passing out materials, collecting materials, cleaning up); for all periods of evaluation, in which homework and tests were being corrected; for all periods in which new material was being introduced; for all periods in which the students and the teacher planned activities together; for all class discussions; and for all periods in which the students worked individually at their desks or in groups. At the end of the hour, the observer added up all the different kinds of statements for each of these six classroom activities and combined them into a grand total for the entire hour.

Flanders (1964, p. 202) states the three principles of teacher influence to which the interaction model applies.

> Restricting student freedom of participation later in the cycle of classroom learning activities increases dependence and decreases achievement.
>
> Restricting student freedom of participation later in the cycle of classroom learning activities does not increase dependence but does increase achievement.
>
> Expanding student freedom of participation early in the cycle of classroom learning activities decreases dependence and increases achievement.

The teacher restricts student freedom of participation when he exercises direct influence (categories 5, 6, and 7 in Table 1-1) through lecturing, giving directions, and criticizing or justifying authority. In these behavior categories the teacher talks more and therefore plays a dominant role in the classroom. Expansion of student participation occurs when the teacher employs categories 1 through 4: He accepts feeling, praises or encourages, accepts or uses student ideas, and asks questions. The phrase *early and late in the cycle* refers to Flanders' particular conception of the order in which events recur in the classroom. Flanders (p. 203) describes this cycle as follows:

> First, an intellectual difference or problem is created; second, the major dimensions of the problem are identified; and third, relationships within the problem are isolated. Fourth, work occurs—such as the gathering of information, the application of a formula, or the trial solution of a problem. Fifth, progress is evaluated and tested. Sixth, the new knowledge is applied to additional problems and interpreted in some meaningful way.

TABLE 1-2

COMMON ELEMENTS OF FOUR PSYCHOLOGICAL TEACHING MODELS.

Basic Teaching Model	Stolurow	Carroll	Flanders
Instructional objectives	a. Subject matter b. Minimum level of final achievement c. Maximum amount of time	Referred to as "tasks," implying behavioral definition	Determined by interaction of teacher and student.
Entering behavior	a. Aptitude level b. Previous relevant knowledge	a. General intelligence b. Aptitude c. Perseverance	Student's feelings, ideas, and present information
Instructional procedures	a. Teacher function b. Professor function	a. Quality of instruction (including materials) b. Opportunity (in time) for learning	Interactions between teacher and student ranging from direct to indirect teacher influence
Performance assessment	Included in teacher and professor functions	Implies initial mastery of the task	Achievement tests and attitude questionnaires used at conclusion of instruction

Steps 1 and 2 represent the early part and steps 5 and 6 represent the late part of the cycle.

The directness or indirectness of the teacher's influence in each part of the cycle affects two aspects of learning: the student's dependence and his achievement. Flanders defines dependence in terms of the degree of concern the student has for pleasing the teacher. A dependent student is more concerned about which method the teacher wants him to use than about which method will solve the problem. According to Flanders, sustained direct influence by the teacher results in increased dependency. Achievement is the difference in pretest and posttest scores. Again, the directness or indirectness of the teacher's influence, in the interaction model, increases or decreases this variable.

We can now compare the interaction model with the basic teaching model. First, the interaction model does not explicitly provide for the statement of instructional objectives or for the adjustment of entering behavior and instructional procedures to different objectives. In his description of the classroom cycle, Flanders refers to the creation "of an intellectual difference or problem." But, since his principles indicate that the teacher should avoid direct influence early in the cycle, when the problem is created and identified and its relationships isolated, we may conclude that the model does not recommend the prior establishment of clear instructional objectives. Second, although the model makes no explicit provision for accommodating differences in entering behavior, the student may be able to adjust the instruction to his own entering behavior since he can control so much of the direction of the learning activity. Also the flexibility of teacher influence, in theory, allows for adjusting the instruction to meet the needs of the students. Third, the model makes no explicit provision for instructional procedures. Rather, it strongly suggests that the most suitable procedures will emerge from the sensitive interaction of students and teacher. Finally, performance assessment, where it is mentioned at all, seems to depend on posttest scores and possible differences in student attitudes. Also, the model does not explicitly provide for using the results of the performance assessment to make changes in objectives, entering behavior, and instructional procedures.

Table 1-2 shows the common elements of the three psychological teaching models and the basic teaching model. Inspection of the table reveals that the models of Stolurow and Carroll easily fit the basic teaching model. Of these two, Stolurow's is the most explicit for all four components. Flanders' is the least explicit.

QUESTION 1-2

In a teaching method developed by Friedrich Herbart (1893), the first step was called *preparation*. In it, the teacher was to inventory the student's *apperceptive mass,* which was composed of clusters of ideas, roughly equivalent to knowledge the student had acquired. The teacher roughly outlined what he might find, questioned the class, and encouraged the student to mention everything that related to the topic. In this way the teacher tried to call into consciousness those ideas which were most crucial for learning (Herbart says *apperceiving*) the new material.

Which of the following teaching models (and which part of the model) does this first step of Herbart's method fit? (a) The computer-based model, (b) Carroll's model for school learning, or (c) Flanders' interaction model?

After you have selected your answer, explain your basis for rejecting the two alternatives.

HISTORICAL TEACHING MODELS

To show the relationship between traditional concepts of teaching and the basic teaching model, I shall now describe three historical models: the Socratic method, the Jesuit classical-humanist method, and a personal-development model.

The Socratic Model

James Jordan (1963, pp. 99–100) uses a selection from *Euthyphro* to illustrate Socratic technique. Socrates begins with a direct request for a definition

> "And what is piety, and what is impiety?" he asks. Euthyphro answers, "Piety is doing as I am doing; that is to say, prosecuting anyone who is guilty of murder, sacrilege, or of any similar crime—whether he be your father or mother, or whoever he may be, that makes no difference; and not to prosecute them is impiety." Euthyphro cites the example of the gods as proof that what he is doing is pious.
>
> After determining that Euthyphro really believes what he says about the gods, Socrates returns to his question, "At present I would rather hear from you a more precise answer, which you have not as yet given, my friend, to the question, 'What is piety?' When asked, you only replied, doing as you do, charging your father with murder." Euthyphro answers, "And what I said was true, Socrates." Socrates returns, "No doubt, Euthyphro; but you would admit that there are many other pious acts?" Euthyphro admits there are, at which Socrates says, "Remember that I did not ask you to give me two or three examples of piety, but to explain the general idea which makes all pious things to be pious. Do you not recollect that there was one idea which made the impious impious, and the pious pious?" Euthyphro remembers and Socrates asks, "Tell me what is the nature of this idea, and then I shall have a standard to which I may look, and by which I may measure actions, whether yours or those of anyone else, and then I shall be able to say that such and such an action is pious, such another impious." Euthyphro then answers, "Piety, then, is that which is dear to the gods, and impiety is that which is not dear to them."
>
> . . . Socrates gets Euthyphro to agree that the gods, like men, disagree over what things are good and evil. From this admission he proceeds, "Then the same things are hated by the gods and loved by the gods, and are both hateful and dear to them?" Euthyphro admits that this is true, and Socrates answers, "And upon this view the same things, Euthyphro, will be pious and impious?" This question obviously destroys Euthyphro's definition of piety for if piety is what the gods love and some gods love one thing and other gods hate the same thing, then the same thing is both pious and impious.

One can observe that Socrates' tutelage of poor Euthyphro consisted of a gentle but inexorable intellectual browbeating.

This passage illustrates several aspects of the Socratic method. First, the primary instructional objective was inquiry. Socrates was less concerned with the acquisition of particular facts and concepts than with the development of skill in asking questions which led to the "truth." Although this passage deals with a definition of piety, Socrates' major purpose was to teach Euthyphro how to arrive at definitions for many concepts. For Socrates, virtue was knowledge. But knowledge was the result of diligent inquiries in which one became personally involved. Second, we see that his method was dialectic—it consisted of a conversation between the teacher and the student. The teacher's role consisted mainly of asking questions; the student's, of organizing his past experiences to answer the questions. Third, the method was not only dialectic, involving teacher-student interaction, but also inductive. Socrates could have begun the lesson by giving Euthyphro the definition of piety which Euthyphro finally arrived at. Instead he asked Euthyphro for his original definition and then enlarged this definition by having Euthyphro recall an array of pious and impious acts. Euthyphro induced the definition of piety by sorting pious and impious acts. The moment of truth arrived when the student grasped the proper relationship of these acts.

Harry Broudy and John Palmer (1965, p. 34) have observed that the Socratic method bears considerable resemblance to psychoanalysis. Socrates usually began with casual questions about the nature of courage, justice, and so on, and gradually showed his students that they were abysmally ignorant exactly where they thought themselves to be most wise. First they became angry with Socrates, then they became angry with themselves. When the anger was turned inward, the students were ready for careful self-examination. For Socrates, education and healing were closely related. Teaching was a kind of love therapy. The student became a disciple whose loyalty was to the master and to his doctrine. Broudy and Palmer observe that in "such a teacher-pupil relationship the character of the teacher and what he teaches are inseparable."

We can now compare the Socratic method with the basic teaching model. Jordan (1963) believes that the Socratic method is not a method of teaching but only a method of inquiry. In terms of the basic teaching model, we can say that Socrates did not formulate specific instructional objectives for his students. Rather, he wanted them to become good inquirers. We can argue, however, that in the process of developing their talents for inquiry the students learned concepts such as courage, moderation, and piety, although, as instructional objectives, the learning of these concepts was subordinate to the development of skill in inquiry. The passage also shows how Socrates adjusted his instruction to the entering behavior of the student by first determining what Euthyphro's present definition of piety was and then making that definition the basis for the instruction which followed. Also in connection with the assessment of entering behavior, Broudy (1963, p. 15) reminds us that Plato, Socrates' successor, believed in the aristocracy of the intellect and reserved long and serious education for those few who could profit from it. As Carroll has indicated, high-aptitude students can profit even from instruction which is not of the highest quality. The instructional procedures of Socrates recall the interaction model of Flanders. By limiting his function to the asking of questions the teacher exercises an indirect influence. Socrates' questions, however, were frequent and insistent and were not necessarily designed to bolster the ego of the student. Socrates' method is similar to what is described later in this book as *discovery learning* (Chapter 11) and *concept learning* (Chapter 10). The instructor helps the student recall examples and nonexamples of the concept (for example, piety) and guides the student toward an adequate definition of it (although this passage ends with the student's concept of piety in shambles). The passage also illustrates performance assessment. Euthyphro proposed two definitions of piety, one in the beginninig and one after the middle of the passage. Socrates assessed the adequacy of these definitions by recalling more examples and nonexamples of piety. Euthyphro then tested the adequacy of his definitions by applying them to these examples, and he discovered, as did Socrates, the shortcomings of his definitions. The passage does not indicate how Socrates assessed increased skill in general inquiry. Perhaps he tried to observe greater skill on the part of Euthyphro in a later inquiry on another concept.

The Jesuit or Classical-Humanist Model

The second historical model, the Jesuit method of education, exemplifies the formal, classical teaching methods of many of our schools and colleges. The Jesuit schools, which flourished from the fifteenth to the nineteenth centuries, were models of classical, humanist education. Broudy (1963, p. 22) describes the Jesuits as "masters of method," with a genius for organizing materials, methods, and teachers into uniformly effective instructional systems. The *Ratio Studiorum,* first published in 1586, is the most detailed description of their method.

Jesuit education was largely a product of the Renaissance, a period of intense revival of interest in the literature of the Greeks and Romans and in their ideals and styles of life. The educated man of the Renaissance was the cultured gentleman at home in many worlds—the royal courts of Europe, the world of wily diplomacy, the new world of trade, and the world of music, painting, sculpture, and literature. Even today many members of liberal arts faculties wistfully dream of their students' attaining this breadth of culture. More specifically, the instructional goals were the acquisition of a high degree of skill in speaking, writing, reasoning, and criticizing. Students gained these skills in the process of mastering Latin and Greek, logic, natural and moral philosophy, metaphysics, theology, and sacred scripture (Fitzpatrick, 1933). Broudy (1963, pp. 22–25) observes that these materials had built-in sets of values, even though the focus was not directly on inculcating them. Critics who see only the avid formalism and intellectualism of the classical schools ignore this value orientation.

The curriculum was fairly standard, and the student had to accommodate himself to the instruction rather than the other way around. We might say that the method selected the student. Those who succeeded under this classical program of studies went on to the universities. Although in the main these students were the children of the old landed aristocracy and the new merchant class, the Jesuits always had an eye for talent, no matter what its socioeconomic trappings. Therefore, children from the lower classes who manifested brightness often found themselves the beneficiaries of the Jesuit schools. The talented aside, the provision for repetition and review in Jesuit education enabled a docile student of even moderate ability to succeed.

The Jesuits had highly developed instructional procedures. The *Ratio Studiorum* contained very specific directions for the teacher. The chief method of presentation was the *prelection*. The teacher studied the assignment in front of the class, and the student was expected to repeat this model performance as precisely as possible. Broudy (1963, pp. 22–23, following Fitzpatrick, 1933, pp. 212–13) quotes the following passage from the *Ratio*, which contains directions for the prelection of an oration or poem:

> If an oration or poem is being explained, first its meaning must be explained, if it is obscure, and the various interpretations considered. Second, the whole method of the workmanship, whether invention, disposition, or delivery is to be considered, also how aptly the author ingratiates himself, how appropriately he speaks, or from what topics he takes his material for persuading, for ornament, or for moving his audience; how many precepts he unites in one and the same place, by what method he includes with the figures of thought the means of instilling belief, and again the figures of thought which he weaves into the figures of words. Third, some passages similar in subject matter and expression are to be adduced and other orators or poets who have used the same precept for the sake of proving or narrating something similar are to be cited. Fourth, let the facts be confirmed by statements of authorities, if opportunity offers. Fifth, let statements from history, from mythology, and from erudition be sought which illustrate the passage. At last, let the words be considered care-

> fully, and their fitness, their elegance, their number, and their rhythm noted. However, let these things be considered, not that the master may always discuss everything, but that from them he may select those which are most fitting.

The Jesuits also retained the medieval disputation for some teaching purposes. The disputation was a formal debate, a kind of formal Socratic dialogue, usually between two students, the defender and the assailant. A master teacher presided over the student debaters, his chief task being to keep the debaters and their audience from muddling their chief points and confusing one another. The rules and the arguments of debating were explicit and had to be learned. Perhaps the only survival of the disputation is the oral examination of doctoral candidates in our graduate schools.

According to Broudy (1963, p. 24), the most important aspect of Jesuit teaching was the method for securing overlapping review. Review of the prelection and other tasks followed immediately upon completion of the work. Students reviewed the work of the week on Saturday; and, for promotion, they reviewed thoroughly the work of the entire year. Students submitted homework assignments at least once a week; grammar students, every day.

The Jesuits made important use of rivalry as a teaching device. They charged each student with catching and correcting every mistake of his opposite number. They also grouped the students into teams, with the success of the team depending on such individual performance. Teachers consistently praised every correct response and blamed every incorrect one, a practice designed both for motivation of the students and for feedback.

The Jesuits built performance assessment intimately into their system. The standard of achievement was mastery of the material and its retention for a year and longer. The teacher or fellow students under the direction of the teacher regularly checked assignments and returned them to the student. The frequent reviews in themselves uncovered what was learned and how well.

Comparing the Jesuit method of instruction with the basic teaching model, you can see that it was explicit for each component of the model. The instructional objectives consisted of good performance in speaking, writing, reasoning, and criticizing. Other objectives, considerably less explicit, were the acquisition of certain attitudes and values. It appears, however, that the Jesuit teachers consciously tried to develop specific performances and hoped that the desirable attitudes and values would evolve from the Greco-Roman materials studied. No conscious variation in objectives and procedures accommodated differences in entering behavior. The Jesuits expected all students to achieve the same objectives and in about the same way. This standardization of objectives and procedures is still characteristic of the classical-humanist curriculum of today. The Jesuit method was most explicit about instructional procedures. Although their methods smack a little of what today we deprecatingly call *rote learning,* the thoroughness of Jesuit teaching often resulted in the students' long-term mastery of a wide range of subjects. American education, when it overadapts to individual differences and shies away from anything rigorously intellectual, often lacks the diligence and the mastery of the classical-humanist school. We have already seen how the Jesuit method provided for performance assessment, the last component of the basic teaching model.

The Personal-Development Model

The progressive education movement was a vital part of the American scene in the first half of the twentieth century. In its long history, which extended back into the nineteenth century, the movement stood and fought for many worthwhile reforms. The very breadth of its objectives and accomplishments makes futile any attempt to epitomize it as a single way of teaching. Its last phase (Cremin, 1964, p. 133)—and the one we are concerned with here—is known as the *life-adjustment movement,* a name first used by the U.S. Office of Education in 1944. The Commission on Life Adjustment Education for Youth, which was established in 1948 and which enunciated some of the philosophy of this movement, originally believed that training in occupational skills was the chief means of assisting the youth of the nation to adjust to the occupational and social world. Later, the psychological dimensions of life adjustment, as exemplified by the mental-hygiene movement in education, became its predominant concern.

Soon after the birth of the Commission, Donald Snygg and Arthur Combs wrote a book which has served as an authoritative reference for those whose major professional concern is the personal adjustment and development of their students. In the first edition (1949) the authors discussed individual behavior and in the revised edition (Combs and Snygg, 1959) they included two chapters—one on goals and purposes, the other on teaching relationships—which related individual behavior to education.

Combs and Snygg suggest only broad instructional goals. Schools, they believe, should give each pupil the opportunity to think of himself as a responsible and contributing member of society. This opportunity will allow the pupil to gain *self-enhancement* (a term the authors prefer to life adjustment) through the discovery of his talents and areas of strength. Self-enhancement leads to an adequate personality, which, in turn, is characterized by a positive view of self, the ability to accept oneself and others, and the ability to relate broadly to one's fellowmen. The authors believe that more definite and specific statements of the desirable behavioral changes should be avoided. Societies change (hence their objection to the term *life adjustment*), and individuals must be able to behave effectively and efficiently under novel conditions. Combs and Snygg (1959, p. 138) state, "For the good of our society and its members it is better to wish for intelligent behavior than for good penmanship or the ability to diagram a declarative sentence or any of the other limited objectives which may or may not be a valuable means of need satisfaction in the future."

The authors offer no clear guidelines for the assessment of and provision for the entering behavior of the student. We are told the chief motive for learning is self-esteem and a feeling of personal adequacy. Teachers should seek activities which increase self-esteem and avoid activities which result in failure and humiliation. To do both successfully, they should teach children only that for which they are ready. A good teacher must be able to adapt method and material to the broad heterogeneity of his students. A less skillful teacher should teach only homogeneous classes.

The authors do give, however, some general guidelines for instructional procedures. Teachers should present material in "such a way that each child will secure a feeling of pride and satisfaction through its mastery" (p. 382). Proper pacing of the work is especially important if each child is to feel successful. In particular repetition should not be imposed; if the child really wants to solve a problem, he will provide his own repetition. When he must learn the material by large amounts of repetition, he is out of step with the work. The authors suggest that good teaching method may only be good human relationships. The teacher should use methods with which he is comfortable: "Effective teaching requires the sensitive use of a human personality as an instrument for assisting other people to new experience and new discovery. It must always be a highly unique and individual matter" (p. 409).

For performance assessment we find a number of caveats or near caveats. Teachers should evaluate achievement by standards appropriate to the age and experience of the pupil. And, since pupil achievement is always unique, teachers should not attempt to make comparisons among class members. Schools should measure success not by the pupils' skill in the verbal description of techniques or even by their use of these techniques in the school but by "the degree to which they voluntarily use them in their daily life outside of school" (Combs and Snygg, 1959, p. 382).

The statement of Combs and Snygg is a philosophy of education more than a model of teaching. As in most educational philosophy, their emphasis is on broad educational goals, particularly the development of personal feelings, attitudes, and values. Their goals slight the learning of subject matter and intellectual skills. The wide appeal of their philosophy is due to the flexibility it promises in adjusting the curriculum to differences in entering behavior. In fact, they strongly suggest that in their scale of values the student precedes the curriculum; therefore, the curriculum should emerge as the gradual manifestation of the needs of the student. Such flexibility, of course, promises great freedom for the students to explore and develop their interests and to satisfy their curiosity, and it also promises great freedom for the teacher to employ whatever instructional procedures further the students' education. Because of their unwillingness to impose upon the student any task for which he does not show an inclination or interest, Combs and Snygg are very indefinite about instructional objectives and procedures. They tell the teacher to rely on his own personality and to make it his chief instrument for instruction. Also, because they give no explicit instructional objectives, no performance assessment is possible. The student himself determines what he has and has not learned. As Lawrence Cremin (1964, pp. 348–49) observes, such freedom was typical of the progressive teaching method, which demanded "extraordinary feats of pedagogical ingenuity to build on the need and interests of students." He continues:

> In the hands of first-rate instructors the innovations worked wonders; in the hands of too many average teachers, however, they led to chaos. Like the proverbial little girl with the curl in the middle of her forehead, progressive education done well was very good indeed; done badly it was abominable—worse, perhaps, than the formalism it sought to supplant.

You should now return to objectives 4–6 (p. 6) and determine how well you have achieved those for the second and third sections of this chapter.

QUESTION 1-3

Othanel Smith (1960) has developed a teaching model which describes what he calls the *ebb and flow* of teaching or the *cycle of giving and taking instruction*. A cycle consists of a teacher phase and a student phase, which mirror each other. In the teacher phase the teacher perceives the student's behavior, diagnoses the student's state of interest, readiness, knowledge, and so on, and, finally, acts. In the student phase the student perceives and diagnoses the teacher's behavior and, finally, acts. Which of the following models is least like Smith's? (a) the Socratic model, (b) the Jesuit model, or (c) the personal-development model? After you have selected your answer, list the characteristics of the model you chose and point out the differences between it and Smith's model.

SUMMARY

This chapter described what a theory of teaching must include. It distinguished a theory of teaching from and related it to a theory of learning and a philosophy of education. The chapter also described the four components of the basic teaching model: instructional objectives, entering behavior, instructional procedures, and performance assessment. It then described psychological teaching models—a computer-based model (Stolurow), a model for school learning (Carroll), and an interaction model (Flanders)—and compared them with the basic teaching model. Finally, it described three historical teaching models—the Socratic model, the classical-humanist model of the Jesuits, and the personal-development model of Combs and Snygg—and compared them with the basic teaching model.

SUGGESTED READINGS

The following articles are the most useful and comprehensive discussions of teaching theory (with its relation to learning theory):

Gage, Nathan L., "Paradigms for Research on Teaching," in *Handbook of Research on Teaching,* ed. N. L. Gage, pp. 94–141. Chicago: Rand McNally & Co., 1963.

———, "Theories of Teaching," in *Theories of Learning and Instruction,* ed. E. R. Hilgard, pp. 268–85, part 1 of the 63rd Yrbk. of the National Society for the Study of Education. Chicago: University of Chicago Press, 1964.

The following works give fuller descriptions of the psychological models I have used:

Carroll, John B., "A Model of School Learning," *Teachers College Record,* 64 (1963), 723–33.

Combs, Arthur, *The Professional Education of Teachers: A Perceptual View of Teacher Preparation.* Boston: Allyn and Bacon, Inc., 1965.

Flanders, Ned A., "Interaction Analysis and In-service Training," *California Journal for Instructional Improvement,* 9 (1966), 14–31.

Stolurow, Lawrence M., and Daniel Davis, "Teaching Machines and Computer-Based Systems," *Teaching Machines and Programed Learning, II: Data and Directions,* ed. R. Glaser, pp. 162–212. Washington, D.C.: Department of Audiovisual Instruction, National Education Association, 1965.

The following works give fuller descriptions of the historical models:

Broudy, Harry S., "Historic Exemplars of Teaching Method," *Handbook of Research on Teaching,* ed. N. S. Gage, pp. 1–43. Chicago: Rand McNally & Co., 1963.

Broudy, Harry S., and John R. Palmer, *Exemplars of Teaching Method.* Chicago: Rand McNally & Co., 1965.

Instructional Objectives

2

This chapter shows you how to make useful statements of instructional objectives and how to analyze these objectives to guide your teaching. The basic contention here is that the most useful statements of instructional objectives refer to observable human performances—student behaviors the teacher can observe and measure. The first section of the chapter distinguishes between explicit and implicit statements of instructional objectives—that is, between those which refer to specific human performances and those which refer to more general educational goals. This section also considers the arguments for and against the use of explicit statements of objectives. In the second section, on task description, I describe how you can convert general statements of educational objectives into specific statements of instructional objectives. The final (third) section deals with task analysis, in which we further analyze the behavioral objectives for teaching and learning purposes. This chapter gives the book its basic psychological orientation, and you should, therefore, read it with great care.

Upon reading this chapter you should be able to meet these objectives:

1. Distinguish between explicit and implicit statements of instructional objectives and identify terminal performance.

2. Describe the arguments for and against the use of explicit statements of instructional objectives.

3. Write explicit statements of instructional objectives, using Mager's three requirements for task description.

4. Identify the missing requirements in faulty task descriptions.

5. List the behavior categories used in two systems of task analysis (Gagné's and Bloom's) and identify and provide examples of instructional objectives for each category.

EXPLICIT STATEMENTS OF INSTRUCTIONAL OBJECTIVES

Robert Gagné (1965a, pp. 1–2) points out that the phrase *educational objectives* can mean quite different things. When the boy in the fourth grade asks why he must study mathematics, you can give him various answers. In Gagné's words, which shall you say to him:

1. You need it in order to learn more mathematics or to learn science?
2. You need it in order to balance your checkbook when you grow up?
3. You need it in order to be successful in almost any job?
4. You need it in order to become an informed and responsible citizen?
5. You need it to appreciate the beauty of numbers?
6. You need it in order to think logically in solving problems?

If the fourth grader asks you how you know his future needs, you can answer with varying degrees of confidence. You can, that is, determine his short-term needs better than his long-term needs. You can more easily show him that he needs to learn multiplication in order to learn division than show him that studying mathematics makes him a more responsible citizen. To convert broad educational objectives into explicit statements of instructional objectives, we need to limit somewhat the possible scope of educational objectives.

Educational Objectives

I shall use *educational objectives* to refer to the broad goals and values which educational systems embrace and which, as you learned in the first chapter, philosophies of education include. *Instructional objectives,* on the other hand, are specific performances students acquire through particular instructional procedures. As teachers our job is to convert educational objectives into instructional objectives.

Despite the winds of controversy which sweep American education, we concur considerably on what our educational goals should be, and several groups have successfully set these down. In 1955, in a document entitled *The Committee for the White House Conference on Education, A Report to the President,* a distinguished group of American educators identified the following educational objectives:

1. A general education as good or better than that offered in the past, with increased emphasis on the physical and social sciences.
2. Programs designed to develop patriotism and good citizenship.
3. Programs designed to foster moral, ethical, and spiritual values.
4. Vocational education tailored to the abilities of each pupil and to the needs of the community and nation.
5. Courses designed to teach domestic skills.
6. Training in leisure-time activities such as music, dancing, avocational reading, and hobbies.
7. A variety of health services for all children, including both physical and dental inspection, aimed at bettering health knowledge and habits.
8. Special treatment for children with speech or reading difficulties and other handicaps.
9. Physical education, ranging from systematic exercises, physical therapy, and intramural sports, to interscholastic competition.
10. Instruction to meet the needs of the abler students.
11. Programs designed to acquaint students with countries other than their own in an effort to help them understand the problems America faces in international relations.
12. Programs designed to foster mental health.
13. Programs designed to foster wholesome family life.
14. Organized recreational and social activities.
15. Courses designed to promote safety. These include instruction in driving automobiles, swimming, civil defense, etc.

In a later report, the Educational Policies Commission (1961, pp. 11–12) expressed this general purpose of American education:

> The purpose which runs through and strengthens all other educational purposes—the common thread of education—is the development of the ability to think. This is the central purpose to which the school must be oriented if it is to accomplish its traditional tasks or those newly accentuated by recent changes in the world. To say that it is central is not to say that it is the sole purpose or in all circumstances the most important purpose, but that it must be a pervasive concern in the work of the school.

Both these statements limit somewhat the possible scope of educational objectives for which we may strive.

Other groups have put considerable effort into developing outlines of educational objectives which reduce these broad objectives to narrower categories more useful to the teacher. The Russell Sage Foundation (Kearney, 1953, and French, 1957) sponsored the development of two such outlines, one for the elementary and another for the high school. The outline for the elementary school stressed four broad categories of behavior: knowledge and understanding—the memorizing or understanding of content so well that it can be easily recalled; motor and intellectual skill and competence; attitude and interest, including basic human needs and drives, the exercise of the will, and the play of the emotions; and action patterns—broad, generalized ways of behaving. The outline divides further into nine broad curriculum areas; three age-grade levels (ages 6 to 15, grades 1 to 9); and "determining conditions," which are "the biological and social context in which the children and the school work together" (Kearney, 1953, p. 91). The outline for the secondary school curriculum contains these educational goals: growing toward self-realization; growing in the ability to maintain desirable small (face-to-face) group relationships; and growing in the ability to maintain the relationships imposed by membership in large organizations. Each of these major categories reduces to several levels of subcategories, with the statements becoming slightly more explicit. For example, "can learn independently and shows desire to do so" finally reduces to (among other statements) "tries to improve his own written work by revising it so that it will convey his intention as clearly as possible." Both these outlines attempt to bridge the gap between broad educational objectives and specific instructional objectives.

Now however we have an ingenious classification of educational objectives which, by dealing with attitudes and values, attempts to bridge this gap more explicitly. In this classification system, David Krathwohl and his associates (1964) place various categories along a continuum indicating the degree of internalization of values and attitudes. These are the five major categories: receiving or attending—awareness, willingness to receive, and controlled or selected attention; responding—acquiescence in responding, willingness to respond, and satisfaction in response; valuing—acceptance of or preference for a value or commitment; organization or conceptualization of a value, or organization of a value system; and characterization of a value or value complex, including generalized set.

In summary, you can see that educational objectives range from very broad statements of goals and values to somewhat more restricted statements suggesting specific human performances. With this distinction between educational and instructional objectives (and the gradations in between) in mind, we can now consider what *explicit statements* of instructional objectives are.

Explicit vs. Implicit Instructional Objectives

Explicit statements of instructional objectives identify the end product of instruction in terms of observable human accomplishment (or performance), which is the outcome of behavior. To determine whether or not a student has learned something, we observe not his behavior but the outcome of his behavior. For example, when a student solves a mathematical problem, the performance is the solution. Thus, explicit statements of instructional objectives designate the solution and not the behavior which produces the solution. We often refer to these end products of instruction as *terminal performances.* Usually these are verbal performances. The following statements are explicit because they refer to specific terminal performances (all of which are verbal):

1. Student is able to name the planets of our solar system.
2. Student is able to distinguish between the Renaissance and the Reformation.
3. Student is able to list the major systems of the body.

In contrast, the following are not explicit statements and do not refer to terminal performances:

1. Student really understands the poetry of John Donne.
2. Student appreciates the beauty of Gothic architecture.
3. Student grasps the significance of the impact of the French Revolution on later political developments in Europe.

We may refer to the second set of objectives as *implicit statements* of instructional objectives because the terminal performances are not specified—how the student will visibly demonstrate his understanding or appreciation of Donne, Gothic architecture, and the French Revolution is not indicated—and because the performances implied are interior states, responses, and processes not open to observation.

The distinction between explicit and implicit statements lies chiefly in the choice of verb. The verbs in the explicit definitions were to name, to distinguish, and to list. These are publicly observable acts. In the implicit statements the verbs were understands, appreciates, and grasps the significance of. These do not indicate how the student will visibly show his understandings and appreciation. Also, much of his understanding and appreciation is neural and cerebral activity which is hardly open to the observation of the teacher. Without denying the importance of implicit behavior for the educational enterprise, this chapter will stress the practical importance of explicit statements of instructional objectives.

The following example will further clarify the distinction between explicit and implicit performance. Compare these two statements:

1. Elvis and Lucille are hopelessly in love.
2. One rarely sees Elvis without Lucille, or Lucille without Elvis.

The first statement describes a joyful (sometimes painful) internal state of two individuals, which can be exemplified in a number of observable acts. Conceivably, Elvis and Lucille may be hopelessly in love because their families, teachers, or community does not approve of their relationship. They may be hopelessly in love because they have no time except for each other—which at least is a hopeless situation for other interested candidates. Or the description may refer to the inevitable quarrels when they are together and the inevitable statements of nostalgia when they are apart—a kind of hopeless compatibility. Or Lucille may be about to die of leukemia or Elvis about to enlist in the Navy—both very hopeless performances.

The second statement, however, refers to explicit behavior—the physical and therefore observable presence of two individuals. Even the word *rarely* implies that we could count the number of times Elvis and Lucille are not seen together. Now we can scarcely deny that Elvis and Lucille may be together for reasons other than love or that they may demonstrate their love in more ways than by a symbiotic existence. Perhaps no one else will have anything to do with them—they may be social outcastes thrown into each other's company. They may be brother and sister or Siamese twins. Or they may be very private in their love, with few or no public appearances. In any case, whether it be love or hate, biological or social necessity, we can at least agree on when and how often we see them together. The performance is explicit.

Now let us analyze two partial statements of instructional objectives for this distinction between explicit and implicit performance.

> 1. The student should know what the Renaissance embraced and how it arose, and appreciate its great cultural significance.
> 2. Given the complete unit of the Italian Renaissance, the student should be able to list and discuss its classical origins and its chief literary and artistic products, and to illustrate its survival in the literary and artistic products of our century.

The important verbs in the first statement are know and appreciate. In the second statement they are list, discuss, and illustrate. The implicit nature of the first statement opens it to considerably more ambiguity than does the explicit nature of the second statement, although, as instructional objectives, both statements leave much to be desired. We know, for example, that the Renaissance included important religious, commercial, political, and social developments which have their legacy in our century. In the first statement, the requirement that the student appreciate the great significance of the period could refer to something as parsimonious as making a general statement that "the Renaissance surely changed the course of events in Europe" or to something as elaborate as undertaking a detailed analysis of social, political, religious, economic, and cultural events of the centuries after the Renaissance in order to identify specific instances of surviving influence. On the other hand, the second statement indicates that what the student should know best is only the cultural part of the historical period. And even this knowledge is limited to cultural products, and does not necessarily include the producers—the artists and the writers. In this instance, to name particular artistic and literary works and to show how they have been influenced by the Renaissance describes performance which involves a very limited appreciation or perhaps no appreciation at all. In any case, in the second statement, as against the first, it is easier to agree on the occurrence or nonoccurrence of the performance in question.

For a third and final illustration of the distinction between explicit and implicit statements, we can turn to the list of objectives which precedes this chapter and try to reduce it to a single statement: Upon reading this chapter, the student will fully understand the importance of stating instructional objectives. Exactly what terminal performance does this statement describe? Does it include only the student's ability to state several reasons why explicit statements are necessary? Does it exclude his ability to describe several methods for making explicit statements and, indeed, to prepare his own statements? Does it include all the statements on p. 31 and more, or possibly none of these at all but quite another set? These questions suggest the ambiguity of the single, general statement. To avoid this ambiguity a list of objectives should refer to observable performance.

Usefulness of Explicit Statements

Now that you can distinguish between explicit and implicit statements and identify terminal performances, we can consider the arguments for and against the use of explicit statements of instructional objectives.

Ralph Tyler (1949, 1950, 1964) and Gagné (1965b) provide three persuasive reasons for the careful definition of instructional objectives. First, such a definition provides guidance in the planning of instruction. A fable created by Robert Mager (1962, p. ix), illustrates this point.

> Once upon a time a Sea Horse gathered up his seven pieces of eight and cantered out to find his fortune. Before he traveled very far he met an Eel, who said,
>
> "Psst. Hey, bud. Where 'ya goin'?"
>
> "I'm going out to find my fortune," replied the Sea Horse, proudly.
>
> "You're in luck," said the Eel, "for four pieces of eight you can

> have this speedy flipper, and then you'll be able to get there a lot faster."
>
> "Gee, that's swell," said the Sea Horse, and paid the money and put on the flipper and slithered off at twice the speed. Soon he came upon a Sponge, who said,
>
> "Psst. Hey, bud. Where 'ya goin'?"
>
> "I'm going to find my fortune," replied the Sea Horse.
>
> "You're in luck," said the Sponge, "for a small fee I will let you have this jet-propelled scooter so that you will be able to travel a lot faster."
>
> So the Sea Horse bought the scooter with his remaining money and went zooming through the sea five times as fast. Soon he came upon a Shark, who said,
>
> "Psst. Hey, bud. Where 'ya goin'?"
>
> "I'm going out to find my fortune," replied the Sea Horse.
>
> "You're in luck. If you take this short cut," said the Shark, pointing to his open mouth, "you'll save yourself a lot of time."
>
> "Gee, thanks," said the Sea Horse, and zoomed off into the interior of the Shark, there to be devoured.

According to Mager, the moral of this fable is that if you are not certain of where you are going, you may very well end up someplace else. Thus, the teacher must determine at the start what the student will be able to do at the finish. A careful statement of this terminal performance enables the teacher to plan the steps the student must take to achieve it. The teacher can provide for all the responses the student must make in order to accomplish the major final responses only after he has adequately described the characteristics of these final responses. You may recall that in the pretutorial phase of the computer-based teaching model the search for the appropriate program is based on the instructional objectives and the entering behavior of the student. One of the possible outcomes of this search is the modification of objectives—by changing the amount of time, the expected level of mastery, or the topics covered. These changes can occur only if the objectives first appear in explicit form. In the same way, instructional procedures cannot accommodate differences in entering behavior unless the teacher determines in some precise form what the student is able to do before instruction and what he is expected to do after instruction. By far the most important reason for using explicit statements of instructional objectives is the guidance they provide the teacher in planning his instructional procedures. Later in the chapter, when I describe task analysis, we will carefully consider the relationship between instructional objectives and procedures.

A second reason for making explicit statements of instructional objectives is that they are useful in performance assessment. In education the original concern for adequate statements of instructional objectives came from men chiefly interested in test construction and curriculum evaluation. They discovered that using ambiguous statements of objectives made it difficult or impossible to construct tests and test items. One has considerably more difficulty constructing test items for objectives which contain the verbs to know and to understand than for those which contain the verbs to solve and to differentiate. In a programed textbook on descriptive linguistics (Gotkin and Goldstein, 1964, p. 1), for example, this is one of the first objectives: Identify whether a set of data represents a sample or a population. Later (p. 243) the authors present this test item:

> List some possible populations that each of the following samples might represent:
> *a.* A bushel of McIntosh apples.
> *b.* Sixty fourth-grade boys.
> *c.* A quart of milk.
> *d.* All members of the New York City chapter of Alcoholics Anonymous.

By correctly identifying possible populations for each of these samples, a student demonstrates his achievement of the instructional objective. The statement of the objective specifically suggests the test item. In this way, the proper statement of objectives and the construction of test items interweave.

A third reason for using explicit statements of objectives pertains more to the student than to the teacher. If the student knows beforehand what he must learn in any given unit of instruction, he can better direct his own attention and efforts. When you contemplate how frequently students are unable to make even an approximate statement of what the teacher is trying to explain, the importance of this practice becomes convincing. Take, for example, the list of objectives for Chapter 1. Although the student cannot define every term in the list the first time he reads it, he does obtain some preliminary idea of what he should look for and be able to do upon completion of the chapter. He knows in summary form and at the outset that, after reading the chapter, he should be able to (1) distinguish between a theory of teaching and theories of learning and philosophies of education; (2) describe the four components of the basic teaching model; and (3) describe the relationship of the model to various psychological and historical teaching models. While reading the chapter, the student can match the responses he makes to the responses given in the list. In programed instruction, the requirement that the student make overt responses throughout the program greatly facilitates this matching process.

A study by Mager and his associate (1961) provides empirical support for the benefits students derive from knowing at the start the specific objectives they should attain. They investigated three groups of engineers being trained on particular engineering tasks. In the first group the instructor selected and ordered all the content. In the second group the students selected and ordered the content which they studied. In the third group the investigators presented the students with a detailed list of the instructional objectives, each one illustrated by the kinds of questions they were expected to answer. They then allowed these students to instruct themselves in any order and by whatever procedures they desired; they reported to the instructor when they were ready to demonstrate their achievement of the objectives. The investigators found that the training time for the third group was 65 per cent less than that for the other groups without any loss in achievement. Thus much learning can occur when the teacher does nothing beyond presenting the student with the list of instructional objectives.

There are several arguments against the use of explicit statements of instructional objectives. The first is that educational objectives concern the development of processes as well as products (Ebel, 1963). Gagné (1965a, p. 6), in repudiating this position, uses two objectives to illustrate it:

> The student should acquire a developing awareness of the magnitude of the solar system and the universe; or the child should become increasingly confident in extemporaneous oral expression.

Evaluating these objectives, Gagné writes:

> It is difficult to know what to say about such statements except that they are weasel-worded. Why is it not possible to say exactly what one wants the student to do in showing his awareness of solar system magnitudes? Why is it not possible to state what kind of extemporaneous oral expression one expects the child to perform? The answer may be, of course, that the latter kind of objectives can indeed be stated, but not all students will attain them. Unfortunately, this is probably true under present circumstances. It would be good, though, if we could amend the statement to read: "Not all students will attain them *with the same speed*." Then they would still remain objectives which any intelligent person could identify, rather than descriptions which if not deliberately hedging are at least ambiguous.

A second argument is that explicit statements involve the danger of overemphasis on conformity. Robert Ebel (1963, p. 34) writes:

> For, if the goals of education are defined in terms of narrowly specific behavior desired by curriculum makers and teachers, what need is there for critical judgment by the student; what freedom is there for creative innovation; what provision is there for adaptive behavior as the cultural world changes?

This position, often defended with notable passion and dedication, contains many uncritical assumptions about the psychology of learning in general and about problem solving in particular, both of which we examine in Part 3 of this book. First, why cannot we define critical judgment, creative innovation, and adaptive behavior explicitly as one or more concrete alternatives the individual may choose in hypothetical situations? Second, does evidence support the assumption that critical judgment, creative innovation, and so on are not based on previously acquired performances and, therefore, cannot result in new performances which can be described in explicit terms? Finally, to claim that the acquisition of knowledge and performances results in slavish conformity to the past presumes a uniformity of achievement which no teacher or school has ever produced or recorded, given the initial variations in the entering behavior of their students. Furthermore, this claim ignores the well-documented observation that those individuals who make creative contributions in the sciences and the arts are those who are the most knowledgeable about their fields.

A third argument is that we cannot determine what the student may be able to do at the end of a unit of instruction. The defenders of this position claim that they are interested in long-range educational outcomes—what the student will be able to do several years after he completes a course of study or after he graduates. They argue that we cannot state the immediate objectives of instruction because we cannot anticipate what the student will do at the end of the instructional period. He may be able to do something the teacher never anticipated. It is better, they argue, to keep our eyes on the long-range objectives. Despite the emotional ardor with which they defend this position, Gagné (1965a, p. 7) believes that it is intellectually insupportable. He writes:

> If one is actually interested in performances which will appear ten years hence, there is nothing wrong with that. Two courses of action are then available. The first is to perform some longitudinal studies to determine what differential factors are in the current educational backgrounds of people who behave desirably and people who behave undesirably at some future time. Alternatively, one could experimentally introduce certain differences in the education of groups of present students, and follow them up after five or ten years to see what kinds of decisions they make. Both of these techniques are of course well known to behavioral scientists, and successful studies have been and are being done to find answers such as these.

As for unexpected changes in performance, changes other than those specified in the statement, Gagné reminds us that we can even specify these, and, in fact, we must specify them if we are to provide evidence that these changes have occurred.

A fourth argument suggests a practical difficulty in using explicit statements of instructional objectives. Ebel (1963, p. 34) writes:

> The virtue of specificity involves the burden of multiplicity. Behavioral definitions tend to be books, not paragraphs, sections, or even chapters. Even in the books, the definitions cannot be completely specific for it is obviously impossible to specify fully and exactly all the particular behaviors that are desired. The virtue of concreteness involves the burden of complexity.

Tyler (1964) believes that at the most useful level of specificity the teacher describes the concrete behavior he wants the student to acquire. These instructional objectives should express a purpose which is meaningful in the larger context of the life goals of the student, and this purpose should be distinguishable from others. Following Tyler's criteria, Gagné (1965a) suggests that teachers seek statements of objectives such as these:

> "Reads a French newspaper," rather than "reads French"; "solves problems requiring the use of sine, cosine, and tangent," rather than "understands trigonometry"; "makes a quantitative description of dispersion errors in observations," rather than "knows statistics."

QUESTION 2-1

The student teacher was preparing a list of instructional objectives for his history lesson. At this point he was interested in identifying terminal performances. The following three items were part of his list:

1. The student should demonstrate his genuine understanding of the French Revolution.
2. The student should be able to name the political leader of the Revolution.
3. The student should be able to explain in concrete terms the causes of the Revolution.

Which of the following is the best evaluation of the list? (a) The list meets all the major requirements of explicit statements of instructional objectives. (b) The list satisfies only one requirement—each statement designates a terminal performance. (c) The list contains only one statement that adequately describes a terminal performance.

After you have made your choice, indicate your basis for rejecting the two alternatives.

Undoubtedly, as Ebel states, explicit statements of instructional objectives involve the danger of unmanageable multiplicity. The remedy, however, is not to adopt nonbehavioral definitions but rather to find a useful level of description of concrete performances.

The overriding objection to general, abstract statements of instructional objectives is not to the broad personal and social aspirations they may embody but to their inability to guide the teacher in making decisions about what to teach, whom to teach, how to teach, and how to determine the success and failure of his own and his students' efforts.

You should now return to objectives 1 and 2 (p. 30) and determine how well you have achieved them.

TASK DESCRIPTION

A task description is a full description of terminal performance. Although it involves more than reference to explicit terminal performance, such references are one of its major elements.

Mager's Procedure

Two experimental psychologists, Robert Mager and Robert Miller, working quite independently in military training programs, have developed two similar methods of task description. An account of both methods may shed more light on the subject than a statement of a single method. In the light of our previous distinction between explicit and implicit behavior, Mager's method is the easier to explain. According to him, a statement of instructional objectives (what I am now calling task description) requires each of the following:

1. Identification of the terminal performance which the instruction attempts to produce.
2. Description of the important conditions under which the behavior is expected to occur.
3. Description of how good a student's performance must be to be acceptable.

Now examine two of Mager's (1962) examples of task description:

> A. Given a linear algebraic equation with one unknown, the learner must be able to solve for the unknown without the aid of references, tables, or calculating devices [p. 26].
>
> B. Given a list of factors leading to significant historical events, the learner must be able to select *at least five factors contributing to the depression of 1929* [p. 27].

Let us apply Mager's three requirements of task description to these two examples. The first requirement, the identification of the terminal performance, should be the easiest of the three for you to apply because it rests on the distinction between explicit and implicit behavior considered earlier. The two examples identify terminal performance as follows:

A. The learner must be able to solve for the unknown. . . .
B. The learner must be able to select . . . factors contributing to the depression of 1929. [Note: I have omitted mention of how many factors.]

You will agree that these are explicit, publicly observable performances.

We have not previously discussed the second and third requirements of task description. Their inclusion, however, further reduces ambiguity about what we are attempting to teach and gives the teacher much more guidance. The second requirement is to describe the important conditions under which the behavior is to occur. The two examples describe these conditions as follows:

A. Given a linear algebraic equation with one unknown. . . . without the aid of references, tables, or calculating devices.
B. Given a list of factors leading to significant historical events. . . .

Note that in the list of objectives for the chapters of this book, the given condition for achievement is the reading of the chapter. Therefore, each list begins with the words "Upon reading this chapter. . . ."

The third requirement is to describe the level of acceptable performance. This may be a somewhat arbitrary standard ranging from 100 per cent mastery (spelling correctly all fifty words in a spelling list) to only minimal mastery (spelling correctly only one of the fifty words in the list). The two examples describe these levels of performance (or standards) as follows:

A. To solve for the unknown. . . . [The implication is 100 per cent mastery.]
B. To select at least five factors. . . . [Five, of course, is a minimum standard.]

We will fully discuss the implications of this last of Mager's three requirements in the chapter on test construction.

Miller's Procedure

Miller's (1962, pp. 187–230) method of task description is somewhat more difficult to describe because it is a product of research on training programs in the Air Force and has not been adapted to the usual school setting. According to Miller there are three elements that are essential in any task description:

1. *Indication,* or the cue which calls for the response. In psychology we call this the *stimulus* or the *stimulus condition.*

2. *Activation,* or the response to be made.

3. *Feedback,* or the indication of how adequate the response has been.

Now examine two illustrations of this method of task description.

> A. When the traffic light turns green, the driver accelerates the car; the car moves across the crosswalk into the intersection.
>
> B. Given the printed instruction *subtract* and two integers, the student writes the symbol representing their difference.

An analysis of these two instructional objectives using Miller's requirements of task description is fairly simple. The indication in the first statement is the traffic light turning green. In the second statement it is the printed instruction and the two integers. These are the stimuli, or stimulus conditions. The activation in the first statement is the acceleration of the car. In the second statement it is writing the correct symbol. These, of course, are the responses the learner must acquire. Feedback in the first statement is the proper movement of the car forward, over the crosswalk and into the intersection. In the second statement the correct answer (in whatever form this is given) furnishes the necessary feedback.

Miller (1962, p. 197) observes that task descriptions can vary in degree of completeness. He considers the following to be a particularly complete task description:

> Must run one mile in ten minutes on straight, level, and smooth concrete roadway, with no wind blowing on a sunny day at 70° F, carrying a thirty-pound load in addition to wearing two pounds of summer clothing and two and a half pounds of normal G.I. boots.

If you do not find contemplation of this task utterly uninviting, you may analyze it for the three requirements described by Miller.

We can readily compare the two methods of task description. As we have presented them here, the difference is chiefly one of terminology.

Miller	*Mager*
Indication	Important conditions
Activation	Terminal performance
Feedback	Standard of performance

Note the high degree of explicitness in all three requirements in both lists. They specifically describe the stimulus conditions under which the student must perform. They indicate the response he is to make in terms of observable performance. Provision for feedback (Miller) or for assessment of student performance (Mager) is exact. Both methods provide for objectivity and precision.

You should now return to objectives 3 and 4 (p. 31) and determine how well you have achieved them. Note that you are required to apply only Mager's method of task description.

QUESTION 2-2

Select the statement below which fills all the requirements of Mager's method of task description:

(a) Given a list of human muscles, the student selects all those which are striated.

(b) The student is able to distinguish between similes and metaphors in poetic passages presented to him.

(c) The student lists 75 per cent of the common characteristics of two biological species.

After you have selected the best task description, indicate what is missing in the two faulty descriptions.

TASK ANALYSIS

The teacher must not only describe but also analyze the tasks he expects the student to perform. In this task analysis the teacher identifies classes of behavior which differ in respect to the conditions necessary for their learning (Gagné, 1965b). In somewhat less technical language, once the teacher has made adequate statements of the instructional objectives (or task descriptions), he must analyze these objectives by fitting them into various classes of behavior. The chief purpose of task analysis is to help the teacher determine the optimum learning conditions for the various tasks the student must learn to perform.

Consider, for example, the following task descriptions:

1. When given examples of various types of geometric figures, the student selects only (and all) those which are triangles.

2. When given a list of French words, the student gives all the correct English equivalents.

These two objectives involve different classes of behavior. The first involves *concept learning;* the second, *verbal learning.* The conditions for learning these two tasks (as you will see in Part 3 of this book) are quite different. In a proper task analysis the teacher would correctly classify the behavior involved in each objective and establish the best learning conditions for each.

A task analysis may also identify the subtasks which must be learned in the process of learning the task proper. This procedure is important because the subtasks may fall into different classes of behavior and require, therefore, different learning conditions. Robert Glaser and James Reynolds (1964) provide an example of how a disingenuously simple instructional objective requires further task description and task analysis. They developed an instructional program for time telling appropriate for six- and seven-year-olds. Ignoring what we have said about task description, they could have settled for this statement of their objective: to teach children to tell time. Such a statement is very ambiguous: It does not define the terminal behavior, the conditions, or the standard of judgment. In it, *time* could have any of the following meanings: (1) the concept of time; (2) the passage of time from midnight, the zero hour, to midnight, the last hour; (3) the units of time, such as seconds, minutes, weeks, months; or (4) the judgment of time units, such as observing that ten hours is longer than ten minutes. They adopted a much more explicit statement of their instructional objective: The child is able to write and to say aloud the time indicated by the clock to an accuracy of one minute. With an adequate task description they proceeded to list the subtasks or subbehaviors the children had to learn in working toward the terminal performance. These are some of the subtasks they identified (C and D are omitted):

SUBTASK A

For Writing the Hour and Minute in Sequence, e.g., 7:35

1. Reading the number on the clock face to which the little hand is pointing.
2. Reading the number on the clock face which the little hand has just passed.
3. Determining the number indicated by the little hand.
4. Writing the number of hours the little hand indicates.

SUBTASK B

Same Purpose as A but Focusing on the Big Hand

1. Writing "00" when the big hand points to top center of clock.
2. Associating the word *o'clock* with 00 and top center of clock (this ties in with subclass D—saying "o'clock").
3. Counting clockwise by one's every single mark from the zero point to determine number indicated by big hand.

4. Counting clockwise by five's every fifth mark from the zero point to determine the number indicated by the big hand.
5. Counting clockwise by five's from zero point and then by one's to determine the number indicated by the big hand.
6. Determining the number indicated by the big hand.
7. Then, writing the number of minutes the big hand indicates.

SUBTASK E

For Saying the Minute and Hours in Sequence, e.g., 35 Minutes After 7

1. Associating *minutes after* with number indicated by the big hand.
2. Associating *hours* with number indicated by little hand.
3. Associating *minutes after* with numbers the big hand indicates when it is off top center.
4. First saying the number the minute hand indicates when it is off top center.
5. Then saying "minutes after" when minute hand is off top center.
6. Then saying number hour hand indicates when minute hand is off top center.

These are only some of the subtasks the children had to learn to reach their instructional objective.

After identifying the subtasks, the teacher must fit each of them into its proper class of behavior. He can then determine which conditions he must establish for the learning of each subtask. We shall now consider two systems for the classification of behavior which have particular educational relevance.

Gagné's Classes of Behavior

The most complete description of Gagné's classes of behavior appears in his *The Conditions of Learning* (1965c). Here he distinguishes eight types of learning, beginning with the simple forms and ending with the complex. Although Gagné refers to these classes as learning types, he is primarily interested in the observable behavior and performance which are the products of each such class. In Part 3, we will treat these learning types together with the conditions necessary for producing them in detail. Here I shall give only a brief description and example of each.

SIGNAL LEARNING. In this type of learning (often also called *classical conditioning*) the animal or individual acquires a conditioned response to a given signal. Pavlov studied such learning in great detail. In it the responses are diffuse and emotional and the learning is involuntary. Examples are the withdrawal of the hand upon sight of a hot object, the salivation of a dog upon hearing food poured into his metal feeding dish, and the tearing of the eyes upon sight of an onion. The signals are the sight of the hot object, the sound of food being poured in the dish, and the sight of the onion. The conditioned responses are withdrawal of the hand, salivation, and tearing of the eyes.

Stimulus-response learning. In this kind of learning, exemplified by animal training, the animal makes precise movements of the skeletal muscles in response to specific stimuli. At first this training usually requires the use of a leash and a choke chain. As the dog learns particular responses for particular jerks of the leash and chain, his master rewards him with pats and praise. Later the master does not have to use the leash and chain; the animal sits, stays, or lies down upon hearing the simple verbal command. Whereas the responses in signal learning are diffuse and emotional, the responses in stimulus-response learning (often called *operant conditioning*) are fairly precise physical movements.

Chaining. In this type of learning (frequently called *skill learning*), the person links together two or more units of stimulus-response learning. Gagné reserves this category for nonverbal sequences. The chief condition for the learning of a chain is the reinstatement of the stimulus-response units in the proper order. In the elementary school, the child acquires many chains. He learns to button, fasten, tie, use a pencil, erase, and cut. Later he learns the chains of physical acts involved in printing and writing. He also learns a number of recreational skills, like catching, throwing, and kicking balls of various sizes and shapes.

Verbal association. This learning is a type of chaining, but the links are verbal units. The simplest verbal association is the activity of naming an object, which involves a chain of two links: An observing response enables the child to identify properly the object he sees; and an internal stimulus enables the child to say the proper name. When the child can not only name an object "ball" but also say "the red ball," he has learned a verbal association of three links. Gagné calls another common verbal association *translation responses;* in these, for example, the individual gives the German or French equivalent of an English word, or one nonsense syllable or English word in response to another syllable or word. The learner frequently acquires verbal associations by verbal mediation—an internal link which helps him associate, for example, the French word and its English equivalent. If the student were learning *hand* in response to the French word *main,* the English word *manual* would provide verbal mediation.

Multiple discrimination. In this type of learning the student must learn different responses for stimuli which might be confused. The student learns to distinguish between motor and verbal chains he has already acquired. In studying French, for example, the student must associate *faim* with *hunger* and *femme* with *woman*. When American boys undertake to identify all the new models of automobiles produced in this country in a particular year, they are engaging in multiple-discrimination learning. They must associate each individual model, with its distinctive appearance, with the correct model name and with no other name. When there is only one model to consider, linking the correct name with the right model illustrates verbal association. When there are several models and names, linking that name with the same model and no other model illustrates multiple-discrimination learning. Teachers, Gagné suggests, engage in multiple-discrimination learning when they devise means for calling each student by his correct name.

CONCEPT LEARNING. In learning a concept we respond to stimuli in terms of abstract characteristics like color, shape, position, and number as opposed to concrete physical properties like specific wavelengths or particular intensities. Gagné uses this example. A child may learn to call a small cube a "block," and also to call similar objects which vary in size and shape "blocks." Later he may learn the concept *cube* and discover that cubes can be made of wood, glass, wire, and other materials, can vary in color, and can be of any size. Or, if a student is given a series of numbers, he is able to select those which belong to the class *odd* as opposed to those in the class *even*. In concept learning, the student's behavior is not under the control of particular physical stimuli but of the abstract properties of each stimulus. Concepts have concrete references even though they are learned with the use of language.

PRINCIPLE LEARNING. In learning a principle we relate two or more concepts. According to Gagné, the simplest principle may be depicted in the form: "If *X*, then *Y*," as in the example, "If a feminine noun, then the article *la*." Or, "If the temperature of the water is above 212° F, then the water boils." Principles are, in effect, chains of concepts. We may represent knowledge as a hierarchy of principles, in which we must learn two or more principles before learning a higher-order principle which embraces them. If the student has learned the component concepts and principles, the teacher can use verbal instruction alone in leading the student to put the principles together.

PROBLEM SOLVING. In the set of events called problem solving, individuals use principles to achieve some goal. When the goal is reached, however, the student has learned something more and is then capable of new performances using his new knowledge. What is learned, according to Gagné, is a higher-order principle, the combined product of two or more lower-order principles. Thus problem solving requires those internal events usually called *thinking*. Gagné suggests these examples. A driver who maps his route through traffic rather than being swept along by it is solving a problem. In replanning his luncheon schedule to accommodate a new appointment, the individual is solving a problem. When the housewife shops selectively for particular items on the basis of price variations, she is solving a problem. Without knowledge of the prerequisite principles, the problems cannot be solved.

We have now completed our description of Gagné's learning types. In Part 3 I describe each type further and carefully consider its application to instructional procedures. We can now turn to another system for classifying behavior which also is relevant to education.

Bloom's Classes of Behavior

For instructional and testing purposes Benjamin Bloom and his associates developed a method of classifying educational objectives, a process I have called *task analysis*. As in Gagné's system, the different classes of behavior are arranged in hierarchical order from the simple to the complex: Behaviors in one class are likely to make use of and build on behaviors in the preceding classes. Bloom and his associates explain their system in the *Taxonomy of Education Objectives* (1956). The system includes two broad categories—(a) knowledge and (b) intellectual abilities and skills—which produce six classes of behavior. I shall describe each class and provide examples of educational objectives for each.

KNOWLEDGE. This class involves the recall of specifics and generalizations; of methods and processes; and of pattern, structure, or setting. Recall simply means bringing the appropriate material to mind, usually without alteration. The *Taxonomy* uses this analogy: If you think of the mind as a file, in a test of knowledge you must find in each problem the signals, cues, and clues which best bring out whatever knowledge you have filed. This class of behavior covers several educational objectives. Here are some examples:

> To define technical terms by giving their attributes, properties, or relations.
>
> To make pupils conscious of correct form and usage in speech and writing.
>
> The recall of major theories about particular cultures.

Bloom categorizes the remaining five classes of behavior as intellectual abilities and skills.

COMPREHENSION. This class is the lowest level of understanding. The student knows what is being communicated and can use the material or idea without necessarily relating it to other material or seeing its full implications. The following examples of educational objectives fit this class:

> Skill in translating mathematical verbal material into symbolic statements.
>
> The ability to grasp the thought of the work as a whole at any desired level of generality.
>
> Skill in predicting continuation of trends.

APPLICATION. This class of behavior requires the student to use abstractions in particular and concrete situations. The abstractions may be general ideas or they may be procedures, technical principles, and theories which must be remembered and applied. These two examples of educational objectives involve application:

> Application to the phenomena discussed in one paper of the scientific terms or concepts used in other papers.
>
> The ability to predict the probable effect of a change in a factor on a biological situation previously at equilibrium.

ANALYSIS. This behavior class requires the student to make clear the relative hierarchy of ideas in a body of material or to make explicit the relations among the ideas or both. Analysis clarifies the materials and indicates how they are organized and how they can vary their effects. These examples of educational objectives involve analysis:

> The ability to recognize unstated assumptions.
>
> Ability to check the consistency of hypotheses with given information and assumptions.
>
> The ability to recognize form and pattern in literary and artistic works as a means of understanding their meaning.

SYNTHESIS. This behavior class requires the student to assemble parts into a whole. It involves the process of arranging and combining pieces, parts, and so on to constitute a pattern or structure not clearly there before. These examples of educational objectives involve synthesis:

> Skill in writing, using an excellent organization of ideas and statements.
>
> Ability to propose ways of testing hypotheses.
>
> Ability to make mathematical discoveries and generalizations.

EVALUATION. This class consists of judgments about the value of material and methods used for particular purposes. The judgments may be quantitative or qualitative, and they may involve the application of standards of acceptability determined by the student or given to him by the teacher. The following examples of educational objectives involve evaluation:

The ability to indicate logical fallacies in arguments.
The ability to compare a work with others of recognized excellence.

The *Taxonomy* includes test questions which apply to each of the six classes of behavior and which ingeniously illustrate both the behavior each class embraces and the type of item which can measure achievement of the objective of each class.

How do the two schemes for classifying behavior compare? The test of any system for classifying behavior is its usefulness for task analysis, which, in turn, should enable the teacher to distinguish various performances and to establish the necessary learning conditions for achieving these performances. If we use this test, we find that Gagné's classes of behavior are more useful than those of Bloom and his associates. Although the *Taxonomy* has greater breadth and variety in the number and type of instructional objectives it embraces, it presents two difficulties for task analysis. First, the educational objectives lists do not meet Mager's requirements for task descriptions, usually because they lack a careful description of the conditions under which the desired performance must occur. For example, the *Taxonomy* lists as an objective the "ability to propose ways of testing hypotheses." Does this mean that when the student is given various experimental procedures and materials he can select and combine those which will be valid and reliable tests of hypotheses? Or does it mean that when presented with a theoretical problem and the available data the student can deduce appropriate hypotheses and procedures for testing them? The general objective may indicate either or both of these more specific objectives, even though each requires significantly different performance. A student could be capable of performing one objective but not the other. Second, each of the formal characteristics listed in the *Taxonomy* does not clearly fall into one distinct class. Gagné (1965b, p. 40), for example, asks how "knowledge of generalization" is distinguished from "interpretation" (which falls under the class *comprehension*) and how both are distinguished from "comprehending the interrelationships of ideas" (which comes under *analysis*). Of course, when the classes of behavior are not distinct, it becomes difficult to classify instructional objectives and to determine their appropriate learning conditions—the major purpose of task analysis.

On the other hand, Gagné's classes of behavior provide for both explicit statements of instructional objectives and for relatively distinct behavior categories. Because his behavior classes are themselves products of research on conditions of learning, they have particular usefulness for task analysis. What we may lose in richness and breadth in Gagné's classification, we gain in greater precision in the design of instruction.

You should now return to objective 5 (p. 31) and determine how well you have achieved it.

QUESTION 2-3

Miss Pegg tried to decide which of Gagné's classes of behavior (or types of learning) her instructional objective involved. This was the objective: Given ten rock specimens, the students will identify the five which are fossils. Which of the following classes of behavior includes this objective? (a) verbal association; (b) concept learning; (c) problem solving.

After you have made your choice, explain your rejection of the two remaining choices.

SUMMARY

This chapter distinguished between educational and instructional objectives and pointed out the relationship of the two. It made a distinction between explicit and implicit statements and described the arguments for and against the use of explicit statements. The second section described two methods of task description and the commonality of the requirements of the two methods. The last section of the chapter defined task analysis and described and compared two systems for classifying instructional objectives. In general, the chapter considered the relationship of explicit statements of instructional objectives to important decisions the teacher must make.

SUGGESTED READINGS

Two very readable articles discuss the relationship between educational and instructional objectives:

Gagné, Robert M., "Educational Objectives and Human Performance," in *Learning and the Educational Process, ed.* J. D. Krumboltz, pp. 1–24. Chicago: Rand McNally & Co., 1965.

Tyler, Ralph W., "Some Persistent Questions on the Defining of Objectives," in *Defining Educational Objectives,* ed. C. M. Lindvall. Pittsburgh: University of Pittsburgh Press, 1964.

A very delightful programed book teaches you how to make adequate task descriptions:

Mager, Robert F., *Preparing Objectives for Programed Instruction.* Palo Alto, Calif.: Fearon Publishers, Inc., 1962.

Task analysis is a much more complicated topic. Substantial discussions appear in the three following articles:

Gagné, Robert M., "The Analysis of Instructional Objectives for the Design of Instruction," in *Teaching Machines and Programed Learning, II: Data and Directions,* ed. R. Glaser, pp. 21–65. Washington, D.C.: Department of Audiovisual Instruction, National Education Association, 1965.

Miller, Robert B., "Analysis and Specification of Behavior for Training," in *Training Research and Education,* ed. R. Glaser, pp. 31–62. Pittsburgh: University of Pittsburgh Press, 1962.

———, "Task Description and Analysis," in *Psychological Principles in System Development,* ed. R. M. Gagné, pp. 187–230. New York: Holt, Rinehart & Winston, Inc., 1962.

PART TWO

ENTERING BEHAVIOR

Part 2 describes the second component of the basic teaching model by dealing with the student as he presents himself for instruction. The student, of course, is a many-splendored organism, and, as such, presents many more facets and capabilities than a teacher could or should cope with. To focus on those aspects of student capacity which have fairly direct relevance to instruction, I use the term *entering behavior*. Chapter 3 defines this term and shows its relationship to the components of the basic teaching model. That chapter also describes entering behavior as learning sets, learning abilities, and learning styles. The basic theme is the need for the teacher to make accurate determinations and assessments of entering behavior when instruction is planned and provided. The three remaining chapters deal with particular aspects of entering behavior. Chapter 4 considers the development and measurement of intelligence to show how maturation and heredity impose limitations on our choice of instructional objectives and procedures and to demonstrate the usefulness of IQ in making instructional decisions. Chapter 5 deals with the attitudes, values, and personality of the student in terms of motivational theory and practice. It describes four broad motivational functions the teacher must perform to maintain or increase student vigor. Finally, Chapter 6 deals with socioeconomic status, especially as this relates to the education of the disadvantaged child.

With the possible exception of Chapter 5 (on motivation) Part 2 does not tell you how to accommodate differences in the students' entering behavior. Such accommodation is the subject matter of the next two parts of the book, on instructional procedures and educational innovations. The underlying, practical assumption for Part 2 is the need for the teacher to base instruction on careful assessments of the entering behavior of the students. Whereas the terminal behavior described in Chapter 2 defines the point at which you end instruction, the entering behavior described in Part 2 defines the point at which you begin instruction. You can begin instruction of your students only after you decide what you want them to be able to do and what they can already do before they engage in a new pursuit of knowledge and skill.

Entering Behavior: A Concept

3

This chapter concerns what the student has already learned, or should have learned, when he presents himself for further instruction. The primary purpose here is to describe what entering behavior includes and how it relates to instructional objectives. The primary emphasis is on a description of entering behavior which is useful for the planning and execution of instruction. The first section of the chapter defines entering behavior and distinguishes it from and relates it to terminal performance. It then compares this concept of entering behavior with similar concepts—readiness, maturation, individual differences, and personality. The second section of the chapter describes categories or classes of entering behavior—learning sets, learning abilities, and learning styles. The final section deals with the assessment of entering behavior and the use of this information in planning instruction.

Upon reading the first section of this chapter (on the definition of entering behavior), you should be able to meet these objectives:

1. List the major characteristics of entering behavior.
2. Distinguish entering behavior from and relate it to terminal performance by pointing out similar and dissimilar characteristics.
3. Distinguish entering behavior from and relate it to readiness, maturation, individual differences, and personality by pointinig out similar and dissimilar characteristics.

4. Illustrate relevant entering behavior for an instructional objective of your own choice.

Upon reading the second section of this chapter (on learning sets, abilities, and styles), you should be able to meet these objectives:

5. List the major characteristics of these concepts: learning to learn, learning sets, learning structures, learning abilities, conceptual tempos, and selection strategies.

6. Provide an illustration of each of the concepts listed in the previous objective.

7. Describe and illustrate the usefulness of each concept as a description of entering behavior for particular instructional objectives.

8. Describe the similarities and differences among these concepts by referring to their characteristics.

Upon reading the third section of this chapter (on the use of entering behavior), you should be able to meet these objectives:

9. Describe the basis for determining what entering behavior is required and provide an illustration of this basis.

10. Describe how entering behavior can be assessed and provide an illustration of this assessment.

11. Describe all the alternative decisions the teacher can make in the case of too much or too little entering behavior.

A DEFINITION OF ENTERING BEHAVIOR

The folly of requiring the student to perform in ways for which he is inadequately prepared is so often repeated we forget that it is entirely avoidable. No matter what feats of will, self-denial, and enthusiasm the student may perform and no matter how much dedication, love, and imagination the teacher may supply, the student cannot acquire new performances based on other performances which he has not acquired. Learning builds on learning in the way success builds on success. When the foundation blocks are missing, future construction, if possible at all, is a very precarious affair. To make your teaching less precarious, you should understand what entering behavior means and how to use it.

Characteristics and Illustrations

Entering behavior describes the behaviors the student must have acquired before he can acquire particular new terminal behaviors. More simply, entering behavior describes the present status of the student's knowledge and skill in reference to a future status the teacher wants him to attain. Entering behavior, therefore, is where the instruction must always begin. Terminal behavior is where the instruction concludes. We can describe teaching as getting the student from where he is to where we would like him to be—as moving from entering to terminal behavior. Together, descriptions of entering and terminal behavior define the limits of instructional responsibility for each discrete act of teaching.

Now you already know that teachers do not usually observe and test behaviors; they observe and test performances, which are the results of behaviors. We could as easily (and perhaps with greater precision) refer to entering behavior as *entering performances* because the teacher is interested in these end products of previous instruction in planning future instruction. I use *entering behavior,* however, because this is the term used in the research literature and in journal discussions. You should remember, however, that, although we say entering *behavior,* we mean entering *performances.*

A list of entering behavior reveals two characteristics: The statements are explicit and refer to specific, observable performances and the list as a whole is generally more comprehensive than the corresponding list of terminal performances. Consider the two lists of entering behavior which follow. The first is for the program on time telling, to which I referred in the previous chapter. The authors gave this description of the terminal performance for that program: "The abilities of writing and saying aloud the time indicated by the clock to an accuracy of one-minute intervals." Now here is the list of entering behavior (Glaser and Reynolds, 1964):

1. Select the smaller of two objects, e.g., the short hand or the long hand of the clock.
2. Follow pointer directions, e.g., "What does the little hand point to?"
3. Follow verbal directions, e.g., "Write the number in the little box" or "Turn the page."
4. Recognize, write, and say numbers from one to sixty.
5. Count by ones up to sixty and by fives up to sixty.

Consider now a second list of entering behavior with the corresponding list of terminal performances (Johnston, 1966). These objectives are for students in a physiology laboratory devoted to the study of the stimulation of muscles and reflexes.

Terminal performance no. 1: To be able to operate the grass model polygraph.

Entering behavior for terminal performance no. 1:

1. Can state purpose of the polygraph.
   a. Can state, define, and describe by example the three basic components of the polygraph.
   b. Can identify the three basic components of the polygraph.
   c. Can identify all the controls on the polygraph.

Terminal performance no. 2: To be able to operate the grass model S5 stimulator.

Entering behavior for terminal performance no. 2:

2. Can state the purpose of the S5 stimulator.
   a. Can state why this type (electrical) of stimulation is used.
   b. Can identify all controls of the S5 stimulator.

Terminal performance no. 3: To demonstrate the various features of skeletal muscle contraction by experimental means and to explain these results and correlate them with what actually occurs in the living animal.

Entering behavior for terminal performance no. 3:

3. Can define and explain
   a. Stimulus (1) subliminal, (2) minimal or threshold, (3) maximal, and (4) supermaximal.
   b. Latent period.
   c. Muscle contraction (1) isometric and (2) isotonic.
   d. Refractory period (1) absolute and (2) relative.
   e. Can recognize experimental isometric muscle recording setup.
   f. Can differentiate from graphs (1) simple muscle twitch, (2) wave summation, and (3) tetanization.

We can now review the first characteristic of a statement of entering behavior: It refers to specific, observable performances. In this respect entering performances are not distinguishable from terminal performances. Note, however, that descriptions of entering behavior (as illustrated in these lists) lack two characteristics of task descriptions: They do not describe the conditions under which the performance must occur, and they do not specify a standard of acceptability. Of course, a list of entering behavior could include all the characteristics of a list of task descriptions; the two lists here, which are typical of many, simply do not. In any case you should remember that, once the student can perform the tasks in the task description of today, that task description becomes the entering behavior statement of tomorrow.

The second characteristic of a statement of entering behavior is its generally comprehensive nature. In the list of entering behavior for the physiology laboratory, you can see that the student is expected to have acquired more entering behavior than he will acquire terminal performances. Even the list of entering behavior for the time-telling program is much more comprehensive than we would expect a list of terminal performances to be. We could not conceive a single program or lesson from which the student would learn all the performances included in this list—from performances as simple as understanding pointer directions to those as complicated as counting by fives and writing the correct time. The nature of teaching itself requires the teacher always to expect that the students have already learned more than he plans to teach them.

Now that we have defined and illustrated entering behavior, we can consider four concepts—readiness, maturation, individual differences, and personality—which relate to it. I will point out how these concepts are similar and dissimilar to the concept of entering behavior.

Readiness and Maturation

Readiness is the adequacy of the student's existing capacity in relation to some instructional objective (Ausubel, 1959). For example, reading readiness refers to performances the student must have acquired before he begins to read: the identification of different marks on the printed page as particular letters, the association of these letters with sounds previously heard, the combination of letters into syllables and words, and so on. When readiness refers to particular performances it is identical to entering behavior. Note that the definition of readiness does not indicate how the student acquired his existing capacity; it merely refers to the adequacy of his capacity.

If teachers always used the term *readiness* to refer to entering behavior, I could have avoided introducing the new term, *entering behavior,* and the risk of sounding jargonish. Readiness, however, is frequently confused with a related but different concept—maturation (Ausubel, 1959). Maturation refers to biological growth which occurs largely under the influence of heredity. When, for example, we observe Elvis' growth in height and weight, his increasing muscle size, and the deepening of his voice, we are observing his maturation. Note that the definition of maturation specifically indicates how it occurs—it is largely the result of hereditary influences. In maturation, certain structural changes must occur before a certain behavior can appear. When the psychologist observes certain capabilities occurring without the benefit of training and observes these same behaviors emerging in all children, he infers that maturation is at work (Martin and Stendler, 1959, p. 99).

What is the relationship between maturation and readiness? Readiness is a product of both training (or learning) and maturation. Several studies show that training is largely wasted if the child has not reached the prerequisite level of maturation. There is, for example, the classical study of Myrtle McGraw (1940) on toilet training. She used two sets of identical male twins to see whether she could speed up their toilet training. One member of each pair was given training from the second month of life. They were placed on the chamber daily at intervals of one hour, for seven hours a day. Their partners were started on toilet training at fourteen and twenty-four months, respectively. At the end of twenty-eight months, McGraw found that the boys whose training had been delayed had achieved as much control as their twins. She concluded that the maturation of certain muscles must precede effective toilet training. Readiness for toilet training, therefore, is based partly on maturation. The study also makes clear, however, that the training must be introduced sometime, that maturation alone will not provide the necessary control. This study and others like it merely indicate when training should be introduced not whether it should be introduced. Thus, readiness is a product of both training and maturation.

When the concepts of maturation and readiness are confused, the schools find themselves in the position described by David Ausubel (1959, p. 246):

> To equate the principles of readiness and maturation not only muddies the conceptual waters but also makes it difficult for the school to appreciate that insufficient readiness may reflect inadequate prior learning on the part of pupils because of inappropriate or ineffective instructional methods. Lack of maturation can thus become a convenient scapegoat whenever children manifest insufficient readiness to learn, and the school, which is thereby automatically absolved of all responsibility in the matter, consequently fails to subject its instructional practices to the degree of self-critical scrutiny necessary for continued educational progress. In short, while it is important to appreciate that the current readiness of pupils determines the school's current choice of instructional methods and materials, it is equally important to bear in mind that this readiness is partly determined by the appropriateness and efficiency of the previous instructional practices to which they have been subjected.

Ausubel implies that where lack of readiness is a product of lack of training, the teacher must increase readiness. Maturation alone will not manifest in the child the readiness to speak grammatically, read skillfully, and compose limericks with consummate poetical skill.

Unlike the term *readiness,* the term *entering behavior* avoids this conceptual confusion since it derives its meaning from the instructional design in which it is embedded. One cannot discuss entering behavior without relating it to specific instructional objectives and procedures. Since descriptions of entering behavior and terminal performances explicitly state the teacher's expectations and responsibilities, by using such descriptions we avoid the vagueness of the term *readiness* and the consequent irresponsibility.

Individual Differences

The psychology of individual differences is largely the study of group differences. This study classifies individuals by age, trait, sex, race, social class, and so on, and observes the differences within and between these groups. For within-group differences or differences within sex, race, and social class, for example, boys are compared with girls, whites with Negroes, and those in the lower class with those in the middle class. Between-group differences may involve comparing middle-class Negroes with lower-class Negroes or ten-year-old boys with ten-year-old girls. The single individual enters this study only to the extent that his particular attributes fit the groups being studied. That is, the study of how Elvis' various attributes are internally related is not the concern of the psychology of individual differences. The study of Elvis in the totality of his attributes is the study of personality, a different branch of psychological inquiry.

Entering behavior, you now know, refers to behavior the student must have acquired before he can acquire a new terminal performance; it refers to the present status of knowledge of a particular student in relation to some future status his teacher wants him to attain. Whereas the study of individual differences may yield information on, for example, the average intelligence of middle-class whites and middle-class Negroes, the description and assessment of entering behavior will tell you exactly what the particular student must and does know in relation to the attainment of a particular instructional objective. In the former case we are dealing with group averages and in the latter with the specific capabilities of a single individual. For our purposes, information on group averages, despite its general interest and importance, is not so useful as a description of what a student must be able to do in order to learn something else.

The measurement of intelligence (which I shall call IQ) is an important segment of the study of individual differences. On the basis of individual and group IQs, as you will see in the following chapter, teachers can make fairly reliable predictions of the general level of academic success students will achieve. These predictions are a direct application of the knowledge of individual differences to educational practice. Now IQ is a very general description of a student's entering behavior; it measures his previous learning of a wide variety of tasks. The questions arise: How accurate a predictor is IQ when we radically improve the quality of instruction, and how does its accuracy compare with that of more specific measures of previous learning?

To answer these questions, consider the following two studies. To determine the relationship of intelligence to instructional method, Lawrence Stolurow (1964) in typical studies set up two different program sequences. For example, he developed two programs to teach fractions. In the first program (the easier one), he ordered the fractions consecutively so that the students could anticipate what fractions would come next. In the second program (the harder one), he presented the fractions in mixed or scrambled sequences. Stolurow then compared the achievement of high- and low-ability groups on both programs. Findings in several such studies have been consistent. With the easier program achievement between high- and low-ability groups differed little. With the harder program, however, the high-ability group obtained scores much higher than those of the low-ability group. Stolurow suggests that the easier program did for the poor-ability group what the high-ability group could do for themselves. He hastens to add, however, that such findings do not imply that intelligence is uncorrelated to learning. They merely indicate that the most efficient instruction for students of low mental ability will produce achievement which has zero correlation with intelligence.

Lewis Eigen and John Feldhusen (1964) conducted a study with normal students in the ninth, tenth, and eleventh grades using a programed text and machine instruction on sets, relations, and functions. The researchers pretested and posttested the students. The researchers also measured how much of the material the students could transfer or apply to novel test situations. Tables 3-1 and 3-2 summarize some of their findings. Acquisition refers to achievement, or how much of the material is learned. Transfer refers to the application of what is learned. The tables concern three variables: acquisition, transfer, and IQ. By partialing out IQ we can observe in the first table the direct relationship between acquisition and transfer. In the second table, by eliminating acquisition we can observe the relationship of transfer and IQ. The correlations in the first table are plainly much higher than those in the second table. More relevant to our discussion here are these correlations of pretest, posttest, and IQ:

IQ and posttest	0.455
IQ and posttest (pretest partialed out)	0.180
IQ and posttest (pretest and scores on the Iowa Test of Basic Skills partialed out)	−0.071
Posttest and Iowa tests (IQ and pretest partialed out)	0.414

The trend is clear: In programed instruction IQ may be a much less reliable predictor of achievement than the previous achievement level of the student in those areas directly related to the content of instruction. This study suggests that a direct assessment of entering behavior

TABLE 3-1

PARTIAL CORRELATIONS BETWEEN ACQUISITION AND TRANSFER WITH IQ PARTIALED OUT (after Eigen and Feldhusen, 1964).

All	0.764
Machine instruction	0.719
Programed text	0.837
Ninth grade	0.819
Tenth grade	0.768
Eleventh grade	0.701

All figures significant beyond the 0.01 level.

TABLE 3-2

PARTIAL CORRELATIONS BETWEEN TRANSFER AND IQ WITH ACQUISITION PARTIALED OUT (after Eigen and Feldhusen, 1964).

All	0.155
Machine instruction	0.301
Programed text	—0.130
Ninth grade	0.130
Tenth grade	—0.012
Eleventh grade	0.437

under optimal instructional conditions is more useful than a general assessment of intelligence. Similarly, the ability to transfer what has been learned by programed instruction is determined more by how much the student has learned than by IQ.

Two chapters which follow, one on the measurement of intelligence and the other on the education of the disadvantaged child, make extensive use of the study of individual differences as an approach to the description of entering behavior. The assumption of those chapters is that knowledge about individual differences helps the teacher locate areas of entering behavior in which students may be deficient. In reading those chapters, however, you must remember that the description of individual differences is not equivalent to the description of entering behavior.

Personality

The psychology of personality is largely the study of hypothetical structures and processes within a person that dispose him to act in certain ways (Lazarus, 1963). A wide range of personality structures and processes have been proposed and, to some extent, investigated. If you are a Freudian, you explain your own and your friends' behavior in terms of conscious and unconscious processes and of the almost interminable, always exciting, and occasionally resolved conflicts among id (libido), superego, and ego. If you are a Rogerian (a follower of Carl Rogers), you believe that the self-concept determines behavior—the individual does not respond to the objective environment but to his perception of that environment no matter how personalized or distorted his perception may be. He sees himself as reformer, realist, and so on, and organizes his behavior to preserve and enhance this self-concept. You can also conceive of personality as the organization of a number of traits of the individual. In this case you describe the behavior of your friends as manifesting various degrees of dominance (or submission), capacity (or incapacity) for status, sociability (or unsociability), self-acceptance (or rejection), and so on. You assume these traits are consistent patterns of behavior in the individual. You emphasize not so much why the individual behaves as he does as how he behaves. You can also explain behavior in terms of the individual's secondary needs, such as the need for acquisition, achievement, dominance, or autonomy. Or you may prefer a different set, such as the need for self-actualization, esteem, love, or safety. The needs theoretically refer to psychological forces which organize our thinking and acting. To distinguish them from physical needs we often call them psychogenic needs. Finally (and my list is far from exhaustive), you can explain the personal behavior of your friends in terms of the psychology of learning by applying such concepts as drive, reinforcement, stimulus (or cue), and response. In Chapter 5, on motivation, I attempt to apply learning concepts to the explanation and management of student motivation.

What is the relationship between entering behavior and the study of personality? Undoubtedly entering behavior is a product of the many personality structures (or something like them) which the study of personality hypothesizes. Since entering behavior refers to present performances which reflect previous learning and since this previous learning both influences and is influenced by various personality structures and processes, we must conclude that a relationship between entering behavior and personality exists. The existence of this relationship does not mean, however, that we can use the terminology of personality theory to describe the entering behavior for particular instructional objectives or of particular students who try to achieve those objectives. As intriguing as your search for your students' self-concepts, ids, traits, and psychogenic needs may be, none of these concepts yields the precise descriptions of student performance which entering behavior requires. In fact, too great a preoccupation with the internal structures and processes of the student, whatever these may be, has often led the teacher away from an objective description of instructional objectives and entering behavior and, consequently, from any precise description of the limits of his instructional responsibilities. Although personality theory and research have considerable clinical importance and popular appeal, at this stage in their development, they are too general and too little tied to observable behavior to be applied in the design of instruction.

Chapter 5 uses the study of personality as an approach to the description of entering behavior to the extent that this study relates to maintaining and increasing student motivation. The assumption of that chapter is that knowledge of personality structures and processes, when tied to observable behavior, may help the teacher define certain of his continuing instructional responsibilities. These instructional responsibilities are described as *functions,* to distinguish them from the instructional *procedures,* which are capable of more specific description and application.

You should now return to objectives 1–4 (pp. 57–58) and determine how well you have achieved them.

QUESTION 3-1

Miss Pegg wants to teach her pupils to select correctly the vowel in all trigrams with the consonants, *b, f, d, t, s,* and *w.* (Examples are bat, den, fun, won, sit.) She makes certain each pupil can recite the alphabet without error and that he can name all printed letters.

Which of the following alternatives is your best prediction of the outcome of Miss Pegg's efforts?

(a) She is likely to succeed because her task is well described and she has made adequate provision for entering behavior.

(b) She has adequately defined neither entering nor terminal performance.

(c) She is likely to fail because she has not adequately defined entering behavior.

After making your choice, point out any inadequacies in Miss Pegg's description of either entering or terminal performance which you think exist.

CLASSES OF ENTERING BEHAVIOR

If you had to describe the entering behavior of your students as minute responses to minute stimuli, the description would be monumental and impractical. If you could classify these stimuli and responses and avoid both the generality of descriptions based on the study of individual differences and personality and the multiplicity of highly detailed descriptions, you would have a practical means for describing entering behavior. Although research on learning sets, abilities, and styles as entering behavior has only recently begun, it promises to distinguish classes of entering behavior which have relevance to and practical application in the design of instruction. This section describes learning sets, learning abilities, and learning styles, and relates each of them to the concept of entering behavior.

Learning Sets

I shall describe two types of learning sets. The first is properly called *learning to learn.* The second is called *learning set* and *learning structure.*

LEARNING TO LEARN. We commonly observe that our capacity to learn new tasks increases when we have practiced similar tasks. Henry Ellis (1965, p. 32) uses this illustration: After a person practices solving linear equations for several days, he improves his speed and accuracy in solving new linear equations. This progressive improvement in performance is known as learning to learn.

A series of experiments by Harry Harlow and his associates (1949), using both monkeys and children as subjects, provided some of the most convincing evidence for the usefulness of this concept. Figure 3-1 illus-

Fig. 3-1. *Apparatus used in experiment on learning to learn (after Harlow, 1949, p. 52).*

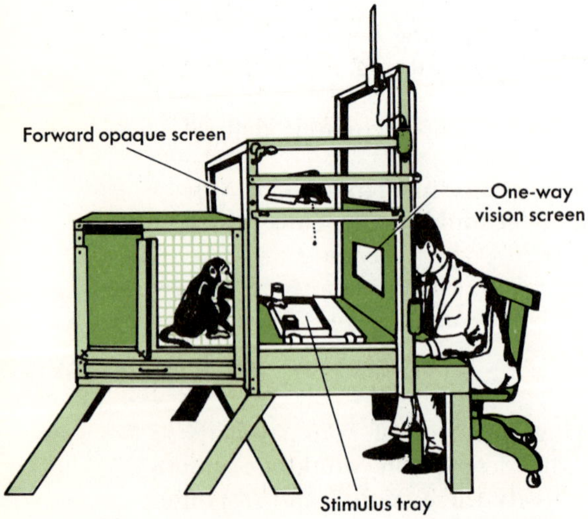

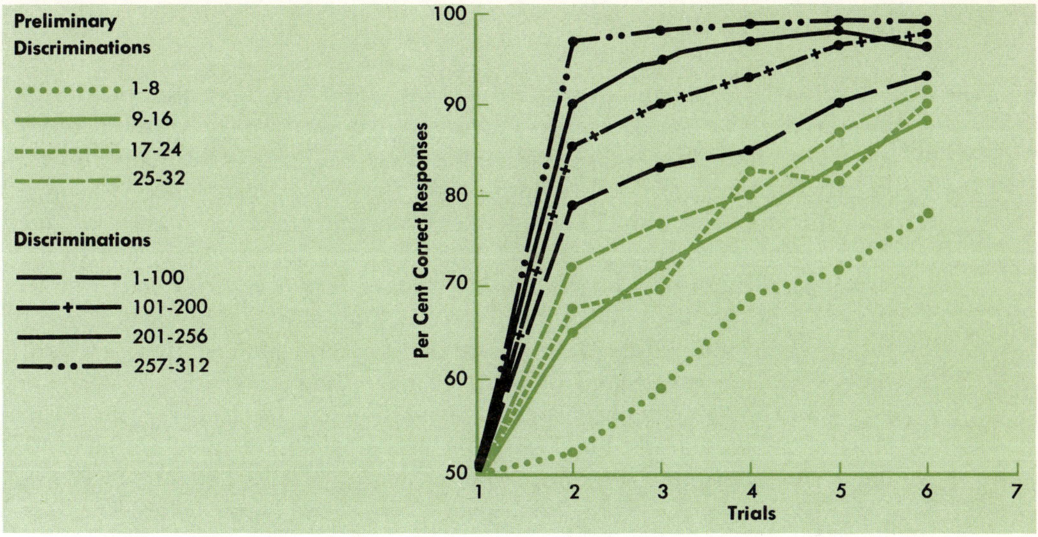

Fig. 3-2. *Learning curves for the same subjects for the first six trials in a series of more than 300 problems (after Harlow, 1949).*

trates the apparatus he used in his experiments with monkeys. The stimulus tray contained food wells which could be covered with various objects (similar to the game of concealing a coin under one of three shells). The forward opaque screen prevented the monkey from seeing which well the food (usually a raisin) was placed in. The one-way vision screen separated the monkey and the experimenter during trials. The objects placed over the wells were two blocks. For each test the two blocks were different in some dimension which could be easily seen —one black, the other white; one cylindrical, the other conical; one striped, the other plain; and so on. In each trial, the monkey was allowed to look under only one block. The best strategy for the monkey would be, for example, to look under the black block if he had failed to find the raisin under the white block in the preceding trial. In one experiment, eight monkeys learned to solve a series of 344 such problems. Figure 3-2 shows the results for the first six trials on different sets of these problems. If you carefully examine the legend for this figure, you will see that the bottom curve shows the performance of the monkeys on the first eight problems. This curve represents their worst performance. Their best performance is represented by the top curve, which shows that they made almost 100 per cent correct choices by the second trial for the last fifty-six problems. The other curves (with one exception) show that the speed and accuracy of the monkeys increased as the number of problems they learned to solve increased. By the end they attained almost total accuracy on the second and third trials. The monkeys had learned to learn.

What did the monkeys learn? You could say that they acquired insight. But we can be more precise. When we (monkeys and people) meet new situations, we must attend and respond to a great many things. Eventually we begin to see similarities between our previous learning and the new situation. The monkeys learned what to attend to and what to ignore in the problems. They learned, for example, not to respond to the position of the block (whether it was right or left) but to the color of the block (whether it was black or white). They also learned to switch. If the raisin were not under the first pattern they selected, they would try the second pattern the next time.

Additional evidence supports these findings on learning to learn. Harlow (1949) found about the same learning curves for children solving series of similar discrimination problems. An earlier study (Ward, 1937) required subjects to learn several lists of nonsense syllables. Lewis Ward found that they learned every succeeding list in fewer trials than they needed to learn those which preceded it. A more recent study (Keppel and Postman, 1966), using paired-associate materials, found that subjects gained skill in learning one pattern of associations by practicing on another pattern—evidence that the subjects were acquiring general paired-associate learning skill.

On the basis of this evidence we may conclude that entering behavior can sometimes be conceived as the general modes of attack available to the student for learning various tasks. If these general modes are to be useful, however, the tasks or instructional objectives must be similar to them—that is, the student must be expected to show about the same terminal performance under about the same conditions. When we introduce wide variation in the conditions or the performances, the advantages of learning to learn dissipate.

LEARNING SET AND STRUCTURES. Robert Gagné and his associates (1961, 1962) developed the more specific idea of learning sets. Gagné defines them as the capabilities the student possesses at any given stage in the learning of a given task. Although these capabilities are internal to the student, they are directly measurable as performances.

You can discover the sets necessary for learning a particular task by working backward from the task to the prerequisite capabilities. Beginning with the final task (the instructional objective), you ask: What capability does the student need if he is to perform this task successfully? The answer identifies a new task which is simpler and more general than the final task from which it was derived. However, the new task is basic to the learning of the final task and, in this sense, is subordinate to it. You continue this process of inquiry with the derived task. Again you ask: What must the student know to be capable of doing this task? The answer gives you the second level of subordinate capabilities. The process continues until you have discovered increasingly simple and more general capabilities which with the higher capabilities, form a hierarchy. These hierarchies are *learning structures* (Gagné, 1965c, pp. 172–203).

Figure 3-3 shows the learning structure for the topic *ordering numbers.* This hierarchy indicates that the most basic learning sets for this task are (1) the child's ability to say the names of the common numbers from one to ten and (2) his ability to hold and make marks with a pencil (both forms of stimulus-response learning). In the next level of the hierarchy the child must be able to print letters and draw geometric forms (a form of chaining). Next, he must know how to count and to name a printed numeral correctly—to say "seven," for example, when he sees 7 (a form of verbal learning). Next he must be able to differentiate one specific object (a marble, for example) from two, two from three, and so on. He must also distinguish between printed numerals (the printed 9 from the printed 6) and between other symbols (+ from ×). This ability to distinguish between confusable numerals and symbols is a form of multiple-discrimination learning. At the next step in the learning structure, the child must have acquired the concepts of *like* and *different* so that he can say that any two (or more) objects, pictures, or symbols are alike or different. He must also know the concepts of *set* and *member of a set.* A set is a variety of collections of specific objects, and a member of a set is a single object in each collection. The child must also know the concepts *adding to* and *taking away,* as well as the concepts of *separation* and *joining.* These concepts are important because the child will be asked later to add something to or take something away from a set or to join together two separated sets or to separate some members of a set from the others. At the next level the child is ready to acquire principles by relating these concepts. The principles may be: The set called *two* is formed by adding a member to the set *one;* the set called *three* is formed by adding a member to *two;* the set called *four* is formed by adding a member to *three.* He learns the principle: Zero is the set which is formed by taking away one member from set *one.* The child learns to add by joining sets: By combining sets *three* and *two* or sets *four* and *one,* the set *five* is obtained. In effect, the child learns that the statements 3 + 2, 4 + 1, and 5 all name the same numbers. Once the child has acquired these principles, he is able to order numbers—that is, he is able to count.

A comparison of learning to learn and learning sets suggests the following conclusions. The capabilities in learning to learn are often those at the base of Gagné's learning structures. These are the most basic and general capabilities the student requires. Learning sets differ from these capabilities in two ways: They are more specific and are defined in relation to particular instructional objectives; and they are

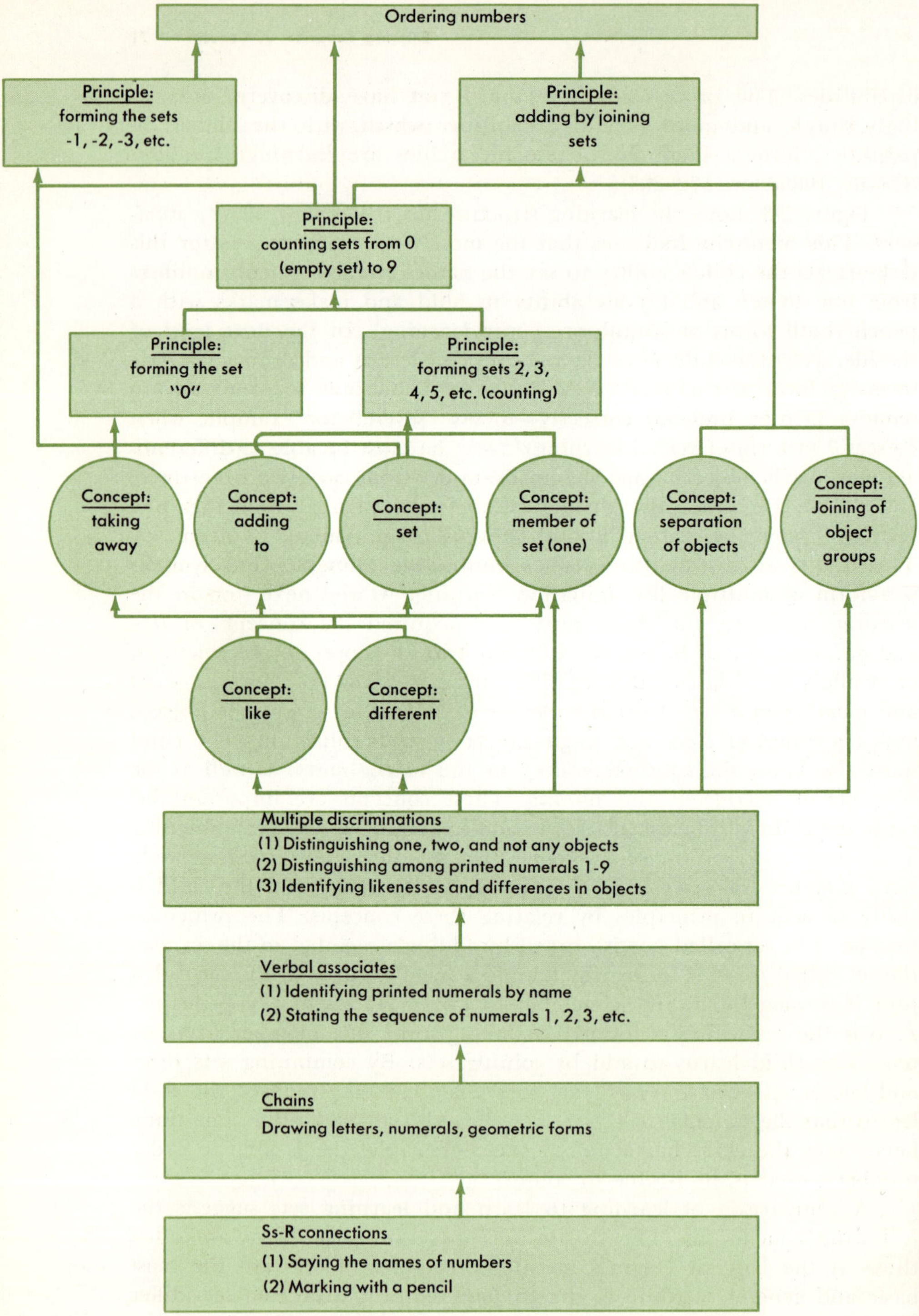

Fig. 3-3. *A learning structure for number operations (after Gagné, 1965c, p. 181).*

hierarchically related. The idea that some learning sets are more basic than, or are subordinate to, other sets is an important expansion of the concept of learning to learn. Both concepts enable us to describe entering behavior as *classes of performances:* printing numerals and symbols, distinguishing between any object or symbol that is alike or different, and adding to and taking away from any set. By describing classes of performances the teacher is often spared the necessity of describing every required detail of performance as entering behavior.

The concept of learning sets and structures applies to the curriculum in English and social sciences as well as to that in mathematics and science. Fred Tyler (1964) suggests that an analysis of the former curriculum in terms of learning structures would answer questions like these: When should the student study restrictive and nonrestrictive clauses? When is the student ready for the *Ode to Immortality* and *Macbeth*? Tyler provides two examples from William James in which the student (James) lacked the necessary learning sets. First, James (1958) misinterpreted what the boatman in *Lord Ullin's Daughter* expected to receive for his services:

> I'll row you o'er the ferry.
> It is not for your silver bright,
> But for your winsome lady.

James, at eight years, concluded that the boatman was to receive the lady as payment, whereas the boatman intended to win merely the lady's favor. Second, misinterpretation is even more likely when the student lacks the learning sets for the figurative use of language, as in this example from *Troilus and Cressida,* in which the lovesick Troilus answers Pandarus, who has just been praising Cressida, Troilus' sweetheart:

> . . . thou answers't, she is fair;
> *Pour'st in the open ulcer of my heart*
> *Her eyes, her hair, her cheek, her gait, her voice.*

One hesitates to conjecture what interpretation of the italicized lines a student who lacks the learning sets for figurative language would provide. Would such a student compassionately suggest medical treatment for an ulcerated heart when psychological help was what poor Troilus needed?

Learning Abilities

Learning abilities are the various processes by which the individual acquires new performances. Arthur Jensen (1960) hypothesizes that individuals differ in learning abilities in a limited number of ways. He gives two examples of such differences: Some students learn better when they pace their own work, while other students learn better when the machine sets the pace; and, although two students may do equally well under spaced-practice conditions, one student may do considerably better than the other under massed-practice conditions. Jensen (1965) found that individuals also differ in their susceptibility to the factors which cause forgetting: retroactive inhibition, proactive inhibition, and response competition (see Chapter 9). According to Jensen (1965) a student's performance on any given task will be a product of the levels of his learning abilities and the degree to which the task involves these abilities. As of now, the basic learning abilities have not been identified or measured—a job for the educational psychologist of the present and future.

Jensen (1963) provides one study which suggests that there are several learning abilities rather than a single, unitary ability and that these abilities sometimes bear little relationship to IQ. Jensen argued that the usual intelligence tests are achievement tests: They tell us more about what the child has learned outside the test situation than about his capacity to learn in a novel environment. He contrived a learning situation which was equally novel for mentally retarded, average, and gifted children of varied socioeconomic backgrounds. The experimental apparatus required the children to push buttons in response to various stimuli—geometric forms such as triangles and squares displayed on a small screen. The children had to learn which of the twelve push buttons would turn on a green light for each of the twelve stimuli. The findings were what one would generally expect. The gifted children performed better than the average children, the average children better than the retarded. Figure 3-4, however, shows some very interesting exceptions within the retarded group. The two top curves show the performances of four of the retarded children on the first and last tests. These four children, whom Jensen calls *fast learners,* scored above average on all the tests. The bottom two curves show the performances of the six slowest learners in the retarded group. Clearly the performance of the retarded group as a whole varied widely. One of the two fastest learners in the entire group of subjects was a retarded child whose IQ was 65! The other was a gifted child whose IQ was 145. The retarded child was below average in scholastic achievement; the gifted child, far above average.

This study lends support to Jensen's notion of learning abilities. For this particular task, some retarded children had the special ability required. On some other learning task the four successful retarded children might have been slow learners. Jensen suggests that retarded children may turn in poor school performances because they lack verbal learning ability. For example, we know that attaching names to objects allows us to refer to those objects in their absence and to use their verbal symbolic form in many abstract contexts. Jensen refers to this as *labeling behavior.* A child who does not have the ability to use labels is severely handicapped in many scholastic functions.

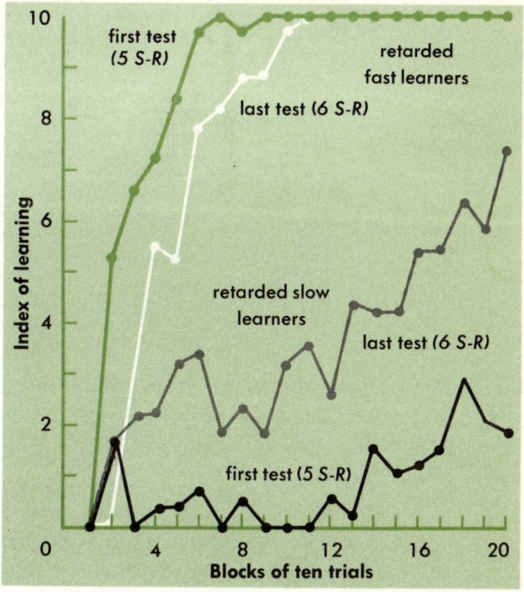

Fig. 3-4. *Learning curves on the first and last tests of four retarded* Ss *who had learning scores above the mean of the gifted group and curves on the same tests of the six slowest learners in the retarded group (after Jensen, 1963, p. 133).*

Learning abilities, as conceived by Jensen, are related to learning to learn, learning sets, and entering behavior. As basic processes which the individual employs in learning a wide assortment of tasks, learning abilities are similar to the concept of learning to learn. Because learning abilities are involved to varying degrees in different tasks, they are similar to the concept of learning sets. Because they are prerequisite capabilities for achieving instructional objectives, learning abilities relate to entering behavior. Since learning abilities occupy an intermediate position between overspecified and overgeneralized descriptions of entering behavior, their identification will quite possibly prove useful in designing instruction.

Learning Styles

Learning styles are personal ways in which individuals process information in the course of learning new concepts and principles. Here I discuss two types of learning styles—conceptual tempos and selection

Fig. 3-5. *Two sample items from Matching Familiar Figures (MFF) test (after Kagan, 1965).*

strategies. In Chapter 10 you will discover how learning styles are related to the learning of concepts. Here they are discussed as aspects of entering behavior.

Conceptual tempos. These are basic dispositions of the individual either to reflect upon his solution of a problem or to make impulsive and unconsidered responses. Jerome Kagan and his associates (1964, 1965, and 1966) have identified children with two different conceptual tempos: The child with the impulsive, or fast, tempo solves a problem with little or no delay. The child with the reflective, or slow, tempo considers alternative problem solutions and, therefore, delays his responses. To determine tempo Kagan used a Matching Familiar Figures (MFF) test and

Fig. 3-6. *Two sample items from Haptic Visual Matching (HVM) test (after Kagan, 1965, p. 137).*

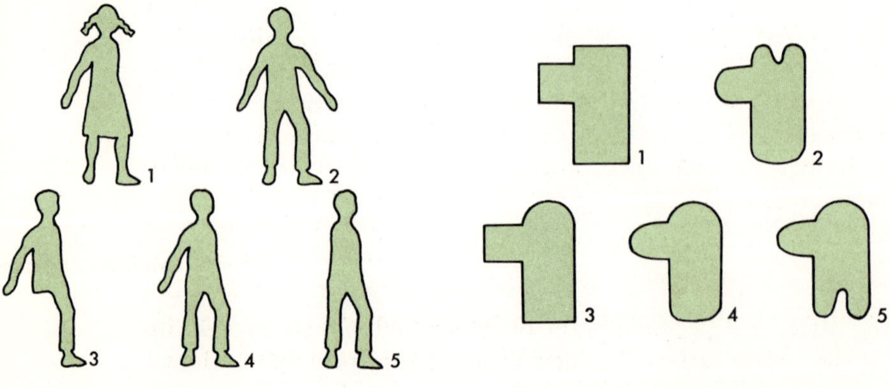

a Haptic Visual Matching (HVM) test. Figures 3-5 and 3-6 illustrate sample items from these tests. In the MFF test the researcher shows the child the drawing at the top and six strikingly similar ones. The child must select the drawing which is identical to the one at the top. The researcher records the amount of time the child uses to make his response. In the HVM test the child explores with his fingers a wooden figure which he cannot see. The researcher then presents the child with five wooden figures he can see. His task is to select the figure that corresponds to the form he explored with his fingers. Again, the researcher records the decision time.

This study of the reflection-impulsivity dimension yielded these results (Kagan, 1965): (1) reflection tends to increase with age, as does accuracy; (2) the tendency to display fast or slow decision times was relatively stable over periods as long as twenty months; (3) the tendency toward reflection or impulsivity shows in the performance of many tasks —such as selecting the correct response from a list of alternatives, providing the correct response in the absence of an alternative, and answering questions in an interview situation; and (4) the dispositions seem to be linked to some basic aspects of the child's personality. Kagan (1965, pp. 154–55) writes:

> At present it is believed that a major determinant of a child's position involves the differential value placed upon two standards espoused by the child's social milieu that are inconsistent. One standard demands, "Get the answer quickly," while the second exhorts, "Do not make a mistake." When problems are difficult, as in MFF or HVM, these standards are mutually exclusive. It is suggested that the impulsive child places a greater value on "quick success" than he does on "avoiding failure.". . . This argument suggests that the reflective child is a low-risk child who avoids situations that are potentially dangerous and productive of failure, humiliation, or harm. The impulsive child prefers a high-risk orientation.

One study (Kagan, Pearson, and Welch, 1966) showed that impulsive children can be trained to be reflective under two specially designed tutoring conditions: a normal nurturant condition, in which the tutor merely comments positively on the child's choices on the two tests: and an adult-identification condition, in which the tutor persuades the child that if he becomes more reflective he will be more like the tutor. In a one-hour training period all children delayed each response for a period of ten or fifteen seconds, answering only when the experimenter told them they were allowed to. The one-hour training in delay did cause the impulsive children to take more time to answer items on tests taken up to a few weeks after the training period. Unfortunately, however, the additional time did not increase their accuracy. And the attempt to get impulsive children to identify with an adult did not produce significantly better results, either.

Kagan believes that the study of reflective and impulsive children has three educational implications. First, the teacher should adjust his procedures and the tempo of his teaching to accommodate the two different modes of learning. He should avoid the tendency to view the reflective child as slower and less bright than the impulsive child. This tendency shows up in bright, impulsive children themselves, who tend to think that they are brighter than bright, reflective children. Second, the teacher should not punish the impulsive child for incorrect answers with sarcasm, laughter, or rejection, especially when he rewards children who offer correct answers quickly. The teacher who behaves in this way handicaps the impulsive child with only average ability. Finally, teachers vary in their teaching tempos, some speaking fast and offering a rapid flow of ideas and others encouraging the child to consider alternatives and placing no premium on speed. The tempo of the teacher should be tailored to the tempo of the child.

SELECTION STRATEGIES. Jerome Bruner and his associates (1956) describe various ways in which individuals can learn concepts. These methods, called *selection strategies,* control the order in which examples and nonexamples of a concept appear. They have three purposes: They maximize the opportunity to obtain useful information about the concept; they reduce the strain of assimilating and keeping track of information; and they regulate the amount of risk we take in reaching a solution —we may take either the risky or the safe course.

Four selection strategies have been identified. In the first of these, *conservative focusing,* the individual uses an example of the concept as a focus and changes one attribute of the example at a time to find those attributes which are essential. Robert Travers (1963, pp. 129–30) uses this example. The student visits a large furniture store and finds a piece of French Provincial furniture, a chair. Wishing to acquire the concept *French Provincial furniture,* he uses the first example as his focus and finds another chair similar in every respect but one, its finish. He discovers that this chair is also French Provincial. He then finds a chair in which only the upholstery is different and discovers that this chair is also French Provincial. By selecting different chairs and varying one attribute at a time, the student will eventually discover the essential and nonessential attributes of French Provincial chairs. This strategy almost guarantees success: It maximizes the opportunity to obtain useful information; it reduces the strain of remembering information through the use of the focus example; and every choice is safe, in the sense that every choice will yield some useful information. *Focus gambling* is a similar selection strategy in that the individual uses a focus example, and dissimilar in that he changes more than one attribute at a time. In Travers' example, the student using this strategy chooses as his next example of a French Provincial chair one that has a higher back, straighter legs, and a different finish (three attributes). If the clerk tells him that he has not chosen a French Provincial chair, he does not know which attributes should be excluded. He has gambled and lost. This strategy holds out the possibility of acquiring the concept with the use of fewer examples than those required in conservative focusing. When the student, however, uses as an example a chair which is not French Provincial, he loses the possible gain in time. In Kagan's terms, impulsive children use focus gambling while reflective children use conservative focusing.

In the two other selection strategies, *simultaneous scanning* and *successive scanning,* the student formulates one or more hypotheses of what the concept may be and then looks for examples. In *simultaneous scanning* the student formulates several hypotheses about the attributes a French Provincial chair must have. Each time he encounters a different French Provincial chair, he decides which hypotheses to keep and which to eliminate. Simultaneous scanning is, as you can see, very exacting for the individual must deal with several independent hypotheses and carry them all in his mind. In *successive scanning* the student tests a single hypothesis at a time. He forms his idea (hypothesis) of the characteristics of a French Provincial chair, and he tests his hypothesis against each chair he encounters. Successive scanning reduces the amount of information which must be remembered, but it also reduces the amount of relevant information each encounter may provide. If he tests one hypothesis at a time, the student must return to chairs he has previously encountered in testing other hypotheses.

Individuals may vary their strategy with the concept or they may retain a particular strategy regardless of the concept they seek to acquire. In the light of Kagan's findings, one is tempted to believe the latter. Travers suggests that the teacher should adjust the selection strategy to the ability of the child. A simultaneous scanning strategy requires more ability than a conservative focusing strategy. Also, in line with Kagan's findings on reflective and impulsive children, the strategies which involve higher risk (simultaneous scanning and focus gambling) may be attractive to impulsive students with fast tempos, while the low-risk strategies may attract reflective students with slow tempos. In any case, selection strategies are one means of classifying entering behavior for instructional objectives which involve the learning of concepts and principles and problem solving. Although Kagan's conceptual tempos and Bruner's selection strategies refer to rather broad areas of entering behavior, both suggest categories for which the teacher can make provision.

You should now return to objectives 5–8 (p. 58) and determine how well you have achieved them.

QUESTION 3-2

Mr. Chips selected this statement as his instructional objective: When presented with examples of the figurative use of language in poetry, the student always correctly indicates the figure of speech employed. In determining the entering behavior for this objective, Mr. Chips did two things: Working backward from the objective, he asked what the student must be able to do before he could achieve the objective, and, in this way, Mr. Chips identified several levels of prerequisite performance; and in choosing examples of the various figures of speech during instruction, he decided which sequences he would allow students to use. Which two different classes of entering behavior was Mr. Chips considering? (a) Conceptual tempos and selection strategies; (b) learning sets and learning abilities; (c) learning to learn and learning abilities.

After making your choice, defend it by pointing out your reasons.

THE INSTRUCTIONAL USE OF ENTERING BEHAVIOR

In this section we briefly consider the problems of incorporating entering behavior in the actual planning of instruction. To do this we must determine what entering behavior is required, assess the entering behavior of the student, and make decisions based on the results of the assessment.

What Entering Behavior Is Required?

After you have made explicit statements of your instructional objectives, you can determine what entering behavior you will require. Essentially instruction should begin with what the student presently knows and should continue to where he is capable of the terminal performance under specified conditions and to a specified standard. Once you have stated your objective, you can decide what you will teach and what you will assume the student already knows. As you will see later, you may always change your instructional objective if, for some reason, it proves to be impractical. You will also see that instruction for new objectives does not begin strictly with new material but rather with the recall of previously learned responses appropriate to the learning of the new material. Finally, different entering behavior is required for different learning. Concept learning, for example, requires as entering behavior the previous learning of verbal associations and discriminations, while principle learning requires as entering behavior the previous learning of concepts. I treat the kinds of entering behavior required for skill, linguistic, concept, and principle learning in detail in Part 3.

Assessing Entering Behavior

After you have determined what entering behavior is necessary for your instructional objective, you must find out whether or not the student has acquired this behavior. This knowledge is best obtained through a test of entering behavior, especially if the list of entering behaviors is extensive. Each prerequisite behavior is the basis for writing three or four test items. You should distinguish a test of entering behavior from a pretest, which measures terminal performance before instruction begins. The pretest is frequently the same as or an alternate form of the posttest. A test of entering behavior, however, measures previous rather than present learning. On many occasions the teacher may wish to administer both a test of entering behavior and a pretest. Or occasionally the test of entering behavior may include items which measure how well the student can perform the component tasks of the terminal performance. It is often wise to include such items to find out whether the student has more entering behavior than you require.

Decisions on Entering Behavior

Once you have stated your objective and have determined and assessed entering behavior, you are ready to make various decisions. If the student has more than enough entering behavior, you may decide either to carry out your instructional plans or to alter your plans and begin instruction at a more advanced point. If the student lacks the necessary

QUESTION 3-3

Mr. B. Wright prepared a test of entering behavior on the topic of kinetic energy. He carefully included three or four items to measure each terminal performance in his list of instructional objectives. He then administered the test to his physics students, and all obtained scores of zero. Which of the following decisions should Mr. Wright make?

(a) He should prepare a new test of entering behavior.

(b) He should adopt a new list of instructional objectives.

(c) He should move ahead with his instructional plans because he has now ascertained that none of the students has knowledge about kinetic energy.

After selecting your answer, explain the basis for your selection and for your rejection of the two alternatives.

entering behavior, several alternatives are available. First, you can increase his entering behavior by review exercises, which will recall material learned earlier but now forgotten. Second, you can provide more instruction than you originally intended to by beginning at an earlier point. Finally, you can change your instructional objective either by choosing a different terminal performance or by lowering the standard. All these decisions are made in the pretutorial phase of the computer-based teaching model (Chapter 1). In any case the results of the determination and the assessment of entering behavior must become an integral part of your instructional plans.

You should now return to objectives 9–11 of this chapter (on p. 58) and determine how well you have achieved them.

SUMMARY

This chapter has developed the concept of entering behavior, the second component of the basic teaching model. We can describe entering behavior, only in the context of particular instructional objectives and particular students. By doing this, we avoid much of the ambiguity of related concepts—readiness, maturation, individual differences, and personality. The chapter also described three ways of classifying entering behavior: as learning sets, as learning abilities, and as learning styles. The most practical classification at this stage of our knowledge is learning sets, which, by using Gagné's procedure, we can translate into learning structures. Finally this chapter considered the practical use of entering behavior and the decisions we can make once entering behavior has been determined and assessed.

SUGGESTED READINGS

These articles will help you develop a proper conception of readiness and its relation to teaching:

Ausubel, David P., "Viewpoints from Related Disciplines: Human Growth and Development," *Teachers College Record,* 60 (1959), 245–54.

Tyler, Fred T., "Issues Related to Readiness to Learn," in *Theories of Learning and Instruction,* ed. E. R. Hilgard, Part I of the 63rd Yrbk. of the National Society for the Study of Education, pp. 210–39. Chicago: University of Chicago Press, 1964.

These articles deal with the different classes of entering behavior:

Gagné, Robert M., "The Acquisition of Knowledge," *Psychological Review,* 69 (1962), 355–65. Here Gagné explains learning sets.

Jensen, Arthur R., "Individual Differences in Concept Learning," in *Analyses of Concept Learning,* eds. H. J. Kluasmeier and C. W. Harris, pp. 139–54. New York: Academic Press Inc., 1966. Here Jensen describes learning abilities.

Kagan, Jerome, "Impulsive and Reflective Children: Significance of Conceptual Tempo," in *Learning and the Educational Process,* ed. J. D. Krumboltz, pp. 133–61. Chicago: Rand McNally & Co., 1965.

The Development and Measurements of Intelligence

4

As the title indicates, this chapter has two sections, the first on the development of intelligence and the second on the measurement of it. The first section presents a brief explanation of Jean Piaget's theory of intelligence, a description of the two school-related periods of development, and a discussion of the relationship of this theory to entering behavior. The work of Piaget and his associates dominates the study of intellectual development, but it does not embrace all the research that has been and remains to be done. However, to give somewhat fuller treatment to Piaget than would be possible if I were to consider also the research of other psychologists and to avoid giving an overly brief explanation of Piaget's work, which would fail to suggest any instructional applications, I have limited our consideration of intellectual development to his theory and findings. The major purpose in presenting Piaget is to suggest ways in which teachers may assess entering behavior (in the intellectual domain), analyze instructional objectives in terms of the various cognitive structures Piaget has described, and select instructional procedures appropriate for both the objectives and the entering behavior.

Whereas you may find the concepts in the first section of the chapter somewhat novel and difficult, you may find those in the second section, on the measurement of intelligence, easier and more familiar. The material in this second section constitutes, by far, most of the chapter. I have several reasons for presenting material on the measurement of intelligence at considerable length. First, the use of intelligence tests is very widespread in American education, and any informed teacher must know their nature, assets, and limitations. In fact, a great deal of the controversy which surrounds the tests pertains to their use and not to the tests themselves. Second, an impressive amount of educational research has attempted to establish relationships between scores students achieve on intelligence tests and scores these same students obtain on a host of achievement, special aptitude, personality, and attitude tests, and on other inventories. Third, the student's IQ has been the basis for many educational decisions on grade and track placement, on majors or courses of study, and on placement in advanced study in high school and college; and it has also been the basis for predictions about ultimate academic success (or failure) and even about success (or failure) in one's career or profession. Fourth, intelligence tests are major diagnostic devices for separating the bright and the dull (sometimes the very bright and the very dull) students. Fifth, intelligence tests within the last fifteen years have been linked very closely to the study of creativity and, consequently, have been subjected to a new kind of criticism. Whereas the old (and still current) argument is that the tests are prejudicial to race and social class, the more recent argument is that they are prejudicial to the bright, nonconformist student. The final, but not the least important, reason for the lengthy treatment of these tests is that they represent a very sophisticated level of psychological and educational measurement, and they have been emulated again and again in the development of other psychological and educational instruments.

Upon reading the first section of this chapter (on the development of intelligence), you should be able to meet these objectives:

1. State the general purpose of Piaget's work, using the terms *function, schema,* and *stages.*
2. Name the two functional invariants and distinguish them from and relate them to each other.
3. Distinguish and relate the concepts of *assimilation* and *accommodation.*
4. Give a biological and a psychological illustration of assimilation and accommodation.
5. Define *schema* in terms of structures and behavior sequences and show its relationship to assimilation and accommodation.
6. List the characteristics of the groupings in the period of concrete operations and give a definition and example of each characteristic.
7. Using the words *possible* and *real,* distinguish between the periods of concrete and formal operations.
8. Referring to the three derived characteristics of the period of

formal operations, distinguish between the two periods of development.

9. List three instructional applications of Piaget's study, referring to intelligence tests, curriculum development, and instructional procedures.

10. Using the characteristics of the periods of concrete and formal operations, illustrate how the teacher may use these characteristics (schemas) for instructional purposes. Also indicate how the application of these schemas is limited.

Upon reading the second section of this chapter (on the measurement of intelligence), you should be able to meet these objectives:

11. Distinguish between intelligence *A* and intelligence *B;* describe a test theory of intelligence in terms of the capacity for reasoning; compare the test theory with Piaget's theory of intelligence in terms of invariant functions, a single factor of intelligence, and a time dimension (or development).

12. Distinguish and show the relationship between general-factor and multifactor theories of intelligence.

13. Distinguish among the three types of intelligence tests: individual tests, group tests, and test batteries; point out the assets and limitations of each type; illustrate appropriate uses of each type.

14. Describe (in terms of correlation and percentage agreement) the relationship between IQ and school achievement; illustrate how narrowing or broadening the sample affects these correlations.

15. Describe stereotypes of bright and dull children and show the relationship of these stereotypes to life expectancies; physical, intellectual, and social development; and occupational level.

16. Describe stereotypes of IQ differences for males and females and show the relationship of these stereotypes to the data on arithmetic reasoning, other skills and aptitudes, and school achievement.

17. Describe the stereotypes of artists or other creative individuals; indicate the shortcomings of the Getzels-Jackson study of IQ and creativity; and describe the probable relationship between IQ and creativity.

18. List the alleged limitations of the notion of general intelligence and the use of IQ tests and show how these allegations are related to misconceptions of *g*, narrow interpretations of democracy and equality, and personal emotional bias.

19. List the practical limitations of IQ tests and show how these could be reduced by the appropriate analysis of intellectual processes; indicate how IQ becomes a better predictor of school achievement as we increase our precision in describing entering behavior and as we improve the quality of instruction.

THE DEVELOPMENT OF INTELLIGENCE

Piaget and his coworkers at the Rousseau Institute and the Centre International d'Epistémologie Génétique, both in Geneva, Switzerland, have given us our most elaborate theory of intellectual development in addition to a considerable amount of supporting data. I have devoted this section to an explanation of some basic theoretical concepts in Piaget's system, a description of the two major periods of intellectual development which correspond to the child's school years, and an examination of the possible applications of Piaget's work to the assessment of and the provision for entering behavior. This brief summary of Piaget's work can hardly do justice to his more than twenty-five books and 150 articles, many of which have not been translated from French (Flavell, 1963, p. 11). Furthermore, Piaget is very difficult to understand and explain because his work requires rather high levels of entering behavior in the areas of mathematics, logic, and epistemology. Here I can only introduce Piaget's system, hoping both to provide enough instruction to enable you to achieve the objectives for this section and to indicate to the interested student where he may find more detailed treatment of Piaget's monumental work.

Basic Aspects of Intellectual Functioning

I begin consideration of Piaget's system with a description of the important basic concepts: functional invariants, organization, adaptation, assimilation and accommodation, and schemas. You should keep in mind several general characteristics of Piaget's system as you consider these concepts. First, Piaget is chiefly interested in the theoretical and qualitative development of what he calls *intellectual structure* (Flavell, 1963, p. 15). He makes a distinction between intellectual function and intellectual structure. Function refers to those general characteristics of intelligent activity which virtually define the essence of intelligence itself. Structure refers to those organized aspects of intelligence which change with age. The developmental changes which structures undergo are the principal focus of Piaget's study. This distinction between function and structure will become clearer when we consider the functional invariants. Second, since Piaget is interested in qualitative development, he has partitioned the growth of intelligence into a number of stages, each of which is qualitatively distinct from the preceding and succeeding stages. These stages always occur in the same sequence and are hierarchically arranged—the intellectual structures which define an earlier stage are incorporated into the intellectual structures of a later stage. With these two general characteristics in mind, we can now turn to some key concepts in Piaget's system.

Functional invariants. Piaget believes that what changes in our intellectual development are the intellectual structures; the intellectual functions remain the same. We do not inherit structures; these must emerge in the course of development. But we do inherit a way of intellectual functioning which, in the words of John Flavell (1963, p. 43), is "a specific manner of doing business with the environment." Because our way of intellectual functioning remains the same throughout our lives, Piaget is able to call the characteristics of that functioning *functional invariants.*

The two functional invariants are *organization* and *adaptation.* Organization describes the fact that intellectual acts are not isolated but coordinated affairs; every act of intelligence is related to the totality (or whole) of such acts. To use a biological analogy, when we digest food, the process is an organized one carried on by an organized being. Whereas organization describes the internal aspect of intellectual functioning, adaptation describes the external aspect. Flavell (1963, pp. 47–48) defines adaptation as an act of intelligence in which accommodation and assimilation are in equilibrium (balance). He quotes Piaget (1952, pp. 7–8):

> Organization is inseparable from adaptation: They are two complementary processes of a single mechanism, the first being the internal aspect of the cycle of which adaptation constitutes the external aspect. . . . The "accord of thought with things" and the "accord of thought with itself" express this dual functional invariant of adaptation and organization. These two aspects of thought are indissociable: It is by adapting to things that thought itself organizes itself and it is by organizing itself that it structures things.

Before illustrating the functional invariants, organization and adaptation, I shall distinguish between the two aspects of adaptation: assimilation and accommodation. Flavell (1963) defines Piaget's concept of *assimilation* in this way:

> Assimilation . . . refers to the fact that every cognitive encounter with an environmental object necessarily involves some kind of cognitive structuring (or restructuring) of that object in accord with the nature of the organism's existing intellectual organization.

In biology, assimilation is the ingestion of food, which is gradually transformed into the organs (structures) of the body. Describing assimilation as a psychological function, J. McV. Hunt (1961, p. 112) states, "Assimilation operates whenever the organism acts in a new situation as it has acted in other situations in the past, whenever it invests anything with familiarity (recognition), importance, or value." Assimilation, in other words, involves the interpretation of something which exists in the external world. *Accommodation,* in the words of Flavell (1963, p. 48), is the "process of adapting oneself to the variegated requirements or demands which the world of objects imposes on one." The most basic type of thinking must come to grips with reality, and reality is not infinitely malleable. Returning to our biological analogy, accommodation enables the organism to adjust to the food it ingests. If the food requires chewing, the organism must provide chewing. And even the digestive processes must adjust to the biochemical properties of the food. Assimilation is closely related to organization as well as to adaptation, whereas accommodation is closely related to adaptation alone. Thus, when the organism ingests food, the body organization assimilates the food and at the same time accommodates itself to the food.

The definitions above view assimilation and accommodation as complementary functions. We may also view them as antagonistic functions: Assimilation of the familiar is primarily conservative, and accommodation to the novel is primarily liberal. Both the complementary and the antagonistic aspects of these functions cause alternate states of equilibrium and disequilibrium in the organism. The initial states of antagonism (or disequilibrium) are gradually resolved into the later states of complementarity (or equilibrium). One may consider the intellectual development of the child as the alternate establishment of states of equilibrium and disequilibrium, with the predominance of states of equilibrium as his intellectual development approaches mature thought. In Piaget's view, the intellectual acts of the stage the child is leaving are in equilibrium, while those of the stage he is entering are in disequilibrium. In equilibrium, we see equal parts of assimilation and accommodation, a balance between the meaningful (assimilation) and the realistic (accommodation), and rapport between the child and his environment.

Flavell (1963, pp. 50–52) uses this illustration to explain the functional invariants:

> An infant comes in contact for the first time with a ring suspended from a string. He makes a series of exploratory accommodations: He looks at it, touches it, causes it to swing back and forth, grasps it, and so on. These accommodatory acts of course do not take place *in vacuo;* through past interactions with various other objects the child already possesses assimilatory structures (schemas) which set in motion and direct those accommodations. Piaget would say here that the ring is assimilated to concepts of touching, moving, seeing, etc., concepts which are already part of the child's cognitive organization. The child's actions with respect to the ring are at once accommodations of these concepts or structures to the reality contours of the ring and assimilations of this new object to these concepts.

> . . . The example of the child and ring can also serve to illustrate the limitations to which structural change is subject in a single organism-reality transaction. In the first place, there are a number of potentially cognizable features of the ring which we may be sure the infant will not accommodate to and will not assimilate. There is nothing in the infant's present structural repertoire which will permit him to accommodate to the ring as an exemplar of the abstract class of circles, for example. Similarly, he cannot apprehend the ring as an object which can be rolled like a hoop, as an object which can be worn as a bracelet, and so forth. In Piaget's terms, the organism cannot accommodate itself to those object potentialities which it is unable to assimilate to something in its present system of meaning. The hiatus between the new and the old cannot be too great. This fact, that new structures must arise almost imperceptibly from the foundations provided by present ones, is always what insures the gradualness of cognitive development.

We cannot refer to the old structures as entering behavior because they are not observable acts or performances. These structures, however, are correlated with behavior in the sense that the child who possesses them is capable of performances which the child who lacks them is not. In a later section of this chapter, I discuss the relationship between the concept of entering behavior and Piaget's theory of intellectual development.

SCHEMAS. We must now consider one final concept. In the previous illustration Flavell refers to schemas, structures, and concepts, and appears to use the terms interchangeably. We can recognize a schema by both its internal and its external aspects. Internally, it is the cognitive structures (or processes) which initiate and control the accommodations the child makes to his environment. Externally, it is a collection of cohesive behaviors or actions. Schemas are named after the behaviors to which they are linked; each developmental stage has its particular schemas. We have, for example, in the earliest stage of development, the schemas of sucking and grasping; in later childhood, the schemas of concrete operations; and, in adolescence, the schemas of formal operations. At the beginning of the chapter I stated that Piaget's chief purpose is the study of the development of intellectual structures. More technically (and with more precision), you can now state that his chief purpose is the study of the development of schemas.

Alfred Baldwin (1967) compares schemas with a single response to a stimulus. We could view the sucking schema, for example, as nothing more than the sucking response to some stimulation inside the mouth. Baldwin (1967, p. 174) however describes it as follows, showing that a schema is a collection of behavior sequences—something much more complicated than a single response to a single stimulus.

> The response involves turning the head when the cheek is stimulated, opening the mouth when the lips are touched, sucking when the inside of the mouth is stimulated, swallowing when the liquid reaches the throat. In the early months after birth, the sucking schema rapidly expands to include searching for the breast when the child is placed against the mother's body, sucking movement performed while the child watches his mother prepare to feed him, and nonnutritive thumb-sucking or sucking and chewing blocks and spoons.

Because schemas refer to organizations and sequences of responses, they are similar to the concept of learning sets and learning styles discussed in Chapter 3. Later, in Chapter 10, you will see that both in nature and development, schemas are similar to concepts and principles.

Later Periods of Development

Now that we have completed our brief consideration of the general purposes of Piaget's system and of some basic theoretical concepts, we are ready to consider those periods (or stages) of cognitive development which embrace the child's school years. If you are interested in the two earlier periods, sensory-motor and preoperational thought, consult the list of suggested readings at the conclusion of this chapter.

PERIOD OF CONCRETE OPERATIONS. During the period from 7 to 11, when the child is in elementary school, his thinking becomes stable and reasonable. Baldwin (1967, pp. 192–93) illustrates some concrete operations the child can perform during this period:

> He can, for example, arrange objects in order of size and fit new ones into the series. He can understand that equality of number of two sets of objects depends upon a one-to-one correspondence between the objects in the two groups. He understands that the number of objects in a group is not changed by purely spatial rearrangements. He can understand many of the simpler relationships between classes of objects; for example, he can realize that a class cannot have fewer members than any of its subclasses. He understands what will happen to the sequence of objects if they are rotated. He can distinguish between the distance between two objects and the length of the path between them. In short, he has acquired a rudimentary conception of time, space, number, and logic, those fundamental conceptions in terms of which our understanding of events and objects is ordered.

According to Piaget, during this period the child understands the relationships among various concrete operational groupings. *Grouping* is a term derived from logic and mathematics and, as such, is difficult to define briefly in nontechnical language. In general, it refers to logical operations. Piaget describes nine distinct groupings for the period of concrete operations. We can say that these nine groupings describe the cognitive structure (or schemas) of the child in this period. Groupings are, therefore, intellectual schemas which possess particular characteristics—closure, associativity, reversibility, and identity.

David Berlyne (1957, pp. 7–8) has defined and illustrated each of these characteristics of groupings:

> 1. *Closure.* Any two operations can be combined to form a third operation (e.g., 2 + 3 = 5; *all men and all women* = *all human adults;* A *is two miles north of* B *and* B *is one mile north of* C = A *is three miles north of* C).
> 2. *Reversibility.* For any operation there is an opposite operation which cancels it (e.g., 2 + 3 = 5 but 5 — 3 = 2; *all human adults* but *all human adults except women* = *all men;* A *is two miles north of* B *and* B *is one mile north of* C = A *is three miles north of* C; but, A *is three miles north of* C *and* C *is one mile south of* B = A *is two miles north of* B).
> 3. *Associativity.* When three operations are to be combined, it does not matter which two are combined first. This is equivalent to the possibility of arriving at the same point by different routes (e.g., (2 + 3) + 4 = 2 + (3 + 4); *all vertebrates and all invertebrates* = *all human beings and all subhuman animals;* a *is the uncle of* b *and* b *is the father of* c = a *is the brother of* d *and* d *is the grandfather of* c).
> 4. *Identity.* There is a "null operation" formed when any operation is combined with its opposite (e.g., 2 — 2 = 0; *all men except those who are men* = *nobody; I travel one hundred miles to the north and I travel one hundred miles to the south* = *I find myself back where I started*).

Berlyne also adds a fifth characteristic, which Flavell (1963, p. 175) has called *special identities.* This characteristic has two versions. First, *tautology* merely indicates that repetition of a classification or relation does not change it. Saying something repeatedly does not add information (e.g., all men and all men = all men). Second, *iteration* indicates that a number combined with itself produces a new number (e.g., 3 + 3 = 6; 3 × 3 = 9).

Flavell summarizes three limitations of the period of concrete operations: (1) The operations are oriented toward concrete things and events in the immediate present—movement toward the nonpresent, or potential, is limited. The child during this period acts as if his primary task were to organize and order what is immediately present—the real does not become a special case of the possible. (2) The child has to relinquish the various physical attributes (such as mass, weight, volume) of objects and events one by one. If, for example, he understands that there is as much clay in object *A* as in object *B* (mass), despite the difference in shape, the child will still need considerable time to understand that the weight and the volume of the clay also remain the same. (3) Each of the groupings which he develops in this period remains an isolated organization and does not form an integrated system of thought. All three of these limitations are removed in the period of formal operations.

PERIOD OF FORMAL OPERATIONS. During the period from 11 to 15, the adolescent acquires the adult capacity for abstract thought. In the previous period the child is only beginning to extend his thought from the actual to the potential (Inhelder and Piaget, 1958). Flavell (1963) uses this analogy: The cognitive structure of the previous period is like a parking lot in which the parking spaces are alternately empty and occupied. The spaces themselves endure, and their owners can and do look beyond the cars which are present toward the future (potential) when other spaces will be occupied and empty.

I shall now summarize the major characteristics of the period of formal operations. These characteristics explain what Berlyne (1957, p. 9) has described as the "adolescent's taste for theorizing and criticizing." The major characteristic of this period, according to Bärbel Inhelder and Piaget (1958), concerns the possible versus the real. In describing this new quality of thought, Flavell (1963, p. 205) writes:

> No longer exclusively preoccupied with the sober business of trying to stabilize and organize just what comes directly to the senses, the adolescent has, through this new orientation, the potentiality of imagining all that might be there—both the very obvious and the very subtle—and thereby of much better insuring the finding of all that is there.

The adolescent, therefore, theorizes about and criticizes the present operation of the world because he conceives of many possible ways in which it could operate and many alternative ways in which it could be better.

From this major characteristic we derive three other characteristics of the period of formal operations. First, the adolescent's thinking is basically *hypothetico-deductive.* To discover the real among the possible requires that the possible be cast as hypotheses, which may be confirmed or rejected. The reasoning of the adolescent, in the words of Flavell (1963, p. 205), may take this form:

> Well, it is clear from the data that *A* might be the necessary and sufficient condition for *X,* or that *B* might be, or that both might be needed; my job is to test these possibilities in turn to see which one or ones really hold true in this problem.

Second, thinking in this period is *propositional thinking.* The adolescent does not consider only raw data but also sentences which contain these data. In the period of concrete operations the child deals with concrete objects and events, which he learns to classify, set in correspondence, and so on. In the period of formal operations he takes the results of these concrete operations, puts them in sentence form, and begins to find relationships among the sentences (or propositions). Berlyne (1957, pp. 7–8) uses these examples of propositional thought: *"Either sentence* p *is true or sentence* q *is true;"* or *If sentence* r *is true, then sentence* s *must be true."* Third, thinking in this period involves *combinatorial analysis.* In considering all the possible solutions to a problem, the adolescent isolates all individual factors and all possible combinations of factors that may figure in the solution. The factors are propositions or statements and the combinations of statements are hypotheses.

Flavell (1963, p. 207) has selected two examples from Inhelder and Piaget (1958, pp. 108–9, 111, and 117) to illustrate the differences in the thinking of children in the periods of concrete and formal operations.

> In experiment I, the child is given four similar flasks containing colorless, odorless liquids which are perceptually identical. We number them: (1) diluted sulphuric acid; (2) water; (3) oxygenated water; (4) thiosulphate; we add a bottle (with a dropper) which we will call *g;* it contains potassium iodide. It is known that oxygenated water oxidizes potassium iodide in an acid medium. Thus mixture (1 + 3 + *g*) will yield a yellow color. The water (2) is neutral, so that adding it will not change the color, whereas the thiosulphate (4) will bleach the mixture (1 + 3 + *g*). The experimenter presents to the subject two glasses, one containing 1 + 3, the other containing 2. In front of the subject, he pours several drops of *g* in each of the two glasses and notes the different reactions. Then the subject is asked simply to reproduce the color yellow, using flasks 1, 2, 3, 4, and *g* as he wishes.

The report on Ren illustrates thinking at the level of concrete operations; that on Cha illustrates the level of formal operations:

> Ren (7;1) tries 4 × *g*, then 2 × *g, and* 3 × *g: "I think I did everything. . . . I tried them all."*—"What else could you have done?"—*"I don't know."* We give him the glasses again: he repeats 1 × *g*, etc.—"You took each bottle separately. What else could you have done?"—*"Take two bottles at the same time"* [he tries 1 × 4 × *g*, then 2 × 3 × *g*, thus failing to cross over between the two sets (of bottles), for example 1 × 2, 1 × 3, 2 × 4, and 3 × 4].—When we suggest that he add others, he puts 1 × *g* in the glass already containing 2 × 3 which results in the appearance of the color: "Try to make the color again."—*"Do I put in two or three?* [he tries with

> 2 × 4 × *g*, then adds 3, then tries it with 1 × 4 × 2 × *g*]. *No, I don't remember any more,"* etc.
>
> Cha (13;0): *"You have to try with all the bottles. I'll begin with the one at the end* [from 1 to 4 with *g*]. *It doesn't work any more. Maybe you have to mix them* [he tries 1 × 2 × *g*, then 1 × 3 × *g*.] *It turned yellow. But are there other solutions? I'll try* [1 × 4 × *g*; 2 × 3 × *g*; 2 × 4 × *g*; 3 × 4 × *g*; with the two preceding combinations this gives the six two-by-two combinations systematically]. *It doesn't work. It only works with"* [1 × 3 × *g*].—"Yes, and what about 2 and 4?"—*"2 and 4 don't make any color together. They are negative. Perhaps you could add 4 in 1 × 3 × g to see if it would cancel out the color* [he does this]. *Liquid 4 cancels it all. You'd have to see if 2 has the same influence* [he tries it]. *No, so 2 and 4 are not alike, for 4 acts on 1 × 3 and 2 does not."*—"What is there in 2 and 4?"—*"In 4 certainly water. No, the opposite, in 2 certainly water since it doesn't act on the liquids; that makes things clearer."* —"And if I were to tell you that 4 is water?"—*"If this liquid 4 is water, when you put it with 1 × 3 it wouldn't completely prevent the yellow from forming. It isn't water; it's something harmful."*

The protocol of the younger child (Ren) shows that he is able to make some of the possible combinations and that he makes the few he thinks of (some with considerable help from the experimenter) in a nonsystematic way. On the other hand, the older child (Cha) in the very beginning thinks of all possible (and feasible) combinations, and he does this in an orderly and systematic way: (1 × *g*) × (2 × *g*), and so on, and then (1 × 2 × *g*) + (1 × 3 × *g*), and so on. The number of if-then statements shows the hypothetico-deductive characteristic of his thinking.

It should be clear by now that during the period of formal operations the adolescent engages in his first scientific reasoning. He is capable of planning truly scientific investigations, and he can vary the factors in all possible combinations and in an orderly fashion. In fact, he appears to be capable of discovering the basic laws of physics with the help of simple apparatus. By observing whether the student attempts to explain a given state of affairs in terms of various combinations of factors and to verify his hypotheses by observing their consequences, the teacher can determine whether the student is operating at the level of formal operations.

Inhelder and Piaget (1958) believe that the development of adolescent reasoning may account for changes in adolescent behavior. Unlike the younger child, who lives in the present, the adolescent lives in the world of the possible and the hypothetical—the world of the future. Since he is capable of reflective thought, he can consider his own future and the future of the society in which he lives. According to Piaget, he develops a special egocentricism, in which he combines an extravagant belief in thought with sweeping disregard for the practicality of the designs and the reforms he proposes. Flavell (1963, p. 224) quotes Inhelder and Piaget (1958, pp. 345–46):

> The adolescent goes through a phase in which he attributes unlimited power to his own thoughts so that the dream of a glorious future or of transforming the world through ideas (even if his idealism takes a materialistic form) seems to be not only fantasy but also an effective action which in itself modifies the empirical world. This is obviously a form of cognitive egocentricism.

This brief description concludes our consideration of the two school periods of intellectual development as identified by Piaget and his associates. In the next section we consider the educational applications of Piaget's psychology, especially as it pertains to entering behavior.

Entering Behavior and Intellectual Development

In Piaget's terms, the educational problem is to discover ways to govern the encounters children have with their environments in order to foster rapid rates of intellectual development and satisfying lives (Hunt, 1961, p. 363). In achieving this solution, however, we must avoid both a fruitless pushing of the child beyond his intellectual resources and a fruitless delay in the introduction of intellectual tasks he is ready to pursue. Instruction must accommodate the intellectual level of the student, and, since we can ascertain this level only by studying his behavior, we can say that it must accommodate his intellectual entering behavior. Flavell (1963, pp. 365–69) has suggested three ways in which Piaget's system can be applied to entering behavior.

First, we may be able to develop intelligence tests based on the intellectual tasks Piaget has used in his extensive research. Presently, at the Universities of Geneva and Montreal, developmental scales of reasoning are being evolved in the following content areas: number, quantity, space, geometry, movement, velocity, time, change, causality, logical deduction, logic of relations, and the child's beliefs about the world (realism, animism, and artificialism). Preliminary evidence indicates that the various responses children give to Piaget's tasks in a given content area do show the age and stage differences his theory describes. Further development of these intelligence tests will make possible the assessment of the entering behavior of the child for the learning of particular cognitive tasks as, for example, the learning of certain mathematical and scientific concepts, principles, and problem solutions. In other words, it may be possible to develop a scale of instructional objectives which has a one-to-one correspondence with a scale of reasoning.

Second, we may be able to plan the curriculum on the basis of Piaget's discoveries. This planning should include both the proper grade placement of particular instructional objectives and provisions for guarding against the student's misacquisitions, which are likely to occur when he attempts to master a new area. Flavell gives these examples of questions which could arise and decisions which could be made: Do Piaget's discoveries suggest that teaching the scientific method should be deferred to early adolescence, when the child is capable of formal thought? Is it possible to teach geometry earlier than usual because the child of 8 or 9 has adequate concepts of spatial representation and measurement? Regarding misacquisitions, the teacher may have to steer the child away from the concept of volume, which pertains only to the interior contents of an object, until the student is able to relate the concept to the surrounding space. British educational psychologists are particularly active in linking curriculum development to Piaget's studies (Lovell, 1959, and Peel, 1959).

The third possible application of Piaget's system is in the proper matching of entering behavior and instructional procedures. Indeed, this may be the most important application. It would require the teacher to perform a task analysis based on the operations described by Piaget. The content of instruction implies the operation the student must perform to learn it. And, since these operations possess certain properties, these properties should be incorporated in the instruction. For example, Piaget believes that both reversibility and associativity are essential aspects of thought. If the teacher wanted to incorporate the property of *reversibility,* he would teach multiplication and division, as well as addition and subtraction in alternation. He would follow a problem like ($5 \times 5 = ?$) with the problem ($25 \div 5 = ?$). If he were considering the economic effects of the War Between the States, he would also consider the economic causes of the War (effect to cause). As for the property of *associativity,* in this system the teacher would show the student different routes to the same problem solution. Flavell suggests the example of deriving the equation for the perimeter of a rectangle. The teacher would lead the student to see the equality of the following expressions: $2(b + h) = 2b + 2h = h + b + h + b = h + h + b + b$, and so on.

The recommendation that the teacher analyze the instructional content in terms of intellectual operations rests on two implicit assumptions. First, as Piaget expresses many times, the student must engage directly with the content he is learning. He must perform real actions on these materials, as concrete and direct as possible. These external actions, according to Piaget, become the internal concrete and formal operations of student thought. In Chapter 11, in which we consider discovery learning, we examine the need for student participation in the learning process. Second, Piaget stresses the great importance of having the student interact with his fellow students to liberate him from his egocentricism. Rationality and objectivity are acquired by pitting one's ideas against those of others and observing the distinctions and similarities. Instruction, therefore, must be conducted on a group as well as on an individual basis.

None of these applications of Piaget's system to education gives specific directions for formulating instructional objectives, assessing entering behavior, and selecting instructional procedures. More specific guidance for the teacher must come from research directed toward finding procedures that are consistent with Piaget's theories and that result in the desired level of thought. Although this research is now underway (see, for example, Smedslund, 1961a and b), some basic theoretical issues must be settled before more direct classroom application of Piaget's findings is possible. In the meantime, since Piaget has given us our only well-developed theory of intellectual development, we should use whatever general guidelines it provides for dealing with the entering behavior of our students.

You should now return to objectives 1–10 (pp. 84–85) and determine how well you have achieved them.

QUESTION 4-1

Mr. I. M. Facile, a science teacher, designed an ingenious apparatus which consisted of a game resembling billiards. The balls were launched from a tubular spring-plunger (as in pinball games), or lever, which could be pivoted in various directions to aim the ball at various points along a projection wall or buffer. The object was to pocket the ball by deflecting it from the wall. Mr. Facile used this game to help students learn the law that the angle of incidence equals the angle of reflection. In presenting this game to children in the third grade, which of the following statements would be most useful in explaining how to make successful shots?

(a) "You have to move the lever according to the target, and vice versa."

(b) "If the lever is straight the ball returns exactly."

(c) "The ball hits the middle of the wall when you hold the lever like this."

After selecting your answer, explain the reasons for your choice and for your rejection of the alternatives.

THE MEASUREMENT OF INTELLIGENCE

This section of the chapter introduces a different theory of intelligence, one which is more traditional than Piaget's and which is the basis for the construction of tests of intelligence. The first three parts of the section deal with theoretical issues pertaining to the construction of tests of intelligence: the comparison of a test theory with a developmental (Piaget's) theory of intelligence; the difference between single-factor and multifactor theories; and the description of various intelligence tests. The last three parts deal with practical issues which arise from the use of the tests in the schools: their value in predicting academic and vocational success; their use as diagnostic devices in assessing individual differences; and their relationship to and value in the assessment of entering behavior for particular instructional purposes.

Test Theory of Intelligence

To explain the theory of intelligence which underlies the construction of intelligence tests, it is helpful to recall a distinction made by Donald Hebb (1949, pp. 294–96) between intelligence *A* and intelligence *B*. Intelligence *A* is our innate potential, or inborn capacity, for development. It amounts to "the possession of a good brain and a good neural metabolism" and is therefore the hereditary factor—the capacity for elaborating perceptions and conceptual activities. Intelligence *B*, on the other hand, is the functioning and the ongoing development of the brain—the average level of performance or comprehension which the child or adult shows. Hebb does not claim that there are two kinds of intelligence, but he does suggest that, although both intelligences *A* and *B* are not observable, intelligence *B* is more accessible to measurement than intelligence *A*. By observing an individual's behavior in many different situations and at different times we can more easily make an estimate of his intelligence *B* than of his intelligence *A*, and, therefore, the test score is more direct measurement of intelligence *B* than of intelligence *A*. Disagreements over the nature of intelligence frequently concern the relation of *A* to *B*. If *A* fully determines *B*, then intelligence is controlled by heredity. If *B*, however, is determined by other factors as well, particularly by experience and learning, then it is distinguishable from hereditary intelligence *A*. Hebb obviously believes the latter.

With the distinction between intelligences *A* and *B* in mind, we can consider three definitions which summarize current conceptualizations of test intelligence (Freeman, 1962, pp. 149–51):

1. Intelligence is the adaptation or adjustment of the individual to his total environment.
2. Intelligence is the ability to learn.
3. Intelligence is the ability to carry on abstract thinking.

The first definition emphasizes the ability of the person to cope with new problems and new situations. The second definition emphasizes the individual's educability. The third definition emphasizes the capacity of the individual for verbal and mathematical reasoning. As you can see, these definitions are not mutually exclusive. For example, an individual would find it difficult if not impossible to solve anything but the most primitive problems of survival without the use of verbal and mathematical symbols or of abstractions. In fact language—verbal abstractions—may be our most basically human characteristic. This relation of abstractions to the solution of problems is the relationship of the first and third definitions. Additionally, the verbal and mathematical symbols or abstractions must be learned (the second definition). The immense amount of overlap indicates both the agreement among psychologists on the definition of intelligence and our inability to discuss intelligence, apart from intelligence tests, in anything but the most abstract terms.

Among the items on intelligence tests, those which usually correlate most highly with the overall scores are the items which measure ability for verbal and numerical reasoning. Perhaps, then, the most empirical and parsimonious definition of intelligence would be: the capacity of the individual for verbal and numerical reasoning. These typical test items require superior ability in verbal and numerical reasoning:

1. Reconciliation of opposites: In what way are ________ and ________ alike? (a) Winter and summer; (b) happy and sad; (c) loud and soft; (d) much and little; and (e) beginning and end (Terman and Merrill, 1937, p. 182).
2. Analogies: (1) Lemons are sour but sugar is ________; (2) You can walk with your legs and throw with your ________; (3) Boys grow up to be men an girls to be ________ (Wechsler, 1949).
3. Arithmetic problems: If a taxi charges 20 cents for the first quarter mile and 5 cents for each quarter mile thereafter, what will the fare be for a two-mile trip?

These items require less ability in verbal and numerical reasoning:

4. The subject repeats after examining the following list of digits: 4–2–9–7–8–3–5–1–6. (Later the subject is required to repeat the list in reverse order.)
5. What is the thing to do when you cut your finger?
6. How far is it from New York to Los Angeles?
7. What is a hieroglyphic? (5–7 from Wechsler, 1949).

Whereas solution of the former items (1–3) requires the use of abstractions, solution of the latter items (4–7) requires the use of only short-

or long-term memory. We expect and we find that subjects who do well on items 1 to 3 also do well on items 4 to 7.

We can now compare the test theory and Piaget's theory of intelligence. First, Piaget's system describes a relationship between intelligences *A* and *B,* while test theory is almost solely concerned with intelligence *B.* The tests make no effort to measure innate intelligence, while Piaget does relate both hereditary and environmental factors to the development of intelligence. What we inherit, he claims, are the invariant functions. What we acquire in actual intellectual development are new and more complex schemas, the products of both heredity (the invariant functions) and environment. Second, test theory tends to view intelligence as a single factor (or small group of factors)—the capacity for verbal and numerical reasoning—which forms a continuous thread throughout the individual's life. Piaget's theory, on the other hand, is cast in terms of the many schemas the individual develops and the several stages of development through which he passes. Besides the functional invariants, the only thread which holds together the various stages is that provided by the hierarchical arrangement of the schemas, so that the schemas of a later developmental period incorporate those of earlier periods. Third, both theories contain a time dimension—implicit in test theory and explicit in Piaget's theory. Piaget's theory is a developmental theory of intelligence and, therefore, describes the qualitative differences in intelligence within various time periods. Test theory implicitly recognizes the time dimension by selecting tasks which are commensurate in difficulty with the age of the child and by comparing the performances of children of the same and different ages. Finally, the intellectual tasks which both theories require are often very similar, often both requiring children to manipulate objects to exemplify a concept or principle. One can well imagine that, when work on the Piaget tests of intelligence is completed, they will bear many resemblances to conventional intelligence tests.

In essence test theory and Piaget's theory supplement each other quite well. Whereas test theory has never developed a very sophisticated view of intelligence and intellectual processes, something which Piaget has now contributed, Piaget's system, until recently, has not produced scales of reasoning which are at once tests of his theory and useful measuring devices.

General-factor vs. Multifactor Theories

We can now resume our discussion of test theory and compare two types which engender almost equal amounts of speculation, research, and pure (unempirical) controversy. The issue over whether we have one intelligence (the general factor) or several intelligences (the multi-factor) climaxed in the feverish work and hearty debates of Charles Spearman (1927) and of L. L. and T. G. Thurstone (1941). In the Churchillian tradition of British doggedness, Spearman defended literally to his death the theory that all mental activities have in common a general factor, which he designated *g*. He described *g* as the mental energy which functions in the mental world just as physical energy does in the physical world. In terms of an old Platonic analogy, *g* is both the charioteer and the horses drawing the chariot. According to Spearman, some activities require more *g* than others. For example, tests which pose problems of relations require more *g* than other tests. In the above test items, these would be items 1 to 3. To defend his view and possibly to accommodate some of the work of his adversaries, Spearman later postulated the existence of highly specific factors, designated *s*, present only in particular activities, and specific to those activities. Each entering behavior of a student, for example, may have its own *s* factor. In Spearman's judgment, however, an intelligence test should measure *g*, and this could be done, he believed, with a single test.

In 1938, L. L. Thurstone, the American psychologist, rose to battle when he proclaimed, "We cannot report any common factor in [our] battery of fifty-six tests." According to Thurstone, the results of these tests indicated that mental ability and activity can be grouped into six factors (six *g*s), each common to a variety of mental operations. Thurstone (p. 9) describes these six factors:

1. The number factor (*N*): This is the ability to perform arithmetic calculations with accuracy and speed.
2. The verbal factor (*V*): This ability is found in tests of verbal comprehension.
3. The space factor (*S*): This ability is required when subjects try to manipulate in their imaginations an object in space.
4. The word fluency factor (*W*): This is the ability to think of isolated words at a rapid rate.
5. The reasoning factor (*R*): This is the ability to induce and deduce a rule or principle involved in series or groups of letters.
6. The rote memory factor (*M*): This is the ability to memorize quickly.

These six factors make up what the Thurstones called *primary mental abilities*. Now, if these abilities are truly independent, we would not always expect individuals who score high, for example, in one or more abilities to score high in the remaining abilities. Unfortunately for Thurstone, this is not the case. For example, subjects who score high on the reasoning factor also score high on the number, verbal, and word fluency factors. In fact, the reasoning factor seems to be very similar to Spearman's *g*. Frank Freeman (1962, p. 166) suggests that these six abilities may be only particular cultural expressions of a single general ability. The inability of the Thurstones to obtain test results which indicated that these factors are independent led them to conclude that in addition to primary abilities there is a second-order general factor. Subsequent studies of primary mental abilities tend to support Spearman's claim for a general factor.

J. P. Guilford (1959) has also developed a multifactor theory of intelligence by dividing intelligence into 120 relatively independent components. He claims to have identified at least fifty of these. He writes, "We may say that there are at least fifty ways of being intelligent. It has been facetiously suggested that there seem to be a great many more ways of being stupid, unfortunately" (Guilford, 1959, p. 477). Guilford advocates a multiple instead of a single IQ score. If we look only at the abilities which Guilford classifies as *content,* we see that he describes four kinds of intelligence: The use of figural information—an ability of mechanics, artists, and musicians—may be regarded as concrete intelligence; symbolic intelligence involves the use of words and numbers; semantic intelligence helps us acquire ideas and facts; and social intelligence, which is largely nonverbal in character, governs our behavior. Perhaps the part of Guilford's theory which has received the most attention is his distinction between convergent and divergent (creative) thinking. We discuss this distinction later in the chapter when we examine the relationship of creativity and intelligence.

In addition to the Thurstone and Guilford concepts, the concept of special aptitudes has also been used in place of the concept of general intelligence. Special aptitudes are independent abilities to perform particular jobs; they are defined in terms of the jobs which require them. Hence, we speak of musical aptitude, mechanical aptitude, and clerical aptitude. Each of these, of course, consists of many basic skills and each skill requires its own measurement. For example, we may wish to measure the aptitude necessary for becoming a bomber pilot. Some of the component skills for this aptitude are dial and table reading, spatial coordination, reading comprehension, rudder control, and finger dexterity. In Chapter 8 you will see how athletic ability also reduces to several component skills. The concept of special aptitudes suggests that an individual must be proficient in a number of skills before he can claim mechanical aptitude, athletic ability, flying ability, and so on. On a transoceanic flight, or indeed any flight, we would be reluctant to entrust our lives to a pilot who has good finger dexterity but is poor in dial and table reading.

Frequently, tests of general intelligence are called *scholastic aptitude tests,* in the sense that they predict future educational or training achievement. To many educators, however, aptitude is merely a euphemism for intelligence. A deficiency in scholastic aptitude does not carry the same stigma as does a deficiency in intelligence. A deficiency in scholastic aptitude may condemn the student to academic hardship but not necessarily to failure in his postgraduation life. Also, to many educators and psychologists scholastic or general aptitude describes only one type of aptitude. They have postulated many others—that is, abilities which are independent of one another and of general intelligence. A deficiency in general aptitude or intelligence, then, describes only one area of the individual's capacities. Common sense, however, prompts many of us to believe that intelligence is a necessary but not a sufficient ingredient for success or, at least, that the possession of intelligence, scholastic aptitude, or whatever, is not a proven handicap in carving out one's destiny in or out of school.

QUESTION 4-2

> The educator, addressing a large audience of parents and teachers, leaned forward on the lectern and stared ahead. He then said in short, measured terms, "It is not what you know but knowing how to find out more that really counts in the child's educational development." To which theory of intelligence might this speaker most easily subscribe: (a) Hebb's notion of intelligence *A;* (b) Piaget's theory; (c) A general-factor theory; (d) A multifactor theory.
>
> After selecting your answer, explain the reasons for your choice and for your rejection of the three alternatives.

Types of Intelligence Tests

Both the general-factor and the multifactor theories of intelligence have produced a number of tests and test batteries which differ in their administration and physical form. In terms of administration, you can distinguish between two major intelligence tests. The individual tests, as the name implies, are administered by a psychologist or trained teacher to a single child at a time. The testing period is approximately one hour, and, during this time, the examiner records the answers which the student (or examinee) makes orally. The examiner also records any significant behavior he observes during the test administration. Throughout the examination the student is required to do little if any writing. Group tests are usually administered by a teacher or counselor to large or small numbers of students or to a single student if the occasion arises. Frequently the tests require less time than the individual tests; this saving in time and money has favored their use over that of the individual tests. Test batteries consist of several tests, which often must be administered over two or more sessions. I shall now describe and compare particular individual and group tests and test batteries.

THE INDIVIDUAL TESTS. Among the individual tests of intelligence, the Stanford-Binet Scales are the best known. The first edition of this test appeared in 1905 and was largely the work of Alfred Binet, the French psychologist, who devised it to identify mentally deficient school children. The three major revisions of the Binet Scales made in 1916, 1937, and 1960 by L. M. Terman, of Stanford University, and Maud E. Merrill are formally known as the Stanford Revisions of the Binet-Simon Intelligence Scale.* They have been based from the beginning on a theory of general intelligence. Binet intended to develop an instrument which measured a student's general intelligence by sampling a variety of intellectual activities. We should not be surprised to learn, then, that every effort, such as Thurstone's, to isolate group factors on the basis of these scales has failed. Test items, however, differ in the extent to which they measure the general factor *g*. The following lists name the various parts of the test for older children and show which parts measure *g* to a high and which to a low extent.

HIGH *g* FACTOR

1. Definitions of abstract words
2. Arithmetical reasoning
3. Differences among abstract words
4. Essential differences
5. Proverbs
6. Sentence building
7. Verbal absurdities
8. Vocabulary

LOW *g* FACTOR

1. Enclosed box problem
2. Memory for stories
3. Papercutting (visual imagery)
4. Plan of search
5. Problems of fact
6. Repeating digits (forward order)
7. Repeating digits (reverse order)
8. Reproducing a beaded chain from memory

Inspection of these lists should suggest two generalizations. First, items which are low in *g* are less complex than items high in *g*. The low-*g*

* Simon was Binet's collaborator; the name of the 1905 test was the Binet-Simon Scale. Other American revisions, by Goddard and Kuhlmann, preceded those of Terman and Merrill.

items involve space perception and spatial relationships (as in the plan of search), visual imagery, and rote memory. Second, items which are high in *g* involve the acquisition and use of language and of the concept of numbers. These items involve acquisition and use of vocabulary; verbal analysis of a situation; comprehension of similarities and differences; verbal and numerical concept formation; and analysis, synthesis, and reorganization of verbal and nonverbal materials (Freeman, 1962, pp. 225–26).

The other widely used tests of individual intelligence are the two Wechsler Scales: the Wechsler Adult Intelligence Scale (known as the WAIS, pronounced to rhyme with base) and the Wechsler Intelligence Scale for Children (known as the WISC, pronounced to rhyme with brisk—see Wechsler, 1949). The first form of WAIS appeared in 1939, but the 1955 revision (see Wechsler, 1955) is currently in use. The WISC, which appeared in 1949, is for children from 5 to 15. The WAIS is for older subjects. For adults, the WAIS is more extensively used than the Stanford-Binet Scale, which is not intended for them. Like the Stanford-Binet Scale, both the WAIS and the WISC are based on a general-factor theory of intelligence. Wechsler hoped, however, that, by combining verbal and nonverbal material, he would develop an instrument which was more diagnostic of both intellectual and personality functions than the former scale. Hence, the Wechsler Scales are divided into two groups of subtests—verbal and performance.

There are six verbal subtests: the information test, which covers a wide range of facts which most individuals in American society can be expected to know (for example, Who discovered America?); the general comprehension test, which depends upon the possession of practical information and the use of past experience (What do you do if you find a letter with stamp and address on it?); the arithmetic reasoning test (see example 3, p. 99); the analogies test (see example 2, p. 99); the test of memory span for digits (see example 4, p. 99); and the vocabulary test of forty words arranged in order of difficulty. Three of the above tests, you will recall, are high in the general factor of intelligence: arithmetic reasoning, similarities, and vocabulary.

There are five performance subtests: a digit-symbol test requires the subject to match symbols with digits—a test of speed, accuracy, and visual memory; a picture-completion test requires the subject to note a missing detail—for example, the nose in a picture of a face; a block-design test requires the subject to copy by the proper arrangement of nine cubes several designs of increasing complexity; a picture-arrangement test requires the arrangement of cards into series which tell a story; and an object-assembly test requires the correct arrangement of the pieces of a disassembled object, such as a hand or an animal.

The Wechsler Scales yield three scores—verbal, performance, and a combination of these—which become the full-scale IQ. Has there been any real gain in adding the performance tests? Recall our earlier definition of intelligence: the capacity for verbal and numerical reasoning. Inspection of the list indicates that the performance tests may be low in *g*. For the WAIS, the performance scores and the verbal scores are moderately related. For the WISC, these relationships are considerably lower. For children of normal intelligence, scores on the Stanford-Binet have more relationship to the verbal than to the performance scores of the WISC. It appears that, as a measure of intelligence, we can put less trust in the performance subtests than in the verbal subtests. Even as a diagnostic device the Wechsler has not fulfilled its purpose, perhaps for the simple reason that a test based on a theory of general intelligence can reveal deficiencies only in general intelligence and not in independent intellectual factors.

THE GROUP TESTS. The schools commonly use group tests of intelligence, which have many of the characteristics of individual intelligence tests. First, like the Stanford-Binet and the Wechsler Scales, they are based on a theory of general capacity and on the assumption that the measurement of this capacity requires a sampling of a variety of mental activities. Group-test items, therefore, closely resemble individual-test items: verbal analogies, word meanings, disarranged sentences, sentence completion, arithmetic problems, information, picture arrangement, absurdities, and so on. Second, the arrangement of items usually runs from easy to difficult so that almost every student is able to obtain some correct responses. Third, the ages and the grade levels of the students determine the items and their level of difficulty. For example, at the kindergarten level the items are nonverbal. At the college level they are almost entirely verbal and numerical. Finally, the raw score is converted into a mental age, which in turn, is converted into an IQ. Unlike the scoring on the individual tests, the scoring on the group tests is rigid and objective and allows no qualitative judgment. (This statement, however, should not imply that the individual tests are subjectively scored.) Table 4-1 lists the sounder group tests of general intelligence, along with their grade levels and their correlations with school achievement tests. The dates following the names of the scales are those of their latest revision. The grade level list shows that one test has different scales for each grade level (the California Test), whereas another has a single scale (the Terman-McNemar). The others fall within this range. The correlations, ranging from 0.42 to 0.87, suggest how well you can predict student performance on school achievement tests. These decimal numbers are called *coefficients of correlation*; * they express the degree of correspondence between intelligence scores and other scores and grades. To estimate the degree of correspondence

* See Chapter 15 for a fuller explanation of coefficients of correlation.

TABLE 4-1

MAJOR GROUP INTELLIGENCE SCALES FOR ELEMENTARY AND HIGH SCHOOL.

Name of Scale	Grade Levels (for use in)	Correlations with School Achievement Tests
California Test of Mental Maturity (revised annually)	1 to 12 and adults (twelve scales)	0.42 to 0.81 (fair to good)
Henmon-Nelson Tests of Mental Ability (1957)	3 to 6, 6 to 9, 9 to 12, college (four scales)	0.64 to 0.85 (average to good)
Kuhlmann-Anderson Tests (1952)	K, 1, 2, 3, 4, 5, 6, 7 to 8, 9 to 12 (nine scales)	0.60 to 0.80 (average to good)
Lorge-Thorndike Intelligence Tests (1952)	K to 12 (five scales)	0.76 to 0.87 (good)
Terman-McNemar Test of Mental Ability (1949)	7 to 12 (one scale)	0.54 to 0.66 (average)

between test scores, you should square the coefficient. Take, for example, the coefficient 0.42. By squaring it you obtain 0.17; for 0.87, you obtain about 0.78. By converting these decimals to percentages, you know that the range of agreement between the IQ scores and scores on school achievement tests is from 17 per cent to 78 per cent. Since each of these scales correlates differently with school grades, educational achievement tests, and performance in various subjects, schools and teachers should clearly know their purposes for administering a test and select that scale which best meets their requirements.

Currently on the market are several group scales for college students. Table 4-2 lists the tests now in use, the types of scores, the performance predicted, and the correlations. These college scales have a high degree of technical precision and interscale correlation. Presently their chief drawback is their inability to distinguish, among the middle 60 per cent of students, those most likely to succeed in college. The homogeneity of this middle group, the lack of test refinement, and the social-emotional factors which influence academic achievement account for the lack of successful predictions. Thus we must consider more than these test scores in selecting college freshmen. Students' school grades, scores on standardized achievement tests, and teacher ratings are useful for this purpose.

TABLE 4-2

MAJOR GROUP INTELLIGENCE SCALES FOR COLLEGE FRESHMEN.

Name of Scale	Types of Scores	Predicted Performance (Criteria)	Correlation
Scholastic Aptitude Test (SAT, revised annually by College Entrance Examination Board)	Verbal and two mathematical	Freshmen average	0.45
College Qualification Test (CQT, 1955–58)	Verbal, numerical, total, science, social studies	First-semester grades in junior college	0.26–0.67
Cooperative School and College Ability Tests (SCAT, 1955–57)	Verbal, quantitative, total, and breakdown for subject area	Freshmen grades	0.43–0.68
Henmon-Nelson (1961)	One score only	First-term grades	0.54

How do the individual and group tests of intelligence compare in merit? The individual tests still maintain their primacy. In the evaluation of the group tests, the major standard is how well their scores correspond to scores on the Stanford-Binet. When we are concerned with the case study of an individual student, the personally administered and scored test gives us more information than an IQ score. The number and variety of the student's responses, his ingenuity, strategy, and style in tackling and solving problems are open to observation and are reported; they furnish important clues to the way he functions mentally. Because the group tests of intelligence leave so much to conjecture, teachers and schools must consider other factors as well as scores on these tests in making instructional decisions.*

THE MULTITEST BATTERIES. Not all psychologists accept a theory of general intelligence. In fact, American educational psychologists have almost eagerly jettisoned this theory. At the conclusion of the chapter we shall discuss possible reasons for their action. Those psychologists who follow in the tradition of the Thurstones and Guilford have at-

* If you recall that intelligence is the capacity for numerical and verbal reasoning, you will realize that school achievement is not the only criterion used in developing these tests. The tests are based on what we call *construct validity*.

tempted to devise tests which measure presumably independent intellectual components. Their assumption is that a battery of several tests will predict student achievement in school and college better than the individual and group tests I have already described. These psychologists also claim that such tests can predict success in nonverbal skills, such as mechanical and clerical skills, and can even predict occupational success. If these claims are true, such prophetic batteries would, of course, be an enormous boon to our harassed school psychologists and school counselors. They could decide to keep Sally out of physics, Harold out of music, and Eric where he belongs, in mathematics and science. They could assign Ralph to premedical training, Gertrude to nursing training, and Marvella to homemaking. The counselors could optimistically assume that every child has his aptitudes and every aptitude its niche.

Of the seven multitest batteries in current use perhaps the most popular and ambitious is the Differential Aptitude Tests (DAT). In preparing this battery researchers tested a sample of 47,000 boys and girls in grades 8 through 12. The DAT include these eight tests: verbal reasoning, numerical ability, abstract reasoning, space relations, mechanical reasoning, clerical speed and accuracy, spelling, and language usage. The authors of the DAT also made follow-up studies of 1,700 individuals who were tested in high school to find out how well the battery predicted their educational and vocational careers. Quinn McNemar (1964) carefully perused the 4,096 correlations in the manual for the DAT test battery. With such exhaustive correlational studies the DAT should have been the answer to the prayer of every counselor. McNemar, however, reached these conclusions: (1) Verbal reasoning is the best single predictor; the language-usage test is a close second. (2) Numerical ability, a test of simple arithmetic operations, is the best predictor of achievement in school mathematics; verbal reasoning, however, correlates better than numerical reasoning with grades in science. (3) The remaining five tests do not distinguish different patterns of academic achievement or occupational choice. General level of performance alone indicates those students who go on to study science, medicine, and engineering and those who become salesmen, beauty operators, and stenographers. The final ironic note is that beauty operators and stenographers do better on the tests of space relations and mechanical reasoning than do musicians and carpenters! The other test batteries do not fare better than the DAT. On the basis of considerable test information we may conclude that multitest batteries and multifactor theories of intelligence do not predict school achievement or occupational choice any better than the old-fashioned tests of general intelligence. Moreover, we should not forget the advantages of giving one test rather than a battery: It takes less time, costs less money, and offers fewer scores to consider.

SUMMARY. With this consideration of a test theory of intelligence, of the distinction between general-factor and multifactor theories, and of the description of three types of intelligence tests, I conclude the discussion of the theoretical issues which pertain to intelligence and intelligence tests. The remaining parts of the chapter deal with practical issues which arise from the use of the tests in the schools. Here we consider the trustworthiness of the tests as forecasters of student achievement, the value of the tests in appraising individual differences, and finally the usefulness of the tests in assessing entering behavior and the design of instructional procedures.

QUESTION 4-3

A high school counselor wants to select an intelligence test which will give him information on his seventy-five advisees in the tenth grade, many of whom want to know whether they should prepare for college. He can select only a single test. Which would be his best selection: (a) the Stanford-Binet Scale; (b) the Scholastic Aptitude Test (SAT); (c) the Differential Aptitude Battery (DAT)?

After selecting your answer, explain the reasons for your choice and for your rejection of the alternatives.

School Achievement and IQ

Beginning in this part of the chapter, we shall frequently refer to intelligence and intelligence test scores as *IQ*. IQ, or Intelligence Quotient, originally referred to a score on the Stanford-Binet which was obtained by applying a formula no longer used. The use of the abbreviation IQ, however, has been retained by psychologists, educators, and laymen, as a convenient way of referring to intelligence or to a score on an intelligence test. In the latest revision of the Stanford-Binet (1960), scores are converted into IQ by referring to tables in the test manual.

A persistent question arising from the use of intelligence tests is this: How much trust can teachers place in IQ as a means of predicting the student's scholastic success or failure? Philip Vernon (1958), the noted English educational psychologist, examined some interesting correlations of IQ and achievement. He reports that by combining the information we obtain from intelligence tests, English and arithmetic tests, and teachers' estimates of ability, and by correlating all this information with school performance over a period of two to five years, we obtain a correlation of 0.86 for a whole age group. For the correlation of intelligence test scores and school performance, again for whole age groups, the correlation is 0.80. These are impressive amounts of agreement—from 64 to 74 per cent. For groups which are narrower in range than the whole age group, the amount of agreement decreases. For example, college freshmen do not represent the whole age group of eighteen-year-olds. Similarly, we would expect lower correlations between intelligence test scores and reading scores for one fourth-grade class than for all fourth-grade classes in an urban school system. We already know enough about the problems of school integration to recall that groups of fourth-graders are not identical the city over.

In Table 4-3 Donald Ross Green shows how correlations change as we narrow our sample from a population of twelve classes in four schools to one class in a single school. The reading scores in the table are called *grade-equivalent scores.* A score of 6.4 means that the student is reading at the level of the average sixth-grader in the fourth month of the

TABLE 4-3

GRADE-EQUIVALENT READING SCORES AT THE BEGINNING OF THE FOURTH AND FIFTH GRADES (after Green, 1964, p. 9).

Group I: Drawn from Twelve Classes in Four Schools			Group II: Drawn from One Class in One School		
	Reading Score			Reading Score	
IQ	Fourth Grade	Fifth Grade	IQ	Fourth Grade	Fifth Grade
118	6.4	7.5	118	6.6	7.5
115	3.6	4.1	118	6.4	7.5
113	5.4	6.2	116	6.7	7.5
111	2.9	4.1	116	5.5	6.1
Range	3.5	3.4	Range	1.1	1.4
108	4.9	5.1	115	4.7	5.8
105	3.0	3.3	113	5.0	5.4
105	5.8	6.5	110	5.0	7.3
100	3.6	4.1	108	4.1	5.3
Range	1.3	1.0	Range	3.6	0.5
97	3.4	4.5	106	4.5	5.1
92	3.5	3.4	98	4.1	4.8
91	3.1	3.7	98	3.1	3.5
81	1.3	1.7	77	4.0	6.6
Range	2.1	2.8	Range	0.5	0.5
Correlation with IQ	0.70	0.74		0.71	0.35

school year. For a student in the fourth grade, this may be a very high level of reading (depending on the school he is in). Note the differences in range between the highest and lowest scores. In group I, for children in the fourth grade with IQs between 111 and 118, the range is 3.5; in the fifth grade the range is 3.4. In group II, however, for children in the fourth grade with IQs between 116 and 118 (itself a narrower range), the range is 1.1; for the fifth grade it is 1.4. Further perusal of the correlations between IQ and reading scores for the two groups shows a similar trend. We expect the lower overall correlation of 0.35 for fifth-graders in group II because the group is drawn from one school. The corresponding correlation for group I is 0.74. This latter correlation is much closer to Vernon's correlation of 0.86 for a whole age group, although group I, of course, does not represent a whole age group.

As Vernon points out, however precise our tests of intelligence may become, their use as screening devices will inevitably result in error. Even if we combine the test scores with other sources of information, we still make mistakes in the selection of students for various educational niches. Using the best criteria we have, let us select the top 20 per cent of a group of one hundred high school graduates for college. The typical result of this selection, in Table 4-4, shows that we would exclude six students who would succeed and that we would include six who would fail.

Vernon does not find convincing the frantic assertion that too large a part of our talented youth does not go to college since the correlation between IQ and success in college is about 0.75. However, if we used IQ alone as our basis for admission to college, about 40 per cent of our students would be unsuitable. If we selected only those students with IQs of 125 and above (the upper 5 per cent), about 25 per cent would still fail. Also, if we sent the upper 75 per cent to college, those with IQs of 90 and above, we would exclude 2 per cent who may have succeeded. We would also include many who would be far happier in vocational schools than in college.

TABLE 4-4

PREDICTION OF COLLEGE SUCCESS (after Vernon, 1958, p. 97).

	Successful in College	Unsuccessful in College	Total
Selected on the basis of tests and previous grades	14	6	20
Rejected on the basis of tests and previous grades	6	74	80
Total	20	80	100

Tests of general intelligence enable educators to reduce the amount of error in their academic prophecies. The tests' value, in this respect, is unquestionable. Alone, though, they are not a sufficient basis for making predictions of school and college success for success is not the result only of intelligence. Even if it were, IQ scores of children fluctuate sufficiently to complicate the matter further. These fluctuations, which we shall discuss later, combined with the changing values and interests of the developing child and adolescent and with a confused social milieu to make unreliable all but short-range predictions based on many sources of information.

In summary, although IQ on the average accounts for less than 50 per cent of the variation in academic performance, no other single factor accounts for so much variation. In this sense, IQ is our best predictor of school achievement, even though more than half of the variation remains unexplained. Even more sobering is the fact that IQ correlates more with high school than with college grades, and more with college than with graduate school grades (Lavin, 1965, p. 58). Our original question concerned how much trust the teacher can place in IQ as a predictor of school achievement (as measured by grades and grade-point average). The answer is, of course, limited faith. Obviously other factors, such as the choice of instructional objectives and procedures based on careful assessments of the students' entering behavior, can significantly affect student achievement. Also, other aspects of entering behavior, such as learning sets, learning ability, and learning styles (which we have already considered) and motivation and socioeconomic status (which we consider in the following two chapters), affect the future success or failure of the student. We will consider what particular use the teacher can make of IQ in the last part of this chapter.

Individual Differences and IQ

In Chapter 3 you learned that the psychology of individual differences is largely the study of group differences. The individual enters this study only to the degree that his particular attributes (IQ, sex, height, and so on) fit the groups being compared. When we refer to an individual's IQ we are describing his relative position in a group. We are not describing, as in the case of entering behavior, the relationship of his specific previous learning to specific instructional objectives or, as in the case of personality, the relationship of one attribute to his other attributes.

In this part of the chapter we shall discuss three areas of individual differences—gifted and retarded students, male and female students, and creative and noncreative students—and relate these differences to IQ. As in the previous part, I will reserve for the concluding section of this chapter discussion of the practical implications of this body of information in the assessment of entering behavior and the selection of instructional procedures.

BRILLIANCE AND DULLNESS. Many individuals have scores which fall at the ends of the distribution of IQ. Those with IQs of 120 and above are often referred to as *gifted,* although this term is occasionally reserved for the very superior students, who have IQs of 140 and above. Those with IQs below 80 are described as *mentally retarded.* Several other appellations fit individuals in these groups: talented, mentally superior, mentally deficient, mentally defective, and so on. American school practice has been to use labels which are more innocuous than descriptive if only because we believe that every child should have an opportunity to appear average or normal. The schools often eschew the use of such terms as genius, mental defective, moron, imbecile, and idiot for the use of the more neutral, compassionate, and ambiguous names. The advantage of using IQ, without any label attached, is that it is both clear and neutral.

The latest revision of the Stanford-Binet shows the distribution for IQs listed in Table 4-5. It is based on a sample of 3,184 native-born, white American children. The actual mean for this sample was 101.8. About two-thirds of the children obtained scores between 129 and 85, or from high average to low average.

The widespread occurrence of mental deficiency in the population has stimulated considerable research (Blackman and Heintz, 1966)

TABLE 4-5

IQ DISTRIBUTION (Merrill, 1938).

IQ	Percentage	Classification
160–69	0.03	
150–59	0.2	Very superior
140–49	1.1	
130–39	3.1	
120–29	8.2	Superior
110–19	18.1	High average
100–9	25.5	
90–99	23.0	Normal or average
80–89	14.5	Low average
70–79	5.6	Borderline defective
60–69	2.0	
50–59	0.4	
40–49	0.2	Mentally defective
30–39	0.03	

focused on the biological or congenital origin of mental deficiency and on the requirements for training programs which will give deficient children the maximum amount of economic and social independence. Much descriptive research attempts only to identify these children. As a group they appear to be below average in physical, social, and intellectual development. They have more physical and sensory defects than does the population as a whole. They have greater susceptibility to disease and shorter life spans. They tend to be below average in all mental functions but especially in verbal and numerical reasoning. For tasks which are monotonous and repetitive, they show the patience of Job. Institutionalization often causes further decreases in IQ, but with proper training and guidance many of them learn to accept and enjoy a fairly restricted occupational and social life.

For the mentally superior children, the description is almost an exact correspondence in reverse. This group appears to be above average in physical, social, and intellectual development. They are healthier and they live longer than average. They achieve a greater degree of social and occupational success. Contrary to the popular stereotype, they suffer from less mental illness than do the intellectually deficient. By far the most distinguishing characteristic of the intellectually superior is their ability to handle verbal and numerical abstractions in almost all contexts. This alone greatly enhances their chances of educational and occupational success. The most extensive study of intellectually superior children was Terman's Stanford Gifted Children Study, which was carried out over a thirty-five-year period, with a sample of 1,528 individuals. Despite its methodological limitations, it indicates their degree of success (Terman and Ogden, 1950). The gifted group excelled in college degrees, graduate degrees, grades, and academic honors. These individuals obtained five to eight times as many Ph.D. degrees as did a comparable sample of college graduates. Table 4-6 indicates the occupational success of gifted men in California in comparison with all California males.

One of the most significant comparisons of the Terman study was that of the 150 men rated most successful with the 150 men rated least successful in adult achievement. The most conspicuous differences between these two groups were the superior educational and vocational level of the parents of the most successful men. Over 50 per cent of the most successful group had fathers who had graduated from college, against 15 per cent of the least successful group. More than twice as many of the most successful men had fathers who were in the professions.

Despite the somewhat convincing nature of the Terman study and other studies of the mentally superior individuals, popular stereotypes of the genius and the curve-raiser persist. The very superior individual,

TABLE 4-6

OCCUPATIONAL CLASSIFICATION OF GIFTED MEN AT THE AGE OF 35 (after Schiller, 1934, p. 67).

Occupational group	Percentage of Gifted Men (N = 724)	Percentage of Employed Males in California (1940) (N = 1,878,559)
I. Professional	45.4	5.7
II. Semiprofessional and higher business	25.7	8.1
III. Clerical, skilled trades, retail business	20.7	24.3
IV. Farming and other agricultural pursuits	1.2	12.4
V. Semiskilled trades, minor clerical	6.2	31.6
VI. Slightly skilled trades	0.7	17.8 (VI and VII combined)
VII. Day laborers: urban and rural	0.0	

in the top 0.03 per cent of the IQ distribution, will hardly seem ordinary to most of us no matter how hard he tries to conceal his intellectual capacities.

In relation to education, is the usual public school environment rich enough or free enough to satisfy the intellectual demands of these individuals? Increasingly, many public school educators are accepting the fact that their schools are not the answer to all the needs of the heterogeneous American population. For students at either end of the IQ continuum, the very special educational environment they require is often not within the organizational or financial means of the general public school. Rather than water down or enrich the curriculum for a few, special agencies with both private and public support can often more efficiently and effectively meet the needs of the child of exceptionally high or low mentality.

Sex and IQ. More significant than differences in male and female intelligence, according to Anne Anastasi (1958, p. 453), is the immense amount of overlap. She reminds us of Samuel Johnson's reply when asked whether man or woman was more intelligent: "Which man, which woman?" This view challenges our stereotypes of men and women. In fact, much evidence points to the wide individual differences found within each sex. For example, Fig. 4-1 shows the distribution of scores of an arithmetic reasoning test for 189 boys and 206 girls in the third and fourth grades. The median for the boys is 40.39; for the girls, 35.81. There is a 28 per cent overlap—that is, 28 per cent of the girls reach

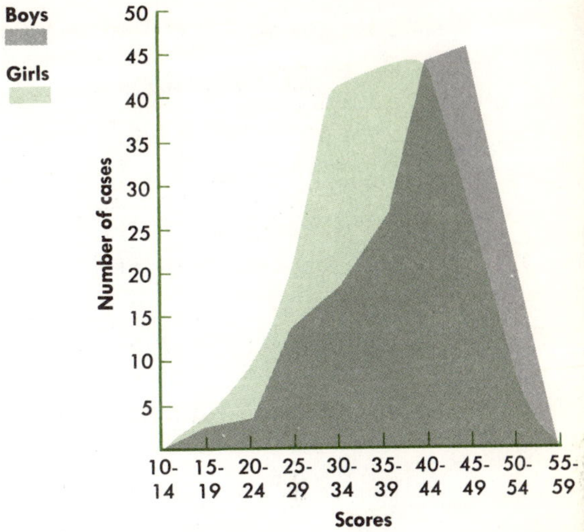

Fig. 4-1. *Distribution of boys and girls on a test of arithmetic reasoning (after Anastasi, 1958, p. 455).*

or exceed the median of the boys. The median is an average: It is the midpoint in a distribution of scores, the point above and below which an equal number of scores occur. By overlap, I mean the common area occupied by the two curves. If the overlap were 100 per cent, the two curves would be identical (they would occupy the same area).

Keeping in mind the great degree of overlap, we can compare the performance of the two sexes in various physical and mental activities. Table 4-7 summarizes these comparative data. Advantage in the major intellectual functions (verbal and numerical reasoning) is well divided between the females and males. Whereas the girls have the verbal advantage, the boys have the advantage in numerical reasoning. In the light of these intellectual differences it is interesting to compare performance of the sexes on the standardized achievement tests and their school performance. On the standardized achievement tests the boys surpass the girls in those subjects requiring numerical reasoning, spatial aptitudes, and the retention of certain information in such subjects as history, geography, and science. The girls surpass the boys in subjects which require verbal abilities, memory, perceptual speed, and accuracy. These differences in test performance are consistent with the differences in aptitudes reported in Table 4-7.

In actual school performance, however, the girls consistently surpass the boys. That is, the girls obtain better school grades, whether the subject is language, literature, arithmetic, science, history, and so on.

TABLE 4-7

SEX COMPARISON OF VARIOUS FUNCTIONS (after Anastasi, 1958, pp. 470–78).

Skill, Process, or Function	The Favored Sex
Gross bodily movement	Males, of all ages
Manual dexterity	Females, of all ages
Perception of details (speed of)	Females
Spatial orientation (Witkins *et al.*, 1954)	Males
Word fluency and mechanics of language	Females
Vocabulary, verbal comprehension, and verbal reasoning	Females (but a smaller difference than in word fluency and mechanics)
Memory of verbal material	Females
Memory of numbers and geometric forms	About the same
Mental imagery—vividness	Females
Spatial and mechanical aptitudes	Males
Numerical aptitude—computation	About the same
Numerical aptitude—reasoning test	Males
Artistic and musical aptitudes —esthetics	Females
—skills	About the same

When compared with boys receiving the same achievement test scores, girls even surpass boys in school grades. This difference in school performance persists throughout high school and college. Anastasi suggests several reasons for the superior school performance of the girls. Their superior verbal ability gives them the advantage both in responding to instruction and in testing, both of which, of course, are predominantly verbal. Also, girls tend to be more docile than boys—less resistant to school routine and more resistant to out-of-school distractions. The predominance of women teachers in elementary schools enables the girls to identify more quickly with school and also predisposes the schools to adapt more quickly to girls than to boys.

Paradoxically, career and success belong to the men rather than to the women. Despite the superior academic ability and achievement of the women, vocational achievement is virtually a male monopoly. In the Terman studies of gifted children, the adult careers of the women were very undistinguished. A very small number engaged in university teaching, creative writing, art, and research, but two-thirds of those with IQs of 170 and above were office workers or housewives. Follow-up testing also indicated that the mean IQ of the women tended to drop at a faster rate than that of the men.

The picture is fairly clear. The stereotypes of the American woman as housewife, mother, companion, and social catalyst make it difficult for the American female of intellectual ability and aspirations to distinguish herself in the professional or semiprofessional world without the risk of losing some of her femininity in the eyes of her would-be male competitors and her conservative female friends. It is not at all uncommon in the American high school and college to see the girl of superior intellectual ability and of average physical appearance displaying more interest in social than in academic achievement. The last veil which the American woman must surrender for her full emancipation is the one that now hides her intellectual capacities.

Creativity and IQ.* The most recent challenge to the concept of general intelligence has come from studies on creativity. Guilford raised the standard of battle in 1950, when he stated that to fathom creativity we must look beyond the bounds of intelligence. He predicted that the correlations between scores on tests of intelligence and on tests of creativity would be moderate or low. The highly intelligent would probably not be highly creative, and the highly creative would not be highly intelligent. A series of creativity studies conducted in the 1960s reached conclusions which tend to support Guilford's prophecy.

Jacob Getzels and Philip Jackson (1962) published a study on creativity and intelligence which has particular relevance to education. Creativity tests were administered to a sample of 533 students with an average IQ of 130. No intelligence tests were newly administered, but previous scores on the WISC, the Henmon-Nelson, and the Stanford-Binet, which had been recorded by the schools, were used. On the basis of the creativity and intelligence tests, the authors made a selection of smaller samples for intensive study. They selected the top 20 per cent of students on the creativity measures and the top 20 per cent on the IQ measures. Those students who were in the top 20 per cent on both the IQ and creativity measures were excluded from the study. The high creatives were compared with the high IQs on total scholastic achievement, motivation for achievement, perception by teachers, personal values, imaginative production, career aspirations, and family background.

Of major concern for this chapter are the relationships which these

* The topic of creativity is given further consideration in Chapter 11, in which we consider instructional procedures for fostering creative thinking.

TABLE 4-8

COMPARISON OF IQ, CREATIVITY, AND ACHIEVEMENT (after Getzels and Jackson, 1962, p. 24).

	Total Population (N = 449)	High IQ (N = 28)	High Creativity (N = 24)
IQ (mean)	132.00	150.00	127.00
School achievement	49.91	55.00	56.27

authors found between intelligence, creativity, and achievement. Table 4-8 reports some of these data. The authors were elated to find that a difference of 23 IQ points between the high-creative group and the high-IQ group was not reflected in the average school achievement of the two groups. On the basis of this evidence the authors felt they were free to conclude that creativity is equal to or more important than intelligence in determining scholastic achievement.

Although some circles have heralded this study as a great breakthrough in our notions about IQ and creativity, others have criticized its many shortcomings. First among these shortcomings, the authors failed to administer an intelligence test at the time they administered the creativity tests. Reliance on test scores of previous years and different scales leaves the study open to many sources of uncontrolled variation. Second, and more seriously, the authors deliberately excluded from their study students who were in the top 20 per cent on both the creativity and intelligence tests, as if they were already committed to the belief that both these qualities could not be found in the same individual. Third, the authors failed to report the basic correlations between creativity, intelligence, and achievement. In the absence of this information, McNemar (1964, p. 879) suggests that we assume the difference between mean creativity scores for the two groups to be the same as the mean difference for IQ, about 23 points. If we make this assumption, we arrive at exactly the opposite conclusion: The high-IQ group did as well in school achievement as the high-creative group despite the mean difference in creativity. A replication of the study which corrected these and other defects did not support the findings of Getzels and Jackson (Yamamoto, 1964).

Many more replications of the faulty design of Getzels and Jackson not quite surprisingly have led to the same conclusions. Paul Torrance

(1962), for example, suggests that by using tests of intelligence we fail to identify 70 per cent of the top fifth of the creative school children. He strongly implies that the correlations between intelligence and creativity are low and that the creativity tests, better than the intelligence tests, identify the gifted. Other writers with the same bias suggest that we identify creativity in preschool children in order to foster its growth and prevent its early extinction.

The lack of valid tests on creativity has surely hampered research on this topic. The ultimate validity of any creativity test must be based on whether it measures the actual creativity prized by our society. Thus far, the makers of creativity tests have not put these measures to such a test. McNemar (1964) suggests that, rather than an inimical relationship between creativity and intelligence, we may expect high positive correlations. In literary, architectural, and scientific work the relationship between creativity and IQ can be depicted as an inverted triangle. At high levels of IQ (near the base) we find wide ranges of creativity. As we move down the triangle to average and lower IQ, we would find very narrow ranges of creativity. McNemar concludes that having a high IQ is not a guarantee of being creative; having a low IQ means creativity is impossible. In summary, then, we have little reason to believe that intelligence tests, as imperfect as they are, are less predictive of creativity than are the current creativity tests.

SUMMARY. We have now concluded our discussion of individual differences in IQ as they relate to the gifted and the retarded, to male and female students, and to creativity. We have seen that having a high IQ is not a guarantee of success and happiness, but it is certainly not a handicap for occupational and social success (for women no less than for men) and for creative achievement in the liberal and scientific disciplines. Much of this part of the chapter has attempted to dispel popular stereotypes held by teachers, students, and laymen regarding the disadvantages of having a high IQ. We consider the instructional implications of these individual differences in the rest of this chapter.

QUESTION 4-4

Your child has an acute attack of appendicitis and you must select one of three doctors: Doctor *A,* who received all As in medical school; Doctor *B,* who received both As and Bs; and Doctor *C,* who obtained a C average in medical school. You can obtain no further information and you must make an immediate decision. Which one do you choose?

Indicate your reasons for choosing a particular doctor and for rejecting the other two.

Entering Behavior and IQ

In this final part of the chapter we shall consider the usefulness of IQ in the planning of instruction, particularly as a means of describing and assessing entering behavior. First, I explain the alleged limitations of IQ as a way of describing the present status of any student and then discuss how many of these criticisms stem from a rather narrow and prosaic interpretation of democracy and equality. Second, I discuss some practical limitations of IQ in the light of our conception of entering behavior and Piaget's theory of intellectual development. Finally, in the context of these limitations, both alleged and practical, I draw some conclusions about how IQ can be used by the teacher.

Alleged limitations of IQ. In an article entitled, "Lost: Our Intelligence? Why?" McNemar (1964) asks why many American psychologists and educators have virtually abandoned the concept of general intelligence. To answer his question, he lists eight attacks on the concept and the tests: the earlier false claims about the stability of the IQ; the failure of IQ tests to make good predictions in individual cases; the early claims that something innate was being measured; the criticism that IQ tests measure only cultural effects; the belief that IQ tests measure only middle-class values; the claim that IQ scores foster unrealistic expectations of school achievement; the opinion that IQ differences are incompatible with democracy and educational freedom; and the belief that stress on general intelligence causes us to ignore other abilities. Such a list of grievances, if true, would almost signal the end of the use of intelligence tests.

We answered some of these criticisms earlier in this chapter. For example, we found the argument and the evidence for specific intellectual abilities other than general mental ability to be at least inconclusive. We saw that tests of creative ability leave much to be desired. We also saw that, although our predictions of school success have a margin of error even when we combine IQ with other evidence, we do remarkably better than chance. Further, it is hard to understand how IQ scores foster unrealistic expectations of school achievement unless they are rigidly applied as the only basis for making educational plans and decisions. By expecting too much from IQ tests, we may very well confuse partial success with total failure. We considered at the beginning of the chapter the questions of the stability of IQ over the life span of the individual and of the genetic component of IQ. Here I can state that the degree of stability found and the evidence for some genetic determination of intellectual capacity have not rested well with many educators, psychologists, and laymen. In Chapter 6 we shall examine the relationship between socioeconomic status and intelligence, and even there we shall find that idealistic sentiment does not square well with available evidence.

At this point, however, I am concerned with the relationship of intelligence tests to our democratic beliefs. We may have no better example of how the behavioral sciences collide with personal and social values than in the current controversy about and attitudes toward intelligence tests. And we also do not have a better example of how political philosophy may assume more weight than empirically supported theory, even for the behavioral scientist. The rationale of intelligence tests is that identifiable differences in human ability exist and that these differences are of practical importance to the individual, the school, and the whole society. Opposed to this rationale is the deep-seated American conviction that all men are created equal and that they are, therefore, entitled to an equal share of the opportunities and the rewards of this world.

Intelligence tests single out an intellectual aristocracy—those individuals who have superior ability to handle verbal and numerical abstractions. This intellectual aristocracy, as we shall see, corresponds roughly with the social aristocracy of wealth and prestige, although many children of the middle class and of the poor have remarkably high degrees of intelligence. If intelligence is largely a product of our genes, we have a biological rather than a social aristocracy. Many Americans find any aristocracy repugnant since the aura of authoritarianism which surrounds aristocracies opposes their vigorously egalitarian beliefs. They are also inclined to reject those tests and that evidence which establish membership in an elite. It is significant that critics of American schools have often pointed out that the public eagerly supports programs which help the mentally deficient but is willing to leave the mentally superior to their own resources.

Part of American ideology also pertains to free enterprise and a laissez-faire philosophy; we believe in open competition. Orville Brim (1965) suggests that, with truly open competition, each generation of the talented elite could rise to the top, and be replaced during the next generation by others not necessarily bearing a blood relationship to them. Yet Brim and his associates have provided evidence that Americans find such a prospect unpalatable. For example, those adults who hold egalitarian views are ones who say most frequently that intelligence tests are unfair.

Opposition to intelligence tests also comes from other sources. Many individuals, for humanistic, social, and psychological reasons, fear and resent the study and measurement of human behavior. They denounce it as an invasion of privacy and as a contribution to the destruction of individual self-determination. Also, many individuals resent intelligence tests because their pride has been hurt by poor test performance. Brim reports that 76 per cent of high school students expect to score average or above, but we know that only 50 per cent will do so. Evidence also shows that, if test performance is sufficiently unacceptable, the students may forget the score, to defend their egos but still direct a residue of resentment against the tests. Furthermore, in high schools and colleges, this resentment increases as the students realize that the tests significantly affect their opportunities for educational and vocational advancement.

We may conclude that many of the alleged limitations of IQ and of the idea of general intelligence are based on misconceptions about general intelligence and about the tests which measure it and on an emotional bias against the tests, which stems from a narrow view of egalitarianism and the natural petulance of those who receive average and low scores.

Practical limitations of IQ. These limitations refer in part to the underlying notion of general intelligence and in part to the restricted use you can make of IQ in planning instruction. First, let us consider the practical limitations of the notion of general intelligence. In the previous chapter you saw that entering behavior can be conceived as learning sets, learning abilities, and learning styles. The evidence there indicated that learning sets and abilities could provide a better indication of what performances the student might acquire than could his IQ. Perhaps the most dramatic instance was the study of Jensen (1963) in which one of the two fastest learners in a group of gifted and retarded children was a retarded child with an IQ of 65. Gagné (1965c) also found that you can very reliably predict performance on subsequent tasks in a hierarchical learning structure and, in this way, predict ultimate performance. Although learning sets and ability are undoubtedly highly correlated with IQ—that is, those students with the most highly developed learning sets and abilities also have the highest IQs—the use of these more refined classes of behavior can effectively improve our prediction of the results of our teaching. Future research may well indicate that multifactor theories have failed to improve significantly the predictions of school achievement because they do not identify the crucial components of a general intelligence factor.

Also you have seen how Piaget's studies of intellectual development have expanded our conception of intelligence. Future research may very well conclude that Piaget's schemas are learning sets and abilities (Whiteman, 1964). Similarly, a general intelligence factor *g* may indicate how efficiently the student is using the schemas or abilities required in verbal and numerical learning tasks. IQ simply refers to general operating efficiency. By studying the processes (schemas, sets, abilities, and styles) which account for IQ, we may considerably improve our assessment of particular areas of entering behavior for the achievement of particular instructional objectives. This is not an argument for throwing out the general measures of intelligence which, as I have noted, correlate very well with specific measures of intellectual components. It is an argument for supplementing IQ scores with assessments of other areas of student entering behavior. We may overcome the practical limitations of the idea of general intelligence by using schemas, learning sets, learning abilities, and styles in making descriptions and assessments of entering behavior.

Second, there are practical limitations to using IQ, as a test score, in the actual planning of instruction. In Chapter 3, in the study of retarded children (Stolurow, 1964), you saw that, when instructional procedures were greatly improved (as in the use of programed instruction), retarded and normal children learned equally well. Similarly, Eigen and Feldhusen (1964) found that tests of achievement in specific subject matter and skill areas were better predictors of how much the students learned in programed instruction than were IQ scores. These studies strongly suggest that instructional procedures are important determinants of achievement and that improved instruction can cancel out the initial advantages of superior IQ. It would appear, as Carroll stated in Chapter 1, that as the quality of instruction improves the student depends less on his general intellectual ability, with the result that students of quite varying IQs can and do succeed equally well under optimal instructional conditions.

Neither type of practical limitation argues for the discontinuation of IQ testing or of the use of IQ scores. They merely suggest that with our newer conceptions of entering behavior, with our improved instructional techniques, and with IQ scores we may significantly improve our predictions of school achievement. Certainly the evidence in this chapter indicates that IQ is a better predictor of achievement, including creative achievement, than are our stereotypes of the gifted, the retarded, men, women, and the creative artist (who is often depicted as a person of pure emotion and madness). If IQ scores are crude predictors then stereotypes are even cruder. No evidence indicates that we should use radically different methods of instruction for, on the one hand the gifted, the males, and the creative, and on the other hand the retarded, the females, and the conformists. None of these broad categories of entering behavior is as useful in the design of instruction as the more precise descriptions of the students' entering behavior which you read about in Chapter 3.

You should now return to objectives 11–19 (p. 85) and determine how well you have achieved them.

SUMMARY

This has been a long chapter. Beginning with the development of intelligence, you read about Piaget's system with its functional invariants, including assimilation and accommodation, and the schemas. Using these key theoretical notions, Piaget has been able to study and describe qualitative differences in periods of development. I described two periods of intellectual development—that of concrete and that of formal operations—and discussed the characteristics of and the differences between them. Finally, I described three applications of Piaget's system to the description and the assessment of entering behavior; these applications concerned new tests of intelligence, curriculum development, and the use of the schemas in task analysis.

The section on the measurement of intelligence first dealt with theoretical issues which pertain to the construction of the tests. We considered the relationship between Piaget's conception of intelligence and the conception of general intelligence as embodied in IQ tests. We considered also single-factor and multifactor theories of intelligence and three kinds of intelligence tests: individual and group tests and multitest batteries. The last three parts of the chapter dealt with practical issues which arise in the school use of the tests. You saw how IQ is our best single predictor of school achievement, but with a 50 per cent margin of error. In the study of individual differences and IQ, you saw that present evidence does little to support current stereotypes of exceptional children, male and female mental ability, and intelligence and creativity. Finally, we dealt with the alleged and practical limitations of IQ tests and scores and with the idea of a unitary intelligence factor. The alleged limitations result from ingrained prejudices which have little supporting evidence. The practical limitations result from the need to develop our notion of intellectual processes. As our understanding of new areas of cognitive entering behavior and our skill in designing instructional procedures improve, we will have the means for supplementing IQ scores as predictors of school achievement.

SUGGESTED READINGS

For the student who is willing to take the time and make the effort, this is the finest summary and criticism of Piaget's system:

Flavell, J. H., *The Developmental Psychology of Jean Piaget*. Princeton, N.J.: D. Van Nostrand Co., Inc., 1963.

Briefer summaries and criticism are found in the following books:

Baldwin, Alfred, *Theories of Child Development*, Chapters 5–9, pp. 171–304. New York: John Wiley & Sons, Inc., 1967.

Hunt, J. McV., *Intelligence and Experience*, Chapters 5–7, pp. 109–307. New York: The Ronald Press Company, 1961.

This book gives the student a more direct contact with Piaget and his coworkers:

Inhelder B., and Jean Piaget, *The Growth of Logical Thinking from Childhood to Adolescence*. New York: Basic Books, Inc., 1958.

This book gives Piaget's views on educational method:

Piaget, Jean, *The Moral Judgment of the Child.* London: Routledge & Kegan Paul, Ltd., 1932. Also in paperback—New York: Free Press, 1965.

The literature on the measurement of intelligence is vast and extensive. Useful summaries and interpretations are found in the following books:

Anastasi, Anne, *Differential Psychology* (3rd ed.). New York: The Macmillan Company, 1958.

Cronbach, Lee J., *Essentials of Psychological Testing* (2nd ed.). New York: Harper & Row, Publishers, Inc., 1960.

Freeman, Frank S., *Theory and Practice of Psychological Testing.* New York: Holt, Rinehart & Winston, Inc., 1962.

Lavin, David E., *The Prediction of Academic Performance.* New York: Russell Sage Foundation, 1965.

Tyler, Leona E., *The Psychology of Human Differences* (3rd ed.). New York: Appleton-Century-Crofts, 1965.

———, *Tests and Measurements.* Englewood Cliffs, N.J.: Prentice-Hall, Inc., 1963.

Motivation: How to Increase Student Vim and Vigor

5

This chapter chiefly helps you to develop a conceptualization of the motivational functions of the teacher. The first of the three sections, which is quite brief, defines motivation in a way which distinguishes it from learning and relates it to entering behavior. The second section introduces the basic theory of and research on motivation. The research reported forms the basis for the four motivational functions of the teacher described in the third section: the arousal, expectancy, incentive, and disciplinary functions. Motivational functions refer to rather broad categories of teacher behavior. I might have (and you may believe that I should have) described motivational procedures—concrete deeds of the teacher which increase motivation. In Part 3 of this book, however, you will discover that almost anything I could have written about motivational procedures can be more aptly and precisely described as learning procedures. What remains are motivational functions, which, if successfully enacted by the teacher, maintain and increase student effort without necessarily initiating or directing learning.

A chapter on motivation must deal with the student's attitudes, values, and, in general, his personality. Although these topics are often given more extensive treatment than they are in this book, everything about them in terms of instructional practice is contained in the description of the four motivational functions of the teacher.

Upon reading the first section of this chapter (on the definition of motivation), you should be able to meet these objectives:

1. List the characteristics of the concept of motivation and distinguish between behavior which is best explained in terms of motivation and behavior which is best explained in terms of habits, abilities, external stimuli, and so on.

2. Describe the relationship between motivation and entering behavior in terms of relative response strength.

Upon reading the second section of this chapter (on basic theory and research), you should be able to meet these objectives:

3. Define arousal in terms of the level of activity and provide illustrations of different arousal levels.

4. Define curiosity and exploratory behavior in terms of stimulus seeking and the conditions which give rise to it and provide examples of this behavior in animals and humans.

5. Define anxiety in terms of arousal and describe its relationship to student ability, learning tasks, and student performance.

6. Define frustration in terms of response competition and describe its relationship to anxiety and performance.

7. Define expectancy in terms of belief about outcomes and describe and illustrate its relationship to discrepancy, valance, and motive to achieve.

8. Distinguish between high- and low-achievement motivation and list the conditions which assist the development of the motive to achieve.

9. Define incentives and explain and illustrate how they increase response vigor; distinguish between positive and negative reinforcers and aversive stimuli and describe their influence in imitative learning.

10. Distinguish between escape and avoidance training and a punishment procedure; explain how punishment is related to intensity of shock, to a rewarded alternative, and to consumatory responses; describe and illustrate two psychological myths about the effects of punishment.

11. Distinguish between the model of motivation offered in this chapter and those of drive-reduction theory, of Freudian theory, and of self-actualizing tendencies.

Upon reading the third section of this chapter (on the motivation of students), you should be able to meet these objectives:

12. Define and illustrate the teacher's arousal function in terms of regulating arousal levels, attracting and holding student attention, and controlling anxiety levels through different teaching procedures.

13. Define and illustrate the teacher's expectancy function in terms of instructional objectives, immediate and remote objectives, changing expectancies, mismatching expectancies, and controlling the level of aspiration.

14. Define and illustrate the teacher's incentive function in terms of feedback of test results, praise and blame, grades, competition, and cooperation.

15. Define and illustrate the teacher's disciplinary function in terms of restitution, the ripple effect, teacher ineptness, instructional objectives, and the urban and suburban setting.

A DEFINITION OF MOTIVATION

The modern teacher is neither a martinet nor a martyr. He may motivate students by combining careful distribution of rewards with mild threats of punishment, somewhat forceful cajolery with benign tolerance of mistakes made in the line of duty, and concessions to immature interests and foibles with frequent reminders of what the student finally must learn. He may be warm and enthusiastic but may still insist on an orderly and businesslike classroom. If the modern teacher no longer slaps faces, thrashes bottoms, or rules the back of hands (at least in most suburban schools), he still furrows a mean brow and grimaces when displeased. He may no longer string gold stars after the names of successful students, but he has learned the advantage of a well-timed smile and a pat on the head or shoulder. To motivate his students, the modern teacher may deliver short sermons on the ultimate salvation and glory of those who persevere and succeed and on the ultimate damnation of those who surrender the task of today to whim and fancy. He may consciously shape himself into the humane and intellectual model he wants his students to imitate. And at times he may share control of the classroom and of the lesson plan with the students, hoping that they will provide conditions which enhance their creative endeavors and satisfy their intellectual curiosity.

As students we have all been exposed to (and perhaps even victimized by) a magnificent array of motivational devices and procedures. For punishment teachers have used the verbal reprimand, either spoken or shouted; the check mark in the roll book; the birch rod; the ruler; and the dunce hat. They have pulled ears and hair, made students stand in corners or corridors, detained them after school, and—the ultimate embarrassment and threat—banished them to the principal's office, expelled them from school, and made them return from exile in the company of their parents. Some teachers have devoted a significant part of their professional lives to creative punishment and have been prevented only by principals and lawyers from using electric shocks and the Chinese water torture. Many teachers earn such renowned reputations as punishers in their early years that their classes are seas of calm and tranquility throughout their later years.

The list of rewards, although not so dramatic, is equally impressive and inexhaustible. Teachers have praised students, both publicly and privately, for work well done; have given the seat or seats of honor to those who distinguish themselves; have publicly displayed notebooks, painting, and projects of superior merit; have awarded the perennial gold stars; and have devised graphs and charts to show how much the students are "growing in knowledge." They have arranged field trips, movies, special projects, and free periods. For some students reward takes the form of positions of privilege—teacher's chief helper, classroom president, aquarium caretaker, bird feeder, school president, and valedictorian. For others the reward is relief—relief that the class, semester, or school year is over; that the project is finished; or that, by law, their education is forever terminated.

Motivation As the Source of Vigor

Motivation is one of the most popular topics in educational, psychological, and business circles. Popular magazines frequently carry inspirational articles which suggest that by being sufficiently aroused or by finding the means of self-arousal an individual can solve all his problems of work, marriage, friendship, child raising, drinking, eating, and sexual relations. Vance Packard (1957, p. 5) reveals how psychology professors (in his opinion) have become merchandisers by using their knowledge to "sell you cake mixes, cigarettes, cars, soaps, and even ideas." These professors, he writes, use MR (motivation research) to find out how people make choices. In this research they employ techniques "designed to reach the unconscious or subconscious mind because preferences generally are determined by factors of which the individual is not conscious" (1957, p. 5). He continues (p. 4):

> What the probers are looking for, of course, are the *whys* of our behavior, so that they can more effectively manipulate our habits and choices in their favor. This has led them to probe why we are afraid of banks; why we love those big fat cars; why we really buy homes; why men smoke cigars; why the kind of car we drive reveals the brand of gasoline we will buy; why housewives typically fall into a hypnoidal trance when they get into a supermarket; why men are drawn into auto showrooms by convertibles but end up buying sedans; why Junior loves cereal that pops, snaps, and crackles.

Packard seems to conclude that the motivation researchers know the answers to all these and other questions and that we are now the passive victims of their artful manipulation. Lay and professional people seem to agree with Packard in assuming that motivation is the sole determinant of behavior. By motivating an individual you release great hidden potential, and by controlling this release you control his behavior. Presumably you can make him buy what you want him to buy rather than what he wants to buy (partly because you know better than he does what he really wants to buy!). It is unfortunate that so many journalists, psychologists, and educators unwittingly present psychology as medieval witchcraft in modern scientific trappings.

Their speculation aside, motivation actually refers to those factors which increase and decrease the vigor of an individual's activity. Thus it determines the levels or degree of his activity. In the following treatment I will not use the concept of motivation to explain the initiation and direction of activity, which are more fully explained in terms of learning. Here I am concerned only with the factors which increase and decrease the vim and vigor of student activity. In educational parlance vigor is often called *effort*. In terms of effort, the study of student motivation searches for those factors which increase the student's effort to make desirable responses. For example, which factors increase Elvis' efforts to run the 100-yard dash, to paint landscapes, and to date girls? And which fail to increase his efforts to balance chemical equations, distinguish metaphors and similes, and trace historical trends? You will note that we are not asking how he acquires (learns) any of these performances. Indeed, we are assuming that he has learned both to balance equations and to paint landscapes. We are asking why he invests more energy in one activity than in the other.

By strengthening an individual's motivation we increase the likelihood of his making the responses he has learned best. We cannot expect the student to make responses he has not learned no matter how ingenious we may be in motivating him. Motivation is also related to learning itself: The amount of effort, energy, and vigor the student invests in any performance will be one factor in determining how well he performs. For example, the fact that Elvis puts more effort (motivation) into dating girls than into distinguishing metaphors and similes forecasts a higher development of his social than of his literary skills (learning).

In the above quotation Packard described the "probers" as looking for the "whys" of our behavior. He goes on to suggest that the whys are found in research on motivation. We now know that Packard's position would assign the entire study of human behavior to the area of motivation. His position represents a vast overcommitment to one among many areas of modern psychology. Why do we behave—at all or as we do? The answer to this question embraces the whole field of psychology. We can distinguish many influences on our behavior other than motivation: (1) Innate structures (genes, for example) influence the direction and level of development; (2) our abilities (intelligence, for example) influence a wide range of behaviors; (3) we manipulate and adapt to the external stimuli, the environment; and (4) our habits—the acts we have learned—control us to some extent also. All these factors stimulate, control, and direct behavior.

Charles Cofer and Mortimer Appley (1964, pp. 825–26) believe that the general statement "without motivation there would be no behavior" is without meaning. Some psychologists point out that the unmotivated organism is inactive, quiescent, and sleepy. This seems to be an assumption of Packard: We are sitting ducks for the persuaders since we passively await their manipulation. No organism is totally inactive however unless it is dead. Motivation does not explain activity vs. inactivity. It explains the levels or degree of an organism's activity—its vigor. The sheer fact that activity occurs is not a psychological problem.

Motivation and Entering Behavior

Miss Pegg presents a list of words to Horatio and asks him to respond with the first three words which come to mind. Miss Pegg says "corn" and Horatio replies "hominy grits." Miss Pegg smiles, pats little Horatio on the head, and asks him to think of two more responses. Horatio simply repeats "hominy grits." A wrinkle or two appear on Miss Pegg's smooth brow (she is combining a little punishment with reward) as she asks Horatio to try harder to think of two additional responses. She remains enthusiastic and warm, recalling how well Horatio has done on other words and other assignments. But Horatio can only think of hominy grits. (It is true that Horatio later thought of another response, "whiskey," but there was something about the smoothness of Miss Pegg's brow and the classroom setting which occasioned his first and only response.) Miss Pegg later taught Horatio several other verbal associations for the word "corn." She suggested "yellow," "shiny," "vegetable," "maize," and even "whiskey" (which she cautioned Horatio no one should ever consume). Miss Pegg had tried to invigorate or increase Horatio's efforts to think of additional responses. She failed because Horatio had essentially only one response he could make.

This rather improbable anecdote illustrates how motivation depends on entering behavior. Entering behavior describes the present status of the student's behavior. It describes the responses he can now make to various stimulus situations. The association between corn and hominy grits was so strong in Horatio's mind that it crowded out all other associations. Under different circumstances Horatio could also have thought of whiskey. The success of Miss Pegg's attempts to motivate him to make more than one response will depend on how much the new associations which Horatio has learned increase in strength over time.

Any procedures a teacher may use to increase student motivation must account for the student's entering behavior. Later in this chapter we shall discuss discrepancies, expectancies, valences, anxiety, frustration, achievement motives, incentives, competition, and punishment. You will quickly discover that student performance varies considerably under each of these conditions. In motivation, as in no other aspect of human behavior, one man's meat is another man's poison. For example, we shall review the evidence which indicates that some students actually achieve better under anxious, risky, competitive, and frustrating conditions than under the opposite ones. Other students' fear of failure makes working under anxious and frustrating conditions an agony. Not all students react to verbal incentives in the same way. Some students feel that they must fail, and praise may only arouse their suspicions and their anxiety. They understand failure. What do they do with success (Van der Reit, 1963)? Students differ in their valences—what they consider to be desirable goals. They differ in their expectancies—what they believe to be realistic success for themselves. The fact that there are no universal prescriptions and universal procedures for increasing student motivation greatly increases the difficulty of teaching. The teacher must make that analysis of the student's entering behavior which suggests the appropriate motivational procedures. The way the teacher makes this analysis and formulates procedures is the subject matter of this chapter.

You should now return to objectives 1 and 2 (p. 129) and determine how well you have achieved them.

QUESTION 5-1

Which of the following behavioral examples best illustrates the concept of motivation?

(a) Hortense has shown steady progress in her ability to relate past and present historical trends.

(b) Horatio has increased his practice time on the electric guitar from one to two hours per day.

(c) Havelock has always shown a keen interest and capacity in the beast stroke.

(d) Henrietta long ago developed the habit of looking up unfamiliar words in the dictionary.

After selecting your answer, explain the reasons for your choice and for your rejection of the alternatives.

BASIC THEORY AND RESEARCH

This section of the chapter introduces the theory and the research on the motivational functions of the teacher described in the following section. Four concepts—arousal, expectancy, incentives, and punishment—help us classify the factors which account for motivation. We may also use these concepts to designate the teacher's motivational functions: the arousal function, the expectancy function, and the incentive function. The exception, of course, is punishment; it seems rather sadistic to designate a punishment function and more humane and practical to describe a disciplinary function. We can now proceed with our discussion of the four factors which account for motivation.

Arousal

Arousal describes the general state of excitability of an organism—the general level of alertness, responsiveness, wakefulness, or vigilance. According to Donald Hebb (1955, p. 249), arousal is an "energizer but not a guide, an engine not a stearing gear." The optimal level of arousal for our most efficient functioning is an intermediate level. We seek mild and avoid strong stimulation. When we describe Hortense as anxious, Elvis as alert, and Abner as asleep, we are referring to high, medium, and low levels of arousal. The curve in Fig. 5-1 shows how our most efficient performance in such activities as memorization, solving

Fig. 5-1. *Hypothetical, inverted U-shape relationship between behavioral efficiency, or level of cue function, and level of arousal (after Hebb, 1955, Fig. 2).*

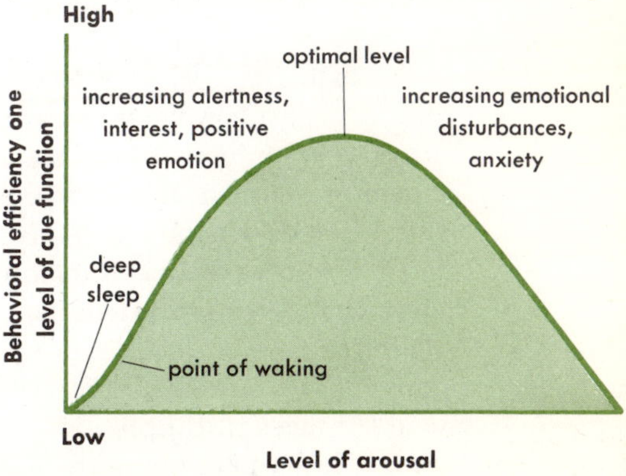

addition problems, and naming letters is at the intermediate level of arousal.

Humans have both internal and external sources of arousal. The external source is the stimulation provided by the environment. Although we cannot discuss here in detail the neural mechanisms which explain arousal, Hebb (1966, p. 209) suggests that stimulation from the environment reaches the cortex through nonspecific pathways. These particular pathways tone up the cortex or, as we say, produce arousal. The internal source of arousal is a down-flow of thought, symbol, and fantasy from the cortex. Evidence for this internal source is the fact that humans do not necessarily go to sleep in a monotonous environment. Our students may day dream to keep themselves aroused when the classroom fails to provide adequate stimulation.

In his discussion of play, boredom, and the search for excitement, Hebb (1966, p. 248) stresses the fact that living things must be active. Ordinarily environmental stimulation and the satisfaction of biological needs keep the brain and the muscles active. He continues (p. 248), "There are times, however, when an animal has no threat to escape, no need of food, no young to care for, no sexual motivation, and no need of sleep. One need remains: to be active physically and mentally." In an economically prosperous society most of the physiological needs are routinely satisfied. "Life can become dull and the need to find excitement pressing—at least part of the time for the majority of citizens" (p. 253). At such times television is a necessity, not a luxury.

In summary we can state that activity is an intrinsic aspect of human nature—to be alive is to be active. The level of activity is called the *level of arousal,* and we ordinarily try to stay at an intermediate level between boredom and excitement. We shall now look at ways in which we escape boredom and seek stimulation through curiosity and exploratory behavior and then at ways in which we avoid stimulation through behavior which reduces anxiety and frustration.

Curiosity and exploratory behavior. In the 1950s investigators showed considerable interest in what appeared to be the spontaneous activity of animals. This behavior did not easily fit a drive-reduction model (explained below) of motivation since the behavior of the animal could not be attributed to any internal deprivation, such as the need for food, water, or sexual intercourse. For example, Harlow and his associates (1950) demonstrated that adult monkeys explore and handle mechanical puzzles and produce puzzle solutions in the absence of a hunger drive. They provided the first group of rhesus monkeys with an assembled mechanical puzzle for twelve days (a situation designed to stimulate curiosity and exploratory behavior—or to produce stimulus seeking). Disassembling the puzzle involved three or four sequential operations, there was no food or water reward. They provided a second group of monkeys with the same puzzle for the same length of time. For this group, however, the puzzle was disassembled—no solution was necessary. Finally, examination day arrived, and both groups were presented new puzzles in their assembled states. The performance of the monkeys in the first group far surpassed that of the monkeys in the second. Harlow later repeated the experiment with hungry monkeys and gave food rewards for successful puzzle solutions. He found fewer solutions under this condition. The hungry monkeys attacked directly that part of the puzzle which obstructed their access to the food, and they ignored the necessary preliminary operations. In the first experiment it appeared that the monkeys attempted to increase stimulation. In the second experiment they appeared to reduce the stimulation of the hunger drive.

Berlyne (1957) studied exploratory behavior in human subjects. Each subject sat alone in a dark room. By pressing a key, he could expose pictures on a slide projector for about one-quarter of a second. The subject could expose a single slide as frequently as he wanted; the next slide would be shown only when the subject indicated his readiness for it. The pictures varied in what Berlyne called *incongruity, complexity, and surprisingness.* An example of incongruity was a picture of an elephant's head attached to a dog's body. Subjects indicated a higher preference for incongruous than for normal pictures. The sequence of six complex pictures started with a simple circle. The following pictures showed the addition of circles until in the last picture a teddy bear was created. Subjects preferred the more complex to the simple pictures. The surprisingness slides were colored geometric figures. One series had twelve pictures. Figures 1 through 6 were red triangles. Figures 7 through 11 were green circles. Figure 12 was a violet square. Figures 7 (the first green circle) and 12 (the violet square) received more key responses than any other figures. Both figures provided new sources of stimulation. Again, as in the case of Harlow's experiment, the subjects appear to be seeking stimulation.

H. W. Nissen (1953) observed the behavior of sexually naive, or virginal, chimpanzees and noted that they tended not to copulate during the mating season. Instead they engaged in other activities, such as scratching, caressing, cleaning, or grooming one another. It would be difficult to claim that these animals were sexually deprived since they had never engaged in copulation before and were not doing so at the time. The grooming behaviors could not be called *secondary drives* since these behaviors occurred before the chimpanzees were sexually mature and between chimpanzees of the same sex. The grooming behaviors could satisfy only the search for new stimulation. Harry Fowler (1965, p. 18) states that a whole general class of behaviors cannot be explained by drive-reduction theorists—behaviors such as peering at a crack in the wall, looking around, twisting a paper clip out of shape, and cracking one's knuckles. These behaviors gradually were labeled *curiosity* and *exploration.*

Experiments were also conducted on *boredom*—also referred to as stimulus deprivation and isolation. Boredom arises from a monotonous environment or the performance of repetitive tasks. It often leads to inattention, and it can have disastrous consequences in automobile driving, military patrolling, and teaching. Experiments on boredom usually reduces the total amount of external stimulation. In an early study, William Bexton, Woodburn Heron, and T. H. Scott (1954) gave college students $20 a day to remain all day (except for eating and toilet needs) in a lighted, soundproof room. Lying on cots, the students wore translucent goggles, which prevented them from seeing objects in clear outline, and cardboard cuffs and gloves, which reduced touch sensitivity. They rested their heads on U-shape, foam-rubber pillows; the only noise was the air-conditioner. The students were free to terminate the experiment at any time. Most of the time they slept. After two or three days they grew increasingly restless. They became so desperate for stimulation they listened with relish to stock market quotations and to a talk for young children on the dangers of alcohol. Although they were required to take difficult tests, they looked forward to the testing periods. They tried to occupy themselves with fantasies of self-induced stimulation. One student terminated the experiment very early even though he took a job requiring heavy physical labor at considerably less pay. As in the studies on exploratory behavior we see the subjects seeking stimulation.

Fowler (1965, p. 33) believes that these studies indicate that organisms respond not only to a change in stimulation but also for a change. Fowler calls curiosity *incentive motivation* (p. 43). The animal learns that upon performing some response he will experience novel and unfamiliar stimuli. For example, monkeys will repeatedly press a button which opens shutters and gives them the opportunity to see other monkeys playing. The anticipated change in stimulation is the incentive for the monkeys' behavior. In terms of expectancy, we could say that the animal expects or anticipates a change by making certain responses. K. C. Montgomery (1954), for example, showed that female rats move to that arm of the Y maze which offers the opportunity to explore a checkerboard maze. They try the opposite arm when the checkerboard maze is attached there.

Boredom may often be the basis for curiosity. Boredom has the characteristics of drive motivation in that the animal is deprived of a change in stimulation by long exposure to familiar or relatively unchanging stimulus conditions. We say that familiarity breeds contempt (although more accurately it breeds indifference). It may also breed the necessity for change or new stimulation. According to Fowler (1965, p

42), bored animals can become curious when they learn to anticipate the changes in stimulation which follow a particular response.

You will note that the common sense view of curiosity is not consistent with Fowler's theory. Fowler views curiosity as an acquired expectation—new stimulation is provided by the performance of a particular act. We do not become curious about the completely unfamiliar and novel. We can hardly be curious about sources of stimulation we are completely ignorant of. When Elvis becomes curious about the effects of firing a paper wad at Miss Pegg, we should not assume that he is necessarily launching a totally new enterprise. The incentive for his firing the paper wad is his excited hope that the performance of such a deviant act will bring a change in classroom routine. For this twisted child, this hope is based on his knowledge of how past misdeeds have provided novel departures from class routines.

Maria Montessori (1964 ed.) observed the spontaneous curiosity and exploratory behavior of children. In educating the senses, Montessori makes *observation* and *liberty* the hallmarks of her method (p. 169). The teacher supplies the child with graded materials and then allows the child a relatively unstructured exploration of the materials. Montessori (p. 169) notes the increased interest of children as they use one of her objects:

> Let us suppose we use our first object—a block in which solid geometric forms are set. Into corresponding holes in the block are set little wooden cylinders, the bases diminishing gradually in millimeters. The game consists of taking the cylinders out of their places, putting them on the table, mixing them, and then putting each one back in its own place. The aim is to educate the eye to the differential perception of dimensions.

According to Montessori (p. 170) the normal child develops "spontaneously a lively interest in this game. He pushes away all who would interfere or offer to help him, and wishes to be alone before his problem." By allowing only one correct solution, the material controls error and permits autoeducation. The student perfects himself through his own efforts. The teacher in no way interferes; she must only observe and "leave her little scholars in liberty" (p. 173). Montessori reports that children will repeat the exercise between five and twenty times before they tire.

The Montessori method utilizes curiosity and exploratory behavior. The child's disassembling of the blocks (his response) presents novel and unfamiliar stimuli which engage his attention and his effort. The very novelty of the problem and the fact that the child can anticipate this novelty each time he disassembles the puzzle strongly motivate him. The liberty to which Montessori refers is simply the opportunity the child has to assemble and reassemble the puzzle. We do not have to postulate from this a passion for freedom and growth and lash out against conventional methods of teaching. No innate spirit, good or bad, moves the child toward wonderment and exploration. To maintain optimum levels of arousal, to escape boredom, to experience slight discrepancies, we are all motivated to seek novelty and adventure.

ANXIETY AND AROUSAL. Anxiety describes the individual's level of emotionality (Table 5-1, p. 141, will illustrate this definition.) We can sometimes distinguish among our friends those who are mainly tense and worried (highly anxious) and those who are "cool" (hardly anxious). We know that anxiety and arousal are related because at the higher levels of arousal we find considerably more emotionality than at the lower levels. Since anxiety is an inferred emotional state of the organism and cannot be directly observed, investigations of anxiety rely heavily on having the individual report his own emotional states under various stress conditions. Educational psychologists have studied test anxiety, or emotional states the student experiences under the stressful conditions of taking a test. George Mandler and Seymour Sarason (1952) believe that students fall into one of two groups: the anxious, or those for whom tests arouse anxiety and who make test-irrelevant responses such as worrying about failing and about their inadequacies, anticipating punishment, and blocking on questions—responses which lead to poor test performance; and those individuals who are without such tendencies and therefore improve their performance (p. 561). These investigators developed a questionnaire, the Test Anxiety Scale (TAS), to measure anxiety in test situations. In responding to the questionnaire the student reports such subjective reactions as worry before and during examinations, heart palpitations, uneasiness, and sweating. These findings emerged from the various studies: (1) Low-anxiety students perform better when challenged by the task and by the prospect that their performance will be assessed; (2) High-anxiety students perform worse under these same conditions; they perform better when they are not threatened with evaluation and faced with a challenging or difficult task.

Later research by Richard Alpert and Ralph Haber (1960) showed that anxiety does not always lead to poor performance. They claim that the TAS does not allow students to report how anxiety may actually enhance their performance. To correct this deficiency Alpert and Haber constructed the Achievement Anxiety Test (AAT), which consists of two sets of items: a *facilitating scale,* which allows the student to report how anxiety improves his test performance, and a *debilitating scale* which describes how anxiety interferes with test performance. Table 5-1 lists the items (without the buffer items) of the two scales. By using both scales they found that they could make a better prediction of grade point average than they could by using either scale alone.

TABLE 5-1

FACILITATING AND DEBILITATING ANXIETY SCALES (Alpert and Haber, 1960, p. 213–14). NUMBERS IN PARENTHESES REFER TO ITEM NUMBERS ON THE ACHIEVEMENT ANXIETY TEST.

Facilitating Anxiety Scale

1. I work most effectively under pressure, as when the task is very important. Always—Never. (2)

2. While I may (or may not) be nervous before taking an exam, once I start, I seem to forget to be nervous. I always forget—I am always nervous during an exam. (9)

3. Nervousness while taking a test helps me do better. It never helps—It often helps. (11)

4. When I start a test, nothing is able to distract me. This is always true of me—This is not true of me. (12)

5. In courses in which the total grade is based mainly on *one* exam, I seem to do better than other people. Never—Almost always. (14)

6. I look forward to exams. Never—Always. (16)

7. Although "cramming" under pre-examination tension is not effective for most people, I find that if the need arises, I can learn material immediately before an exam, even under considerable pressure, and successfully retain it to use on the exam. I am always able to use the "crammed" material successfully —I am never able to use the "crammed" material successfully. (19)

8. I enjoy taking a difficult exam more than an easy one. Always—Never. (21)

9. The more important the exam, or test, the better I seem to do. This is true of me—This is not true of me. (24)

Debilitating Anxiety Scale

1. Nervousness while taking an exam or test hinders me from doing well. Always—Never. (1)

2. In a course in which I have been doing poorly, my fear of a bad grade cuts down my efficiency. Never—Always. (3)

3. When I am poorly prepared for an exam or test, I get upset, and do less well than even my restricted knowledge should allow. This never happens to me—This practically always happens to me. (5)

4. The more important the examination, the less well I seem to do. Always—Never. (6)

5. During exams or tests, I block on questions to which I know the answers, even though I might remember them as soon as the exam is over. This always happens to me —I never block on questions to which I know the answers. (10)

6. I find that my mind goes blank at the beginning of an exam, and it takes me a few minutes before I can function. I almost always blank out at first—I never blank out at first. (15)

7. I am so tired from worrying about an exam, that I find I almost don't care how well I do by the time I start the test. I never feel this way—I almost always feel this way. (17)

8. Time pressure on an exam causes me to do worse than the rest of the group under similar conditions. Time pressure always seems to make me do worse on an exam than others do—Time pressure never seems to make me do worse on an exam than others do. (18)

9. I find myself reading exam questions without understanding them, and I must go back over them so that they will make sense. Never —Almost always. (23)

10. When I don't do well on a difficult item at the beginning of the exam, it tends to upset me so that I block even on easy questions later on. This never happens to me —This almost always happens to me. (26)

Research on anxiety which uses anxiety tests and scales is mainly concerned with studying anxiety as a personality trait. Charles Spielberger (1966, p. 12) states that anxiety can also be a state. As such, it is the stimulus conditions which cause defenses to be set up to avoid the state. Subjectively, these states are feelings of apprehension and tension. As a personality trait, anxiety is an acquired disposition for the individual to perceive a wide range of objectively nondangerous conditions as threatening. The anxiety trait and the anxiety state are related to each other: The reactions typical of the anxiety state are experienced most often by individuals with the anxiety trait. When we refer to anxiety as arousal, we are referring to anxiety as a state. When we distinguish between students who tend to be anxious, and those who tend to be nonanxious, we are referring to anxiety as a trait.

In a series of studies on the relationship of arousal (or of the anxiety state) to complex learning, Spielberger (1966, pp. 361–96) observed these results: (1) High-anxiety students obtained superior test scores on a learning-recall test when relativity few recall errors were possible; low-anxiety subjects obtained superior test scores when relatively more recall errors were possible. (2) Of those students in the broad middle range of IQ, the low-anxiety students performed better than the high-anxiety students; high anxiety had no effect on the performance of low-ability students and tended to facilitate the performance of the very brightest students. In a follow-up study on the long-term effects of anxiety on academic performance, Spielberger found that the percentage of high-anxiety, able students who failed was four times greater than the percentage of low-anxiety, able students who failed. (3) In serial rote learning (see Chapter 9), low-anxiety students were superior in performance early in learning, while high-anxiety students were superior later in learning. (4) In the learning of concepts, high-anxiety, high-intelligence students performed better than low-anxiety, high-intelligence students; high-anxiety, low-intelligence students performed less well than low-anxiety, low-ability students.

The conclusion, based on the studies now available, is certainly not that anxiety must always be avoided or reduced in teaching situations. Able students may profit more than less able students from anxiety. On occasion the teacher should deliberately increase anxiety, particularly for students with high IQs. Further study may reveal that increasing the anxiety of low-anxiety students of high IQ may result in performances which rival those of their anxious intellectual peers.

Frustration and arousal. Frustration is a conflict situation in which the individual must complete one task or turn to another. In the classroom the student faces frustrating situations when either he wants to or feels that he must engage in activity which competes with hi achievement of the instructional objective. Teachers face frustration when they must engage in activities which compete with the attention they could give to their teaching objectives. Current research on frustration (Lawson, 1965), interestingly enough, indicates that the frustrating (or conflict) situation may sometimes increase the individual's efforts to complete the task. When this occurs, the frustration becomes a challenge—the individual increases his determination to finish what he has started. Perhaps this increased vigor of response or rededication to the job has led the theorists to believe that frustration leads to aggression (Dollard *et al.*, 1939).

The research question and, indeed, the question all of us want to answer is why frustration causes some individuals to pursue a task with renewed zeal and other individuals to surrender to other tasks which compete for their attention. Ian Waterhouse and Irvin Child (1953) designed a series of studies to help answer this question. They assigned college students complex and routine intellectual tasks. The complex tasks were those found on intelligence tests; the routine tasks required such performances as writing the letter *a* as many times as possible in two minutes. Subjects in a frustrated group were told from time to time that their performance was very poor; those in a neutral group were given the impression that their performance was realistically successful. To obtain information on possible competing responses, the students answered a questionnaire and reported their typical reactions to frustration. Illustrative statements were: "I tend to brood over my failures" and "I am inclined to be very critical of myself when I fail." The results of the questionnaire divided the students into high-interference and low-interference groups. When both groups were frustrated as described above, the effects were notably different: The performance of the high-interference group decreased, while the performance of the low-interference group increased.

Whether frustration assists students in achieving instructional objectives depends on their entering behavior. Frustration in almost every case will invigorate student behavior, but it will not necessarily cause the student to invest his effort in classroom tasks. It will elicit those responses in the student which have the greatest strength. Since frustration is part of the human condition and none of us escapes it, the teacher must find ways of channeling the effects of frustration toward achievement rather than toward either nonachievement or the achievement of alternative or irrelevant objectives. At present we know only that some individuals find achievement more difficult than others and that the teacher, like a good doctor, must adapt the treatment to the patient. For some students the difficult, the new, and the demanding will kindle what William James (1892, p. 51) has called their *pugnacity*. For the less pugnacious student the teacher must devote his efforts to strengthening the weaker task-relevant responses. In no case does the current research indicate that the teacher should retire either frustration or anxiety (if this were possible) from his repertory of teaching procedures.

SUMMARY. The individual maintains an arousal level which avoids both boredom, or an absence of stimulation, and intense excitement, or a surplus of stimulation. Through curiosity and exploratory behavior, he seeks stimulation to maintain a suitable level of arousal. You saw examples of stimulus seeking in the behavior of monkeys solving mechanical puzzles in the absence of a food reward, in the behavior of individuals preferring incongruous to normal pictures, in the grooming behaviors of virginal chimpanzees, in the students' preferences for unknown items, and in the spontaneous activity of Montessori's school children. An impressive amount of evidence shows that we perform some acts only because they will produce relatively novel and unfamiliar situations and experiences. The degree of arousal and the kinds of tasks efficiently performed in high-arousal states vary from student to student. Some students find anxious and frustrating circumstances motivating. Others find them debilitating. The relationship between IQ and high arousal strongly suggests that when the student possesses the appropriate entering behavior in sufficient strength, high anxiety or high frustration will not impede and may even facilitate performance. When the prerequisite entering behavior is lacking or weak, however, the student may very well experience the punitive effects of increased anxiety and frustration without experiencing the benefits.

Expectancy

Expectancy is a momentary belief that a particular outcome will follow a particular act (Vroom, 1964, p. 17). Expectancies can range from the subjective certainty that something will occur to the subjective certainty that something will not occur. We may be aroused when there is a discrepancy between what we perceive and what we expected to perceive. We become angry when we perceive someone doing something we neither like nor expected. Hortense becomes angry when Darrell fails to date her, and Darrell becomes angry when Lucille, whom he does date, becomes boisterous and unmanageable at a party. Miss Pegg smolders if Johnny colors when she expects him to read. When he colors his reading book, there is an even greater discrepancy between what Miss Pegg perceives and what she expects, and there is greater anger. Hebb tells us that the more intelligent we are the better able we are to detect discrepancy and the more emotional we become. He uses a mechanical analogy: "The more complex the equipment, the greater the number of things by which its operation may be disturbed, the greater the aberration from

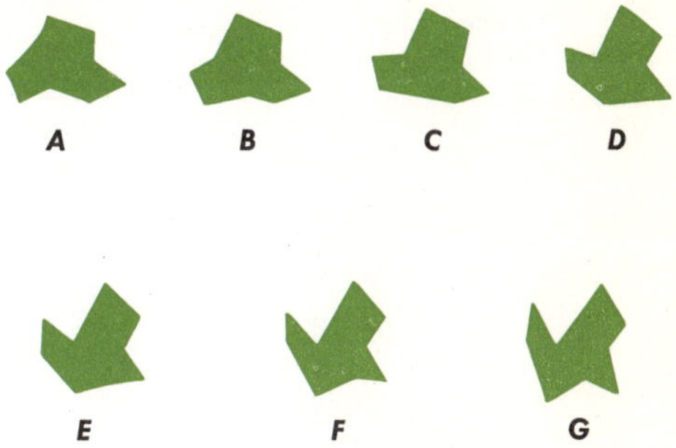

Fig. 5-2. *Seven geometric shapes used as stimuli (after Conners, 1964, p. 460).*

normal function may be, and the longer it may take to get it back in working order" (1966, p. 239).

Discrepancies between perception and expectancies are sources of arousal. When we become overly familiar with our surroundings they lose their power to arouse us. This may be why we have the adage "there's no shoe like an old shoe," which reminds us not to sacrifice the familiar even though it no longer excites us. In any case, when the environment provides us exactly what we expect, we are no longer aroused by it. Hence we can sleep in a noisy environment of familiar sounds and suddenly awake at the sound of an unfamiliar footstep.

What determines whether we will be pleased or frightened by departures from our expectations? David McClelland (1953, p. 28) suggests that the size of the discrepancy determines the feeling we experience. A large discrepancy results in unpleasantness. A small discrepancy results in pleasantness. Keith Conners (1964) determined which nonsense shapes (see Fig. 5-2) students found most esthetically pleasing. The students believed that they were subjects in an ESP experiment designed to find out if ESP could affect their esthetic preferences. In the experimental group the students first studied and drew one of the nonsense figures attached to the outside of the viewing box. This figure is called an *adaptation stimulus;* it is an anchor of expectancy—of what the students expect to see next. Then the students viewed the stimulus objects in random pairs. Adjacent figures were more similar (less discrepant) than figures farther apart. Preference was determined by how much time the student looked at one figure as compared with the time he looked at the other and by his verbally expressed preference. The graph, Fig. 5-3, shows the students' preferences. Preference was highest when the size of the discrepancy was small (between shapes *A* and *B*) and lowest when the size of the discrepancy was large (between shapes *A* and *G*, for example).

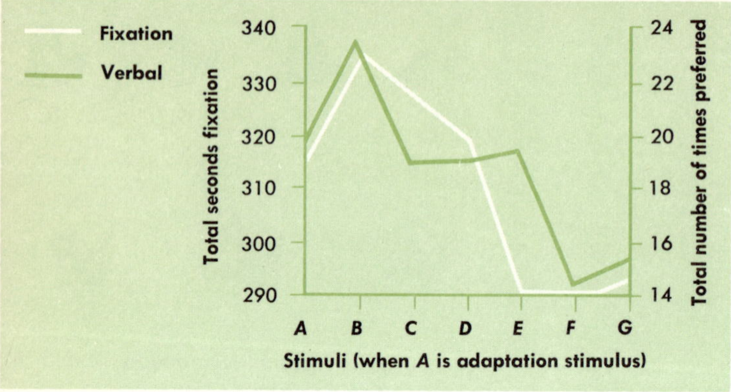

Fig. 5-3. *Student preferences (measured in fixation time) for various sizes of discrepancy (after Conners, 1964, p. 460).*

Conners' findings may explain our growing acceptance of modern abstract painting. The size of the discrepancy between what we see in the modern painting and what we expected to see narrows as we become more accustomed to visual abstraction. His study may also explain why we should not attempt to sweep the school with revolutionary innovation. When the size of the discrepancy between conventional and innovative practice is large, it may produce unpleasant reactions in both teachers and students. The findings on discrepancies may also explain adult reactions to adolescent fads and fashions. The discrepancies in adolescent dance, dress, and manners are small and pleasant for the adolescent. For the adult the discrepancies are large and sometimes shockingly unpleasant.

Valence—the individual's anticipated satisfaction, or his emotional preference for certain outcomes (Vroom, 1964, p. 15)—is associated with the concept of expectancy. Given two possible outcomes, the individual can prefer *X* to *Y*, *Y* to *X*, or remain indifferent to either outcome. More concretely, Elvis can prefer a date with Harriet to a date with Hilda, a date with Hilda to a date with Harriet, or not care to date either girl. Desiring an outcome (valence) is not the same as enjoying an outcome once we attain it. The eyes are frequently bigger than the stomach. Elvis may prefer Harriet to Hilda only to discover later that he does not enjoy Harriet. He may even discover that he enjoys an outcome he did not desire—that a date with Hilda is more satisfying. The anticipated satisfaction is called *valence*. The actual satisfaction is called *value*.

The vigor with which the individual acts is a product of both expectancy and valence. If a person is indifferent to an outcome (low valence) he will not act even though he is almost guaranteed success (high expectancy). We find students in our schools who expect little satisfaction in academic achievement (low valence) even though they have the ability which assures them academic success (high expectancy). We sometimes call them *underachievers.* We also find the reverse conditions of high valence and low expectancy: the students who want to achieve but are unable to do so. These students are unmotivated because they do not invest much effort in highly desired outcomes which they have little chance of attaining. Their anticipated failure produces only a polite modicum of effort.

Before summarizing the discussion of expectancy, we will consider a rather extensively studied type of expectancy and valence—the motive to achieve.

THE MOTIVE TO ACHIEVE. The teacher must help the student who lacks the desire to achieve to acquire the desire or the motive. Exactly what we mean by motive to achieve will become clearer as we review a fascinating program of research in social psychology conducted by McClelland, John Atkinson, and their associates (McClelland *et al.,* 1953; McClelland, 1955; Atkinson, 1958). They studied the achievement motive in this way (adapted from Brown, 1966, p. 424).

> You are presented with a picture of a boy about eighteen. He is sitting at his desk in a classroom occupied by other students. A book lies open before him but he does not look at it. He rests his forehead on one hand and gazes out toward the viewer. As the viewer of this picture you are asked to write an imaginary story and answer these four questions: (1) What is happening? Who are the persons? (2)What has led up to this situation? (3) What is being thought? What is wanted? By whom? (4) What will happen? What will be done? You are asked to spend one minute on each question. You are told that this is a test of creative imagination. Atkinson (1958) gives us these examples of high- and low-achievement imagery from his research.

HIGH-ACHIEVEMENT MOTIVATION

1. This chap is doing some heavy meditating. He is a sophomore and he has reached an intellectual crisis. He cannot make up his mind. He is troubled and worried.
2. He wants to present a clear-cut synthesis of these two conflicting philosophies, to satisfy his ego and to gain academic recognition from his professor.
3. He will screw himself up royally. Too inexperienced and uninformed, he has tackled too great a problem. He will give up in despair, go down to G_____, and drown his sorrow in a bucket of beer.

LOW-ACHIEVEMENT MOTIVATION

1. Ed has been troubled by his father's drunkenness and his maltreatment of Ed's mother. He thinks of this often and worries about it.

2. Ed is thinking of leaving home for a while in the hope that this might shock his parents into getting along.
3. Ed will leave home but will only meet with further disillusionment away from home.

Utilizing these examples and others, we can define *achievement motivation* as the expectancy of finding satisfaction in mastering challenging and difficult performances. In education we sometimes call it the pursuit of excellence. In history and sociology we call it the Protestant Ethic (Weber, 1904). As Max Weber suggested, students may have the expectancy of divine salvation (in Calvinistic doctrine predestination reduced uncertainty almost to zero). High achievement is merely the demonstration of the fact that he belongs to the Elect, to those who are promised salvation.

McClelland (1965) lists twelve propositions for developing new motives in adults. These motives are based on his research on training programs designed to develop the achievement motive in such individuals as businessmen in India, where achievement motivation is not a part of the traditional culture. I have taken the liberty of modifying McClelland's propositions to accommodate your entering behavior.

1. Educational attempts to develop a new motive will best succeed when the individual has many reasons in advance to believe that he can, will, or should develop a motive.
2. Educational attempts will best succeed when the individual understands that developing the new motive is realistic and reasonable.
3. The individual is likely to develop the motive when he can describe and clearly conceive the various aspects of the motive.
4. Change in thought and action will most likely occur and endure when the individual can link the motive to related actions.
5. The new motive is most likely to influence the thoughts and actions of the individual when he can link it to events in his everyday life.
6. The new motive will influence thought and action when the individual sees the motive as an improvement in his self-image.
7. The motive is likely to influence thought and action when the individual can see and experience the new motive as an improvement on the prevailing cultural values (e.g., Indian businessmen can see the motive to achieve as superior to the motive to withdraw).
8. The motive is likely to influence thought and action when the individual commits himself to achieving concrete goals in life related to the newly formed motive.
9. The motive is likely to influence thought and action when the individual keeps a record of his progress toward achieving goals to which he is committed.

10. Changes in motives are likely to occur in an atmosphere in which the person feels warmly but honestly supported and in which he is respected by others as a person capable of guiding and directing his own future behavior.
11. The more the setting dramatizes the importance of self-study and lifts it out of the routine of everyday life, the more changes in motives which are likely to occur.
12. If the new motive is a sign of membership in a new reference group, changes in motives are likely to occur.

McClelland has not had enough time to determine the long-term effectiveness of his course. His study of eighty-six businessmen in India over two- to three-year periods indicated that about two-thirds profit and one-third remain unaffected. Amount of profit was determined by a coding system which recorded whether each individual had shown unusual entrepreneurial activity, such as would result in receiving an unusual salary raise or promotion or in initiating a new business venture.

McClelland's course suggests that teachers may teach students how to develop the motive to achieve, especially those students who are notably deficient in the desire to meet challenges, to master, and generally to succeed. In such a course, the pedagogical problem is not only to accommodate the present entering behavior of the student but also to develop new entering behavior which, in turn and with time, will enable the students to accomplish advanced instructional objectives.

James (1892, p. 51) referred to achievement motivation as pugnacity and as ambitious impulses. His words are an appropriate way of ending our discussion of achievement motivation and teaching:

> Pugnacity need not be thought of merely in the form of physical combativeness. It can be taken in the sense of general unwillingness to be beaten by any kind of difficulty. It is what makes us feel "stumped" and challenged by arduous achievements, and is essential to a spirited and enterprising character. We have of late been hearing much of the philosophy of tenderness in education; "interest" must be assiduously awakened in everything, and difficulties must be smoothed away. *Soft* pedagogics have taken the place of the old steep and rocky path to learning. But from this lukewarm air the bracing oxygen of effort is left out. It is nonsense to suppose that every step in education *can* be interesting. The fighting impulse must often be appealed to. Make the pupil feel ashamed of being scared at fractions, of being "downed" by the law of falling bodies; arouse his pugnacity and pride, and he will rush at the difficult places with an inner wrath at himself that is one of his best faculties. . . . The teacher who never rouses this sort of pugnacious excitement in his pupils falls short of one of his best forms of usefulness.

Summary. Expectancies, you saw, can be a source of arousal, especially when there is a manageable discrepancy between what we see and what we expected to see. Instructional objectives are the expectancies that are the teacher's main concern. But he must also be concerned with the expectancies and valences of the student. The student must be made to desire instructional outcomes (valence) which he has a good chance of reaching (expectancy). The vigor with which the student pursues instructional objectives is a product of both expectancy and valence. The motive to achieve describes a particular relationship of expectancy and valence: the expectancy of finding satisfaction (valence) in mastering difficult and challenging performances. McClelland and his associates have been studying the conditions under which this motive best develops. Among these are the following conditions: The student gives reasons for developing the motive, understands that the motive is realistic, can link the motive to deeds and to daily events in his life, commits himself to concrete goals, keeps a record of progress, has honest and warm support, engages in self-study, and feels that he belongs to a successful group.

Incentives

Incentives are actual goal objects. For human beings they can be concrete or symbolic rewards. They incite, arouse, and move to action when they are associated with certain stimuli which signal their presence. For example, we are motivated by the various signs that we shall obtain money as well as by the money itself. Although Clark Hull (1952) and Kenneth Spence (1956) were primarily concerned with the development of drive theory (which I discuss briefly below), they also believed that some activities of the organism can be motivated by the goal object or incentive, itself. A rat will run a maze not only because it is hungry but also because it expects or anticipates food when it reaches the goal box. The mechanism which underlies this anticipation is too complex to discuss here. We observe, however, that the rat's mouth waters and its jaws begin to chew even before it obtains the food. And this anticipatory activity increases its running speed. The larger the incentive the more vigor we find in the rat's responses. The rat runs the maze faster when given several hundred food pellets than when given only a few. It presses a bar more frequently for a food mixture containing saccharine and less frequently for a mixture containing citric acid (Murray, 1964, p. 13). Similarly, we can expect the student to invest more effort for a goal or prize he really covets than for one in which he is only mildly interested. The vigor of his activity is affected by the nature of the incentive. Edward Murray (p. 9) also suggests these examples:

> A man may not feel particularly hungry when he smells the delicious aroma of a chicken frying on the stove. The smell, sight, or

> taste of the food is said to operate as an incentive. In social situations the motivating effect of the goal is much more apparent than that of internal factors. Motivation is aroused by incentive pay, by the sight of a pretty girl, and by a television commercial.

Positive and negative reinforcers can be viewed as incentives (Skinner, 1953). In Chapter 7 I will define and summarize the importance of reinforcers in learning. I will treat them here more briefly. A positive reinforcer is a positive reward. A negative reinforcer is a negative reward —a stimulus which gives us relief from an unpleasant state of affairs. Examples of positive reinforcers are praise, prizes, smiles, and money. Examples of negative reinforcers are the relief from noise which follows closing the window, the signal which marks the end of a dreary television commercial, the anesthesia which reduces or eliminates dental pain, and the laryngitis in the vocal cords of a nagging wife. Both reinforcers strengthen the responses which precede them. Skinner observes that if you give flowers to your girl after you have quarreled with her, you may very well strengthen her tendency to quarrel. Better to give her the flowers after she has been sweet to you. Elvis faithfully practices his basketball because he receives the attention and the praise of the high school girls. He also knows that steady practice avoids the wrath of the coach (a negative reinforcer).

Skinner describes punishment as the removal of a positive reinforcer and the addition of an aversive stimulus. You not only take your flowers back but also slap your girl friend. This procedure produces emotional states (you can be sure), but it does not eliminate the troublesome response. Your girl may not continue to argue, but she also may not agree and she may very well cry. If you kiss her when she cries she may very well cry more, and if your relationship survives this crisis you will probably face more quarrels and tears. Below, Richard Solomon (1964) disputes Skinner's description of the effects of punishment.

The control of behavior, in Skinner's formulation, is clearly outside the organism and is consistent with our previous discussion of incentive motivation. The individual's expectation of obtaining a reinforcer and of avoiding aversive stimuli could account for the increased vigor of response which organisms often demonstrate as they approach attractive goal objects they have previously experienced.

Albert Bandura (1962) has studied the relationship of incentives to imitative learning in children. The children, divided into three groups, viewed a film in which an adult model showed four novel aggressive responses. The first group saw the film model severely punished. The second group saw the model generously rewarded with approval and food. The third group saw the model receive no treatment (neither reward nor punishment) for his aggressive acts. The children were later placed in a situation in which they could imitate the model. The first group, which

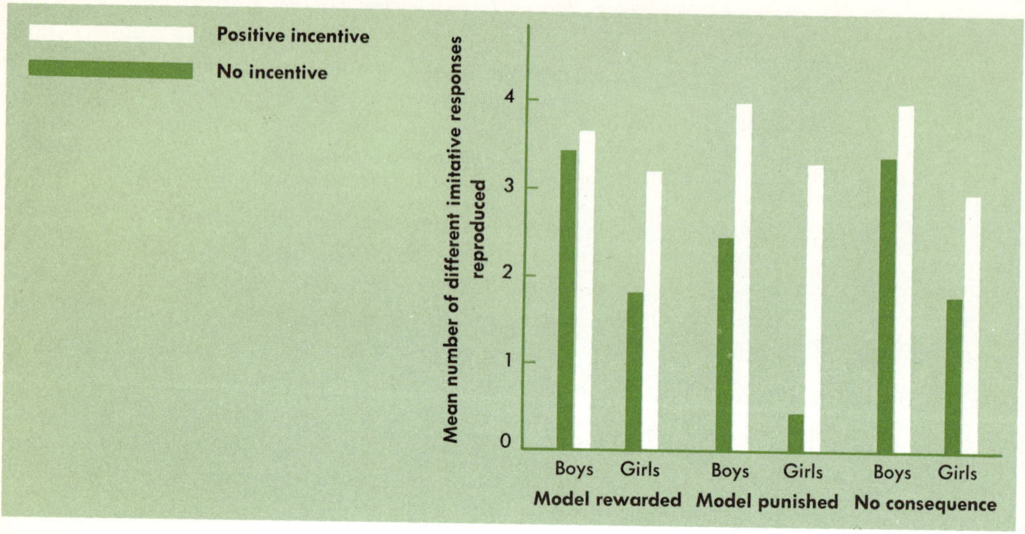

Fig. 5-4. *Mean number of different imitative responses reproduced by children with and without incentives (after Bandura and Walters, 1963, p. 58).*

saw the model punished, made fewer aggressive responses than did the other two groups. The boys were more aggressive than the girls, especially in the first group. In terms of expectancy, the child's observation of who received rewards may have influenced his expectation of reward if he behaved in the same manner. In the second phase of this experiment the children in all three groups were given attractive incentives for being aggressive. All previous performance differences were wiped out, including the sex difference. Figure 5-4 shows the difference between the incentive—no incentive performances.

SUMMARY. Incentives are among the factors which increase the vigor of our behavior. They operate in two ways. First, they are goals or pleasant anticipations of repeating past experiences in the near future. Second, they strengthen responses which precede their delivery. Some evidence suggests that children identify with the adult who is rewarded in their presence and alienated from the adult who is punished or left unrewarded. The following part of the chapter has more to say about punishment.

Punishment

Solomon (1964) defines punishment as a stimulus the individual seeks to escape or avoid. Given a choice between punishment and no stimulus at all, the individual will choose no stimulus. Experimenters use three procedures in studying the effects of punishment: escape training, avoidance training, and a punishment procedure. For all procedures the experimenter may use an apparatus such as an alley runway, six feet long, with a start box (to contain a rat) at one end and a goal box at the other. In escape training the rat receives a shock as soon as the gate of the start box is raised; the rat quickly learns to run down the alley. In avoidance training the rat is given, for example, five seconds to reach the goal box after the start box gate is opened. He learns to run quickly enough to avoid the shock. In the punishment procedure the rat is first taught to run to the goal box to obtain food. After this behavior is well established, the rat is given a shock in the alley and goal box through an electrified grill. The rat quickly learns not to leave the start box. There is an interesting distinction between escape and avoidance training on the one hand, and the punishment procedure on the other hand. In the former case the rat is taught what to do, while in the latter case he is taught what not to do. You will later see interesting parallels in the control of human behavior.

According to Solomon, the effects of the punishment procedure differ according to the nature of the response involved. Moreover, to make even the crudest prediction of the effect of punishment on a response, you must know how that particular response was inserted in the individual's repertory of responses. Punishment, therefore, must be addressed to the entering behavior of the student. Let us consider the effects of punishment on responses previously established through positive reinforcers. Here the results of the punishment procedure depend largely on the intensity of the punishing agent. Solomon (p. 240) reports these findings:

> As the intensity of shock applied to rats, cats, and dogs is increased from about 0.1 milliampere to 4 milliamperes, these orderly results can be obtained: (a) *detection* and *arousal,* wherein the punisher can be used as a cue, discriminative stimulus [Chapter 6], response intensifier, or even a secondary reinforcer; (b) *temporary suppression,* wherein punishment results in suppression of the punished response, followed by complete recovery, such that the subject later appears unaltered from his prepunished state; (c) *partial suppression,* wherein the subject always displays some lasting suppression of the punished response, without total recovery; and (d) finally, there is *complete suppression,* with no observable recovery.

The ambiguous results of many punishment experiments can be attributed to the different intensities and durations of punishment.

Evidence also shows that if the individual receives a shock together with positive reinforcement during reward training, the punishment procedure may actually strengthen the response. The association of reward and punishment produces stronger responses than the use of reward alone. Barclay Martin (1963) refers to an unpublished study which involved the rewarding and punishing of puppies. The reward-only puppies were petted and fondled by the experimenter. The punished-rewarded puppies were also petted and fondled, but, about five times a week, they were punished by switching, rough handling, and electric shocks. To test the effects of these two treatments, a human sat in a corner of the room and an observer recorded the amount of time the puppies spent near the human. The punished-rewarded puppies spent considerably more time near the human than did the reward-only puppies. This result is interesting because the usual effect of punishment is for the individual to avoid the punishing person and object. Martin suggests that the combination of reward and punishment may cause more arousal than reward alone and that occasional punishment may even heighten the anticipation of reward. The positive effects of punishment, however, would not prevail if the punishment were too intense and frequent, if it were not gradually introduced, and if the reward training which preceded the punishment were not sufficient. Martin's findings support the statement that disciplinary techniques should involve the combination of reward and punishment.

Punishment is extremely effective when the individual is offered a rewarded alternative to the punished response (Whiting and Mowrer, 1943). This procedure is used in housebreaking a dog. The dog learns to suppress urination and defecation inside the house (indoor stimuli) as long as these functions go unpunished outside the house (outdoor stimuli). This use of the punishment procedure, according to Solomon (1964), can produce a highly reliable dog or child. He has even observed that puppies raised in the laboratory, if punished by a newspaper swat for eating horsemeat and rewarded for eating pellets, will starve themselves to death when given opportunity to eat only the taboo horsemeat. They will readily eat the pellets when they are available. The use of punishment with a rewarded alternative is the basis of the disciplinary technique which I later describe as restitution.

We have now considered the effects of punishment on previously rewarded response. What are the effects of punishment on *consummatory responses*—responses necessary for biological survival, such as eating and sexual behavior? Contrary to ordinary expectation, these responses can be easily suppressed by punishment. Sexual behavior in males can be suppressed by weak punishment (Beach *et al.*, 1956). Eating in dogs and cats can be permanently suppressed by even a mild shock delivered through the feeding dish or the feet (Masserman, 1943). The punishment may act as a conditioned stimulus (see Chapter 7) warning the individual that punishment will ensue if he makes a particular response.

Solomon (1966) feels that the many psychological myths about the effects of punishment stem from two sources. First, there is the traditional emphasis in the psychology of learning, exemplified in the writing of both Thorndike and Skinner, that positive reinforcers (or satisfiers) are more effective than punishment in controlling behavior. For this reason no punishments were used in Skinner's *Walden Two* (1948). Second, there is the belief that, although punishment may effectively suppress undesired responses, the devastating side effects threaten the emotional balance of the individual. Solomon thinks this belief has been accepted at face value without supporting evidence (p. 250):

> Anyone who has tried to train a rat in a T maze, using food reward for a correct response and shock to the feet for an incorrect response, knows that there *is* a period of emotionality during the early training, but that, thereafter, the rat, when the percentage of correct responses is high, looks like a hungry, well-motivated, happy rat, eager to get from his cage to the experimenter's hand, and thence to the start box. Evidently going through a conflict is not a condition for neurosis. The rat is reliable, unswerving in his choices. Is he neurotic? Should this be called subservient resignation? Or a happy adjustment to an inevitable event? Is it a fixation, an evidence of behavioral rigidity? The criteria for answering such questions are vague today.

According to Solomon both the Skinnerian doctrine that punishment is inadequate in suppressing responses and the Freudian doctrine that almost permanent trauma results from punishment hold up only under particular conditions. They are not universal dicta on the effects of all punishment.

SUMMARY. As in the case of anxiety and frustration, the experimental evidence does not warrant the exclusion of punishment procedures from the repertory of techniques the teacher may use to control the behavior of students. Under particular conditions a punishment procedure may be very effective—particularly when the individual is permitted to make an alternative response which is desirable and incompatible with the punished response. The practical implications of the experimental findings on punishment are discussed below as the teacher's disciplinary function.

Relationship of Arousal, Expectancy, Incentives, and Punishment

We can now point out the relationship of these four motivational factors. In general, arousal is a product of learned expectancies. Past experience shows us that by making (or not making) certain responses under certain conditions we can attain valued goals. The smell of fried chicken stimulates our expectations of finding the chicken on the table and consuming it. The combination of environmental stimuli and learned expectancies hastens our steps to the dining room. The goal object (the chicken) is the incentive because it influences future behavior by increasing the vigor of that behavior the next time. A completely novel incentive cannot motivate behavior. A completely novel punishment cannot suppress behavior. Once, however, we obtain an incentive we enjoy, we not only discover how to obtain it (a product of learning) but also learn to note the signs that its attainment is possible and perhaps even imminent. We then begin to make responses which bring us closer to the incentive. At Christmastime children become peculiarly aware both of the facial expressions of parents and of locked closet doors as indications of hidden treasures. They respond to these cues by discussing with their parents how their lives will be enriched by the anticipated gift if they receive it. The children even begin to improve their behavior if the rewards are associated with winning and maintaining parental approval. Under Christmastime conditions the children have learned to expect certain outcomes and these learned expectations motivate their behavior.

A Theoretical Model

We have presented the following view of motivation:

1. Motivation results in increased vigor of performance. Since the human organism is always active, the theoretical problem is not to explain how to arouse the individual from his torpor but how to increase the vigor of particular responses.

2. Arousal is the general state of alertness of the individual. Optimum levels of arousal avoid the extremes of monotony and intense stimulation.

3. Expectancy, as a motivational factor, is a momentary belief that a particular outcome will occur. Arousal may be a product of a small mismatch between what we see and what we expected to see. The discrepancy can be pleasant if it is in the direction of our expectancy. Expectancy depends on valence. The individual does what he wants because he expects to obtain something. Expectancy alone is not enough.

4. Incentives are goal objects which become associated with certain stimuli and responses. The associated stimuli (the smell of fried chicken associated with its later consumption) trigger off anticipations, and these learned anticipations motivate our behavior.

5. Depending on how the responses are first acquired, punishment may effectively suppress undesirable responses. Suppression is most likely to occur and endure when the individual is allowed to make an alternative response to the one which is punished.

This model of motivation avoids reference to such concepts as drive, libido, and self-actualizing tendencies, which you probably studied in introductory psychology (see Murray, 1964). Hull (1951) uses the concept of drive to explain how needs initiate activity. Drives are stimuli which arise from unsatisfied physiological needs for food, water, oxygen, and so on. Hull describes several basic drives, such as hunger, thirst, sexual intercourse, and pain avoidance. The drives cause general restlessness or activity, and they are reduced only when the individual eats, drinks, has sexual intercourse, avoids or escapes pain, and so on. Secondary drives are associated with primary or basic drives. The drive-reduction theory, as Hull's theory is called, has been criticized considerably because it conflicts with almost two decades of research on curiosity and exploratory behavior as well as with later research on drive reduction. Research on sexual behavior illustrates the point. Organisms, both human and animal, after no prolonged period of sexual deprivation, may be aroused. Frank Beach (1956) has shown that hormonal readiness (a physiological need state) must combine with sexual stimulation (which in human beings can be fantasized) to arouse sexual behavior. A male rat who is hormonally ready requires the presence of an oestrus female. Even then the rat does not engage in copulation until after an extensive period of preplay, which may serve to arouse the male. The hormonal state does not act as a drive; it sensitizes the male to the stimuli provided by the available and willing female. The motivational image of the individual, as reflected in current research and theory, is shifting from that of a deprived individual driven to satisfy basic needs only to win a moment's peace in his long struggle for survival to that of an individual who seeks stimulation to satisfy certain expectations which arise out of his past experience and to avoid the monotony of a familiar environment.

The Freudian image of man as the victim of an abundance of psychosexual energy does not square with current motivational research any better than does the drive-reduction theory. In fact Freudian theory may simply be the obverse side of the coin. Whereas drive-reduction theory assumes that motivation originates in a deprived or deficient organism, Freudian theory assumes that the energy of the organism is potentially available but that it is held in check by the superego, a censoring mechanism which enforces the taboos and moral codes of society. Both theories rather severely restrict the scope of human behavior. In Freudian theory you have the choice of surrendering to internal psychosexual forces, becoming a social outcast, and possibly destroying yourself and others or of sublimating your drives and living in a state of mild frustration. In drive-reduction theory your only hope is to eliminate the drive, which is impossible. If, however, our behavior is controlled by expectations and if these expectations are learned by modifying or eliminating other expectations, we can change our behavior.

Our motivational model does not require us to assume that human nature, unspoiled by law and civilization, is intrinsically good, rational, and individualistic. It does not require us to believe in innate or self-actualizing tendencies, which propel the individual toward self-fulfillment, toward doing what he can do best, and toward actualizing (and, in this sense, realizing what he is potentially (Maslow, 1954). And our motivational model does not require us to accept a hierarchy of needs or the belief that once lower needs (physiological and safety needs) are satisfied the organism is free to pursue his needs for love, security, belonging, esteem, and self-actualization. For one thing such a view of need gratification is a misinterpretation of the physiological view of homeostasis, which is a dynamic and not a fixed state of physical equilibrium (Cofer and Appley, 1965, pp. 303–66). Moreover, little evidence supports a hierarchical view of needs and self-actualizing tendencies. In reviewing this evidence, Cofer and Appley (pp. 685–90) suggest that "giving love does not seem to cure psychosis, neurosis, and delinquency" (p. 690). We add that giving love is not enough to help students reach important instructional objectives.

You should now return to objectives 3–11 (p. 129) and determine how well you have achieved them.

QUESTION 5-2

Mr. X. Seiting attempted to increase the vim and vigor of his students' efforts in studying logarithms. He particularly tried to pose challenging and difficult problems for his high-IQ students and interesting but easier problems for his average students. He occasionally gave both groups the opportunity to investigate alternate solution methods which they thought of. Which of the following classes of factors appears to be Mr. Seiting's chief motivational concern? (a) arousal; (b) expectancy; (c) incentives; (d) punishment.

After selecting your answer, explain the reasons for your choice and for your rejection of the alternatives.

ON THE MOTIVATION OF STUDENTS

We have now reviewed the theory of and the research on motivation. The research which translates the theory into classroom practice, for the most part, does not now exist. At this point in the development of educational psychology we can only deduce from the available theory and data some general functions the teacher should perform to increase the motivation of the student. In describing these functions below I utilize the basic teaching model and the motivational concepts you have now learned. These are the teacher's motivational functions:

1. To engage the student in learning. This is the *arousal* function.

2. To describe concretely for the student what he will be able to do (his new capabilities) at the conclusion of the instruction. This is the *expectancy* function.

3. To provide rewards for present achievement in a way which stimulates future achievement. This is the *incentive* function.

4. To use rewards and punishment to control deviant behavior. This is the *disciplinary* function.

The Arousal Function

Arousal, according to Hebb (1966, p. 209), is a general level of behavioral excitability. In education we prefer to define arousal as the student's general level of alertness or attentiveness. As teachers we may be faced with the problem of raising the level of arousal when the student is about to go to sleep or of lowering the level when the student is about to erupt emotionally. The student will perform best when he is neither sleepy nor frantic—when he is simply alert. In any case an initial responsibility of the teacher is to win and to maintain the attention of the students. In the holy name of education, almost anything the teacher does to do this—ringing bells, blowing whistles, rapping the desk or the head of the nearest underaroused or overaroused student—is justified, although we learn by experience that some techniques have worse side effects than others. In the end, however, attention must be paid! James (1892; 1958 ed., p. 25) describes the arousal function in this way:

> . . . in teaching, you must simply work your pupil into such a state of interest in what you are going to teach him that every other object of attention is banished from his mind; then reveal it so impressively that he will remember the occasion to his dying day; and finally fill him with devouring curiosity to know what the next steps in connection with the subject are.

In the daily classroom routine the teacher must guard against monotony and boredom. He should always provide the student with enough to think about and to do. What the student does, however, must not be so regular and repetitious that it reduces his level of arousal. You will recall that, in the experiments on sensory deprivation in which the students spent several days lying on cots with nothing to do, their tolerance for the monotony and the lack of stimulation they were forced to endure was very short lived. Fowler suggests that curiosity is born out of boredom. Bored students invest considerable ingenuity and social deviancy in transforming a dull into an uncontrollably exciting classroom. The stimulation which the teacher fails to provide the students provide for themselves. James (1892; 1958 ed., p. 84) makes these suggestions to teachers who wish to attract and hold the attention of their students:

> If the topic is highly abstract, show its nature by concrete examples. If it be unfamiliar, trace some point of analogy in it with the known; if it be inhuman, make it figure as part of a story. If it be difficult, couple its acquisition with some prospect of personal gain. Above all things, make sure that it shall run through certain inner changes since no unvarying object can possibly hold the mental field for long. Let your pupil wander from one aspect to another of your subject if you do not wish him to wander from it altogether to something else, variety in unity being the secret of interesting talk and thought. The relation of all these things to the native genius of the instructor is too obvious to need comment here.

Teaching methods can capitalize on the student's need for new stimulation and on his propensities to be curious and to explore. We have referred to Montessori's method of observation and liberty. Bruner (1961) suggests that, when the student is allowed to approach learning as an act of discovery, he will engage increasingly in learning with the autonomy of self-reward.* In Bruner's sense the student provides for his own stimulation and in this way performs his own arousal function. Robert White (1959) uses the term *competence motivation* to describe the child's "intrinsic need to deal with the environment" (p. 318). Competence motivation explains such acts as grasping and exploring, crawling and walking, attending and perceiving, talking and thinking, and manipulating and changing the surroundings. We have referred to such activity as curiosity and exploratory behavior.

Bert Kersh (1963) investigated the motivational effects of discovery learning. He provided high school geometry students with three ways to learn complex rules of addition. The directed-learning group used a programed learning booklet which reduced the material to a series of small steps. Each step contained the answers to the questions and the solutions to the problems. The guided-discovery group used a Socratic method which required each student to make inferences about the rules without help. A control group memorized the rules and obtained no explanation for them. Kersh found that the guided-discovery group used the rules (his measure of motivation) more often than did the directed-learning group. Kersh concluded that interest is a result of learning by discovery.

* Discovery learning is described in Chapter 11.

Torrance (1963) wanted to know which teaching conditions helped students to produce as many and as clever and unusual ideas as possible. The first of four groups of students used brainstorming procedures designed to facilitate the production of ideas by suspending initial discussion and criticism. This group was motivated to produce as many ideas as possible. The second group also learned the brainstorming procedures but was motivated to produce clever and unusual ideas. The last two groups did not learn these procedures, but instead were offered prizes on the basis of their performance. The third group was directed to produce as many ideas as possible, and the fourth group, to produce clever and unusual ideas. Torrance's results confirmed his expectations: (1) The special training in brainstorming produced more ideas than did the promise of prizes; (2) the directions to produce clever and unusual ideas produced more of these ideas than did the direction to produce as many ideas as possible. These findings indicate that the freer, or more open, conditions of brainstorming and originality of response produce greater response vigor, or motivation, than do the more closed conditions of responding for mere quantity and prizes.

Flanders (1951), whose interaction model you read about in Chapter 1, investigated the relationship of personal-social anxiety and instructional method. He experimentally produced two learning climates designed to arouse different levels of anxiety. In the learner-centered climate the teacher's comments and interaction conveyed acceptance of and support for the students. The teacher used public standards of evaluation known to the students before they were invoked. In the teacher-centered climate the teacher's comments and interaction were directive and demanding, and the standards were private and unknown to the student. Anxiety was measured by increase in pulse rate and sweating, and the students could move a lever which recorded their positive and negative feelings. Flanders' results show the anxiety reactions students have to the use of rewards and punishment. Flanders discovered that the learner-centered students were more task-oriented, had less anxiety, and felt less emotional disturbance. The teacher-centered students felt more hostile, aggressive, apathetic, and generally more emotionally disturbed. Unfortunately, we have no comparable studies on the levels and types of anxiety produced by teachers who concentrate their efforts on the achievement of instructional objectives as contrasted with those produced by teachers who concentrate their attention on their interpersonal relations with their students.

Highly structured teaching situations are not necessarily debilitating for all students. Howard Kight and Julius Sassenrath (1966) used programed instruction to study the relationship of achievement motivation, anxiety, and teaching method. Programed instruction (Chapter 12) is the most highly controlled teaching situation we now have. These investigators found that students with high achievement motivation (we discuss this motivation below) or high test anxiety required less time to complete the program, made fewer errors, and remembered the material better than did students with low achievement motivation and low test anxiety. The authors suggest that students with high achievement motivation profit from the immediate knowledge of results provided in programed instruction. High-anxiety students find the highly structured teaching in programed instruction a less anxious situation than they find loosely structured teaching.

AROUSAL FUNCTION. The arousal function is the teacher's effort to engage the student in learning. It involves the initial responsibility of winning the student's attention and the continuing responsibility of regulating the level of arousal to avoid both sleep and emotional eruption. To meet these requirements, the instruction must provide in the teaching situation a certain measure of freedom to wander from one aspect of the subject to another (in the words of James). Discovery-learning and brainstorming methods provide this freedom. Regulation of the level of arousal includes the control of anxiety and frustration. Not all students suffer the debilitating effects of anxiety and frustration, some evidently find them invigorating. The teacher must have sufficient knowledge of the entering dispositions of his students to provide the necessary increases and decreases in individual levels of arousal.

The Expectancy Function

The expectancy function requires the teacher concretely to describe for the student what he will be able to do when a particular class, lesson, or project is completed. In performing this function, the teacher must modify, substitute, or eliminate the student's expectations in such a way as to increase his efforts to accomplish the new instructional objectives.

INSTRUCTIONAL OBJECTIVES AS EXPECTANCIES. Statements of instructional objectives must be concrete enough for the student to know exactly what outcomes the teacher expects. In making these statements, the teacher should avoid words like *appreciation, comprehension,* and *desire to understand.* The emphasis, as you learned in Chapter 2, should be on *action*—some performance capability the student will acquire. For example, the teacher could begin his lesson with the vague and lofty pronouncement that his purpose is to develop in the students a deep understanding of and appreciation for human motivation. Students are not unaccustomed to such abstract statements of instructional goals, and they have learned that they can ignore them without harmful consequences. Instead, the teacher could make this concrete statement: "At the end of today's lesson, when you are given various examples of human behavior you will be able to identify those examples which are best explained by motivation rather than by habit." This latter statement provides the student with considerably more focus for his efforts and even with the promise that he will do something later he cannot do now.

It is also desirable to illustrate exactly what the objective means. In the example above, the teacher could describe two or more instances of human behavior which might or might not illustrate the concept of motivation. In one instance the teacher might describe how much energy Clyde expends on football and how little he expends on mathematics. In the other instance he might describe Hilda's ability to memorize poetry and to retain what she has learned. Which instance is the better illustration of motivation? The students might guess now, but the teacher can promise them that they will know later. If the illustrations of the objectives are phrased in terms of the students' present interests, the statement of the instructional objective should provide increased student motivation to achieve the objective.

The teacher's expectancy function requires him to select objectives which accommodate student entering behavior. To the extent that the teacher requires students to use skills and knowledge they now lack in the attainment of new skills and knowledge, he will produce the motivational effects of failure we will describe below. The teacher must make the students' expectancies the terminal behavior the instructional objectives promise. The teacher's repeated failure to deliver what he has promised will certainly undermine the confidence of the students in themselves and in the teacher. Students arrive at our classroom doors with different valences and different discrepancies. They are bored by and curious about different things. The teacher cannot impose on all children a uniform lesson plan or instructional procedure; these must be modified to accommodate individual students. I am not advising that the school and the curriculum simply dissolve before the sea of individual differences the student body represents. The school and the teacher should know what they want to teach, but they must remember that successful teaching requires accommodation to the present level of student capability.

Immediate, intermediate, and remote expectancies. Instructional objectives represent the intermediate expectancies, or the outcomes the student can attain at the end of a lesson, session, project, and so on. In Chapter 2 we discussed task analysis, the process of reducing instructional objectives to their component subtasks. Subtasks represent immediate expectancies. Whenever the instructional objective (the major task) requires considerable effort and time on the part of the students, the teacher should concretely describe and illustrate the subtasks so that student effort does not wane along the way. The students ordinarily must have a continuing sense of accomplishment. Only the most advanced scholars in their laboratories and studies can sustain their efforts over long periods of time even when they are faced with a paucity of results. Most of our students become more quickly impatient with error and slight gains.

Remote goals represent the student's long-range expectancies for home, family, friends, and career. The choice of these goals and the manner and the energy with which they are pursued largely reflect the student's basic beliefs about what will bring him satisfaction and happiness. In a democratic society the students can choose from myriad goals. Like all expectancies, remote goals influence the amount of energy we invest in various academic and nonacademic enterprises. The teacher who knows the remote expectancies the student cherishes (rightly or wrongly) can relate remote to immediate and intermediate expectancies. The inspiring teacher may be the one who convincingly relates what the student learns today to what the student deeply desires to do in his later life. The mass media develop in a student all kinds of expectations about the joys and adventure of adult life. Out of what he sees on television and reads in magazines, the student develops his remote expectancies (Cremin, 1965). The teacher must expend considerable effort in all phases of his teaching to impress upon the student the realization that the adult prerogatives he deeply desires require that he learn to do many things which he cannot do now but which he can learn to do with the proper expenditure of effort.*

Changing expectancies. Expectancies, we have said, are learned anticipations of the consequences of our behavior. They are indeed a product of our past experience. This fact suggests two ways in which expectancies can be modified: (1) The actual past experience of success and failure is the primary basis for predictions of the success and failure of our future efforts. The amount of effort students invest in academic, athletic, and social activities is largely determined by the amount of success and failure each realm of activity has provided them in the past. In this way success breeds success and failure breeds failure. Students thread their ways through gargantuan college catalogs and often select those courses—the so-called *snap* or *breeze* courses—which promise them the highest probability of success. To change their expectancies and to develop new ones, the students must have some solid base of success. Students who have never drunk from the sweet cup of academic success must be provided academic success at the level of their entering behavior before they will raise their expectancies to include more difficult outcomes in the future. (2) The teacher can also control a student's expectancy by

* Relating remote expectancies to instructional objectives may be a particularly burdensome task, unconvincing to the student and unrewarding for the teacher. Success in bridging the gap, however, whenever attained, becomes a source of motivation.

telling him what the likelihood of success and failure will be. Our advising and counseling of a student often consist of this very function. We look at his previous grades, his general intelligence, and the courses and programs he desires to or must take, and we make some estimates of his probable success. The student, of course, will expend most of his energy where he has the greatest promise of success.

Since expectancy depends on valence, or anticipated satisfactions, the teacher must also find ways of increasing valence. Victor Vroom (1964, p. 23) suggests at least two ways of doing this: (1) When the student is unfamiliar with the possible outcomes he can attain, the teacher can give him information which increases his desirability for one outcome rather than for another. If Elvis can have a blind date with either Hortense or Marilyn, by describing the more satisfying physical and personal attributes of Marilyn, we can increase the vigor of Elvis' efforts to date her. Teachers frequently point out to students how the particular execution of an assignment leads to better results than do alternative ways the students can think of. For example, by telling the student about the wide range of literary and personal expression possible through the use of certain literary and linguistic conventions, the teacher can increase the student's valence for acquiring the new verbal capabilities. (2) The teacher can also arouse appropriate motives. For example, he can arouse the student's motive to achieve by describing the fruits of the mastery of some area of knowledge—his life will never be the same, and it will be greatly enriched! The fact that the student will be able to do something which he cannot now do and that he will do it well is often a great incentive.

Mismatching expectancies. The discrepancy hypothesis (p. 144) states that a moderate, positive degree of discrepancy between what we experience and what we expect to experience can be a source of satisfaction. Hunt (1961, pp. 267–72) refers to the process of establishing a nondiscrepant situation—in which experience and expectation fit perfectly —as *matching*. For example, in the Berlyne experiment on incongruity (p. 137), a proper match would attach an elephant's head to an elephant's body. In the basic teaching model, a proper match would result in the instructional objectives', procedures', and materials' fully accommodating the student's entering behavior. Hunt believes that a perfect match results in stultifying boredom. To avoid this the teacher has to introduce incongruity, complexity, and "surprisingness" into his lessons. New materials must have the proper blend of the familiar and the unfamiliar to attract and hold the attention of students. A study in a school setting (Gewirtz, 1959) supports the idea of increased motivation through mismatching. When children were given puzzles to solve, some were successful and some were not. Asked to select similar or different puzzles for their next trials, most of the unsuccessful children selected the same puzzles, while some of the successful children selected different puzzles. Television advertising exhibits considerable ingenuity in mismatching with Jolly Green Giants, Hawaiian punches, and Superman. Incongruity has been a major source of American humor from Charlie Chaplin to Phyllis Diller. The tobacco industry has exploited the incongruity of a gentleman's offering a lady a Tiparillo and of the lady's contemplating acceptance of the offer. The discrepancy is kept within tolerable and even pleasing limits by the daintiness of the cigar, its ivory tip, the elegance and solidity of the gentlemen and the ladies and of the setting in which the proposal is contemplated. (In the early commercials the offer was never overtly made or accepted, but we were privileged to observe what the gentleman and lady were thinking.) The fact that we remember, sometimes with affection and humor and sometimes with humor alone, those teachers whose behavior we described as different, queer, hilarious, inspiring, and just plain interesting may attest to the motivational value of incongruity and mismatching.

Level of aspiration. The effect of expectancy on student performance has been observed in several studies of level of aspiration, which, in the context of this chapter, we may call *level of expectancy*. In these studies students are asked how well they expect to do on their next performance. Then their actual performance is compared with their expected performance. In a very provocative study Pauline Sears (1940) divided elementary school children into three groups based on their grades and how successful they felt they were in school: (1) a success group with high grades and high feelings of success; (2) a failure group with low grades and little feeling of success; and (3) a mixed group who were successful in reading but unsuccessful in arithmetic. In the first phase of the experiment each child did ordinary reading and arithmetic assignments. After each assignment the child was asked how many seconds it would take him to do the next task. The amount of time the child indicated (a measure of his expectancies) was compared with the amount of time he took to complete the original task. This difference yielded a discrepancy score. Sears found that (1) the success group lowered their estimate of the amount of time it would take them to complete the next task, which amounted to a slight but realistic increase in their level of expectancy; (2) the failure group was erratic, setting their goals above, below, and at the same level as their original performance with seven of twelve subjects in this group setting their goals higher and sometimes unrealistically high; and (3) the mixed group was more like the success group in reading (the school subject in which they had been more successful) and more like the failure group in arithmetic.

In the second phase the children performed similar tasks, which afforded them a second trial. Fifty per cent in each group were told tha they were very successful in their second trials, and 50 per cent were told that they had done very poorly. How did this treatment affect the children? (1) The children who were told that they were very successful set goals which were realistic related to their past performance (low discrepancy scores). (2) The children who were told that they had done very poorly set very erratic goals—as the failure group had done in the first phase of the experiment.

A number of studies on level of expectancy have lead to these conclusions:

1. Past success conditions students to make realistic increases in their expectancies.

2. Past failure, over long periods of time, conditions students to lower their expectancies, almost as if to guard themselves against failure by never expecting success.

3. Some students unrealistically raise their expectancies almost as if the hope of success alone would bring success.

Success, it seems, develops a modest self-confidence which often leads to more success. Failure results in more variable behavior—despair and resignation or an optimism which seems born out of defeat. This research supports the importance of the teacher's expectancy function: The student's every effort does not have to meet with success, but he must experience enough success to keep his wagon hitched to a star of reasonable height. By modifying students' expectancies in accordance with these findings, teachers can increase the vigor of student effort.

Jerald Bachman (1964) has found that a person's expectation of success is greatest when he thinks he has the appropriate training and when he has the freedom to use this training. On the basis of his findings Bachman speculates about the mechanisms which may explain why repeated failure reduces motivation. An individual may cope with failure by general dissatisfaction with the situation and eventually withdrawal; by lowering the estimate of his own ability and developing the feeling that he cannot perform a given task; by deciding that he has little control over the situation—which makes the situation, rather than his inability, responsible for the failure; and finally by discrediting or distorting the evidence of failure—which may be the mechanism employed by the undaunted optimists in Sears's study.

Summary. The expectancy function requires the teacher to maintain or modify the student's expectation of success or failure in reaching the instructional objectives. It requires the teacher to describe concretely for the student what he will be able to do when a particular class, lesson, or project is completed. The teacher must relate intermediate expectancies to immediate and remote goals of the students to engage the student's full effort in learning. The teacher must sometimes change expectancies and, to increase behavioral vigor, deliberately mismatch them. Mismatched expectancies are a source of humor, and humor can be a source of motivation. Expectancies also concern the student's history of success and failure; the teacher may have to protect the student whose long history of failure has affected his levels of aspiration. Undoubtedly, a major source of motivation in any enterprise we undertake is the prior feeling and belief that we are equal to the task. The expectancy function requires the teacher to have sufficient knowledge of the past school failure and success of individual students to distinguish among realistic, pessimistic, and extravagantly optimistic expectancies. When there has been much failure, the teacher may have to provide much success.

The Incentive Function

The teacher rewards achievement in such a way as to encourage further effort on the part of the student. This statement describes the teacher's incentive function. The incentives are goal objects or symbols which the teacher uses to produce this increased vigor. They may be feedback of test results, spoken or written praise and encouragement, grades, or the fruits of successful competition. We shall discuss each of these below.

Incentives work their effects forward in time since they result in learned anticipations. Having obtained a particular goal object, the individual begins to associate the responses he made and the stimuli he met with every future approach to the goal. These responses and signs increase the vigor of his performance. The second time, the rat runs a little faster for the cheese in the goal box, the child hastens to the candy counter, and Elvis' heart beats faster as he pulls his car into Clarabelle's driveway. If Johnny solves a difficult problem in balancing chemical equations, in his later attempts to solve similar problems he makes responses and meets stimuli that assure him that he is on the right path. This learned anticipation of the correct solution increases the vigor of his efforts.

Feedback of test results.* At this point we wish to consider the motivational effects of performance assessment. Test results must be fed back to the student with sufficient frequency and in a form that will enable him to confirm his expectancies. Unconfirmed outcomes leave the student ignorant of his possible success and deny him the satisfaction of

* The research on the effects of feedback on learning are discussed in detail in Chapters 7 and 8.

accomplishment. Continuous withholding of feedback can have very deleterious effects on student motivation and learning. American students ordinarily show keen interest in their test results. Results which somewhat exceed their expectations give them considerable satisfaction, which becomes a source of motivation for future learning. For learning and motivation purposes, testing should be more systematic and more frequent than it is in most schools. American schools are still influenced by the European practice of testing after long periods of time, sometimes from one to four years or more. The use of comprehensive examinations to assess student learning over long periods of time may encourage students to study materials in a way which guarantees their long-term retention. The more frequent testing in American education may motivate only short-term retention. Comprehensive examinations, however, are not a suitable substitute for the short-term feedback students need to bolster their efforts for continued study.

We may also arrange instructional materials and procedures in ways which permit students to develop checkpoints and standards for assessing their own achievement. In our discussion of curiosity and exploratory behavior, we referred to the discovery learning of Bruner, Kersh, and Montessori (p. 160). These studies indicate that we can teach students to generate their own instructions and strategies of learning. As students learn to engage in independent study and acquire skill in establishing their own standards—as any scientist, author, and artist must do—they have less need for feedback from the teacher or from a systematic program of tests. Our desire to produce independent scholars, however, should not obscure the fact that this achievement is frequently the result of long and dedicated teaching.

PRAISE AND BLAME. Elizabeth Hurlock (1924) made one of the earliest studies of the effects of incentives. In the first of the experimental sessions with elementary school children, the children took an intelligence test. Feedback on the test was handled in three ways: (1) Children in the praise group were told that their scores were very high and their papers very neat; (2) children in the blame group were told that their scores were very low and their papers sloppy; and (3) children in the control group received neither praise nor blame. In the second session these children were given another form of the same intelligence test. The scores for the second test showed that (1) the performance of both the praise and blame groups improved; (2) both groups did about equally well; and (3) both groups did better than the control group, which had received neither praise nor blame. In a later experiment (1925) Hurlock used three groups of children who took a short arithmetic test each day for five days. All groups (but one) worked in the same room and could witness all three experimental treatments: (1) Children in the praise groups were called by name before the class and praised for their work;

(2) children in the blame group were publicly reproved for their work; (3) children in a third group were simply ignored; and (4) children in a control group worked in a separate room and received no praise or blame. Again Hurlock found that the performances of the praise and blame groups improved. She discovered, however, that continued blame over a five-day period reduced performance and continued praise increased performance. The control group did the worst, performing more poorly than even the children in the ignored group. Hurlock concluded that praise is a better incentive than blame because the effects of praise are more enduring. An alternative explanation of the results of the second experiment is simply that the reproved children stopped trying because their efforts were never rewarded (Cofer and Appley, 1965, p. 771).

In reviewing the praise-blame studies of Hurlock and others, Wallace Kennedy and Herman Willcutt (1964) suggest the need to control the entering behavior of the subjects in the experiments. For example, other investigators have found that praise does not help severe underachievers. Blame does not impede the performance of Negro students performing under Negro examiners. Finally, blame does not impede the performance of very bright adolescents. These later findings make it necessary for teachers to observe the effects that praise and blame have on various students. The teacher's incentive function requires him to use incentives which will increase student effort on subsequent tasks. The teacher must confirm the effectiveness with which he performs this function by observing the effects of the incentives he uses on subsequent student behavior.

Grades as incentives. American educators have made frequent at tempts, some successful, to discontinue the use of standardized gradin systems. Some schools have substituted pass or fail for the conventiona letter grades. Frequently, however, the pass grade is modified to pas with high honor, pass with honor, and just plain pass. You can also fai satisfactorily or fail dismally. When all these words have been addec we have virtually returned to the conventional grading system of fiv letters. Grades evidently have enough incentive value for students tha schools and teachers continue their use and even reintroduce them onc they have been discontinued.

There have been several interesting studies of the effects of grade written comments, and grading policies. Ellis Page (1958) conducted most ambitious and provocative study involving 2,139 students in sevent four classrooms. Cooperating teachers were asked to mark the objectiv tests of these junior and senior high school students in three ways: (the no-comment group received only their test scores and the equivaler letter grade; (2) the free-comment group received personalized commen which conformed to the teachers' own feelings and practices; and (3) tl specified-comment group received the following stereotyped commen for each letter grade.

A: Excellent! Keep it up.
B: Good work. Keep it up!
C: Perhaps try to do still better.
D: Let's bring this up.
F: Let's raise this grade!

All groups received test scores and letter grades. The student subjects were totally naive; none of them was aware or suspected that he was an experimental subject. In the second phase of the experiment the students were given a second test to determine the effects of these three grading practices. Both the free-comment and the specified-comment groups did better than the no-comment group. The free-comment group did better (but not significantly better) than the specified-comment group. The F students who received the free comment showed the greatest improvement. The effects of the comments did not depend on student ability or school year. Page concluded that teachers should take the time to write encouraging comments on student papers.

Faculties frequently debate which grading policy most strongly motivates students to improve their performance. Teachers use absolute standards and normal curves. They mark students leniently or strictly. They establish fixed quotas for each letter grade. When they have a choice, the students look for the easy markers among the faculty. Every teacher believes that his own grading policy is the best (whose is better?) and that his policy inspires the student to or coerces him into notably high achievement. The hard school of pedagogy believes that strict policies spur student effort and result in high-quality work. The soft school believes that strict standards strike terror in the hearts of students and cause resignation and discouragement. Lewis Goldberg (1965) has attempted to resolve this debate by studying the effects of five grading policies on college-student motivation. Students were assigned a grade on the first midterm examination on the basis of one of these grading policies: strict, lenient, bimodal, normal, and rectangular. Table 6-2 shows the percentage of students who received each letter grade. These percentages define each grading policy. The students were told that their course grades would be determined by the course examinations using these percentages: first midterm—10 per cent; second midterm—40 per cent; and final—50 per cent. After the first midterm, only letter grades were reported to the students; individual test scores were withheld. Goldberg discovered no appreciable differences in performance on the second midterm as a result of the five different grading policies. He believed that his findings "should force proponents of a particular grading policy to make a thorough reappraisal of their beliefs. And, while instructors may wish to defend their own grading practice on *administrative* and/or *informational* grounds, they should now be wary

TABLE 5-2

PERCENTAGE OF STUDENTS ASSIGNED EACH LETTER GRADE FOR FIVE GRADING POLICIES (after Goldberg, 1965).

Grading Policy	Percentage of students who received A	B	C	D	F
Strict	0.00	0.05	0.25	0.40	0.30
Lenient	0.30	0.40	0.25	0.05	0.00
Bimodal	0.20	0.30	0.00	0.30	0.20
Normal	0.10	0.20	0.40	0.20	0.10
Rectangular	0.20	0.20	0.20	0.20	0.20

of including *motivational* rationales as part of their arguments" (pp. 22–23). If grading policies do not produce different motivational effects, then teachers should emphasize giving that type of detailed feedback to students which does enhance their motivation and learning.

COMPETITION: THE EMULOUS PASSION. In a competitive instructional situation, rewards are unequally distributed and given only to those students whose achievement is of recognized superiority. Traditional grading practices, for example, are competitive since relatively few students receive marks of distinction. Few receive scholarships, fellowships, and memberships in honorary societies. Entrance to particular colleges and universities has become increasingly competitive. It is paradoxical that, while the American school has become sentimental and egalitarian in its formal educational ideology, it has also become fiercely competitive in practice as the race for admission to the freshmen classes of crowded colleges and universities continues unabated. The competition has become so ignominious that educators and laymen attribute to it student suicide, student corruption (cheating), and parental intimidation and bribery of recalcitrant teachers and deans. The rewards for the victors—high grades, choice colleges, and so on—have sometimes resulted in superior performance of dubious merit—when, for example, students take snap courses to maintain high grade-point averages rather than taking difficult courses of recognized intellectual and vocational merit.

The function of the American school is to teach everyone who enters its halls at the level of his entering behavior. Students of lower capabilities should not be subjected to competition which always leads to failure and humiliation. This prescription, however, does not mean that groups of students of similar capabilities, whatever their level of entering behavior, should not have the occasional satisfaction of triumphing over their rivals. When we say that the American school is competitive we refer to the activities of those few students who enter the academ arena of national merit scholars and valedictorians. For the bulk of American students, who never enter this arena, the school is neither competitive nor cooperative. It does not seem inconsistent to suggest that the school should continue to pay tribute to its ranking scholars, who compete for the seats of honor at graduation, while providing smaller arenas of competition and prizes for less able students.

Competition and cooperation. Research on competition and cooperation is inconclusive and does not furnish an adequate basis for determining the conditions under which competition aids individual student achievement. M. M. Gross (1946) investigated whether students would achieve and cheat more when they competed with themselves to surpass their previous levels of performance (the first group) or when they competed with each other (the second group). The experimenter provided the occasion for cheating by allowing the students to score their own daily tests, which gave them the opportunity to change their answers. In the first group the students kept their own progress records. Students in the second group were told how their scores compared with other scores in the class. Gross found (1) an equal amount of cheating in both groups, (2) equal levels of achievement, and (3) that bright students cheated less and achieved more than did the less bright students. However, competition probably had very little to do with the results of this experiment. The less able students cheated because this was the easiest way for them to obtain right answers. The daily feedback from the quizzes probably contributed more to the students' levels of achievement than did the competition.

Perhaps more to the point is the experiment of Morton Deutsch (1960) in which he compared the effectiveness of competitive and cooperative groups in solving puzzle problems and human-relations problems. The students in the cooperative groups had to arrive at joint solutions to the problems; they were rated as a group. Students in the competitive groups could work together but had to arrive at individual problem solutions; they were rated as individuals. Deutsch found that the cooperative groups surpassed the competitive groups in almost every respect: The communication was friendlier, more open, and more effective; the cooperative groups exhibited a greater diversity, coordination, and sharing of effort and responsibility; and they were more orderly and productive. In assessing these results, we must remember that Deutsch was comparing the effectiveness of competitive and cooperative groups. When Dorothy Marquart (1955) compared the relative effectiveness of group and individual solutions to puzzle problems, she discovered that the group was no more successful than the best individual problem solver in it. We should not generalize the results of group competition to individual competition.

James Coleman (1961) suggests that we substitute interscholastic competition in academic subjects for our present interscholastic competition in athletics. The intellectual should be able to contribute to his community and to the prestige of his school in the way the athlete now does. The student body, he contends, only rewards students who are members of a team which has done something to bring glory to old Alma Mater. Interscholastic academic competition would convert the present position of the adolescent scholar from one of opprobrious curve-raiser to one of respected and adulated member of the student body. One worries, however, whether interscholastic competition for academic honors would sometimes have the same abrasive effect on the quality of academic performance that interscholastic competition has had on the quality of athletic performance.

James (1892) writes that "to veto and taboo all possible rivalry of one youth with another, because such rivalry may degenerate into greedy and selfish excess, does seem to savor somewhat of sentimentality, or even fanaticism" (p. 50). The evidence we have examined does not indicate that we should try to eliminate competition from the school (if this were at all possible) any more than we should try to eliminate anxiety, frustration, and punishment. Students who enjoy challenge and risk may profit from the very same classroom conditions which make achievement difficult for students who are anxious and have low levels of expectancy. Rather than establishing conditions which favor one group over the other, it seems considerably more sensible to provide each student with his most congenial motivational environment. If time, energy, money, and resources make individual treatment impossible, we should recognize these limitations for what they are rather than espouse universal teaching prescriptions which inevitably prejudice the cause of large parts of the student body.

Summary. The incentive function requires the teacher to reward student achievement in such a way as to encourage further effort in the pursuit of instructional objectives. We have discussed the incentive value of test results, spoken or written praise and encouragement, grades, and competition and cooperation. The feedback of test results is a particu larly useful incentive because it may not only increase student vigo but also play an important part in learning procedures and in per formance assessment, two components of the basic teaching model. Al these incentives can become punishment when improperly applied When the feedback of test results shows the student that he has learne very little indeed, when spoken or written praise becomes reproof, whe grades become further evidence of failure, and when competition be comes the final humiliation before one's peers, the use of these incentive leaves much to be desired. The misuse of incentives, which is ofte inadvertent, no more warrants their abolition from the classroom than does the fact that some students obtain high and others obtain low scores on IQ tests warrant their abolition. In one sense the classroom is a microcosm of the society in which it is embedded, and no modern industrial society, whatever capitalist, socialist, or communist labels it parades behind, has failed to find the use of incentives and competition an aid to social progress.

The Disciplinary Function

The disciplinary function requires the teacher to control deviant behavior through the use of rewards and punishment. Punishment, we have seen, refers to a stimulus which the student will avoid or seek to escape. If he is given a choice between punishment and no stimulus at all, he will choose no stimulus. In the modern American classroom punishment is often limited to verbal reprimands and threats: "You are not to speak before raising your hand!" or "One more scene like that, Elvis, and you are banished from this classroom!" There are also the physical stimuli—ear pulling, arm squeezing, knuckle beating, and head rapping. Punishment should be distinguished from *nonreward,* in which the behavior (Terrence's grumbling dissatisfaction to himself) is ignored —neither rewarded nor punished.

Restitution. Punishment, you saw, can involve restitution, which requires the student to perform properly what he originally performed improperly. It combines the suppression of one response and the substitution of another. Terence restates in decent language what he originally blurted out in abusive language. After pulling Harriet's hair, Elvis restores her feminine dignity with an apology and a favor. In restitu-ion, the substitute response must be rewarded. The teacher should ipprove Terence's demonstration of linguistic propriety, and Harriet and the teacher should show Elvis that good girls yield more easily to courtesy and charm than to verbal abuse and attack. Restitution, which nvolves reward as well as punishment, is preferable to punishment alone because it focuses on learning new socially acceptable responses rather than on stamping out antisocial responses. Restitution establishes a situation of response-competition (the deviant response competes with the social response) in the hope that the rewarded social response will eventually win out.

Restitution, however, is only effective when the student has a social esponse he can substitute for the antisocial one. It is not inconceivable hat the home background of the student has been so inadequate that e cannot distinguish between social and antisocial responses. For the udent to learn through restitution in these cases, the teacher must suggest concrete alternative responses. If most of the communication he hears at home is what novelists call colorful and vivid, Terrence may not be able to distinguish between abusive and decent language. He may have to learn some neutral words before he can make restitution.

Any disciplinary technique involves two operations (Bandura and Walters, 1963, p. 189): the presentation of a punitive (aversive) stimulus (punishment) and the withdrawal or withholding of a positive reinforcer (reward). For example, the parents may describe to the child the horrible things which will happen to him if he further alienates them. The aversive stimulus is the threat of horrible happenings. The positive reinforcer (which is being temporarily withdrawn and withheld and conditionally promised) is parental love. The mother may promise her love to the child (positive reinforcer) while spanking him (aversive stimulus). The teacher may pull Terence's ear (aversive) while promising him respect for his work (positive). Bandura and Richard Walters state that disciplinary techniques differ in their emphasis on the punishment and reward components. When, for example, the emphasis is almost wholly on the withholding or withdrawing of love, the technique emphasizes the reward component. Bandura and Walters (p. 221) suggest that disciplinary techniques should emphasize rewards which are withdrawn or withheld until the child complies with adult demands or makes restitution. When such disciplinary methods are used by warm and affectionate parents, children seem to develop self-control and the requisite amount of social conscience. Disciplinary methods which emphasize punishment often result in the avoidance of the person who does the punishing.

THE RIPPLE EFFECT. This effect describes the way students who witness a disciplinary technique used against their classmates are affected by the technique (Kounin and Gump, 1958). The metaphor *ripple* implies that the effects of the technique spread out in concentric waves from the disciplined student to his witnessing classmates. When Miss Pegg tells Leroy that she will make "an example of him," she is assuming that the rest of the class may profit by anticipating what happens when a certain deviant act occurs. She is using the ripple effect.

The ripple effect can work to the teacher's advantage or disadvantage. Jacob Kounin, Paul Gump, and James Ryan (1961) have studied the effects on students of what they call *desist techniques.* An audience of children witnessed three desist techniques and were later asked to describe their reaction to each one. These were the techniques: (1) The teacher was punitive and grim. She said to the student, "Hey you, who do you think you are?" She pulled the student toward his seat and said, "Now sit down. If you ever do that again, I'll really make trouble for you." This technique emphasizes punishment, or the use of negative reinforcers. (2) The teacher using this technique was matter-of-fact. She said to the errant student, "Don't do that again. Please sit in your seat now." The "please" implied the use of a positive reinforcer, and the request to sit down specified the alternative response the student could make. (3) The teacher indicated awareness of the deviant behavior, but chose to ignore it. The student audience rated the various techniques as follows: (1) They like the third teacher best; (2) they thought the second teacher was the fairest; (3) they thought the first teacher was best able to keep discipline in a class of tough kids; (4) they believed that misbehavior would most likely occur for the third teacher; (5) they believed that the first teacher made too much of an issue of the misbehavior and produced the most discomforting reactions (ripple effect); and (6) most important of all, they believed that the students would pay more attention afterward to the second teacher than to the other two teachers. Since the major purpose of disciplinary techniques is to assist students to achieve instructional objectives, the matter-of-fact technique of the second teacher has much to recommend it.

William Gnagey (1965) suggests several ways in which the teacher can use the ripple effect to increase his control over the class: * (1) Use nonthreatening techniques whenever possible to avoid negative reactions to the teacher and the lesson. (2) Make clear who the deviant is, what the misbehavior is, and the proper alternative. "Leroy, if you pull Harriet's hair again, you will remain after school for three weeks" is very clear as to deviant and deviation but does not specify an alternative behavior, an apology to poor Harriet. (3) Increase firmness (the I-mean-it quality) by lowering or raising your voice, moving close to the culprit, or staring him into compliance. (4) Focus attention on the learning task and not on teacher approval. Gnagey (pp. 10–13) illustrates this suggestion: (a) "I hear a noise in back of this room. We will never finish learning how to do square root if that din continues!" is preferable to (b) "I hear noise in the back of this room. Mrs. Cooper doesn't like noisy children in her room." Finally, (5) know your subject matter. Students are less inclined to misbehave when they are learning something if only because the learning supplies constructive competing responses. All of these techniques, because of the ripple effect, have beneficial effects on both the misbehaving student and his classmates.

Jean Grambs and William Iverson (1952, p. 310) remind us that disciplinary problems often arise from the ineptness of the teacher. They list several ways in which teachers can display a lack of teaching skill; these actions will result in student misbehavior: conducting classes in a dull, monotonous way; speaking in a rasping, irritating voice; giving

* It may be more precise to say *to arrange the conditions which cause* the ripple effect rather than *to use* the ripple effect. The latter is an abbreviated way of stating the former.

vague assignments; giving assignments too difficult for the students; giving assignments too easy for the students; proceeding with oral work when there is noise inside or outside the room; failing to give attention to conditions of light and heat; being confused about classroom routines, such as distributing supplies; being subject to student pressures at unpredictable times; failing to make the steps of learning clear; giving tests on material not covered in class; and rewarding only one kind of aptitude. They also list the types of social ineptness on the part of the teacher which may result in disciplinary problems: using sarcasm, failing to answer reasonable questions, being insensitive to stuttering and other special problems of the students, being inconsistent—for example, telling a student who has arrived late to ask another student for help and then reprimanding him for talking, being impolite and rough, making personal references about students, being unfair and having favorites, making disparaging remarks about minority groups, and gossiping about students in public places. The students often develop their own system of rewards and punishment for the misbehaving teacher. If the students do not, the principal does and the school board does.

In describing the teacher's disciplinary function, we should recall that establishing police control over the class should not be the major preoccupation of the teacher. Teachers sometimes develop excellent enforcement policies which involve clear rules about hand raising, gum chewing, and swearing. Their patrol of aisles, halls, and cafeterias emulates that of the civilian and military police. The totality of their control and their physical omnipresence are often the marvel of the student body. Out of boredom or curiosity a foolhardy student will sometimes challenge one of these lion-hearted teachers. The teacher may welcome the challenge because everyone will then witness the magnificence of his disciplinary system in full operation. When the preoccupation, however, has been so totally with control and discipline, one wonders how much thought this teacher has given to what the students will learn while and after control has been established. A teacher's concern about discipline should not compete seriously with a well-conceived lesson plan. Generations of student teachers and beginning teachers have made rather bitter comments about their teacher-training programs because they never learned how to control the class. The obvious answer to this charge is that everything in educational psychology from the formulation of instructional objectives to the assessment of performance should contribute to the control of the class. We resort to punishment when other efforts fail. The quality and success of your planning efforts ought to bear at least joint responsibility with the teacher-training program for the breakdown of control.

Finally, because all of us in education are idealists and missionaries we sometimes find it difficult to bow before the cruel realities of our schools. We must acknowledge that teachers in large urban and suburban schools often find a high incidence of antisocial behavior. To protect life, limb, virtue, and sanity they must sometimes resort to suppression and punishment. By doing so they are occasionally able to establish enough order to assist the students in achieving some minimal objectives.

SUMMARY. The disciplinary function requires the teacher to control deviant behavior through the use of rewards and punishment. Punishment is an unpopular word in American psychology even though the experimental evidence reviewed earlier in the chapter indicates that it is an effective means of learning and impulse control. Research on infrahuman and human subjects indicates that a punishment procedure which involves both the suppression of the undesired response and the provision of an alternative rewarded response may be a most effective procedure, especially when the undesired response has been previously rewarded. This artful combination of punishment and reward as a disciplinary technique is called *restitution*. Evidence shows that classmates identify with their punished fellows, so that the act of punishment has a ripple effect. The effect can operate to the advantage of the teacher if desist or nonthreatening techniques are used whenever possible. These cause a minimum of discomfort to the disciplined student's classmates. Punishment, of course, should never be used as a defense of our own pedagogical ineptness. But it should not be avoided at all costs. Both experimental evidence and ordinary observation confirm the belief that punishment can produce rather dramatic, permanent, and desirable changes in behavior. The beliefs that punishment is not so effective as reward and that it causes permanent trauma are undoubtedly vast overstatements of very ambiguous studies. The evidence we now have does not indicate that we should banish punishment from the teacher's repertory of motivational techniques any more than we should exclude the use of anxiety, frustration, incentives, and competition, even if such banishment were humanly possible.

You should now return to objectives 12–15 (pp. 129–30 and determine how well you have achieved them.

QUESTION 5-3

Miss Dee Litefull spent considerable effort devising analogies between past and present historical events. In diplomacy she compared Queen Elizabeth I with President De Gaulle, St. Francis of Assisi with beatnik and hippie leaders, and the leaders of the Crusades with the leaders of the peace demonstrations. Which of the four motivational functions do Miss Litefull's analogies best illustrate? (a) Arousal function; (b) expectancy function; (c) incentives function; (d) disciplinary function.

After selecting your answer, explain the reasons for your choice and for your rejection of the alternatives.

SUMMARY

Motivation refers to factors which invigorate student behavior. For *invigoration* you may read *increased effort.* Motivation is closely related to entering behavior: When students are motivated, they make the strongest responses they have learned. No amount of motivation can trigger or direct responses the students have not learned.

The factors which produce motivation are grouped into four classes: arousal, expectancy, incentives, and punishment. These factors, of course, are interrelated and interdependent. Arousal is the general level of alertness of the individual. The optimum levels of arousal are related to stimulus seeking, anxiety, and frustration. Expectancies are momentary beliefs about the probability of the occurrence of particular results. Expectancies are often products of discrepancies, and they are closely related to valences—what the individual wants as well as what he expects. Incentives are goal objects which become associated with certain stimuli and responses; they trigger anticipations. Punishment involves the suppression of an undesired response—the individual learns what not to do.

These four factors (or classes) form a motivation model distinct from that of drive-reduction theory, Freudian theory, and theories about self-actualization. From this model we derive the four motivational functions of the teacher. The arousal function requires the teacher to engage the student in learning. The expectancy function requires him to describe concretely what the student will be able to do at the conclusion of instruction. The incentive function requires the rewarding of present achievement in such a way as to encourage future achievement. Finally, the disciplinary function requires the teacher to use a combination of rewards and punishment in controlling student behavior.

SUGGESTED READINGS

This book gives an introductory, well-written overview of motivational theory, research, and controversy:

Murray, Edward J., *Motivation and Emotion.* Englewood Cliffs, N.J.: Prentice-Hall, Inc., 1964 (paper).

These books are for the serious student who wants comprehensive reviews and analyses of the vast research and theory on motivation:

Bindra, Dalbir, *Motivation—A Systematic Interpretation.* New York: The Ronald Press Company, 1959.

Brown, Judson S., *The Motivation of Behavior.* New York: McGraw-Hill Book Company, 1961.

Cofer, Charles N., and Mortimer H. Appley, *Motivation: Theory and Research.* New York: John Wiley & Sons, Inc., 1964. This is the *most* comprehensive.

These books are very provocative discussions of curiosity and exploratory behavior:

Fowler, Harry, *Curiosity and Exploratory Behavior.* New York: The Macmillan Company, 1965 (paper). This is a good introductory review and synthesis of the research.

Berlyne, Daniel E., *Conflict, Arousal, and Curiosity*. New York: McGraw-Hill Book Company, 1960. This is a more advanced treatment.

For other aspects of motivation, as indicated by their titles, the following books are authoritative and challenging:

McClelland, David C., *The Achieving Society*. Princeton, N.J.: D. Van Nostrand Co., Inc., 1961.

Spielberger, Charles D., *Anxiety and Behavior*. New York: Academic Press, Inc., 1966.

Vroom, Victor H., *Work and Motivation*. New York: John Wiley & Sons, Inc., 1964.

This stimulating discussion links theory and research to teaching practice:

Sears, Pauline S., and Ernest R. Hilgard, "The Teacher's Role in the Motivation of the Learner," *Theories of Learning and Instruction,* ed. E. R. Hilgard, Part 1 of the 63rd Yearbook, National Society for the Study of Education, pp. 182–209. Chicago: University of Chicago Press, 1964.

This pamphlet gives some rather practical suggestions for discipline (based on the little available research):

Gnagey, William J., *Controlling Classroom Misbehavior*. Washington, D.C.: National Educational Association, 1965 (a pamphlet).

The Education of the Disadvantaged Child

6

Two current social movements will have permanent effects on American public education. The civil rights movement is a vivid, effective renewal of our democratic commitment to educate all our children to their fullest social and intellectual potential. The current educational reform attempts to meet a very clear challenge: to design for students poorly equipped for learning, school programs that do not compromise intellectual honesty and substance. According to Cremin (1965, pp. 74, 82) the educational reformers are resting their case on the assumption, as yet untested, that "culture can be democratized without being vulgarized" and that "the way to nurture taste is to make the good so widely available that the cheaper ceases to satisfy." Continuing his description of these reformers, Cremin writes (p. 59):

> They simply refuse to honor the view that only 20 per cent of our children can profit from academic courses and that the remaining 80 per cent need either trade training or something called "life adjustment education." Indeed, their real contention is that all children need the "new math" and the "new English" if they are to make any intelligent adjustment whatsoever to modern life. This is not to say that they are foolish enough to argue that every child can master the sciences and the humanities in the same way; it is rather to argue that every child can master the sciences and humanities in some intellectually honest way.

The importance of the current reform movement requires the schools and the teachers to make careful inventories of the entering behavior of and instructional procedures for the disadvantaged child. Because these inventories have proved difficult to make and their results difficult to apply, the problems of educating the disadvantaged child require extended consideration. Since we are only beginning to discover what behavioral equipment the disadvantaged child has when he enters the school and since we must make this assessment of entering behavior before we can determine the appropriate instructional procedures, this chapter appears in Part 2 (on entering behavior) rather than in Part 3 (on instructional procedures). You will discover, however, that the last section of the chapter does describe procedures which have been utilized and recommended for the education of the disadvantaged child.

The chapter has three sections. The first describes the family and social background of the disadvantaged child, evaluates the available descriptions of him in terms of the soundness of the social-class concept, describes the studies of socioeconomic status and IQ, and, finally, discusses the usefulness of these correlational data for describing and accommodating entering behavior. The second section describes the learning conditions under which the disadvantaged child develops. In it, a theoretical model of the growth of intelligence illustrates the divergent effects of enriched and impoverished environments. The section then reviews the available research on the effects of impoverished environments on perceptual learning and linguistic and cognitive development, and discusses the usefulness of these studies for describing and accommodating entering behavior. The third (concluding) section deals with programs, practices, teachers, and guidelines. It summarizes the current state of the art by describing recent programs and practices. The section then discusses the research on teachers of disadvantaged children, hypothetical models of ideal teacher characteristics, and the dilemmas often faced by the teacher. The section concludes with a list of guidelines derived from the theory and research of the previous sections; these guidelines can be used in planning instruction for disadvantaged children.

Upon reading the first section of this chapter (on social conditions), you should be able to meet these objectives:

1. Distinguish the disadvantaged from the nondisadvantaged child by describing the disadvantaged child's entering behavior and his economic, racial, and ethnic characteristics.

2. Distinguish between the concept of social class and the concept of socioeconomic status (SES) and provide illustrations of each.

3. Describe the relationship between SES and school achievement, motivation, and IQ.

4. Describe the relationship between Negro and white IQ.

5. Describe the relationship between Negro learning ability and IQ.

6. List the limitations of culture fair IQ tests.

7. Distinguish between correlational and experimental studies and give two illustrations of each.

8. Describe three uses of the correlational studies on SES for assessing the entering behavior of disadvantaged children.

Upon reading the second section of this chapter (on learning conditions), you should be able to meet these objectives:

9. Describe the effects of impoverished environments on the problem-solving ability of Scotty puppies and the brain chemistry of rats and also the effects on the early cognitive stimulation of children.

10. Describe the impoverished home environments of disadvantaged children by referring to visual, verbal, and auditory stimulation and in terms of memory span, use of positive reinforcers, and speech sequences.

11. Define cumulative deficits in terms of school learning and illustrate possible irreversible effects.

12. Describe Jensen's model for the growth of intelligence in terms of the relationship of heredity and enriched and impoverished environments.

13. Describe the relationship among environmental change, achievement, and IQ by referring to particular studies (the Scottish surveys, Klineberg, Wheeler, and Bloom) and point out the effects of early environment.

14. Describe the effects of impoverished environments on perceptual learning by referring to habits of attending and listening.

15. Describe the effects of impoverished environments on language development by referring to the disadvantaged child's ability to comprehend more than he expresses.

16. Distinguish between restricted and elaborated language codes by listing the characteristics and providing illustrations of each code.

17. Describe the effects of impoverished environments on cognitive development in terms of verbal mediation: labeling, syntactical mediation, word-object stability, feedback, and learning styles.

Upon reading the third section of this chapter (on programs, practices, teachers, and guidelines), you should be able to meet these objectives:

18. Make a crude distinction between programs and practices and illustrate the distinction you make.

19. List five types of programs.

20. Describe the two comprehensive programs of New York City by referring to the schools and the students involved (number, type, and so on) and to the services provided; describe the results of these two programs.

21. Describe the Perry Preschool Project by indicating what the program consisted of and distinguishing the three Waves; describe the results of the program.

22. Describe the use of puppets, stories, synonymity, and commercial aids in teaching the disadvantaged child.

23. List Reissman's characteristics of the ideal teacher for disadvantaged children and indicate points of disagreement between him and the teachers in the Groff (1962) study.

24. List the distinguishing characteristics of Negro and white teachers as reported in the Gottlieb (1964) study.

25. Describe the hypothetical teacher models of Webster and Goldberg and show their similarities and differences.

26. Show how the research on the teacher's social class does not support conclusions on the school's middle-class values and on the use of these values in judging the performance of disadvantaged children.

27. Name three limitations of teacher influence in solving the educational problems of disadvantaged children and describe the dilemmas the teachers face.

28. List five guidelines for the instruction of disadvantaged children and show their relationship to research reported in this and the previous chapter.

SOCIAL CONDITIONS

The first part of this section describes the family and social background of the disadvantaged child. Here I define what we mean by the *disadvantaged child;* I describe his economic, racial, and ethnic characteristics, and discuss some of the research on child-rearing practices as it relates to our topic. Next I consider the validity of the concept of social class as it applies to American society in general and to descriptions of the lower class in particular. Finally I describe the studies of the relationship between socioeconomic status and IQ, including those studies which compare Negro and white IQs. This section on social conditions broadly delineates the problem of educating the disadvantaged child. The section on learning conditions, which follows, defines the problem in ways more useful for the assessment and accommodation of his entering behavior.

Family and Social Background

Definition of disadvantaged. The disadvantaged child is one who is reared in a preschool environment which fails to develop the entering behavior necessary for beginning his formal education in the public schools. Many other terms are currently used to describe this child: poor, lower-class, of lower socioeconomic status, underprivileged, and socially and culturally deprived. Educationally he has sometimes been described as retarded, slow, and underachieving. The choice of term is a sensitive issue because each suggests somewhat different deficiencies and different sources of blame: the child, the parents, the school, and the society. To avoid any implication of deficiencies in the children and their parents the term *culturally different* has been suggested (Haubrich, 1963). Hilda Taba (1964) notes that the educational terms describe the difficulty while the other terms describe the source of the problem.

Economic characteristics: how poor is poor? Helen Witmer (1964) describes the economic distress of disadvantaged children. They are reared in families which have average annual incomes of $3,000 per year. About one-third of this income is spent on food ($5 per week for each person), $65 per month is spent on rent, and $25 per week is left for everything else, including clothing, medical care, and recreation. In 1962 about 20 per cent of American families were poor—9.3 million out of 47 million families. More than one-half of the poor families (4.7 million) had incomes under $2,000. In 1961, about 17 million children were living in poverty; that is, 25 per cent of all American children were growing up in families whose incomes were clearly inadequate. The poor are very poor and very numerous.

Some poor are poorer than others. If we take race, we find that 47 per cent of nonwhite families are poor compared with 14 per cent of white families. If we take families with female heads, we find that 63 per cent of these families are poor compared with 13 per cent of the families with male heads. If we take rural families, we find that 26 per cent of these families are poor compared with 11 per cent of urban families. Finally, if we take the South, we find that 30 per cent of these families are poor compared with 11 per cent of the families in the rest of the country. When the disadvantage of belonging to a nonwhite race is added to the disadvantage of having a woman as chief wage earner, the likelihood of poverty rises from 41 per cent to 81 per cent.

Racial and ethnic characteristics. Robert Havighurst (1964) identifies the following characteristics of disadvantaged persons: (1) They are often southern Negroes who have recently migrated to northern cities; (2) they are often southern whites who have migrated from the rural south and southern mountains to northern cities; (3) they are often

Puerto Ricans living in northern cities; (4) they are often Mexican farmers who have migrated to the West and Midwest; and (5) they are often European immigrants from eastern and southern Europe.

Social class characteristics. Before we consider the evidence for and the arguments against the existence of social classes in American society, I shall summarize the characteristics of the lower class as reported by various writers. Disadvantaged children are sometimes described in terms of the social class to which they presumably belong. For example, Davis (1948) describes the physical and socially aroused anxieties of lower-class people. Their physical anxieties derive from the uncertainty of having food, the fear of eviction, the fear of being cold and in the dark, and the fear of getting too little sleep. When they have food, they eat too much; and, when they have money, they spend too much to reduce anxiety and to protect themselves against an uncertain future. Davis states (p. 27) that "in their lives it is all or nothing, or next to nothing." Their socially aroused anxieties derive from a vast number of taboos and group standards regarding the right amount of food, the proper furniture, and the proper house. Fortunately, for the poor, not all is bleak. Davis believes that they enjoy two areas of experience which are acute sources of anxiety for the middle class: sexual relations and physical aggression. While middle-class children are punished for their sexual and aggressive behavior, lower-class children are rewarded. Davis does concede that the instability of lower-class marriages may mean that the lower-class individual does not have a sexual partner for as many days each month as does the middle-class person, "but one (the lower-class person) gets and gives more satisfaction over longer periods when he does have a sexual partner" (p. 33). In comparing three- and four-year-old boys and girls, John McKee and Florence Leader (1955) found significantly more aggressive and competitive behavior in lower-status than in higher-status children. They suggest that the higher incidence of this behavior in these children may be due to lack of parental supervision as well as to more parental reward.

Frank Riessman (1962) describes disadvantaged children and their families: They are traditional, patriarchal, superstitious, and religious; they are ineffective readers, poorly informed, suggestible, and suspicious of newfangled ideas; they are opinionated about morality, punishment, custom, diet, education, the role of women, and the role of intellectuals; they feel socially alienated; they are not individualistic, self-centered, or self-expressive; they are poor patients in psychotherapy; they have a greater need for getting by than getting ahead; they are egalitarian (but not always politically liberal), anti-Communist, attracted to strong leaders, prejudiced, and intolerant; they are very interested in family and personal comforts; they are informal, easy, and comfortable, with an "affectionate bite of humor"; they expect individuals to rise above their official positions; they are attracted to excitement, news, gossip, new gadgets, and new goals; they are pragmatic and anti-intellectual; they perform manual labor best; and they are attracted to masculinity—even the Negro mother is a strong masculine type. Riessman believes that anti-intellectualism is their most salient characteristic.

There is some disagreement over the hedonism of lower-class people. Jules Henry (1965) believes that their lives are a "flight from death": a desperate effort to concentrate on those experiences, including the taking of drugs and the drinking of alcohol, which give them vivid reassurances of being alive. Anthony Davids (1966), using two personality tests, found that underachieving boys of superior academic potential for the study of science, when compared with equally able but achieving peers, placed more emphasis on heterosexuality, good looks, pleasure seeking, and a lack of inhibition. The underachieving boys, however, also had a greater need for succorance, or for soliciting sympathy, affection, and emotional support from others.

David and Pearl Ausubel (1963) believe that Negro children lack adult figures with whom to identify and that they lack expectations of future success. Even before he enters school the Negro child realizes the inferior status of his race and prefers to play with white dolls and white playmates. He finds it difficult to identify with a black mother and father, and he therefore fails to identify with any adult. His chief socializing agent is his peer group, and, in the case of the Negro boy, this association results in precocious maturity. In the years before adolescence the Negro child develops low levels of expectancy as he learns of the opportunities denied his caste. He is ambivalent about middle-class values because he is loyal to his own parents and race. Richard Cloward and James Jones (1963) found that lower-class individuals do not see education as a means of upward mobility not because they devalue education but because they do not expect to rise very far in the occupational world.

Child rearing. Melvin Kohn (1959) studied the relation between social class and parental values. He interviewed the parents of 400 fifth grade children. Using an index of social status, he divided them into middle-class families, which were almost entirely professional, and working-class families, which included small shopkeepers, clerks, salespeople, foremen, and skilled workers. He presented the parents with a list of seventeen behavioral characteristics appropriate for children of this age (see Table 6-1) and asked them to select the three most important characteristics. Table 6-1 shows the commonality and the differences in the maternal values of the two classes. They agreed considerably on the importance of honesty, consideration, obedience, dependability, and manners for both girls and boys. If we look at the differences between classes, the middle-class parents valued self-control and consideration in their children. The child should behave properly because he wants to

TABLE 6-1

PROPORTION OF MOTHERS WHO SELECTED EACH CHARACTERISTIC AS ONE OF THREE "MOST DESIRABLE" IN A TEN- OR ELEVEN-YEAR-OLD CHILD (Kohn, 1959, p. 340).

Characteristics	For Boys Middle Class	For Boys Working Class	For Girls Middle Class	For Girls Working Class	Combined Middle Class	Combined Working Class
1. That he is honest	0.44	0.57	0.44	0.48	0.44	0.53
2. That he is happy	.44*	.27	.48	.45	.46*	.36
3. That he is considerate of others	.40	.30	.38*	.24	.39*	.27
4. That he obeys his parents well	.18*	.37	.23	.30	.20*	.33
5. That he is dependable	.27	.27	.20	.14	.24	.21
6. That he has good manners	.16	.17	.23	.32	.19	.24
7. That he has self-control	.24	.14	.20	.13	.22*	.13
8. That he is popular with other children	.13	.15	.17	.20	.15	.18
9. That he is a good student	.17	.23	.13	.11	.15	.17
10. That he is neat and clean	.07	.13	.15*	.28	.11*	.20
11. That he is curious about things	.20*	.06	.15	.07	.18*	.06
12. That he is ambitious	.09	.18	.06	.08	.07	.13
13. That he is able to defend himself	.13	.05	.06	.08	.10	.06
14. That he is affectionate	.03	.05	.07	.04	.05	.04
15. That he is liked by adults	.03	.05	.07	.04	.05	.04
16. That he is able to play by himself	.01	.02	.00	.03	.01	.02
17. That he acts in a serious way	0.00	0.01	0.00	0.00	0.00	0.01
N	90	85	84	80	174	165

* Social-class differences statistically significant, 0.05 level or better, using chi-square test.

and not because his parents require him to. Working-class parents placed a greater value on neatness, cleanliness, and obedience to externally imposed standards. Kohn concluded that for the middle class and the working class social class is a reliable indicator of values.

Some evidence indicates that lower-class parents are adopting the child-rearing practices of middle-class parents. Urie Bronfenbrenner (1961) refers to middle-class practices as love-oriented and psychological.

Among these are the following: (1) greater parental permissiveness toward the spontaneous desires of the child; (2) freer parental expression of affection; (3) less reliance on direct methods of discipline (physical punishment, scolding, and threats) and more reliance on indirect, psychological techniques (reasoning and appealing to guilt); (4) fathers becoming more affectionate and less authoritarian and mothers becoming the chief disciplinarians, even for the boys. Parents tolerate the child's impulses, desires, and expressions of feeling; they reason with the child, isolate him, appeal to his guilt, and show disappointment. They make clear to him the behavior they expect. We have very little direct evidence on how the use of these techniques over the past twenty-five years has affected the behavior of middle-class children. Bronfenbrenner suggests that the middle-class, democratic family may produce young people who do not take initiative, look up to others for direction and decision, and cannot be trusted to fulfill obligations. The lower middle-class boys may come out ahead since they receive inadequate discipline and emotional support and, therefore, show more leadership, higher levels of aspiration, and more competitiveness.

SUMMARY. The disadvantaged child lacks the school entering behavior usually acquired in preschool development. To identify this child further we have considered his economic, racial, ethnic, and class characteristics together with the child-rearing practices of his parents. In these descriptions of social-class characteristics and child-rearing practices we have assumed that there is a readily identifiable class structure in American society and that for each social class there are distinct value systems and modes of behavior. Most discussions of and much research on the disadvantaged child have assumed the existence of such a structure. Many investigators however have questioned this assumption, have reanalyzed old data, and have obtained new data which strongly indicate that the social-class structure which may have existed before World War I no longer exists today. We now turn to a consideration of social class and its application to American society.

Social Class: Where Is It?

Four conditions must exist in a community before we can affirm the existence of social class (Brown, 1965, p. 114). (1) The population must be conscious of classes and agree on the number of classes. (2) Styles of life within the classes must be strikingly uniform and, between classes, clearly unique. (3) Social interaction must be sharply patterned on class. (4) Data on each of these factors must indicate the same boundaries between classes. We will apply these four conditions to the above descriptions of the lower class to see whether we can establish the existence of this class.

Consciousness of class. Are members of a community conscious of belonging to particular classes? Very probably not. When sociologists ask residents of a community to talk about social life and when the sociologists do not refer to social class, they often fail to obtain references to it. "What kinds of differences are there among people in San Francisco?" the sociologist may ask. Most answers refer to income, occupation, race, and so on. Gross (1953) found that when he asked the residents in Minneapolis "What class do you belong to?" one-third of the respondents said there were no classes in Minneapolis. American Negroes are not conscious of belonging to a social class but of belonging to a caste which, like castes in India, has had little or no upward social mobility. There is no class consciousness in the sense of the old English yeoman's identification with the soil or of the old English landed aristocracy's identification with positions of power, wealth, and prestige.

Style of life. Are there striking differences between the middle-class and lower-class styles of life and do all members of those classes have uniform styles? Again the answer is probably no. Unquestionably we have prestige rankings based on occupations, but we have no sharp breaks between class lines. As one rises in occupational and financial status in American life, he does not suddenly change his style of life as would an English yeoman who became a great landowner. If the head of the American household earns much money the family has more and better quality possessions. Life style is not a product of class membership but a reflection of income and occupation (Brown, 1965).

Social interaction. This criterion requires the members of a class to confine social interaction almost exclusively to their own class. No such exclusiveness exists in American life. Roger Brown (1965, pp. 126–27) re-examined the data on the study of Elmtown (Hollingshead, 1949) and found that, although the highest frequency of interaction was within each class, there was frequent interaction among classes. For marriages in New Haven for the same or adjacent class, the frequency was 83 per cent not 100 per cent—which indicates interaction across as well as between adjacent classes.

Identical data boundaries. The last criterion for judging social class requires that the data of the three other standards—class consciousness, life style, and social interaction—all indicate the same boundary. There is, however, considerable discrepancy. Although we know that a prestigious occupation, high income from respectable sources, a fine house, and a fashionable address all form a homogeneous collection, the American newspapers delight in reporting the enormous wealth but somewhat discordant life styles of Hollywood actors, Nevada gamblers, and New York racketeers. These people, with the discrepancy between their wealth and their manners, are the Asian and European stereotypes of Ugly Americans. Only in such areas as the Middle East and Latin America do we find that striking convergence of wealth, power, and prestige which verifies the existence of social classes.

Many studies of social-class values use significant differences between classes to infer characteristics within classes. Both logically and statistically, of course, this is a very questionable procedure. To illustrate this point, Kathryn Johnsen and Gerald Leslie (1965) reanalyzed the data of Kohn's study of social class and parental values, which we described above. Their presentation of Kohn's data shows the close similarity of the values of the two classes (Table 6-2). Kohn concluded that the major emphasis of middle-class mothers was the development of self-control in their children. Table 6-2 shows that the percentages for self-control were only 22 per cent for middle-class mothers and 13 per cent for working-class mothers. Also, 20 per cent of the middle-class mothers chose obedience, which Kohn had concluded was a major concern only of working-class mothers. These researchers rephrase Kohn's findings as follows (p. 351): "Contrary to previous expectations, 78 per cent of the middle-class mothers thought at least three characteristics more important than self-control. Among the working-class mothers, 80 per cent thought three other characteristics more important than self-control." In this latter analysis of Kohn's data we see uniform social-class values vanish.

Another characteristic often attributed to the lower class is sexual permissiveness (see p. 187). Johnsen and Leslie (1965) shows that, in studying a characteristic such as this, the way you ask a question in an interview or questionnaire determines the responses you obtain. Asking a variety of questions on the topic often bring a wide range of responses. Table 6-3 lists six different items, all on sexual permissiveness. You can

TABLE 6-2

CHARACTERISTICS CONSIDERED MOST DESIRABLE IN A TEN- OR ELEVEN-YEAR-OLD; PARTIAL SUMMARY OF M. L. KOHN'S 1959 FINDINGS (Johnsen and Leslie, 1965, p. 351).

Trait	Per cent of mothers choosing trait	
	Middle class	Lower class
Honesty	44	53
Happiness	46	36
Consideration	39	27
Dependability	24	21
Self-control	22	13
Obedience	20	33
Neatness and cleanliness	11	20

TABLE 6-3

PERCENTAGE DISTRIBUTIONS OF RESPONSES TO SIX ITEMS ON SEXUAL PERMISSIVENESS, $N = 264$ (Johnsen and Leslie, 1965, p. 354).

Item	Distribution of Response		
	Permissive	Intermediate	Strict
1. A mother should teach her children that curiosity about sex should not be satisfied in play with other children.	1.8	31.3	66.8
2. A mother should allow her children to satisfy their curiosity about the opposite sex	25.7	61.5	12.8
3. A mother should teach her children that it is wrong to be curious about sex.*	87.2	11.7	1.1
4. How much have you allowed your children to run about the house without their clothes on?	14.7	73.5	11.7
5. Many mothers report that their young children and their playmates will take off their pants, look at each other, giggle, etc. at times. How much of this do you allow?	1.9	24.6	73.5
6. You have just discovered your preschool daughter playing with a little boy of the same age. They have their pants off and are talking about differences in their bodies. What are you most likely to do?	27.7	58.3	14.0

* Strong disagreement with the item as stated is interpreted as reflecting the newer permissive normative pattern.

see that the proportion of permissive responses ranges from 1.8 per cent to 87.2 per cent. The researchers suggest that the most significant finding is that parents are considerably confused over how to convey to the child the acceptance of sex per se without accepting the child's sex play—a peculiarly modern family dilemma. Detailed items on obedience and aggression toward the mother also suggest the same parental confusion. To generalize class characteristics from such studies is therefore impossible. And, since all the value terms used to describe the middle and lower classes refer to similarly complex behaviors, these descriptions can only be considered high-flown abstractions.

Robert Nisbet (1959) refers to the statement sometimes made that Marx, because of a religious turn of mind, transmuted the theological myth of the war between good and evil into the economic myth of the war between the proletariat and the capitalists. American sociologists have carried this transmutation one step further in assuming the necessary conflict between the lower class (the good) and the middle class (the evil). Some sociologists, whose zeal is more powerful than their data, have tried to find more positive values in the lives of the lower class than in the lives of the middle class. Their attacks on middle-class values have sometimes called forth the defense of these values. James Heald (1965), for example, considers some of the allegations leveled against middle-class teachers, who are described by their critics as victims of the tensions, anxieties, neuroses, and psychoses of the middle class. Heald (following Havighurst and Taba, 1949) lists, among others, the following values of these teachers: community responsibility, cleanliness and neatness, honesty, self-reliance, sexual morality, and thrift. Such a list is nothing to be ashamed of, even though Heald suggests that it may be criticized for what it omits rather than for what it includes. My contention, however, is that the middle class has no monopoly on such values. And, as Havighurst (1964, p. 216) states, research shows that the lower class has no special advantages either: "There is substantial doubt that socially disadvantaged children in our big cities have *any* positive qualities of potential value in urban society in which they are systematically better than children of families who participate more fully in the mass culture."

I rest my case with these words. No convincing evidence proves the existence of social classes in modern American life. All Marxian arguments to the contrary, we are truly the classless society. We have no clear consciousness of class, no sense of class solidarity, no highly distinctive styles of life, and no highly exclusive patterns of social interaction. The President's daughter can marry the son of a small-town businessman, and the spectacle delights the nation and confirms our belief in upward mobility. Big Labor is as strong as Big Business, and Big Government may be stronger than both. Privilege, power, and wealth are not the monopoly of one class.

Finally, descriptions of social class do not help the teacher define the entering behavior of disadvantaged children. We can assume no uniformity of moral values, child-rearing practices, character formation or preschool educational experience. Although often the product of humanitarian zeal, the myth of social classes leads more often to the stereotyping and patronizing of disadvantaged children than to informed efforts to give them the pedagogical assistance they require. Debate over whether the wiser course is to convert the middle class to lower-class values and life style or to convert the lower class to middle-class values and life style have no solid basis and often distract us from the real problem of assessing and providing for the entering behavior of the disadvantaged child.

Socioeconomic Status, IQ, and Race

Is it any more useful for the teacher to know the child's socioeconomic status than it is to know his social class? Socioeconomic status, which we henceforth designate SES, does not require us to make assumptions about class consciousness, life styles, and social interaction. Whereas social class emphasizes discontinuities in American life, SES assumes a continuous ranking from high to low on the basis of occupation, education, income, and so on. Also, SES emphasizes the upward mobility of American society, while social class emphasizes clear class boundaries that are rarely crossed. We can describe some rather striking divergencies of American education, wealth, and life styles on the basis of SES without assuming the uniformity and social rigidity which the class concept requires.

We may define SES in many ways. One of the best-known methods is the Index of Social Characteristics (the ISC) of Lloyd Warner and his associates (1949). The ISC (in revised form) is based upon weighted ratings of four characteristics: occupation, source of income, house type, and dwelling area. Ratings on each characteristic range from 1 (very high) to 7 (very low). Occupation carries the most weight, with income, house type, and dwelling area following in that order. Warner later discovered that consideration of occupation alone resulted in about the same SES as did consideration of all four characteristics. Unfortunately, Warner and his associates claim that ISC ratings can be converted into social-class designations. Our discussion above indicates that this is a great conceptual leap. We can describe the continuity and the mobility of American society much more faithfully in terms of SES than in terms of social class.

Considerable research has attempted to determine the extent of the relationship between SES and IQ. Some of these studies have focused directly on this relationship; others have examined the relationship between SES and school achievement, motivation, race, and so on. The study of SES and IQ has raised questions about the fairness of using the standard IQ tests for measuring the intelligence of disadvantaged children. In this part of the chapter we shall first consider the studies and the controversy over the use of the tests and then consider the usefulness of the research results in assessing and providing for the entering behavior of the disadvantaged child.

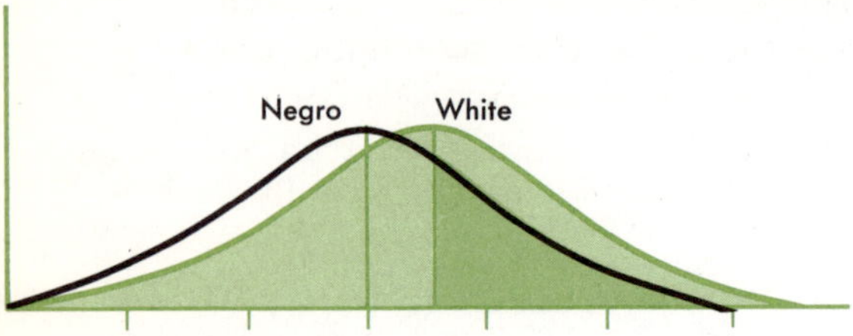

Fig. 6-1. *Schematic distribution illustrating 30 per cent overlap (after Anastasi, 1958, p. 549).*

Overlap of negro-white iq. The comparison of Negro and white intelligence is easy to make. Figure 6-1 compares the intelligence test scores of Negroes and whites in the United States. You can see the familiar phenomenon of overlapping. Anastasi (1958, p. 549), on the basis of this overlap, points out that, if a Negro were chosen at random from a group of Negroes, thirty out of one hundred times his score would equal or surpass that of the average white person. If you were to assume that the Negro were inferior to the average white, you would be wrong thirty out of one hundred times. In psychological and educational research we reject a finding if we can be in error five out of one hundred times. This overlap should make it clear that we cannot generalize from the group to the individual student. Although most Negroes score below whites, almost one-third do not. We can see that significant group differences have little practical value when applied to individual students.

SES, race, and iq. Is IQ related to SES better than to race? A number of studies have made this comparison. Ada Arlitt (1921) studied 343 elementary school children in a single school district. Most of the children had native American parents. Children of the other "races" had Italian and Negro parents. Establishing the children's SES on the basis of their parents' occupations, she found that 40 per cent of the low SES children had IQs below 90 and only 4.6 per cent had IQs above 110. About 50 per cent of the average SES children had average IQs and 25 per cent had IQs above average (that is, above 110). About 75 per cent of the superior SES children had IQs above average, and 76 per cent of these had IQs above 120. These data are consistent with findings on SES which we discussed earlier (p. 195). Arlitt also compared Italian and Negro children with white children of inferior and very inferior SES. All the children in this comparison lived in the same section of the city. She discovered that the difference in average IQ was reduced from 33.9 points to 8.6 points. She concluded that there is more likeness among children of the same SES but different race than among children of the same race but different SES. Her findings are consistent with those of Carrell Horton and Perry Crump (1962), who found that SES and the educational level of the parents were more highly correlated with IQ than with race.

The more recent findings of Deutsch and Bert Brown (1964) extend our knowledge about the relationship of SES to Negro and white intelligence. They studied a sample of 543 elementary school children of both races in the first and fifth grades. They divided the children into three SES levels on the basis of information about their homes and housing conditions, their daily routines, and the aspirations of both parents and children. They used an IQ test composed of pictorial and numerical items which the children had to pair, classify, and so on.

Deutsch and Brown found (1) no significant differences in IQ between the first and fifth grades for either the white or the Negro children; (2) highly significant differences between Negro and white IQs at both grade levels; and (3) highly significant differences between SES and IQ, with the higher IQs correlating with the higher SES levels. Table 6-4 indicates the direction and the size of these differences by mean. This table supports two conclusions: Negro children at each SES level score lower than white children (a finding consistent with previous studies); and Negro-white IQ differences increase at each higher SES

TABLE 6-4

MEAN IQ SCORES FOR NEGRO AND WHITE CHILDREN AT THREE SES LEVELS (after Deutsch and Brown, 1964, p. 26).

Group	Means	N
SES I (Low)		
White	97.24	104
Negro	91.24	157
Total	93.63	261
SES II		
White	105.59	68
Negro	94.87	111
Total	98.94	179
SES III (High)		
White	114.92	52
Negro	102.57	51
Total	108.81	103
Total race groups		
White	103.88	224
Negro	94.32	319

level—the whites show more gain in IQ points at higher SES levels than do the Negroes.

These investigators believe that this latter finding lends support to their participation hypothesis. They describe this hypothesis as follows (p. 27):

> The hypothesis we would advance has to do with increased participation in the cultural mainstream, and the differing conditions under which Negroes and whites participate. . . . The weight of color and resulting minority status, it is postulated here, results in much less participation by the Negro, while the lowest class status operates similarly for the white as well as for the Negro. In other words, it is much more difficult for the Negro to attain identical middle- or upper-middle-class status with whites, and the social class gradations are less marked for Negroes because Negro life in a caste society is considerably more homogeneous than is life for the majority group.

Although they used SES in their study, Deutsch and Brown express their hypothesis in terms of social class. Their findings, however, support the participation hypothesis even more when interpreted in terms of SES. Their study shows that caste differences can exist even when class differences no longer prevail. The homogeneity of Negro life is not due to their class but to their caste status. If social classes truly functioned effectively in American life, we would expect Negroes to be more like their class peers than like their racial peers. The differences between SES and IQ for Negroes and whites strongly indicate that caste influences prevail over class influences, a finding inconsistent with a belief in the existence of social classes.

During World War II, and since then, the Armed Forces have used the Army General Classification Test (the AGCT), a reliable group intelligence test, to measure IQ. Naomi Stewart (1947) made an analysis of the scores obtained by a representative sample of 81,553 white enlisted men during World War II. Figure 6-2 shows the data for fifteen occupations. This sample is not representative of the civilian population, especially since it omits officers, who have higher occupational status. For example, it includes no data on doctors and engineers. Yet Fig. 6-2 tells us fairly well what we would expect: The higher the civilian occupation of the soldier, the higher his IQ. You should note the considerable overlapping however. Differences between adjacent groups are not significant, but differences between widely separated groups are significant. You should also note that the range of scores generally increases as you descend the list—a factor which makes it more difficult to predict IQ in the lower than in the higher status occupations.

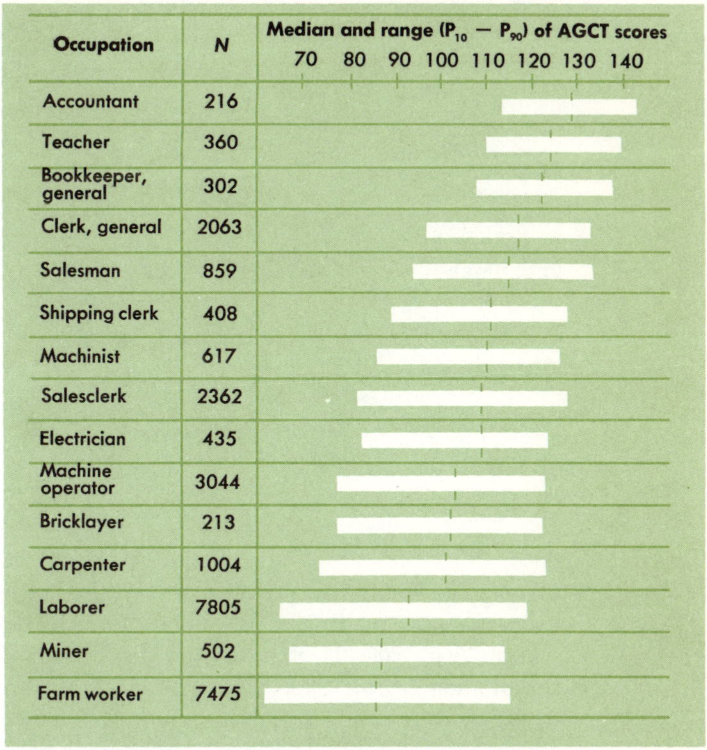

Fig. 6-2. *AGCT score in relation to civilian occupation (Stewart, pp. 5–13, 194, after Anastasi, 1958, p. 516).*

SES AND ACHIEVEMENT. Does the same pattern appear when we compare SES and reading achievement (as one measure of academic achievement)? To determine this relationship, Alan Wilson (1963) used children in the high sixth grade in fourteen schools in Berkeley, California. He divided the community into the Hills, the Foothills, and the Flats. The Hill parents were primarily in professional, executive, and white-collar occupations. The Flats contained working-class homes. The Foothills were heterogeneous. Table 6-5 shows the relationship between SES (in terms of father's occupation) and the reading achievement scores. Wilson also included the relationship of sex and what he calls *school strata,*—whether the school was in the Hills, Foothills, or Flats. Reading across the table (left to right) and reading down the table (top to bottom) give you two distinct but related impressions. By reading down each column you see that occupation (or SES) does make a difference, but that it makes less difference in the Hill schools than in the other schools.

TABLE 6-5

MEAN READING ACHIEVEMENT-TEST SCORES OF HIGH SIXTH GRADE STUDENTS, CLASSIFIED BY SEX, SCHOOL STRATA, AND FATHERS' OCCUPATIONS (Wilson, 1963, p. 223). (The numbers in parentheses refer to the number of students in each category.)

	Boys			Girls		
Father's Occupation	Hills	Foothills	Flats	Hills	Foothills	Flats
Professional and executive	107 (94)	100 (21)	—* (2)	107 (93)	108 (15)	—* (1)
White-collar and merchant	106 (46)	93 (31)	81 (18)	102 (55)	69 (38)	81 (16)
Manual and artisan	—* (3)	91 (55)	71 (72)	103 (11)	93 (46)	84 (87)

* Means are not reported for cells containing fewer than ten cases.

Also, the largest differences in the scores of boys and girls occur in the schools of the Flats. Reading across the table you can see substantial differences in reading achievement for the students attending different schools (e.g., 106, 93, 81). Wilson suggests that these latter data indicate the homogenizing effects of schools. You can answer the question of whether these data argue in favor of school desegregation. The table also shows that the Hill girls and boys have about equal achievement, while the Flats girls are clearly superior to the Flats boys.

The trend of these data is supported by research on SES and on almost any other variable related to school achievement. David Montague (1964) found that high SES children were clearly superior to low SES children in scores on an arithmetic concept test. But there was a much greater range of scores for the low SES children—6.51 points as compared with 2.98 points for the high SES children. Jerome Siller (1957), studying white sixth grade children, found that high SES children did better than low SES children on all tests of conceptual ability, particularly those involving verbal material. The high SES group also selected more definitions of an abstract type than did the low SES group. Siller's tests included classification, analogies, and abstract-concrete similarities.

SES AND MOTIVATION. Studies which compare SES and motivational variables, such as anxiety, educational aspiration, and self-concept, show about the same relationship—the positive attributes are more closely associated with high than with low SES students. John Feldhusen and Herbert Klausmeier (1962) found, among girls and boys in the fifth grade that low IQ children were more anxious than children of average or high IQ. Also anxiety was significantly related to arithmetic achievement in low IQ children. Since most low IQ children are also low SES children we can infer a positive relationship between SES and anxiety for low SES children. This study suggests that even in the fifth grade the long history of school failure for low SES children begins to have its emotionally erosive effects. And we are not surprised to find too that low SES students have anxious and pessimistic expectations for educational and occupational success. Albert Hieronymus (1951) found that SES, more than IQ, was related to the attitudes of junior and senior high school students toward education and to their expectations of occupational success. Expectation varied with SES but not with ability. Using a motivational scale constructed at Michigan State University, Robert Green and William Farquhar (1965) discovered that the scale predicted achievement for Negro male high school students better than did tests of intelligence and that the self-concept test (one part of the scale) predicted achievement better than did the other tests.

Since so many disadvantaged children are Negro, the study of Negro intelligence, particularly its relationship to white intelligence, SES, and the nature of the intelligence tests themselves, has been a matter of continuing interest and controversy. It is to these studies of Negro intelligence that we now turn. The implications of these studies for entering behavior will be considered at the end of the first section of this chapter.

Culture-fair IQ tests. A strong protest against the use of standardized intelligence tests for Negro and other low SES children was first made in the late 1940s (see Davis, 1948). The verbal emphasis of these tests, the critics contended, reflected the values and the culture of the middle class. Since that time there have been several attempts to develop culture-fair and even culture-free intelligence tests not prejudicial to children of any SES. Allison Davis and Kenneth Eells (1953) have constructed a culture-fair test known as the Davis-Eells Games. Presumably the test items, the vocabulary, and the grammatical constructions do not favor any single SES. The test content is equally familiar or unfamiliar to all children. These tests have not proved useful. As Jensen (1968) has observed:

> These particular tests do not correlate very satisfactorily with school achievement, occupational level, or other real-life criteria generally regarded as indicators of intelligence. Even if it were possible to devise an intelligence test that would make absolutely no discrimination among social classes, the factors that cause school failure and other undesirable outcomes of poor learning would, of course, continue to operate.

We also have the remarkable finding that children who score well on the standard tests also score well on the culture-fair tests. Even when the tests are kept nonverbal (although none are completely nonverbal), as in the case of picture vocabulary tests which merely require the child to point to the picture which corresponds to the word the examiner has spoken, the high SES children score above the low SES children.

LEARNING ABILITY VS. IQ. Ernest Haggard (1954) revised forty items of standard IQ tests so that the items would be equally meaningful to children of high and low SES. Here is an example of a revised item:

> Item no. 24 (standard)
> Cub is to bear as gosling is to
> 1( ) fox, 2( ) grouse, 3( ) goose, 4( ) rabbit, and 5( ) duck.
> Item no. 24 (revised)
> Puppy goes with dog like kitten goes with
> 1( ) fox, 2( ) goose, 3( ) cat, 4( ) rabbit, and 5( ) duck.

The children in his experiment, who were eleven years old, were pretested on the standard or on the revised items. They were then subjected to various practice and motivational conditions and posttested on the same type of items. Haggard discovered that both high and low SES children made greater gains on the revised items than on the standard items. The high SES children, however, gained relatively more on the standard test, while the low SES children gained relatively more on the revised test. Findings such as these strongly suggest that standard intelligence tests are measuring past learning rather than learning ability (see Chapter 3, p. 74).

Two later studies of Negro intelligence also found differences between learning abilities and IQ. Ira Semler and Ira Iscoe (1963, 1966) in their first study required southern white and Negro children (eight to nine years old) to learn pairs of objects and to associate them with colored pictures. This task emphasized present learning abilities rather than past learning as measured by IQ tests. Although the Negro children had significantly lower IQ scores, as measured by the WISC, the Negro and white children did not significantly differ in their learning of the object-picture task. In the second study, they administered the Progressive Matrices (PM) and the WISC to seven- to nine-year-old white and Negro children. As in the first study, the white children had higher IQ than the Negroes at all age levels. They found that the white children had higher PM scores at the seven-year level but not at the eight- and nine-year level. In explaining their findings for both studies, Semler and Iscoe conclude that the object-picture pairing in the first experiment and the new learning required in the PM involve materials and tests equally common in the environments of white and Negro children; they therefore capitalize on learning abilities and minimize or eliminate the advantages gained from SES and IQ, or previous learning.

SUMMARY. The studies of SES and IQ give us this description of Negro intelligence. There is a 30 per cent overlap in Negro and white intelligence. If you were to guess that a particular Negro had an IQ which was not equal to or was below the average white IQ, you would be wrong one out of three times. Recent evidence, although not clearly consistent with previous findings, indicates that you would not greatly improve your guess of a particular Negro's IQ by knowing his SES since improved SES seems less well related to Negro than to white IQ. You could make a more accurate guess of the Negro's comparative performance on two different tests if you knew that one test emphasized within-test learning and that the other emphasized previous learning. You would predict, in this case, that the Negro would do better on the former test. These findings make any highly generalized statements about Negro intelligence, the effects of SES, and Negro test performance quite untenable. The question then arises: How can we use these findings on SES, race, and intelligence in the planning of instruction? This is the next question we consider.

Entering Behavior: SES, IQ, and Race

The usefulness of studies of the relationship of SES, IQ, and race for the assessment of and the provision for entering behavior involves the more general problem of the usefulness of correlation studies in teaching practice. I treat this general problem more extensively in Chapter 16 than I can treat it here. At this point I want to make a crude but useful distinction between correlational and experimental studies, to show their relationship to instructional planning, and, finally, to relate all this to the studies on SES, IQ, and race.

CORRELATIONAL AND EXPERIMENTAL STUDIES. Correlational studies are hose which investigate, for example, the relationship between sex and ntelligence, IQ and academic achievement, SES and IQ, or SES and race. n a study of the relationship between sex and IQ, the investigator may neasure the IQ of a sample of boys and girls, determine the averages of he two sexes, and finally express this relationship as a coefficient of cor-elation or in some other way. Let us say that he finds that the boys' verage is higher than the girls'. Should he conclude that boys are more ntelligent than girls? This may or may not be a sound conclusion. With nly this evidence, the conclusion is very risky. Since so many other actors relate to sex, one of these factors may have produced the difference a IQ scores. Similarly, an investigator may find cases of lung cancer. fter considering several possible causes, he finally selects cigarette noking as the most probable one. If he finds a high degree of relationship can he conclude that smoking causes cancer? Again, he is on shaky ground. Many factors in smoking do not result in lung cancer. A substance contained in the smoke and not cigarette smoking itself may be the culprit.

The difficulty with correlational studies is that the investigator must take things as they are and try to disentangle them. Experimental studies, on the other hand, allow the investigator to select a possible "cause" and actually to introduce it in a way which enables him to observe its effects directly. In an experimental study of lung cancer, for example, the experimenter may paint the skins of rats with a substance which may cause cancer, making sure to eliminate other substances as possible causes of the effect. If the experimenter does indeed note that this substance causes cancer, his conclusion has a firm base. Whereas most of the studies of IQ in Chapter 4 were correlational, most of the studies of motivation in Chapter 5 were experimental. In the studies of IQ and school achievement, for example, we considered other factors, besides IQ, which may account for successful achievement—one of these factors being the quality of instruction. In the experimental studies of the effects of punishment on previously learned responses, we observed directly the avoidance, escape, and desist responses. We can be more certain about the effects on animal behavior of introducing punishing stimuli than we can be of the effects of IQ on school achievement.

The ultimate objective of any science, including educational psychology, is to make the world more predictable. Experimental studies enable us to make better predictions than do correlational studies. Does this mean that correlational studies have no value? Certainly not. In the history and the development of both the natural and the behavioral sciences, correlational studies, undertaken early, have narrowed the range of possible causes which experimental studies later investigate. The correlational studies of lung cancer and smoking, for example, have played an important part in narrowing the search for the causes of cancer. In fact, where the correlations between cigarette smoking and lung cancer have been very high, for example, for those individuals who smoke two or more packs of cigarettes each day, the correlational study itself has had high predictive value.

The chief distinction between the two studies is this: Correlational studies establish relationships which point to one of many causes; experimental studies establish the one cause among many causes. More succinctly, correlational studies suggest causes; experimental studies isolate causes. As aids to instructional planning, in which the teacher must select and introduce various materials and procedures to obtain particular results, experimental studies are a more valuable source of teaching knowledge than correlational studies. In the basic teaching model, the teacher systematically arranges instructional conditions to bring about particular effects.

Usefulness of correlational studies. In the light of this distinction between correlational and experimental studies, we can return to our original question about the usefulness of the studies of SES, IQ, and race in assessing and providing for entering behavior. Knowledge of the relationship of SES, IQ, and race to school achievement and motivation may provide the teacher with some general guidance in a positive or a negative direction. First, the teacher knows that he can make more reliable guesses about the intelligence and achievement of students of very high and very low SES than he can about children in the middle SES range. Unfortunately, at least for making predictions about future performance, most children are in the middle. Second, the great degree of overlap in the scores of children in adjacent SES should discourage attempts to stereotype children on the basis of parental occupation, income, education, and so on. The overlap should at least warn the teacher that he cannot generalize from a group average to a specific student either in assessing the student's entering behavior or in predicting his future performance. Third, the tendency for groups of low SES children to have as entering behavior a wider range of ability and achievement than do groups of high SES children strongly suggests that the low SES students may require more individual instruction than that which they often receive. Finally, correlational studies, as you will see in the section which follows, enable us to launch experimental studies of the learning conditions of disadvantaged children and to locate environmental deficiencies which retard their educational progress. After the correlational studies help us locate the students who are most likely to have deficiencies in entering behavior, both the investigator, through formal study, and the teacher, through informal observation and experimentation, must look for specific deficiencies and try various ways to remove them.

Summary. This first section of the chapter has dealt with the social onditions of the disadvantaged child. We have seen that his deficiencies n entering behavior are accompanied by poverty, racial and ethnic miority status, and inferior SES. We further saw that inferior SES is acompanied by poor school achievement, poor motivation, but not necesrily by impaired learning abilities. Although we have little reason to elieve that the disadvantaged child is locked in a so-called *lower class,* ith its own life style and values, we do have preliminary evidence that e Negro, because of his color, is locked into a caste system from which it difficult to escape. Studies of the social conditions of the disadvantaged ild are often correlational in nature and have the usual limitations of ch studies. Their usefulness for teaching lies largely in the general guidance they provide in locating the disadvantaged children in our classrooms and in suggesting where we may look for strengths as well as weaknesses which can be developed or removed in the course of instruction.

We can now take a closer look at the entering behavior of the disadvantaged child by reviewing studies of the learning conditions of his home and early environment.

You should now return to objectives 1–8 (pp. 183–84) and determine how well you have achieved them.

QUESTION 6-1

A study of the relationship of SES and word usage indicated that low SES children have more difficulty than high SES children in the correct use of verbs but are equal to high SES children in the correct use of nouns. On the basis of this study which of the following teaching procedures is best warranted?

(a) The procedure described in this study for teaching verbs should be adapted for classroom use.

(b) Care should be taken to avoid teaching the use of verbs and to emphasize teaching the use of nouns.

(c) Previous verb usage should be carefully assessed in introducing new reading materials.

(d) Since the study shows that the low SES children's difficulty with verbs is the chief cause of their difficulties in self-expression, other parts of speech may be freely used.

After selecting your answer, give the reasons for your choice and for your rejection of the alternatives.

LEARNING CONDITIONS

In this section of the chapter we shall describe the learning condi tions of the disadvantaged child, particularly those conditions of hi preschool years. Whereas the studies in the previous section were cor relational, the studies in this section are mostly (but not entirely) ex perimental. First, I shall briefly describe the impoverished learnin conditions of this child. Second, we shall inspect Jensen's model of th growth of intelligence and the effects of impoverished and enriched en vironments. Third, we shall inspect some longitudinal studies of th development of intelligence to show the effects of impoverished enviror ments over time. We shall then consider the effects of these environment on particular areas of learning: perceptual learning, language develo ment, and cognitive development. We shall conclude with a discussio of the use of experimental studies for assessing and providing for th disadvantaged child's entering behavior.

Impoverished Early Environments

The serious detrimental and, perhaps irreversible, effects of early deprivation were first observed in experimental studies of animals. I shall briefly illustrate and review those studies and then describe the early environment of the disadvantaged child.

ENRICHED AND IMPOVERISHED ENVIRONMENTS: EXPERIMENTAL STUDIES. Several studies have investigated the effects of various environmental conditions on the ability of animals and humans to learn. Hunt (1964, pp. 216–17) describes an experiment of William Thompson and Heron (1954) which illustrates the usual experimental procedures and results. In this experiment the problem-solving ability of Scotty puppies reared as pets in human homes from weaning was compared with that of their litter mates reared in isolation in laboratory cages.

> In one of these tests, the dog is brought into a room while hungry. After being allowed to smell and see a bowl of food, the dog is permitted to watch as this food is removed and put behind a screen in one of the opposite corners of the room. Both pet-reared and cage-reared dogs go immediately to the spot where the food disappeared. After the same procedure has been repeated several times, the food is then placed, while the animal watches, behind a screen in the opposite corner of the room. . . . Now when the dog is released, if he is pet-reared he goes immediately to the screen in the left corner for the food. But, if he is cage-reared, he is more likely to go to the screen in the right corner where he had previously found food.

David Krech, Mark Rosenzweig, and Edward Bennett (1962) found changes in brain chemistry as well as in learning after exposure to enriched and impoverished environments. In their study, rats lived in enriched and impoverished environments for thirty days. Under the impoverished condition, the rats lived in individual cages in which they could not touch or see another rat. Under the enriched condition, the rats lived in cages containing ten animals; each of these cages contained a maze and various toys. The animals exposed to the enriched environment performed better than their isolated litter mates on maze problems, and they had significant increases and decreases in the cholinesterase activity of the cortex and subcortex.

Hunt (1964) also refers to studies which have shown that the unhampered opportunity of children to throw and manipulate objects in a wide variety of situations and to see a variety of sights and hear a variety of sounds is of the greatest importance in determining the degree of skill the children will manifest later. These opportunities may be lacking in the early environments of disadvantaged children.

Considerable evidence favors the early cognitive stimulation of the child. Fowler (1962) refers to studies which show the excellent adjustment and accomplishments of gifted children who grew up in intellectually stimulating environments; of average and low IQ children under five who were given lengthy intellectual training without ill effects; and of children whose cognitive training in nursery school made them superior in both learning and adjustment in first grade to those children who lacked this training. Fowler believes that emphasis on the social training of the child to the virtual exclusion of cognitive training is partly a result of an ingrained belief that madness and genius are related. He writes (p. 142):

> We wonder, in short, whether our modern anxiety over the damage [which] childhood cognitive stimulation *may* induce is sufficiently anchored in reality. In the probably well-founded criticisms of severe methods formerly (and perhaps even now occasionally) used, was there reason to assail the process of early cognitive instruction, per se? Is it possible that reformist zeal, fed liberally by the discoveries of Freud and others, may have resulted in methods and conditions being profoundly confused with subject matter, that is, cognitive material as such? Research to date, although requiring much extension, appears to harmonize very well with such an interpretation.

Impoverished home environments. Deutsch (1963b) believes that the lack of a variety of new and interesting things to see and to hear results in disadvantaged children's inability to sustain attention and to acquire perceptual skills. Their environment lacks many things: (1) Visually, the environment lacks objects. Those objects available are repetitious and dull in color, and few can be manipulated. (2) The nonverbal orientation of the environment results in the underdevelopment of auditory skills. Poor readers, Deutsch reminds us, have more difficulty than good readers in auditory discrimination. (3) Adults do not relate the present to the past, and, consequently, the children do not develop memory. Lawrence Leshan (1952) reports that disadvantaged children have vague and indefinite notions of the future and little sense of pattern and regularity. (4) Adults do not give approval or disapproval for jobs the children complete or leave uncompleted. The tasks themselves are usually physical in nature, have short time spans, and relate only to concrete objects and services. (5) Disadvantaged children do not know how to use adults as sources of information and as a means of satisfying curiosity. (6) Their language development is retarded because they do not learn the correct labeling of the environment (see p. 219). (7) Their speech sequences are limited in time and poor in syntax. Deutsch believes that the major deficits are in perceptual rather than in verbal learning.

Cumulative deficits. The deficits of the disadvantaged child are cumulative because of the ever widening gap between his present capabilities and the difficulty of the school tasks he encounters. Unable, for example, to perform simple grammatical operations he is subjected to the increased complexity of sentences, vocabulary, and thought from the first through the twelfth grades. Ausubel (1965) suggests that some of the early effects of impoverished environments may be irreversible because the organism's plasticity decreases with age. He states (p. 11), "By the time an individual reaches adolescence, differential factors of interest, relative ability, specialization of training, motivation, success and failure experience, and cultural expectation operate selectively to develop certain potential abilities and to leave others relatively underdeveloped."

A Model for the Growth of Intelligence

Jensen (1966b, 1968) gives us a very illuminating picture of the effects of impoverished and enriched environments and the relationship of heredity, environment, and intelligence. Figure 6-3 is his theoretical model of the growth of intelligence. Genes and prenatal development account for 80 per cent of our intelligence. About 20 per cent, representing a range of twenty IQ points, is left for the environment. The arrows represent individuals with different amounts of innate intelligence; *A* and *C* were born with more intelligence than *B* and *D*. The large rectangles are the environments these four individuals must pass through. The broken lines indicate the various stages of environmental influ-

Fig. 6-3. *A model of growth of intelligence (Jensen, 1966).*

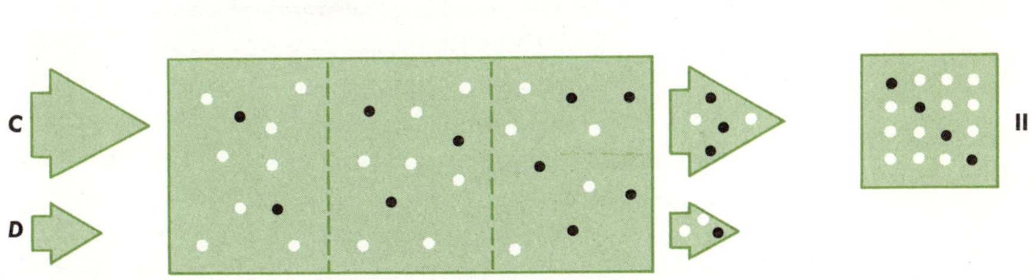

ence. The dots represent the various elements of the environment. The greater the number of dots, the richer the opportunities for learning. The white dots refer to what we will later describe as perceptual learning. The black dots represent that learning which has broad application to all future learning (the *g* factor in IQ tests). You can observe that the number of black dots increases in each succeeding sector of the environment since learning must build on previous learning. Let us say that at the age of eighteen, the four individuals emerge. The elements they have acquired depend on two factors: the richness of the environment and their original intellectual capacities.

Finally, these four individuals are placed in two test situations. Test I is a standard intelligence test with a heavy *g* loading. Test II is a specialized achievement test in spelling or arithmetic. Test I measures the acquisition of black dots and Test II, of white dots. How will these individuals rank in intelligence and achievement? Although individuals *A* and *C* began with the same intellectual capacity, *A* will achieve higher scores. *B* and *D* will have about the same scores, but *B* will be ahead in black dots. Jensen suggests that you consider *A* and *C* as one set and *B* and *D* as another set of identical twins. Both pairs are separated and are raised by foster parents in different environments. The upper rectangle represents a high SES environment, and the lower rectangle a low SES environment. The average test performances of *A* and *B* will be much closer to those of their foster parents than to those of their natural parents.

Although the environments in Fig. 6-3 provide only 20 per cent of intelligence, this percentage may represent a range of twenty to thirty IQ points. Jensen (1968) observes:

> But even this difference of twenty or thirty IQ points that can be effected through the environment can mean the difference between functional illiteracy and literacy, between educational attainment equivalent to less than an eighth grade education and college education, between an unskilled job and a skilled job, between unemployment and gainful occupation, and in some cases it can even mean the difference between the designations "mentally retarded and "normal." Though the 20 per cent of the variance in intelligence attributed to environment may not seem like a great deal alongside the 80 per cent attributable to heredity, it is clearly enough to have significant consequences. It is these effects of environmental factors and their mode of operation that are of greatest interest from the standpoint of the psychology of learning.

Enriched environments may most benefit those with IQs in the range of 70 to 90. When the IQ is below 70, the deficiency is usually of an organic nature. When the individual has an IQ over 90, the environment generally does not lack the essential ingredients for intellectual growth. Jensen (1966b) makes an analogy between intellectual growth and nutrition. Since the diet of a normally healthy child is probably not deficient, the addition of vitamin and mineral capsules will bring little improvement. Even the improvement of the diet of the undernourished child involves more than feeding him more food. The essential foods must be found. Similarly, psychologists must discover the essential ingredients of intellectual growth.

One last reference to Fig. 6-3. Jensen asks what would happen to individual *C*, for example, if you were to place him in an enriched environment after he had passed two-thirds of the way through the impoverished environment. This situation is analogous to that of the disadvantaged child when he leaves his home and enters the school. Individual *C* would not be able to acquire all the elements that individual *A* had acquired. *C* can catch up with *A* only by going back to a stage at which he could acquire all the elements prerequisite to the acquisition of the elements in the later stages. You will recall that to acquire more black dots you must have already acquired other black dots.

Although Jensen's model is theoretical, it does illustrate how an impoverished environment may retard intellectual development and eventually produce cumulative deficits.

Effects of Environmental Change

Supporting evidence for some aspects of Jensen's model is found in several correlational studies. Here I will describe studies which measured changes in IQ and their relationship to changes in the environment. Also, by combining several of these correlational studies, you will see the serious effects of early deprivation.

ENVIRONMENTAL CHANGE AND IQ. Many studies have investigated the effects on intelligence test scores of improvement in cultural and educational opportunities. In some of these comparable samples of the same population were studied at different points in time, separated by as many as ten or more years. The most celebrated of these studies are the Scottish Surveys of 1932 and 1947, as reported by the Scottish Council for Research in Education (1953). In 1932 intelligence tests were administered to nearly all eleven-year-old Scottish children (87,498). In 1947 the tests were given to children of the same age (70,805). The average scores showed a small but significant improvement over the fifteen-year period. In another study, Lester Wheeler (1942) compared the intelligence of East Tennessee children over a ten-year period. During that time the schools in the area had improved their circulating libraries, the training of their teachers, the availability of free textbooks, and so on.

Wheeler found that the average mountain child had gained ten points in IQ, or nearly one point per year during the ten-year period. In a third study, Read Tuddenham (1948) compared soldier intelligence in World Wars I and II. The average IQ score for World War I soldiers was 62. For World War II soldiers the average score was 104. It is also highly significant that 83 per cent of World War I soldiers scored below the average of World War II soldiers. Tuddenham attributes these dramatic differences to the varying amounts of education of the two groups. Soldiers in the first war had an average of about eight years of education; those in the second war, an average of ten years.

In a classic series of studies on Negro intelligence, Otto Klineberg (1950) demonstrated the relationship between Negro intelligence and length of residence in New York City. He studied about 3,000 Negro children, ages 10 and 11, in Harlem. The subjects were matched for age, sex, and SES. The only difference was the amount of time they had lived in New York City. Table 6-6 summarizes the data of the study. The National Intelligence Test, which he used, is primarily verbal and reflects very well differences in amount of formal education.

TABLE 6-6

RELATION BETWEEN LENGTH OF RESIDENCE IN NEW YORK CITY AND NATIONAL INTELLIGENCE TEST SCORES OF NEGRO SCHOOL CHILDREN (adapted from Klineberg, 1950).

Years of Residence	Number of Cases	Mean Score
1–2	130	72
3–4	123	76
5–6	136	84
7–8	112	90
Over 8	157	94
Northern-born	1017	92

Studies of identical twins reared apart in enriched and impoverished environments and studies of so-called *wild* or *ferral* children who were later civilized also indicate the beneficial effects of enriched environments on intelligence. Although these studies have not involved Negro subjects, we have no reason to expect that the results would be different for Negroes than for whites.

Effects of early environment. In an impressive analysis of several studies of stability and change in human characteristics, Benjamin Bloom (1964) marshals evidence which indicates that deprivation in the earl years of childhood can have far greater consequences than deprivation in later years. Bloom based his conclusions on several types of studies: identical twins reared apart in enriched and impoverished environments; children originally reared in isolated environments and then educated in enriched environments (as in Wheeler's study); Negro children and the length of their residence in the North; and institutionalized retarded children presented with preschool stimulation. In Table 6-7 we see what Bloom calls the "hypothesized effects of different environments for three age periods." You can see that one-half of the development of intelligence occurs in the first four years. Early deprivation, therefore, can be much more serious than deprivation in the ten years from eight to seventeen. You can also see that Bloom is hypothesizing that a change from a deprived to an abundant environment can mean the gain of 20 IQ points. Such a change, in the realities of our occupational world, can mean the difference between a profession and a semiskilled laboring job. In Table 6-8 you can see that the effects of the early environment on school achievement follow the same pattern. One-third of school achievement is determined before the child enters school.

TABLE 6-7

HYPOTHETICAL EFFECTS OF DIFFERENT ENVIRONMENTS ON THE DEVELOPMENT OF INTELLIGENCE IN THREE SELECTED AGE PERIODS (Bloom, 1964, p. 72).

		Variation from Normal Growth in IQ Units			
Age Period	Per cent of Mature Intelligence	Deprived	Normal	Abundant	Abundant-Deprived
Birth–4	50	–5	0	+5	10
4–8	30	–3	0	+3	6
8–17	20	–2	0	+2	4
	—	—	—	—	—
Total	100	–10	0	+10	20

Bloom's analysis shows the great importance of the early home environment, the nursery school, and the kindergarten. Much of the child's intellectual development occurs before he enters the first grade. We also see that another 17 per cent of the growth takes place between six and thirteen, which indicates that the elementary school years are the most crucial period of achievement.

We shall need much more detailed studies and precise measures of environment before we can establish exact relationships between environmental conditions and intellectual and educational development. Bloom believes that measures of SES, social class, and occupational and

TABLE 6-8

ESTIMATED PERCENTAGES FOR THE DEVELOPMENT OF LEARNING AS BASED ON VARIOUS MEASURES OF ACHIEVEMENT (Bloom, 1964, p. 110).

	Per cent of Age 18 Development	
Age	Each Period	Cumulative
Birth– 6	33	33
6–13	42	75
13–18	25	100

educational levels of parents will not give us the information we need. Bloom refers to an unpublished study by Rich Dave (1963) of six variables in the home environment: "achievement press," language models, academic guidance, stimulation to explore various aspects of the larger environment, intellectual interests and activities, and work habits emphasized. Dave obtained a correlation of 0.80 between ratings of home environment on these variables and achievement test battery scores of the children. The usual correlations between SES and achievement are less than 0.50. From these results, we can see how studies are becoming more precise in identifying those environmental factors which enhance or block the growth of intelligence.

SUMMARY. Thus far our description of the learning conditions of the disadvantaged child gives this composite picture: an environment which lacks optimal stimulation and a variety of new and interesting things and events to see, to hear, and to think and talk about; a cumulative deficit between the disadvantaged child's entering behavior and advanced instructional objectives; a possible irreversibility in the effects of early deprivation; and an optimistic possibility of significantly raising the child's IQ by changing his environment in the preschool years.

With this broad picture of the learning conditions of the disadvantaged child in mind, we can examine the studies of the effects of these conditions on three key areas of development: perceptual development, linguistic development, and cognitive development. The study of these areas promises the clearest and most useful description of the entering behavior of the disadvantaged child.

Perceptual Learning

The earliest form of learning must take place without the benefit of previous learning. Information feeds to the brain through our visual and auditory senses and, in this way, the environment gains control over areas of the brain (Hebb, 1949). Jensen (1968) has reviewed some of the evidence we have for perceptual learning. Individuals who were blinded by cataracts at birth and who later had these cataracts removed were unable to use their eyes to judge distance, depth, size, shape, perspective, and so on. Although some of the patients were intelligent and successful students, they were unable to recognize a square without carefully counting the corners. They were unable to recognize the familiar forms of doctors and nurses. The patients lacked what is called *perceptual constancy*, or the ability to recognize an object as the same object under a variety of viewing conditions. Perceptual constancy, for example, enables us to recognize a person we know whether we approach him from the rear, the side, or the front. This recognition is probably the result of hundreds of exposures to the same object. Although most of these exposures occur in the earliest years of lives, adults are also capable of perceptual learning. Jensen refers to the experience of laboratory assistants who work with monkeys. At first they cannot distinguish the monkeys. After they have gained experience, however, the monkeys look as different to them as human beings do. Perceptual learning has enabled them to learn those "monkey" characteristics which distinguish individual monkeys.

The development of attention is also involved in perceptual learning. Attention is the central process of the brain which screens, selects, and steers the information we receive through our senses. When J. M. G. Itard (1932) tried to educate Victor, the Wild Boy of Aveyron, he had to teach Victor to pay attention. Victor had so much trouble distinguishing speech sounds from background noises that it was easier for him to understand printed than spoken words.

Cynthia Deutsch (1964) suggests that disadvantaged children may have more trouble hearing than seeing. We know that repetitious or excessive stimulation causes the organism to become inattentive (see the discussion of optimal stimulation, p. 136). In hearing we often call this inattention *tuning out*. Deutsch suggests that the child raised in a noisy environment with little organized and sustained conversation may fail to distinguish and recognize speech sounds. This child fails to learn to pay attention to others' talking and he also fails to learn any skill, such as reading, which is dependent on auditory learning. Auditory learning should occur before the first grade, before bad listening habits develop. This learning requires a quiet environment, which concentrates auditory stimuli, reduces visual stimuli, and avoids too much repetition and variety. The ordinary nursery school, she suggests, may provide too many distractions and too much noise for disadvantaged children to acquire auditory learning.

In conclusion, we can say that preliminary evidence indicates that perceptual learning in the disadvantaged child is lacking or seriously underdeveloped. His impoverished environment offers only fitful and fragmented exposure to objects and experiences or no exposure at all. Without adequate perceptual learning the disadvantaged child is seriously hampered in more advanced learning, that is, in his linguistic and cognitive development. It is to this development that we now turn.

Language Development

The emphasis of disadvantaged children on physical activity is both cause and result of their verbal underdevelopment. Riessman (1962) describes their preference for motoric and physical activity. Even their primary religious expression involves handclapping and singing. Their preference for physical forms is reflected in their participation in and enjoyment of sports and in their physical forms of discipline. Riessman notes several characteristics of the language of the disadvantaged child. He uses adjectives better than verbs; he understands more language than he uses; he has the verbal ability to fantasize; and he expresses himself best in spontaneous and unstructured situations, which precipitate a freer flow of language because the child is not required to make particular responses. For example, the disadvantaged child shows considerable ability to express himself in this situation. He is presented with a large toy clown whose nose lights up when the child talks. The child freely selects his topic and may repeat himself. When the child is silent and the clown's nose fails to light up, the child is told that the clown is sad.

Evidence also indicates that disadvantaged children comprehend more than they communicate. Arnold Carson and A. I. Rabin (1960) measured comprehension with a picture vocabulary test which required the children merely to point to a specific picture each time a word was read from the vocabulary list. To measure communication these children were required to give definitions for the vocabulary words of the WISC (see p. 105) and also for the vocabulary words of the picture test. The children were fourth, fifth, and sixth grade Negro and white children. Some of the Negro children were born and reared in the North, and some were born in the South but reared in the North. Interestingly enough, the results showed that the children could understand more than they could communicate. On all tests, the whites did better than the northern-born Negroes, who did better than the southern-born Negroes. Whereas the whites were able to give the critical feature and function of the word they defined, the northern-born Negroes often gave vague responses and southern-born Negroes many "don't know" responses.

Language codes. Basil Bernstein (1961) makes the most intriguing analysis of the language of disadvantaged children. He distinguishes between the *restricted code* (or language) of the disadvantaged person and the *elaborated code* of individuals of higher SES. These are the characteristics of the restricted code (p. 169):

1. Short, grammatically simple, often unfinished sentences with a poor syntactical form stressing the active voice.
2. Simple and repetitive use of conjunctions (so, then, because).
3. Little use of subordinate clauses to break down the initial categories of the dominant subject.
4. Inability to hold a formal subject through a speech sequence; thus a dislocated informational content is facilitated.
5. Rigid and limited use of adjectives and adverbs.
6. Infrequent use of impersonal pronouns as subjects of conditional classes.
7. Frequent use of statements where the reason and conclusion are confounded to produce a categoric statement.
8. A large number of statements and phrases which signal a requirement for the previous speech sequence to be reinforced: "Wouldn't it? You see? You know?" etc. This process is termed "sympathetic circularity."
9. Individual selection from a group of idiomatic phrases or sequences will frequently occur.
10. *The individual qualification is in the sentence organization: It is a language of implicit meaning.*

The restricted code seriously limits the scope of expression and thought. Thoughts are strung together somewhat like beads on a frame and do not follow a planned sequence. Much information is repeated, as in the following illustration of the speech of a sixteen-year-old English boy of normal intelligence (Bernstein, 1961, p. 171):

> It's all according like these youths and that if they get into these gangs and that they most have a bit of nark around and say it goes wrong and that and they probably knock someone off I mean think they just do it to be big getting publicity here and there.

The elaborated code has the following characteristics (p. 172):

1. Accurate grammatical order and syntax regulate what is said.
2. Logical modifications and stress are mediated through a grammatically complex sentence construction, especially through the use of a range of conjunctions and subordinate clauses.
3. Frequent use of prepositions which indicate logical relationships as well as prepositions which indicate temporal and spatial contiguity.
4. Frequent use of the personal pronoun "I."
5. A discriminative selection from a range of adjectives and adverbs.

6. Individual qualification is verbally mediated through the structure and relationships within and between sentences.
7. Expressive symbolism discriminates between meanings within speech sequences rather than reinforcing dominant words or phrases, or accompanying the sequence in a diffuse, generalized manner.
8. It is a language use which points to the possibilities inherent in a complex conceptual hierarchy for the organizing of experience.

The elaborated code, according to Bernstein, makes the intended meaning of the speaker explicit. It also supplies him with many more alternatives for elaborating and expressing his thoughts. Middle-class children have access to both codes, working-class children, only to the restricted code. The problem with the restricted code is not the lack of vocabulary since the evidence indicates that the number of adjectives and adverbs does not vary in either code when speakers are matched for age and very high nonverbal IQ. Bernstein also notes that, despite the warmth and vitality of the restricted code, it tends to be impersonal because the personal meaning of the speakers is never explicit. Bernstein believes that the use of the restricted code has far-reaching consequences for the disadvantaged child (1961, p. 174):

> In the learning of this linguistic form, the child is progressively oriented to a relatively low level of conceptualization. It induces a lack of interest in processes, a preference to be aroused by, and to respond to, that which is given immediately, rather than responding to the implications of a matrix of relationships. In turn, this will affect what is to be learned and how it is learned and so influence future learning. There will be a tendency to accept and respond to authority which inheres in the form of the social relationship which maximizes the identifications with aims and principles of the local group rather than with the complex differentiated aims of the wider society. Finally, and of greatest importance, it is the language of implicit meaning in which it becomes progressively more difficult to make explicit, and to elaborate verbally, subjective intent.

The disadvantaged child experiences in school the consequences of knowing only the restricted code since the teacher uses the elaborated code. What is an opportunity for linguistic development for one child is a situation of linguistic change for the disadvantaged child. The teacher's job, according to Bernstein, is to preserve for the disadvantaged child the appeal and dignity of his accustomed code while making available to him the possibilities of expression in the elaborated code.

In summary, the study of language development shows that the disadvantaged child is verbally underdeveloped. Although some evidence indicates that under certain conditions he can express himself freely and comprehend more than he communicates, his verbal underdevelopment is a pervasive functional characteristic. His use of the restricted rather than the elaborated code limits not only what he can express but also the ways in which he thinks. Although Bernstein's description of language codes lacks empirical support at this time, it does suggest in broad outline the kind of language limitations under which the disadvantaged child must labor in and out of school. I describe next the limitations which his verbal underdevelopment imposes on his cognitive development.

Cognitive Development: Verbal Mediation

Language is basic to the development of thought. One aspect of language which appears to have crucial importance in cognitive development is the use of verbal mediators. Jensen (1966b, p. 101) defines verbal mediation as "talking to oneself in relevant ways when confronted with something to be learned, a problem to be solved, or a concept to be attained." We think out loud only when problems become difficult. Most mediation is subvocal and unconscious. I shall describe two forms of mediation: labeling and syntactical mediation.

LABELING. An experiment of Vera John and Leo Goldstein (1964) illustrates the use of labels as mediators. They studied the test performance of high and low SES Negro students in the first and fifth grades. The test consisted of sixteen sample drawings which could be grouped into functional pairs, such as *sailor* and *boat,* or into logically consistent piles, such as *means of transportation* or *animals.* After he sorted the cards, the child was asked for the basis of his sorting. One concept was represented by pictures of four men at work: a policeman, a doctor, a farmer, and a sailor. Here are some of the children's explanations for their piles (p. 272):

Low SES children	*High SES children*
1. Because the doctor nurses these other people	1. Because they are all men
2. Because the man and big Bill (the policeman) like each other	2. All the same
3. Because they look the same	3. They are both [sic] people

Inspection of these sample responses shows that the high SES Negro children produced the appropriate name or label, while the disadvantaged Negro children attended to nonessential details.

SYNTACTICAL MEDIATION. This type of mediation is called *syntactical* because it depends on the grammatical structure of the language. Jensen (1966b) illustrates that when normal subjects are asked to learn a list of paired words, they use additional words to link the pairs. For example, if you were asked learn this list of pairs

HAT—TABLE
TREE—HOUSE
CAT—BED
etc.

you would use additional words to link together hat and table, tree and house, and so on. Young children and mentally retarded children do not use mediators and, therefore, take longer to learn the list. If, however, the words are imbedded in sentences, then learning is almost immediate for all subjects. The following sentences give examples of imbedded words (Jensen, 1966b, p. 108):

The HAT fell off the TABLE.
The TREE stands beside the HOUSE.
The CAT ran under the BED.

When incomplete sentences are employed the mediators are less effective. For example (p. 109), "The dirty HAT on the sleeping COW" is not so effective a mediator as "The dirty HAT rested quietly on the sleeping COW."

WORD-OBJECT STABILITY AND FEEDBACK. Why do disadvantaged children often fail to develop verbal mediation? The normal child learns words and labels by the repeated association of touching and seeing the object and of hearing the name of the object. They hear the name spoken by their mothers, fathers, brothers and sisters, relatives, and by other children. They experience the association of the name and the object as they view television. In low SES homes, John and Goldstein (1964) suggest that the label and the object fail to become associated for two reasons: Low SES homes do not provide the stable conditions which keep object and name properly tied together; and the low SES child is given little or no correction when he misapplies a label to an object.

In pursuing the study of word-object association, through the use of a picture vocabulary test which required the child to point to the correct picture when he heard a particular label, John and Goldstein found that low SES Negro children have more trouble with action words than with rural and other unfamiliar words. Examples of action words are: digging, typing, pouring, and building. Rural words are: leaf, bee, bush, and nest. Unfamiliar words (for these children) are: kangaroo, caboose, and accident. Why did the children have the most trouble with the action words? The reason may be that the disadvantaged child has not had adequate experience in fitting a label to the various forms of action he has observed. He may have experienced digging or building in many different situations with many different individuals, but the connection between the action and its label was never made clear to him. Also, if the child were to misapply the label and if he were not corrected, or if he were not rewarded for the correct application of the label, the essential conditions for learning the proper use of action words would be lacking. Figure 6-4 indicates the postulated relationship between corrective feedback, stability of the word-referent relationship, and the type of label the child learns. He will find Coca Cola and ball easiest to learn, key and teacher more difficult, and the action words the most difficult to learn.

Bruner (1961) believes that the disadvantaged child lacks both the richness of environment for developing models and strategies of thought and the corrective feedback necessary for their maintenance. Through

Fig. 6-4. *Stability of word-referent relationship (after John and Goldstein, 1964, p. 270).*

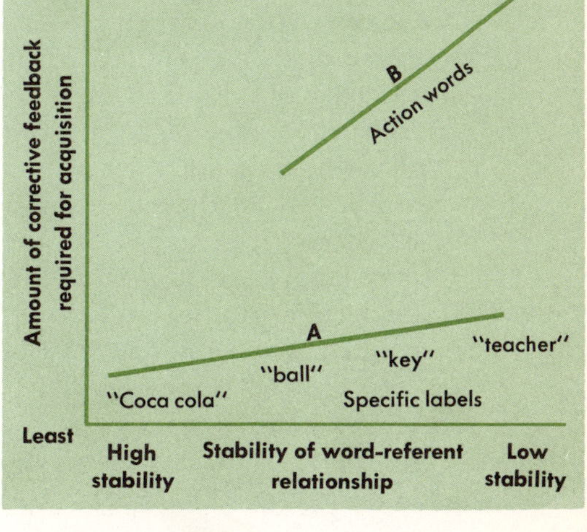

models we conserve information in the form of concepts and through strategies we learn to make inferences or to go beyond the information given.

In summary, evidence indicates that the cognitive development of the disadvantaged child is hampered by a lack of verbal mediators, as indicated by his difficulty in attaching labels to objects and people and by his difficulty with syntactical mediation. We can attribute many of these deficiencies to the lack of word-object stability and feedback in his early experience. Evidence also shows that the disadvantaged child fails to develop learning sets, learning abilities, and learning styles—categories of entering behavior which play a major part in school learning.

Entering Behavior: Perceptual, Linguistic, and Cognitive Development

How useful are the studies of the perceptual, linguistic, and cognitive development of the disadvantaged child in assessing and providing for entering behavior? Recalling the distinction between correlational and experimental studies, you know that many of the studies of these three aspects of development have been experimental, particularly the study of verbal mediation. These investigations point to fairly specific areas of behavior in which deficiencies may occur and in which training may be required. For example, the disadvantaged child may require special training in the use of labels, in learning the advantages of referring to objects by name. We can assess his entering behavior in terms of the language codes he uses and teach him to use and to recognize the advantages of the elaborated code. The school environment can deliberately provide the word-object stability absent in the background of the disadvantaged child. It can also provide him with systematic feedback in his initial attempts to use verbal mediators so that he can separate their correct from their incorrect applications. It can develop his perceptual learning by providing him with opportunities to manipulate and to experiment with the materials used in Montessori instruction. We must also train him to attend and to listen.

The study of the perceptual, linguistic, and cognitive development of the disadvantaged child not only indicates possible deficiencies in entering behavior but also provides some hints on the procedures we may employ to supply the entering behavior which is lacking. For example, the studies of Jensen and his associates show how we may give mediators to children who lack or fail to use them. Educational psychologists however will have to develop these mediational procedures under school learning conditions before they will be fully applicable by the teacher. But even before they report this research, the enterprising teacher of the disadvantaged child can experiment with the use of labels, syntactical mediation, language codes, and so on.

This early stage of research on the developmental deficiencies of the disadvantaged child strongly indicates that careful and detailed identification of these deficiencies and carefully planned programs of remediation and development will lead to greater improvement in school learning conditions than will literary speculations about middle-class value systems, personality disturbances, and the enhancement of self-concepts. In the section which follows, you will examine some of the programs and practices which have been tried.

You should now return to objectives 9–17 (p. 184) and determine how well you have achieved them.

QUESTION 6-2

Mr. Peabody has a class of disadvantaged children. To teach them the concept *sailor,* he shows them various pictures of men at work. Several show men in white hats and bell-bottomed trousers, working on or about sailing vessels. Other pictures show policemen, firemen, carpenters, and farmers at work. Which of the following procedures should Mr. Peabody adopt to teach this concept?

(a) Have the children repeat "sailor" each time they see a picture of a sailor.

(b) As each picture is presented, ask the children, "Is this a sailor?" and have them reply "yes" or "no."

(c) Have the children identify the other workers by name, but have them say only "yes" when they see a picture of a sailor.

(d) Supply each child with a set of pictures and have him sort them into sailor and nonsailor piles.

After selecting your answer, give the reasons for your choice and for your rejection of the alternatives.

PROGRAMS, PRACTICES, AND TEACHERS

This section of the chapter deals with the practical implications of the theory and the research we examined in the earlier sections. First, I shall describe some programs and practices that have been and are being tried. Second, I shall describe the characteristics of the teacher of the disadvantaged child as these characteristics have emerged from both research and theoretical speculation. Finally, I shall list some conditions which teachers and schools should provide the disadvantaged child. In beginning this section you should remember that no matter how critical the need has become in recent years for solutions to the educational problems of the disadvantaged child, we lack the research which can provide these solutions. Much of the present research has been informal, exploratory, and sometimes slightly frantic. In any case, it is difficult to list concrete procedures for use with the disadvantaged child when the research itself has rarely described what these procedures should be.

Programs and Practices

Unfortunately the research literature we have thus far does not develop a clear distinction between programs and practices. In ordinary usage we tend to describe fairly extensive curricular changes as *programs,* and the introduction of special procedures and materials within the old course and curriculum structure as *practices.*

PROGRAMS. Doxey Wilkerson (1965) distinguishes five programs: comprehensive programs, reading improvement programs, use of multiracial reading materials, preschool programs, and dropout programs.

New York City has offered two comprehensive programs which have received much publicity: the pioneer Demonstration Guidance Project, which began in 1956–57 and ended in 1962 (see Hillson and Myers, 1963), and the Higher Horizons Program, which started in 1959 (see Wrightstone *et al.,* 1964). The Demonstration Guidance Project involved 717 students originally in a junior high school in a depressed area of New York City. The students were primarily disadvantaged Negro and Puerto Rican children. They represented the upper half of the student body of their school, although all of them were below average in intelligence and school achievement. At both the junior and senior high school levels the project provided the following services among others: a modified curriculum, small classes, remedial instruction, cultural activities, counseling, clinical services, and relations with parents. By the end of the project (1961–62), without counting students who moved away or transferred to other schools, 329 remained in the project and 71 left school—a dropout rate of 22 per cent. Of those who remained 258 had graduated by 1962. Wilkerson (1965) summarizes the findings of the project report (the comparison groups were preproject students from the same junior high school and they graduated during 1957–59 from the same senior high school): (1) The project classes earned 108 academic diplomas; the preproject classes, 43. (2) Forty-four project high school students finished high school with no failures; only fourteen preproject students did. (3) Thirty-seven project and only eleven preproject students had grade averages of 80 per cent or better. (4) In a senior high school graduating class of between 800 and 900 students, individual project students ranked as follows: first, fourth, and sixth in the class of 1960; fourth in 1961; and second, fourth, and ninth in 1962. The highest ranking students in the preproject classes were 51st in 1957, 65th in 1958, and 226th in 1959. (5) Of the project students 168 were admitted to institutions for further study; only 47 of the preproject students were. Ninety-six (or 89 per cent) of the project students who received academic diplomas entered college. (6) Students and teachers in the project evaluated it positively.

The Higher Horizons Program was a larger program of similar pattern. In 1962 it involved 64,000 children in grades 3 to 10 in fifty-two elementary and thirteen junior high schools. The program included "all disadvantaged pupils rather than just the more academically able" (p. 428). The program was decentralized and under the direction of the local teaching staffs. Finally, cost for each student was smaller than that in the Demonstration Guidance Project. More or less comparable (control) schools were chosen for the evaluation of the Program. Wilkerson (p. 428) observes, however, that the Higher Horizons and the control schools differed in these ways: the HH schools tended to have smaller classes, lower rates of transiency, larger proportions of regular teachers, and more counseling in the junior high schools. The evaluation of the program showed that students in the experimental schools were superior to those in the control schools in a single area of school achievement—arithmetic on the elementary level. The students in the experimental schools were not superior in growth in mental ability or in reading. At the elementary level, the experimental schools had less truancy and higher attendance, and, at the junior high level, they had a lower suspension rate than did the control schools. Wilkerson observes that on most of the criteria used in the evaluation, including scholastic, personal, and social development, the experimental school students showed no clear superiority over the control school students, although most teachers and principals valued the program, especially the principals. It is hard to ascertain whether the more modest gains of the Higher Horizons Program as compared to those of the Guidance Demonstration Project are due to the more careful evaluative procedures in the former, the greater effectiveness of the latter, or the difficulties faced by the Higher Horizon Program in serving many more students.

In her review of programs for disadvantaged children, Wilkerson (1965, pp. 435–36) describes a project which embodied many desirable characteristics of programs for disadvantaged children—the Perry Preschool Project in Ypsilanti, Michigan. The project report (Weikart, Kamii, and Radin, 1964) describes the project as an "experiment with replications to assess the impact of a cognitive program upon the educability of functionally retarded, culturally deprived, Negro preschool children." The program consisted of a morning preschool, home visits in the afternoon to involve mothers in the learning activities of their children, and group meetings for the parents of the children in the program. The three experimental groups of children were called *Waves:* Wave 0, composed of thirteen four-year-olds, spent one year in preschool, one year in kindergarten, and were in the first grade during 1964–65; Wave 1, composed of ten three-year-olds, entered in the fall of 1962, spent two years in preschool, and were in kindergarten during 1964–65; and Wave 2, composed of thirteen three-year-olds, entered in the fall of 1963 and were in the second year of preschool during 1964–65. On the basis of the Stanford-Binet Scales and a Cultural Deprivation Rating, children in the Waves were matched with children in control groups. Table 6-9

TABLE 6-9

RESULTS ON PERRY PRESCHOOL PROJECT—IQ SCORES.

Group	Average gain in IQ, first year in program	Differences when compared with control groups and level of significance
Wave 0	12.8	8.9 (0.01)
Wave 1	11.5	12.8 (0.05)
Wave 2	20.3	18.0 (0.001)

shows the gains in Stanford-Binet scores for the three Waves and the differences after one year between the experimental and the control groups. It shows dramatic gains in IQ after only one year in the program. These gains, however, were not maintained by those children who were in the program a second year. The children made comparable gains in language development. It will be interesting to find out from the follow-up research whether the children maintained these gains after they entered elementary school.

PRACTICES. James Olson and Richard Larson (1965) describe the practices they developed for teaching twenty disadvantaged kindergarten children in Racine, Wisconsin. Table 6-10 lists the particular language skills (one of four major areas of their program) they tried to develop. They used puppets to dramatize well-known stories and to allow the children to project their speech without personal exposure.

Eunice Newton (1960) stresses the techniques of synonymity in teaching language to disadvantaged children. Synonymity is the teacher's restating of a difficult term or word in many different and familiar ways. For example, when a passage contains reference to the "deleterious effects of narcotics," the teacher should immediately paraphrase the original passage to "harmful, or injurious, or detrimental effects of narcotics."

Disadvantaged children have trouble with mathematics because the abstract nature of the subject and their need for concrete experienc Herbert Fremont (1964) suggests several concrete representations whic may be used: automated programs, commercial aids, mathematical gam

TABLE 6-10

A FRAMEWORK FOR CURRICULUM DEVELOPMENT: KINDERGARTEN (after Olson and Larson, 1965, p. 554).

Developmental Areas Differentiating Culturally Deprived	Persisting School Situations	Classroom Activities
Language development	Receptive language	This column was completed by the classroom teacher as daily lesson plans
	Auditory skills	
	Listening to get meaning from auditory symbols	
	. . . for learning	
	. . . for fun in conversation	
	Visual skills	
	Interpreting interpersonal meaning from facial and bodily expressions	
	Recognizing relationships between symbolic and concrete concepts and objects	
	Gaining familiarity with traditional cultural symbols	
	Flag	
	Santa Claus	
	Mottoes	
	Slogans, etc.	
	Expressive language	
	Verbal expressive	
	Development of understandable articulatory habits	
	Using words in sequence	
	Adapting speech to different social situations	
	Motor expressive	
	Drawing	
	Writing	
	Rhythms	

nd puzzles, manipulative devices, and homemade flash cards. He also uggests the use of a personal folder which contains all the test papers, ritten work, ditto work, and other items of interest completed by the hild. In his mathematics course the children showed great pride in wning a workbook in which they could write. Fremont also used visits the stock exchange and guest speakers from the business and financial world. Natalie Mintz and Fremont (1965) used large department store catalogs to teach multiplication and division of decimal fractions, meaning of per cent and equivalent per cent, conversion of per cent to fractions (and the reverse), and general problem-solving techniques. The children filled out the order blanks, which listed each catalog item, to learn mathematical computations. The unit culminated in the actual purchase of a single item—a fish tank for the classroom.

SUMMARY. Evaluations of programs and practices for disadvantaged children, according to Wilkerson (1965), should contain precise descriptions of the educational procedures employed, clear statements of the hypotheses which specify the effects of these procedures, definitions of appropriate tests of such hypotheses, and the relevant data collected and interpreted through technically adequate procedures (see Chapter 16). In Wilkerson's opinion, most evaluations have failed to meet these criteria (p. 439):

> The general premise that the educational handicaps commonly ob- served among socially disadvantaged children can be overcome in large measure through appropriate school experiences is well an- chored in psychological and sociological theory, but how best to bring about these experiences is still open to question. Evidenc from preliminary evaluation of preschool programs strongly suggest the validity of this general approach; but even in the preschoo area it still has not been determined precisely which types of ex- perience yield the best developmental outcomes, and the ultimat test of elementary school performance is yet to be made. The ger erally inconclusive evidence from evaluations in most other area of compensatory education may be a function of theoretically un sound programs, of ineffective implementation of programs tha are sound, of technically inadequate procedures of evaluation, c of some combination of these. The profession and the lay publ are in no position yet to make firm judgments and long-term cor mitments for or against most programs in this field.

There are indications now that theory is guiding practice and that com petent techniques are guiding research in later programs and practice On this sober note, we can turn to a consideration of the teachers of disadvantaged children.

The Teachers

GENERAL DESCRIPTIONS. There has been considerably more spec lation than research on the desirable characteristics of teachers of d advantaged children. In describing the effective teacher, several write have relied on intuitive judgment. Riessman (1962) renders the f lowing portrait. The teacher should be consistent and dependable, as well as informal, warm, and down-to-earth. He should openly disagree with the anti-intellectualism of his disadvantaged students, but this should be done honestly and directly and without snobbery or manipulation. He should be one who wants "to teach children history" or other subject matter not one who wants "to teach history to children." He should identify with the underdog, be more physical than word-ridden, and be dedicated to his work. He should not treat the Negro child with informality because the child sees this as disrespect. Reissman believes that more of these teachers should be recruited from minority groups. Patrick Groff (1962) submitted a list of these and other characteristics suggested by Riessman to 294 teachers of disadvantaged children in a large metropolitan area and found that they disagreed with several of Riessman's points. They did not believe that the teacher should treat the Negro child with formality or that the child saw informality as disrespect; that teachers tend to talk down to the child; that the best teachers are those who are physical rather than word-ridden; and that more teachers of disadvantaged children should be recruited from the minorities.

Riessman also suggests school procedures and organization. Among these, the class should not be run like a prison, but the routine should be unvarying with simple, clear rules enforced to promote learning. The children should be taught to listen. Role playing should be used to develop verbal skills. The teacher must show the child in every way that he expects the child to learn, and he must bring the child beyond initial withdrawal and hostility. Groff's study, however, showed that teachers disagreed with the following statements made by Riessman: that physical punishment fails to deter the aggressive behavior of disadvantaged children; that the teachers should imply that they have and demonstrate their superior physical strength; that the teachers cannot take a gentle approach; and that disadvantaged children should not be segregated on the basis of ability and achievement.

A comparative study of Negro and white teachers revealed some important differences in their characteristics. David Gottlieb (1964) studied eighty-nine elementary school teachers in a midwestern city. Most of their students were low SES Negroes. Gottlieb found these differences: (1) More Negro than white teachers came from larger cities and obtained their degrees from urban universities; (2) 47 per cent of the Negro and 30 per cent of the white teachers were under thirty-five, and the Negro teachers were more likely to be married; (3) fathers of the Negro teachers were mostly in manual occupations, while fathers of the white teachers were mostly in professional and managerial positions; (4) the Negroes were more satisfied with their teaching experience although this satisfaction decreased as length of teaching experience increased); (5) the white teachers wanted more realistic professional training, but the Negro teachers wanted more knowledge of subject matter; (6) the white teachers attributed job dissatisfaction to student lack of ability, poor student motivation, and discipline problems, while the Negro teachers emphasized large classes, poor equipment, inadequate supplies, and improper curriculum; and (7) the Negro teachers tended to see the children as "happy, energetic, and fun-loving," while the white teachers saw the same children as "talkative, lazy, and rebellious." Inspection of these findings suggests that white teachers tend to emphasize the shortcomings of their pupils, while Negro teachers tend to emphasize the inadequate physical conditions under which they work. The attitude of the Negro teachers in this study suggests more optimism and job-mindedness than the attitude of the white teachers.

Hypothetical models. Hypothetical models of teachers of disadvantaged children have been recommended as a basis for research. Staten Webster (1966) bases his model on the assumption that middle-class teachers find difficulty in disadvantaged schools because their experience in these schools is their first encounter with a subculture. This encounter produces a conflict in attitudes, values, and desired social and academic behaviors. Webster suggests several hypotheses to explain why some teachers remain and others leave assignments in disadvantaged schools. Those who remain (1) will have less discrepancy between their own family SES and the SES of the families of the disadvantaged children; (2) will obtain higher scores on a test which measures amount of exposure to divergent ethnic, cultural, and SES groups; (3) will show more knowledge of the subculture; (4) will have higher scores on measures of optimism concerning what the school can do, child-centered orientation, restrictive classrooms, and acceptance of lower-class values, attitudes, and behaviors; (5) will show higher levels of social initiative in interacting with people; (6) will show less need for others to initiate social interaction with them; and (7) will obtain lower scores on a scale of dogmatism. Two additional hypotheses concern the behavior of the disadvantaged child and how this behavior will complement that of the hypothesized teacher. Inspection of Webster's list indicates the great emphasis he places on the teacher's social relations with the disadvantaged child and others.

A second hypothetical model of the successful teacher of disad- vantaged children also emphasizes the teacher's knowledge of the chi dren's backgrounds but stresses somewhat more the teacher's ability t deal realistically with the children. Miriam Goldberg (1964, pp. 167 69) believes that the successful teacher respects disadvantaged childre "not because he sees them through the rose-colored lenses of the r mantic—finding 'beauty' and 'strength' where others see poverty an cultural emptiness." Instead, this teacher meets the children on a perso to-person basis. He sets the rules, fixes the boundaries, and establishes the routines with a minimum of discussion. When he does these things, he is impersonal, undeviating, strict, but never punitive. "Within these boundaries the successful teacher is businesslike and orderly, knowing that he is there to do a job. But he is also warm and outgoing." The teacher informs the child that he expects more than the child thinks he can produce, but he does not set high and remote standards that cause frustration. He gives only honest and not sentimental praise. Finally, he is a showman "coming to his task with an extensive repertory of carefully constructed scripts and props into which he breathes a sense of drama and high interests to capture the imagination of his pupils and hold their attention." Goldberg summarizes her model of the successful teacher in a single phrase: *ordered flexibility*.

Social class. There has been considerable interest in investigating the impact of the teacher's social class on his behavior in the classroom. Howard Becker (1952), for example, in a study based on interviews of ixty teachers of poor children, located three problem areas which he ttributes to the social-class conflict between teachers and disadvantaged hildren: (1) the actual teaching itself, for which the children seemed o lack interest, ability, and previous training; (2) the disciplinary probems which arose when they tried to control unrestrained and physically ggressive children; and (3) the problem of moral acceptability—the lum children, according to Becker, offended the teachers' moral sensiilities by word, action, and appearance. They were shocked, for exmple, by the children's "sexual maturity."

Among the basic tenets of the research on the social class of teachers re these two: Teachers are drawn from the American middle class and, erefore, hold middle-class values; and the teachers' use of middle-class alues in judging classroom performances is prejudicial to lower-class hildren. After a careful review of the research, W. W. Charters (1962) ould find little support for these assumptions. The standards and the alues of the school, he suggests, are not the result of middle-class inuence but of organized attempts to perform a job which requires work, unctuality, control of aggression, avoidance of conflict, and relative uiet. Charters also questions the view that the lower-class child is punhed for what he is and not for what he does. This view rather awkardly implies that the teacher is appropriately punishing and rewarding e behavior of the middle-class child but not the behavior of the lowerass child—that he is punishing the lower-class child because he bengs to the lower class. As my discussion of social class earlier indicated, l these questions about the influence of social class on teacher and ident behavior could be avoided by recognizing the unsoundness of e concept of social class.

It is very easy to exaggerate the influence of the teachers and the school in the solution to the problems of disadvantaged children. Eleanor and Leo Wolf (1962) point out some limitations of this influence. First, the schools cannot create aspirations on the part of the overwhelming majority of disadvantaged children if the surrounding society gives the lie to such goals. Second, the schools can do little to compensate for the effects of fatherless families. Contacts with male teachers will not supply father images. Third, the school can assume only a limited number of social welfare functions. The actual time for classroom instruction is already very low. Teachers conduct save-stamps sales; sell and distribute milk; collect lunch money; check vision; patrol halls, playgrounds, and lunch rooms; and keep records. The local elementary school is often the focal point of all neighborhood organization. The authors also point out the unfortunate tendency to scapegoat the classroom teacher and to confront her with contradictory admonitions. If the teacher's expectations are too high, they are condemned as unrealistic. If the expectations are too low, they are condemned because they reinforce the child's lack of self-esteem and reflect the teacher's middle-class prejudice. Teachers report that they are accused of relaxing standards if they alter the grading system, and they are accused of prejudice if they use the same standards as before. On the one hand, the failure of disadvantaged children is attributed to their lack of work habits and of values which stress order, neatness, and punctuality. On the other hand, when teachers display or demonstrate these characteristics, they are reproached for their middle-class rigidity and propriety.

SUMMARY. As yet we have no generally accepted characteristics for teachers of disadvantaged children. Whereas some writers have advocated a fairly open, informal, and egalitarian relationship between teacher and child, others have emphasized an authoritarian, formal task-centered relationship. Available evidence suggests that Negro teachers seek improvement in the physical conditions under which they must teach while white teachers seek improvement in the attitudes of their students. Since it is often easier to change the physical environment of the school than to change the attitudes of teachers and students, the Negro teachers appear to be more optimistic than their white counterparts. One hypothetical model of teachers of disadvantaged children emphasizes the quality of the interpersonal action between teacher and student; another model emphasizes ordered flexibility, which requires the teacher to establish the boundaries and the rules and yet to remain warm and responsive. Also, a description of individual behavior in terms of social-class background is as unsound and misleading for teachers as it is for students. Teachers have only limited influence over disadvantaged children, although expectations about what changes they can produce are often unrealistic.

It may be useful to shift future research and discussions from consideration of desirable teacher characteristics to consideration of desirable teaching techniques. In terms of the basic teaching model, the best teacher for the disadvantaged child is one who selects appropriate instructional objectives, makes careful assessments of entering behavior, selects and devises effective instructional procedures, and assesses the performance of his students to uncover the relative success or failure of his instructional efforts.

How to Teach the Disadvantaged Child

Inspection of the research on the relationship of SES to IQ, race, and achievement and on perceptual, linguistic, and cognitive development suggests five general guidelines for planning instruction for the disadvantaged child.

1. PROVIDE THE CHILD WITH THE NECESSARY COGNITIVE STIMULATION. Deutsch (1964) suggests that cognitive growth may be the best therapy and the best means of self-realization (p. 262):

> The overgeneralized influence on some sections of early childhood education of the emphasis in the child guidance movement upon protecting the child from stress, creating a supportive environment, and resolving emotional conflicts has done more to misdirect and retard the fields of child care, guidance, and development than any other single influence. The effect has especially operated to make these fields ineffective in responding to the problems of integrating and educating the nonwhite urban child. These orientations have conceived of the child as being always on the verge of some disease process and have assigned to themselves the role of protecting the child in the same manner that a zookeeper arranges for the survival of his charges. Too frequently a philosophy of protectiveness that asks only about possible dangers has prevailed over any question of potential stimulation of development.

Cognitive growth occurs in many aspects of the child's development, cluding the following: (a) the development of language, particularly ntinuous, sustained, connected, and relevant discourse; (b) perceptual aining, which increases the child's skill in distinguishing and responding to the various dimensions of objects and to speech sounds; (c) memory aining, which facilitates the child's association of past, present, and ture events; and (d) the development of verbal mediation as a way of creasing the child's general learning efficiency.

2. BEGIN HIS FORMAL EDUCATION IN THE PRESCHOOL YEARS. Programs r disadvantaged children should begin in the preschool years for three

reasons: First, the preschool years are the best ones for cognitive growth. Ways of learning concepts, habit patterns, and interest areas are probably all established at fairly early ages. Fowler (1962) suggests that after the child has developed one cognitive style he may have difficulty developing a more useful one. In the case of the disadvantaged child, his early emphasis on a style which stresses impulsive, concrete, and physical behavior may inhibit his later attempts to develop a style which emphasizes problem-solving, abstract, and verbal behavior. Second, an increasingly complex and technological society requires all children tc begin their cognitive development as early as possible. Third, the pre school can serve as a bridge between the two cultures which the disad vantaged child experiences—the culture of the home and of his regior of the city and the culture of the school. Taba (1964) believes that the spanning of these cultures is so difficult for these children that thei experience should be described as culture shock.

3. Utilize motivation derived from curiosity and explorator behavior and use tangible incentives. Ausubel (1963) presents this cas for stressing what he calls *cognitive drive*—the tendency of humans t explore, manipulate, and cope with the environment—in programs fo disadvantaged children: Disadvantaged children are not motivated b the promise of future jobs and improved social status because they ar skeptical about ever attaining these goals. Since, in any case, most of th learning which occurs in the school cannot be justified in terms of pre aration for a career or for meeting the demands of daily living, the be way to motivate these unmotivated students is to ignore their motiv tional state for the present and to continue teaching them material substance as effectively as possible. Ausubel does not rule out the u of tangible incentives, such as career advancement, but merely stress motivation derived from the learning materials and experiences the selves. Indeed, Glenn Terrel, Kathryn Durkin, and Melvin Wiesl (1959) found that low SES children learned more when they were giv a material incentive (a small piece of candy) than when they were giv a nonmaterial incentive (a light flash which indicated that they sponded correctly). High SES children (ages 5 to 11) stated that th would rather "do something for the fun of it" than be "promised given something for doing it." It is likely that Ausubel's cognitive dri is itself a product of learning and of a successful history of learni Disadvantaged children should then learn cognitive drive as they lea the use of verbal mediators.

4. Provide a sequential and hierarchical arrangement of lea ing experiences. In our consideration of entering behavior in Chap 3, we discussed learning sets and learning structures (pp. 70–71) defined learning sets as component behaviors a student must acqu before he reaches the terminal behavior, and I defined learning structu

as particular orders in which the learning sets are placed. Since the disadvantaged child may lack crucial learning sets, the organization of instructional materials becomes a major consideration. The learning structure informs the teacher of the learning sets which must be found in the entering behavior of the students or which must be acquired as the student progresses toward the terminal behavior. Deutsch (1964) suggests that the materials of Montessori may supply the necessary learning structures. For example, for teaching size and differences in size, her materials are all the same shape and color so that attention focuses on size rather than on a competing element. Ausubel (1963) believes that programed instruction (in nonmachine form) may be ideally suited for disadvantaged children because the learning of subsequent items is carefully based on the learning of previous items.

5. Provide consolidation of learning. Consolidation is the final mastery of materials. It requires the student to repeat, review, and practice what he has learned since one-time exposure to materials is usually insufficient for the successful learning of disadvantaged children. These operations are particularly important in difficult parts of assignments. Frequent testing and feedback also promote consolidation.

Summary. These five guidelines for teaching the disadvantaged child emphasize cognitive growth as his best means for achieving self-realization. The teacher can stimulate this growth with the proper materials and training and under certain conditions: when the child begins his formal education in his preschool years; when motivation of the child is a product of curiosity, exploratory behavior, and incentives; when learning experiences are arranged in orderly and hierarchical fashion; and when provision for consolidation of previous learning is made.

You should now return to objectives 18–28 (p. 185) and determine how well you have achieved them.

QUESTION 6-3

Mr. Dew Moore must advise new teachers of disadvantaged children about suitable instructional procedures. Which of the following statements could he most wisely make?

(a) Take care *not* to impose middle-class values on these children.

(b) Kindle their interest in new subject matter before they are actually exposed to this subject matter.

(c) Accept no child for instruction who has not had the benefits of preschool training.

(d) Provide for sequences of the learning materials in terms of learning sets rather than in terms of logic.

After selecting your answer give reasons for your choice and for your rejection of the alternatives.

SUMMARY

Many of the difficulties the disadvantaged child meets in the pursuit of the instructional objectives of the school arise from deficiencies in entering behavior. This chapter has attempted to describe these deficiencies and to discuss how they may be handled.

The first section dealt with the social conditions under which the disadvantaged child is reared and educated. He is an economically poor child who often belongs to a racial or ethnic minority. Although he cannot be realistically described in terms of social-class origin, he can be described in terms of socioeconomic status and the relationship of this status to IQ, race, achievement, motivation, and learning ability. Studies of these relationships are correlational in nature and suggest one of the several causes of low IQ, low achievement, and so on. Although these studies do not link cause and effect as well as experimental studies, they do suggest to the teacher where he may look for strengths and weaknesses in the entering behavior of disadvantaged children.

The second section dealt with the learning conditions under which the disadvantaged child is often reared. Here we saw the nature of his impoverished home environment, the cumulative deficits which this impoverishment causes, and the rather dramatic effects which can occur if changes are made in the preschool years. Jensen's model of the growth of intelligence shows the relationship of impoverished and enriched environments to heredity and intellectual development. The effects of impoverished environments on perceptual learning, linguistic development, and cognitive development were described. Impoverished environments cause deficiencies in auditory learning, in attention and in verbal mediation. They result in the use of restricted rather than elaborated language codes. The procedures for eliminating these deficiencies are not fully devised and will require further exploration and research. The experimental research in these areas promises, however, to facilitate greatly the assessment of areas of entering behavior crucial for school learning.

The third section dealt with programs, practices, teachers, and guidelines for instructing disadvantaged children. The review of programs and practices indicates that the state of the art is in the initial stages and that we presently have no firm basis for unqualified endorsement or rejection of various instructional practices and programs. There are no generally accepted characteristics for teachers of disadvantaged children, although certain qualities of personal interaction and ordered flexibility may be important. Often quite incompatible and unrealistic expectations are imposed on these teachers. The research reviewed in this and in the preceding chapter suggests certain guidelines for teaching disadvantaged children. These guidelines pertain to cognitive stimulation, preschool training, motivation, learning sets, and the consolidation of learning.

SUGGESTED READINGS

These edited volumes include speculative essays, critiques, and research on disadvantaged children:

Frost, Joe L. and Glenn R. Hawkes, eds., *The Disadvantaged Child: Issues and Innovations*. Boston: Houghton Mifflin Company, 1966 (paper).

Passow, A. Harry, ed., *Education in Depressed Areas*. New York: Teachers College Press, Columbia University, 1963 (paper).

———, Miriam Goldberg, and Abraham J. Tannebaum, eds., *Education of the Disadvantaged: A Book of Readings*. New York: Holt, Rinehart & Winston, Inc., 1967.

Webster, Staten W., *The Disadvantaged Learner*. San Francisco: Chandler Publishing Company, 1966 (paper). In three parts, under three separate bindings.

This source gives the most authoritative review by several authors on the characteristics, language development, psychological appraisal, and learning disabilities of and educational programs for disadvantged children:

"Education for Socially Disadvantaged Children," *Review of Educational Research,* 35 (1965), 373–442.

This book is the best collection of theoretical speculation and research on the language development and other phases of the psychological development of disadvantaged children:

Deutsch, Martin, Arthur R. Jensen, and Irwin Katz, eds., *Social Class, Race, and Psychological Development*. New York: Holt, Rinehart & Winston, Inc., 1968.

Although the bibliography is rapidly growing, one published bibliography attempts to collect the relevant literature:

Bloom, Benjamin, Allison Davis, and Robert Hess, *Compensatory Education for Cultural Deprivation*. New York: Holt, Rinehart & Winston, Inc., 1965. This book also contains a summary of the problems of cultural deprivation.

These works give summaries of current educational programs and recommendations for educational changes:

Jewett, Arno, *et al.*, *Improving English Skills of Culturally Different Youth*. Washington, D.C.: U. S. Department of Health, Education, and Welfare, 1964.

Programs for the Educationally Disadvantaged, Bulletin No. 17. Washington, D.C.: U. S. Department of Health, Education, and Welfare, Office of Education, 1963.

PART THREE

INSTRUCTIONAL PROCEDURES

Part 3 introduces you to the third component of the basic teaching model—instructional procedures—to tell you how to teach skills, concepts, principles, and problem solving. Several factors determine the proper selection or design of instructional procedures. You are already familiar with two of these factors: instructional objectives and entering behavior. Obviously, before the teacher can decide how to teach, he must determine what to teach—the instructional objectives. Generally, these objectives should have priority over the procedures except in those unusual cases in which we can find no adequate instruction to meet particular objectives. In ordinary practice, however, the teacher should not allow his preferences for particular procedures solely to dictate his choice of objectives. Moreover, before the teacher can decide how to teach, he must determine whom he is teaching—the entering behavior of his students. General the students should have priority over the procedures except in those almost hopeless cases in which we can find no adequate instruction for particular students. In ordinary practice the teacher cannot and does not allow his preferences for particular procedures solely to determine whom he will and will not teach. A fondness for particul procedures can become a fetish and a bane to learning.

Part 3 introduces additional factors which may guide your sel ion or design of instructional procedures. We call these factors he *conditions of learning* and distinguish between internal and ex-ernal conditions (Gagné, 1965c). The *internal conditions* are the level f the student's entering behavior—his present capabilities. Part 2 nalyzed internal learning conditions, that is, entering behavior. *External conditions* of learning are outside the student in what we hall later call the *stimulus situation.* Even though we assume that Ella Mae has the same entering behavior for memorizing the alphabet nd for adding fractions, the appropriate external learning conditions or these two objectives are quite different. Although repetition is e chief condition for memorizing the alphabet, adding fractions equires that and other external learning conditions.

As the level of learning complexity increases (from memorizing e alphabet to adding fractions, and so on), the conditions for arning change correspondingly. To organize the materials in art 3, I have used Gagné's (1965c) categories of learning, which were escribed in Chapter 2. You will recall that Gagné formed a hierarchy these categories, with the simplest learning near the base and the ost complex near the apex. Following Gagné's arrangement, there-re, we first consider classical and operant conditioning and then oceed to skill learning, language learning, concept learning, principle learning, and problem solving. In this organization of material the learning type determines the internal and external conditions discussed. In Chapter 7, I introduce certain basic external learning conditions common to many learning types, and, in the later chapters, I apply them to the various learning types. By having the learning *type* determine our consideration of the conditions of learning, we are maintaining the priority of instructional objectives (what to teach over instructional procedures (how to teach).

Our present level of knowledge in educational psychology does not permit us to make specific suggestions for teaching particular objectives. In fact, such specific applications are probably not the goal of most research in the field. The teacher finds it more useful to know how to match classes of conditions with classes of objective The educational psychologist, for example, is not interested in telling you what you must do to teach the specific concepts of monarchy, revolution, gravity, and isotopes. He is able, to some extent, however, to tell you the necessary classes of conditions—contiguity, practice, reinforcement, and so on—for teaching most concepts. As a teacher your task is to infer the specific procedures and materials you will use from the learning types involved and their associated conditio

Basic Learning Conditions and Types

7

This chapter describes the conditions necessary for the learning dis-
:ussed in the remaining chapters of Part 3. These conditions are ex-
ernal—they exist outside the student in the stimulus situation—and
is such are distinct from internal learning conditions—the student's
entering behavior. Successful performance is the result of the happy
onfluence of external and internal learning conditions.

The chapter has four sections. The first defines learning and the
earning event. The second (and major) section defines the basic learn-
ng conditions: contiguity, practice, reinforcement, generalization, and
liscrimination. The third section describes the two basic learning types
—classical and operant conditioning. The final section considers the
elationship of basic learning conditions to instructional procedures.

The chapter uses the language of the connectionist-reinforcement
earning theories (Hill, 1963, pp. 27–30). Research based on these the-
ries forms the major part of psychological knowledge. My choice of
heory and language merely reflects the opinion that connectionist-
einforcement theories and vocabulary more than cognitive theories and
ocabulary lend themselves to the explicit description of the conditions
f learning and teaching. Those of us who view psychology as a natural
:ience look to future research to resolve some of the issues between the
vo learning theories. In the meantime the teacher and the educational
sychologist should borrow from the psychology of learning whatever
ems useful for the psychology of instruction, avoiding any ideological

attack, defense, and counterattack. The progress of scientific psychology shows that research settles more issues than do invective and debate.

Upon reading the first section of this chapter (on a definition of learning), you should be able to meet these objectives:

1. Define learning in terms of change, reinforcement, and practice.
2. Distinguish learning from performance, native response tendencies, maturation, and temporary states of the organism.
3. Define the learning event in terms of stimulus, response, and learner, and provide illustrations of learning events.

Upon reading the second section of this chapter (on the basic learning conditions), you should be able to meet these objectives:

4. Distinguish between internal and external conditions of learn ing (see also the introduction to Part 3).
5. Define contiguity in terms of occurrence of stimulus and re sponse and describe its importance in various learning types.
6. Define practice in terms of repetition and describe its importanc in various learning types.
7. Define reinforcement in terms of a procedure for presenting reinforcer; give illustrations of the procedure.
8. Distinguish between positive and negative reinforcers and giv illustrations of each.
9. Give illustrations of the trans-situational nature of reinforcer
10. Define reinforcement in terms of a feedback procedure; list fou feedback procedures and illustrate each.
11. Define extinction in terms of reinforcers and competing r sponses.
12. List the four major conditions of reinforcement and illustrat the major effects of each condition on learning.
13. Describe the importance of reinforcement as a condition fc various learning types.
14. Define generalization in terms of a response to a new stimult and illustrate this behavior.
15. Define discrimination in terms of a different response to two (more stimuli and illustrate this behavior; distinguish between S^D ar S^Δ and provide behavioral illustrations involving both stimuli.
16. Give illustrations to show what is meant by overgeneralizatic and overdiscrimination.

Upon reading the third section of this chapter (on two basic learning types), you should be able to meet these objectives:

17. Describe the necessary learning conditions for classical conditioning and the order in which they are provided; distinguish between the nature of conditioned and unconditioned responses; give an illustration of classical conditioning.

18. Describe the necessary learning conditions for operant conditioning and the order in which they are provided; give an illustration of operant conditioning.

19. Describe the major distinction between classical and operant conditioning and give an illustration of this distinction.

Upon reading the fourth part of this chapter (on learning conditions and instructional procedures), you should be able to meet these objectives:

20. Define instructional procedures in terms of learning conditions, ypes, and objectives.

21. Illustrate a *class* of learning conditions by selecting a particular ondition.

22. Describe and illustrate the advantages and disadvantages of ısing classical and operant conditioning as teaching models for various nstructional objectives.

BASIC CONCEPTS

Before discussing the basic learning conditions we should clearly efine learning and the learning event. This section, therefore, defines earning and distinguishes it from performance, native response tendenies, maturation, and temporary states of the organism. The learning vent comprises the learner, the stimulus situation, and the response.

A Definition of Learning

Learning is a relatively permanent change in a behavioral tendency nd is the result of reinforced practice (Kimble and Garmezy, 1963, p. 33). The reinforced practice (which I will explain shortly) is the cause f the learning. The learning actually occurs between the cause and the sult. Figure 7-1 indicates the relationship between the three parts of e definition. We use the term *behavioral tendency* in the definition

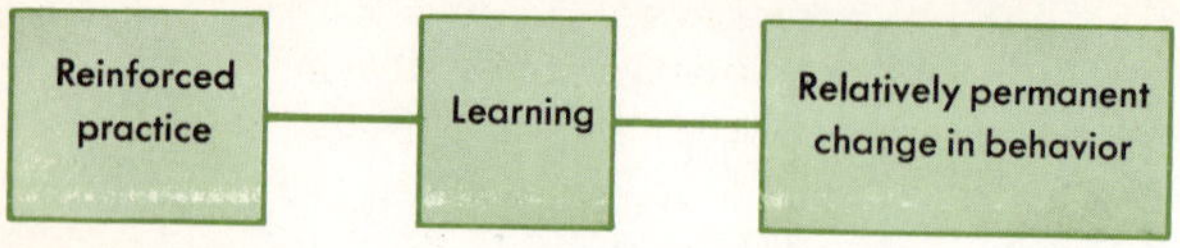

Fig. 7-1. *The concept of learning (after Kimble, 1964).*

to keep the distinction between learning and performance. In Fig. 7-1, the relatively permanent change in behavior refers to a change in performance. We can observe a performance but we cannot observe learning. We infer that a person has learned when he can do something later which he could not do before. When Elvis shouts "Down!" Hound Dog sits down. We know that Hound Dog has learned because he never before did anything at this command except stare soulfully at Elvis. Not everything we learn, however, results in a change of behavior or performance. A student may master all the knowledge in a textbook on teaching, but, before he teaches, he will not have the chance to change his performance by using this knowledge. If some day he is teaching a concept and he provides all the necessary illustrations, his learning will then affect performance. The learning, or change in behavioral tendency, however, occurred earlier.

When Elvis says "Paw!" Hound Dog sits and presents his right paw as if to shake hands. For this performance he receives a morsel of food (a piece of hominy grit which Hound Dog relishes). How did Hound Dog learn to perform what appears to be a most unnatural act for a dog? We cannot describe the full procedure, but it involved both internal and external learning conditions. Hound Dog had to learn to sit when commanded to do so. This was necessary entering behavior or, if you like, a necessary internal learning condition. When Hound Dog was sitting, Elvis uttered the command, "Paw," lifted the dog's paw, and shook it vigorously, trying not to knock poor Hound Dog off balance. He then rewarded the dog with the choicest piece of hominy grit. Elvis repeated this procedure several times a day for several days, and soon Hound Dog cordially presented his paw whenever Elvis walked in the door. In terms of our definition of learning, the practice consisted of lifting Hound Dog's paw and shaking it in response to the command over a period of several days. The reinforced practice consisted of the candy reward Elvis presented each time he held the dog's paw. The change in behavior consisted of Hound Dog's presenting his paw to Elvis. Now Hound Dog may not present his paw to just anyone, and he may still prefer to bark at strangers who darken Elvis' door (not all learning changes performance). Still the behavioral tendency to raise his paw in greeting has been strengthened, and the actual performance of this act tells us that Hound Dog has learned.

There are many obvious examples of human learning—learning to drive a car or to operate a typewriter, memorizing the lines of a play, acquiring new vocabulary. All these acts are new performances which we acquire with reinforced practice. There are less obvious examples of learning. We learn our prejudices, our preferences, our social attitudes and skills. In the terminology of a previous chapter, we learn our expectancies and our valences. We do not inherit the preference to live next door only to those of our own race. We acquire or learn this preference. Expecting success or failure in our studies, wanting fame or knowledge or both, buying hardtops or convertibles, pursuing go-go girls or no-no girls—all these preferences are products of learning.

Some areas of behavior do not furnish examples of learning. First among these are the native response tendencies. We do not learn the knee jerk, the eye blink, breathing, and nausea. We once called these tendencies *instincts.* We can just as well call them *reflexes.* In any event, we are born with these capabilities, and we do not acquire them through practice and reinforcement. Some borderline behaviors may be a product of both instinct and learning. The best example is the tendency of newborn ducklings, at a critical period shortly after birth, to follow the first moving and quacking object they meet (Lorenz, 1937). Usually this object is their mother, but it is possible to get them to follow an artificial duck with a tape recorder inside which emits quacking sounds (Ramsay and Hess, 1954). This following behavior is called *imprinting;* once the ducklings have been imprinted with the artificial duck it is very difficult to get them to follow any other duck. We cannot ascertain at this time how much of this behavior is the result of instinct and how much the result of learning.

The second area of behavior which does not furnish examples of learning is maturation—growth tendencies which are relatively independent of specific learning conditions. Human and animal growth in height and weight is not learned behavior. The swimming of tadpoles and the flying of birds simply occur at the moment of anatomical maturation. But do we learn to walk? We cannot walk until our legs are strong enough to support our weight and we have developed the proper neural structures. But not every child walks the same way, and we can even distinguish between familiar and unfamiliar footsteps in adults. Similiarly, the child cannot talk before proper vocal and neural devolpment, but not all children speak the same language, and those who speak the same language do so in different ways. In other words, as in the case of native response tendencies, we do not have sufficient knowledge to make a clear distinction between learning and maturation.

The third area of behavior includes the temporary states of the organism due to fatigue, habituation, or drugs. If an endless line of visitors comes to his home the day Abigail gets married, Hound Dog will certainly not raise his paw at every command and for every guest. The poor dog would be tired. But the next day he will faithfully await Elvis' arrival at the door, and his paw will be raised in greeting. The sheer repetition of a response, after a time, disinclines its immediate repetition. But the resulting change in behavior is attributable to fatigue and not to learning. Habituation changes our behavior in the direction of reduced responsiveness. For example, many individuals fall asleep on the New York subways even with the usual screeching, rocking, and jerking of the trains. We also grow accustomed to the traffic moving below our apartment windows at night. Most likely we do not learn to ignore these and other irrelevant noises. Innate mechanisms automatically take over and produce the adaptation necessary for us to get our sleep or to pay attention to more relevant noises. Finally, drugs produce or inhibit behavior changes, usually just temporarily. Under the influence of considerable amounts of vodka or gin (which are depressants), we may forget the line of Hamlet's soliloquy we so desperately need to remember to entertain our friends. After our return to normality, memory returns (sometimes to our regret), and, without any intervening reinforced practice, we can recite the soliloquy if we are still inclined to and if anyone is around to listen. Even with drugs, however, the case is not clear; it is possible that certain organic compounds or drugs can influence learning and memory.

You should note that the definition of learning states nothing about improvements in behavior. Most of our learning consists of such improvements—when, for example, we learn new vocabulary, new concepts, new ways of dealing with individuals of other races, and more effective teaching procedures. We can as easily strengthen behavioral tendencies potentially injurious to ourselves and others, as in the case of excessive smoking, excessive eating, and excessive drinking (see Dollard and Miller, 1950). We can acquire a taste for racial hatred, for drugs, and for neurotic behavior. Indeed, even pigeons can be trained to peck at each other at the sound of a buzzer and to soothe ruffled feathers at the flashing of a green light (Skinner, 1938).

The Learning Event

Which elements in a situation are essential for learning? Three elements together constitute the learning event (Gagné, 1965c): the learner the stimulus or stimulus situation, and the response. A *learner* consists of sense organs, a central nervous system, and muscles. His previous learning is his entering behavior, or his internal conditions of learning. A *stimulus* (plural: stimuli—to rhyme with pie) is an event in the environment; a stimulus situation is several events in the environment. A *re sponse* is simply a part of our behavior. Rain is an environmental event—a stimulus—which leads to the responses of grabbing raincoats and opening umbrellas. A fall in temperature is a stimulus; the appearance of goose pimples is a response. Consider this statement: Lucille's lips pucker when she sees a lemon. The lemon is the stimulus. The pucker is the response.

One of the easiest ways to depict learning is as follows. When a stimulus is first presented, there is no response. When it is presented the next time, there is a response. Miss Pegg shows the class a picture of a hyena and asks the class to name the animal. There is no response. She tells them that it is a picture of a hyena—she presents the stimulus. When she presents the picture a second time, everyone responds "hyena." This response indicates a change in the performance of these learners from the time before they were in the stimulus situation to the time after they were in the situation. From this change in performance we infer the occurrence of learning. Your behavior will presumably change as a result of reading this chapter. Before you read this chapter you may have defined learning as the acquisition of knowledge. After reading this chapter you may define learning as a relatively permanent change in a behavioral tendency as a result of reinforced practice. Your performance will have changed, and we will infer that you have learned.

By taking the learning event into consideration, we can easily plan instruction. A clear teaching plan ought to foresee which stimuli will result in the student's making which responses. Stimuli are all teaching materials and media—textbooks, films, lectures, programed lessons, television, discussion questions, and so on. The responses are the new performances the teacher expects the student to acquire. Considering how frequently instructors present materials to students without a clear conception of the new responses they expect the students to make, we can see how much clarity the use of the learning event introduces into instructional planning. In Chapter 2, we called the responses the instructor plans for *terminal behavior*—that behavior the teacher wants the student to show at the end of instruction. You will recall that in a detailed task analysis, the responses the student is expected to make lead to the terminal behavior.

From this discussion of learning, performance, response, and terminal behavior you can easily see that the terms overlap in meaning. In discussions of teaching, we almost always are referring to observable behavior changes, whether we call them learning, achievement, performances, responses, or terminal behavior. You will recall that to develop a clear concept of learning, we distinguished between learning and performance or behavior. As teachers we can observe and measure achievement, performance, and behavior, but we can only infer the occurrence or nonoccurrence of learning. In the ensuing discussion, therefore, even though I will refer to learning I ordinarily will mean achievement, performance, behavior, or response.

SUMMARY. Learning has been defined as a relatively permanent change in a behavioral tendency, the result of reinforced practice. Learning, an inferred state of the organism, should be distinguished from performance, an observed state of the organism. Learning events consist of stimuli, learners, and responses. In the chapters in Part 3 I will frequently refer to learning events.

You should now return to objectives 1–3 (p. 242) and determine how well you have achieved them.

QUESTION 7-1

> Miss Pegg, a nursery school teacher, watched the children develop increased skill in movement. LeRoy, who two months ago was unable to sit securely on the tricycle seat, has been peddling the tricycle with aplomb and peer approval for the last month. Which of the following best explains LeRoy's change in behavior? (a) learning; (b) maturation; (c) native response tendencies; (d) habituation.
>
> After selecting your answer, give the reasons for your choice and for your rejection of the alternatives.

THE BASIC CONDITIONS

External conditions of learning—contiguity, practice, reinforcement, generalization, and discrimination—are important in the various learning types. In this section, I shall describe and illustrate each of these conditions and briefly relate each to the learning for which it is important. The chapters following this give more detailed consideration to these conditions and to their relationship to the various types of learning. In those chapters you will see that not all these conditions are equally important in each learning type. Whereas practice (for example, repetition) is important in simple learning, contiguity is important in both simple and complex learning.

Contiguity

One of the basic learning conditions is contiguity—the almost simultaneous occurrence of the stimuli and the responses. In the typical Pavlovian experiment the ringing of the bell—the stimulus—was contiguous with the salivation of the dog—the response. Miss Pegg presents a flash card which bears the word *cat,* and the children say "cat." The flash card is the stimulus, and "cat" is the response. One learning theor

(Guthrie, 1952) holds that the only necessary condition for learning is contiguity, or the simultaneous occurrence of the stimulus and the response.* In planning your teaching you will often provide for such a simultaneous occurrence. When we teach the child to associate the word *doll* with the object, we must present the stimulus object at the time the child says "doll," the response. In the previous chapter we noted the absence of contiguity in the homes of disadvantaged children. These children fail to associate words and objects because the word is not uttered by the child or the adult when the object is presented. As teachers we are always interested in having the students build up associations between particular stimuli and responses. One of the necessary learning conditions for developing such associations is contiguity.

Contiguity is an important condition in most learning. Classical conditioning involves contiguity of the conditioned and the unconditioned stimulus. Operant conditioning involves contiguity of the response and the reinforcing stimulus. Skill learning involves contiguity in the occurrence of the various links in the motor chain. Concept learning involves contiguity in the presentation of examples and nonexamples. Principle learning involves contiguity in the recall of the component concepts. Finally, problem solving involves contiguity in the recall of the component principles.

Practice

The definition of learning refers to reinforced practice, another basic external condition of learning. Practice is the repetition of a response in the presence of the stimulus. Unless other learning conditions are ideally provided, we probably learn very little (of relative permanency) from the first response we make to a particular stimulus. We usually must practice or repeat *S-R* (stimulus-response) associations to retain them for relatively long periods. The current educational emphasis on cognition and meaningful learning has made practice or repetition an unpopular learning condition. To many educators practice recalls the monotonous drills required by the teacher in the country schoolhouse. Practice becomes less necessary when the student has the entering behavior particular instructional objectives require. For example, those of you who studied learning in introductory psychology have less difficulty with the concept than those who are studying it for the first time. The ease with which you learn new things is largely a result of what you know at the start. For relatively novel stimuli and novel responses more practice is required than for those which are familiar. If I were to ask you to learn

* In Edwin Guthrie's theory, responses are conceived as movements (see Hilgard and Bower, 1966, pp. 74–106).

pairs of associated words, such as sand–box, bed–rock, mind–matter, and I presented the words both in English and in French, most students would require much less practice with the English list than with the French list because they already know the single English words and must only learn the associations. For the French list, most students would have to learn the single words and the associations. Of course, the student whose entering behavior includes a knowledge of French would require less practice than the student who did not have this knowledge. The teacher's provision for student practice should not be based on personal preference or on philosophical grounds but on the student's need for practice to attain the instructional objective (see Chapter 8).

Practice is of diminishing importance as a condition as we move from simple to complex learning. In classical conditioning, operant conditioning, skill learning, and verbal learning it is of crucial importance. In concept learning, principle learning, and problem solving it is of minor importance if the other learning conditions are properly provided. Later discussions will describe the major ways in which practice may be changed: the amount (in time) of practice, the number of practice periods, and the distribution of practice.

Reinforcement: Its Nature

Reinforcement is a major condition for most learning. You will see that we can vary reinforcement procedures to provide different effects. The effects, of course, are the learning types we want our students to acquire. Because of the breadth of the concept and because it is an important condition for most learning, I give reinforcement extended treatment in this chapter.

In this section we discuss reinforcement as a procedure. First we consider the procedure of providing the reinforcing stimulus, and then we consider the somewhat more complex procedure of providing informational feedback. Finally we discuss extinction, the procedure of withholding a reinforcer or of giving opposing responses. In the following section we discuss the conditions of reinforcement: immediacy, frequency, amount, and number.

Overwhelming evidence supports this generalization: Rewarded responses tend to be repeated in given situations; unrewarded responses tend to be discontinued. This statement, known as the law of effect, was first enunciated by the great American educational psychologist Thorndike (1911) as follows:

> Of the several responses made to the same situation, those which are accompanied or closely followed by satisfaction to the animal will, other things being equal, be more firmly connected to the

> situation, so that when it recurs, they will be more likely to recur; those which are accompanied or closely followed by discomfort to the animal will, other things being equal, have their connection weakened, so that, when it recurs, they will be less likely to recur.

The statement indicates the fundamental hedonism of the psychology of learning, a tradition which continues today. Much of Thorndike's experimental work was done with cats. By pulling a string which in turn opened a door, they escaped from their cages and obtained rewards in the form of raw fish. The cats' response was pulling the string, and the satisfaction following this response was the fish or the freedom of life outside the cage. If the cat received a mild electric shock (a state of "discomfort") each time it pulled the string instead of receiving fish and freedom, it would be less likely to make the correct response. Thorndike's formulation of the law of effect did not include a description of what happens when responses are followed by neither satisfaction nor discomfort, a topic we will consider below.

In the reinforcement procedure, an organism is presented with a particular stimulus—a reinforcer—before or after it makes a response. In a given situation the organism will tend to repeat responses for which it is reinforced and to discontinue responses for which it is not reinforced. We can distinguish a reinforcer from other stimuli because it has this particular effect on behavior.

Many examples illustrate the use of the reinforcement procedure. Let us take as an example a reinforcer which follows the response. Hound Dog raises his head and majestically presents a series of barks (a signal to Elvis that he intends to go outside). Elvis opens the door and, without a thank you, Hound Dog makes his exit. The door, according to our definition, is the reinforcer; opening the door, a procedure, is reinforcement; and the response being reinforced is Hound Dog's barking by the door. In Thorndike's sense, opening the door is a satisfier. Several experiments have utilized similar procedures with human subjects. William Verplanck (1955) reports a study in which subjects, who were unaware of how their behavior was being influenced, were reinforced for making opinion statements. Opinion statements were those the subjects began with words like "I think. . . ," "It seems to me. . . ," and "I believe. . . ." As reinforcement, the experimenters nodded their heads, smiled, paraphrased what the subject said, and made statements of agreement such as "You're right" and "I agree." The subjects tended to make more opinion statements as a result of the reinforcement. When the reinforcers were withdrawn or the experimenters disagreed with or failed to paraphrase the statements of the subjects, the number of opinion statements sharply decreased.

We can also provide the reinforcer before the response. Ivan Pavlov, the Russian psychologist, employed this procedure. He presented meat or meat powder to a dog to cause salivation. The meat powder was the reinforcer, and the salivation was the response. Later in this chapter, when we compare signal learning (classical conditioning) and operant conditioning, you will see that this difference in procedure is the chief distinction between two basic learning types.

In human behavior we can easily find examples of the procedure which presents the reinforcer after the response is made. Harriet, in the second grade, correctly spells rat, bat, and fat. For these responses she receives three gold stars, a practice conforming with Miss Rhea Ward's classroom policy. The responses are the correct spelling of the three words. The reinforcers are the gold stars. The procedure of presenting the gold stars after these correct responses is reinforcement. Elvis punches Rodney in the mouth, and their classmates cheer. We have the response —the punch—and the reinforcer (for Elvis, but not for battered Rodney) —the mob cheers of their classmates. The law of effect predicts that Harriet will continue to spell these words correctly and that Elvis will probably throw more punches at Rodney and perhaps at others. It also predicts that Rodney will do everything in his power to avoid Elvis' aggression.

POSITIVE AND NEGATIVE REINFORCERS. We can distinguish between positive and negative reinforcers. James Holland and B. F. Skinner (1961, pp. 52–62) present many familiar examples of positive reinforcers. A funny television program is a positive reinforcer. Presenting the program is positive reinforcement. In a trickier situation, the husband who brings candy to his wife to end an argument may later find that his wife argues more frequently. Since receiving candy is a satisfier for his wife and since the candy followed her disagreement with her husband, the law of effect predicts that she will start more arguments to win more favors from her husband. The candy is a positive reinforcer. What the husband should do is wait until she is nice to him again and then present the candy. The teacher who dismisses the class when it is rowdy may increase the amount of rowdy behavior since dismissal is probably a positive reinforcement for the rowdy children. Positive reinforcement is the procedure of presenting stimuli. The stimuli themselves (gold stars, cheers, and candy) are the positive reinforcers.

Many examples illustrate negative reinforcers and negative reinforcement. We close windows and doors to avoid hearing loud noises. The loud noises are the negative reinforcers. Closing the windows and doors is the procedure we employ to eliminate them—the procedure of negative reinforcement. We avoid seeing an ugly sight by turning our faces. We avoid wrong answers by giving right answers. Ugly sights and wrong answers are negative reinforcers. We also turn off television commercials or absent ourselves from the room to avoid hearing them. The commercials are the negative reinforcers. The various means of avoiding them are negative reinforcement. Negative reinforcement is the procedure of terminating stimuli. The stimuli which we try to terminate (noise, commercials, ugly sights, and so on) are the negative reinforcers.

Trans-situational reinforcers. Reinforcers are trans-situational because they strengthen all or most learnable responses in a given species. A reinforcer which is effective in improving spelling will also be effective in improving arithmetic. Money is the best example of a trans-situational reinforcer. In modern urban society, in which we have little opportunity to assess the entering behavior of people we meet for the first time, we often say that "money talks." The amount of money one seems to have and to spend becomes the sole criterion of status and personal worth. In effect, we assign money a wide reinforcing value. To have money (or only to have the appearance of having money) is to carry within one's self trans-situational reinforcement. The fact that reinforcers are trans-situational spares the teacher the problem of finding a new reinforcer for each response. However, the reinforcers which students find rewarding are products of their past histories. Fortunately, students, as heirs of the same culture, have sufficiently common histories to react positively to about the same reinforcers. No matter how often dissident social elements condemn our bourgeois way of life, most of us continue to enjoy money, praise, status, and success.

Reinforcement as feedback. In this procedure the student is given knowledge of his correct responses. Whereas the term *reinforcement* connotes the hedonic aspect of reward, the term *feedback* stresses the informational aspect of the teacher's function. When Harriet spells fat correctly, the teacher may give her gold stars (which may please Harriet no end), but the more important fact is that Harriet knows she has been correct in her spelling. Usually students expect reinforcers for their efforts, whether or not their efforts have paid off. Harriet might believe that she will obtain gold stars if she merely utters whatever letters come to mind. As yet we have no way of separating the reward function from the informational function. Until we devise such a procedure, we cannot dismiss the importance of reinforcement in school learning.

A study by Travers and his associates (1964b) illustrates various ways in which feedback may be provided. Elementary school children had to learn the English equivalents of German words. The German words appeared on flash cards with two English words, and the children were to select the correct English alternative. The experimenters used four feedback procedures: If the child selected the correct alternative, he was told, "That's right"; when he was incorrect, he was told, "No, that's wrong." If the child selected the correct alternative, he was told nothing; if incorrect, he was told, "No, that's wrong." If the child selected the correct alternative, he was told, "That's right"; if incorrect, he was told, "No, that's wrong; [German word] means [English word]." If the child selected the correct alternative he was told nothing; if incorrect, he was told, "No, that's wrong; [German word] means [English word]." The results indicated that the last two procedures were superior to the first two. In interpreting these results, Travers observes that the last two procedures introduced more redundancy into learning the correct English equivalents—that is, the repetition of the English word increased learning.

In an earlier study Keith Van Wagenen and Travers (1963) investigated the importance of the student's making an overt response and being reinforced for it. In the typical classroom situation only one student responds, and the others remain observers. The investigators tried to determine whether the nonparticipating students, the observers, learned as much as the participating students, those who made responses and obtained direct feedback. In more technical language, they compared the effectiveness of direct learning with that of vicarious learning (the learning of the nonparticipants). They designed an ingenious classroom situation which allowed the teacher to interact with some children but not with others. They used the same materials described in the previous experiment, flash cards with German words and English alternatives. The teacher held up a card and said, "John, this word is *baum*." John had to select the correct English alternative. If he said "tree," the teacher said "Right"; if he made a wrong selection, the teacher said nothing. Van Wagenen and Travers found that the children who interacted with the teacher (the direct learning group) learned and retained more of the correct English words than the children who did not interact with the teacher (the vicarious learning group). The experimental procedure allowed the children in the direct learning group to respond only every fourth time because each such group was composed of four children and only one could respond each time. It was possible, therefore, to determine how well the children in the direct learning group retained items on which they interacted with the teacher and how well they retained items on which they did not interact. Figure 7-2a shows that the children learned more items when they actively responded and obtained feedback (the direct learning condition). Figure 7-2b shows how well the vicariously learned items were retained by children who learned one-fourth of the items directly (condition *A*) and by those who learned all the items vicariously (condition *B*). You can see little difference between the two groups. The child in the direct learning group benefited from being there only for those items on which he interacted with the teacher.

Knowledge of the importance of supplying feedback has sparked several technological innovations, including programed instruction and computer-assisted instruction. Although the desirability of supplying feedback is amply supported by research, classroom observation quickl

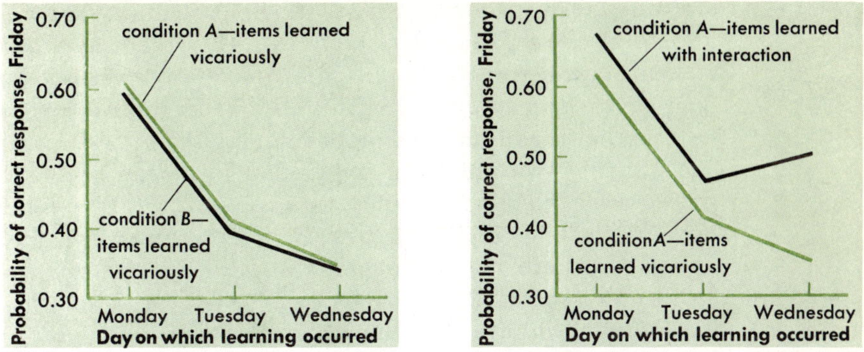

Fig. 7-2a. *Test performance on Friday for direct learning group (after Van Wagenen and Travers, 1963).*

Fig. 7-2b. *Test performance on Friday for vicariously learned items of direct and vicarious learning groups (after Van Wagenen and Travers, 1963).*

reveals the insuperable difficulties the teacher faces in attempting to provide feedback for twenty-five or more students. Patrick Suppes (1964, p. 83) describes the teacher's dilemma:

> Let us suppose . . . that the class consists of only twenty-five children. If the class is working on this particular page [of a workbook containing problems] together, the teacher cannot hope to monitor the 250 problems being done, and, on the spot, have each child make appropriate corrections. Some of the elementary school mathematics teachers with whom I have worked have told me that in order to do a good job in the first and second grade it is necessary to spend at least one hour after each school day correcting the children's workbooks. Some of them have insisted that a more realistic estimate would be two hours. I have watched teachers who have gone through this laborious process of marking each child's work on each problem and requiring him to correct his errors the next day. . . . The impression of teachers who have tried this procedure has been positive, but I cannot cite any controlled data.

uppes believes that technological methods will have to be introduced nto the classroom to provide students with all the overt correction effiient learning requires.

Extinction. In this procedure a reinforcer is withheld to weaken a esponse. In the experimental laboratory, if an animal is not reinforced with food) for pressing a bar which controls a feeding mechanism, the nimal will press the bar somewhat more rapidly at first. Each nonreinforced occurrence, however, decreases the probability of the response. We can expect correct student responses which are not overtly reinforced to weaken or to become extinct. Unfortunately, we do not have the classroom research to support this assumption. In human learning, however, the situation is considerably more complex than it is in animal learning. The student can think he is right—that is, he can reinforce his own response—even when he is wrong. Or his response can be right, and he can think it is wrong. In the absence of reinforcement from the teacher, we cannot be certain that extinction will weaken correct responses, but we can suspect its operation in many cases. The teacher may also use extinction. If being informed of the incorrectness of his response is punishing and upsetting to the student, the teacher may reinforce the student's correct responses and ignore the incorrect responses. Admittedly, the procedure is risky because we do not know how the student will interpret the teacher's silence. Many students believe that no news is good news.

Another way to weaken or to eliminate a response is to make two responses incompatible. A husband who reinforces his wife when she makes life comfortable for him will find a decrease in the frequency of her outrageous demands on him. The husband's compliments presumably become incompatible with the wife's complaints. In the classroom, the teacher reduces the frequency of inattentive behavior by reinforcing the task-related responses of the student. If, however, in the adolescent classroom, the students obtain social reinforcers from their classmates for nonwork behavior, the teacher will find the management of the classroom difficult. The social reinforcers have become incompatible with the teacher's reinforcers. The teacher must control the reinforcers in the classroom in such a way as to make incompatibility of response work in favor of achieving instructional objectives.

Conditions of Reinforcement

Several conditions of reinforcement influence the strength of the response or the adequacy of the performance: (1) the immediacy of the reinforcer, (2) the frequency of the reinforcement, (3) the amount of the reinforcer, and (4) the number of reinforcers.

IMMEDIACY OF THE REINFORCER. Experimental studies show that the reinforcer must almost immediately follow the response if the organism is to associate the response with the stimulus. The delay should usually be no longer than one or two seconds. The case is not so clear in human learning because language can bridge the gap between response and reinforcement. One study actually disclosed that a delay in feedback and reinforcement was related to improved retention (Brackbill, Wagner, and Wilson, 1964). The experimenters required subjects to pair an English word with the correct one of two French words. The experiment used both informational feedback on the correctness of the choice and marbles and toys as rewards for correct responses. Some groups of children received a ten-second delay in feedback; and other groups, no delay. The groups with the delayed feedback retained more of the material after seven days than did the groups with the immediate feedback. This result is clearly inconsistent with the findings for animal learning. It is also possible that further findings may show that younger students require less delay than older students.

Learning cannot occur efficiently without the student's obtaining feedback on the quality of his efforts. The importance of the student's receiving adequate feedback for his responses is not diminished by the uncertainty about how quickly the feedback should be provided. At no level of the educational system from preschool to graduate school is the absence or neglect of feedback pedagogically defensible. Unless the teacher makes systematic plans for feedback before moving on to new materials, he may easily ignore this important condition of learning. This then is a very practical reason for providing immediate feedback.

FREQUENCY OF REINFORCEMENT. In partial reinforcement, the subject is rewarded only a fraction of the time for making responses. Evidence from extensive studies of partial reinforcement in animal learning indicates that responses resist extinction more when they have been reinforced on a partial rather than on a continuous pattern. Pigeons, for example, will continue to peck a disc when only one response in a thousand is rewarded. There have been extensive studies of various reinforcement procedures known as *schedules of reinforcement* (Ferster and Skinner, 1957). In some schedules the organism is reinforced for varying amounts of work or after varying amounts of time. In other schedules the organism is reinforced for fixed amounts of work or after fixed amounts of time. In general, responses on the variable schedules show more resistance to extinction than responses on the fixed schedules.

The applicability of these findings on partial reinforcement to teaching is questionable. The school curriculum, usually so crowded with instructional objectives, hardly leaves time to reinforce responses made even for the first time. It is true that in the natural setting responses we have already acquired are not reinforced each time we make them and yet they persist. In fact, dedication has been defined as the persistence of a response in the absence of reinforcement (Holland and Skinner, 1961). In the school setting, however, the findings on partial reinforcement do not excuse the teacher from reinforcing correct responses when they first occur. How often the teacher should reinforce these responses after they have been acquired is a question we cannot answer now.

AMOUNT AND NUMBER OF REINFORCERS. Response strength increases as the number of reinforcements of that response increases. When a limit is reached however, each successive reinforcement adds smaller and smaller amounts of response strength. Since these limits hold in animal learning, we have every reason (and yet little supporting data) to believe that they hold and are reached sooner in human learning. The tedium often reported by students who have used teaching machines and programed materials is the result of more reinforcement of correct responses than they believe necessary. The amount of the reinforcer also affects behavior. In one study (Wolfe and Kaplan, 1941), a chicken ran faster to get four quarter-grains of corn than to get one whole grain, suggesting that the additional activity involved in consuming the four quarter-grains contributed something to the reward value. The applicability of this finding to teaching is uncertain, although it may puritanically suggest that our students will not appreciate what they learn unless we require them to expend the maximum effort.

SUMMARY. We have now considered the nature and the conditions of reinforcement. Discussing first the nature of reinforcement, I explained that reinforcers can be introduced before or after the desired response, can be positive or negative, and are trans-situational. As feedback, reinforcement is the procedure in which the student is given knowledge of his correct responses. Available evidence indicates that active responding combined with direct feedback is superior to passive responding with indirect feedback. Finally, I described extinction as a procedure in which a reinforcer is withheld to weaken a response or in which two responses are made incompatible. I next considered the conditions of reinforcement. Here I discussed the practical importance of immediate feedback, the efficacy of partial reinforcement, and the relationship of the amount and the number of reinforcers to student effort.

As a basic learning condition, reinforcement is important in most learning. In the form of the conditioned stimulus, it has major importance in classical conditioning. As the reinforcing stimulus, it has major importance in operant conditioning. As both kinesthetic and informational feedback, it plays a crucial role in skill learning. As feedback for the correct discriminations the student makes between examples and nonexamples of a concept, it is important in concept learning. As feedback for the correct interrelating of concepts and principles, it is important in principle learning. It may be least important in problem solving since the correct solution generates its own feedback. In fact we may conclude that the importance of reinforcement diminishes somewhat in the three higher learning types since successful learning at these levels generates its own feedback. The student, in other words, when he undertakes some complex learning, knows the correct form of the class, relationship, or solution he seeks. Indeed, he achieves a large measure of scholarly independence when he knows what tests to apply to assess the adequacy of his own performance.

We can now turn to our last two conditions, or basic phenomena, of learning, what we shall call generalization and discrimination.

Generalization

Both generalization and discrimination are perhaps better defined as phenomena than as conditions of learning. They more properly refer to behavior which occurs under particular learning conditions than to the conditions themselves. I have taken the liberty of calling them learning conditions because they are so closely associated with the basic conditions of contiguity, practice, and reinforcement and because they are basic to all learning. Many learning and educational psychologists prefer to describe even complex learning in terms of stimulus generalization and discrimination (see Glaser, 1962, Staats and Staats, 1963). Whatever your preference, it does appear that we can better understand all learning by understanding generalization and discrimination.

Frequently we observe that a child, when confronted with a new stimulus, makes a response he had previously learned to make to another stimulus. We call this behavior *generalization* (or stimulus generalization). When a child is told to call a particular color red, he is also learning to call other similar hues red. The child, however, does not make the same response to blue and yellow. When children learn not only that they have fathers but also that there are fathers of other children, fathers of fathers (or grandfathers), fathers of countries, fathers of inventions, and even fathers of various kinds of psychology, these children are generalizing. When Harriet discovers the similarity between hat, sat, fat, and cat, she recognizes other three-letter words ending in *at*. Harriet is generalizing. If we could not generalize, we would have to learn discrete responses for each discrete stimulus, and our behavior would appear to be something less than human.

Generalization gradients (curves) show that the tendency to generalize increases with the similarity of the new stimuli to the training stimuli. Figure 7-3 shows one such gradient. Experimenters trained pigeons to peck a disc illuminated with a green light. After they learned to peck at the green light, the experimenter gradually changed the color of the disc. In Fig. 7-3, the arrow and the letters *CS* (for conditioned stimulus) indicate the green light. The closer the hues are to green, the greater the frequency of pecking responses. Pigeons apparently see similarities among colors in much the same way as humans do.

Generalization is an important aspect of human behavior—either appropriate or inappropriate. Our social stereotypes result from generalization. Some conservative individuals see a Communist in every reformer. They see groups and individuals who favor the legalization of abortion, the abolition of nuclear warfare, the liberalization of the

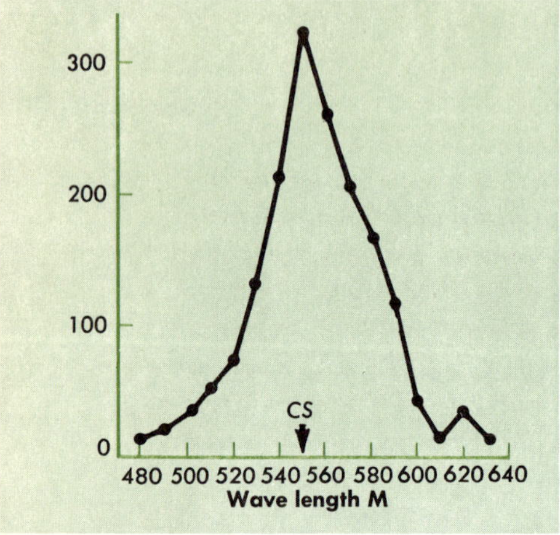

Fig. 7-3. *A generalization gradient obtained from pigeons. The CS was a greenish light. The pigeon was tested to lights ranging from blue to red. Unpublished data, Norman Guttman and Harry I. Kalish (after Kimble and Garmezy, 1963, p. 145).*

divorce laws, the spread of information on birth control, and the preservation of wild life as either dupes of or conscious participants in the vast international Communist conspiracy. Similarly, others see as hopelessly middle class those individuals who uphold the value of duty; honor; obedience; self-denial in food, drink, and sex; hard work; and material success. Even our fear responses generalize. Although we feel pain (the prick of the needle with the anesthesia) for only a few moments in having a cavity filled, we generalize our fear responses to the dentist's waiting room (where we sit in our own perspiration), to his pretty and courteous receptionist, to the antiseptic smells of the inner offices, to all the implements lying on the tables, to the dental chair, and to white coats. Even the white coat of a waiter or a barber can conjure up memories of painful experiences at the hands of the dentist. Each of these examples illustrates what we commonly call *overgeneralization.*

Discrimination

In discrimination behavior the individual makes different responses to two or more stimuli. A child, for example, can learn to select the color red and not to select pink. To the extent that he learns to pick red and to ignore pink, he has learned to discriminate. Lewis Lipsit (1961) studied discrimination learning of fourth grade children. The experimental apparatus included three windows with five different colored bulbs behind them. The children could press one of three buttons. If they pressed the correct button, the window light went out and a signal light went on. Incorrect response merely turned out the stimulus lights. Under one of the experimental conditions, the children were presented with the colors red, pink, and blue. Response to one of the buttons under these colors was rewarded (the signal light went on). Responses to the other two buttons were unrewarded (all the lights went out and no signal light went on). These children had to discriminate the right button from the wrong buttons. In terms of our definition of discrimination, the children were learning to make different responses to two or more stimuli.

As we become more discriminating, the environment exercises more control over our behavior. If the child learns to add when he sees a plus sign and to subtract when he sees a minus sign, these two signs (stimuli) exercise control over his behavior. When Hortense enters the Museum of Modern Art and is able to distinguish a painting by Picasso from one by Matisse and to point out to her companions the distinguishing characteristics, the stimuli of the paintings are controlling Hortense's behavior. When we ask a student to distinguish between two breeds of dogs and he correctly calls one a German Shepherd and the other a Collie, he can discriminate between these two breeds.

A useful way to describe discrimination learning is by the designations S^D and S^Δ. An S^D (ess-dee) is a discriminative stimulus—the occasion on which the response is reinforced. It is the go signal, like the green traffic light. In the S^Δ (ess-delta) situation, the response is not reinforced. It is the stop signal, like the red traffic light. We may visualize our behavior as being under the alternate control of S^Ds and S^Δs. Clarence likes Molly and always wants to be with her or at least to talk with her on the phone. He dials her number (S^D), and Molly answers (her voice is his reinforcer). He asks her for a date (S^D), and Molly accepts (more reinforcement). He continues to talk about the latest social scandals of the campus. Molly tells him that she is busy preparing for her midterm examinations (her mild complaint is an S^Δ). Clarence goes on to ask Molly what she thinks of the latest rock-and-roll group to appear on campus. He receives no response (another S^Δ). With a slight tenseness in his voice, he asks Molly if she is serious about the date they have made (an S^D, but if he is not careful it could become an S^Δ). In a rather formal manner, she confirms her acceptance. Then she repeats that she is very busy (an S^Δ). This time Clarence notes the nature of the stimulus, and, with heart palpitating and the knowledge that a little love is better than none, he says good-bye (a possible S^Δ for Molly). Molly replies good-bye (a final S^Δ for Clarence).

It is also possible but not very useful for the teacher to analyze his teaching materials as patterns of S^Ds and S^Δs. We can, for example, analyze the print signals we have learned to use in reading in terms of these two stimuli. The new chapter headings, the paragraph indentations, the boldface type, and the capital letters at the beginning of sentences essentially represent go signals or S^Ds. The periods, the commas, and the ends of chapters and paragraphs represent stop signals or S^Δs.

It is more useful for the teacher to realize that teaching materials and methods provide stimuli (S^Ds) to which the students should respond and stimuli (S^Δs) to which the students should not respond. The teacher provides both types to develop the proper discriminations. When Daisy sees a plus sign (an S^D), she knows that she adds the adjacent numbers. When she sees a minus sign, she does not add the numbers if her directions are to add and not to subtract. In this instance the minus sign is an S^Δ. When teaching children the names of the capitals of the various states, we often find that the largest cities in those states are S^Δs. New York, Los Angeles, and Chicago are incorrect responses to the question on capitals, while Albany, Sacramento, and Springfield are correct responses. The students eventually learn to discriminate between the stimuli *capital* and *largest city.* In teaching you the distinction between a positive and a negative reinforcer, I tried to supply S^Ds. The S^D for the positive reinforcer was the verb (and its equivalents) *present.* A positive reinforcer is a stimulus which is presented. The S^D for the negative reinforcer was the verb (and its equivalents) *terminate.* A negative reinforcer is a stimulus which is removed or terminated. In making this distinction, we make each verb an S^Δ for the opposite reinforcer, so that the word *present* is an S^Δ for the response *negative reinforcer.* These examples suggest the very fine-grain analysis of instructional procedures and materials the use of S^Ds and S^Δs makes possible. In our later discussion of programed instruction, we shall see the extensive use of these two stimuli.

Just as one can overgeneralize, so can one overdiscriminate. Making correct, even subtle, discriminations can be the mark of the scholar or the pedant, the gentleman or the dandy. The distinction in either case is sometimes difficult to make; it may depend on how useful the discriminations made prove to be. Sometimes old ideas parade under new names which add very little if anything in meaning. In psychological jargon we can refer mysteriously to high libidinal erotic tendencies combined with low superego resistance when we mean nothing more than sex without guilt (a very old idea). The need for love becomes the need for nurturance, and the need to give love becomes the need for succorance. If the new terms add anything to the description of human behavior, individuals rarely agree on exactly what it is. Similarly, in the interests of courtesy to and comfort for one's guests, one should supply ample silverware for each place setting. When, however, the hostess supplies each guest with so many implements of silver that good taste becomes massive confusion, we have a case of overdiscrimination. A ring and cuff links are proper gentlemanly attire, but the dandy may include an array of jewelry, hair lacquers, ascots, and colognes which betray more than the usual discriminations in male adornment.

Travers (1963, p. 123) refers to the tendency in the classroom to stress discrimination and to suppress generalization. He states that "many teachers will mark unusual metaphors and figures of speech as 'unclear' and will suppress generalization in the literary field. Despite the efforts to the contrary on the part of many school officials, the prosaic development of precise discriminations generally takes precedence as an objective over free, creative, and often undisciplined expression." The current emphasis on learning the basic structure of various subject matter and on creative thinking may often overlook the fact that generalizations must derive from the discriminations the student has learned. Both the scholar and the college sophomore, an aspiring scholar, generalize about literature, science, history, and human behavior, yet we have little difficulty in distinguishing the two products. The discriminatory accuracy of the scholar, although sometimes labored and over disciplined, is quite distinct from the broad and sometimes fortuitously brilliant strokes of the sophomore. For purposes of motivation, however, but not necessarily for the acquisition of knowledge, we perhaps should allow the student his private avenues in the pursuit of some instructional objectives.

Summary

The discussion of generalization and discrimination concludes the section on basic learning conditions and phenomena. I have postponed the discussion of other important learning phenomena, particularly retention and transfer, until we reach the description of the learning types with which they are most closely associated. In this section we have described contiguity, practice, reinforcement (both its nature and conditions), generalization, and discrimination. Contiguity, the almost simultaneous occurrence of stimulus and response, appears to be an important condition for most learning. Practice, the repetition of a response in the presence of the stimulus, diminishes in importance as we move up the hierarchy to complex learning. Reinforcement, as a procedure for introducing a stimulus or feedback, varies in importance in accordance with the nature of the reinforcer (as in the case of reward or information) and the conditions of reinforcement, as well as with the learning type. As an external condition of learning, it may diminish in importance as the student learns to generate his own reinforcers. Generalization and discrimination, as basic learning phenomena, can explain both simple and complex learning. In the description which follows of the two basic learning types, you will see generalization and discrimination at work. It is equally possible, and in the opinion of many educational and experimental psychologists entirely legitimate, to explain skill, verbal, concept, and principle learning in terms of generalization and discrimination. Whether such explanations are intellectual *tours de force* or the basis of distinctions useful for the teacher remains to be seen.

In the remainder of Part 3 I shall frequently refer to these basic learning conditions. As we discuss each learning type, we shall consider what conditions the teacher must arrange to facilitate the learning embodied in his instructional objectives. Since these conditions represent classes of external stimulus situations, you will see that they can be provided in many different ways. The third section of this chapter considers the first two learning types, classical and operant conditioning.

You should now return to objectives 4–16 (p. 242) and determine how well you have achieved them.

QUESTION 7-2

Mr. Dromboski, in teaching the concept *dog* to children in the second grade, adopted this procedure. He used a series of pictures, exposing a pair of pictures each time. One picture always showed a dog. The other showed another animal, such as a fox, wolf, or coyote. Which of the following best describes Mr. Dromboski's procedure? (a) Reinforcement; (b) discrimination; (c) practice; (d) generalization.

After selecting your answer, give the reasons for your choice and for your rejection of the alternatives.

TWO BASIC LEARNING TYPES

The two basic learning types are classical and operant conditioning. They stand in the same relationship to complex learning as the electron and atom do to complex molecules. Because human learning is most frequently complex learning, we have difficulty finding pure examples of classical and operant conditioning. By understanding these simple learning types, however, we can easily observe how the conditions of learning relate to complex learning. Furthermore, familiarity with basic learning gives us the vocabulary we need to analyze complex learning in terms of the conditions and components the teacher can manipulate. Undoubtedly you will ask, as every student legitimately asks, "What does classical and operant conditioning tell me about how to teach?" Perhaps the most honest answer is that they tell you little. They do, however, make their contribution to understanding the complex learning I shall describe in the ensuing chapters, and this learning has direct relevance to instruction.

In this section we shall look first at classical conditioning and then at operant conditioning. You will see that they are chiefly distinguished by the conditions under which they occur.

Classical Conditioning

The necessary entering behavior for classical conditioning is the unconditioned reflex—an inborn response to stimuli. It is unconditioned in the sense that it is unlearned. Many examples illustrate unconditioned reflexes in animals and humans: salivating of the dog at the sight of food, blinking of the eye in response to a puff of air, jerking of the knee in response to a tap below the knee, being nauseous in response to various noxious stimuli, being frightened and startled in response to loud noises, and so on. In human behavior, many of our emotional responses are the result of classical conditioning.

Pavlov exhaustively observed and measured the two external learning conditions necessary for this learning—contiguity and practice. The almost simultaneous presentation of two stimuli provides contiguity. One stimulus is called the *unconditioned stimulus,* and the other, the *conditioned stimulus.* In the familiar example of Pavlov's dogs, the dogs salivated at the sight of food. The food is the unconditioned stimulus. The conditioned stimulus could be any number of events. Pavlov used the ringing of a bell, the sounding of a tuning fork, or the flashing of a light. Originally each of these events is a neutral stimulus. It becomes a conditioned stimulus when it is paired with the unconditioned stimulus (food). In the typical classical-conditioning procedure the conditioned stimulus (e.g., the ringing of a bell) precedes the unconditioned stimulus (e.g., the food) by about one-half second, a very brief interval.

The second external learning condition is practice. The pairing of the unconditioned (the food) and the conditioned (the bell) stimuli must be repeated. The amount of practice necessary depends on how strong the response to the unconditioned stimulus is. In any case the response to the conditioned stimulus (salivation in response to the ringing of the bell) becomes stronger with the number of pairings of food and bell. The result of the procedure, of course, is that the dog will salivate in response to the bell even in the absence of the food. Diagramatically, the procedure is this:

Bell (conditioned stimulus) . . . . Salivation
Food (unconditioned stimulus) . . . . Salivation

When the dog's response (salivation) is made to the bell, the response is called a *conditioned response.*

A favorite conditioning experiment involves the eye blink. When a puff of air reaches the pupil of the eye, the eye blinks. This is an unconditioned reflex—an inborn and not a learned behavior. In one variation of the procedure, a clicking noise is presented just one-half second before the air puff reaches the eye. This procedure satisfies the condition of contiguity. Repeated a number of times the air puff and the click meet the condition of practice. The air puff is the unconditioned stimulus, and the click is the conditioned stimulus. When the eye blink occurs in response to the click, the eye blink is the conditioned response.

To avoid oversimplification we should note that the conditioned blink (or response) is not the same as the unconditioned blink (or response). The unconditioned blink is a more rapid response and occurs in about one-fifth the time of the conditioned blink. We may learn an *anticipatory* blink, which occurs before the puff of air reaches the eye. Gagné (1965, pp. 61–63) refers to classical conditioning as *signal learning* because, in the example of the eye blink, the conditioned blink anticipates the puff of air—it signals a puff of air to come. In other conditioned responses, both the rapidity and the magnitude differ from those of the unconditioned response. The dog's salivation is less in amount when the response is conditioned rather than unconditioned.

In human learning, as I indicated above, it is difficult to find pure examples of classical conditioning. We learn to respond to signals, bells, buzzers, alarms, signs, and warnings through classical conditioning. Emotional responses, made originally to unconditioned stimuli, are often made to conditioned stimuli. Experiments show that the specific fears of children and adults are the result of classical conditioning (Dollard and Miller, 1950). The fear of water, for example, may be the result of falling into water and being temporarily submerged. The unconditioned fear of drowning becomes the conditioned fear of water.

Operant Conditioning

A somewhat more complicated learning type is called *operant conditioning,* or trial-and-error learning (a misleading label), or instrumental learning. The necessary entering behavior is the availability to the organism of particular responses. A pigeon must be able to peck a rat to press a bar or lever, a human being to smile or scratch his head These responses are called *operants* because they operate on the environment. When the pigeon pecks a disc, the rat presses a bar, or you scratch your head, you have changed the state of the environment by your response or operant. The objective of operant-conditioning procedure is simply to increase the frequency of the response—to have more pecking, pressing, and scratching. If Margaret never smiled, you could no increase the frequency of her smiles. If she smiled only once, you have a chance. If you can get your girl to kiss you once, with operant conditioning you may be able to increase the frequency of her kisses. But there must be the first time.

Three external learning conditions must be provided in operant conditioning: reinforcement, contiguity, and practice. Fred Keller (1954, p. 6) gives this illustration of the conditions for this learning:

> This time our subject is a little girl, about seventeen months old, and the experimental situation is an ordinary living room, modified slightly to serve a laboratory purpose. Our observations begin as the little girl runs into the living room from the hallway and attempts to engage the attention of her mother, who sits by the window reading. Failing in her efforts, the child turns away. As her eyes wander over the room, they suddenly alight upon a new feature. Through a narrow gap between the sliding doors to the dining room, a small T-shaped handle projects itself. Just beneath the handle is a tin dish, easily within the child's reach. Approaching these objects quickly, but warily, the child touches the handle with her finger, and looks into the dish. As she does so, a small pellet of chocolate drops into the dish from a tube, the other end of which is out of sight in the dining room. Startled by this, the little girl momentarily withdraws from the dish, but returns to pick up the pellet and eat it. A few seconds later, she grasps the bar firmly and pulls it downward an inch or so, causing a second pellet to be discharged into the dish. From this time on, with rapidly growing efficiency, she operates this lever mechanism, eating each pellet as it comes, until the chocolate finally loses its appeal.

This description illustrates each of the external conditions of learning. First, the chocolate pellets are reinforcement, or, in Thorndike's terms, a satisfier. Second, contiguity is provided when the reinforcer is presented almost without delay once the girl responds by pulling the bar downward. Third, practice is provided since the girl pulls the bar several more times and is reinforced each time. The practice enables the girl to isolate the particular act which results in the reinforcement.

Operant conditioning is a more complex learning type than is classical conditioning, and we more easily find illustrations of it in human behavior. Gagné (1965c, p. 84) suggests these examples in the behavior of children: reaching and grasping for toys or other objects, smiling at particular people, posturing the body and limbs, vocalizing particular sounds and words. In adult learning, the pronunciation of unfamiliar foreign words is an instance of operant conditioning. Once the correct pronunciation is made (the operant), the correct response must be reinforced, the response and the reinforcement must be contiguous, and the response must be practiced under these conditions.

Diagrammatically, the procedure for operant conditioning is this:

R (pulling the handle) . . . . *S* (chocolate pellets)

In a later section of the book, when we discuss programed instruction, you will see how manipulating the reinforcement procedure allows us to produce varied and complicated responses, as in animal training acts. You will see, however, that in shaping a response we must still observe all conditions for operant conditioning.

Differences in Classical and Operant Conditioning

Gregory Kimble and Norman Garmezy (1963, p. 139) use these examples in comparing the two learning types. Example *A:* A dog is conditioned to lift his paw when he hears a bell. The bell is paired with an electric shock delivered to the dog by an electrode attached to its paw. Example *B:* The dog is trained to lift his paw at the sound of a bell. Again there is a shock to his paw, but the shock comes from a grill upon which the animal is standing. By lifting his paw the animal can avoid the shock. The first example illustrates classical conditioning. The second example, operant conditioning. In classical conditioning the bell and the shock are paired on every trial. In operant conditioning the dog can avoid the shock by lifting his paw. The difference then is in the reinforcement procedure: In classical conditioning the reinforcer (the unconditioned stimulus) occurs on every trial. In operant conditioning the reinforcer occurs only when the animal makes the correct response. In more precise language, we say that in operant conditioning the reinforcer is contingent (depends) upon the animal making the correct response. Whereas in classical conditioning the presentation of the reinforcer determines the response, in operant conditioning the response determines the presentation of the reinforcer.

You should now return to objectives 17–19 (p. 243) and determine how well you have achieved them.

QUESTION 7-3

> Mr. I. M. Sternski has devised a disciplinary technique which he claims is very effective. Whenever a student breaks a classroom rule, a light flashes near the student's desk and he receives a relatively mild electric shock. On other occasions Mr. Sternski merely flashes the light without delivering a shock to the student. Which of the following best describes Mr. Sternski's technique: (a) classical conditioning; (b) operant conditioning; (c) both; (d) neither.
>
> After selecting your answer, give reasons for your choice and for your rejection of the alternatives.

LEARNING CONDITIONS AND INSTRUCTIONAL PROCEDURES

In this final section of the chapter we shall explore the relationship of external learning conditions to instructional procedures—methods of arranging the learning conditions in ways appropriate for the learning required by the instructional objectives. In contrast to internal learning conditions, which are the student's entering behavior, external conditions are the stimulus situation the teacher arranges. The proper confluence of entering behavior and external conditions enables the student to achieve the instructional objectives.

The learning conditions described in this chapter are classes of conditions and learning phenomena. Particular instances of contiguity, practice, reinforcement, and so on exhibit both similarities and differences. Consider, for example, contiguity. In skill learning, this condition is met when adjacent *S-R* links occur at the proper time and in the proper order. In concept learning, the condition of contiguity is met when examples of the concept are presented simultaneously or in serial order. In principle learning, contiguity occurs in the recall of component concepts and principles. Your task as a teacher is to provide the necessary conditions in both practical and effective ways. The remaining chapters in Part 3 tell you how to make these provisions.

Can the basic learning types—classical and operant conditioning—also be translated into practical teaching procedures? We have the following, somewhat primitive examples. Mr. D. Termand wants the class to learn to come to attention when he assumes a typical teaching position behind his lectern. At first the students do not respond to this stimulus. Mr. D. Termand, lonely and ignored behind his lectern, is a neutral stimulus. He can become a conditioned stimulus by slamming his gavel against the lectern to make an impressively loud and disturbing noise. Our responses to very loud noises are largely unconditioned reflexes. One response is to attend at once to the loud noise. So, to produce a change in behavior from no attention to attention, Mr. Termand gets behind the lectern and within one-half second begins beating the gavel against the lectern. By pairing the noise of the gavel with his position behind the lectern, he provides contiguity of conditioned and unconditioned stimuli. By repeating this procedure for several days, he provides practice. Soon, either light taps of the gavel or the assumption of his pedagogical posture behind the lectern commands the students' instant attention.

The teacher also may analyze teaching materials in terms of unconditioned and conditioned stimuli. For example, before you read the section on reinforcement, you knew the meaning of the word *reward.* I could have defined learning as the result of rewarded practice (I did not do so for particular reasons). In this case, your response to the term reward would be unconditioned (you would not have been learning anything new about the word). However, by defining learning as the result of reinforced practice, I expected you to substitute *reinforcer* for *reward* and to realize that reward has a much broader meaning than does reinforcer, which refers to a particular procedure. If I gave you the statement: Learning is the result of ______ practice, eventually I would want you to respond "reinforced." When you did so, the statement would be a conditioned stimulus and your response a conditioned response. Much teaching involves substitute learning—substituting a foreign word for an English word, a more rigorous procedure for a less rigorous procedure, a technical term for a lay term, and so on. In planning your instruction you should analyze your materials and procedures in terms of unconditioned (previously learned) and conditioned (to be learned) stimuli. As in the case of discrimination learning, such a procedure provides a fine-grain analysis and organization of your materials and procedures. Such an analysis and such a construction of instructional materials were originally employed in programed instruction (see Chapter 12). The program frame was the stimulus, the student's response to the frame was the response, and the confirmation of the response was the reinforcement or feedback. Using this conception of the learning event, one could construct a series of frames and eventually a program. Many programers today continue to design programs in terms of basic phenomena of learning and, for example, refer to frames as representing generalization and discrimination sequences (Taber *et al.,* 1965, pp. 117–21).

We can now return to the original question about translating classical and operant conditioning into practical teaching procedures. The fact is that these translations or adaptations can be made, informally by the classroom teacher and formally by the educational researcher, with an important qualification: As teachers we should use classical and operant conditioning models only when our instructional objectives indicate that those learning types are required. The purpose of task analysis, you will recall, is to classify instructional objectives under various learning types. Most (but surely not all) instructional objectives of the school involve more complex learning than classical and operant conditioning and thus also require different learning conditions. There is no practical virtue, on the one hand, in reducing complex human learning to its most basic elements or, on the other hand, in conceiving of the simplest learning in terms of complex interrelationships, when by a more precise analysis of our instructional objectives, we can distinguish several learning types, ranging from simple to complex, and can determine the appropriate learning conditions for each.

You should now return to objectives 20–22 (p. 243) and determine how well you have achieved them.

SUMMARY

Part 3 considers the third component of the basic teaching model, instructional procedures. Each chapter in this part describes the procedures for providing instruction for the various learning types. The present chapter, for example, described the procedures for classical and operant conditioning. Future chapters are devoted to skill learning, language learning, concept learning, principle learning, and problem solving. The present chapter also introduced you to the basic external learning conditions—those conditions outside the student in what is called the stimulus situation. Internal learning conditions are the student's entering behavior, the subject matter of Part 2 and the recurrent material of Part 3.

The first section defined learning and the learning event. It distinguished learning from performance and from maturation, native response tendencies, fatigue, habituation, and drug effects. The second section described the external conditions of learning: Contiguity is the almost simultaneous occurrence of the stimulus and response. Practice is the repetition of the response in the presence of the stimulus. In the third condition, reinforcement, the organism is presented with a particular stimulus before or after it makes a response. Contiguity, practice, and reinforcement are classes of events. Particular instances of these conditions vary with the learning they are designed to produce. In school learning, for example, reinforcement is often a procedure for supplying the student feedback on the correctness of his responses. Extinction is a procedure of withholding a reinforcer to weaken a response or of making one response incompatible with another. This section also described two phenomena of learning: In generalization a response made to a new stimulus is one previously made to another stimulus. In discrimination, the individual makes a different response to two or more stimuli. Both generalization and discrimination are basic learning phenomena and have been employed in describing complex human learning.

The third section described two basic learning types. Both classical and operant conditioning involve all the basic learning conditions and phenomena I have described. The reinforcement procedure distinguishes them. In classical conditioning the reinforcer occurs on every trial, while in operant conditioning the reinforcer occurs only when the organism makes the correct response. Although many daily examples illustrate both, they are not the learning usually required by the instructional objectives of the school. Their major practical importance is their contribution to our understanding of complex human learning.

The final section of the chapter defined the relationship between learning conditions and instructional procedures. Instructional procedures are methods of arranging the conditions of learning in ways appropriate for the learning required by the instructional objectives. Since the basic learning conditions are really classes of conditions, we must tailor them to the learning they are to produce. We can use classical and operant conditioning, as basic learning types, for fine-grain analysis of instructional procedures and materials. They have been used in the construction of programed instruction. It is unwise, however, to reduce all forms of learning to these basic types when we can distinguish other learning which requires different internal and external learning conditions.

SUGGESTED READINGS

Several very important volumes on the psychology of learning, in hard-cover and paperback editions, will help the serious student to find out about the research in this area:

Hilgard, Ernest R. and Gordon H. Bower, *Theories of Learning* (3rd ed.). New York: Appleton-Century-Crofts, 1966.

Kimble, Gregory A., *Hilgard and Marquis' Conditioning and Learning.* New York: Appleton-Century-Crofts, 1961.

Pavlov, I. P., *Conditioned Reflexes: An Investigation of the Physiological Activity of the Cerebral Cortex,* trans. and ed. G. V. Anrep. London: Oxford University Press, 1927.

Skinner, B. F., *Science and Human Behavior.* New York: The Free Press of Glencoe, 1953.

Several volumes on learning were especially written for teachers, trainers, and other educators. These are among the leading volumes:

Gagné, Robert M., *The Conditions of Learning.* New York: Holt, Rinehart & Winston, Inc., 1965.

Hill, Winfred F., *Learning: A Survey of Psychological Interpretations.* San Francisco: Chandler Publishing Co., 1963.

Travers, John F., *Learning: Analysis and Application.* New York: David McKay Co., Inc., 1965.

Travers, Robert M., *Essentials of Learning: An Overview for Students of Education.* New York: The Macmillan Company, 1963.

The following are general introductory texts on learning; some are programed:

Geis, George L., William C. Stebbins, and Robert W. Lundin, *Reflex and Operant Conditioning.* New York: Basic Systems, Inc., 1965. A programed textbook.

Holland, James G. and B. F. Skinner, *The Analysis of Behavior.* New York: McGraw-Hill Book Company, 1961. A programed textbook.

Mednick, Sarnoff A., *Learning.* Englewood Cliffs, N.J.: Prentice-Hall, Inc., 1964.

The following books discuss types or categories of learning and the problems associated with the classification of learning:

Gagné, Robert M., *The Conditions of Learning.* New York: Holt, Rinehart & Winston, Inc., 1965.

Melton, Arthur W., ed., *Categories of Human Learning.* New York: Academic Press Inc., 1964.

These books of readings emphasize the psychology of learning:

De Cecco, John P., ed., *Human Learning in the School.* New York: Holt Rinehart & Winston, Inc., 1963.

Harris, Theodore L. and Wilson E. Schwahn, eds., *The Learning Process.* New York: Oxford University Press, Inc., 1961.

Staats, Arthur W., ed., *Human Learning.* New York: Holt, Rinehart & Winston, Inc., 1964.

The Teaching and Learning of Skills

8

'his chapter continues our consideration of the third component of ıe basic teaching model. In the first chapter in this section you learned ɔout basic learning conditions and about two basic learning types. In ıis chapter you will learn about a more complex type of learning—the :quisition of skills. The chapter, as you will discover, concerns motor ills as distinct from verbal skills, which we consider in Chapter 9. For asons which will become apparent later, however, I have avoided the e of the term *motor skills* in the title of this chapter. In the discuson which follows you will see how the simpler learning types and basic arning conditions contribute to the learning of skilled behavior.

The organization of this chapter is briefly as follows. In the first the three major parts, you will learn what a skill is and how we acıire skills. In the second part, you will learn about the physical abilis which make it possible for us to learn a skill. Finally, in the third rt, you will learn how to teach your students a skill. As in the previous apters, we derive the instructional functions from basic theory and earch on skill learning.

Upon reading the first part of this chapter (on the definition of lls and the nature of skill learning), you should be able to meet these jectives:

1. Describe the two trends in skilled activity in the 1960s by reing both to the nature of the activity and to the change in research phasis and illustrate these trends, using contemporary skills.

2. Describe the three characteristics of skilled activity in terms of chains, coordination, and response patterns and illustrate these characteristics, using a skill you will teach.

3. Define constancies in terms of behavior patterns and list the three ways in which we classify *S-R* chains.

4. Describe the three phases of skill learning in terms of their distinguishing characteristics and illustrate these phases, using a skill you plan to teach.

5. Describe the two aspects of contiguity important in skill learn ing and their relationship to whole and part-whole methods; illustrate how you would provide contiguity in a skill you plan to teach.

6. Describe three ways in which practice is important in skill learn ing and distinguish between distributed and massed practice and thei advantages; illustrate how you would provide for practice in teachin your skill.

7. Distinguish between the two types and modes of feedback an provide illustrations of each; describe the effects of withholding an delaying feedback and provide an illustration of the effects of both pro cedures; define feedback as prompting and give an illustration of thi procedure; describe the relationship of the two modes and the two type of feedback to stages of skill learning and provide illustrations of th relationship.

Upon reading the second section of this chapter (on psychomoto abilities), you should be able to meet these objectives:

8. Indicate two ways in which entering behavior for skill learnin can be described and give one illustration of each way.

9. Distinguish psychomotor abilities and skills and illustrate you distinction.

10. Distinguish the physical proficiency abilities from the notion general physical ability by referring to the various areas of the forme define physical abilities in terms of hierarchical structures.

11. Distinguish the manipulative-proficiency abilities from the n tion of general manual dexterity by referring to particular manipulati abilities.

12. Describe the relationship between psychomotor abilities a learning in terms of early and late stages of learning and illustrate h you would use your knowledge of this relationship for task analysis a for assessing entering behavior.

Upon reading the third section of this chapter (on instruction skills), you should be able to meet these objectives:

13. List the four categories you can use in analyzing a skill; indicate how skills can be analyzed as *S-R* units; provide an illustration of both methods (using the categories and the *S-R* units). (Step 1.)

14. Describe the three ways in which entering behavior can be assessed and illustrate your use of one of these ways. (Step 2.)

15. Describe the two purposes for arranging preinstruction for skill components and illustrate how you would do this. (Step 3.)

16. Describe the various ways in which skills may be presented and demonstrated and describe and illustrate the conditions under which each way can be best employed. (Step 4.)

17. Describe the various methods for providing for contiguity, practice, and feedback and indicate the basis for choosing each particular method; illustrate how you would provide for each of these basic learning conditions in a skill you will teach. (Step 5.)

THE NATURE OF SKILL LEARNING

The Study of Skills

Research in the field of skills lacks a pioneer who had a high de-ree of creativity, engaged in a wide variety of studies, and promulgated trong opinions which his followers could accept as dogma (Irion, 1966). No one, for example, has the stature of Ebbinghaus, Freud, Cattell, Binet, Thorndike, Hull, or Skinner. Arthur Irion (1966) suggests that he history of research on motor skills is largely the history of experi-nental psychology. Irion also suggests that the absence of dogma may ave had beneficial effects since attention could center on research prob-ems rather than ideological debates. An unfortunate effect of the ab-ence of any great luminary figure and of a loudly trumpeted theoretical redo has been that research on motor-skill learning in the school setting increasingly difficult to find. Although the field lacks any great pio-eer, A. T. Welford (1962) suggests that the scientific study of human ill began with Bessel, an astronomer, who, during the 1820s, studied ne reaction times of himself and his colleagues to find out how they ffered in their observations of star-transit times. But surely Bessel ever intended to be the father of research on skill learning.

In the twentieth century we have seen a remarkable change in the ecific skills which we learn. The change is largely the result of tech-ological innovations and the earnest pursuit of leisure-time activities. echnology has introduced new machinery into the armed forces and dustry at an increasingly rapid rate. We are now witnessing the rapid troduction of machinery into the home and the school. The use of is machinery requires the skills to build, install, repair, and properly operate it. Most of us feel that we do quite well if we learn only to operate the new gadgets with which industry either enriches or clutters our lives. We are indeed confronted with an impressive array of tape recorders, stereo–high-fidelity sets, dishwashers, sewing machines, musical instruments, duplicating machines, airplanes, automobiles and motorcycles, still and movie cameras, and slide projectors which promise to keep our lives busy and which require the learning of new skills. As new skills are introduced, old ones are retired; some of us painfully learned manual gear shifting only to have it replaced with automatic transmission. With the growth of leisure time we have turned with new zest to athletic and social activities, from the relatively uncomplicated bowling and badminton to the totally consuming golf and tennis. To swimming we have added water skiing, scuba diving, and even surfing. The composing of, rendering of, and dancing to rock-and-roll music have become increasingly innovative if not always recognizably skillful. In our less social moments we (at least collectively) spend more time reading and writing than we once did.

These changes in human skills in modern society represent two major trends: a shift in emphasis from motor skills, performed while standing or in motion, to sedentary skills, and in research a shift in emphasis from skill learning and training in the armed forces to those in industry. Regarding the first trend, Paul Fitts (1962, pp. 77–78) notes the tendency today for skilled work to be done while the individual is seated. This is particularly true for both clerical and industrial jobs, and it is also true for the arts and crafts which occupy our time at home. In fact the increased concern (often more verbal than motor) with physical fitness, athletic activities, and weight control may partly reflect the increasingly sedentary nature of the jobs we perform and the hobbies we pursue. According to Fitts (1962, p. 78), the skills which are growing in importance are those in which the individual must keep track of several sources of information (stimuli), organize this information, and sort out the effects of his own earlier actions from the effects produced by outside agents. Flying an airplane is an example. The panel of dials, the position and feel of the plane, and the radio messages represent many sources of information. The effects of the pilot's manipulation of the controls must be separated from the effects produced by the aircraft itself and the effects of the atmosphere. Although flying an airplane may not be the best example, most skills performed when the body is at rest are easier to learn than skills performed when the body is in motion.

Regarding the second trend, Welford (1962) notes that the emphasis in applied research on skills is gradually shifting from the armed forces to industry. Large-scale developments in the scientific study of skills did not occur until World War II. During that time it became necessary to operate complicated military equipment, especially devices used in high-speed aircraft. These tasks became so complex that no amount of selection and training of military personnel could ensure adequate performance. Research had to uncover the factors which made the performance of the skill easy or difficult, especially when the skill had to be used under pressure, speedily, and with the adversary staring down the throats of our men. Now much of the applied research facilitates the operation of complex industrial electrical equipment.

The Definition of Skills

A skill has three characteristics: It represents a chain of motor responses; it involves the coordination of hand and eye movements; and it requires the organization of chains into complex response patterns.

Response chains. First, a skilled performance involves a chain of motor responses. Motor responses, as distinct from verbal responses, are muscular movements. The movements of the fingers, arms, legs, and toes are examples. Each movement can be viewed as an individual stimulus-response (*S-R*) association. A skill is a series or chain of such movements, with each link an individual *S-R* unit which acts as a stimulus for the next link. Gagné (1965c, p. 88) uses this illustration, which involves the starting of a car engine by a novice driver:

> *S* (start the engine)—*R* (looking forward and to the rear).
> *S* (sight of clear road)—*R* (testing for gear in neutral).
> *S* (gear in neutral)—*R* (turning the key to activate starter).
> *S* (sound of motor catching)—*R* (release of key).
> *S* (key released)—*R* (depressing the accelerator).

The *R*'s in the above example refer to the muscular movements or the motor responses. These responses must be executed in a particular sequence. If you depress the accelerator before releasing the ignition key, you create an impressive screeching noise to remind you of the proper *S-R* sequence. The releasing of the key (which is also a response) acts as a stimulus for the next response—the depressing of the accelerator.

The stimulation for each *S-R* link in a chain is partly kinesthetic. Kinesthetic stimulation is internal muscular tension, which we often refer to as the right "feel." When the golf club and baseball bat are properly positioned and swung, we experience certain feelings in the wrists and arms which tell us that our execution of the motor act is proper. When we first learn to shift, most of us rely on visual (or external) cues to tell us that the gear is in the proper position. After we become quite skilled at shifting, we rely almost entirely on kinesthetic stimulation and feedback to guide our shifting behavior. You will see below that this gradual change from reliance on external cues to reliance on internal cues characterizes most skill learning.

The amount of body movement involved in skilled behavior can vary considerably. Fitts (1964, p. 245) describes three categories: Some skilled behavior involves gross body movements, such as walking, running, jumping, swimming, balancing, and dancing. Other forms of skilled behavior involve only segments of the total anatomy, as in grasping, reaching, and manipulating objects with the fingers. Finally, for most of us today, skilled behavior often requires the manipulation of tools or objects or the control of machines, as in writing, typewriting, playing a musical instrument, sewing, driving a car, piloting an aircraft, playing tennis, tossing a ball, and doing assembly work.

Movement coordination. Second, you can view skilled behavior as the coordination of hand and eye movements (Bilodeau and Bilodeau, 1961). Frequently motor skills are called *perceptual-motor* skills to emphasize the coordination of perception (the eye) and motor acts (the hand). Swinging golf clubs, tennis rackets, and baseball bats requires high degrees of hand and eye coordination. In verbal skills, which we will consider in another chapter, the emphasis is on the tongue rather than on the hand or eye. Although we can use this distinction to separate the fields of motor learning and verbal learning, you will see tha the two areas have much in common with each other and even witl more complex learning types—the learning of concepts and principle (Fitts, 1964).

Response patterns. Third, you can view skilled behavior as th organization of *S-R* chains into larger response patterns. When we dis cuss many complex human skills (e.g., piloting an aircraft), we almos have to describe response patterns since there are so many individua *S-R* units and *S-R* chains. We sometimes describe the *S-R* chains whic constitute the large response patterns as subtasks or subroutines. I swimming, for example, the arm strokes, the breathing, and the le kicks are subtasks or subroutines. Each of these subroutines represen one or more response chains. Considerable evidence shows that th chains which make up complex human skills are hierarchically organize into larger response patterns; we must learn particular *S-R* units an *S-R* chains before learning others, and we must learn all the subordina chains before we can perform a particular skill. The skill is the tot response pattern. The timing, the anticipation, and the smooth flo of response which we observe in the accomplished musician, swimme and race car driver indicate that the learning of the *S-R* units and *S-* chains has welded them into a single response pattern.

William Bryan and Noble Harter (1897, 1899) provided some the earliest evidence for the theory that skills are hierarchical respon patterns. They observed that as students became more skilled in learning and using the Morse code, the students seemed to hear and to tap patterns of dots and dashes for the individual letters directly. Later the students dealt with whole words and even short phrases. William Book (1908) observed the same development of response patterns in students learning to type. Book called the lowest level of the hierarchy the *letter association stage*. In this stage the student must look at each letter in the copy, say or think of the letter, mentally locate the letter on the keyboard, place the proper finger on the key, and again pronounce the letter or initiate the final letter-making movement. In the second stage, the syllable and word association stage, the student looks at words or syllables slightly ahead, uses an abbreviated mental spelling, and strikes off groups of letters and words. Finally, in the expert stage, the student reads the copy a number of words ahead of the movement of his hands, keeps his eyes continuously on the copy, initiates and directs his finger movements by the incipient or actual pronunciation of words, and centers his attention completely on the work. The third stage represents the highly organized response pattern which comprises the response chains learned in the two earlier stages.

Typewriting skill is unique in that it consists of a number of discrete acts rather than of a single unitary act. A study by M. A. Vince (1953) illustrated how continuous responses (or response chains) can be amalgamated into a single response pattern. Students had to learn a skill which involved drawing a line through a series of circles inscribed on a moving band. The students had to watch for the circles through a narrow slit. Figure 8-1 shows the basic pattern of circles. The direction of the pattern changed at the six corners, the student had to learn to anticipate each corner and to respond accurately in drawing the connecting line. Vince noted three stages in the learning of this skill. The

Fig. 8-1. *Pattern of circles (after Vince, 1953).*

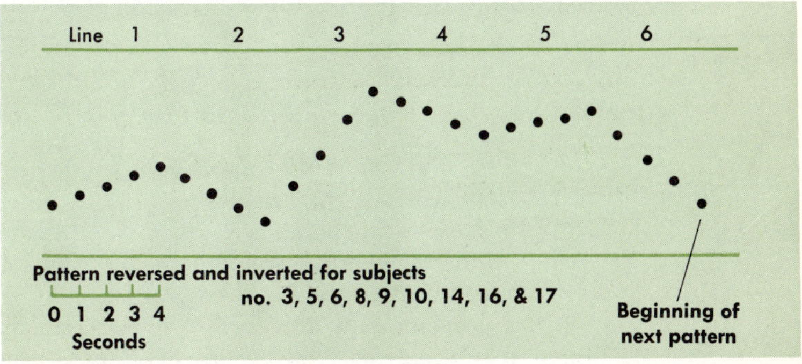

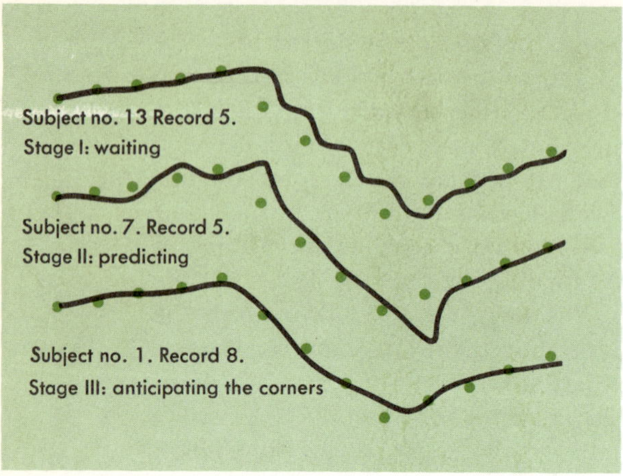

Fig. 8-2. *Learning stages (after Vince, 1953).*

students used a waiting response in the early part of the experiment, when the position of the next circle was not known and when a mistake had been made. In the early part they also used a predictive response, which led to overshooting at points where the direction of the pattern changed. At this stage the students had to learn the key points in the pattern. In the final stage the students learned to anticipate correctly the corners of the pattern—a task which involved accurate prediction and response to the slope of the line of the circles. Figure 8-2 shows the three stages of learning. The student could not learn this skill by responding to each circle separately. He had to develop a correct notion of the whole pattern of circles. As part of the experiment the students reported their own thoughts as they were learning this skill. Almost all mentioned the pattern as being important. When one student was asked the number of circles she had seen, she stated, "They were more or less in units of four. I have just thought of that!" In this way she revealed her awareness of the pattern.

According to George Miller, Eugene Galanter, and Karl Pribam (1960, pp. 88–9), the student tackles the learning of a new skill with a verbal plan or strategy—a crutch he uses until he learns to walk. They refer to the look-remember-hunt-hit-check plan for typing:

> The entire pattern of movements, guided continually by perceptual feedback, can then be represented in other plans as if it were a unitary, independent act. The same procedure of welding these new unities together to form larger skilled units may repeat at the higher level, until eventually the typist is planning whole paragraphs and the aviator is planning whole trips, secure that when the time comes to execute the plan the subdivisions will be prepared to carry out orders in a rapid, efficient manner.

According to these writers, the plans of the beginner and of the expert may bring the same result, but they are different in nature. The expert's version of the plan is involuntary, inflexible, and usually locked in. The plan is often so automatic for him that he is unable to explain how he executes his performance. The beginner's plan is voluntary, flexible, and communicable. Until the beginner's plan becomes automatic, he is not free to work the skill he is learning into a larger plan—that is, into a more complex skill. The notion that complex skills (or plans) are the result of the learning of subordinate skills (or plans) is consistent with the idea of hierarchically organized response patterns.

Now that you know how to define a skill, we can turn to a fuller consideration of how skills are learned.

Classification of Skills

Fitts (1962, 1964) has developed a means for classifying skills. One basis for his classification is called *skill constancies*—uniform patterns found in highly skilled behavior. Constancies can be described as (1) gross body movements and (2) the extent of external pacing of the activity. Constancies also vary in the level of complexity, of which Fitts (1962, p. 179) describes three. At the lowest level, the body is at rest prior to the beginning of the skilled action. The student initiates a behavior pattern which he carries out in relation to a fixed object. Examples of this level of constancy are driving a golf ball, threading a needle, and picking up a pencil. These constancies (or uniform behavior patterns) are fairly easy to describe and measure. At a more complex level, the student begins the skilled activity either when the body is in motion and the external objects are fixed or when the external objects are in motion and the body is not in motion but is set to go. The basketball forward is executed when the body is in motion; the batter in baseball is fixed (or set) when swinging at a pitched ball. The uniform patterns at this level are harder to describe. At the most complex level both the student and the external objects undergo change just prior to the execution of the skilled activity. Fitts suggests these examples: a man trying to keep his balance on the deck of a pitching ship and at the same time training his eyes (or perhaps a gun) on an aircraft flying overhead, and a football quarterback throwing a running pass. In both instances, both student and object are in motion before the performance of the skill. At this level it is very difficult to identify constancies.

We can also classify skilled activity in terms of certain *S-R*–chain characteristics—coherence, continuity, and complexity (Fitts, 1964, pp. 46–47). Chains are coherent to the degree that successive responses are dependent. Spoken English, walking movements, and the succession of notes in classical music are all highly coherent. Less coherent are the movement patterns involved in skating, swimming, and handwriting.

Chains are continuous to the degree that the responses are continuous with few pauses in between. Steering a car is a continuous task. Hitting a baseball is a discrete task. Typing is also a discrete task—except that responses follow each other with great rapidity. Finally, the level of complexity of the *S-R* chains depends on the number of different stimuli and responses possible in a given block of time and space. Learning the English alphabet is less complex than learning the Chinese alphabet. Reading the instrument panel of an automobile is less complex than reading the panel of an aircraft.

Phases of Skill Learning

Fitts (1962, pp. 186–89) identifies three phases—the cognitive, the fixation, and the autonomous—through which the student passes in learning a complex skill. The phases, of course, overlap; they are not distinct units. Moving from one phase to another is a continuous (not a discontinuous) process.

In the *cognitive* phase the students attempt to intellectualize the skill they are to perform. In the terms of Miller, Galanter, and Pribam (1960), the students develop plans which guide the execution of the skill. During this phase, according to Fitts, the instructor and the students try to analyze the skills and to verbalize about what is being learned. The instructor describes what to expect and what to do. He describes procedures and gives information about errors, which occur with great frequency in this phase. In showing the importance of the proper instructional management of this phase, Fitts (p. 187) refers to the studies on pilot training made by A. C. Williams, Ralph Flexman and their associates at the University of Illinois (see Williams, 1949 and Flexman, 1950). They discovered that they could reduce from eight to four the average number of hours required to learn to solo by providing certain basic learning conditions. Relevant to this phase of skill learning, they developed a number of procedures to enhance understanding of flight problems and flight procedures. Among other learning conditions they gave knowledge of results (reinforcement), they established appropriate expectancies, and they talked through the maneuvers. In most adult learning this phase is short—lasting for hours or days.

In the *fixation* phase the correct behavior patterns are practiced until the chance of making incorrect responses is reduced to zero; the behavior becomes fixed. This stage lasts for days or months. At the most basic level the student is learning to link together the basic units of the chain. At a more advanced level he is learning to organize the chains into an overall pattern. Fitts (1962, p. 188) uses these examples. For the aircraft pilot, this phase extends from the first time he flie

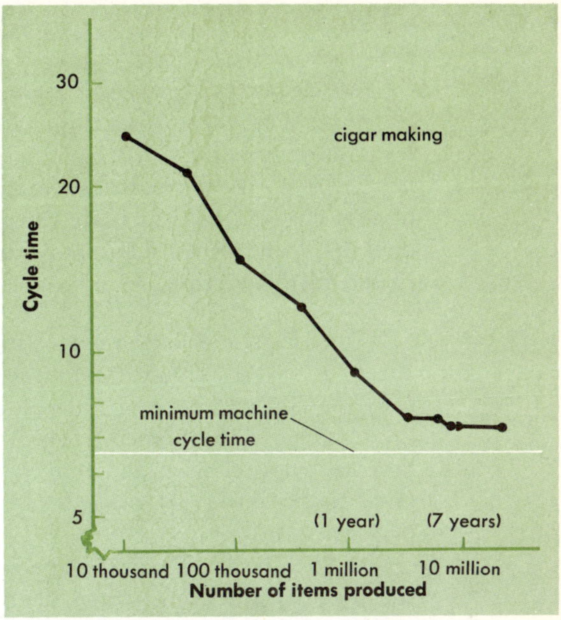

Fig. 8-3. *Gradual improvement in the performance of an industrial task over several years of work (after Crossman, 1959).*

alone (the first solo) through the time he obtains a private license and perhaps through his first one hundred hours of flying. For the typist this phase extends from the point at which he learns the position of the different keys and how the fingers are used in striking them to the point at which he graduates from the first typing course and reduces errors to fewer than 1 per cent.

Finally, the *autonomous* phase is characterized by increasing speed of performance in skills in which it is important to improve accuracy to the point at which errors are very unlikely to occur. In this phase the student also increases his resistance to stress and to the interference of outside activities which he is able to perform at the same time. This is the stage achieved by the expert, for whom the performance of the skill has become involuntary, inflexible, and even locked in. The available evidence indicates that performance can improve over millions of cycles of practice (Fitts, 1964, p. 165). Fitts refers to a study by E. R. F. W. Crossman (1959) which shows that gradual improvement may continue over several years of practice. Figure 8-3 shows the results of long periods of practice on an industrial task.

Basic Learning Conditions

Much research has been devoted to the conditions important in skill learning. The most important are contiguity, practice, and feedback (or knowledge of results). In this part of the chapter you will find out how each of these conditions influences skill learning. In the last part of this chapter, in which we develop a series of steps for the teaching of skills, we shall consider the practical implications of the research discussed in this section.

CONTIGUITY. We defined contiguity as the almost simultaneous occurrence of the stimulus and the response. At the basic level of skill learning continguity is the simultaneous occurrence of the *S-R* units in the chains. At the higher levels of skill learning contiguity is the simultaneous occurrence of the chains which constitute the overall skill pattern. In lay terms, we often refer to contiguity as *timing, coordination,* or *proper order.*

Two aspects of contiguity are important in skill learning. One is the proper sequence of the *S-R* units and the chains. Unless these units and chains occur in the proper order we cannot perform the skill. Use of a little bizarre imagination shows what would happen if the novice driver, in stopping his car, failed to remove his foot from the accelerator before applying the brakes. Many lumpy foreheads remind us of the consequences of not observing the proper order for stopping a car: remove foot from accelerator and then gradually apply the brakes. Of course, the veteran driver learns to anticipate his stops and uses a pumping motion which alternately accelerates and decelerates the car by the careful application and release of pressure on the accelerator and the brakes. The sequence of *S-R* units here is more complex than that executed by the novice driver.

Training procedures for helping the student learn the *S-R* units and the chains in the proper order have been an area of research and even lively debate. The interest and the controversy have centered around whether the student should perform the entire skill or first practice the parts of the skill. The first procedure is called the whole method, the second is called the part (or part-whole) method. A study by F. J. McGuigan and Eugene MacCaslin (1955, p. 658) illustrates the two procedures. They were interested in teaching army recruits how to fire a rifle. This task has several subtasks which the trainee must learn:

1. To assume certain well-defined postures for firing in the standing, kneeling, sitting, and prone positions.

2. Either to wrap (hasty sling) or to loop (loop sling) the rifle sling about his arm as the position demands, to give him greater stability.

3. To move the sight adjustment to alter the strike of the bullet.

4. To load and unload his weapon.

5. To align his sights on the target to obtain the proper sight picture.

6. To control his breathing—to take a breath and to hold it until he has fired.

7. To squeeze the trigger gradually to avoid stimuli to which an anticipatory startle or flinching response might be anchored.

In the *part training method,* the trainees received instruction on the first subtask (assuming proper postures). Then they received training on the second subtask (wrapping and looping the sling) while practicing the first subtask. In this way contiguity was provided. Then they received instruction on the third subtask (moving the sight adjustment) while practicing the first two subtasks. This procedure was continued until all the subtasks were put together in their proper order for the act of firing. In the *whole training method,* the trainees first watched a half-hour demonstration of the entire sequence of subtasks. In the training periods which followed they received instruction and practice on all the subtasks and on firing. In this particular study the investigators found that the whole method was superior to the part method. Their findings were consistent with those of an earlier study by Clyde Knapp and Robert Dixon (1952), who found that the whole method was superior to the part method in teaching students how to juggle.

Thomas Gilbert (1962a) suggests that a reversal of the part method may be the best training procedure. In Gilbert's reverse-contiguity (called *mathetics*) the trainee begins with the last subtask and works back to the first one. In rifle training, for example, you first teach the student to squeeze the trigger. Mastering this act should be reinforcing to the student and dispose him to learn the responses which lead to the proper firing of the rifle. You then teach him to control his breathing. As soon as he learns to hold his breath while firing, you allow him to squeeze the trigger again and thereby reinforce proper breath holding. You then teach him to align his sights on the target. When he does this, you immediately allow him to control his breathing and fire the rifle again. In this way the student works backward to the first subtask on our list. One may have some doubts about allowing untutored students the privilege of firing rifles, but one cannot deny that the act of firing has the major reinforcing effect in the learning of this skill. John Cox and Lynn Boren (1965) compared Gilbert's training method with whole method of training and found that both methods were equally effective. They concluded that Gilbert did not consider that an adult human (unlike a rat) can hold a goal in mind and that this mental image of the goal can reinforce each response which he believes promotes attainment of the goal.

In summarizing the evidence on the part vs. the whole method James Naylor (1962) concludes that for skills which are not difficult and which are not highly organized, the use of the part method to practice those parts in which the student is weakest is the most efficient procedure. For skills which are of moderate and high degrees of difficulty and which are highly organized, the whole method is the most efficient procedure. Using Fitts's classification of skills, we may conclude that the part method is the better one for teaching those skills in which the constancies are least complex—that is, those in which the body is at rest prior to the beginning of skilled action, as in driving a golf ball or threading a needle. When either body or external objects or both are in motion, the whole method is the better training procedure. We can also conclude that highly coherent, continuous, and complex chains may be learned better by the whole method.

The second aspect of contiguity important in skill learning is the need to execute the *S-R* links in the chains or the chains in the overall response pattern in close time succession (Gagné, 1965c). If you recall that each link in the chain and each chain in the pattern acts as a stimulus for the subsequent responses, you see how delay can disrupt the performance of the skill. Delay is failure to present the stimulus needed for the next response in a series of responses. Because of the interdependence of the *S-R* units and chains in skill learning, the absence of contiguity can be seriously disruptive. Skilled professionals emphasize the importance of timing, which, in part, is the need for contiguity in the learning and performance of particular skilled activities. Some skills, of course, have delays built into their execution. Gagné (1965c, p. 94) uses this example. In using a coin-operated machine we must learn to delay pulling the lever until we hear the coins fall into the coin box. But even here the pulling of the lever should be contiguous with the noise in the coin box; the lever must be pulled (if you are to get what you paid for) before someone else uses the machine.

Practice. A second condition of major importance in the learning of skills is practice, an external learning condition. Practice, I have said, is the repetition of a response in the presence of a stimulus. It sets the stage for corrective feedback and confirming reinforcement. In the learning of skills practice is a way of (1) rehearsing those particular subtasks which are only partially learned; (2) coordinating the subtasks so that they are performed in the proper sequence and with appropriate timing; (3) preventing extinction and forgetting of the subtasks; and (4) developing the skill to the autonomous stage of learning. Considerable evidence in skill learning proves that practice leads to perfect performance.

In this section of the chapter we consider some of the basic research on practice, reserving for the last part of the chapter consideration of the practical implications of this research for teaching. This research does not concern the need for practice. Radical educational philosophies to the contrary, we can confidently assume that practice is a necessary condition for the attainment of a high level of performance in complex skills. The research presented here raises this question: Is it better to practice a task with as little interruption for rest as possible or is rest beneficial to the learning and performance of skills? In more technical language, the issue is the relative benefits of massed and distributed practice. *Massed practice* provides little or no interruption for rest. If you reserve all your studying in a course for one study session before the final examination, you are massing your practice. *Distributed practice* allows for rest periods. If you reserve a period of time each week to study the material in each of your courses, you are distributing your practice (study) in those courses.

The classic experiment by Irving Lorge (1930) illustrates the two

Fig. 8-4. *The effect of distribution of practice upon mirror drawing. Notice that, apart from the very first trials, there is almost a constant difference between the different groups (after Lorge, 1930).*

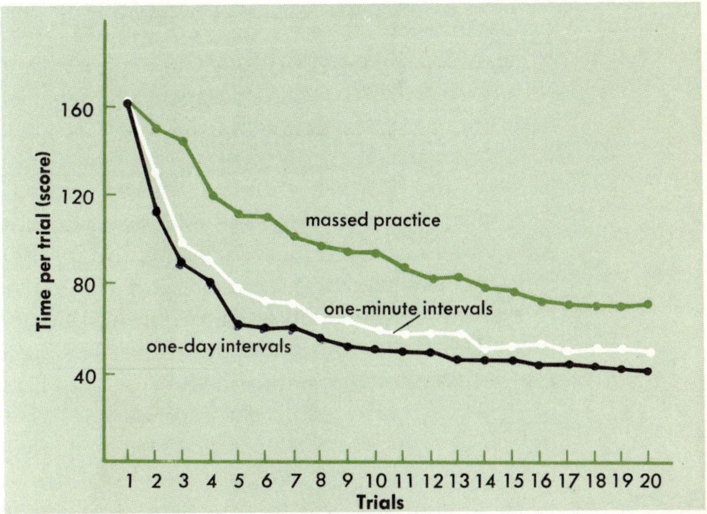

kinds of practice. Among other tasks, three groups of students had to learn to draw a figure using only a mirror image of the figure and of what they were drawing—a task, of course, for which the students had little previous practice. The first group had twenty trials (attempts) to make the drawing with no rest between trials (massed practice). The two remaining groups were provided distributed practice. One of these groups had twenty trials with one-minute rest periods between trials. The other group had twenty trials with one-day rest periods between trials. The measure of performance was the amount of time required to complete the drawing on each trial. Figure 8-4 shows the results. On trials 3 and 4 the groups with distributed practice showed a very rapid drop in the amount of time per trial. The group with massed practice, however, showed no corresponding drop. Lorge's findings are typical of experiments which compare the effects of massed and distributed practice: The differences in favor of distributed practice are consistent and large.

Lorge's experiment raises another question: Does the length of the rest period make an important difference in the learning and performance of the skill? In his experiment a rest period of one minute had about the same effect as a rest period of one day (see Fig. 8-4). Mary Kientzle (1946) performed an experiment to find at what point in time the rest period no longer pays off. She used a different task—printing the alphabet upside down so that when the paper was turned through an angle of 180 degrees the alphabet could be read from left to right in the usual manner. The rest periods varied from zero seconds (massed practice) to seven days. Figure 8-5 shows the effects of the different rest periods. You can see that after forty-five seconds there are few increases in performance. The sharpest gains are made between zero seconds and ten seconds. Confirming the findings of Lorge, this experiment makes it clear that a rest of a few seconds produces most of the maximum possible gain in distributed practice.

These experiments leave unanswered the following question: Which is more important—the practice (or work) or the rest periods? Gregory Kimble and Edward Bilodeau (1949) studied performance of a simple task to answer this question. They required students to overturn cylindrical blocks in a large board containing circular holes. Table 8-1 lists the four experimental groups, the various lengths of the work and the rest periods. These investigators found that shortening the rest period was much more important than lengthening the work period. But they also found that the length of the rest period must depend on the length of the work period. Furthermore, as James Deese (1958, p. 190) reminds us, we cannot arbitrarily decide how long the work periods must be for this depends on the nature of the task. He suggests, for example, that it would not be wise to interrupt someone solving a puzzle before he had reached the solution.

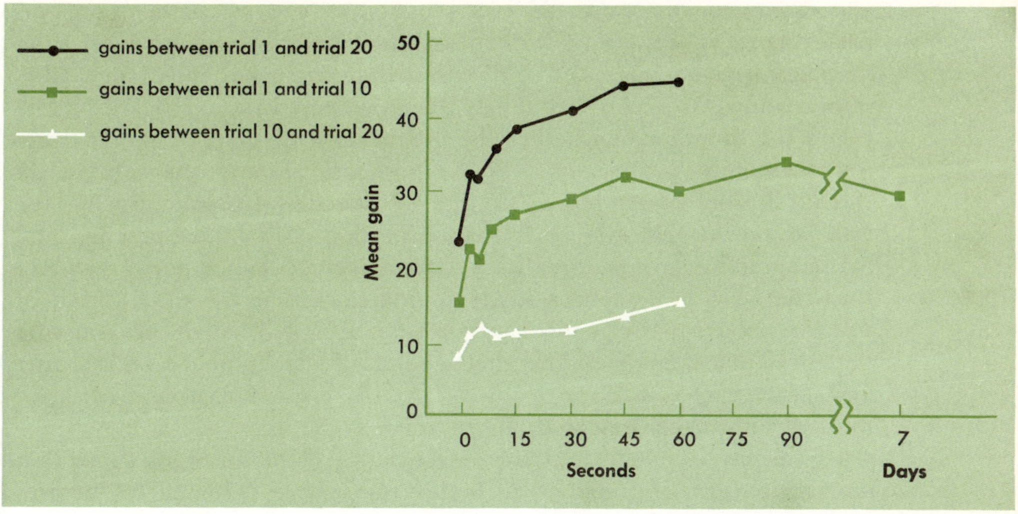

Fig. 8-5. *Mean gains under varied distributions of practice. (Legend: filled circles, gains between Trial 1 and Trial 20; empty circles, gains between Trial 1 and Trial 10; triangles, gains between Trial 10 and Trial 20; after Kientzle, 1946).*

These experiments left one further question unanswered: What is the effect on learning and performance if the total amount of time is kept equal for all experimental subjects with some spending more time on practice and others spending more time at rest? Carl Duncan (1951) designed an experiment that compared these conditions. One group practiced continuously (massed practice), receiving three times as much practice as the other group. The other group periodically stopped for a rest period (distributed practice). Surprisingly enough, Duncan discovered that the group with distributed practice, even though it had only one-third as much practice, produced the better performance. He

TABLE 8-1

LENGTH OF REST AND WORK PERIODS IN EXPERIMENT OF DISTRIBUTED PRACTICE (after Kimble and Bilodeau, 1949, p. 151).

Group	Work period, seconds	Rest period, seconds
1	10	10
2	10	30
3	30	10
4	30	30

also discovered that after an equal period of rest for both groups the performance of the group with distributed practice remained superior.

Research on massed and distributed practice has raised one additional issue. An experiment by L. R. Doré and Ernest Hilgard (1938) raised the question of whether the distribution of practice affects learning or merely performance. The experiment showed that almost all the inhibition which builds up during practice dissipates during the rest period so that the performance of both distributed-practice and massed-practice groups equalizes. Arthur Irion (1966) suggests however that the weight of modern evidence indicates that the distribution of practice affects performance and not learning, although he concedes that present evidence on the effects of distributed practice on learning and performance is not conclusive and that more complete evidence must await further research.

We may conclude that for performance of motor skills some rest, or distribution of practice, is better than none. The effects of rest periods undoubtedly vary with different skills. It would be interesting to use Fitts's classification of skilled performances to find out what this variation may be. Later, you will see that the detrimental effects of massed practice do not occur in verbal learning so consistently as they do in skill learning. In verbal learning, the findings are much more complex and may even indicate no substantial difference in the effects of massed and distributed practice (see Chapter 9). In skill learning, however, we may conclude that distributed practice is superior to massed practice.

FEEDBACK. Our third basic condition for skill learning is feedback. In the discussion which follows you will see why the term *feedback* is more useful than the term *reinforcement* in the description of skill learning. Whereas reinforcement stresses the hedonic or reward effects of learning, feedback emphasizes the informational aspect of learning. In the experimental literature feedback is often called *knowledge of results*. I will use this definition: Feedback is the information available to the student which makes possible the comparison of his actual performance with some standard performance of a skill.

John Annet (1964) distinguishes two types of feedback, intrinsic and extrinsic. *Intrinsic* feedback is the information the student obtains through his own actions. When, for example, he rolls the ball down the bowling alley and knocks over ten pins, the effect of his actions (the knocking over of all the pins) becomes intrinsic feedback. *Extrinsic* feedback is the information the teacher gives to the student about the effectiveness of his actions. The bowling instructor may point out that the student is rolling the ball with too much curve or that he is not giving enough spin to the ball. As we move from the fixation to the autonomous stages of skill learning, we rely less on extrinsic and more on intrinsic feedback. In this way our skill learning becomes self-evaluative.

Margaret Robb (1966) distinguishes between two modes of feedback—external and internal. Information received through the external sensory organs—that is, through vision, hearing, touch, smell, and taste—belongs to the *external* mode. Information obtained from the internal receptor organs, as in the case of kinesthetic feedback, is *internal* feedback. For example, in the forehand drive in tennis, the student places his feet approximately shoulder-width apart and flexes his knees slightly. If the student determines the correctness of his position largely through vision—that is, by looking at his feet and knees—he is using the external mode of feedback. But, if he relies on the feeling for the correct position without visual inspection of his posture, he is using the internal mode of feedback. The accomplished execution of a skill requires the student to rely more and more on internal feedback (Fitts, 1951). Gagné and Edwin Fleishman (1959) point out that only when internal feedback has been dependably sorted out does the golfer execute a consistent swing.

Robb (1966) describes a study in which she controlled both the type and the mode of feedback to observe the effects on the rate of learning a simple arm-movement pattern. The major purpose of her study was to find out whether the students relied mainly on internal feedback after this skill was highly practiced. During their practice periods the students in the experimental groups received extrinsic feedback in the form of scores of their practice performance and intrinsic feedback in the form of on-going information while performing the skill. Subjects in the control group were trained only with internal feedback—that is, they were not allowed to use vision in learning the arm-movement pattern. The final test in this study required all students to perform the skill without visual (external) feedback. Robb found that the students in the experimental groups were able to perform the skill as well as students in the control group. Through extensive practice, the experimental subjects had also learned to rely on internal feedback, even though they were not told to do so.

What evidence do we have that any feedback is important in skill learning? There are two major sources of such evidence: experiments in which feedback has been withheld and experiments in which feedback has been delayed. Some experiments, of course, study both effects. First I will describe an experiment in which feedback was withheld. J. L. Elwell and G. C. Grindley (1938) taught students a coordinated movement of two hands by which they could direct a spot of light on the bull's-eye of a target. One hand regulated vertical and the other hand regulated horizontal movement. The amount of error in the movement of either hand was indicated by the amount of deviation of the

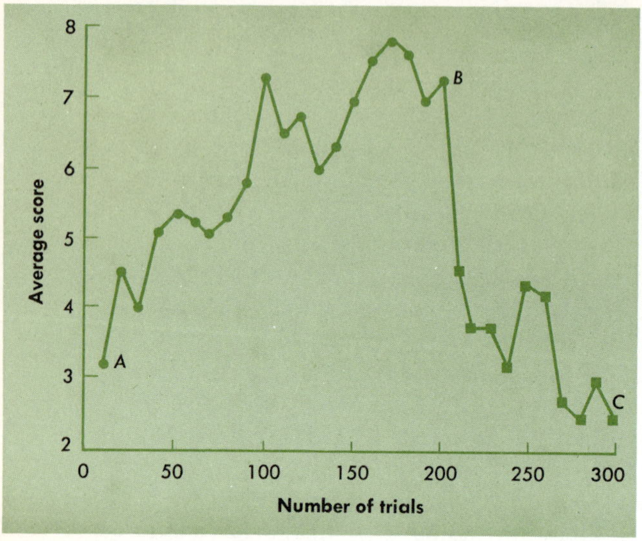

Fig. 8-6. *Average of performance of ten subjects in Exp. I (feedback removed at B; after Elwell and Grindley, 1938, p. 45).*

spot of light from the bull's-eye—a form of intrinsic feedback. At a particular point in the experiment this feedback was withdrawn (i.e., the students could no longer see the target). Figure 8-6 shows the dramatic drop in performance at point *B*, at which feedback was withdrawn. The withdrawal of the feedback also affected motivation. Students expressed displeasure, became bored, lost keenness, and began to arrive late for experimental sessions. In discussing the results of their experiment, Elwell and Grindley state that feedback not only has a directive effect in the learning of a skill but also can be conducive to the development of a conscious attitude to perform the skill with accuracy.

Whereas the previous experiment showed the effects of complete withdrawal of feedback, several experiments show the effects of delaying feedback. One of the earliest of these was performed by Lorge and Edward Thorndike (1935). Students had to learn to toss two wooden balls back over their heads at an unseen target of concentric circles. For one group the informational and motivational aspects of feedback were not separated since the students received money in proportion to the accuracy of their tosses. The feedback was extrinsic—announcements were made to the students about the accuracy of their throws. Another group received no feedback; another received immediate feedback; and four groups received feedback after one, two, four, or six seconds. An

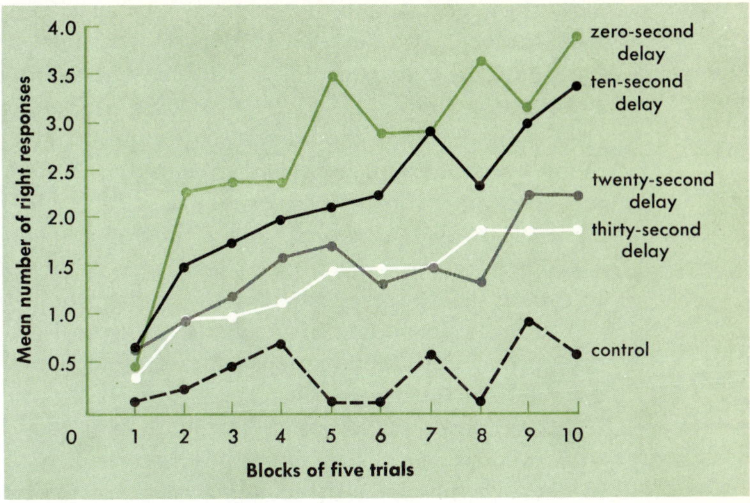

Fig. 8-7. *Mean number of "right" responses of the control and experimental groups for successive blocks of five trials (after Greenspoon and Foreman, 1956, p. 227).*

additional group received feedback for a previous throw after they had made an intervening throw. Only this latter group and the group which received no feedback failed to show improvement. However, less improvement resulted from a four- to six-second delay than from a one- to four-second delay. A similar study by Joel Greenspoon and Sally Foreman (1956) considerably lengthened the periods of delay. The students had to draw three-inch, straight, horizontal lines while blindfolded and while their arms and hands were removed from the table. They had to draw fifty lines with thirty-second intervals between trials. They were given the following extrinsic feedback: If the line were more than 3¼ inches, they were told "long"; if less than 2¾ inches, they were told "short"; and if between 2¾ and 3¼ inches, they were told "right." Of the five groups, one received immediate feedback; another no feedback; and three groups received feedback after delays of ten, twenty, or thirty seconds. Figure 8-7 shows the correct number of responses for the five groups. Increasing the length of delay of feedback reduced the rate of learning. Short delays of ten seconds or less seemed to have little effect. After ten seconds, the deterioration in performance was quite sharp.

Feedback also acts as a form of *prompting*—giving information to the student before or at the same time he makes his response. In the experiments I have described most of the extrinsic feedback was supplied after the student made his response. Annet (1964) reminds us that feedback really comes between responses. The fact that information comes before the next response in a series may be as important as the fact that information comes after the preceding response. In one study Annet (1964) showed that the advance information given to the students was more effective than feedback given after responses were made. In a series of maze-learning experiments, subjects had to learn a series of right-left choices presented on a moving paper band viewed through a slit in a screen. They traced the paths with a stylus. One group had to choose before seeing whether the choice would be correct. This group was entirely dependent on feedback. A second group was allowed to see the correct path before making their selection. Both groups were required to make two perfect runs. This task took the first group (with feedback) three to five times longer than it took the second. Providing sufficient advance instructional guidance to help students avoid mistakes in the first place has been a major concern of programed instruction (see Chapter 11). In any case, you must remember that feedback after the performance is only one way to present the student with the information necessary to carry out the desired actions. It may not always be the most efficient instructional procedure.

From these three experiments on the withholding and the delay of feedback you can see that feedback, as a form of reinforcement, affects motivation as well as learning. This was explicitly the case in the experiment by Elwell and Grindley in which the students' interest waned noticeably after feedback was withdrawn. Although experimentally it is difficult to separate the motivational and informational aspects of feedback (Postman, 1947), Alphonse Chapanis (1964) has made an attempt. He chose a very simple task, punching random digits into a teletype tape, which hardly required skill or informational feedback to learn. Three of his groups had counters in plain sight which they could use to record work output. In the case of only one of these groups was attention directed to the counter; they were told to record the numbers on the counter only for the purpose of attendance. Any differences in performance would have to be attributed to work incentive or to the motivational aspects of the available feedback. Chapanis found no significant differences among these three groups or between these groups and a control group, which had no counter available.

Annet (1964) believes that the following evidence supports the conclusion that the informational aspect of feedback is important in learning and the motivational aspect important in performance: (1) Both reward and punishment act as emphasizers since we recall quite readily responses which are either rewarded or punished; (2) emphasis (pleasant or unpleasant) on right responses is more effective than emphasis on wrong responses; (3) feedback increases effort and directs attention

(4) reward and punishment influence either beneficially or detrimentally the way the student tries to learn a skill; and (5) reported success and failure can both increase and decrease effort.

In summary, what may we conclude about the effects of feedback on the learning of skills? First, feedback is the single most important variable governing the acquisition of skills (Irion, 1966). Robert Ammons (1954) states that feedback is perhaps one of the most dependable and thoroughly tested principles in modern psychology. The principle holds for animals and men, children and adults, groups and individuals and for a wide variety of motor, monitoring, and other general-performance tasks.

Second, on the basis of the evidence presented in this chapter we may also conclude the following: (1) Extrinsic and external feedback are important in the early stages of skill learning, while intrinsic and internal feedback are important in later stages; (2) feedback should be immediate or very nearly immediate; (3) giving the student advance information on the performance of a skill may be more efficient than using only feedback for information; and (4) the motivational aspects of feedback may affect performance, or the amount of effort the student will invest in practicing the skill.

Summary

This consideration of feedback as a basic learning condition concludes our discussion of the nature of skill learning. In this part of the chapter we observed some modern trends which pertain to skill learning: (1) Emphasis is shifting from motor skills performed with the body in motion to less complex sedentary skills, and (2) the research emphasis is shifting from military to industrial skills.

In defining a skill we identified three characteristics: Skills are chains composed of *S-R* units, involve hand-eye coordination, and are hierarchically organized into response patterns. We described three basic conditions for the learning of skills: contiguity, practice, and feedback. Contiguity requires both the proper sequencing of the subtasks and their execution in rapid time succession. Depending on the skill, both the whole and the part-whole methods provide the necessary contiguity. In the case of practice, the evidence strongly favors some form of distributed practice in the performance of motor skills, but distributed practice may be superior to massed practice only in the performance and not in the learning of the skill. Finally the evidence shows that feedback is the single most important variable in skill learning.

You should now return to the list of instructional objectives for the first section of this chapter (p. 243) and determine how well you have achieved them.

QUESTION 8-1

> In providing instruction in beginning swimming, Mr. Kinetic was particularly concerned that, in the early demonstrations of the skill, the student see the relationship among arm, leg, and foot movements and between these movements and breathing. About which of the following learning conditions was Mr. Kinetic most concerned? (a) reinforcement; (b) contiguity; (c) practice; (d) feedback; (e) discrimination.
>
> After selecting your answer, give reasons for your choice and for your rejection of the alternatives.

PSYCHOMOTOR ABILITIES

Entering Behavior

Successful learning of skills is determined not only by the external conditions of learning but also by the entering behavior of the student. In discussing his model of skill learning, Fitts (1964, pp. 259–60) describes the entering behavior of the student in this way:

> An adult, or even a child of a few years of age, never begins the acquisition of a new form of skilled behavior except from the background of many already existing, highly developed, both general and specific skills. Thus the initial stage of our model is not that of a random network but an already organized system [the student] possessing language skills, concepts, and efficient subroutines [skill subtasks] such as those employed in maintaining posture, walking, and manipulating. The number of such highly developed skills in an adult is certainly in the hundreds, each having its own executive program [plan] and library of subroutines, many of the subroutines being shared with other skills. Learning to swim provides a typical example of a skill that is already learned against a complex background of already existing habits.

In this statement Fitts emphasizes the fact that new skill learning must be built on old skill learning. The new learning consists largely of coordinating into a single pattern less complex skills that the student has already mastered. In swimming, for example, the student may have already learned proper breathing, arm movements, and leg movements in connection with other athletic activities. To learn to swim he must simply combine these three subroutines into an overall pattern. Indeed, one of the major characteristics of complex skilled performances is the response patterns which they comprise.

The entering behavior of the student, at the most basic level of skill learning, consists of the *S-R* units which constitute the links in the chain (Gagné, 1965c, p. 87). The student must have previously learned the individual *S-R* connections or he will be unable to learn a chain on the first attempt. And, as indicated by Fitts, the student must also have acquired entire chains, which Fitts calls *subroutines.*

Definition of Psychomotor Abilities

We can also define entering behavior in terms of the student's psychomotor abilities, which have been identified and studied in an extensive research program by Fleishman and his coworkers (1962, 1964). According to Fleishman, a psychomotor ability is a general trait of the individual which is related to performance of a wide variety of skills. The distinction between ability and skill is fairly clear: A skill is performance of a specific task. For example, operating a turret lathe is a skill which depends on the basic psychomotor abilities of manual dexterity and motor coordination. These same abilities, however, are needed in other skills. Manual dexterity is needed in assembling electrical components, and motor coordination is needed in piloting an aircraft. Flying an aircraft and trouble shooting a circuit are skills. Reaction time, finger dexterity, and speed of arm movement are psychomotor abilities. These abilities change very little in the adult. At any given stage they are analogous to a wiring diagram that the individual brings with him to a specific task. This wiring diagram describes his psychomotor entering behavior.

Fleishman and his coworkers have identified several of these abilities. They can be roughly grouped into two classes: those which pertain to the area of physical proficiency and those which pertain to the area of manipulative skills. We will now describe the abilities Fleishman has identified.

Abilities in Physical Proficiency

Fleishman (1964) has identified fourteen physical abilities in five broad areas: strength, flexibility-speed, balance, coordination, and endurance. In the outline which follows I list the fourteen factors, describe them, and list the tests which measure them.

A. STRENGTH AREA

1. Explosive strength
   Ability to expend maximum energy in one explosive act.
   Tests: broad jump, vertical jump, and medicine-ball put.
2. Dynamic strength
   Ability to move or support the weight of the body repeatedly over a given period of time.
   Tests: pull-ups (chin), rope climb, and dips (requiring student to suspend himself between parallel bars).

3. Static strength
   Ability to exert continuously a maximum force for a brief period of time up to the maximum.
   Tests: the dynamometer tests applied to hand grip and to arm, leg, and back muscles; lifting heavy weights.

B. FLEXIBILITY-SPEED AREA

4. Extent flexibility
   Ability to flex or stretch the trunk and back muscles as far as possible in either a forward, lateral, or backward direction.
   Test: yoga exercises.
5. Dynamic flexibility
   Ability to make repeated, rapid, flexing movements in which the resiliency of the muscles in recovering from strain and distortion is critical.
   Tests: squat thrusts and deep-knee bends.
6. Speed of change of direction
   Ability to quickly change direction, usually while running.
   Tests: shuttle runs, dodging runs, and potato races.
7. Running speed
   Ability to make long and short dashes.
   Tests: ten-yard and fifty-yard dashes.
8. Speed of limb movement
   Ability to move arms or legs as rapidly as possible when skill is not involved.
   Test: breaking photoelectric beam with rapid arm movements.

C. BALANCE AREA

9. Static balance
   Ability to maintain bodily equilibrium in some fixed position.
   Test: standing on one foot.
10. Dynamic balance
    Ability to maintain balance while performing a task like rail walking.
    Test: balancing oneself on a large ball.
11. Balancing objects
    Self-explanatory.
    Test: balancing ball on back of hand.

D. COORDINATION AREA

12. Multilimb coordination
    Ability to coordinate the simultaneous movements of two hands, two feet, or hands and feet in operating various devices.
    Test: two-hand coordination test.

13. Gross body coordination
Ability to control gross activity of the whole body.
Test: cable jump.

E. ENDURANCE AREA

14. Endurance (no subfactors)
Ability to maintain maximum effort over long periods of time.
Test: doing as many pull-ups as possible.

These are the fourteen physical proficiency abilities identified at the present time. Further research will probably uncover others. The analysis of physical proficiency strongly suggests two hypotheses: There is no such thing as general physical ability; and there may be a hierarchical structure of ability in the various areas described above. The first hypothesis recalls those theories of intelligence which postulate several independent factors rather than a single *g* factor. The evidence which Fleishman and others have marshaled to support this conclusion has been considerably greater and more convincing in the area of physical ability than that which others have presented in the area of mental ability. The fact that there are physical abilities and not a unitary physical ability imposes upon the school and the teacher the responsibilities of properly assessing the physical entering behavior of the students and of establishing instructional objectives and designing instructional procedures which are appropriate for them. Differences in entering behavior may require the assignment of students to different sections and different remedial treatments. The often-popular policy of cultivating the star athletes and neglecting the rest of the school population seems particularly unwarranted in the light of our knowledge about the several physical proficiency abilities and the probability that most individuals have sufficient ability at least in some areas to warrant careful attention to the physical education of the entire student body.

The second hypothesis pertains to the hierarchical structure of physical ability. Fleishman (1964, p. 32) suggests that the hierarchy in Fig. 8-8 may exist in the flexibility-speed area. The diagram indicates that the most general factor is general flexibility-speed, the ability of the muscles to endure strain and distortion with some emphasis on the rapid recovery from this strain, which allows an immediate repetition of the movement. Contributing to the general factor are two broad, second-order factors, extent flexibility and dynamic flexibility. Finally, there are the narrow third-order factors, and, in the case of one of these, speed of limb movement, fourth-order factors apply to the arms and legs. Such hierarchies, if supported by further research, have teaching usefulness since they make possible a careful analysis of the student's

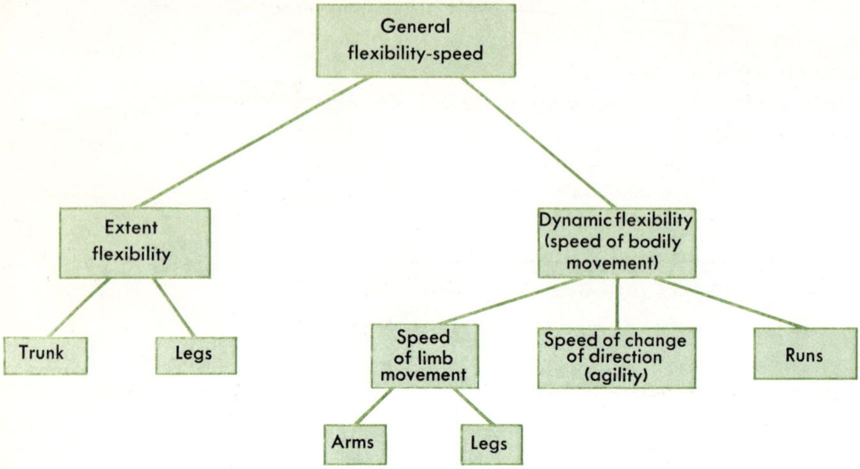

Fig. 8-8. *A possible hierarchical factor structure hypothesized to describe the flexibility-speed area (after Fleishman, 1964, p. 32).*

entering behavior for various instructional objectives which require more than one physical ability. For example, if the student lacks speed of limb movement, the teacher can predict that the student will have difficulty in tasks requiring dynamic flexibility and general flexibility-speed. If we could prescribe activities which would develop speed of limb movement in both arms and legs, we could provide the student with the entering behavior he needs for tasks requiring the broader physical abilities. Fleishman's research thus far does not indicate whether physical abilities are relatively static and genetic (they seem to be in the adult) or whether modification of them is possible.

Abilities in Manipulative Proficiency

The abilities described here are necessary in the performance of particular laboratory skills. Walter Hempel and Fleishman (1955) found that these abilities, which contribute to the performance of fine manipulative skills, are quite independent of the physical proficiency abilities. Fleishman and his coworkers have identified eleven of these manipulative abilities. The tests of these abilities involve laboratory equipment which, with one or two exceptions, cannot be described or illustrated here. The reader can find illustrations and descriptions of the equipment and tests in Fleishman (1964, pp. 16–26).

1. Control precision
   Ability to make fine, highly controlled muscular adjustments. Tests: complex coordination and rotary pursuit. (See Fig. 8-9.)

2. Multilimb coordination
   Ability to coordinate the movements of a number of limbs simultaneously.
   Tests: rudder control and complex coordination.
3. Response orientation
   Ability to make the correct movement in relation to the correct stimulus, especially under high-speed conditions.
   Tests: discrimination reaction time and direction control.
4. Reaction time
   Speed with which the individual is able to respond to a stimulus when it appears.
   Test: discrimination reaction time. (See Fig. 8-10.)
5. Speed of arm movement
   Speed with which an individual can make a gross, discrete arm movement when accuracy is not required.
   Test: two-plate tapping.
6. Rate control
   Ability to make continuous, anticipatory motor adjustments relative to changes in speed and in direction of a continuously moving object.
   Test: single-dimension pursuit.
7. Manual dexterity
   Ability to make skillful, well-directed, arm-hand movements in manipulating fairly large objects under speed conditions.
   Test: Minnesota Rate-of-Manipulation Test.
8. Finger dexterity
   Ability to make skillful, controlled manipulations of tiny objects using primarily the fingers.
   Test: Purdue Peg Board.
9. Arm-hand steadiness
   Ability to make precise arm-hand positioning movements when strength and speed are minimized.

Fig. 8-9. *Rotary-pursuit test. The subject tries to keep the stylus tip in contact with the target, which is set near the edge of a revolving turntable. His score is the total time on target during the test period (after Fleishman, 1964, p. 17).*

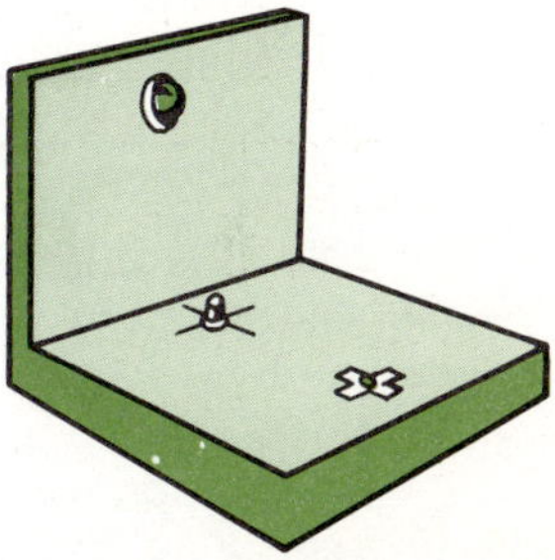

Fig. 8-10. *Reaction-time test. The subject presses the button as rapidly as possible when the light comes on. Score is the cumulated response times to the total series of signals (after Fleishman, 1964, p. 21).*

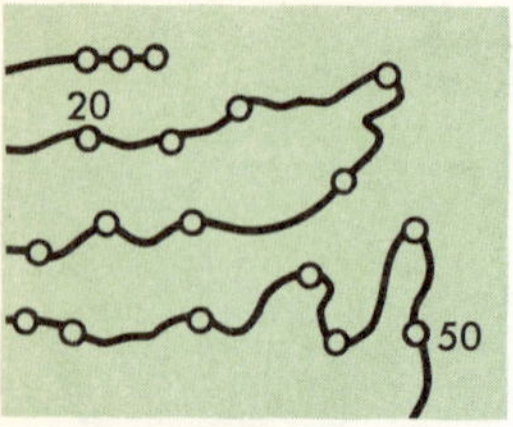

Fig. 8-11. *Page section from "Pursuit aiming test." Examinee is required to place one dot in each 1/8-inch circle, going around the pattern as rapidly as possible. Score is the number of dots placed in the time limit (after Fleishman, 1964).*

Test: track tracing.

10. Wrist-finger speed
Ability to make the movement required in rapid tapping of a pencil in relatively large areas.
Test: tapping.

11. Aiming
Ability required to dot-in very small circles when there are a large number of circles and when the test is highly speeded.
Test: Pursuit aiming.
(See Fig. 8-11.)

As in the area of physical proficiency, in the area of manipulative abilities the identification of several such abilities strongly supports the hypothesis that there is no general manual dexterity. A student may have fast reaction time and speed of arm movement and have poor finger dexterity and manual dexterity. We need no longer crudely classify students as the manually able and the manually disabled since the identification of several abilities permits a more precise assessment of entering behavior. Again, as in the case of physical education, the teacher can use the results of this assessment in two ways: He can predict how successful the student will be in learning skills which require various combinations of these abilities; and he can provide the remedial instruction which will enable the student to develop the abilities needed to perform the particular skills he is required to learn. The teacher, of course, uses this information about the student's entering behavior to achieve particular instructional objectives—the learning of particular skills. Accordingly, the statement of instructional objectives must include a task analysis which indicates exactly which manipulative abilities are required in the performance of the task. The teacher must try to obtain an appropriate match of the student's abilities and the abilities required by the skill.

Psychomotor Abilities and Learning

One of the most important findings in the research on skill learning is the following: As the student moves through the various stages of skill learning, the particular combination of abilities which the skill requires changes (Fleishman and Hempel, 1954, 1955). The combination of abilities required early in the training may be quite different from the combination required later. To study how these changes occur, Fleishman and Hempel (1955) had students practice on the discrimination reaction-time task (Fig. 8-12). Figure 8-13 shows the results of this study. The percentages in the left margin indicate the contribution of each ability to the performance of the skill. You should note that the sizes of the labeled areas represent the percentage contributed by each ability at each stage (trial) of learning. As we move from the first to the fifteenth trial these percentages change for each ability. You can see, for example, that an ability called spatial relations contributes 36 per cent in the beginning but only 11 per cent at the end. Also, reaction time and rate of arm movement, which are barely represented in the initial performance of the skill, increase in importance, and, together, at the end of practice, contribute over 30 per cent to the performance of the skill. Manual dexterity contributes in the beginning and at the end of practice, but decreases in importance during the middle part. Discrimination reaction time, which is a major factor in the performance of this task, increases in importance as practice continues.

Fig. 8-12. *Discrimination reaction-time task. The subject throws one of four switches in response to rapidly changing light patterns. Score is the cumulative response time (after Fleishman, 1964, p. 19).*

Why do these changes occur? According to Fleishman and Hempel (1954), in the early stages of practice of the discrimination reaction-time task, the ability to learn the spatial relationships of the different stimuli to the different responses makes an important contribution to the performance of the skill. In this example, the different stimuli are rapidly changing light patterns. The different responses are throwing one of four switches. Once the students learn the spatial relationships to a sufficiently high degree, so that further improvement is neither necessary nor possible, other features of the task assume increasing importance. Rate of arm movement, in which the proper sequence of movements must be quickly completed, becomes the important ability.

The point is that the combination of abilities required later in practice differs from the combination required earlier in practice. Any prediction about the student's ultimate success based on the initial combination of abilities alone would be very misleading. As the ability requirements of the task change during practice, individual differences in these abilities affect the student's learning and performance. For example, we can predict that a student with good spatial ability but slow rate of arm movement will make much faster progress in the beginning than in the concluding phases of learning the discrimination reaction-

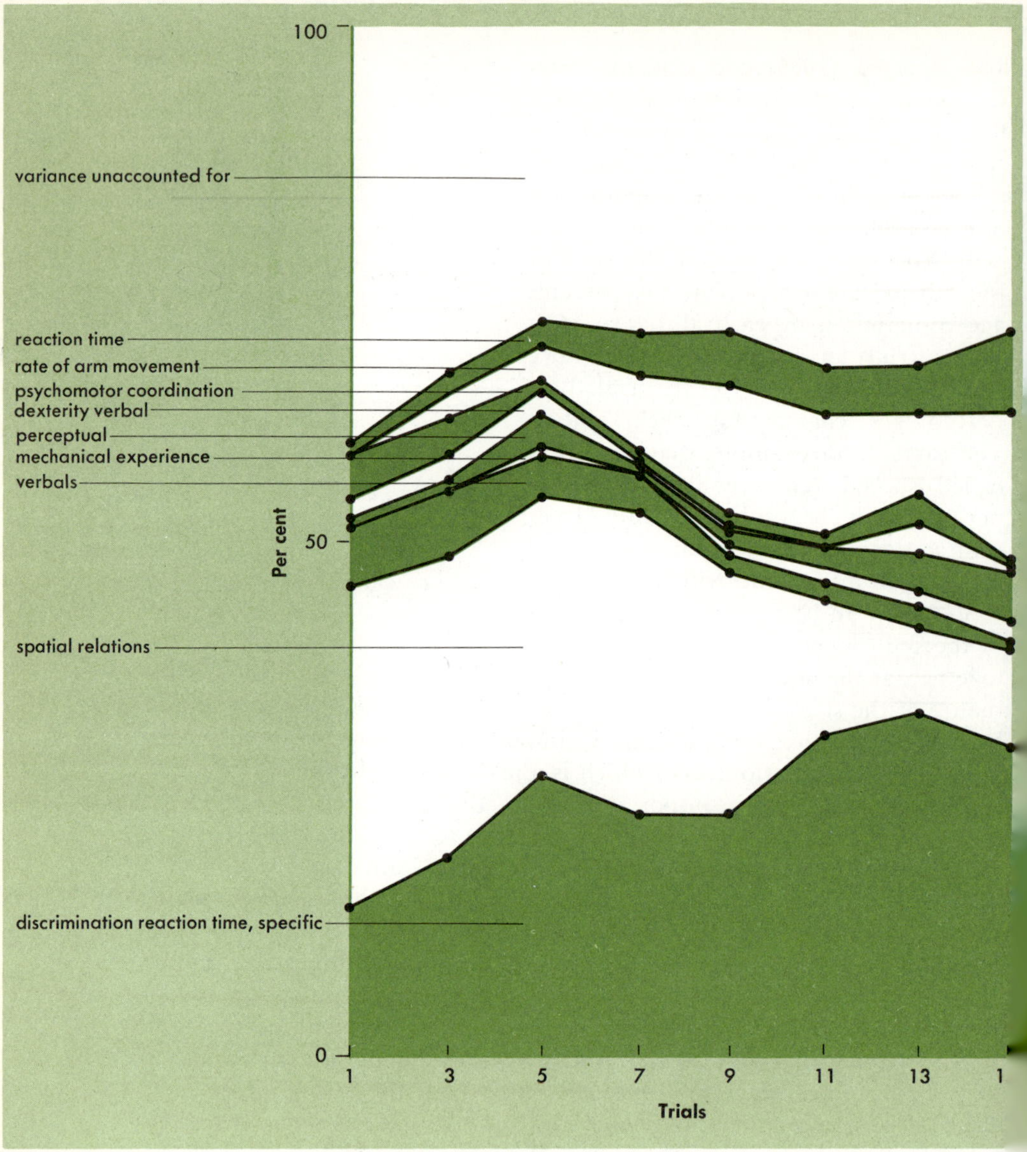

Fig. 8-13. *Percentages of variance represented by loadings on each factor at different stages of practice on the discrimination reaction time task (after Fleishman and Hempel, 1955).*

time task. In assessing the entering behavior of the student the teacher must know all the abilities the practice of the skill requires so that he can determine where each student will make his most rapid and his slowest progress and so that he can supply the necessary help for the periods of slowest progress. Rarely can the student make the same rate of progress in all stages of skill learning.

Summary

We can now conclude our discussion of psychomotor abilities, the second part of this chapter. The discussion was related to our consideration of entering behavior in skill learning. First, the teacher must know that students use general and specific skills which they have already acquired, and that sometimes they have not acquired enough. To learn a new chain of *S-R* units they must have previously learned each *S-R* link in the chain. In more complex skills, they must have learned the subtasks or chains which constitute the skill.

Second, psychomotor abilities also determine the extent of skill learning. These abilities are general traits related to performance of a wide variety of tasks. They fall into two classes: those that pertain to the area of physical proficiency—in which fourteen abilities have been identified; and those that pertain to the area of manipulative skill—in which eleven abilities have been identified. Research on these abilities strongly suggests that there is no general physical ability and no general manual dexterity. It is also possible that certain areas of physical ability are hierarchically organized. The teacher can use his knowledge of psychomotor abilities to obtain an appropriate match of the student's abilities and the abilities required by the skill. In arriving at this match, the teacher must be aware of an additional factor: Abilities required earlier in the learning of a skill differ from those required later. Any predictions about learning outcomes and any provision for instruction must be based on the variations in psychomotor abilities the different stages in skill learning require.

You should now return to the list of instructional objectives for this section and determine how well you have achieved them.

QUESTION 8-2

Mr. Potemkin, the tennis instructor, used the following screening test to determine which students he would accept for beginning tennis. He asked them to appear at the tennis courts for three consecutive days and to perform certain arm and foot movements typical of the initial steps in learning tennis. Which of the following statements is the best appraisal of this screening test?

(a) It is a suitable test of the entering behavior of the student and of the entering behavior required for this skill.

(b) It is less suitable as a screening device than as a careful observation of their performance of a skill they have already acquired.

(c) It is unsuitable as a screening device because it is unrelated to the entering behavior required by this skill.

(d) It is not so suitable as separate tests of each component ability required in tennis.

After selecting your answer, give the reasons for your choice and for your rejection of the alternatives.

INSTRUCTION IN SKILLS

In this third (and final) part of the chapter, I shall deduce from our discussion of skill learning and psychomotor abilities the steps you should take in teaching skills to your students. Some of these steps, unfortunately, have less empirical support than others, but all are at least suggested by the basic research I have already described. To illustrate these steps I shall use a skill in a popular sport—the forehand drive in tennis.

Step 1. Analyze the Skill

Your first teaching function is to do a task analysis of the skill you plan to teach. Frank Verducci (1967) made the following analysis of the forehand drive:

> A. Body position: (1) The body is at right angles to the net with the left foot and shoulder toward the net; (2) the feet are placed approximately shoulder-width apart; (3) the knees are slightly flexed with the body weight carried on the balls of the feet.
> B. Backswing: (1) The head of the racket moves back first with elbow close to the body; (2) as the racket moves back, the weight is shifted to the rear foot; (3) the racket head is brought straight back parallel to the ground; (4) the racket head is higher than the wrist; (5) the elbow is slightly bent; and (6) the eyes watch the ball.
> C. Forward swing: (1) The forward swing is a continuous movement of the arm and racket; (2) the swing causes the path of the racket head to be a straight line pointing slightly upward; (3) the racket head should be even [with] or higher than the wrist throughout the forward swing; (4) throughout the swing, the arm is slightly bent and fairly close to the body; (5) the body weight shifts from the right to the left foot; (6) the body should rotate forward along with the shifting of the weight; and (7) the wrist should be fairly firm.
> D. Position of the ball at impact: (1) The ball is opposite the forward foot at racket's length when impact occurs; and (2) the face of the racket is perpendicular to the ground.

Earlier you learned that skills can be described in terms of their constancies, continuity, coherence, and complexity (p. 274). In the forehand drive, the constancies are the position and movement of the body and racket and the position and movement of the ball. The task analysis of the forehand drive clearly describes all these positions and movements. You can see that the execution of the forehand drive is more complex than that of the drive in golf because the tennis ball is in motion, and, under certain conditions, both the ball and the body are in motion. In any case, a task analysis of a skill must include a description of the relative position and movements of body and objects.

The sequences in which these movements are executed are as important as the movements themselves. These sequences can be described in terms of coherence, continuity, and complexity. The analysis of the forehand drive shows that it is a highly coherent skill—the proper execution of one movement is highly dependent on the proper execution of prior movements. At a basic level, for example, you can see that the forward swing depends on the backswing. But even within the forward swing, the positioning of the racket depends on the proper positioning of the arm, which, in turn, depends on the proper shifting and rotation of the body. The forehand drive is also a highly continuous task—with no pauses between backswing and forward swing and, as the task analysis states, with a continuous movement of the arm and the racket. Finally, this task analysis indicates that the forehand drive is not a complex task since the eyes must focus on only a single object—the ball. More complex tasks require a greater division of attention, as in the case of watching the instrument panel of an airplane. You can now see that a task analysis of a skill should include a description of coherence, continuity, and complexity.

Ernest Jokl (1966, p. 20) suggests that a task analysis begin with the observation of successful performers. He refers to an interview in which a professional basketball player analyzed the hook shot:

> Bradley's hook shot consists of the high-lifted knee of the Los Angeles Lakers' Darral Imhoff, the arms of Bill Russell of the Boston Celtics, who extends his idle hand far under his shooting arm and thus stabilizes the shot, and the general approach of Kentucky's Cotton Nash. Bradley carries his analysis of shots further than merely identifying them with pieces of these players. "There are five parts to the hook shot," Bradley explained. He picked up a ball and stood about eighteen feet from the basket. "Crouch," he said, whereupon he crouched and demonstrated the other moves. "Turn your head to look for the basket, step, kick, and follow through with your arms." Once, when he was explaining this to me, the ball curled around the rim and failed to go in.
> "What happened?" I asked him.
> "I didn't kick high enough," he said.
> "Do you always know exactly why you've missed a shot?"
> "Yes," he said, missing another one.
> "What happened that time?"
> "I was talking to you. I didn't concentrate. One of the secrets of shooting is concentration." [John McPhee, *The New Yorker,* January 23, 1965, p. 42.]

This informal description of the hook shot describes some of the constancies—crouching, turning the head, stepping, kicking, and following through. Except by implication, it does not describe the proper position of the arms and hands. For those constancies described, we have some idea of coherence and continuity. We see, that is, the order in which movements must be made and that they are essentially continuous. Also, since the eyes are focused on the basket (and attention is undivided), the task is not complex.

We may also analyze a skill in terms of *S-R* units, as we did in the example of the novice driver starting the car. An analysis of the forehand drive in terms of *S-R* units is as follows:

> *S* ("Position body to the net") -*R* (body positioned at right angle to net). . . *S* (sight of body at right angle) -*R* (feet placed shoulder-width apart). . . *S* (sight of feet in proper position) -*R* (knees slightly flexed). . . *S* ("Swing racket backward") -*R* (moving head of racket back first). . . *S* (sight of racket moving back) -*R* (shifting weight to rear foot). . . *S* (sight of moving ball) -*R* (beginning forward swing). . . and so on.

The analysis of a skill as a single chain of *S-R* units becomes difficult when body and objects move simultaneously, as in the forward swing. The analysis into *S-R* units is probably the best way of identifying the basic components of a skill, but it is not always the best way of showing their relationship. For the most thorough analysis of skills we should first identify the *S-R* units and then use constancies, coherence, continuity, and complexity to describe the relationship of the components.

Step 2. Assess the Entering Behavior of the Student

Your second teaching function is to determine the adequacy of the student's preparation for learning the skill. This assessment of entering behavior can take three forms. First, if your analysis of the skill is in terms of chains of *S-R* units, you must determine whether the student has acquired all the links of the chains—all the specific *S-R* units. Since every link is the stimulus for the succeeding link, the absence of one link means that the skill cannot be performed. For example, in the forward swing, as the arm moves forward, the body weight shifts from the right to the left foot and also rotates to a forward position. A student who does not (or cannot) shift his weight from right to left foot will also fail to rotate his body. Or, if he does rotate his body without shifting weight, he will be in a most awkward position for hitting the ball and will miss it. In shifting the car gears, a student who does not know the position of an intermediate gear (such as second gear) will fail to reach the final gear in the proper sequence.

Second, if your analysis is in the form of component skills necessary for the learning of a complex skill, you must determine if the student has learned all the components. The forehand drive has several component skills: the proper grip of the racket, the proper basic stance, and the proper footwork. The absence of any of these prerequisite skills will make the learning of the forehand drive a difficult if not an impossible task.

Finally, in your analysis of entering behavior, you should assess the physical and manipulative psychomotor abilities of the student. I have already described the purpose and nature of this assessment so that our discussion here will be brief. This assessment must consist of a measurement of the psychomotor abilities of the student, an analysis of the abilities required by the skill or various components of the skill, and an attempt to bring the task requirements and the student abilities together in a way which makes learning possible. The results of this assessment will present the teacher with several courses of action: (1) When the student lacks or is underdeveloped in the necessary abilities, the teacher can provide him the opportunity to develop the abilities to the level necessary for learning the particular skill. An analysis of the abilities required in the forehand drive may indicate that speed of change of direction is an important ability in the advanced practice of this skill. If the student lacks this ability, the teacher can provide him with exercises which will develop it. (2) In this same situation the teacher may decide to abandon teaching the skill for which the student lacks the necessary physical abilities and to teach him those skills for which he is prepared. Students often choose this course for themselves when they invent ways of avoiding certain physical activities either by exercising choices which the curriculum gives them or by developing certain physical incapacities to evade curricular requirements. (3) Finally, the teacher can use the results of the assessment for planning his instruction. Knowing the student's level of psychomotor abilities and the ability requirements of the skill in various phases of learning, the teacher can predict where the student will have his greatest success and difficulty and consequently plan to assist him when he needs help.

Step 3. Arrange for Training in the Component Units, Skills, or Abilities

This step has two purposes: It provides the student with the opportunity to learn missing *S-R* links or component skills or to develop (as I stated in step 2) the prerequisite psychomotor abilities; and it provides the student with the opportunity to learn the skill components (or some of them) so well that he can focus his attention on the new aspects of the complex task he is learning. To illustrate the second purpose the student who, in learning the forehand drive, continues his practice on grip, stance, and footwork to the autonomous stage of learning can give his undivided attention to arm, body, and racket position and coordination. In swimming, a student who has practiced kicking to an advanced stage of learning can devote his attention to breathing or to the coordination of all the component skills of swimming. It is more than coincidence that we practice those component skills we have learned best when we undertake the learning of a new complex skill. It is also good teaching practice to allow the student to develop mastery over skill components where and when he can as a way of moving him on to more complex performance.

Step 4. Describe and Demonstrate the Skill for the Student

This step marks the actual teaching of the overall task or skill. According to Fitts (1964, p. 260), in skill learning the student usually listens to instructions, observes demonstrations, tries out different component skills which he already has available, and then somehow starts learning the new skill.

The purpose of describing and demonstrating the skill is to develop a plan for the execution of the task. In two studies (Guilford and Lacey, 1947, and Smode and Fitts, 1957) of instructors of aviation cadets and physical education students, all the instructors mentioned the importance of providing description and demonstration early in the training. In performing this step the instructors used movies, lectures, and demonstrations by experts, and had the students watch themselves in a mirror. They stressed the importance of these activities early in the skill learning. In another study, Dorothy Davies (1945) found that early verbal instruction helped students to learn archery. One group was given a description of the skill and methods for practicing it. A second group was permitted to learn by trial and error. The study continued over one semester, and the groups were provided an equal number of practice sessions. At the end of the semester Davies found that the group which had received instruction was far superior in performance. Students in the second group often adopted inadequate practice methods with which they laboriously persevered throughout the semester. The students in this group never learned the necessity of working on the components of the skill to raise their scores. Almost all their attention was on aiming the arrows at the target and chalking up points. Davies concluded that one of the chief advantages of verbal instruction is that it directs the student's attention to practice techniques more adequate than those he is likely to adopt by himself.

Verbal instructions should be at a minimum in the early stages of skill learning. Aileene Lockhart (1966) believes that most physical education teachers talk too much! She suggests that the initial explanation be brief and deal with the skill in general terms. Descriptions should direct the student's attention to only the essential aspects of a skill. To some extent the student must invent his own means for getting his muscles to carry out the skill the instructor describes and demonstrates. Miller and his associates (1960) consider the following detailed description of a skill an example of bad teaching:

> On take-off the throttle should be opened slowly so that rudder control can be introduced smoothly to overcome the tendency of the plane to turn as a result of increased torque. Open the throttle continuously so that it is completed by the time you count to five; when you reach three start to apply some right rudder.

They explain that this description is bad teaching because it makes the student feel very busy. Although counting may work for some students, others may find that it interferes with their performance of other parts of the skill. One student found his own means. He pushed the throttle forward to the panel while keeping extended one finger of the hand on the throttle. When the extended finger hit the panel, he began to apply the right rudder.

The opportunity for the student to obtain feedback from his own movements is missing in descriptions and demonstrations. When the student's finger hit the panel, he received the feedback he needed. Robb (1966) found that students who passively watched a skilled performance of an arm-movement pattern and then engaged in active practice did not gain so much skill as another group which had continual active practice and visual feedback.

Several studies have examined the use of motion pictures in teaching various skills. Roy Priebe and William Burton (1939) used slow motion pictures of champions in teaching the high jump. Edward Ruffa (1936) used motion pictures to teach five track events to high school boys. Thurston Adams (1939) taught the tennis serve to college students in this way. Finally, Dale Nelson (1957) used a slow motion picture loop in teaching golf. These studies indicate that skills which involve gross body movements can be taught through the use of motion pictures. According to Lockhart (1966) the evidence strongly suggests that the chief value of motion pictures is in the early stage of learning and in the autonomous or final stage of learning. When the student has reached high levels of proficiency in skill practice, he is able to attend to details in the films which he would have ignored earlier. The chief advantage of the motion picture is that it reveals the elements of time and motion which are crucial in the performance of the skill.

Mark May (1946) found that to combine the advantages of demonstration and feedback the films should enable the students to participate verbally. May suggests a liberal pause between sentences of the commentary; this device allows the observers time to formulate their own verbal cues. In the group discussion immediately following the film, each student should review verbally and orally the directions he has heard. These directions should then be checked by running the picture a second time before the students begin their practice. Finally, each student must be given an opportunity to try his hand at the skill under the supervision of the teacher.

The student's own descriptions of the skill may be an important aid to learning. N. G. Ozolin (1958) allowed his experimental groups to learn the terminology connected with stunts by writing the words down and studying them. The control group gave no special attention to terminology. Ozolin found that the special training in terminology was especially helpful in the learning of the more complex exercises. Lockhart (1966) refers to an unpublished study by Bonnie Purdy in which student description or verbalization was the major variable. Students in both groups were learning beginning archery. Students in the verbalization group listened to instructions on correct address, position of bow arm and shoulder, and so on, and then repeated those instructions to a partner. Students in the other group simply practiced after listening to the instructor. Although the differences between the groups were not significant, the performance of the verbalization group fluctuated less than did that of the control group. One advantage of student verbalization is that the instructor can determine whether the student has received the directions as they were given. Joan Johnson (see Lockhart, 1966) discovered that students often form incorrect ideas of the movements in the beginning and use these ideas throughout practice. She also found that colorful words (e.g., the racket *swishes*) were easily remembered and acted upon.

We can now summarize what you have learned about the description and demonstration of skills (step 4). Most instructors stress the importance of performing this step early in the learning of the skill. One of the chief advantages is that the student is directed to the most efficient means of practice in the beginning. It is important to remember, particularly in teaching beginning students, that verbal instruction should be kept to a minimum and should deal with only the most essential aspects of the skill. To a considerable extent the student must develop his own techniques and sources of feedback. The motion picture has the advantage of revealing time and motion in skill performance. The use of the motion picture must allow students to develop their own verbal descriptions, to review these descriptions, and finally to practice the skill under the teacher's supervision. In developing their own descriptions of the skill, the students stabilize their performance and give the teacher an opportunity to discover any erroneous interpretations before practice is underway. For most teachers, the danger is that they will say too much rather than too little. Beginning students need a set of specific directions with little or no analysis of the task or of the methods for performing it.

Step 5. Provide for the Three Basic Learning Conditions

In teaching skills, we combine the three learning conditions—contiguity, practice, and feedback—into a single step because we must usually provide them concurrently rather than sequentially. More simply, much of your success in teaching a skill will depend not only on how well you provide for each of these learning conditions but also on how skillfully you can combine them into a single teaching situation.

5A. PROVIDE FOR CONTIGUITY. To meet this condition you must teach the student proper coordination and timing. For proper coordination the student must learn the proper order, or sequence, of the units or subtasks of the skill. For proper timing, the adjacent units in a chain or adjacent subtasks in a hierarchy must occur simultaneously, without delay and unnecessary pauses. Previously we discussed three methods for providing contiguity: the whole method, the part method, and the reverse-part method of Gilbert. The decision on which method to use must rest largely on your analysis of the task and assessment of the entering behavior of the student. Highly organized skills have high coherence and continuity—that is, their components interact. For these skills the whole method is a means of simplification. Less highly organized skills have low degrees of coherence and continuity. For these skills part learning allows the student to become proficient in the subtasks. In considering the entering behavior of the student, you should realize that the whole method is better when your assessment indicates that the student will find the task difficult. When the student possesses the prerequisite ability, the part method will be more useful. The choice of method also should determine the conditions of practice. The whole method is more efficient with distributed practice; the part method is better with massed practice.

Instructors of aviation cadets and physical education students (Guilford and Lacey, 1947, and Smode and Fitts, 1957) stress the need for providing contiguity. They refer to it as the need for the student to develop coordination. In pilot training, the coordination of hand and foot movements is important. In learning to hit a golf ball, the coordination of body, shoulder, arm, and wrist action is important. In learning the forehand drive in tennis, the coordination of body, arm, and foot action is important. Coordination, of course, involves timing. These instructors stress the importance of the student's learning the proper timing both of movements which occur in sequence and of movements of the body in relation to external objects (e.g., the tennis ball). They also emphasize the importance of developing rhythm. Lawrence Lindahl (1945) found that identification of and training in the co-ordination of hand and foot movements in the use of a machine for slicing thin discs from tungsten rods reduced training time, improved both the quantity and quality of work, and reduced costly breakage in the machine in a few weeks.

5B. Provide for practice. In the opening part of this chapter we concluded that distributed practice was more useful than massed practice in the learning of psychomotor skills. Furthermore, we found that the effects of distribution are powerful and reliable, that there are optimum limits to the rest period, and that shortening the practice period is more important than lengthening the rest period. We also saw that massed practice may affect performance but not learning—that, after a suitable amount of rest after massed practice, what was originally lost in performance may be regained. We know very little about how the distribution of practice affects skills of varying constancies, coherence, continuity, and complexity.

The major teaching problem is scheduling the practice and the rest periods in ways consistent with these findings. Here, again, very little applied research has concentrated on how this can be done with skills taught in the school. The practice schedule must conform to the school schedule, which often routinely determines the amount of time to be spent on any course and, by necessity, the amount of rest, or time between student exposures to the same courses. Somehow the teacher must develop a practice schedule which meets the requirements of the task, the entering behavior of the student, the amount of time he has for direct tuition, and the schedule of the school. In addition, the taxpayer will be considerably concerned if he discovers that students are spending as much or more time at rest than on practice. At best, a rest period in the school means that the student is working on some task unrelated to the task he has been practicing. The absence of true rest periods may complicate the scheduling problems of the teacher who now finds himself juggling rest and practice periods for two or three tasks and finding intricate ways of interweaving them.

Here are some practical guidelines the teacher may use in determining the number and length of practice and rest periods. (1) The nature of the task should determine to some extent the length of the practice period. In teaching the forehand drive, we would find it unnatural to teach the backswing one day and the forward swing another day when the two movement patterns are so highly coherent. In teaching the breaststroke in swimming, we would not teach the movement of the right arm one day and the movement of the left arm the next day when the coordination of arm movements is so important in this maneuver. Possibly some highly complex tasks (like trouble shooting) cannot be rehearsed in one practice period and must be extended over two or more periods. The instructor then must find a dividing point which fits the school schedule but does not seriously disturb the learning of the skill. (2) During the rest periods students can practice tasks they have already learned in preparation for tasks they are beginning to learn. Of course, fatigue becomes a major concern when the skills involve gross body movement. In physical education rest must mean rest. (3) Provision can be made for students to practice on their own time and after school hours on schedules they develop with the instructor. Most complex physical and manipulatory skills require practice beyond that provided by formal instruction. (4) Massed practice is better than no practice at all. For learning, it may be equal in effect to distributed practice. The teacher may have to provide periods of massed practice when the school schedule does not permit distributed practice.

If your instructional objective requires the student to reach the autonomous phase of skill learning, a great deal of practice is required. Fitts (1962, p. 195) states the following:

> The importance of continuing practice far beyond the point in time where some (often arbitrary) criterion is reached cannot be overemphasized. . . . Individuals who have not had a great deal of practice beyond the stage of initial satisfactory performance probably do not experience the beneficial increase in resistance to stress, fatigue, and interference that comes from overlearning.

Although we have very little research on the effects of practice at the very advanced levels of skill learning, we do have the testimony of outstanding performers. Eva Bosakova, the Olympic gymnastic champion of Czechoslovakia, describes her practice periods, which began at the age of fifteen under the tutelage of her father:

> He prescribed daily thirty-minute periods of work on the beam, during which it was necessary to remain on the apparatus constantly in action, walking, hopping, turning, and again walking without rest. I spent hundreds of hours and uncounted kilometers walking and running on the beam. . . . I constantly searched for new methods, elements, and dynamic combinations for my exercises. In the process I gained complete confidence, accustomed myself to unfamiliar movements, and lost all fear of falling. Each individual exercise period lasted more than one hour. During this time I went through my whole routine five to seven times. Afterward I worked on individual elements of the exercises and their connections, selected passages and their combinations. At the height of my career, it took me from about six to eight months to acquire mastery of a new exercise such as those prescribed for Olympic games. [Jokl, 1966, p. 19.]

Unless the instructor allows the student to develop a skill to the autonomous phase of learning, the necessary expenditure of time, effort, and energy may well deter the student from continued practice of the skill.

A considerable amount of research supports the beneficial effects of mental practice. Wilbur Twining (1949) compared three practice conditions for students learning to throw rope rings over wooden pegs. The first group threw 210 rings on the first and on the twenty-second day—this was the no-practice group. The second group threw 210 rings on the first day and twenty rings each day up to and including the twenty-second day—this was the live-practice group. A third group threw 210 rings the first day. After this they mentally rehearsed their first day's activity for fifteen minutes daily until the twenty-second day, when they again threw 210 rings. In group I no significant learning occurred. Group II showed 137 per cent improvement, and group III showed 36 per cent improvement. Mental practice was much better than no practice but not so beneficial as physical practice. Verdelle Clark (1960) obtained essentially the same results in teaching the one-hand foul shot in basketball. Instruction for the mental-practice group was restricted to the reading each day of mental-practice work sheets. They had to imagine each day that they were shooting five warm-ups and twenty-five foul shots. Clark found that physical practice was more effective than mental practice. However, consistent with the findings of Twining, he found highly significant gains in learning even with mental practice. Also mental practice was slightly more effective for the novice than for the varsity players. A recent study by John Jones (1965) lends further support to these findings. We may conclude that mental practice, which is a form of student verbalization, has beneficial effects on skill learning and that most of the benefits are derived in the early phases. In reviewing studies of mental practice, John Lawther (1966) claims these advantages: (1) It is a means of reviewing previous performance and planning the next trials; (2) it is a means of planning the order of movements in simple skills; (3) it reduces the amount of extinction in the next performance; and (4) it preserves mental alertness and mental set for a quicker start at the next practice session. Lawther also claims that mental practice is important at autonomous levels of skill learning (along with increased physical practice) to maintain awareness of feedback and precise adaptation to cues.

We shall consider briefly three further aspects of practice. First, Poppelreuter's law of practice states that the best results in skill learning occur when speed is retarded until a reasonable level of accuracy has been obtained and then is increased gradually. William Solley (1952) in subjecting this law to an experimental test found evidence to warrant this restatement: In skills in which speed is the predominant factor for successful performance, the most efficient results are obtained by early emphasis on speed; in skills in which both speed and accuracy are important, equal emphasis on speed and accuracy yields the best results. Second, Robb (1966) studied the effects of slow practice, in which students go through the movement pattern of a skill slowly before practicing at the standard rate. She found that this method hindered the students' learning of a simple skill. She concludes that slow practice should not be used in skills in which the timing requirements are important. Third, in the use of mechanical guidance with the student's cooperative effort, the teacher, in the practice of skills, guides the student through a rough approximation of the movement pattern he must learn. Although the studies of this method do not entirely agree, considerable evidence shows that mechanical guidance should be used only in the initial stages of practice and that it is best used with the very young, with the very old, or with students who have great difficulty in learning the skill (Ragsdale, 1950). It should probably not be used until the student has made some preliminary responses for himself. Excessive reliance on mechanical practice robs the student of the opportunity to use internal and intrinsic feedback.

In summary we may conclude that the teacher should make some provision for distributed practice within the framework of the school schedule and the available time the student has outside school. If feasible scheduling proves impossible, you are reminded that massed practice is better than no practice at all. It is very easy for a skill to go underpracticed. Without the proper provision for continued, strenuous practice, students never obtain the benefits of the autonomous stage of skill learning. Mental practice has beneficial effects, for different reasons, on both early and late stages of skill learning. We also have pointed out the limitations of emphasizing accuracy at the price of speed, of practicing slowly when timing is an important skill characteristic, and of providing mechanical guidance. Practice must remain an important element in planning programs for skill learning. Paul Hunsicker (1963) observes that even though students have different capacities for physical skills, they must all be pressed to improve the level of development they have attained.

5c. Provide for feedback. In the first part of this chapter I illustrated the primary importance of feedback in skill learning. The type of feedback most beneficial to the student depends largely on the phase of skill learning. Let us consider first the early phase, in which extrinsic and external feedback play the major roles. Since the teacher ordinarily provides extrinsic feedback, the early phase of skill learning requires close supervision. The teacher must point out discrepancies between the student's performance and a standard performance of the skill. In reporting their observations teachers frequently direct the attention of the student to external cues and discriminations in movements which the student tends to ignore. In the forehand drive, for example, the forward swing is executed with the racket head even with or higher than the wrist. The arm is slightly bent and held fairly close to the body. In providing extrinsic feedback the teacher reports to the student when the racket head falls too low and when his arm is too far from his body. In this early phase of learning the teacher must often demonstrate several times the proper execution of the movement and compare this execution with that of the student. The teacher combines the use of extrinsic and external feedback in early skill learning. When, for example, the student visually inspects the position of the racket head and the movements of his arm, he is relying on an external mode of feedback. The teacher should direct the student's attention to whatever external modes are available and useful. For example, by directing the student's attention to the racket's swish in the tennis serve, an auditory mode of feedback is employed.

As the student progresses through the fixation and the autonomous phases of skill learning, he relies on intrinsic and internal feedback. In using intrinsic feedback, he observes the effects of his movements. In the forehand drive, he observes the speed of the ball and the direction in which it moves. From the very consequences of his execution of the skill he is able to interpret flaws in movements, timing, and overall coordination. The student's increasing reliance on intrinsic feedback enables him eventually to take over the evaluation function performed by the teacher in the early phase of skill learning. In using internal feedback, the student loses his original self-consciousness and is less inclined to rely on visual inspection of his posture and movement for information on the acceptability of his performance. Instead he relies more and more on kinesthetic stimulation. He develops a feel for the correct movement of the tennis racket and of his arm. We do not have any direct way to develop each student's awareness of the feel for the proper movements (Robb, 1966). Whenever the proper movement is practiced, internal feedback is unavoidably provided. For this reason, specific devices for developing or strengthening the awareness of internal feedback appear to be unnecessary. As Miller and his associates (1960) suggest, the student must develop his own tactics for getting the proper movements into his muscles.

Summary

We have concluded this chapter with a description of the five steps you must take in teaching skills to your students. The first three are preparatory to the actual teaching of the overall skill. The first step requires you to analyze the skill in terms of *S-R* units and chains or in terms of a hierarchy of patterns of chains. These chains we have called *subtasks or component skills.* We may also analyze the skill in terms of constancies, coherence, continuity, and complexity. The most thorough task analysis combines the use of each of these methods. The second step requires you to assess the entering behavior of the student. Here again you are presented with a choice of analytical methods. You can assess entering behavior in terms of *S-R* units, of component skills (or subtasks), or of psychomotor abilities. In using the knowledge gained in the assessment of the student's psychomotor abilities, the teacher must also make an analysis of the abilities required by the skill the student is about to learn. Then the teacher must match student ability and task demands. The third step requires you to arrange for student practice of the components of the skill you are about to teach.

The actual teaching of the overall skill gets under way with the fourth step, which requires you to describe and demonstrate the skill and to help the student develop a plan for the execution of it. Both description and demonstration require that the teacher emphasize only the essential characteristics of the performance. Motion pictures are especially useful in demonstrating movement and timing. Whatever the form of the demonstration, it should eventually provide for student verbalization and later for student practice of the skill. The fifth step requires you to provide for three basic learning conditions. You can provide contiguity by a whole or a part method and even by a reverse-part method. Practice should ordinarily be distributed if it is feasible to arrange spaced practice sessions. Mental practice has distinct advantages over no practice and is a useful supplement to physical practice. Finally, the teacher has the responsibility of providing feedback. The need for extrinsic and external feedback in the early phase of skill learning imposes this immediate responsibility.

Return to the list of instructional objectives for part three of this chapter (p. 275) and determine how well you have achieved them.

QUESTION 8-3

In teaching his students the skill of rolling the bowling ball down the alley with the maximum striking accuracy, Mr. Tuition took the following steps. First, he analyzed the skill in terms of *S-R* units, constancies, continuity, coherence, and complexity. Second, he assessed the entering behavior of the students in terms of prerequisite *S-R* units, component skills, and psychomotor abilities. Third, he provided training in the component units, skills, and abilities. Then he used verbal instruction and films which described the skill and showed an expert rolling the ball down the alley. Finally, he taught the students the proper coordination and timing, using the whole method, and provided them with suitable practice schedules. Which of the following steps was *in*adequately provided for? (a) analysis of the skill; (b) assessment of entering behavior; (c) training in component skills; (d) description and demonstration; (e) basic learning conditions.

After selecting your answer, give the reasons for your choice and for rejection of the alternatives.

SUMMARY

This chapter concerned the teaching and learning of skills. In the future we will have to learn different skills than those we have learned up to now, skills that are less complex and more sedentary in nature. Skilled behavior can be described and analyzed in a number of ways: as chains of *S-R* units, as hand-eye coordination, and as hierarchically organized response patterns. Skills can also be classified on the basis of constancies, coherence, continuity, and complexity. Skill learning has three phases: the cognitive, the fixation, and the autonomous. The basic conditions for learning skills are contiguity, practice, and feedback. Contiguity provides the proper sequence and timing of movements. Distributed practice is usually better than massed practice, but massed practice is better than none. The importance of the different types and modes of feedback varies with the nature of the skill and the phase of learning.

The second section dealt with entering behavior and psychomotor abilities. New skill learning is based on old skill learning and often requires coordinating into a single pattern less complex skills. Psychomotor abilities, as distinct from skills, are individual traits important in the performance of several skills. There is no general physical ability or manual dexterity but rather a number of relatively distinct abilities for each of these general areas. Abilities required early in learning may differ from those required later in learning—a fact teachers must consider in assessing entering behavior.

The third section dealt with instruction in skills. First, you must analyze the skill you will teach in terms of constancies and sequences of movements (coherence, continuity, and complexity). You may also (although it is not always practical) analyze the skill as a single chain of *S-R* units. Second, you must assess the entering behavior of the student in terms of specific *S-R* units, component skills, and psychomotor abilities. Third, as preinstruction, you must provide training in component units, skills, and abilities to allow the student to acquire missing links or parts and to learn these links and parts so well that he can concentrate on their coordination. Fourth, you must describe and demonstrate the skill so that the student can develop his own plan for its execution. Verbal instructions are usually combined with live or filmed performance in this step. Finally, you must provide for contiguity, practice, and feedback. In providing contiguity you can use the whole, the part, or the reverse-part method. You can use either distributed or massed practice and even mental practice. The type and mode of feedback varies with the phases of skill learning. Whereas extrinsic and external feedback are important in early skill learning, intrinsic and internal feedback are important in late skill learning.

SUGGESTED READINGS

Unlike other topics we have considered, the teaching of skills suffers from a dearth of literature. The most serious recent discussions of the basic research are in the following articles and books:

Bilodeau, Edward A., ed., *Acquisition of Skill.* New York: Academic Press

Inc., 1966. The chapters are on the history of skill research, selective learning, individual differences, mechanisms of motor responding, facilitation and interference, information feedback, retention, tracking behavior, cybernetic theory, and motor skills and verbal learning.

Fitts, Paul M., "Factors in Complex Skill Learning," in *Training Research and Education,* ed. R. Glaser, pp. 177–98. Pittsburgh: University of Pittsburgh Press, 1962.

———, "Perceptual-Motor Skill Learning," in *Categories of Human Learning,* ed. A. W. Melton, pp. 244–85. New York: Academic Press Inc., 1964.

Fleishman, Edwin A., "The Description and Prediction of Perceptual-Motor Skill Learning," in *Training Research and Education,* ed. R. Glaser, pp. 137–76. Pittsburgh: University of Pittsburgh Press, 1962.

Irion, Arthur L., "A Brief History of Research on the Acquisition of Skill," in *Acquisition of Skill,* ed. E. A. Bilodeau, pp. 1–46. New York: Academic Press Inc., 1966.

In the field of physical education, the following books and articles report research or are based on research:

Espenschade, Anna S., *What Research Says to the Teacher: Physical Education in the Elementary Schools.* Washington, D.C.: National Education Association, 1963.

Fleishman, Edwin A., *The Structure and Measurement of Physical Fitness.* Englewood Cliffs, N.J.: Prentice-Hall, Inc., 1964.

Hunsicker, Paul, *What Research Says to the Teacher: Physical Fitness.* Washington, D.C.: National Education Association, 1963.

Paterson, Ann and Edmond C. Hallberg, eds., *Background Readings for Physical Education.* New York: Holt, Rinehart & Winston, Inc., 1965. See especially Sec. 3, "Psychological Backgrounds," pp. 211–321.

"A Symposium on Motor Learning," *Quest,* Monograph VI (Spring 1966). A publication of the National Associations for Physical Education of College Women and Men.

The chief research journal in physical education is the *Research Quarterly.*

The Teaching and Learning of Verbal Knowledge

9

This chapter deals chiefly with the psychology of verbal learning and its applications to teaching. As used in this chapter, the term *verbal knowledge* refers merely to the language or verbal component in most human learning. It does not refer to concepts, principles, or problem solving, the subject matter of the two chapters which follow. The major purpose here is to acquaint you with the conditions of learning you must provide whenever your instruction involves the use of language. Since almost all school instruction, irrespective of grade level, subject matter, or skill, requires the use of language, all teachers should be able to describe and provide the necessary internal and external conditions fo verbal learning.

The chapter has two additional and related purposes. First, sinc 1952, when John McGeoch and Irion published their second edition o *The Psychology of Human Learning,* investigators of human learnin have shifted their emphasis from the study of animal conditioning t the study of verbal learning (Kausler, 1966; Mandler, 1967). Althoug as you will see in this chapter, the same basic learning conditions an processes are studied, knowledge of their effects on human verbal learn ing has greatly expanded our general knowledge of human learning Your skill in providing appropriate learning conditions for your stu dents will be enhanced by your knowledge of human verbal learning Second, research on verbal learning and language has revealed the clos relationship of verbal learning to concept learning and to learning rul of grammar (Underwood, 1964a; Miller, 1962, 1965; and Mandler, 1967

As this chapter reveals, modern studies of verbal learning do not view the human subject as a passive but as an active organism whose entering behavior significantly determines the course of his verbal learning. Your knowledge of the research on verbal learning can help you to assess and accommodate the entering behavior of your students and to provide the necessary conditions for other learning.

The chapter has four major sections. The first describes the nature of verbal learning and its relationship to the learning types described in the two preceding chapters, basic *S-R* and skill learning. It also describes Jensen's theory of the development of verbal learning. The second section describes the internal and external conditions necessary for verbal learning: meaningfulness, verbal mediation, instructions to learn, practice, reinforcement, and retention. Under retention we consider the processes of retaining and forgetting as explained by interference theory. Finally, this section discusses the relationship between verbal learning and its measurement. The third section deals with the steps you must take in promoting the verbal learning of your students. The steps are inferences drawn from the research discussed in the second section of the chapter.

The final section deals with linguistics, transformational grammar, and instruction. Here the emphasis is on the nature of language, particularly the grammar, as distinct from the learning of language, the emphasis of the preceding sections. In this section we will consider the implications of linguistics and transformational grammar for the teaching of reading and foreign languages.

Upon reading the first section of this chapter (on the nature and development of verbal learning), you should be able to meet the objectives:

1. Distinguish verbal learning from and relate it to *S-R* learning (operant conditioning) and skill learning.

2. Describe the materials and the three procedures used in the study of verbal learning and give examples of each. non sense syllable

3. Define the various developmental levels (there are seven) of verbal behavior, using Jensen's notation, and give examples of each level.

Upon reading the second section of this chapter (on the conditions of verbal learning), you should be able to meet these objectives:

4. Describe two common views of rote learning in terms of verbal associations and discuss the possible intellectual worth of rote learning.

5. Define meaningfulness in terms of different verbal associations and, using three English words, illustrate your definition.

6. Describe the spew hypothesis in terms of experience and availability of verbal responses and illustrate your definition.

7. Describe the effect of meaningfulness on rate of learning and illustrate this effect.

8. Define retention and forgetting in terms of the amount of material and time.

9. Describe the effect of meaningfulness on retention and illustrate this effect.

10. Define verbal mediation in terms of talking to yourself.

11. Distinguish between pictorial and verbal mediators by giving examples of each.

12. Describe the effect of verbal mediation on verbal learning.

13. Distinguish between incidental and intentional learning in terms of instructions to learn and of their relative effects on verbal learning.

14. Describe and illustrate the general effect of the amount of practice on the amount of learning.

15. Distinguish between massed and distributed practice in verbal learning and describe and illustrate the conditions under which each is more effective.

16. Define overlearning in terms of task mastery and describe and illustrate the conditions under which it is most effective.

17. Distinguish between whole and part practice and describe and illustrate the conditions under which each is more effective.

18. Describe the effect of reinforcement on verbal learning by comparing it with other conditions of verbal learning.

19. Distinguish between confirmation and prompting procedures and describe and illustrate the conditions for their effective use.

20. Define interference in terms of response competition and illustrate its effects on retention.

21. Distinguish between retroactive and proactive inhibition by describing and illustrating the conditions which result in each type.

22. Describe and illustrate the relationship between proactive inhibition and entering behavior.

23. Describe the effect of chunking on the retention of long verbal sequences and illustrate this effect.

24. Describe the serial-position effect in terms of what is retained and forgotten and illustrate this effect in the spelling of long English words.

25. Describe and illustrate the effects on retention of the five methods of measuring retention.

Upon reading the third section of this chapter (on instruction in verbal knowledge), you should be able to describe and illustrate each of the following instructional steps:

26. Step 1: Describe for the student what you expect him to learn.
27. Step 2: Examine the instructional tasks and materials for their meaningfulness.
28. Step 3: Assess entering behavior for the availability of meaningful responses and verbal mediators.
29. Step 4: Provide appropriate practice conditions.
30. Step 5: Provide knowledge of correct results.
31. Step 6: Provide conditions which maximize retention.
32. Step 7: Use suitable methods of measurement.

Upon reading the fourth section of this chapter (on linguistics and teaching), you should be able to meet these objectives:

33. Describe three major characteristics of human language and relate them to expandable and flexible form and meaning.
34. Define phoneme in terms of sound units and give three examples of phonemes.
35. Define morpheme in terms of phoneme and give three examples of morphemes.
36. Describe (in terms of novel sentences) what transformational grammar tries to explain.
37. Define kernel sentences in relation to other sentences.
38. Define noun and verb phrase in terms of sentence structure and give examples of each type of phrase.
39. Illustrate an appropriate and an inappropriate application to sentences of a single transformational rule.
40. Illustrate the preschool child's knowledge of grammar by using a particular grammatical rule and some nonsense words.
41. Describe the major reason why linguistics now has limited applications to teaching by referring to teaching methodology.
42. Distinguish between Fries' method and Pitman's (Initial Teaching Alphabet) method of teaching grapheme-phoneme relationships by illustrating each procedure.
43. Illustrate the child's knowledge of grapheme-phoneme relationships through the use of pseudowords.
44. Describe the three characteristics of the audiolingual method of teaching foreign languages and distinguish it from the direct method.

45. Describe the major function of the language laboratory and illustrate how it could be modified to provide for reinforcement of student responses.

THE NATURE AND DEVELOPMENT OF VERBAL LEARNING

In this section of the chapter we consider the nature of verbal learning as distinct from and related to the learning types previously described. We also consider the materials used in the study of verbal learning, and we examine Jensen's theory of the development of verbal learning or, more properly, verbal behavior. Here we see how simple associations can become complex verbal hierarchies.

The Nature of Verbal Learning

At its most basic level, verbal learning may be considered the process of forming verbal associations. Gagné (1965c) uses this example: A child is presented with a three-dimensional object and told it is a tetrahedron. If the appropriate conditions are present, when the child sees this object the next time he will be able to say that it is a tetrahedron. At the most basic level, then, verbal learning is naming—attaching a name to an object. Later we shall refer to naming as *labeling* behavior. According to Gagné, verbal learning (at this level) is like skill learning in that it involves a chain of at least two links. The first link is the presentation of the object (the stimulus) and the observing of the object (the response). In the second link, the observing response results in certain internal stimuli which give rise to the verbal response —the utterance "tetrahedron." Gagné (p. 98) diagrams the simple act of naming:

$$Ss \longrightarrow R \quad \sim \quad s \longrightarrow R$$

object   observing   tetrahedron   "tetrahedron"

The small *s*'s refer to internal stimuli.

The diagram indicates how verbal learning is related to basic *S-R* learning. The observing response which enables the child to distinguish a three-sided triangular object from other three-sided objects is acquired through operant conditioning. The second link, which connects the internal stimuli to the actual utterance of the word, is also acquired through operant conditioning. As you will see shortly in the description of verbal development, both these links are necessary entering behavior for naming or labeling. You will also see that considerably more complex verbal associations are possible, involving longer chains and verbal hierarchies. Verbal learning resembles skill learning in that both involve the chaining of responses. In both chains each link is an individual stimulus-response association and acts as a stimulus for the next link. The major distinction between skill and verbal chains is the type of response. Skill chains involve motor responses; verbal chains involve syllable and word responses.

To give you a fuller conception of the nature of verbal learning, I shall now describe the materials and procedures used in its study.

Verbal Learning: Materials and Procedures

MATERIALS. The materials often used in research on verbal learning try to exclude meaning as an influence since the object is to study how individuals combine elements into the usual language structures (Deese and Hulse, 1967). The materials frequently do not consist of ordinary words, phrases, or sentences. A widely used verbal material is the nonsense syllable, invented by Hermann Ebbinghaus (1850–1909) in his early studies of memory. Originally, nonsense syllables consisted of a vowel between two consonants—for example, BAB, TUC, and YAB. Ebbinghaus (1885) found 2,300 consonant-vowel-consonant nonsense syllables in the German language. Using nonsense syllables eliminates meaningfulness as a factor in verbal learning. It was found later, however, that nonsense syllables as English words vary in meaningfulness (Glaze, 1928). Some nonsense syllables are easier to learn than others because they bear closer resemblance to English words. For example the nonsense syllables BIZ, SEN, and MAK are more meaningful than WEZ, XIY, and CIJ. To have stricter control over meaningfulness, recent investigators have used consonant syllables which contain no vowel, such as MHZ, KBH, and WDQ. Even these syllables differ in meaningfulness however. For example, BKD and WHP are considerably more meaningful than MHZ and KBH. Despite all of our fears of meaningless rote learning, total meaninglessness is indeed a hard state to achieve.

Other materials are used in the study of verbal learning. Ordinary English words are often presented as a single list, as in serial learning, or as pairs of words, as in paired-associate learning. Occasionally both nonsense syllables and words are mixed.

PROCEDURES. We shall now briefly consider the three procedures used in presenting the materials: immediate free recall, serial learning, and paired-associate learning.

Immediate free recall. Here the subject is asked to recall what he has learned after one exposure to verbal material. Investigators may present the words one at a time and request the subject to recall as many words as possible in any order they occur to him. The verbal materials may consist of one or more lists. The words in the lists may be essentially unrelated or they may be closely associated (Deese, 1959).

It is even possible to vary the order of the words in the list with each successive presentation of it (Waugh, 1961).

Serial learning. Here the subject has less freedom in recall. He is expected to recall the words in the order in which they were presented. The usual method is to present the words one at a time and to have the subject anticipate the next word in the list—the serial anticipation method. When the complete list of words has been exposed, one trial is completed. If nonsense syllables are used, the subject must spell the item. If English words are used, he only pronounces the item. Later in the chapter we will consider the serial-position effect involved in serial learning.

Paired-associate learning. This procedure is similar to learning the English equivalents of a list of foreign words. In the study of verbal learning, the verbal units in the pairs can be nonsense syllables, words, or both. This list of paired associates combines nonsense syllables and words:

CFY—KID
XBN—GAT
DSU—CAT
etc.

Later in our discussion you will see examples of lists in which only nonsense syllables or words are paired. The first word in the pair is called the *stimulus term* (CFY, XBN, and DSU). The second word is called the *response term* (KID, GAT, and CAT). Later you will also see that the factors which influence the learning of the response term do not always apply to the learning of the stimulus term.

The Development of Verbal Behavior

The importance of the reasearch on verbal learning which employs these materials and methods can be easily underestimated. Jensen (1968) writes:

> The psychological consequences of verbal behavior are extremely profound in ways and degrees scarcely appreciated by those unfamiliar with recent research. To the extent that a person is prevented, by whatever reason, from falling heir to these consequences of his human potential for verbal learning, he will fall short of his potential as a human being.

As one way of organizing our knowledge of verbal behavior, Jensen (1966) has proposed a theory for its development. Table 9-1 lists the

TABLE 9-1

TYPES OF VERBAL LEARNING (after Jensen, 1966, 1968).

Learning Type	Age Development Begins
1. S_v-R	One year
2. S-R_v	Two years
3. R_v-R or V-R	Three years
4. S-V-R	Three years
or S- r-s -R (see p. 340)	Three years
5. S-V-R-V_c	Three years
6. S-V-V-R	Three years
7. V-V-V (verbal hierarchies), converging to V	

Note: R_v refers to an overt verbal utterance, and V refers to a covert verbal utterance.

·arious types of verbal learning which Jensen describes and the approxi-nate ages at which these learning types develop.

S_v-R LEARNING. Verbal learning begins when the child hears words n connection with other stimuli in his environment. Before the age of ·ne the child's environment presents a confusion of noise. The child ıakes little or no distinction between human speech and other sounds e hears. In S_v-R learning, the child begins to distinguish human speech ·om other sounds in his environment. In Jensen's notation, S_v refers › a *v*erbal *s*timulus—a syllable, a word, a phrase, and so on. R refers › the physical movement the child makes in response to the verbal imulus (or V_s). The movement may involve touching, grasping, or therwise manipulating some object. For example, mother may tell ercival (age 1) to get the ball, and Percival, distinguishing the sound ›all" from the clatter of other household noises, responds by fetching ıe ball and bringing it to his mother. Ball is the S_v (verbal stimulus), ıd Percival's action is the response (R). At Percival's age, children ·spond to words about four times faster than they respond to other ›unds in their environment. It is not clear why this is so, but it is ›ssible that the reinforcing effects of making proper responses to verbal imuli are sufficiently strong to cause a rapid development of this be-ıvior. S_v-R learning represents, then, the simplest form of verbal be-ıvior.

S-R_v LEARNING. In the second and third years of Percival's (or any ıild's) life, he progresses to more sophisticated verbal behavior. (After ι, even Hound Dog is capable of S_v-R learning.) In S-R_v learning,

Percival acquires the ability not only to fetch the ball at his mother's command but also to utter the word "ball" when he sees the ball or has the ball presented to him. In this example, the ball (as object) is the stimulus (*S*) and Percival's utterance of the word "ball" is the response (R_v). To distinguish verbal responses (that is, speech or utterance) from physical movements, Jensen uses the notation R_v instead of *R*. Between two and three years of age the child is obsessed with pointing to objects, hearing the parent label the object, and then imitating what the parent has spoken. It would almost appear that the child is attempting to catalog everything in his environment. Presumably, at this stage in his development, the child has learned to discriminate between various objects. His verbal learning now consists of discriminating certain sounds and associating these sounds with particular objects The child's responses constitute labeling behavior which may be seriously lacking in the development of disadvantaged children.

R-R_v AND *V-R* LEARNING. In the third or fourth year the child' movements come under the control of his own verbal behavior. A earlier stages the child's movements are mostly involuntary actions. H responds rather indiscriminately to many stimuli in his environment and these stimuli control his behavior. At this later stage, however, th child can think the word "run" and start propelling his body throug space. Or he can audibly say "run" (really saying it to himself) an start running. Similarly he can control his walking, crawling, grasping and other manipulatory behavior. At this stage he is no longer tie solely to the physical environment. With his ability to say and thin various words he has the capacity to direct his behavior. His move ments, however, are not entirely divorced from his environment. R_v- learning consists of making an overt response to his own spoken respons Percival says "bite" (R_v), and indeed he does bite (*R*) you. *V-R* learnin consists of making an overt response to his own thoughts. Percival thin "bite" (*V*), and he then proceeds to sink his teeth into your flesh.

S-V-R LEARNING. To show the proper relationship among enviro ment, verbal response, and movement, Jensen describes the *V-R* level *S-V-R* learning. *S* is the environmental stimuli, *V* is the verbal respon (which the child speaks to himself), and *R* is the physical movemen which finally result. For example, Percival sees his big, red ball; thinks or states to himself that he will run after it (*V*); and he does r after it (*R*). He could just as well have thought "crawl," "roll," "throw "pinch," or "eat"—all covert verbal responses (*V*) which may be esthe cally less appealing but within the possibilities of Percival's verbal b havior. At the level of R_v-*R* and *V-R* or, more fully, *S-V-R* learning, can begin to distinguish between animal and human behavior. For t most part animal learning does not progress beyond S_v-*R* learnin

Hound Dog, you may remember, is a slave to the physical stimuli of his environment. He cannot think or say "paw," and, on his own volition, raise his paw. He must wait for the signal (S_v) from Elvis; without this verbal stimulus Hound Dog is helpless. Human beings, however, can and do respond not only to environmental stimuli but also to words and symbols which these stimuli evoke.

The addition of the V_c in *S-V-R-*V_c learning does not indicate another learning type but simply another aspect of *S-V-R* (or *V-R*) learning. V_c refers to a verbal confirming response or feedback. Percival sees his big, red, soft ball (*S*). He thinks that he would like to bite it (*V*), and he does (*R*). He then says, "Yum, yum!" (V_c). Percival's approval of his own response, biting the ball, is simply a form of self-reinforcement. His words evoke various responses, and these responses bring certain consequences. If the ball were hard and Percival cracked a tooth in the process of biting it, the V_c would be negative, and Percival might in time give up biting hard balls (or any ball) and limit his consumption to food. The addition of V_c to the *S-V-R* notation indicates the relationship of reinforcement, particularly self-reinforcement, to the development of verbal behavior.

S-V-V-R LEARNING. Words may also become linked to words in ways which facilitate the association of stimulus and response. Later in the :hapter, you will read about the teacher's mediation function in making hese associations, and you will see how mediation operates. (At that ime I shall also explain the notation, *S-r-s-R,* which also appears in Table 9-1.) In the laboratory study of verbal learning, the subject is ometimes given a particular word and asked to respond with the first vord which comes to mind. For example, if we give the subject the vord *table,* he will most likely respond *chair.* If we give him the word *nan,* he will respond *woman.* Among individuals with the same culural background, the first responses are very similar. The notation *-V-V-R* indicates such connections between verbal responses as well as onnections between environmental stimuli and verbal responses. To ake a crude example, Percival sees the ball (*S*), decides to touch the all (*V*), which in turn suggests that he bite the ball (the second *V*), nd he bites it (*R*). Touch is highly associated with bite in Percival's ender experience.

VERBAL HIERARCHIES. The last notation in Table 9-1 shows that two ords not directly associated with each other may be directly associated ith a third word. For example, take the words *table, chair,* and *bed.* able and chair are strongly associated with each other, but neither is rongly associated with bed. All three words, however, are associated ith the word *furniture. Furniture,* in this example, is a higher-order, : more general, word. The relationship of all four words is a verbal hierarchy, with *furniture* at the apex and the words *table, chair,* and *bed* below. These networks of verbal associations undoubtedly play major roles in our intellectual lives. They are basic to our so-called *verbal intelligence.*

Summary

In describing the nature of verbal learning we saw that it both resembles skill learning, because it involves chains of stimulus-response associations, and is distinct from skill learning, because it involves verbal rather than motor responses. Because each link in the chain is a stimulus-response association, operant conditioning must provide the necessary entering behavior. Materials used in the study of verbal learning are selected on the basis of their meaninglessness. The nonsense syllable permits the best control, but ordinary English words are also used. The three procedures used in the study of verbal learning are immediate free recall (the least structured procedure), and serial and paired-associate learning. The development of *S-V-R* learning distinguishes between animal and human behavior. At this stage, the child begins to respond to words as well as to objects. The development of verbal behavior eventually reaches the level of the formation of verbal hierarchies.

Now that we have described the nature and the development of verbal learning, we can turn our attention to the conditions of verbal learning—the prerequisite entering behavior and the stimulus conditions of the learning event.

You should now return to objectives 1–3 (p. 323) and determine how well you have achieved them.

QUESTION 9-1

Percival sees Hound Dog wagging his tail. Percival thinks "touch hound dog" and he proceeds to touch the dog. What level of verbal development has Percival reached? (a) S_v-R learning; (b) S-R_v learning; (c) *S-V-R* learning; (d) *S-V-V-R* learning.

After selecting your answer, give the reasons for your choice and for your rejection of the alternatives.

THE CONDITIONS OF VERBAL LEARNING

This section considers two internal conditions (aspects of the st dent's entering behavior) which have major effects on verbal learnin meaningfulness and verbal mediation. Several external conditions al influence verbal learning: (1) instructions to learn, (2) practice, (3) inforcement, (4) interference, and (5) methods of measurement. We shall consider first the internal and then the external conditions of verbal learning.

Meaningfulness

Meaningfulness, among all the conditions of verbal learning, has the strongest influence over the rapidity of learning (Underwood, 1964b). Because of its importance we shall consider several aspects of meaningfulness: its relationship to rote learning; its empirical definition; the spew hypothesis; and its relationship to rate of learning and retention.

Rote and meaningful learning. Many slogans are able to galvanize educators into action, but no slogan has more revolutionary and dramatic appeal than this one: Down with Rote Learning! Up with Meaningful Learning! Benton Underwood (1964a, pp. 51–52) characterizes commonly held opinions of rote learning:

> Rote Learning! Let us imagine some free associations which these two words might elicit from people in psychological and educational circles, restricting the responses to those which meet standards of good taste. It is likely that the following would be among the most frequent responses: "dull," "Ebbinghaus," "narrow," "verbal learning," "sterile," "nonsense syllable," "memory drum," "serial list," and so on. Two notions might be culled from such associations. First is the notion that rote learning is closely associated with verbal learning, an association which is quite appropriate. The second notion is that rote learning is felt to be dull, narrow, sterile, and in a manner of speaking, deals with a form of learning that is almost intellectually demeaning.

This harsh image of rote learning undoubtedly has a long lineage. Mere verbal repetition, which requires students to memorize poetic passages from Shakespeare, Donne, Keats, and Browning, the great speeches of Jefferson and Lincoln, and the verses of patriotic songs, had fallen into considerable disrepute by the beginning of this century. The educational reformers of that time were quick to point out the rather obvious stupidity of having students recite with the bombast and dramatic gesture of the elocution teacher eloquent passages from Shakespearean soliloquies and Lincolnian public addresses. The students did not understand them, slavishly parrotted them, and soon forgot them. For the reformers meaningful learning had to replace rote learning. Underwood (1959, p. 112) cites this extreme example of the former policy:

> . . . The student would memorize the multiplication tables in rote fashion. He would be supposed to acquire this knowledge over a period of time and as a consequence of having to use multiplication in contrived situations, such as, say, play store. Undoubtedly no practice of this policy has been quite this extreme, but it seems clear that there has been a marked de-emphasis of rote acquisition.

Definition of meaningfulness. The ambiguity of the words *meaning, meaningfulness, understanding,* and so on has caused several centuries of controversy in philosophical, educational, and, more recently, psychological circles. We have treatises on the meaning of meaning, on meaning as subsumption, on meaning as subjective interpretation of experience, on linguistic meaning, and on meaning as cognitive structure. You can take your choice of these and others still. From this pot pourri I have chosen a definition consistent with the emphasis of this book on the importance of quantifying behavior as a means of studying it. Laboratory research on verbal learning, as distinct from armchair discussions of meaningfulness, has defined meaningfulness in terms o measurable behavior. Clyde Noble (1952), for example, defines it a the number of different associations elicited by a verbal unit—a nonsense syllable or an English word. This is how Noble proceeded. He gave college students a list of ninety-six words and asked them to write al the associated terms, things, places, and events they could think of in one minute. For example, given the word *king,* in one minute the stu dent could record these responses: queen, King Cole, ruler, Sky King kingdom, England, imperial, and kingfish. Noble selected his list partl from the Thorndike-Lorge (1944) list of the 20,000 most frequently use words in the English language. He also chose words which occurre very infrequently. His list, therefore, contained such words as *kitche* and *army* (high-frequency words) and *lemur, grapnel,* and *stoma* (lov frequency words). Table 9-2 lists some of the words and indicates the frequency. The words at the head of the list evoked more associatior from the students than did the words at the end. What Noble disco ered (and Table 9-2 shows) is that the words with the highest numb of associations are also the words which occur with the greatest fr quency in the language. *Kitchen, army, money,* and *dinner,* for exampl which head the list, occur with very high frequency. *Stoma, grapne flotsam,* and *carom* appear at the end of the list and also are not amor the 20,000 most frequently used words.

When we define meaningfulness as the number of different associ tions elicited by a verbal unit we are defining it as *frequency or fami iarity.* The more frequently a word occurs in the language, the great its familiarity, and the greater the ease with which it can be attach to other words. In this sense some words are more meaningful th

TABLE 9-2

MEANINGFULNESS OF WORDS AND FREQUENCY OF OCCURRENCE IN THE ENGLISH LANGUAGE (after Underwood, 1959, p. 114).

Word	*T-L*	Word	*T-L*	Word	*T-L*
1. kitchen	*AA*	21. region	*A*	41. argon	—
2. army	*AA*	22. quarter	*AA*	42. sequence	6
3. money	*AA*	23. leader	*AA*	43. pallor	2
4. dinner	*AA*	24. mallet	3	44. tankard	1
5. wagon	*A*	25. kennel	6	45. bodice	2
6. office	*AA*	26. keeper	23	46. vertex	—
7. heaven	*AA*	27. fatigue	19	47. rostrum	—
8. jelly	19	28. unit	29	48. ovum	—
9. jewel	41	29. effort	*AA*	49. tartan	1
10. insect	40	30. quarry	11	50. endive	—
11. village	*AA*	31. quota	3	51. jetsam	—
12. garment	40	32. yeomen	11	52. lichens	7
13. zebra	2	33. zenith	4	53. percept	—
14. captain	*AA*	34. ordeal	5	54. capstan	—
15. typhoon	—	35. pigment	4	55. lemur	—
16. youngster	21	36. naphtha	1	56. nimbus	—
17. uncle	*AA*	37. pallet	2	57. carom	—
18. income	46	38. entrant	—	58. flotsam	—
19. zero	11	39. jitney	—	59. grapnel	—
20. hunger	37	40. rampart	4	60. stoma	—

Note: The sixty words are from Noble (1952); they are given in order of meaningfulness. The *T-L* column indicates the frequency of occurrence of that word in the Thorndike-Lorge count (1944). *AA* is most frequent, such words occurring more than one hundred times per million words. *A* words are those that occur from fifty to one hundred times per million. A number refers to the actual frequency per million. A dash indicates that the word does not occur in the 20,000 most frequently used words.

thers: *Kitchen* and *army* are more meaningful than *stoma* and *grapnel.* 'his definition lacks in pretentiousness what it gains in explicitness. or the experimental purposes for which it was invented, it has worked ery well.

SPEW HYPOTHESIS. This hypothesis, based on Noble's definition of eaningfulness, is as follows: The frequency with which words have een experienced determines their availability as responses in new as-ciative connections (Underwood and Schulz, 1960). We have already own how the words which occur most frequently in the language evoke e greatest number of associations. But even more strikingly, the order which verbal responses are made to these words is determined by the nount of experience the subject has had with each response. An in-resting experiment illustrates this point (Cromwell, 1956). Each sub-ct was given eight blank cards and asked to write the names of eight different individuals who possessed the same first name. The experimenter gave the first name to be used. For example, if he gave the name *John,* each subject wrote down the names of eight Johns whom he knew. The eight cards were numbered so that the experimenter could determine later the order in which the names were written. Following this phase of the experiment the subjects ranked each of the eight people on these characterisics: (1) how well they liked the person; (2) how much contact they had had with the person; (3) how long it had been since they had seen the person; (4) how well they knew the person. Rue L. Cromwell was interested in how the order in which the names were written was related to frequency of contact. The correlation was 0.96, almost perfect. We can conclude that frequency of contact was related to the frequency with which the name was spoken and therefore to the various response strengths represented in the order in which the names appeared on the eight cards.

MEANINGFULNESS AND RATE OF LEARNING. A well-established principle is the following: The higher the meaningfulness, the more rapid the learning (Underwood, 1964b). Which of the following two lists, for example, would you find easier to learn?

LIST A	LIST B
LWD—PANF	LWD—HORSE
SPX—LEMUR	SPX—FRENCH
BDQ—GOYJO	BDQ—GO-GO

Fig. 9-1. *The relationship between ease of learning and meaningfulness of English words (Kimble and Garmezy, 1963, p. 222).*

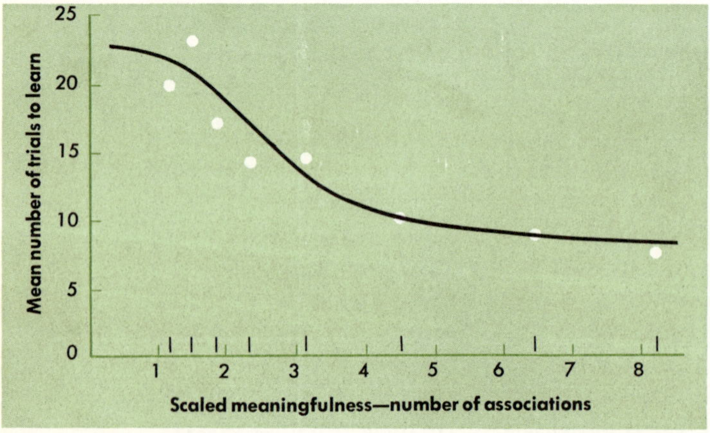

Most students would learn list *B* faster than list *A* because of the greater familiarity (i.e., meaningfulness) of the response terms in list *B*. Several studies supply the evidence upon which this principle is based. Using Noble's procedure for measuring meaningfulness, Kimble (1963) required students to learn eight different lists of different average levels of meaningfulness. Figure 9-1 shows the results of his study. List 1, which was the least meaningful, required between twenty and twenty-five trials (and considerable patience) to learn. List 8, the most meaningful, required between five and ten trials.

Rapid learning also results in slow forgetting, and slow learning in rapid forgetting (Underwood, 1949). This finding is contrary to the popular notion that students who learn rapidly forget just as rapidly, while the plodding student makes slower but surer progress. Although it would be pleasing to find the advantages more democratically distributed, the evidence is all in favor of the rapid learner.

Meaningfulness and retention. Before we can discuss this relationship, we must define *retention*. Retention refers to the amount of material remaining over a period of time. If I asked you to memorize five important dates in English history (1066, 1215, 1588, 1815, and 1914), and, if, several weeks later, I asked you to list these dates, you might have forgotten one or two. Retention would refer to the three or four dates you could recall. *Forgetting* refers to the amount of material lost over a period of time. The total learning material equals the amount of material retained plus the amount forgotten. Some individuals like to say that they have forgotten more than they learned in school and college. This, of course, is not possible. If you never learned one of the historical English dates you cannot, in all honesty, say that you have forgotten it. With regard to our formal education it may be more accurate to say that we have forgotten more than we have remembered (or retained). You should be aware of the distinctions in these definitions. It is quite possible that you have forgotten many dates which you once learned. We have all had the experience of cramming for examinations. As if the examination were a ritualistic act of purgation, shortly after it we find it quite impossible to recall the most obvious facts and ideas. There was more learning than retention.

We can now examine the relationship between meaningfulness and retention. The principle is this: Not only is meaningful material more rapidly learned than meaningless material, but also it is remembered for longer periods of time. Figure 9-2 shows the retention of different materials over a period of one month. You can see that "substance with insight" (presumably more meaningful) was remembered longer than ordinary prose and nonsense syllables. Although the comparison is not made, we know that prose is remembered longer than lists of unrelated English words (e.g., fish, books, metal, geometry).

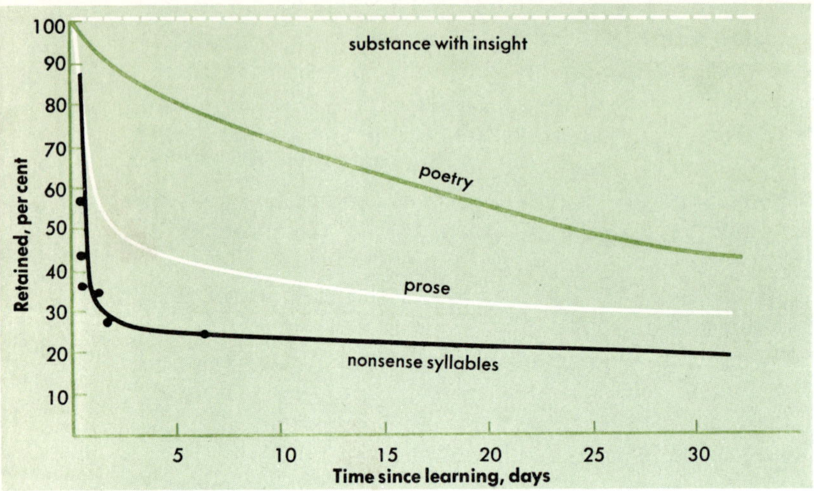

Fig. 9-2. *Retention curves for different materials from five to thirty days (after Guilford, 1952, p. 408).*

A study of how much course content was retained one year after the completion of a course in zoology (Tyler, 1934) classified materials on the basis of various examination questions. Table 9-3 lists the questions. You can see that retention of the first three questions, which dealt mostly with factual information, approximated retention of nonsense syllables and unrelated words in Fig. 9-2. Retention of the last two questions, which required application of principles and interpretation, resembled retention of the more meaningful material in Fig. 9-2. The retention of material in the zoology course probably represents the long-term outcome of many similar courses: After one year much of the factual information is forgotten, but there is a gain in scores on questions dealing with conceptual material. The gain in retention of conceptual materials may reflect the student's continued use of this area of his knowledge. Tyler's study, unfortunately, has been used by some authors as a rationale for dispensing with the teaching of technical terms and information. In most disciplines such dispensation is neither feasible nor desirable. The teacher's function, I shall argue below, is not the elimination of meaningless course materials but the finding of procedures which make relatively meaningless materials relatively meaningful.

SUMMARY. This chapter treats meaningfulness as one of the conditions of the student's entering behavior. It is an aspect of both the materials the student attempts to learn and his previous experience wi

TABLE 9-3

A COMPARISON OF EXAMINATION SCORES DURING THE SEMESTER AND ONE YEAR LATER (after Tyler, 1934).

Type of Examination Exercise	Mean Scores Beginning of Course	Time of Course Examinations	One Year Later	Per Cent of Gain Lost One Year Later
1. Naming animal structures pictured in diagrams	22.2	61.8	31.4	76.8
2. Identifying technical terms	19.7	83.1	66.5	26.2
3. Recalling information				
a. Structures performing functions in type forms	13.3	39.3	33.9	20.8
b. Other facts	21.4	62.6	54.1	20.6
4. Applying principles to new situations	35.2	64.9	65.1	Gain 0.7
5. Interpreting new experiments	30.3	57.3	64.0	Gain 24.8
Average for all exercises in the examination	23.7	74.4	63.3	21.9

those materials. Meaningfulness was defined as the number of different associations elicited by a verbal unit. It is, in this sense, word frequency or familiarity. The spew hypothesis, utilizing this definition of meaningfulness, states that the frequency with which words have been experienced determines their availability as responses in new associative connections. Meaningfulness influences both learning and retention. The higher the meaningfulness the more rapid the learning and the longer the materials are retained.

We shall now turn to another condition of entering behavior for verbal learning: verbal mediation.

Verbal Mediation

DEFINITION. Verbal mediation is talking to yourself in relevant ways when faced with something to be learned or a problem to be solved (Jensen, 1966). Most mediation is inaudible and unconscious. In fact, we are always slightly embarrassed when we are caught talking aloud to ourselves, although we all do it especially when the problems we are trying to solve are particularly difficult. In fact, when our problems "drive us out of our minds," we may ignore others completely and talk aloud to the only person who understands us—ourselves. In Table 9-1, which listed various verbal behaviors Percival had attained, we left one notation mysteriously unexplained: *S- r-s -R*. This notation, the more standard way of representing *S-V-R* learning, describes this situation: The stimulus (*S*) gives rise to an implicit response (*r*), which in turn acts as an internal stimulus (*s*) for the overt response (*R*). The *r* and *s* appear as small letters because they represent internal events (occurring in the brain) which are not directly observable. We can now use the new notation to analyze Percival's behavior. He sees the big, red, soft ball (*S*). He says to himself, "Bite the ball!" (*r*). This response (which you cannot hear because it occurs in Percival's brain and is not spoken aloud) becomes an internal stimulus (*s*), which in turn triggers Percival to bite the ball (*R*). The *V* (an internal verbal response) in the *S-V-R* notation and the *r-s* in the *S- r-s -R* notation represent the same thing: internal verbal mediation.

An experiment by Miller (1935) shows how something you say to yourself (*V* or *r-s*) can act as an internal stimulus for a public act. In this experiment the subject received a shock just after the letter *T* was presented but received no shock after the figure 4 was presented. Each time the *T* or the 4 was presented the subject had to say "T" or "four." In the next phase of the experiment the subject was presented with a series of dots. He was directed to think to himself of *T* when one dot was presented and to think to himself of 4 when the next dot was presented, and so on in an alternate manner. Every time the subject thought of *T*, he made the same response that he made to the electric shock. He did not make this response when he thought of 4. In terms of our notation (*S- r-s -R*), the *T* is the stimulus (*S*), thinking of *T* is the internal verbal repsonse (*r*), this response becomes an internal stimulus (*s*), and the subject makes the response to the electric shock (*R*). This is another example of how our internal verbal behavior controls our public acts.

Pictorial and verbal mediators. Some mediators are pictorial rather than verbal. Gagné (1965c) suggests the following example. If we require a student to learn the pair of words *hat—fix,* he can use a verbal or a pictorial mediator. He might think of Dick's hatband (a pictorial mediator) and learn the pair in this fashion: *hat—Dick's—fix*. The word *Dick's* also rhymes with fix, so it also acts as a verbal mediator. Another student might imagine a battered hat which needs fixing. In this case a purely visual image serves as the mediator. In Fig. 9-3 Gagné gives examples of both verbal and pictorial mediators (or links) for learning the English equivalents of French words. The verbal links are English

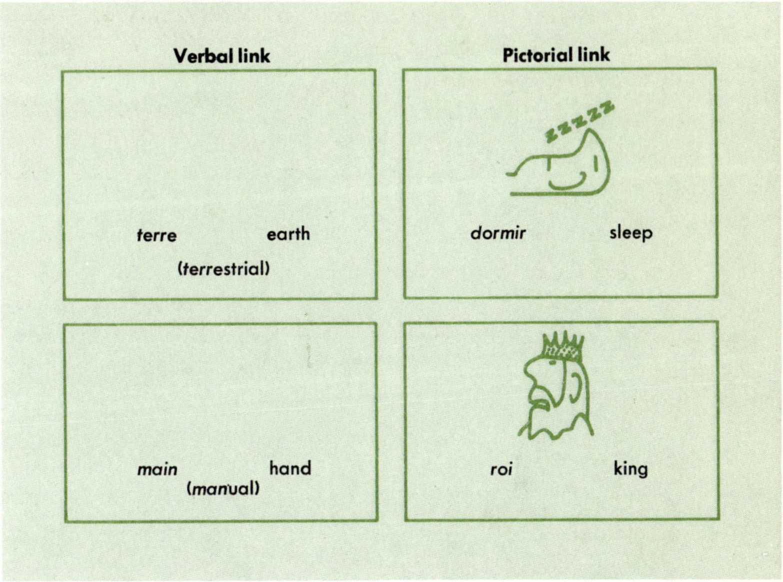

Fig. 9-3. *Examples of verbal and pictorial mediators in learning English equivalents of French words (after Gagné, 1965c, p. 101).*

words similar to the French words, as in the case of *terrestrial* for *terre*. The pictorial links seem more peculiar and idiosyncratic but, on the whole, most people find that they work better than verbal links.

THE EFFECT OF VERBAL MEDIATION. This effect was demonstrated in the classic study by Wallace Russell and Lowell Storms (1955). They wanted to find out exactly how verbal mediation could make learning easier. Table 9-4 lists the words and nonsense syllables they used in their study. Reading from left to right, note that the words above the line are all similar in meaning—for example, *wish—want—need*. The words below the line are not all similar in meaning: The words in the first two columns are similar, but the word in the last column is not—for example, *justice—peace—house*. Similarly, above the line we have *trouble—bad—good,* all similar in meaning, and below the line we have *thief—steal—sleep,* in which sleep is not similar in meaning to the first two words. To build the chains of associations above the line in Table 9-4 the following procedure was used. Given the word *stem,* the subject gave the first word he could think of—*flower*. Given the word *flower* next, he again gave the first word he could think of—*smell*. In this way the experimenters determined before the experiment proper the verbal associations the subjects had already formed.

TABLE 9-4

NONSENSE SYLLABLES AND WORDS USED IN BOTH PARTS OF STUDY ON VERBAL MEDIATION (after Russell and Storms, 1955, p. 290).

Nonsense Syllable	First Chained Word	Second Chained Word	Final Chained Word
CEF	Stem	Flower	Smell
DAX	Memory	Mind	Matter
YOV	Soldier	Army	Navy
VUX	Trouble	Bad	Good
WUB	Wish	Want	Need
GEX	Justice	Peace	House
JID	Thief	Steal	Sleep
ZIL	Ocean	Water	Doctor
LAJ	Command	Order	Cabbage
MYV	Fruit	Apple	Hand

In the experiment proper each subject had to learn two lists. The first list consisted of nonsense syllables paired with words in the second column of the Table. For example, the subject learned CEF—STEM, DAX—MEMORY, and MYV—FRUIT. In the second list the subject had to pair the nonsense syllable with the word in the last column. For example, he learned CEF—SMELL, DAX—MATTER, and MYV—HAND. Now the question was: Would the subjects, in learning the second list, find the pairs above the solid line easier to learn than the pairs below the solid line? In other words, would mediators which were similar in meaning make learning easier than mediators dissimilar in meaning did? More concretely, would CEF—SMELL be easier to learn than MYV—HAND? The investigators' expectations were confirmed. In the second list the pairs above the line were learned in fewer trials than were the pairs below the line.

TYPES OF VERBAL MEDIATORS. As yet we know comparatively little about the types of verbal mediators and their effects, even though this knowledge would be very useful for the teacher. One study classified mediators into single-step and multiple-step associations (Underwood and Schulz, 1960). Table 9-5 shows the word pairs the students learned; they were composed of nonsense syllables and three-letter English words. The table also lists the associations the students reported they used in learning these paired associates. Perusing the comments of the students, you will note a variety of mediators. Among others, the students used (1) letter identity, (2) sound identity, and (3) similar meaning. Each student used several types. If he tried to use only one, he would probably be quite unsuccessful since the word pairs require a shift. Th

TABLE 9-5

VERBAL MEDIATORS USED BY STUDENTS IN LEARNING PAIRED ASSOCIATES
(after Underwood and Schulz, 1960, pp. 299–300).

Single-step associations. For each association we will give the pair of items learned by the subject, and his reported association.

CFY—KID:	C and K similar in sound.
XBN—GAT:	GAT is odd word, X is odd letter.
DSU—CAT:	D to dog to CAT.
CFY—DOG:	C to cat to DOG.
XBN—RAT:	X suggested poison—poison RAT.
TPM—AND:	T associated with symbol (&) for AND.
RZL—SAT:	R to rum to SAT.
RZL—SAT:	R and S in alphabetical order.
DSU—BAN:	U—BAN (brand of coffee).
RZL—KID:	RZL suggested Russell; Russell is a KID.
CFY—THE:	remembered because first one in list.
KHQ—FAN:	KHQ to radio to radio FAN.
IGW—MAN:	W inverted looks like M, hence MAN.
IGW—MAN:	IG to IGnorant to IGnorant·MAN.
RZL—BOY:	RZL looks like lazy; hence, lazy BOY.
RZL—CAT:	Z is hissing sound of CAT.

In some cases, a mediator would be used, but the subject could not report how he got from the mediator to the response. It is possible that these should be classed as no association:

IGW—AND:	IGW elicited International Geophysical Year; don't know how this suggests AND.
RZL—BAT:	made right out of R; just associated right with BAT.
TPM—PIG:	tympany to PIG.
OVJ—BAT:	OVJ became JOV and just tied BAT to it.
DSU—HAT:	DU means fraternity house; associated this with HAT.

Multiple-step mediation.

RZL—BAT:	someone she knows on baseball team with initials R. Z.
DSU—HAT:	D is last letter in heaD; HAT goes on HEAD.
DSU—HAT:	Desilu Productions—to theater—to theatrical HAT.
DSU—HAT:	Desilu; Lucy wears HAT.
OVJ—MAN:	OVJ to OVA to woman to MAN.
TPM—AND:	TPM signifies time; AND is pause in time.
TPM—AND:	TPM to WPM—words per minute on typewriter; AND is word commonly written on typewriter.
IGW—FAN:	IGW to igloo to cold to FAN.

study also showed that the multiple-step associations were not so useful as the single-step associations.

SUMMARY. In addition to meaningfulness, verbal mediation is a condition of entering behavior necessary for verbal learning. Verbal mediation is talking to yourself in relevant ways when faced with something to be learned or a problem to be solved. Most mediation is inaudible and unconscious. Mediators may be both pictorial and verbal, but pictorial mediators work better for most individuals. Some convincing evidence indicates that verbal mediation greatly facilitates verbal learning. I described some of this evidence in this chapter. Chapter 6, on the education of the disadvantaged child, described the learning difficulties of students who do not have available or do not use verbal mediation. Finally, I described here different mediators: letter identity, sound identity, and similar meaning.

Before discussing the applications to teaching of our knowledge about the effects of meaningfulness and verbal mediation, we shall examine several external learning conditions: instructions to learn, practice, reinforcement, interference factors, and methods of measurement.

Instructions to Learn

Originally incidental learning (discussed below) was explained in terms of *set to learn*. Although set was an ambiguous concept, it described an apparent state of readiness induced by instructions given to the experimental subject (Gibson, 1941). Because of the ambiguity of the concept of set, the concept of *instructions to learn* has replaced set in discussions of incidental learning (McLaughlin, 1965).

INCIDENTAL VS. INTENTIONAL LEARNING. The problem in both the laboratory and the classroom is to focus the attention of the student on particular stimuli among the deluge of stimuli which bombard him. Although students frequently do not learn what we intend to teach, they often incidentally learn other things and sometimes they learn things we would prefer they did not learn at all. The distinction between this intentional and this incidental learning is not sharp, but the effects of both have been the subjects of extensive laboratory research (see Postman, 1964). According to Leo Postman (1964), in incidental learning, the instructions do not prepare the student for a test on the materials. In intentional learning, the students are told before learning the materials that they will have a test. These two laboratory situations are not unlike classroom situations we all experience.

There are actually two types of incidental learning situations. In type *A*, the student is exposed to materials but is given no instruction to learn. After his exposure to the materials, he is given a surprise test. In type *B*, the student is directed to learn a specific task but at the same time he is exposed to materials which are not covered in the directions. The test he is given tries to discover how much he learns of the tasks not covered in the directions.

The incidental-learning situation referred to as type *A* is illustrated in an experiment by Postman and Virginia Senders (1946). The students, Harvard and Radcliffe undergraduates, were given a thirty-five–word mimeographed selection from Chekov's short story *The Bet*. The material was very detailed and had dramatic appeal. The subjects were divided into six groups. The experimenter told the students in the incidental-learning group (group *A*) to read the selection for purposes of timing because he was interested in their reading speed. Consistent with our definition of incidental-learning situations (type *A*), these students were exposed to material but given no instructions to learn. The experimenter gave the students in the other five groups specific instructions to learn, by telling them that the study was a memory experiment and that they were to read the selection carefully. After this general direction, the experimenter gave each of the remaining five groups a different task. Group *B* was told that it would be tested for general comprehension of the material, *C* for the specific sequence of individual events, *D* for details of content, *E* for details of wording, *F* for details of physical appearance. In general, the intentional learners obtained higher test scores than the incidental learners. Also, the directions varied in effectiveness. For example, the students who were told that they would be tested for details of content also did better on test items on general comprehension of the material. But the major result (the one you should remember) is that the students who were given directions to learn specific materials did better than the students in the incidental-learning situation, who received no directions to learn.

The incidental-learning situation referred to as type *B* is illustrated in the following situation (Postman, 1964). The subject is given a list of words, with each word in a different color. He is then instructed to learn the words. No mention is made of the colors. In another example of a type *B* situation, the subject is instructed to learn a series of words. Digits and geometric forms are exposed along with the words. In the two situations, the students are tested for their learning of the colors, digits, and forms rather than of the words.

It is important to note that the distinctions between incidental and intentional learning are quantitative and not qualitative. In a review of the relevant research, Barry McLaughlin (1965) concludes that incidental learning is usually a misnomer. No experimental evidence supports the belief in a distinct learning process which occurs without motive, self-instruction, or instructions to learn. He states (p. 374): "Whether such learning does occur is an unanswered, and perhaps unanswerable, question."

SUMMARY. In an incidental learning situation, the experimenter does not provide instructions which prepare students for a test on the materials they are to learn. The students can be given no directions at all or they can be directed to learn one and be tested on another task. Intentional learning provides for the prior announcement of the test and the learning task. The differences between incidental and intentional learning are only quantitative. Because individuals can and do supply their own directions and motivation when these are not provided externally, in the strict sense of the term there may be no such phenomenon as incidental learning.

Practice

A second external learning condition for verbal learning is practice. Research on skill learning gives a fairly clear picture of the effects of practice. Research on verbal learning, however, has not resulted in the same degree of certainty about these effects. Even students and teachers question the value of practice in knowledge acquisition. The general rebellion against the Puritan Ethic on university and college campuses has made disreputable what many individuals have learned from their own experience and what laboratory studies almost without exception corroborate: The longer a person works at learning the more he will learn (Underwood, 1964b). How to get students to increase the vim and vigor of their efforts is the problem of motivation, but the beneficial effects of that effort, once it is invested, are above question.

It is not practice itself but the conditions of practice which pose problems for the experimenter and the teacher. We shall consider first the effects of massed and distributed practice, then the effects of overlearning, and finally the effects of part and whole practice.

MASSED VS. DISTRIBUTED PRACTICE. The learning of tasks can be concentrated into one time period or spread over several time periods. The familiar example of massed practice—the concentration of the learning in one time period—is the student cramming for examinations. All his study for a particular course is concentrated in one time period, usually a day or two before the examination. In distributed practice periods of learning alternate with periods of rest. In teaching Hound Dog to obey his commands, Elvis uses distributed practice. He trains Hound Dog for three periods of fifteen minutes each day for several days.

Although not many teachers or students took the statement seriously, most textbooks in the past rather flatly reported that more learning resulted from distributed than from massed practice. The statement, of course, is a vast oversimplification, as you already know, because many conditions influence how much and how fast we learn, and practice is only one of these conditions. Despite the reiteration of the statement, however, teachers often ignored the necessity for review and students continued to cram for their examinations. Both students and teachers made a practical discovery which the textbooks ignored: Massed practice took less time than distributed practice. After all, distributed practice requires learning time plus spaced time. Massed practice requires only learning time. It is possible that the conditions under which distributed practice is superior to massed practice are so specialized that they are of little practical importance (Underwood, 1964b).

What are these special conditions? In reviewing ten years of research on the effects of massed and distributed practice on verbal learning, Benton Underwood (1961) arrived at this conclusion: The interval between practice periods (in distributed practice) must be shorter when error tendency is high than it must be when it is low. For example, in learning a list of paired associates, if the student tends to forget the response terms, the intervals of practice should be shortened; long intervals will result in forgetting. If the probability of forgetting is very high, massed practice should replace distributed practice.

Evidence also indicates that massed practice is better for learning and that distributed practice is better for retention (Underwood, 1964). Everyone has observed that cramming for examinations often results in high test performance and in rapid forgetting after the test. Theoretically, distributed practice is beneficial because the intervals allow time for unwanted or erroneous responses to drop out or to become extinguished (Underwood, 1961).

Overlearning. Overlearning is an example of massed practice. In this procedure the teacher requires the student to practice a task beyond initial mastery. For example, a teacher ordinarily does not require the child to discontinue the recitation of the alphabet after the child has turned in his first perfect performance. The teacher encourages the child to repeat this marvelous feat several more times not only to satisfy the child's exhibitionist cravings but also to calm his teacher's fears about the inevitability of forgetting. We overlearn many skills such as dancing, skating, typing, and bicycling. Certainly our reading, writing, and speaking skills are overlearned.

Overlearning can reach a point of diminishing returns (Kreuger, 1929). At this point additional practice increases retention only slightly —the effort surpasses the gain. As Fig. 9-4 indicates, Kreuger used three degrees of overlearning. In 0 per cent overlearning, the subjects learned a list of nonsense syllables until they could recite them the first time without error. Strictly speaking, this is not overlearning but simply initial mastery of the task. In 50 per cent overlearning, if the student required

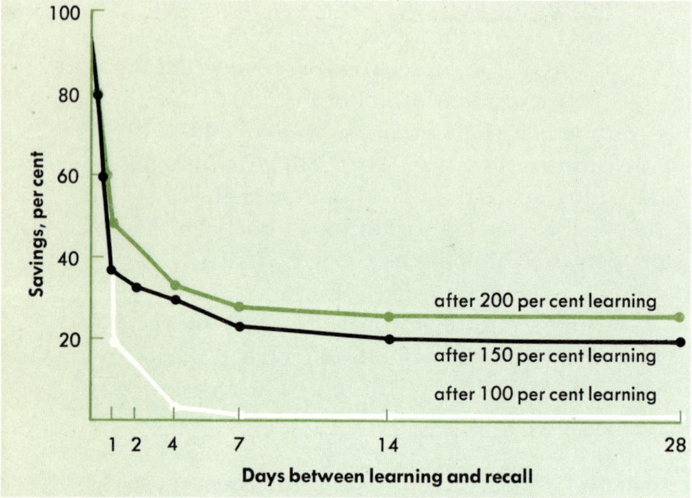

Fig. 9-4. *Three degrees of overlearning and their effects on retention (after Kreuger, 1929, pp. 76–77).*

ten trials for original mastery, he would recite the list five more times. In 100 per cent overlearning, he would recite the list ten more times. Figure 9-4 shows that there are striking gains for 50 per cent overlearning and that 100 per cent overlearning adds little to these gains.

Part vs. whole practice. In the preceding chapter I described the effects on skill learning of part vs. whole practice. When verbal material is learned as a whole, the entire task is practiced once before any part of it is repeated. When the material is learned by parts, each part is learned before they are combined. One part method, the progressive-part method, requires practicing material by combining several units into fewer units (McGeoch, 1942). In this method parts 1 and 2 are mastered separately and then combined to form a whole. Part 3 is next learned separately, then practiced with parts 1 and 2, and so on, until all the parts of the original material have been combined. This is the way we often have memorized poetry of several stanzas. We master stanza 1. Then we master stanza 2. Next we recite stanzas 1 and 2 together. Then we master stanza 3. Next we recite together stanzas 1, 2, and 3. We continue this procedure until we have mastered all the stanzas of the poem. This method is time consuming but often very effective.

Studying the relative effectiveness of the part and the whole methods focuses attention on their relative efficiency: Which method requires less time for gaining mastery? In reviewing the most recent evidence, Deese and Stewart Hulse (1967) conclude that the relative effectiveness of the part and the whole methods in verbal learning depends on the internal organization of the materials to be learned. If dividing the material into parts makes the task of learning the material simpler, the part method should be used. If, however, this division makes the task of learning the material more difficult, the whole method should be used. They use this example (p. 304). You must memorize two lists of words. List *A* contains these words: *north, man, red, spring, woman, east, autumn, yellow, summer, boy, blue, west, winter, girl, green, south.* List *B* contains these words: *north, east, south, west, spring, summer, autumn, winter, red, yellow, green, blue, man, woman, boy, girl.* Although both lists contain the same words, they differ in internal organization, with list *A* containing little apparent organization and list *B* being organized into directions, seasons, colors, and humans. You could easily learn list *B* by the part method because it divides easily into four parts and these parts easily recombine. In the case of list *A,* however, if you divide it into two parts by splitting it in the middle, you would have difficulty recombining the halves since no internal organization tells you which kinds of words belong where. Thus, the choice of the part or the whole method depends on the internal organization or structure of the materials to be learned.

SUMMARY. Since practice is the condition which describes the amount of work output, there is strong empirical support for the common sense observation that the longer a person works (practices) at learning the more he will learn. We have examined here three practice conditions: massed vs. distributed practice, overlearning, and part vs. whole practice. Evidence indicates that intervals for distributed practice must be shorter when the material is difficult and the probability of erroneous responses is high. If the likelihood of forgetting responses is very high, massed practice should replace distributed practice. Some evidence also indicates that massed practice is better for learning and distributed practice is better for performance—a principle which may apply equally well to both skill and verbal learning. When we want our students to acquire secure mastery of materials and verbal skills, we can employ overlearning, which is learning beyond original mastery. Finally, the choice of the part or the whole method of practice must depend on the internal organization of the learning material. Some materials divide into parts and recombine into wholes much more easily than others. The part method can be used effectively with such materials.

We are now in a position to examine the effects of reinforcement on verbal learning.

Reinforcement

Another condition of verbal learning is the reinforcement of correct responses. Such reinforcement is often called *confirmation*—the student's correct responses are confirmed. This confirmation, of course, is a form of feedback, or knowledge of results. We provide confirmation in two ways. First, if the student is learning a list of words, we present him with a printed copy of the list after he has attempted to reproduce the words. Second, if the anticipation method of learning is used, the the student must guess the next word in the list and then be presented with that word within a limited time. The exposure of the correct word is a form of reinforcement, or feedback.

In his theory of verbal development Jensen also refers to confirmation, or the verbal confirming response (V_c). After the student has balanced a difficult equation, he can peruse his work and say to himself, "Very good! Indeed, excellent!" The quoted words are the verbal confirming response. You can see that the student in this case is reinforcing himself.

The current study of verbal learning places relatively little emphasis on the effects of reinforcement (Underwood, 1959). According to Underwood most of the verbal learning observed in the laboratory is not dependent on immediate reward. Only the informational feedback on the correctness of responses remains.

In Chapter 12, on programed instruction, we shall consider the relative effectiveness of what are called *confirmation* and *prompting procedures*. In a recent study, James Hawker (1964) made this comparison of the two procedures. Each student was to learn a list of paired associates, but each stimulus term had four response terms. He was to select the correct response term for each stimulus word. In the confirmation procedure, the student was presented with a set of items and required to push the switch under the response term he thought correct. If he were correct, the light over the response term would flash. In the prompting procedure the light over the correct response term flashed each time the student was presented with a new set of items. He was required to push the switch under that item and go on to the next set. In the prompting procedure the student had no opportunity to make errors. On a free-recall test, Hawker found no significant differences in numbers of correct responses. He did find, however, that prompting was more effective than confirmation in the first block of trials and also resulted in faster performances.

It appears then that, although confirmation can be a useful condition of verbal learning, it is possible to substitute other and sometimes more useful procedures for it. However, the student must be kept informed of the correct response whether this information is presented before or after he makes his response.

Interference Factors

Interference factors, unlike those conditions of verbal learning discussed above, are conditions of forgetting rather than of learning and retention. First I shall define the major theory of forgetting, called *interference theory*. Then I shall examine two sources of forgetting—from associations learned later in time (retroactive inhibition) and from associations learned earlier in time (proactive inhibition). Finally I shall examine the effects of the amount of material learned and the serial-position effect.

THE THEORY OF INTERFERENCE. We have two consistent findings for verbal learning: Learning new associations causes one to forget old associations learned earlier in time and to forget the new associations as well. In effect, associations compete, with one association interfering with the retention of others. Interference is the competition of old and new responses which results in forgetting. We shall shortly examine some illustrations.

The theory that forgetting is the result of interference rather than of a mysterious fading away of traces in the brain originally came from a study of J. G. Jenkins and Karl Dallenbach (1924). These investigators studied the differences in retention following periods of sleeping and of waking. They required the two subjects in the experiment to recall lists of ten nonsense syllables after various periods of ordinary waking activity and after sleeping. The waking and sleeping periods were one, two, four, and eight hours in duration. With the self-sacrifice which has ennobled the scientific profession, the two subjects slept in the laboratory with the experimenter. Before they went to bed they learned the lists of nonsense syllables. Then they were awakened at the intervals indicated above. Apparently the subjects were not irritated with these interruptions of their slumber and, in spite of considerable drowsiness, were able to recall the lists. Only one interval (one hour, two hours, and so on) was used each night so that the subjects had to sleep in the laboratory for four nights. For the waking part of the experiment, the subjects returned to the laboratory during the day at the appropriate times (the same intervals as those used for the sleeping part) and were tested for recall of the lists. Figure 9-5 shows that recall after sleeping was considerably higher than recall after waking. The first two intervals show a similar drop in retention for both sleeping and waking, but the forgetting continues for the waking state in the later intervals. The experiment indicated that the intervening activity between learning and recalling the lists and not the mere passage of time was the cause of the forgetting. That teachers will ever gain sufficient control over the waking lives of their students to put these finding into practice seems very dubious.

RETROACTIVE INHIBITION. Many experiments deliberately introduce possible sources of interference to observe their effect on retention. The sources of interference, as we saw earlier, are two: from associations

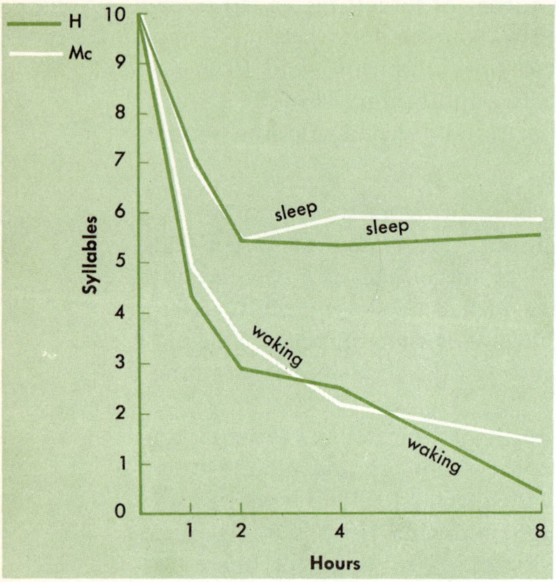

Fig. 9-5. *Differences in retention after sleeping and waking periods. H and Mc are the two subjects in this experiment (after Jenkins and Dallenbach, 1924, p. 610).*

learned earlier and from associations learned later. This is the design for observing the effects of associations learned later on associations learned earlier:

Experimental group	Learn list *A*	Learn list *B*	Test list *A*
Control group	Learn list *A*	Unrelated activity	Test list *A*

This design essentially repeats the experiment on retention after sleeping and waking. In terms of that experiment, the lists which the subjects learned are designated list *A*. The waking activity is equivalent to learning list *B*. The sleeping is equivalent to the unrelated activity of the control group. The recall after sleeping and waking is identical to testing list *A*. Using this design, we discover that the control group has better retention of list *A* than the experimental group because, for the experimental group, learning list *B* interferes with the retention of list *A*—the associations of the two lists compete. The control group eliminates this competition because it has a single list to learn. Interference which arises from associations learned later in time is called *retroactive inhibition*. Such interference, of course, is not retroactive in time (we cannot undo what has been done) but it is retroactive in effect, that is, in the effect it has on the recall of the materials learned earlier.

Proactive inhibition. The second source of interference is from associations learned earlier in time. This source is called proactive inhibition. The following experimental design illustrates it:

Experimental group	Learn list *A*	Learn list *B*	Test list *B*
Control group	Unrelated activity	Learn list *B*	Test list *B*

In these experiments the control group again shows greater retention than the experimental group but for a different reason: Here the list learned earlier interferes with the retention of the list learned later. As in retroactive inhibition, there is response competition, but the source of the interference has shifted. Early investigators believed that retroactive inhibition was the major source of forgetting. Underwood (1957) uncovered an interesting flaw in the early research. He noticed that different studies of forgetting reported very different amounts of forgetting, ranging from 25 per cent to 80 per cent, after one hour. The original forgetting curves of Ebbinghaus were particularly discouraging because they seemed to indicate that after the first hour and certainly after one day our minds become essentially tabulae rasae and forgetting is almost complete. In the studies of retention which Underwood persued, subjects were required to learn several different lists of nonsense syllables. Underwood discovered a very clear relationship between the number of lists learned by the subjects and the amount of forgetting reported by the investigator. Figure 9-6 shows this relationship. When the subject learned a single list, he retained almost 80 per cent after one hour. When he learned over twenty lists the retention rate resembled that in Ebbinghaus' studies, with less than 20 per cent recall after one hour. We can be much less pessimistic today than we could have been in his day about how much we remember and how much we forget.

The major cause of forgetting appears to be proactive inhibition. In defending this assertion, Underwood (1964b, p. 146) states:

> Assume that a student, ten years of age, learns a given task and the retention of this task is tested one month later. The fact that proactive inhibition is assigned a major role in the cause of forgetting is based on the assumption that, during the first ten years of the student's life, he will have acquired more habits that will interfere with the task to be recalled than he will acquire during the one-month interval between learning and the retention test.

The emphasis on proactive inhibition stresses the importance in verbal learning of the student's entering behavior. The assessment of that behavior must include an appraisal not only of its status (the responses

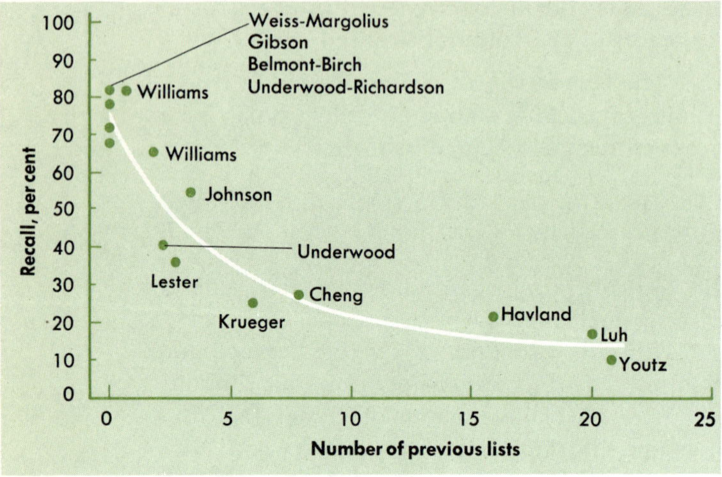

Fig. 9-6. *The percentage of material retained after one hour and the number of lists previously memorized by the subject (after Underwood, 1957, p. 53).*

which are and are not available) but also of its potentially interfering effects on subsequent learning. More succinctly, not everything we have learned in the past makes it easier to learn new things in the present since learning is not an additive process, the simple accretion of knowledge; we are both the slaves and the masters of our previous learning. Underwood (1964b) goes on to suggest that some individuals may be able to resist interference better than others. Such a variable should also be included in the assessment of entering behavior.

Length of the sequence. This refers to the amount of material presented to the student. The length of verbal sequences may vary from a simple sequence of two links (*dog—chien*) to long sequences which include all the lines of a Shakespearean play. Miller (1956) presents evidence that the span of immediate memory is about seven links (or bits of information). After seven links we recode the materials we are learning into chunks of information. Since the memory span is a fixed number of chunks, we can increase the amount of information we retain by building larger and larger chunks. Deese (1958) uses this example. You are asked to remember this number after a single reading 010110100110101011011100111001110 0. How much can you remember Almost everyone would try to recode it. Most individuals would try to reorganize the series into sequences of three: 010–110–100–110, and so on. A more efficient method is to recode by assigning numerical name to groups of three numbers. For example, 100 could be coded as *fou* and 110 as *five*. Using the second method, you would have fewer names than individual digits to remember. Nonsense syllables are harder to memorize than English prose because the prose is already organized into chunks; we must reorganize the nonsense material.

SERIAL-POSITION EFFECT. This effect describes the fact that the easiest parts of a sequence (or list) to learn are the beginning and the end and the most difficult part is that just past the middle. Subjects recalling a list of twelve nonsense syllables, for example, make the greatest number of errors in about the seventh position. Jensen (1962) found that spelling errors show the serial-position effect. That is, errors in spelling are generally more frequent in the middle of the word, with the fewest errors at the beginning and the end. Figure 9-7 shows the serial-position effect for nonsense syllables. Figure 9-8 shows the curve for English words of various length. You can see that the curves are very similar in shape.

SUMMARY. Interference is the competition of old and new responses which results in forgetting. In retroactive inhibition what is learned later in time interferes with the retention of what was learned earlier. In proactive inhibition what was learned earlier in time interferes with the retention of what is learned later. From the standpoint of entering

Fig. 9-7. *The number of errors made at each position in a list of nonsense syllables in serial learning (after Hovland, 1938, p. 275).*

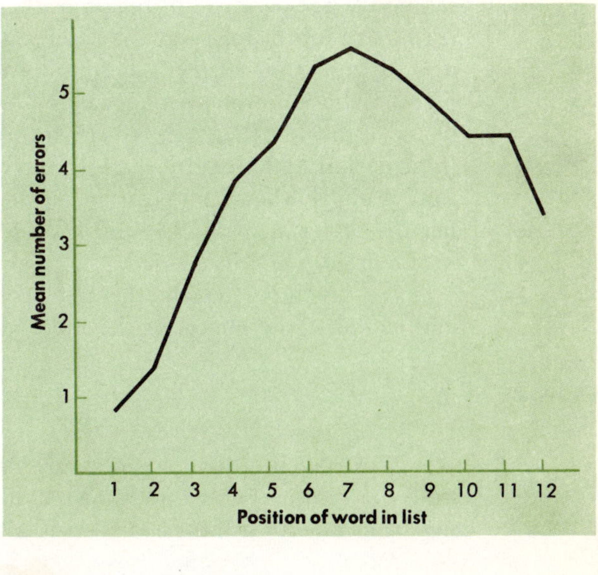

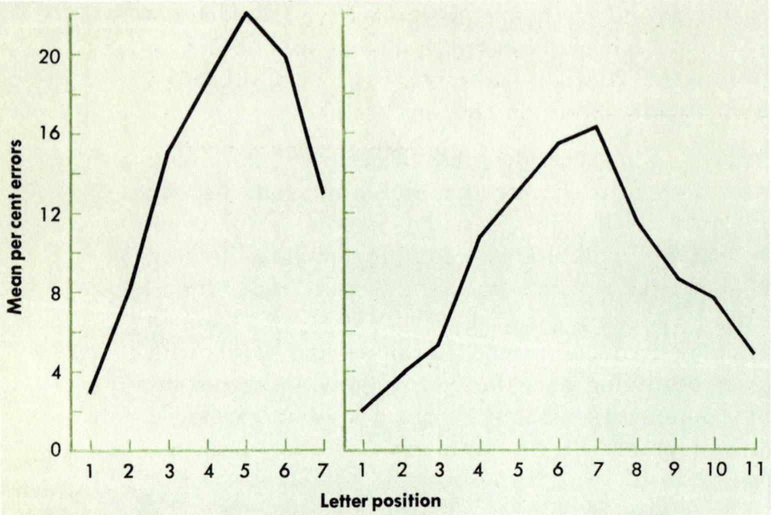

Fig. 9-8. *Serial-position curves for errors in seven- and eleven-letter words. The curve for seven-letter words is based on a total of 1,546 spelling errors made on twenty-four words by 150 eighth graders. The eleven-letter curve is based on a total of 2,262 spelling errors made on forty-eight words by 89 junior college freshmen (after Jensen, 1962, p. 107).*

behavior, proactive inhibition is the major cause of forgetting. This conclusion is at odds with the traditional belief that what was learned subsequently (retroactive inhibition) rather than what was learned previously (proactive inhibition) was the chief source of forgetting. Present evidence also suggests that extinction is the process underlying interference. Concerning the amount of material (or length of the sequence or list), evidence indicates that we recode information we learn into chunks of information and thereby increase our capacity to retain bits of information. Finally, the serial-position effect describes the tendency to remember the material in the beginning and the end and to forget the material in the middle of a list.

We can now turn to the last external condition of verbal learning and examine the effects of the method of measurement on retention.

Methods of Measurement

The way in which we measure retention of verbal learning affects what we retain. Figure 9-9 shows five retention curves for periods varying from twenty minutes to two days for the five methods of measuring retention which I shall describe below. You should notice that the recognition method produces the highest and the anticipation method the lowest score. The curve for the savings (relearning) method should follow the pattern of the other curves and fall between the curves for the anticipation and reproduction methods. A methodological flaw in the study resulted in the distortion of this curve.

I shall now describe each of the five methods of measurement designated in Fig. 9-9.

REPRODUCTION. This method (which you may have referred to as the *recall method*) requires the student to reproduce the material he has learned. You have taught the student five crucial dates of American history: 1776, 1789, 1849, 1860, and 1918. Using the reproduction method, on the midterm examination you require the student to list these dates and the associated events. Or, after a review of the history of verbal learning, you ask this question on an essay examination: List the psychologists who have made important methodological and theoretical contributions to the study of verbal learning. The essay examination, properly conceived, employs essentially the reproduction method: The student is required to reproduce what he has learned.

RECOGNITION. This method requires the student to select from a series of items those which are the responses he has learned. Multiple-choice examinations are the most common examples of the recognition method. The student is presented with this test item: The (American)

Fig. 9-9. *The method of measuring retention affects the amount of retention (Luh, 1922, p. 22).*

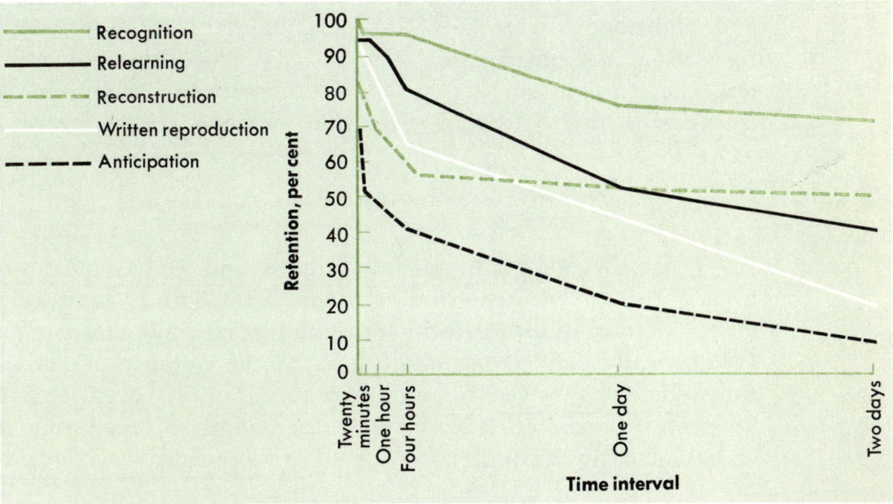

Civil War began in (1) 1776, (2) 1789, (3) 1849, (4) 1860, (5) 1918. The student recognizes (he selects) the correct response (1860).

Reconstruction. This method requires the student to unscramble a set of scrambled items. You ask the student to do the following: Arrange in proper chronological order the following historical events: (1) the French Revolution, (2) the American Civil War, (3) the American Declaration of Independence, (4) World War I, and (5) the California Gold Rush. By recalling the approximate dates for these events, the student can reconstruct the proper order.

Anticipation. This method, you have seen, is used in laboratory research on verbal learning. It requires the student to recall the next item in a series. Using a special mechanical contrivance which exposes one word at a time, the student must anticipate the next word in the list. If we use the dates instead of words, when the student sees 1776 he is expected to anticipate 1789. When he sees 1789, he anticipates 1849, and so on. After he learns the list of dates, you test him to find out how many he can recall in the proper order.

Savings. The savings (or relearning) method requires the student to learn a set of materials to mastery (an errorless performance) and then to relearn the materials. Using a fairly simple calculation, the teacher determines how much less time was required for relearning than for original learning. It is a somewhat surprising finding that relearning takes less time when the subject does not recognize the materials as being familiar.

If you now return to Fig. 9-10 (and remember the correction for the methodological flaw), you can observe the following. After one or two days, the amount of retention is greatest for the recognition method and diminishes as we move through the reconstruction, reproduction, relearning, and anticipation methods. To state this finding in another way, the most demanding or sensitive measures of retention are the relearning (or savings) and anticipation methods.

Summary

I have treated both meaningfulness and verbal mediation as aspects of the student's entering behavior. They both refer to the repertory of verbal associations with which the student enters the learning situation. I empirically defined meaningfulness as the number of verbal associations elicited by a verbal unit. As a condition of verbal learning it influences the rate of learning and the length of retention. I defined verbal mediation as talking to yourself in ways which are relevant to some thing you are learning or to a problem you are solving. The evidence which shows how verbal mediators facilitate learning and how their absence in disadvantaged children inhibits learning indicates their general importance in verbal learning.

We also examined several external conditions of verbal learning. First, the supplying of instructions to learn can vary from the situation in which the teacher supplies no information before learning begins on what will be tested to the situation in which the teacher supplies specific information. When no instructions are supplied, the students appear to supply their own. Second, practice is an important condition. Massed and distributed practice, overlearning, and part and whole practice all have their facilitating and inhibiting effects on verbal learning. Third, reinforcement does not appear to be a major condition of verbal learning, and evidence indicates that under particular conditions a prompting procedure may be equally or more effective than a confirmation or reinforcement procedure. Fourth, several factors result in interference and forgetting. What has been learned earlier is very often a source of interference for what is learned later (proactive inhibition). The process underlying proactive and retroactive inhibition appears to be the process of extinction. Attempts to retain discrete bits rather than chunks of information also result in forgetting. Finally, it is often easier to retain the beginning and the end of verbal materials than to retain the middle portions. The fifth (and last) condition, the method of measurement, also influences how much we retain. The savings (or relearning) and anticipation methods are the most sensitive for measuring retention of verbal material.

In the following section of the chapter we shall consider the implications of the internal and external conditions of verbal learning for the design of instructional procedures.

You should now return to objectives 4–25 (pp. 323–24) and determine how well you have achieved them.

QUESTION 9-2

Mr. Werdee wants his students to distinguish between three land masses: a peninsula, an island, and a continent. He presents several drawings of each and directs his students to make the following associations: peninsula—finger; island—button; and continent—pfug. Each time they see a drawing they must respond with the word associated with the land mass. Which of the following conditions of verbal learning is Mr. Werdee particularly providing? (a) meaningfulness; (b) verbal mediation; (c) instructions to learn; (d) reinforcement.

After selecting your answer, give the reasons for your choice and for your rejection of the alternatives.

INSTRUCTION IN VERBAL KNOWLEDGE

The claim is made that the experimental psychologist often ignores behavior which does not fit his theories and measures. Underwood (1964a) relates an anecdote which illustrates this point. In his laboratory the experimenter records why the subjects sometimes fail to complete the task. Once the record bore this notation: "About half way through the experiment the subject rose from his seat, muttered, 'To hell with it,' and walked out of the room." For another subject the notation was: "Subject dismissed; insisted on talking to the experimenter when he was supposed to be learning." Underwood facetiously comments (p. 75):

> Perhaps we are not alert enough to such happenings. Perhaps the investigator of the sleepy rat could, by modifying the situation somewhat, produce an ideal device for studying sleep-inducing stimuli. Perhaps the subject who stalked out of the experimental room rather than continue learning would give us a lead for the study of frustration and withdrawal behavior. Perhaps the talkative subject has provided us with a hypothesis on the memory drum as an instigator of social behavior.

Underwood (1959, p. 109) believes, however, that the phenomena of verbal learning which this chapter has described derive from studies which closely approximate the conditions of the classroom:

> Speaking of laboratory studies is only a manner of indicating a situation where there is some control of conditions and an active variation of some particular factor or factors. The important point is that the danger involved in generalizing from laboratory to the classroom for verbal learning studies may be less than anticipated for in fact the classroom is often the laboratory.

This section of the chapter deals with the instructional implication of the verbal-learning research we have now examined. As in the cas of skill learning, I present these implications as a series of teaching step which conform to the basic teaching model. These are the steps: (1 Describe for the student what you expect him to learn. (2) Examine th instructional task and materials for their meaningfulness. (3) Assess en tering behavior for the availability of meaningful responses and verba mediators. (4) Provide the appropriate practice conditions. (5) Provid knowledge of correct responses. (6) Provide conditions which reduc interference. (7) Use suitable methods for measuring retention.

Step 1: Describe for the Student What You Expect Him to Learn

This step derives from the research on incidental vs. intentional learning. The experiment of Postman and Senders (1946) showed that intentional learners obtained higher test scores than did incidental learners. In taking this step you should inform the students, prior to the time they begin to study, what aspects of their performance will be assessed. In effect, you should state for them the instructional objectives.

A classroom study by Ausubel and his associates (1957) illustrates the importance of telling students before they study what their tests will comprise. Students were given a passage of three or four pages on opiate addiction. In the first phase of the experiment the students were told that they would be tested on the materials at the end of the period. They were not told, however, that they would be retested two weeks later on the same materials. In the second phase of the experiment, which occurred the following semester, a second group of students was given the same passage to read. They were also told that they would be tested at the end of the period, and, in addition, that they would be tested two weeks later. They received this latter information after they had studied the passage. The results showed no significant differences in the scores of the two groups on either the immediate or the follow-up test. Telling your students what they will be tested on after they have studied does very little good.

We now need to look at an experiment in which students are told beforehand how their performance will be evaluated. It is a situation close to your hearts in that it involves student teachers and grades in educational psychology and student teaching. Merlin Wittrock (1963) informed one group of student teachers that the final course grade they received in educational psychology and student teaching would be determined by the amount of improvement in the performance of their high school students. A second group of student teachers did not receive this direction. The high school students of both groups were given tests to determine how much they knew about social studies, government, history, and English at the beginning of the semester, and they were tested later to determine how much more they knew at the end of the semester. The student teachers, therefore, were to be graded on the basis of the gains or the losses (a tragedy for everyone concerned) of their high school students. The experimental groups were the students of those teachers who received the direction. The control groups were the students of nondirected student teachers. The results were impressively clear: The students in the experimental groups did considerably better than those in the control groups, especially in English. Further evidence indicated that students in the control groups had more favorable attitudes toward their student teachers than did students in the experimental groups. I allow you to guess why.

In taking step 1, two common instructional practices should be avoided. First, the practice of launching the instructional ship in unchartered waters with no destination specified can only diffuse the students' attention and cause them to attend to irrelevant and sometimes competing aspects of the instructional materials. Although we know that incidental learning occurs without specific direction, we also know that particular learning occurs more frequently and more easily when instructions on what to learn are explicit. The romantic educator laments the student's passage from childhood to manhood and would rather let him wander through the halls of academe learning (incidentally) whatever he can. There is considerable doubt that the progress of civilization is so utterly accidental and that such relatively untutored children ever learn much that is worthwhile. Second, the ignominious practice, more common in colleges and high schools than in elementary schools, of teaching one set of materials and testing on quite a different and unrelated set should be avoided. Students are born gamblers, and, if they think they can save energy and time, they are sometimes willing to play this guessing game with the teacher. One's education ought to be more than a gamble (it is a gamble even when teachers do what they are supposed to do), and we ought to invest more time and ingenuity in easing the learning of our students than in outwitting them.

Step 2: Examine the Instructional Task and Materials for Their Meaningfulness

I defined meaningfulness as word frequency or familiarity—the mor frequently a word occurs in the language, the greater its familiarity and therefore, its meaningfulness. This definition suggests that some of th verbal materials you use in your teaching will be more meaningful tha others. Studies have been made of the most frequently used words i the English language, and the resulting lists are available to the teache (e.g., Thorndike-Lorge, 1944). Such lists are often used in the prepara tion of reading materials for the elementary grades. They can also b appropriately used in the preparation of verbal instructional materia both written and oral, at all educational levels.

One way of performing this step is to make a list of words whic occur in the materials you will use and for which you do not plan t provide explicit instruction. These are words you are assuming to b in the students' entering behavior. A check of your list with a publishe word-frequency count will indicate the likelihood of the students' being familiar with the word. In this way you may discover that the students' entering behavior is below the level that you expected and that you will have to select more familiar words or provide instruction which will raise the level of entering verbal behavior.

Step 3: Assess Entering Behavior for the Availability of Meaningful Responses and Verbal Mediators

In assessing the availability of meaningful responses, the teacher is attempting to make relatively meaningless materials meaningful. Or, if you prefer less technical language, the teacher is making unfamiliar materials familiar. The definition seems obvious—no one would expect otherwise of any competent teacher. Considerably less obvious are the procedures the teacher must use to perform this function. The performance requires two things: to assess the student's entering behavior to discover not only which responses are available but also their relative availability and to present the new (presently meaningless) materials in terms of meaningful responses now available to the student. As you learned in Chapter 3, the assessment of entering behavior involves testing the student's knowledge of material which is related to the new material you are about to introduce but for which you will not provide instruction. If the results of your testing indicate (and in most classrooms this would not be surprising) that the student lacks the prerequisite entering behavior, then you must teach the prerequisites first. Once the student has acquired the necessary entering behavior, you can proceed to the next step; that is, you can present the new materials in terms of meaningful responses—those which are available and relatively strong. The actual instruction you provide must bridge the old and the new meanings. Totally meaningless materials (if they exist) require considerably more time to learn. When the teacher does introduce highly novel materials (as in mathematics and some uncommon foreign languages), he should provide the additional time required for familiarization.

Mr. U. Knowitt wants his students to learn to use appropriately the colon and the semicolon in the writing of their weekly themes. He also wants to perform step 3 conscientiously. He first administers a short test to discover how skilled the students are in using these and other, more familiar marks of punctuation. The test results indicate that the students have mastered the use of the period and the comma (if "mastery" of the comma is possible). He then gives them some reading material containing colons and semicolons and asks them to explain their use. In this way Mr. Knowitt has assessed the entering behavior of the students and now has some information he can use in planning his instruction. In introducing the use of the colon and semicolon, he reviews what the students know about periods and commas. He points out the similarity of the use of the colon to that of the period, and of the use of the semicolon to that of the comma. The semicolon, like the comma, is often used to separate phrases and clauses in a series, especially when the phrases are lengthy and when the clauses form complete sentences. In other words, the semicolon indicates less connectedness than does the comma. The colon is a more formal stop than the period. For example, lengthy quotations within a text are often introduced with a colon. Mr. Knowitt gives several examples of the use of periods and colons and of commas and semicolons, carefully pointing out the similarities to capitalize on the knowledge of punctuation the students have already acquired. Later, of course, he must teach the distinctions in the use of the relatively unfamiliar punctuation marks. In any case, Mr. Knowitt has performed step 3: He assessed the entering behavior of his students to discover the relative availability of punctuation responses, and he presented the new material in terms of these responses. Of course, the familiarization function is not divorced from other functions the teacher must perform. Life, especially the life of the teacher, is never so simple as we can make it in textbook illustrations.

We can now consider the assessment of entering behavior for the availability of verbal mediators (the rest of step 3). This step consists of the following procedures: (1) determining which verbal and pictorial mediators may be useful for the instructional task; (2) assessing entering behavior to find out which of these (and others) may be available; and (3) supplying mediators which may be useful in the learning of the task.

Charles Spiker (1963) describes an experiment in which children learned to distinguish drawings of four faces through the use of verbal mediators. In the pretraining period, some of the children learned distinctive names for the faces, such as *wug* and *kos.* The other children learned similar names, such as *zim* and *zam.* In the experiment proper the children were asked to identify new examples of the four faces. Those children who had learned (in fact, overlearned) the distinctive names (mediators) were able to distinguish the faces more easily than were those who had learned similar names. The experiment showed that not any mediator will do, and, for a given task, some mediators are better than others. In the next chapter you will see how effectivel mediators have been used in the teaching and learning of concepts.

Step 4: Provide the Appropriate Practice Conditions

In the performance of this step the teacher must (1) provide opportunities for the student to make the necessary responses, (2) schedul practice on a massed or a distributed basis, (3) determine the degree of mastery the student must attain, and (4) provide either part or whole practice. I described the experimental bases for making these decisions in the preceding section.

First, you can provide the student with the opportunity for making the responses he is expected to learn in several ways: recitation, discussion, and programed instruction. When we discuss programed instruction (Chapter 12), we will consider the research on overt vs. covert responses. Here we will confine our attention to recitation and discussion. The recitation method is characterized by assignment, study, and report (Wallen and Travers, 1963, p. 483). In American public schools it is considered the traditional method of instruction, although little experimental evidence supports it. Recitation allows the individual student to practice overt responses. It may well be true that the hoary practice of choral recitation, in which the whole class roars the right answer to the teacher's question, leaves much to be desired. The difficulty with choral recitation, apart from its generally noisy aspect, is that Elvis and Ella Mae may be able to hide their ignorance behind the impressive roar of their classmates. All the research we have on overt responding assumes individual monitoring of each student's responses.

There has been considerably more research on the discussion method, especially the comparison of the relative effectiveness of the discussion and the lecture methods for the learning of factual information (Wallen and Travers, 1963, p. 481). Most of these studies find no significant differences between the two methods. The effect of the discussion method on the retention of learning has rarely been investigated: One study (Ward, 1956) found greater retention of material for students of high academic ability with discussion procedures and greater retention for students of low ability with the lecture method. The difficulty with group discussion is the same difficulty we find with choral recitation: There is little opportunity to monitor individual student responses. The discussion method has the further disadvantage of providing only limited opportunity for students to make overt responses: While one student talks, all the rest must listen. Unless the teacher provides oral instruction on a one-to-one basis, programed instruction is one of the few instructional procedures which provides each student in a group of students with the opportunity to respond and to obtain knowledge of results for each response.

Second, you must decide how to schedule the students' practice. Should you provide massed or distributed practice? The best practice schedule makes the most efficient use of the students' and the teacher's time and yields the greatest amount of learning and the longest periods of retention. The criteria are clear, but the procedures for meeting them are not. Certainly, when there is very little time for the learning of new material, massed practice is more efficient than distributed practice. In distributed practice, you recall, the teacher must allow for learning (practice) time and intervals between practice. When you are interested in having your students retain fairly large amounts of material for long periods of time, you should provide distributed practice. If you use a schedule of distributed practice, you must also decide what you will have the students do during the practice intervals. If the intervals are to be effective, the students cannot be occupied with learning related material, which only interferes with the retention of the practice material. The intervals can, of course, be occupied with the learning of relatively unrelated material or with recreational activities. One could even develop a rather valid argument for periodic recreational activities in the classroom to facilitate student learning.

If you plan your instruction in sufficient detail and with scrupulous respect for time, the practice of old material possibly can be combined with the introduction of new material. Travers (1963) suggests that the teacher utilize multiplication in the solution of daily problems in and out of school rather than simply drilling the student on the multiplication tables. The student has many opportunities to practice his reading skills in perusing material of his own choice as well as in reading class assignments. Practice, however, cannot be left to chance. Unless you arrange for practice in spelling, reading, writing, speaking, and playing the violin, there will often be no practice. Surveying the crowded school curriculum, one is often tempted to recommend a reform in which we teach a few things well, with practice, rather than myriad things poorly, without practice.

Third, you must decide which instructional tasks should be overlearned, and you must allow the student to practice these tasks beyond mastery. The tasks scheduled for overlearning should be those which are mandatory entering behavior for the learning of a wide array of future tasks. Certain linguistic and mathematical skills and concepts must often be overlearned so that they can be automatically applied in more advanced learning. In this course in educational psychology it is mandatory that you overlearn the components of the basic teaching model. If you do not, your understanding of the course organization will certainly be poor. Overlearning can sometimes be provided by a spiral treatment of the particular learning task. That is, you can return again and again to the same task and require the student to practice it in continuously changing contexts.

Fourth, you must decide whether to require part or whole practice. You should base this decision on the structure of the learning material. Students can learn material which logically divides into parts and recombines into wholes by part practice. Other materials may require whole practice. The standard, again, is learning the most in the least amount of time. A poem with several stanzas, for example, has readily recognized parts and an overall structure in which the parts readily fit. An impressionistic essay, on the other hand, which tries to portray a general mood or attitude, may require reading and practice in its entirety since it lacks any discernible structure. Even impressionistic or existential poetry may defy profitable part practice.

Step 5: Provide Knowledge of Correct Responses

In this step you must provide prompting or confirmation (reinforcement) of correct responses. In prompting, you provide the correct answers before the student responds. In confirming, you provide the correct answers after the student responds. Some evidence indicates that prompting may be more effective than confirmation in early practice and that both procedures may be equally effective in late practice. With these and any other procedures, however, the student must have some means of discovering the correct answers and the opportunity to compare his own answers with them.

Step 6: Provide Conditions which Reduce Interference

In this step you must reduce the influence of factors which cause interference and forgetting. On the basis of the research we have considered, these general recommendations can be made: (1) The performance of this step requires the type of task analysis which reduces the major task to a series of component tasks. Such an analysis makes explicit for the teacher the steps the student must take and the order in which he must take them to master the task. In this sense, once the teacher has completed the task analysis, he has completed the major part of the sequence. (2) After the task analysis, the teacher must present the subtasks in such a way as to avoid interference. In the case of proactive inhibition, interference results when the learning of an earlier subtask interferes with retention of a subtask learned later. Retroactive inhibition occurs when the learning of a later task interferes with retention of a subtask learned earlier. (3) The teacher must find those points in the material he presents which are frequently sources of interference or confusion. Our present knowledge of the effects of stimulus-and-response similarity should assist the teacher in identifying sequences likely to interfere with the retention of materials. (4) We know that highly dissimilar stimuli and responses prevent forgetting. Through the use of various devices, such as color, symbols, and drawings, the teacher may introduce dissimilarity into potentially confusing materials. An oversimplified example is the following: To aid students to learn and remember the differences between *ie* and *ei* in words like *receive, either, believe,* and so on, *ie* could be printed in red and *ei* in blue. Devices of this nature help to reduce retroactive inhibition. (5) The major source of forgetting is proactive inhibition—what the student has previously learned in our own and other classes. With a fairly standard curriculum for all students, we could identify sources of proactive inhibition. With so much diversity in the entering behavior of our students however, we must identify sources of interference for individual students. As in the case of assessing entering behavior for meaningful responses, research on proactive inhibition confirms our emphasis on the careful assessment of the entering behavior of the student as an important basis for planning instruction.

Step 7: Use Suitable Methods of Measurement

You recall that the method of measurement affects how much is retained. How do you decide which method to use? The basis for this decision should be the standard of acceptability specified in the statement of the instructional objective. If the objective requires, under given conditions, that the student only recognize the correct response in a list of alternatives or reconstruct a list by unscrambling it, you should use only those methods of measurement. If the standard of acceptability requires recall, relearning, and anticipation, then you should use these more rigorous methods. Ordinarily we reserve the use of the relearning and anticipation methods for the laboratory, but we can easily adapt them to the classroom. You should also remember that each of these methods gives you a slightly altered picture of the effectiveness of your instructional procedures. For the most exacting tests of your procedures, for those moments in your career when you achieve supreme confidence in and a scientifically dispassionate view of your own teaching, you can use the more rigorous methods of measurement.

Summary

I have described seven steps you should take in teaching verbal knowledge—the verbal component in instructional objectives.

Step 1: Describe for the student what you expect him to learn.
Step 2: Examine the instructional task and the materials for their meaningfulness.
Step 3: Assess entering behavior for the availability of meaningful responses and verbal mediators.
Step 4: Provide the appropriate practice conditions.

Step 5: Provide knowledge of correct results.
Step 6: Provide conditions which reduce interference.
Step 7: Use suitable methods of measurement.

In the last section of this chapter we shall focus on the nature of language and its implications for teaching. The first two sections emphasized verbal (or language) learning and its implications for teaching.

You should now return to objectives 26–32 (p. 325) and determine how well you have achieved them.

QUESTION 9-3

Miss Pegg wants her students to learn the French equivalents of English names of anatomical parts (arm, elbow, leg, knee, and so on). Before requiring the students to recite the whole list of paired associates, she gives them extended practice on each pair of English and French words. Which of the following instructional steps is Miss Pegg performing? (a) Providing a statement of the instructional objective (step 1); (b) examining the task for its meaningfulness (step 2); (c) providing for knowledge of correct results (step 5); (d) providing conditions which reduce interference (step 6).

After selecting your answer, give the reasons for your choice and for your rejection of the alternatives.

LINGUISTICS AND TEACHING

In this final section of the chapter we shall examine the nature of anguage as viewed by the linguist and psycholinguist (the psychologist vho studies language) and see what implications their studies have for eaching. The first part of this section deals with the nature and the ›urpose of language—as a communication vehicle, as a series of language ınits, and as transformational grammar. The second part deals with he teaching of reading and foreign languages.

The Nature of Language

Dolphins and bees, for example, have language or communication ut, as far as we know, their languages lack the unique combination of :atures of human language. Susan Ervin-Tripp (1964) lists three par-cular features which combine to produce human language: the combina-on and the recombination of a limited number of elements; the creation f arbitrary meanings for combinations which are conventional in a ›cial group; and the reference to distant objects and events and to in-ngible concepts. These three characteristics make human language expandable and flexible in form and in meaning. The first characteristic, combination and recombination, makes language expandable in form, so that we can always create sounds, words, and grammatical parts and rules. We continually engage in the rather marvelous act of composing sentences which have never been uttered before, a feat unmatched even by computers with the largest capabilities. The second and third characteristics make language expandable and flexible in meaning. We can invent new terms or give old terms new meanings which are quickly accepted and used by various social groups. The whole nation is frequently delighted by the expansion of vocabulary which accompanies our exploration of space and our attempts to make a safe landing on the moon. The Russians are able to describe their space program in their language. Even the Chinese and French have nuclear and missile programs which their languages if not their foreign policies accommodate very well. All nations, with all their languages, are engaged in a universal discourse on international government and law, which demonstrates the flexibility of all languages. Also, many of the things we talk about—world government, world peace, and an era of human equality—are distant and not always tangible concepts. Unlike animal communication, human communication is not limited to discussion of the present. We can talk about the past and the future and the highly abstract. In education, language accommodates scientific subjects and the physical and creative arts as easily as it accommodates literature and history.

Language Units

The structural linguist analyzes language into basic components. Although there is no universal agreement on what the structural units are, two types of units have received considerable attention—phonemes and morphemes.

Phonemes. These are the basic sound units of a language. More particularly, they are bundles of mutually exclusive sounds (Eric Hamp, 1967). In English, for example, *p* has four sounds: A breathed *p* appears at the beginning of words like *peace;* an unbreathed *p* occurs in words such as *spit* and *span;* an exploded *p* occurs in a word like *cup;* and a glottalized *p* is heard when we say the word *peace* immediately after we have taken a drink of water. Each of these is a distinct sound, but in English we have bundled these sounds together into one phoneme for *p*. That is, we will recognize the phoneme within the range and limits of these four sounds. Similarly, in English we recognize distinctive sounds not heard in other languages. The Spaniard, for example, does not hear the *d* sound in the middle or the end of the word as a ditinctive phoneme. For this sound most Spaniards use a voiceless *th*. The characterization which we give foreign languages is the result of hearing those languages through our own patterns of phonemes. When we say that German sounds "guttural," we have only observed a phonemic pattern different from our own, such as *shl* and *tzt* in *shlange* and *jetzt* and the liberal use of the phoneme *ch*. When we call Italian the "lilting" language, among other things we have noticed the double consonant clusters in words like *fratello* and *madonna*. Both the German and the Italian consonant clusters are usually lacking in English. All known languages now employ between twelve and eighty phonemes, and in English (depending on your dialect) we employ between forty and forty-five. Hamp (1967, p. 12) describes phonemes as follows:

> The sounds have no intrinsic meaning of their own; they are merely the smallest contrasted units that can be isolated in a stream of speech. They may be likened to bricks which, though each has its own color, consistency, and character, may be put together to build a wall, a sewer, a well, and even a statue.

Henry Gleason (1965) observes that if you listen carefully when you ask an English-speaking child to utter nonsense, you will notice that it is English nonsense. It is interesting to note that the phonemes do not occur with equal frequency. Nine English phonemes account for 50 per cent of the spoken language. The *i* in *hit* is used one hundred more imes than the *z* in *azure*.

Morphemes. These language units consist of phonemes and convey meaning. A morpheme is any form which cannot be divided into two r more forms (Carroll, 1964). Carroll uses these examples: In the words *lighthouse, redbook,* and *unreconstructed,* the morphemes are *light, house, red, book, un-, re-, construct,* and *-ed.* Of the two types of morphemes, *free forms* are those which can stand alone, such as *fish, gold, oy,* and *goldfish. Bound forms* cannot stand alone and occur in ordiary speech with some accompanying form. Examples are *un-, -struct,* nd *con-*. Hamp points out that many but not all words are free forms. nd all free forms are not single words. *The,* for example, is a word, ut it is not a free form because it cannot stand alone. Also, *the house* not a single word, but it is a free form. For the linguist the spaces etween words are simply an accident of history. The word *the* could onveniently be attached to the words it precedes.

Originally the linguist saw these units as combining in various ways produce the grammar or syntax of the language. For example, if he und out how frequently free forms and bound forms occurred and scovered that the bound forms occurred with much higher frequency, he would then state the rules which governed their combination. In this way, he would assemble the forms into a grammar, or a description of the basic structure of the language. Current linguistic theory, however, sees a very different relationship between basic language structure and grammar.

Transformational Grammar

Modern linguists object to the analysis of language in its constituent parts because this analysis obscures aspects of the language about which the native speaker is fully aware. The native speaker, for example, realizes the relationship between sentences which may be quite different in structure. Gleason (1965) states that the native speaker of English would match these sentences without difficulty and in the same way as any other native speaker:

Where are you going?	That is a book.
What is that?	I like that one.
Which one do you like?	I am going tomorrow.
Are you going tomorrow?	I am going home.

The relationship of these sentences does not depend on meaning but on grammar. These sentences are related by rules called *transformations.* All the rules (or transformations) for the English language link together large sets of sentences.

The idea of a transformational grammar was set forth by Noam Chomsky (1957), who tried to explain why the native speaker is able to produce and understand sentences that have never before been written or spoken. Transformational grammar assumes that language is a system of rules and that the application of these rules makes possible the formation and comprehension of new sentences. Knowledge of the language is based on the intuitive mastery of the rules. The rules, in a sense, generate sentences: Applying the rules in a carefully prescribed manner creates only grammatical sentences.

Kernel sentences. Basic to this conception of grammar is the ide of kernel sentences—those underlying sentences of the language from which all other sentences derive. Here are two examples:

Hound Dog came in.
Elvis played hooky.

Kernel sentences have two main structures, a *noun phrase* and a *ver phrase*. In the preceding sentences the noun phrases are *Hound Do* and *Elvis*. You will note that *Elvis* is a single word, but it is still a nou phrase. The verb phrases are *came in* and *played hooky*. You may believe that the linguist has been guilty of term swapping. After all, is not noun phrase a fancy name for subject, and verb phrase for predicate? The distinction is that noun and verb phrases refer to structure, while subject and predicate refer to functions of structures. You recall that the subject is usually defined as the performer of an action, and the predicate as the action. Many sentences, however, contain no performer-action relationship. Some of these may even be kernel sentences, like the following:

Harriet appeared ecstatic.
Archibald was funny.

Single transformations. Using an example of Gleason (1955), let us consider single transformations. Below are two columns of sentences. The sentences in the first column have been changed into the sentences of the second by the application of a rule.

1. John is writing a letter.	John isn't writing a letter.
2. Jim has been trying to do it.	Jim hasn't been trying to do it.
3. James will come tomorrow.	James won't come tomorrow.
4. Ruth was a beautiful girl.	Ruth wasn't a beautiful girl.
5. Mary could have been there.	Mary couldn't have been there.

This rule covers these transformations: Add *n't* as a suffix to the first word in the verb phrase. Sentence 3 contains a minor complication, since *will* and *n't* do not yield *won't*. But this can be shown to be quite regular. Here, then, is a single rule for negative transformations.

Transformations operate on particular sentence structures and not on others. For example, in these sentences the rule which governs changing a noun phrase to an object position applies:

We saw Elvis on Tuesday.
Elvis we saw on Tuesday.

It does not apply to a noun phrase in these positions:

We wanted the name of the boy with Elvis.
Elvis we wanted the name of the boy with.

n the negative transformation above, the rule about adding *n't* to the irst word does not always apply:

His father walked home.
His father walkedn't home.

Words like *walked* must be changed to *did walk,* and the *n't* added to the *did.*

Chomsky's transformational grammar is of major importance in studying the relation of language and thought. The transformational rules are a product of the structure of the language and of the psychological processes within the speaker. Jacques Mehler (1963) has found that the recall of English sentences is related to the applications of these rules. Miller (1962) has explored the relationship of memory to syntactic categories (roughly, parts of speech) and the relation of these categories to the understanding of sentences. In our later discussion of human thought we shall describe his research. We have already referred to the work of Jensen (Chapter 6) which showed that syntactic mediation aids in the learning and retention of words.

KNOWLEDGE OF GRAMMAR IN CHILDREN. Some evidence indicates that the child masters language structure and the transformational rules before he enters school. His mastery, of course, is intuitive in that he can seldom state the rules he is using to create and understand new sentences. Jean Berko (1958), for example, designed a study to find out how much mastery children had of these rules: forming plurals of nouns, forming two possessives of nouns (singular and plural), using the third person singular of verbs, and using the progressive and past tense. All are sophisticated rules, particularly for the children she studied, who were in either preschool or the first grade. To be certain that the child had not memorized the correct linguistic form, she used nonsense words. She could

Fig. 9-10. *Child to give the plural of* wug *after seeing this card (after Berko, 1958, p. 154).*

not, for example, ask the child the plural of *witch* because he might have memorized *witches.* Instead she asked the plural of *wug,* a nonsense word. Figure 9-10 shows one of the cards presented to the child as a test of his knowledge of the rule for forming plurals. Here is one of the questions for testing the rule for past tense:

> The card showed a man with a streaming pitcher in his hand and bore this question:
> This is a man who knows how to spow. He is spowing. He did the same thing yesterday. What did he do yesterday. Yesterday he ———.

And one for testing the rule for the third person singular:

> The card showed a man shaking an object and bore these words:
> This is a man who knows how to naz. He is nazzing. He does it every day. Every day he ———.

For five of the nonsense words, well over half the children made the correct responses, which indicated their knowledge of the rule. Berko concluded that if a child's knowledge of English consisted of no more than storing up many memorized words, the child would refuse to answer because he had never, for example, heard of a *wug.* The children's consistent and orderly answers for the grammatical structures, however, indicated their knowledge of the rules.

Children of three to four years appear to be aware of parts of speech. Brown (1961) presented pictures which depicted action for verbs, mass "count" nouns, and containers for particular nouns. In the case of he verb, for example, the child would be shown a picture and told that e could see *sibbing* (a nonsense verb). He would then be asked to hoose one of three pictures which also showed *sibbing.* The child was xpected to point to the one picture of the three which depicted motion. This study showed that very young children have knowledge of arts of speech and that they use this knowledge as a clue to the meang of words.

Also, response terms of adults presented with a list of words for ree association belong to the same part of speech as the stimulus terms, hile those of young children do not. Adults, for example, respond *ble* to the word *chair* (two nouns). Children respond *eat* to the word *hair* (a verb and noun). Ervin-Tripp (1961) found that with increasg age (starting from seven to twelve), children respond with the same art of speech.

Linguistics and Teaching

It has been "embarrassingly fashionable" to discuss the contributions of linguistics to the teaching of the language arts. John Carroll (1964, p. 179) writes:

> One's embarrassment comes from the fact that despite certain very definite and positive contributions that linguistics can make to these endeavors, these contributions are of relatively small extent. Once we accept such fundamental tenets of linguistics as the primacy of speech over writing, the structure of the language code as a patterning of distinctive communicative elements, and the arbitrariness of standards of usage, and work out their implications in detail, we find that we are still faced with enormous problems of methodology in the teaching of such subjects as English, reading, and foreign languages.

With this caveat, we shall now consider the contribution of linguistics to the teaching of reading and foreign languages.

Instruction in Reading

Structural reading. The basic tenet of Charles Fries (1963) is that we should shift from a word-centered to a structure-centered view of language. Fries describes three stages of learning to read: (1) In the transfer stage, the child must learn to respond rapidly and accurately to the visual patterns of the printed page. This stage should be accomplished by presenting the child with two letters or two simple words at a time and asking him to respond by saying that they are alike or different. (2) The child should overlearn the printed shape of letters and words until he can respond to meanings implicit in the letters and shapes. The child should not be taught the connections between phonemes and graphemes (the printed forms) but should be allowed to discover the connections himself. Fries (unlike Sir James Pitman whose method is discussed below) uses only capital letters to accomplish this end. (3) Finally, the child should learn "vivid imaginative realization" of the values involved in the action or experience he reads about For this the child should read poetry. Fries's method shows the linguisti emphasis on learning language structure and on deriving meaning from knowledge of structure.

Convincing evidence indicates that a child who learns to read wel is forming useful spelling-to-sound habits which relate English phoneme to graphemes. In fact, linguists can predict pronunciation from spelling. The child masters the phonemes of his language before he begin to read. In learning to read he must discover how phonemes, or sound correspond to graphemes, or the written sound. Possibly the child learr grapheme-phoneme rules in the way he learns transformation rules. In any case, he is able to use both rules long before he is able to state them. Eleanor Gibson and her associates (1962) constructed pseudowords on the basis of spelling-to-sound rules. The pseudowords are of two types: (1) those which are pronounceable and follow the rules and (2) those which are unpronounceable, ignore the rules, but consist of the same letters as the pronounceable words. Among the pronounceable words are *dink, vuns, glox, sulb,* and *lods.* Some of the derived unpronounceable words are *nkid, nsuv, xogl, lbus,* and *dsol.* Gibson found that the curve for the pronounceable words was consistently higher than the curve for the unpronounceable words. Figure 9-11 shows the results of the study. The percentage of correct response rises sharply between the first and second exposure and increases very little thereafter. These findings strongly suggest that the proper unit for use in analyzing the processes of reading and writing is not the alphabetical letter but the spelling pattern which has a stable relationship with the phonemic pattern. The reading of words becomes inseparable from the hearing of words.

THE INITIAL TEACHING ALPHABET. With considerable ardor, Pitman and his associates encourage the use of a reformed alphabet for use in beginning reading (Harrison, 1964). Pitman has developed an alphabet in which one sign represents one sound and one sound only (see Tables 9-6 and 9-7). There is, for example, only one sign for the letter *g.* Pitman uses lower-case letters; if a capital is required, the lower-case letter is written large. He writes digraphs (two letters with a single

Fig. 9-11. *Percentage of correct responses for pronounceable* (P) *and unpronounceable* (U) *words (Gibson* et al., *1962, p. 562).*

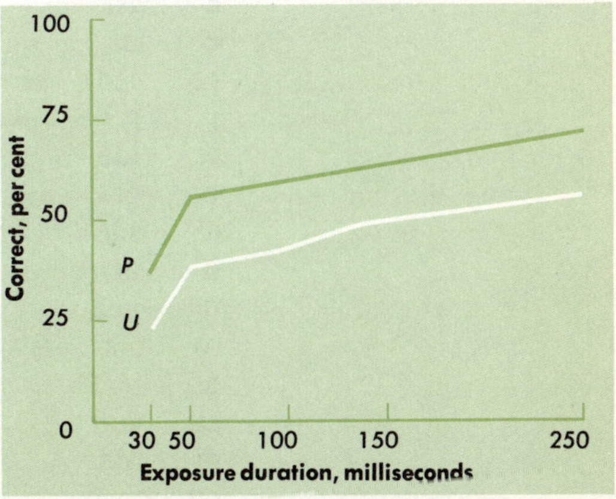

TABLE 9-6

THE INITIAL TEACHING ALPHABET (Harrison, 1964, pp. 110–11).

b	bee	bat	bat
c	kee	cut	cut
d	dee	det	debt
f	ef	fit	fit
g	gay	got	got
h	hay	hunt	hunt
j	jay	jest	jest
k	kay	aks	axe
l	ell	lip	lip
m	em	mous	mouse
n	en	nævy	navy
p	pee	pens	pence
r	ray	rist	wrist
ɹ	er	fiɹst	first
s	ess	sord	sword
t	tee	tiet	tight
v	vee	velvet	velvet
w	way	wun	one
z	zed (or zee)	zeebra	zebra
ƨ	zess	horseƨ	horses
ch	chay	chuɹch	church
ŋ	ing	briŋiŋ	bringing
ʃh	ish	ʃhaft	shaft
th	ith	thaut	thought
ƭh	thee	ƭhis	this
wh	whay	whær	where
ʒ	zhee	meʒuer	measure
y	yay	yot, sity	yacht, city
æ	aid	cæs	case
a	at	caʃh	cash
ɑ	ahd	cɑm	calm
a	ask	casl	castle
e	et	net	net
ee	eed	neet	neat
i	it	nit	knit
ie	ide	niet	night
o	ot	not	knot
œ	ode	nœt	note
u	ut	tuf	tough
ue	ued	tuen	tune
ω	oot	tωk	took
ωω	ood	tωωth	tooth
au	aud	taut	taught
ɔi	oid	tɔi	toy
ou	owd	toun	town

TABLE 9-7

A SPECIMEN OF PRINTING IN THE INTERNATIONAL TEACHING ALPHABET (Harrison, 1964, p. 104).

a spesimen ov i.t.a. printiŋ

ie hav just cum from a scωl whær ŧhe nue reediŋ iz taut. ie met ŧhær a littl girl ov siks. ʃhee iz ŧhe œldest ov a larj family liviŋ on an œldham housiŋ estæt. tω yeerz agœ ʃhee woz a ʃhie nervus chield, tω frietend tω tauk. ʃhee haz wun priezd personal pozzeʃhon—a dog-eerd anthology ov vers, given tω her bie an œlder chield. ŧhat littl girl ov siks haz just red tω mee very buetifωlly wurdzwurth's daffodilz. ie askt her whie ʃhee chœz ŧhat pœem. ʃhee replied ŧhat ʃhee luvd daffodilz.

tωdæ ʃhee speeks wiŧh charm and confidens. ŧhe œnly critisizm ov her reediŋ ov ŧhe pœem miet bee ŧhat ʃhee red it raŧher kwickly, tω neerly at ŧhe speed ov sielent reediŋ. ʃhee found ŧhe pæj in ŧhe bωk bie lωkiŋ up ŧhe pœet's næm in ŧhe alfabetical indeks.

œnly ŧhe sircumstansez ov ŧhat story ar novel. ŧhe acheevment ov ŧhat littl girl ov siks yeerz iz ov itself færly commonplæs in œldham nouadæz.

octœber, 1963

speech sound) as one letter. For example, *mishap,* in which *s* and *h* have different sounds, can be distinguished from *bishop,* in which the *sh* has one sound. When the child is ready, the conventional alphabet replaces the new alphabet. Pitman and his followers have furnished some preliminary evidence that the use of the new alphabet with beginning readers enables them to learn to read conventional materials in less time than conventional reading programs require (Downing, 1964). Important is the fact that the forty-five characters of the new alphabet roughly reflect the English phonemes and try to preserve their sound value while the child is learning to make the transition from speaking to reading.

Instruction in Foreign Languages

Although there has been growing insistence that children learn foreign languages in our schools, very little research supports the feasibility of such a policy. Sometimes the available evidence has been ignored by those educators who are attempting to shape public school policy. One fact that has been ignored, for example, is the wide spread of individual differences in language aptitude, even among students of average and superior intelligence. Here, however, we shall limit our attention to the contribution of linguistics to the teaching of foreign languages.

THE AUDIOLINGUAL METHOD. George Scherer and Michael Wertheimer (1964) describe this method in this way:

> The audiolingual method is characterized by intensive drills in speaking and listening through dialogues which are memorized and pattern drills which are thoroughly learned by the student. Instead of encouraging free conversation at first, the teacher uses directed dialogues which employ the learned patterns. While the foreign language is used as much as is practically possible in the classroom, English may be employed for the explanation of structure and, in varying degrees, for the teaching of meaning. Although grammar is not taught as an end in itself, the materials are constructed so that the students can arrive at its comprehension by induction. After the examples have been drilled, the grammar is discussed and clarified.

The audiolingual method is distinct from the direct method of language instruction, which bans English entirely and excludes formal grammar.

Scherer and Wertheimer (1964) conducted an intensive evaluation of the comparative merits of audiolingual (AL) and traditional (T) language instruction using beginning students of German. At the end of two years of study, these were the results: (1) The groups were equal in listening ability; (2) the AL group was far superior in speaking; (3) the groups were equal in reading; (4) the T group was superior in writing; (5) the groups were equal in English-to-German translation; and (6) the T group was far superior in German-to-English translation. In brief, the new method did not result in equal or superior performance in reading, writing, listening, or translation. The AL students, however, did report a more positive attitude than did the T students toward German and themselves while speaking German. The results of the study hardly support a radical change in foreign language teaching.

THE LANGUAGE LABORATORY. In the past decade there have been several attempts to provide more opportunity for students to hear and speak the foreign language they are studying. The language laboratory has been the most popular technical innovation for providing this opportunity. The language laboratory, as Carroll (1960) remarks, is a misnomer since it is no more like a laboratory than a music practice room or a gymnasium is. It is essentially an opportunity for the students to hear the language spoken by a native and to practice speaking the language themselves. Traditional language teaching, unless the circumstances are ideal, does not usually allow as much time for oral and auditory experience as the student needs to develop speaking skill. Carroll remarks (p. 138), "Trying to teach a spoken foreign language without it [auditory stimulation] would be like trying to teach music appreciation solely from printed musical scores."

In the language laboratory, the student usually listens to a tape recording of a native speaker talking in a particular language. The tapes have spaces which allow the student to repeat what the speaker has said and then to listen once more to what the speaker said the first time. Lawrence Mace and Evan Keislar (1965) have found convincing evidence that the passive listening to tapes in the language laboratory is not enough. A more effective procedure requires the student to make overt responses which are evaluated for their accuracy. In their study, each student received discrimination training in the sounds of the language. The native voice spoke a pair of words, one of which was the correct pronunciation of a French phoneme. The student selected the word he thought correct and was then told the correct answer. He then heard the word again. Finally, the speaker said one word of each pair; the subject circled his choice of which word it was in the booklet and then was given the correct answer. This procedure provided for student participation and instructional feedback. In a later study, Mace (1966) found that training in speaking should precede training in listening to develop listening comprehension. This sequence reverses the ordinary procedure of the audiolingual method.

Many students in the past with traditional methods and many students in the present with a combination of traditional and audiolingual methods have learned and will continue to learn and even master foreign languages. The heralded technological changes for education have revolutionized foreign language instruction no more than they have any other part of the school curriculum.

Summary. This section dealt with linguistics and teaching. Human language is unique because it is expandable and flexible in both form and meaning. It is composed of structural units such as the phoneme and the morpheme. Phonemes are the basic sound units of the language. Morphemes are phonemes which convey meaning. Transformational grammar explains why the native speaker is able to produce and understand sentences that have never been written or spoken before. It assumes that languages are systems of rules and that the application of these rules makes possible the formation and comprehension of new sentences. Kernel sentences are the underlying sentences of the language from which all other sentences derive. Some evidence indicates that the child intuitively masters language structure and transformational rules before his formal education. The application of linguistics to teaching appears at this time to be limited because of our lack of knowledge about teaching methodology and the language arts. Fries argues for discovery learning on the part of the child in linking phonemes and graphemes. According to him, beginning reading should emphasize visual patterns. The research of Gibson and her associates shows that the reading of words is inseparable from the hearing of words. The Initial Teaching Alphabet attempts to simplify beginning reading by making graphemes phonemic. As yet little or no evidence supports the use of the audiolingual over the direct method of foreign language instruction. The language laboratory provides the obvious advantage of allowing the student to hear the language spoken by a native speaker and to practice speaking the language himself.

You should now return to objectives 33–45 (pp. 324–25) and see how well you have achieved them.

QUESTION 9-4

Which of the following conclusions is best supported by the research on linguistics and on teaching described in this chapter?

(a) The child who learns to read well is forming useful spelling-to-sound rules.

(b) When combined with the language laboratory, the audiolingual method is more effective than the direct method of foreign language instruction.

(c) The child's mastery of grammatical rules is largely a product of his early school years.

(d) The Initial Teaching Alphabet is an effective means of teaching grapheme-phoneme relationships.

After selecting your answer, give the reasons for your choice and for your rejection of the alternatives.

SUMMARY

The first section of this chapter dealt with the nature and the developmen of verbal learning. Verbal learning resembles skill learning in that it involve chains of stimulus-response associations. It is distinct from skill learning in tha it involves verbal rather than motor responses. Verbal chains can vary in lengtl from those which have only two links to those which have many. The material used in the study of verbal learning vary from nonsense syllables, or relativel meaningless material, to words and phrases, or relatively meaningful materia Immediate free recall, serial learning, and paired-associate learning are the pro cedures used in this study. We can trace the development of verbal behavio through several levels—distinguishing human speech from other environmenta sounds, naming objects in the environment, physically responding to interna verbal responses, confirming the response, linking words together, and, finally, forming verbal hierarchies.

The second section described the effects of several conditions of verbal learning. Meaningfulness and verbal mediation have powerful effects and are linked to entering behavior. Instructions to learn, practice, confirmation (or reinforcement), interference, and method of measurement also affect verbal learning and are linked to external conditions. Meaningfulness is based on the number of verbal associations elicited by a verbal stimulus. Verbal mediation is talking to yourself in ways which are relevant to something you are learning. Instructions to learn can vary from no instructions, as in the case of incidental learning, to explicit instructions, as in the case of intentional learning. Conditions of practice can also vary: We have massed and distributed practice, overlearning, and part and whole practice. We can provide reinforcement through confirmation or prompting. There are several sources of interference: Retroactive inhibition results from sources occurring later in time; proactive inhibition, from sources occurring earlier in time. There appears to be more interference due to proactive inhibition than to retroactive inhibition. Stimulus similarity within and between learning materials produces interference, and so does the serial-position effect. Finally, the method of measurement also affects how much is retained.

The third section described the instructional steps for providing verbal knowledge. These steps require the teacher to supply the students with statements of instructional objectives, to examine learning tasks for their meaningfulness, to assess entering behavior for meaningful and mediating responses, to provide appropriate practice conditions, to provide knowledge of correct results, to provide conditions which reduce interference, and to use suitable methods of measurement.

The final section dealt with linguistics and teaching. Here we considered the nature of human language, its structural units, and the rules of transformational grammar. The child may master the application of transformational rules long before he is able to verbalize them. We considered the applications of linguistics to the teaching of reading and foreign languages. These applications are limited because of the underdevelopment of the theory and the methodology of teaching the language arts. Apart from linguistics, the language laboratory provides the student the important opportunity to hear native speakers of the language and to practice speaking the language himself.

SUGGESTED READINGS

These are published symposia and books of readings on many aspects of verbal learning and the psychological study of language (psycholinguistics):

De Cecco, John P., ed., *The Psychology of Language, Thought, and Instruction*. New York: Holt, Rinehart & Winston, Inc., 1967.

Kausler, Donald H., ed., *Readings in Verbal Learning*. New York: John Wiley & Sons, Inc., 1966.

Saporta, Sol, ed., *Psycholinguistics*. New York: Holt, Rinehart & Winston, Inc., 1961.

Smith, Frank, and George A. Miller, eds., *The Genesis of Language*. Cambridge, Mass.: M. I. T. Press, 1966.

These articles explore the relationship of research on verbal learning to instructional practice:

Underwood, Benton J., "Verbal Learning in the Educative Process," *Harvard Educational Review,* 29 (1959), 107–17 (also in De Cecco, 1964).

———, "Laboratory Studies of Verbal Learning," in *Theories of Learning and Instruction,* ed. E. R. Hilgard, Part 1 of the 63rd Yrbk. of the National Society for the Study of Education, pp. 133–52. Chicago, 1964.

These articles explore the relationship of verbal learning to concept learning, principle learning, and problem solving:

Mandler, George, "Verbal Learning," in *New Direction in Psychology,* Vol. III, pp. 1–50. New York: Holt, Rinehart & Winston, Inc., 1967.

Underwood, Benton J., "The Representativeness of Rote Verbal Learning," in *Categories of Human Learning,* ed. A. W. Melton, pp. 48–78. New York: Academic Press, Inc., 1964.

These works discuss linguistics and transformational grammar and their possible educational relevance:

Carroll, John B., *Language and Thought.* Englewood Cliffs, N.J.: Prentice-Hall, Inc., 1964 (paper).

Gleason, H. A., Jr., *Linguistics and English Grammar*. New York: Holt, Rinehart & Winston, Inc., 1965.

Postal, P. M., "Underlying and Superficial Linguistic Structures," *Harvard Educational Review,* 34 (1964), 246–66.

See the following books for foreign language teaching and research:

Lado, Robert, *Language Teaching: A Scientific Approach.* New York: McGraw-Hill Book Company, 1964 (paper).

Scherer, George A., and Michael Wertheimer, *A Psycholinguistic Experiment in Foreign-Language Teaching.* New York: McGraw-Hill Book Company, 1964.

The Teaching and Learning of Concepts and Principles

10

In this chapter you learn about more complex learning types than the basic learning types and skill and verbal learning. The learning of concepts and principles is more complex because it requires as entering behavior the previous learning as well as an extension of that learning. You will see, therefore, that the basic learning conditions of contiguity, reinforcement, and practice still apply to the learning of concepts and principles. You will also see that skill and verbal learning are necessary prerequisites.

The chapter has three sections. The first deals with the nature and uses of concepts and principles. In it I define concept and principle, their relationship to levels of intellectual development, and, primarily in the context of the school and classroom, their uses. The second section deals with the teaching of concepts. Here I describe nine instructional steps concerning expected performance, selection of attributes, provision of verbal mediators, provision of positive and negative examples, order of presentation of the examples, identification of further examples, verification of concept learning, definition of the concept, and, finally, practice and reinforcement. The third section deals with the teaching of principles. Here I describe eight instructional steps concerning expected performance, identification of component concepts, recollection of previously learned concepts, proper ordering of the component concepts, demonstration of the principle, full statement of the principle, verification of principle learning, and practice and reinforcement. This brief résumé of the steps for concept and principle teaching should reveal the close similarity of their learning conditions.

Upon reading the first section of this chapter (on the nature and uses of concepts and principles), you should be able to meet these objectives:

1. Define concept in terms of a class of stimuli and give three examples of concepts in the subject areas you plan to teach.
2. Define attribute in terms of concepts and designate the attributes of your three illustrative concepts.
3. Define attribute value in terms of attributes and designate the attribute values of your three illustrative concepts.
4. Give the number of attributes of your three illustrative concepts.
5. Define attribute dominance in terms of obviousness and designate the relative dominance of the attributes of your three illustrative concepts.
6. Distinguish among conjunctive, disjunctive, and relational concepts in terms of the relationship of their attributes and give two examples of each type of concept.
7. Define principle in terms of concepts and other principles and give three examples of principles in the subject areas you plan to teach.
8. Express your three principles as if-then statements.
9. Indicate the relationship between the teaching of concepts and principles and the student's level of intellectual development by describing two concepts and principles you plan to teach at each level.
10. Demonstrate the relationship between concept learning and preschool experience by using a particular concept.
11. Illustrate six uses of concepts in school learning in terms of reducing environmental complexity, identifying objects, reducing the need for constant learning, providing direction for activity, facilitating instruction, and serving as stereotypes.

Upon reading the second section of this chapter (on the teaching of concepts), you should be able to describe and illustrate each of the following instructional steps:

12. Step 1: Describe the performance expected of the student after he has learned the concept.
13. Step 2: Reduce the number of attributes to be learned in complex concepts and make important attributes dominant.

14. Step 3: Provide the student with useful verbal mediators.

15. Step 4: Provide positive and negative examples of the concept in terms of appropriate number and realism.

16. Step 5: Present the examples in close succession or simultaneously.

17. Step 6: Present a new positive example of the concept and ask the student to identify it.

18. Step 7: Verify the student's learning of the concept.

19. Step 8: Require the student to define the concept.

20. Step 9: Provide occasions for student responses and the reinforcement of these responses.

Upon reading the third section of this chapter (on the teaching of principles), you should be able to describe and illustrate each of the following instructional steps.

21. Step 1: Describe the performance expected of the student after he has learned the principle.

22. Step 2: Decide and indicate which concepts or principles the student must recall in learning the new principle.

23. Step 3: Assist the student in the recall of component concepts.

24. Step 4: Help the student to combine the concepts in the proper order.

25. Step 5: Require the student to demonstrate the principle fully.

26. Step 6: Require the student to give a full statement of the principle.

27. Step 7: Verify the student's learning of the principle.

28. Step 8: Provide for practice of the principle and for reinforcement of student responses.

THE NATURE OF CONCEPTS AND PRINCIPLES

In this section of the chapter you should learn what a concept is and what a principle is, their relationship to level of intellectual development, and their important uses in school learning.

The Nature of Concepts

Here I will define and illustrate a concept, describe the characteristics of concepts, and distinguish among three types of concepts.

WHAT IS A CONCEPT? A concept is a class of stimuli which have common characteristics. These stimuli may be objects, events, or persons. We ordinarily designate a concept by its name, such as book, war, and student, or beautiful women, dedicated teachers, and hallucinatory drugs. All these concepts refer to classes (or categories) of stimuli. Some stimuli do not refer to concepts: Elizabeth Taylor, Miss Pegg (the elementary school teacher), Tolstoy's *War and Peace,* the Vietnam War, and the annual Tournament of Roses. These are particular (not classes of) stimuli, persons, or events. A concept is not a particular stimulus but a class of stimuli. The difference is between all beautiful women and Elizabeth Taylor. The concept *beautiful women* includes (undoubtedly) Elizabeth Taylor, but it includes many other women as well. The concept *beautiful women* excludes all ugly women and even plain and unfetching women. In this chapter, when we talk about concepts, you should remember that we are not referring to particular stimuli but to classes of stimuli.

Concepts are not always congruent with our personal experience, but they represent human attempts to classify our experience at least crudely. Not all of us (particularly the women) agree on who the beautiful women are, although there is considerably less argument about including some women than there is about including others. The concept is a very broad one, and it can include women of varied sizes, colorations, and shapes. Similarly, the concept *book* may include something as monumental as the *Oxford English Dictionary* or something as trivial and flimsy as a comic book. The *state* can include Luxembourg and China and, in another sense, Rhode Island and Texas. A student may be an individual who grows a beard, strums a banjo, smokes marijuana, and occasionally attends class. He may also be an individual who dresses plainly, visits the library frequently, carries books, and studies regularly. In classifying both individuals as students we have to ignore the nonessential characteristics of their behavior and concentrate on only the essential ones. Romantic artists and educators have lamented the fact that the classification of the stimuli of our environment destroys the fine nuances of nature and feeling. They argue that what we feel is good whether we or others call it love or passion. We cannot argue with the romantics about the appreciation of the nuances of experience. We can and will insist, however, on the need for all of us to classify the confusion of our world and to render it more amenable to our control and satisfaction.

CONCEPT ATTRIBUTES. An attribute is a distinctive feature of a concept and thus varies from concept to concept. For example, let us use a laboratory concept, *blue squares,* which has two attributes: color and form (or shape). Color, of course, can vary from concept to concept and, therefore, qualifies as an attribute. We can indeed have blue circles, blue triangles, and blue parallelograms. We can even have chartreuse octagons! A more ordinary concept is *lake*. The chief attribute which distinguishes a lake from an ocean and sea, on one hand, and from a pool and pond, on the other hand, is size. A lake is usually smaller than an ocean or a sea and usually larger than a pool or a pond. There are undoubtedly other attributes of *lake* (river drainage, fresh water, and so on), but size is one of its major attributes. Size qualifies as an attribute because it can vary from concept to concept.

Attribute values. Values are the particular variations an attribute many undergo. We have established color as an attribute. It may have several values: red, white, blue, maroon, and fawn. Similarly, form may have several values: rectangular, trapezoidal, square, and circular. Concepts vary in the number of values their attributes have. Some concepts have attributes with only two values. A human being (a concept) can be a man or woman, dead or alive, and married or single. Other concepts may have attributes with a range of values. The color of an orange (the fruit) can vary from red-orange to orange-yellow. The color, however, must not vary so much that we confuse an orange with a lemon or grapefruit. Fortunately, when an attribute has a wide range of values, we can use other attributes to identify the stimulus in question. In identifying an orange, for example, we also observe the attributes of shape, size, and texture.

Number of attributes. The number of attributes varies from concept to concept. *Blue squares* has only two attributes—color and form. *Small blue squares* has three attributes—size, color, and form. An *orange* has four attributes: color, size, form, and texture. Some very complex concepts have a dozen or more attributes. Making a list of the attributes for the concepts *democracy* and *human rights* may require the exhaustive consideration of long treatises. As the number of attributes increases the difficulty of learning the concept increases. Scanning the values of a dozen attributes, for example, is strenuous and time consuming. Bruner and his associates (1956) suggest that, when operating under ordinary time pressures, the individual tends to reduce the amount of strain involved in perusing several attributes by reducing the number of attributes to which he attends. He can do this by attending to some attributes and ignoring others or by combining a large number of attributes into a smaller number of patterns. We shall use the concept of *tort* below to show how the teacher can reduce the number of attributes to be learned in complex concepts.

Dominance of the attributes. Dominance refers to the fact that some attributes are more obvious than others. We know that physical location is more dominant (or obvious) than the attributes of color and form. Also color-form concepts such as *red squares* are more dominant than number-color concepts such as *one red.* Thus, dominance refers to the concept as well as to its attributes. Dominant concepts have dominant attributes. James Archer (1962) studied the effects on concept learning of increasing or decreasing the obviousness of attributes. In the high-obvious condition he used figures which were recognizably different in height and shape, and in the low-obvious condition he used figures which were about the same in height and shape. He found that when the attribute of size or shape was both important for recognizing the concept and obvious, the mastery of the concept was easy. Mastery of the concept was most difficult when the attributes were not obvious. In a similar experiment Lee Sechrest and Judith Kaas (1965) used triangles of various shades of red (dark, medium, and light), of various heights (short, medium, and tall), and of various sizes (thin, medium, and fat). The cards which displayed these triangles had borders of one, two, or three lines. Thus each of the four attributes had three values. The students had to learn the concept *bif. Bif* was a light red, fat triangle. In learning this concept they could ignore the attributes of height and the number of lines in the border. The experimenters found that, when they used cards which had similar attribute values (e.g., light red and medium red), the students had increased difficulty learning the concept. When they used dissimilar values (e.g., light red and dark red), the students learned *bif* more easily. John Wallace (1964) discovered that students learn concepts with dominant attributes with significantly fewer examples than those they need to learn concepts with obscure attributes.

Through your own experimentation you will discover the variation in dominance and the attributes of the concepts you plan to teach. Informally, teachers observe that students usually attend to certain points in their description of a concept but ignore other points that are equally important. In learning the concept *state capital* children may attend to the attribute of location (usually near the center of a state) and ignore size (the fact that capitals are often small cities). Teachers must give aural or visual emphasis to attributes which are obscure and yet important in identifying the concept. In defining concepts teachers traditionally resort to vocal inflection, hand and arm gesticulation, underscoring, diagraming, drawing, and so on, to make obscure attributes obvious. Unless this emphasis is provided the student will learn some attributes and not others and, thereby, fail to learn the complete concept.

Types of concepts. Attributes combine in three different ways to produce three types of concepts: conjunctive concepts, disjunctive concepts, and relational concepts. I shall now define and illustrate each of these.

Fig. 10-1. *An array of concepts with four attributes, each exhibiting three values. Plain figures are uncolored, striped figures are light green, solid figures are green (Bruner and associates, 1956, p. 42).*

Conjunctive concepts. In a conjunctive concept the appropriate values of several attributes are jointly present. Figure 10-1 shows an array of cards which illustrate various concepts. One of these concepts is *three red circles.* It is a conjunctive concept because it has three attributes (number, color, and form) and each attribute has a particular value (respectively, three, red, and circle). How many cards in Fig. 10-1 are examples of this concept? In only three cards are the appropriate values (three, red, and circle) of each attribute jointly present. Another conjunctive concept is *one red.* The attributes are number and color and the values are one and red. How many examples of this concept can you find in Fig. 10-1? Most concepts which come readily to mind are conjunctive concepts. *Dog,* for example, has attributes of color, size, shape, texture, and behavior. The values of these attributes indeed vary —from those of the fawn-colored Great Dane to those of the white miniature poodle. The classification of a particular animal as a dog requires the joint presence of the appropriate value of each attribute. Despite the considerable variation in values which exist in the attributes of *dog,* most of us can readily distinguish dogs from cats, horses, cows, and other domesticated animals. Conjunctive concepts are often the easiest to learn and to teach because of the additive quality of their attributes and values. More simply, attributes and values are added together to produce a conjunctive concept. The student must simply learn a list of attributes and appropriate values.

Disjunctive concepts. In a disjunctive concept, the appropriate values of one attribute or of another attribute or of both are present. In such a concept, attributes and values are substituted for one another. *Two figures and/or two circles* is a disjunctive concept. You can see that the attributes are form and number and that the value of the number remains the same. The concept is disjunctive because the value of the form can change—it can be a circle or any form. How many cards in Fig. 10-1 illustrate this concept? A much more difficult disjunctive concept is *three red circles or any constituent thereof.* In Fig. 10-1 fifty-seven cards illustrate this concept. These cards include three figures, red figures, circles, three red figures, red circles, or three circles. A more ordinary example of a disjunctive concept is a *strike*—a pitch which crosses the plate between the batter's knees and shoulders or a pitch which the batter strikes at and misses. In football the *extra point* after a touchdown is made by successfully kicking the ball between the goal posts or by carrying or by catching the ball over the goal line. In baseball a *walk* occurs when four balls have been pitched or when a pitched ball strikes the batter. Disjunctive concepts are often difficult to learn because of the seemingly arbitrary equivalence of their attributes. Disjunctive concepts are, in effect, rules which the student must learn to apply to equivalent stimulus situations. Most of our thinking tends to be conjunctive—the inclusion of stimuli in one class excludes them from other classes. As teachers we must often invest greater effort and ingenuity in the teaching of disjunctive concepts than in the teaching of conjunctive concepts.

Relational concepts. A relational concept is one that has a specifiable relationship between attributes. In Fig. 10-1 the following concepts are relational: (1) all cards containing the same number of figures and borders; (2) all cards containing fewer figures than borders; and (3) all cards containing fewer borders than figures. The number of figures and the number of borders are the attributes of these three concepts. The statement of the relationship of these attributes describes the concepts. As in the case of disjunctive concepts, each of these descriptions is a rule which can be used to select cards from the array in Fig. 10-1. Bruner (1956) suggests that income tax brackets after deductions are relational concepts: They depend on the relationship between the number of dependents and the net amount of income. *Distance* and *direction* are relational concepts. Distance specifies the relationship between two points; it refers to the separation of these points. *Direction* also specifies a relationship between two or more points; it refers to the movement from one to another point. Carroll (1964) discusses several relational concepts which are difficult for students to learn: time, many, few, average, longitude, mass, and weight. Relational concepts are more difficult to learn than conjunctive concepts. Since the concept does not adhere in the attributes themselves but in the particular relationships of the attributes, it is easy for the child (and even the adult) to become confused. For example, both the concept *distance* and the concept *direction* have as their attributes points in space and time. What distinguishes them is the difference in the relationship of the same attributes.

SUMMARY. Thus far in this chapter we have discussed the nature of concepts. You have learned that concepts are distinguished by their attributes and the values of their attributes. You have also learned that some concepts have more attributes than others and that some attributes are more dominant or obvious than others. Concepts with a few obvious attributes are easier to learn than concepts with several obscure attributes. As a teacher you must determine the number and relative dominance of the attributes of the concepts you teach and use this information in planning your instruction. Important attributes which lack dominance must be given special emphasis. Large numbers of attributes can be reduced by ignoring some and focusing attention on others or by combining the attributes into a smaller number of patterns. Identifying the type of concept you are teaching makes clear the relationship of the attributes and the possible level of difficulty of the concept. Conjunctive concepts are generally (but not always) easier to learn than disjunctive or relational concepts. The student, of course, should learn the same relationship of the attributes which you used in identifying the type of concept with which you are dealing.

The Nature of Principles

Now that you can define and identify concepts it is easy to define principles.

WHAT IS A PRINCIPLE? A principle is a statement of the relationship between two or more concepts (Gagné, 1965c, 1966). Principles are sometimes called rules or generalizations. These are some examples: (1) Four plus ten equals fourteen; (2) all men are created equal; (3) learning is the result of reinforced practice; (4) three-dimensional objects have six sides; and (5) the active voice is used when the subject performs the action of the verb. These statements and phrases are not principles: (1) Hortense likes Elvis; (2) Elvis claims he is stronger than any boy at Horatio High; (3) evergreen trees; (4) the Democrats won the last election; and (5) who's afraid of Virginia Woolf? The first set of statements qualify as principles because they state relationships among concepts.

The first statement, for example, states the relationship among five concepts: four, plus, ten, equals, and fourteen. The second statement relates four concepts: all, men, created, and equal. Count the concepts in the three remaining statements. The second set of statements are not principles: *Hortense* and *Elvis* are not concepts. *Likes* is a concept, but the statement describes no relationship between this and any other concept. *Evergreen trees* is not a principle; it is a concept. In the last statement, *afraid* is the only concept; *who's* and *Virginia Woolf* refer to particular individuals. For practice in stating principles, try to convert the second set of statements into principles.

It is sometimes helpful to think of statements of principles as if-then statements. For example, if you add four and ten, then you obtain fourteen; if you are a man, then you have been created equal (to all men); if there is reinforced practice, then learning results; if an object has six sides, then it is three-dimensional; and if the subject performs the action of the verb, then you use the active voice. The advantage of phrasing a principle as an if-then statement is that the statement then indicates the proper ordering of the component concepts. Only the proper arrangement of the concepts results in satisfactory learning of principles.

Now that we have defined concepts and principles, we shall briefly consider their relationship to the student's intellectual development.

Intellectual Development and Concepts and Principles

In the sections which deal with the teaching of concepts and principles, we shall consider the prerequisite behavior for learning them in terms of less complex learning. Here we want to focus on that aspect of entering behavior which pertains to intellectual development as described by Piaget (see Chapter 4) and to preschool concept learning.

Limits imposed by developmental periods. The learning of concepts and principles requires the student to engage in what Piaget calls *abstract thought.* According to Piaget the child's stage of development determines the level of thought of which he is capable. In the context of school learning we should not expect children from the ages of seven to eleven (the period of concrete operations) to have the adult's capacity for abstract thought (formal operations). You recall the chief characteristics of the two periods (pp. 90–95): In the period of concrete operations, the child's thinking is oriented toward concrete objects in his immediate environment; he relinquishes the physical attributes of objects one by one, and each grouping remains an isolated organization. In the period of formal operations, the child's thought concerns the possible as well as the real. He is capable of hypotheticodeductive and propositional thinking.

What implications do these periods of intellectual development have for the teaching and learning of concepts and principles? The child in the period of concrete operations can learn concepts which require the classification of concrete objects and events. In acquiring new concepts he can employ his rudimentary concepts of time, space, number, and logic. His intellectual operations or groupings of this period show the characteristics of closure, associativity, reversibility, and identity. The child in the period of formal operations can handle principles as well as concepts since principles, as if-then statements, are a form of propositional and hypotheticodeductive thinking. If-then statements require the student to think of possible combinations of concepts and, in the period of formal operations, he can consider these combinations in an orderly and systematic way. It would appear therefore that the younger child, in the period of concrete operations, is not ordinarily capable of engaging in the scientific thought which the older child, in the period of formal operations, often can engage in with considerable skill. Although teaching can contribute to the development of abstract thought in children in both periods of development, the rigors of abstract thought required in the learning of concepts and principles must be reserved for older children.

PRESCHOOL CONCEPT LEARNING. In assessing the entering behavior of the younger child we must also be aware that much of his learning occurs before he begins his formal education and that the elementary school depends on this previous learning to a large extent. For the most part the child learns concepts from direct experience, and, since this experience is always limited, he learns them incompletely. Carroll (1964, p. 195), to illustrate this point, reports that children often have incorrect or incomplete concepts for *tourist* and *immigrant:*

> . . . All tourists may be obviously American whereas all the immigrants may be obviously Mexican. . . . The tourist may be well dressed, the immigrants poorly dressed, and so on. If the natural environment is like a grand concept-formation experiment, it may take the child a long time to attain the concepts *tourist* and *immigrant;* indeed, the environment may not be as informative as the usual experimenter since the child may not always be informed, or reliably informed, as to the correctness of his guesses. No wonder a child might form the concept that a tourist is a well-dressed person who drives a station wagon with out-of-state license plates!

The school must take these incomplete concepts with which the child enters his formal education and add all the relevant and eliminate all the irrelevant attributes. In school, if not in his direct experience, the child can learn that Americans emigrate to other countries and become both immigrants and foreigners in their newly adopted land.

As yet we have no studies of the concepts and principles with which most American children enter school and of the concepts they should learn first and those they should learn later. Several studies are underway which promise to provide some of this information. Project Talent (Flanagan, 1964) has developed a comprehensive battery of tests which measure conceptual development in areas such as general information, English, verbal memory, arithmetic computation and reasoning, introductory and advanced mathematics, and spatial visualization. The International Study of Achievement in Mathematics (Husén, 1967), by comparing outcomes of educational systems in twelve countries, gives us some indication of the level of mathematical development we can expect in our students. Continuation of these studies and inauguration of others will be invaluable in planning the curriculum of the elementary school.

Gagné (1965c) suggests that when the child enters kindergarten he may know these concepts: above and below, on top of, underneath, next to, the middle one, start, stop, go, come, sit, stand, and so on. He may not know concepts such as these: the one before, the next one, double, like, unlike, grapheme-phoneme correspondences, and number names for quantities. In the case of disadvantaged children we must be especially careful to avoid unwarranted assumptions about what they have and have not learned.

Uses of Concepts and Principles

The great importance of concepts and principles in the development and education of the student has not always been fully recognized. Bruner and his associates (1956) write:

> Psychology has been celebrating the role of "emotional factors" and "unconscious drives" for so long now that man's capacity for rational coping with his world has come to seem some residual capacity that shows its head only when the irrational lets up. . . . Man is not a logic machine, but he is certainly capable of making decisions and gathering information in a manner that reflects better on his learning capacity than we have yet been ready to grant.

This statement reflects an important shift which has occurred in educational psychology in the last two decades—from an emphasis on social adjustment and personal development to an emphasis on intellectual development and achievement.

Let us now consider the various ways in which concepts are useful in the student's education and one way (as stereotypes) in which they are not always useful but are at least influential.

Concepts reduce the complexity of the environment. You recall that concepts are not particular but classes of events or stimuli. If we were forced to respond to each stimulus we encountered as unique, the complexity of the world would overwhelm us. This complexity is especially evident with the present knowledge explosion, which forces us to develop efficient categories of information to spare ourselves the distraction of fine detail. The fact that we can group events into classes is an important source of mastery over our environment. Bruner and his associates (1956, p. 1) point out that there may be more than 7 million distinct colors and that we see a fair proportion of them in one week. If we had to respond to each of these colors individually, we would be reduced to intellectual impotence:

> Consider only the linguistic task of acquiring a vocabulary fully adequate to cope with the world of color differences! The result of this seeming paradox is achieved by man's capacity to categorize. To categorize is to render discriminably different things equivalent, to group objects and events and people around us into classes, and to respond to them in terms of their class membership rather than their uniqueness. . . . In place of a color lexicon (dictionary) of 7 million items, people in our society get along with a dozen or so commonly used color names. It suffices to note that the book on the desk has a "blue" cover. If the task calls for finer discrimination, we may narrow the category and note that it is in the class of things called "medium blue."

Archer (1966, p. 46) suggests that reducing the complexity of the world takes on the character of motivation or striving. The individual tries not only to reduce complexity in chaotic environments but also "to seek and search out peculiarities and differences in the elements in its environment in order to optimize its environmental complexity." Archer also believes that this motivation to reduce environmental complexity is related to age and intelligence. He uses this example. When a child learns that his pet is a dog, his tendency is to classify all four-footed animals as dogs, whether they be cats, horses, or cows. At a later age, however, the child becomes more sensitive to the differences which make dogs dogs and cats cats. At this point he shows a need to appreciate differences in his environment as well as to reduce the complexity of his environment. Archer suggests that the highest levels of intellectual sophistication are reached when the individual can with ease both reduce environmental complexity and appreciate the subtle differences among the elements within his environment—a feat accomplished frequently by the artist.

The learning of concepts and principles, therefore, enables the student to grasp, in an array of environmental stimuli, similarities and differences which he would otherwise have great difficulty coping with. Education, in this sense, gives the student environmental mastery which he would otherwise lack.

Concepts help us to identify the objects of the world around us. This use is closely related to the first use we have described. Indentification involves placing an object in a class and, therefore, reducing the complexity of the environment. Identifications are never absent from our experience. Bruner (1956, p. 12) reminds us that we even classify sounds as "that sound which comes from outdoors at night" or "those porcupines chewing on an old tree stump." Archer (1966) believes that this use also takes on the character of a drive—the child is tempted to try out his concepts and to identify as many dogs as he can. This use can be extended in that concepts that the child first learns affect the nature and extent of the concepts he subsequently learns. Archer (1966, p. 47) writes:

> Until the child is able to specify his concept of "dog" he will probably have considerable difficulty distinguishing between dogs and cats. However, until he has successfully differentiated the two concepts of "dog" and "cat" he will probably have considerable difficulty distinguishing foxes, wolves, hyenas, and domesticated dogs. And, of course, the real world will not leave him alone; after our imaginary child has finally figured out all of these beasts, it will be his misfortune to encounter a Tasmanian tiger.

The use of concepts to identify objects in the world around us points out the importance of concepts as entering behavior. As Gagné (1965c) suggests, concepts and principles may be related to the world and to each other in hierarchical fashion; if the child does not learn concepts and principles low in the hierarchy, the learning of those higher in the hierarchy becomes difficult or impossible.

Concepts and principles reduce the necessity of constant learning. We do not have to be taught *de novo* that the object before us is a mammal. Once we have learned the attributes of mammals, we can apply the concept *mammal* over and over again without further learning. In the schools, concepts and principles, by reducing the necessity of constant learning, enable the student to progress through a discipline and to acquire increasing amounts of knowledge. As we grow older, however, we may develop a resistance toward breaking old patterns of thought and toward learning new ways of organizing knowledge (Bayley, 1966).

Concepts and principles provide direction for instrumental activity. By using concepts and principles we know in advance the actions we can take; placing the object or person in the right class enables us to arrive at important decisions. This use is probably very important in problem solving, which is discussed in the following chapter. In problem solving, it is possible that we try different classes for an object until we find one that it fits in and one that solves the problem.

CONCEPTS AND PRINCIPLES MAKE INSTRUCTION POSSIBLE. The steps described for the teaching of concepts and principles are largely embodied in a set of verbal instructions. These instructions would not be possible if the student had not already learned some concepts and principles. As we move from elementary school to high school to college and finally to the university graduate school, instruction becomes increasingly verbal because the assumption is made (and often warranted) that the student has mastered concepts and principles and that the words which refer to them are sufficient for evoking them when their recall is important. Specific words arouse concepts and principles in our students and save us the effort of covering all the old territory to introduce a new area of knowledge. The atmosphere of the graduate school appears very rarefied to the unsophisticated because the great store of concepts at the command of graduate professors and students reduces the need to deal with the concrete environment. When the layman refers to the "ivy tower" and the "unrealism" of the university, he fails to understand the complex relationship of concepts and concepts, of principles and principles, and of both concepts and principles to environmental stimuli.

Of course, teachers and students may lose sight of the fact that the great value of concepts is that they refer to the concrete environment. Gagné (1965c, p. 139) writes:

> Learning can become oververbalized, which means that concepts learned are highly inadequate in their references to actual situations. . . . The danger of verbal superficiality, and the necessity of avoiding it, is recognized in a number of educational doctrines. "Learning by doing" is one of these. Another is the recognition of the importance of the laboratory and the demonstration in science teaching. The concepts of science deal with the real world and therefore must be based on "operations" that are equally concrete.

In the following chapter, when we discuss inductive and deductive teaching and what we currently call *discovery learning,* we shall discuss also the value of carefully anchoring the learning activities of our students in concrete experience. Here we wish only to point out that concepts and principles can become an obstacle to instruction when the student has an inadequate grasp of them and does not know their relationship to the concrete environment.

CONCEPTS CAN BE STEREOTYPES. Frederick McDonald (1965) defines a stereotype as a rigid or inaccurate concept impervious to experience.

In discussing stereotypes we are not referring to a use of concepts so much as to the responsibility of the teacher to take the incomplete social stereotypes with which the child enters the school and to make these concepts complete or, at least, adequate. If the child excludes members of some races, religions, and nationalities from the general concept *human being,* some instruction is strongly indicated. Or, if the child lists the attributes of one race as intelligent, socially responsible, sanitary, and achieving and the attributes of another race as stupid, irresponsible, dirty, and lazy, the teacher can provide a wider array of positive and negative examples for both races than the child may have experienced before. Certain emotional auras surround many of our concepts and principles, and these auras seem less amenable to new learning than those which, as teachers, we often prefer. The concepts of motherhood, children, God, and brotherhood, for example, are not cold lists of attributes. The emotional aspect of our concepts may be a product of early classical conditioning and consistent reinforcement, as in the case of our fears and appetites, and therefore they may be difficult to extinguish. In the North and in the South we all know very well that there are dirty white men and clean Negroes, but many of us continue to exclude these examples from our concepts of white man and black man. The teacher can present information to the student in objective and relatively impersonal ways and hope that the student will incorporate the new positive examples into a more accurate concept than he now has. In the final analysis, however, concepts (even stereotypes) reside in individuals and are always idiosyncratic. Carroll (1964, pp. 183–84) writes:

> Concepts . . . reside in particular individuals with particular histories of experience that lead them to classify those experiences in particular ways. My concept of "stone" may not be precisely your concept of "stone" because my experiences with stones may have included work with pieces of vitreous rock that you may have seldom seen. To a large extent, how I sort out my experiences is my own business and may not lead to the same sorting as yours.

In attempting to improve the social stereotypes of our students we must always remember the great range of personal experience and entering behavior which those stereotypes represent. Complex social concepts and principles often result from opinion and not from information. The over-zealous teacher can find himself in the untenable position of trying to get the student to surrender his own for the teacher's own stereotypes.

Summary

In this section we have considered the nature of concepts and principles, their relationship to the intellectual development of the student and their uses in school learning. Among the uses of concepts we have considered stereotypes or concepts based on a nonrepresentative array of examples.

First, I defined a concept as a class of stimuli which have common characteristics. Concept attributes are distinctive features of a concept and vary in value, number, and dominance. The value is the particular variation an attribute may undergo. The number of attributes varies from concept to concept. Dominance is the fact that some attributes are more obvious than others. Attributes combine in various ways to produce three types of concepts: conjunctive, disjunctive, and relational. In a conjunctive concept the appropriate attribute values are jointly present. In a disjunctive concept the appropriate values of one attribute or another attribute or both are present. A relational concept has a specifiable relationship among attributes. A principle is a statement of the relationship between two or among more than two concepts. This relationship can often be expressed as an if-then statement.

Second, the teaching and learning of concepts must be related to the student's level of intellectual development. In teaching concepts during the period of concrete operations (ages 7 to 11) the teacher must remember that the child's thinking is oriented toward concrete objects in the immediate environment, that he relinquishes the physical attributes of objects one by one, and that each grouping (or schema) remains an isolated organization. In the period of formal operations the older child is capable of hypotheticodeductive and propositional thinking. Although the teaching of concepts can and does occur during both periods, the teaching of principles proceeds more easily during the later period. Because the child's school learning of concepts is limited by his preschool learning, the school must often provide corrective experience to exclude irrelevant and include relevant attributes. A comprehensive national survey of school achievement promises to provide teachers with information on which concepts students should learn first and which they should learn later.

Third, I suggested several educational uses of concepts and principles: (1) Concepts reduce the complexity of the environment. (2) Concepts help us to identify the objects of the world around us. (3) Concepts and principles reduce the necessity of constant learning. (4) Concepts and principles provide direction for instrumental activity. (5) Concepts and principles make instruction possible. Finally, the teacher must sometimes provide corrective experience for an additional use of concepts: stereotypes. As concepts, stereotypes can sometimes be changed when the student is provided with a wider array of positive and negative examples than those which he has previously experienced.

You should now return to objectives 1–11 (p. 386) and determine how well you have achieved them.

QUESTION 10-1

Use the key which follows in classifying the item below:

Key: (a) attributes
(b) attribute values
(c) conjunctive concept
(d) disjunctive concept
(e) relational concept
(f) principle

1. two long-haired students
2. several
3. two dogs and/or cats
4. color, size, shape, and weight
5. two, red, enormous
6. a concept refers to a class of stimuli

After selecting your answers, give the reasons for each one.

THE TEACHING OF CONCEPTS

I shall now describe the teaching of concepts as a series of nine steps which conform to the four components of the basic teaching model. Steps 1 and 2 pertain to instructional objectives. Step 1 requires a statement of the objective, and step 2, a type of task analysis. Step 2 provides the student with the appropriate entering behavior. Steps 3 through 6 and step 9 are specific instructional procedures for concept teaching. Steps 7 and 8 deal mainly with performance assessment.

Step 1. Describe the Performance Expected of the Student After He Has Learned the Concept

In the case of concept learning, the expected performance is th correct identification of new examples of the concept. For the concep *direct object,* this could be the expected performance: When given nev examples of direct objects in English sentences, the student will cor rectly identify them. You will note that this description of termina behavior requires a performance quite different from rattling off thi definition: A direct object is a noun or pronoun which receives the ac tion of a verb. The student might very well memorize the definitio and fail to identify direct objects. And, conceivably, the student coul correctly identify direct objects and not give a very good definition. W shall discuss later the advantages of learning the concept and learning the definition of the concept. The point here is that the description of the expected behavior should not include the requirement that the student give a definition of the concept.

Describing terminal behavior has two purposes. First, the teacher has a means for assessing the adequacy of the performance and for determining the need for further instruction. The teacher at a given point in time may not desire that the students be completely able to identify and use the concept. In the beginning, for example, the teacher may be quite satisfied to have the students recognize direct objects only in simple English sentences. Later he may want the students to recognize direct objects in compound sentences in both dependent and independent clauses. Still later he may want the students to use direct objects in various sentence contexts. The prior description of the students' expected performance clearly indicates to the teacher and to the students the degree of adequacy the students are to attain at a particular time. Second, the students have a way of assessing their own performance and of determining when their learning is complete. The students' self-assessments then become a way of generating their own reinforcement.

Step 2. Reduce the Number of Attributes to Be Learned in Complex Concepts and Make Important Attributes Dominant

In this step what you learned about the values, number, dominance, and relationship of attributes can be put to pedagogical use. This step requires you to make an analysis of the concepts you decide to teach your students. The determination of the values and the number of attributes can be made before instruction is underway. The determination of the dominance of the attributes requires experimentation on your part and observation of which important attributes students are likely to ignore. After you have made these determinations, you must devise procedures for teaching the concept. Two general procedures reduce the number of attributes of complex concepts: You can ignore some of the attributes and focus on those you think most important or you can code the attributes into fewer patterns.

Carroll (1964) lists the attributes of one complex concept—*tort*. *Tort* is a legal term which refers to a wrongful act, injury, or damage for which a civil action can be brought. A careful analysis of the various laws and decisions relating to torts shows that the concept has these attributes: (1) battery; (2) false imprisonment; (3) malicious prosecution; (4) trespass to land; (5) interference to chattels; (6) interference with advantageous relations; (7) misrepresentation; (8) defamation; (9) malicious intent; (10) negligence; (11) causal nexus; (12) consent; (13) privilege; (14) reasonable risk by plaintiff; and (15) breach of contract.

To discover the relative dominance of these attributes, we would have to allow the students to examine various civil actions, some of which involved torts and others which did not. By observing how the students applied the concept, we could discover which attributes in the list they favored and which they ignored. These observations would tell us on which attributes additional emphasis was necessary.

Beyond considering the number and the dominance of the attributes, we would have to determine their relationship. In as complex a concept as *tort,* the relationship of the attributes is both conjunctive and disjunctive. In the above list the first eight attributes are disjunctive in that a tort can have any or all of these attributes. That is, a tort can be a battery, a false imprisonment, a malicious prosecution, a trespass to land, an interference to chattels, an interference with advantageous relations, a misrepresentation and/or a defamatory act. The next two attributes (9 and 10) are also disjunctive: The act (whichever it is) can be done with malicious intent and/or with negligence. And the last four attributes (12, 13, 14, and 15) are also disjunctive: The act can be done without the plaintiff's consent or without privilege on the part of the plaintiff or without reasonable risk by the plaintiff or it can be an act which is not a breach of contract. Attribute 11 (causal nexus) indicates that the wrongful act must be the cause of the injury claimed by the plaintiff. The concept is also conjunctive because the attributes can be grouped as follows: Attributes 1 through 8 refer to the wrongful act; attributes 9 and 10 refer to the motivation or irresponsibility of the defendant; attribute 11 indicates the causal relationship of the first ten attributes to the last four attributes; and the last four attributes (12 through 15) specify the agreements and responsibilities of the defendant and the plaintiff before or during the act. The conjunctive grouping of the attributes of *tort* suggests the way the teacher could code them and thereby reduce them in number. The first eight attributes could be coded (grouped) under types of acts; the next two under motivation and irresponsibility of the defendant; and the last four under prior and concurrent responsibilities and agreements of defendant and plaintiff. With this grouping, the students would have only four patterns of attributes (if we call attribute 11, causal nexus, a pattern) to remember. Alternatively, the teacher could ignore some attributes and concentrate on others. Some acts, for example, may qualify as torts more often than other acts. Misrepresentation may occur much less frequently than battery. Also, the absence of a breach of contract may be much more important than the absence of privilege on the part of the plaintiff since contracts are so common in legal proceedings. The choice of which attributes to ignore requires that the teacher have considerable familiarity with the concept and its ordinary uses. For a complete understanding of the concept, the student would have to learn all the attributes listed.

Step 3. Provide the Student with Useful Verbal Mediators

Here we are concerned that the student has the prerequisite verbal associations before he undertakes the learning of the concept. In this step you can see how verbal and concept learning are related. Considerable evidence indicates that the learning of certain names or labels (as verbal mediators) facilitates the student's learning of a concept. Some studies even indicate the type of verbal association which can be most helpful.

An impressive amount of evidence has been gathered by Wittrock, Keislar, and Carolyn Stern (1963, 1964, and 1965) on the verbal mediators most helpful in concept learning. To illustrate the materials used in their studies, we will discuss first the experiment of Stern (1965), who was interested in finding out whether giving children the class cue (explained below) was better than giving them the name of an example of the concept. Figure 10-2 illustrates the material she used for two of the concepts, *mammal* and *tree*. The figure indicates that the children had to match the picture in the top row with one of the pictures in the bottom row. One group of children received the class label as a verbal mediator. That is, they were told that the picture in the top row was a mammal or a tree. The other group received the name of the example of the concept. They were told that the picture in the top row was a dog, a horse, a rabbit or a maple, a palm, a fir. After this training period the children took various tests in which they had to identify new examples of the concepts, new concepts of the same type, and a new category of concepts. Stern found that the students who learned the class labels did better than the other group in tests on a new set of concepts. Both groups did equally well in tests which measured their ability to identify new instances of the concepts.

In an earlier study with somewhat more conclusive results (Wittrock, Keislar, and Stern, 1964), kindergarten children were given three months of pretraining in which they learned the French names of two common objects and animals, that each French name had an initial *la* or *le* sound, and that *la* and *le* stood for *articles*. After the pretraining, the children were presented with a picture and asked to match it with one of five pictures (as in the Stern experiment). The children were divided into four groups each of which was given a different verbal mediator or no mediator at all. Group 1 was given no mediator. These children were merely told, "Something you have learned will help you find the right answer." Group 2 was given a general mediator. They were told that recalling the article would help them find the right answer. Group 3 was given the class mediator (as in the previous Stern experiment). They were told, "The top picture is a *la* (*le*) word. Find a *la* (*le*) picture on the bottom which goes with it." Group 4 was given a specific mediator: "The name of the top picture is [French word]."

Fig. 10-2. *Sample sequence of slides from the eight-concept program (after Stern, 1965, p. 237).*

The class mediator represented an intermediate amount of instructional guidance—more guidance than that provided by the general mediator and less guidance than that provided by the specific mediator. The results showed that the children who received the class mediator (intermediate guidance) retained the concepts longer and recognized more new examples of the concepts. In a later study (Wittrock and Keislar, 1965), the class mediator and the specific mediator were equally effective in teaching concepts like those in Fig. 10-1. Both studies rather effectively dispute the popular myth that young children can learn concepts best with little or no instructional guidance.

The first and second steps I have described for the teaching of concepts primarily concern the first component of the basic teaching model. Both steps involve decisions about what you will teach and what the students will learn. More simply, these steps concern instructional objectives. The third step primarily concerns entering behavior. In this step we establish the verbal associations (if they are not already learned) necessary for learning the concept. We are beginning to realize that verbal learning and concept learning have much in common (Underwood, 1966). Gagné (1965c) uses the concept *edge* to illustrate this point. The student must be able to respond *edge* when the teacher points to three different edges. The responses are what enable the teacher to ascertain whether the student has the appropriate verbal response available. In the experiment by Wittrock and his associates (1964), the appropriate verbal associations (*la* and *le*) were taught so that there was little doubt that the students would use them in their concept learning. The following steps for the teaching of concepts primarily concern the external conditions of learning and relate particularly to the third component of the basic teaching model.

Step 4. Provide Positive and Negative Examples of the Concept

In discussing this step, I shall use the word *example* rather than *instance* or *exemplar* since *example* is used more frequently in discussions of teaching. A positive example of a concept is one which contains the attributes of the concept. A negative example is one which does not contain any of the attributes. For example, positive examples of the concept *bird* are robin, canary, hummingbird, and snowy egret. Negative examples are dog, cat, snake, fly, bee, and even bat. The research on concept learning indicates that provision of positive and negative examples is a major condition of learning. We can even say that the use of positive and negative examples is a necessary condition for the learning of concepts.

Psychologists have developed various models to depict and explain how the student utilizes positive and negative examples in learning a concept. To describe one of these models, we must consider some of the conditions under which concepts can be learned. If, in teaching the concept *dog,* you are using cards which bear drawings of various breeds of dogs, you can present the cards in three different ways. You can present one card (bearing a drawing of a German shepherd), tell the student that this is an example of a dog, and leave that card in view as you present positive and negative examples of dogs. You can present a series of positive and negative examples with no positive example remaining in view. You can leave every card, both positive and negative examples, in view as you present them. Under all three conditions you inform the student immediately of the correctness or incorrectness of his responses. Our question concerns how the student uses the examples you present. Solis Kates and Lee Yudin (1964) suggest that the student's implicit responses may follow this sequence: (1) He makes a guess; (2) he tests his guess against the current example and the shown or remembered example; (3) he retains his guess if it agrees with the shown or remembered example; (4) he changes his guess if it does not agree; and (5) he may possibly change his method of arriving at guesses about the correct concept.

You can also view the student's learning in terms of discrimination and generalization. In learning the concept *dog,* he must discriminate between the cards which bear drawings of dogs and those which bear drawings of other animals. He is discriminating among the attributes which define the concept and the attributes which do not. Since *dog* is a conjunctive concept, we can say that by discrimination the student is learning what to exclude from his list of dog attributes. He excludes, for example, beaks, feathery tails, wings, and certain feline characteristics. If his discrimination learning is successful, he is able to distinguish among dogs, cats, birds, cows, jackals, and so on. But he must also learn to apply his list of dog attributes to a wide variety of breeds of dogs—from the small, ingratiating schnauzer to the rather bulky Saint Bernard. That is, the student must be able to generalize. By generalizing he learns what to include in his list of dog attributes. Thus, through the processes of discrimination and generalization (exclusion and inclusion), the student learns the attributes of dogs or, if you like, he learns the concept *dog.* By presenting the student with positive examples (to be included in his concept) and with negative examples (to be excluded), we facilitate his making the proper discriminations and generalizations.

How many positive and negative examples? Gagné (1965c) suggests that you use enough positive examples to represent the range of the concept you are teaching. He uses the concept *edge* to illustrate his point. *Edges* are parts of (1) three-dimensional objects, such as books, desks, and chairs; (2) flat, thin objects, such as a piece of paper, a handker chief, and a bedsheet; and (3) drawn two-dimensional pictures, as in the case of the figures in this book. In teaching the concept *edge* you must present positive examples of these three edges. If you present examples of only two the student's concept will be inadequate. To be certain that you represent the entire range, you must consider the various attributes and attribute values of the concept and the relationship of these attributes. Then you must select those positive examples of the concept which you will present to the student.

We must be less explicit about the number of negative examples you should use. This number will be an outgrowth of your experience in teaching the concept, which should reveal the negative attributes the student incorrectly includes in his concept. Using Gagné's example once more, we see that the student must distinguish an edge from the side of a three-dimensional object, from the corner, the top, and the curved surface. All negative examples of the attributes which usually confuse the students should be presented and, if necessary, explained.

Relative merits of positive and negative examples. Although we can learn a concept with all positive or all negative examples, the degree of concept mastery and the amount of time and effort involved often discourage us from limiting ourselves to only one type. Kenneth Smoke (1933) compared the merits of learning concepts from only positive examples and from both positive and negative examples. One concept was *mib*—a triangle with a line extending at right angles from its shortest side. The positive examples of mib contained all the necessary attributes. The negative examples violated one, and only one, attribute (e.g., the line might extend from the longest side of the triangle). Although Smoke discovered no difference in the amount of time it took students to learn the concept with positive examples alone or with both positive and negative examples, most subjects preferred having both. Smoke believes that the negative examples discouraged snap judgments and prevented the students from coming to erroneous conclusions. A later study by LeRoy Olson (1963), which used materials from physics on reciprocal motion and levers, confirmed the findings of Smoke. Janellen Huttenlocher (1962) allowed students to learn a conjunctive concept with positive examples only, negative examples only, or a mixture of positive and negative examples. He controlled the amount of information, so that each example contained the same amount. (This control was lacking in the two previous studies.) Huttenlocher found that students learned the concept better in the mixed series than in the positive series. The series which contained only negative examples was the most difficult to learn. Loy Braley (1963) compared the merits of teaching an easy concept with all negative examples and of teaching a relatively difficult concept with all positive examples. Examples of the two concepts were presented side by side so that each student could learn both. Surprisingly enough, Braley discovered that the students learned the more difficult concept much more rapidly than they learned the easier concept. He concluded that it is difficult for students to use information they gain from negative examples until they have acquired some reasonably well-defined positive representation of the concept. The use of negative examples alone places a considerable burden on the memory of the learner. He must remember all the attributes he has seen in the negative examples and then eliminate the irrelevant attributes as he progresses toward the solution of the problem. Such *exclusion strategies,* as Braley calls them, are used in trouble shooting by mechanics, who must locate a malfunction by eliminating one by one the systems which are functioning properly. If you recall how frequently mechanics arrive at the wrong conclusion and make an unnecessary repair, you will begin to see how difficult this elimination process can be.

In support of Braley's conclusion, Yudin and Kates (1963) studied the value of using negative examples when the student had before him at all times a positive example of the concept. With the provision of this positive example (called a *focus instance)* they found no differences in concept learning under these three conditions: when the subjects were shown (1) all positive examples, (2) all negative examples, and (3) a mixed series of positive and negative examples. Negative examples, they concluded, help in concept learning only when some positive example accompanies them. Finally, Arnold Buss (1950) found that the example the students use determines what they learn. If they practice on negative examples, they learn these better than positive examples and vice versa.

Realism of the examples. Since Alexis de Tocqueville wrote on the topic, considerable fear has been expressed that the American student will learn abstractions in rote fashion and that these abstractions will have little or no relevance to his experience. Even before John Dewey, American education had a pragmatic bent. Teachers have tried to overcome the isolation of the classroom by packing their students into wagons and buses and sending them into the real world outside. These fears about insular classrooms are warranted to some extent. There is not much possibility that children will memorize definitions which have no relevance to their experience as long as the school attempts to broaden and inform that experience. Yet it is always possible that concept learning will be so divorced from the stimuli to which it refers that it becomes empty verbalism. Cronbach (1963) uses this example. The teacher might define sea chantey as a "rhythmic song, sung in chorus by a ship's crew." For a child who has never heard a sea chantey, this definition would convey only a pallid image. Preferably the teacher would (and most music teachers do) provide recordings of sea chanteys (positive examples) and related songs (negative examples) and have the students make the proper discriminations. It is probably unnecessary, however, to put the children on the bus, head for the nearest wharf, and, by some laborious prearrangement, have the local college choir, dressed in crew garb, sing sea chanteys to the children. The children might very well miss the whole point of the field trip and learn more about the ship and the crew than about sea chanteys. Klausmeier and William Goodwin (1966) suggest that one trip to the turkey farm to see hundreds of turkeys with the same attributes is not better than showing pictures of two turkeys, two hens, and so on.

Possibly realistic situations present us with more information that we can easily handle. Travers and his associates (1964a) prove that drawings or animated moving pictures which show only the important attributes of the concept are considerably more effective than direct experience. Travers (1946) points out that human beings have only a limited capacity to use information. When the brain receives more information than it can use, it compresses that information—discarding some of it and attending to those parts of it which are most useful. In visual displays the boundaries of objects provide more information than do other parts. Consequently, line drawings and cartoons are powerful (even if artificial) transmitters of information. Travers (1964, p. 4) criticizes the emphasis on realism in the design of instructional materials, particularly educational films:

> The nervous system cannot deal with the environment in all of its wealth of detail. It handles it by simplifying it, and it is through such simplified inputs and the resulting perceptions and conceptualizations that man learns to cope with a very complex universe. Through simplified presentations in learning situations, the teacher can be sure that the compression process is effective. When this is done the selection of the important element of the message is not up to the learner, who may fail. The separation is made for him. Unfortunately, some producers of instructional movies are, at the present time, doing precisely the reverse. Movies are being produced with visual displays highly embellished with color and complex artistic adornments, and the sound channel is cluttered up with music and other sound effects. The evidence seems clear that such a procedure is not the way to transmit information effectively.

Melvin Marks and Charles Ramond (1951) suggest that the real situation may disrupt or inhibit awareness of those elements which are necessary for concept learning. They state (p. 428), "We know that people do better in school problems than in real-life problems. Perhaps the academic halls have an atmosphere conducive to analysis."

SUMMARY. What can we say about the number, type, and realism of the examples used in teaching concepts? The presentation of a mixed series of positive and negative examples is usually more effective than the presentation of a purely positive or a purely negative series. Presentation of only negative examples makes concept learning extremely difficult. As for number, you should present enough positive examples to represent the range of attributes and attribute values of the concept. In the case of negative examples, you should present at least enough of these to eliminate irrelevant attributes which students are likely to include as part of the concept. Finally, direct experience or realistic examples are usually not preferable to simplified presentations of the concepts, such as line drawings, cartoons, diagrams, and charts. These presentations help achieve the effects of step 2 above, which directed you to simplify the learning of the concept by focusing on its major attributes.

Step 5. Present the Examples in Close Succession or Simultaneously

In this step we are concerned with the order in which the examples as a whole and the types of examples (positive and negative) are presented to the student. The learning condition which this step seeks to provide is contiguity—the almost simultaneous presentation of the examples of the concept. A study by Kates and Yudin (1964) indicates the presentations you can make: *successive presentation,* in which one example is shown at a time and removed after twenty seconds; a *focus condition,* in which two examples are presented together—the focus example (which is always positive) and the new example (which is positive or negative); and *simultaneous presentation,* in which each new example is shown with all the previous examples remaining in view. They found that simultaneous presentation was better than the focus condition, which, in turn, was better than successive presentation. Apparently, simultaneous presentation is superior because the student does not have to rely upon memory for previous examples. Other research tends to support this conclusion and to indicate the superiority of procedures which keep in view the examples presented earlier (Dominowski, 1965). Successive presentation is probably the most common teaching practice, however, because our teaching habits sometimes prompt us to focus the student's attention on one thing at a time. It is a very simple matter, however, to plan our verbal, visual, and auditory presentations so that the student has available all the information he needs to learn the concept. In teaching the concept *dog,* we should leave in view pictures of cats, birds, horses, and dogs while presenting new pictures. In this way we maximize contiguity and reduce the information load on the memory. The evidence is less conclusive about the order of the types of examples. Should the positive examples or the negative examples come first in a mixed series of examples? Carl Hovland and Walter Weiss (1953) found that the order did not affect learning efficiency. More recently, however, Huttenlocher (1962) found that a series of negative examples followed by positive examples facilitated concept learning.

Step 6. Present a New Positive Example of the Concept and Ask the Student to Identify It

In this step you are providing both contiguity and reinforcement. Whereas the previous step emphasizes discrimination (or the distinction between positive and negative examples), this step emphasizes generalization, or the ability of the student to make the conceptual response to a new but similar pattern of stimuli. In teaching the concept *dog,* for example, you might have shown pictures of Dalmatians, Saint Bernards, poodles, German shepherds, English Bulls, and terriers. In this step then you present a picture of a sad-faced cocker spaniel. If the student is able to identify the new example of a dog, he has learned the concept. To provide reinforcement the student must be informed about the accuracy of his response.

The additional steps I shall describe are not designed for original concept learning but are your means of verifying, preserving, and extending the learning which has already occurred in steps 4 and 5.

Step 7. Verify the Student's Learning of the Concept

Here you should present several new positive and negative examples of the concept and ask the student to select only the positive examples. You can now show pictures of basset hounds, Doberman pinschers, Weimaraners, and otterhounds (all dogs) along with pictures of wolves, foxes, jackals, and bobcats. The available evidence does not indicate whether this step is necessary for concept learning. It is important in concept teaching because it is our means for assessing the student's performance (the fourth component of the basic teaching model). It also provides the student with additional opportunities to make responses for which he can obtain his own or the teacher's reinforcement or both.

Step 8. Require the Student to Define the Concept

Much concept learning is prelingual (before the acquisition of language) or alingual (without the use of language). The child, for example, learns to discriminate and generalize among dogs, cats, birds, and horses as well as among mother, father, sister, and brother long before he can give us an adequate definition of these concepts. In most of the concept-learning experiments I have described in this chapter the student was required to identify a concept, often by selecting the correct card. Sometimes he had to respond "yes" to positive examples and "no" to negative examples. In neither case was he required to define the concept. On the basis of the procedures we used in teaching *dog*, we could not expect the elementary school child to give this definition: any of a large and varied group of domesticated animals related to the fox, wolf, and jackal. In fact this definition embodies little of what he would have learned about the attributes of dogs.

Some experimental evidence indicates that students can learn to identify concepts without being able to define them correctly. Donald Johnson and Charlene O'Reilly (1964) taught students the difference between a gunkle bird and a bunkle bird (two laboratory concepts) by having them learn that all gunkle birds had black tails. The cards which the students were shown contained pictures of birds with several other attributes of different values: red, yellow, and blue wings; orange, green, as well as black tails; pointed, long, and hooked beaks. In the pictorial group the students had to classify as gunkle or bunkle birds a series of pictures of birds with these attributes. The verbal group had to classify verbal phrases which described birds with the same attributes as those in the pictures. The third group, a pictorial-definition group, had to classify the same pictures used by the first group, but they also were asked after every five cards, "How do you tell a gunkle bird?" The first and second groups were asked this question only after they had completed their examination of all the cards and phrases. Johnson and O'Reilly found that the pictorial-definition group gave twice as many good definitions as did the pictorial group. They also found that the classification task was learned fastest by the verbal group. The investigators concluded that a small amount of practice of the definition, even when the students are not told how good the definition is, improves the quality of definitions. They also argue that if thorough concept learning includes the ability to use the concept in communication, special attention should be given to learning the definition. The teacher cannot assume that the student's ability to define the concept follows from his ability to identify the concept. We should also recall that some concepts in science, mathematics, and other disciplines are difficult to describe in words. It is probably most necessary to provide special training for concept definition when that definition is particularly difficult to formulate.

Step 9. Provide Occasions for Student Responses and the Reinforcement of These Responses

It is somewhat misleading to call this a *step* because response and reinforcement are integral parts of steps 4 through 8. By including them in our list however, we are able to give them more detailed consideration and to remind you of their importance. In concept learning reinforcement primarily provides informational feedback, which enables the student either to separate positive and negative examples and to compose his list or to define the relationship of the various attributes. We know that the consistency with which reinforcement is provided affects the learning of concepts (Rhine and Silun, 1958). Some evidence indicates that 100 per cent reinforcement speeds the learning of the concept more than partial reinforcement does (Carpenter, 1954). Delaying the reinforcement even by as little as forty minutes impairs the learning of concepts (Sax, 1960).

The type and the intensity of the feedback (reinforcement) affect concept learning. In his study, Wallace (1964) used two types of negative feedback—auditory and verbal. These examples illustrate the three levels of intensity of verbal feedback: mild—"Wrong!"; moderate—"Wrong, I didn't think it would be this hard!"; and strong—"Most college students get this one very quickly. I don't understand why you can't get it!" Auditory feedback was provided by the ringing of a doorbell attached to a muffin pan and placed in a large galvanized tub. Auditory feedback also varied in intensity from mild to moderate to strong. Wallace found that the more difficult concepts (as compared with the easier ones) were learned with fewer examples when the intensity of the feedback was strong. Also, mild verbal feedback was less effective than mild auditory feedback. Wallace suggests that auditory feedback may be more effective than verbal feedback because it is relatively impersonal and does not discourage guesses about which the student is relatively uncertain. In a previous experiment Sechrest and Wallace (1962) found that negative verbal feedback discouraged what they call *hypothesis spewing*—making more than one guess in learning a concept. Of course, if the student views any verbal feedback as punitive, he may not even venture his first guess. If he suspends all overt guessing, he receives less feedback, and it will take him longer to learn the concept.

Shifting the mode of response also inhibits concept learning. Nancy Wilder and Donald Ross Green (1963) asked students to observe the growth of two plants, one in the sun and the other in poor light, over a two-week period, without discussing the changes with their fellow students. After two weeks, the plants were placed side by side, and the students were asked to describe their differences. One group drew pictures of the differences. A second group wrote about them. After forty minutes, the students were presented with two begonia plants which had been grown under the same conditions, and they were again asked to describe the differences. At this point the students were divided into four groups: Group I wrote their descriptions both times; group II wrote the first time and drew the second time; group III drew both times; and group IV drew the first time and wrote the second time. They found that shifting the response mode from writing to drawing (or the reverse) inhibited the expression of the concept.

Further occasion for reinforcement is provided in practicing the concept beyond the original learning situation. While studying other animals the student can be reinforced for the correct identification and use of the concept *dog*. After he has applied the concept to a variety of new examples, he has thoroughly learned the attributes and can, from that point, reinforce his own use of the concept.

In summary, student responses and reinforcement of these responses are crucial learning conditions for concept learning. The primary purpose of reinforcement is to provide informational feedback to the student on the correctness of his responses. Since this feedback is crucial, any inconsistency, delay, or failure to provide it will impair student learning. However, because the student knows which terminal behavior he must acquire, he can to some extent monitor his own learning. Since reinforcement has motivational aspects, negative verbal feedback may impair concept learning by discouraging the student from making early guesses which can be confirmed. The teacher should remember to focus on the reinforcement of the student's responses and not on the student. The mode of the response should not be shifted, at least in the early learning of the concept. It is quite possible, however, that the shift from spoken to written responses is less inhibiting than the shift from drawing to writing or writing to drawing. Various mechanical and electronic devices may maintain consistency of response mode and informational feedback better than we can now do under ordinary classroom conditions. These same contrivances may also provide students with more occasions for reinforced practice than we can now provide.

Summary: An Illustration of Concept Teaching

To summarize the nine steps for concept teaching we shall describe how Miss D. Voted taught her students the concept *tourist*. Miss Voted (step 1) began her lesson with these words: "Today I want to teach you the concept *tourist*. By the end of the lesson you should be able to identify quickly any examples of *tourist* which I present to you." Miss Voted had analyzed the concept (step 2) and decided that it was a simple conjunctive concept with three attributes—activity, purpose, and residence. Each attribute had a particular value: For activity, it was travel and sightseeing; for purpose, it was pleasure; for residence, it was keeping the same permanent residence. These were the attributes and attribute values the students had to learn. Miss D. Voted thought of other attributes such as mode of travel, mode of dress, passports, and visas but she decided that these were not major attributes and that their introduction could confuse the students. She then made certain that her students had the necessary verbal association (step 3). She wrote the word *tourist* on the board and asked the students to say the word; they did so with impressive choral response. Next, Miss D. Voted presented her positive and negative examples of *tourist* (step 4). Her examples were verbal descriptions printed in large letters on large cards which all the students could see and read. Each card was left in view after it was presented (step 5). Before presenting each card she reminded the students that they were looking for a *class* of people. Her first card bore these words: Mr. Phog lives in San Francisco but he is on vacation and he is visiting Rome to see friends and the city. Miss Voted asked, "Is Mr. Phog a tourist?" The class in complete unison responded "yes." Miss Voted smiled and said they were correct. She then presented a second card which bore these words: Mr. Michael Angelo left Italy in 1898 and has raised his children in the United States. Is he a tourist? The students shouted "no." Harriet Smart added that Mr. Angelo was an immigrant. Miss D. Voted smiled, and the children knew they were right and that Harriet was right and smart. She then presented a card which described an American visiting another country; the students recognized this person as a tourist. Miss D. Voted also presented several negative examples, such as commercial pilots who flew between cities and countries, ambassadors and envoys who retained their original citizenship and residences but who were not traveling primarily for pleasure, Americans who changed their permanent residence to other countries, and even a man without a country. She had several more positive examples of *tourist,* such as individuals moving within a country to sightsee and visit friends, moving from one country to another for the same purpose, and even moving from one region of the world to another, as in the case of the jet set. Each time she presented a card she waited for the students to indicate whether the description referred to a tourist, and she told them in each case whether they were correct. By the end of her presentation, all the cards were in view.

Miss D. Voted was now ready to proceed to the next step (6). She presented a new positive example of tourist. It was Mr. Angelo and he was returning to Italy to visit friends and relatives, to sightsee, and to relax along the Adriatic Sea. Is Mr. Angelo a tourist? The class (with a few students remaining silent) said "yes," and Harriet added "definitely!" Miss Voted said they were correct. She then presented several new positive and negative examples of *tourist,* using different nationalities, different regions, and different purposes for travel (step 7). She threw in a few more examples (for Harriet) of individuals who were both tourists and immigrants at different times in their lives. Then Miss Voted asked the students to write a definition of a tourist (step 8). She asked them to keep in mind how a tourist is different from an immigrant. In evaluating these definitions Miss Voted simply compared her list of attributes with those attributes contained in the students' definitions. She reinforced all correct definitional responses and indicated all inaccuracies. Finally, she reminded her students of the original instructional objective. She then administered a test of terminal performance which contained several new positive and negative examples of *tourist*. She immediately scored the tests, and the students discovered that they all did very well and that Harriet obtained a perfect score (step 9).

We can now list the steps you should take in teaching a concept:

Step 1: Describe the performance expected of the student after he has learned the concept.

Step 2: Reduce the number of attributes to be learned in complex concepts and make important attributes dominant.

Step 3: Provide the student with useful verbal mediators.

Step 4: Provide positive and negative examples of the concept.

Step 5: Present examples in close succession or simultaneously.

Step 6: Present a new positive example of the concept and ask the student to identify it.

Step 7: Verify the student's learning of the concept.

Step 8: Require the student to define the concept.

Step 9: Provide occasions for student responses and the reinforcement of these responses.

You should now return to objectives 12–20 (pp. 386–87) and determine how well you have achieved these objectives.

QUESTION 10-2

In presenting cards which contained positive and negative examples of *tourist*, Miss D. Voted left each card in view after it was presented. Why did she do this?

(a) To keep the students aware of their expected performance.
(b) To provide the students with useful verbal mediators.
(c) To provide contiguity in the presentation of the material.
(d) To verify the students' learning of the concept.

After selecting your answer, give the reasons for your choice and for your rejection of the alternatives.

THE TEACHING OF PRINCIPLES

I shall now describe the teaching of principles as a series of eight steps which conform to the four components of the basic teaching model. Steps 1 and 2 chiefly pertain to instructional objectives. Step 1 requires a statement of the objective, and step 2 requires a task analysis. Step 2 also specifies the prerequisite entering behavior, while step 3 assists the student in the use of the appropriate entering behavior. Steps 4 and 8 provide the essential learning conditions of contiguity, practice, and reinforcement. Steps 5 through 7 pertain chiefly to performance assessment.

For the sake of brevity I shall use a single principle in the illustration of these steps: The plural of most nouns is formed by adding *s* to the singular form of the noun. (We shall not worry at the moment about the plural form of nouns that end in *s, sh, ch, x,* or *z*.)

Step 1. Describe the Performance Expected of the Student After He Has Learned the Principle

As in the case of concept learning, this step allows the student to monitor his own performance and to generate his own reinforcement. For our principle, the statement could be as follows: When given the singular form of several English nouns, you will form the plural by adding *s*.

Step 2. Decide and Indicate Which Concepts or Principles the Student Must Recall in Learning the New Principle

In this step, you must analyze the principle to determine what the component concepts are, and you must assess the entering behavior of the student to determine whether he has mastered these concepts. For our illustrative principle, the student needs to know these concepts: plural, most, nouns, formed by adding, *s,* and singular form. Unless the student has mastered each of these he cannot learn the relationship the principle specifies. Supporting evidence for the necessity of knowing component concepts is found in an experiment by Howard Kendler and Robert Vineberg (1954). The component concepts were *size* and *shape*. In the first part of the experiment the students were taught in three different ways: Group 1 learned the two component concepts; group 2 learned one of the two component concepts (shape); and group 3 learned neither of the component concepts but learned instead two irrelevant concepts. In the second part of the experiment they had to learn a principle, or compound concept. They were presented with a large gray triangle and a small orange circle and required to sort several cards which bore similar figures by matching them with the triangle or the circle. For example, if they were presented with a card with a large orange square, they were to match it with the large gray triangle because both figures are the same in size (large) and in shape (with straight lines). A card with a small black crescent was to be matched with a small orange circle because both figures are the same in size (small) and shape (with curved lines). Group 1 took an average of twenty-three trials to learn the test concept, while the next best group (group 2) took almost twice this number, and group 3 (which had learned neither component concept) took four times as many trials!

Your performance of step 2 in principle teaching is complicated by the fact that the learning of one principle is often dependent on the prior learning of another principle. There are, in effect, hierarchies of principles. Gagné (1965c, p. 151) states, "In hierarchies of principles two or more principles may be prerequisite to the learning of a superordinate principle. Once the latter is learned, it may combine with another principle to support the learning of still another higher-level principle, and so on. A hierarchy may be called a structure of organized knowledge about a topic." Gagné and his associates (1961, 1962, 1963) have found that the order in which topics are presented figures prominently in the students' achievement of the instructional objectives.

Figure 10-3 is a hierarchy of principles in the topic of nonmetric geometry. The student has to learn not simply to recognize points, lines, and curves, but also to show that the existence of each of these entities is dependent on the application of certain principles. The figure is interesting because it depicts how concepts are organized into principles and how principles are interrelated. Gagné (pp. 151–52) explains Fig. 10-3 in these words:

> At the lowest level, the boxes numbered VI and V represent *concepts* that must be known at the start. VIa is the concept *separation (of entities into groups)*. VIb is *point*. Va is *set of points*—a new name for what most uninstructed students would simply call a "line." Beginning with these fairly simple concepts, which must be acquired in the manner described for type 6 [concept] learning, the learner is ready to attain a new set of interrelated *principles*. First he learns to identify and draw a straight line (IVa), which is a set of points extending indefinitely in both directions. Later, he learns the principle which defines *line segment,* namely, that part of a line which consists of two points and the set of points between (IIIa). Then, he learns to identify and draw a *ray,* the set of points formed by a point on a line and one of the half lines made by this point (IIIb). Later still, he learns to define and make a *triangle;* this is made up of three points not on the same straight line and the line segments that join these points (IIa). Picking up another thread of principles that build on each other, the student has also learned about *intersections* of lines and parts of lines (IVb, IIb, IIc). Finally, putting together these ideas of a *triangle* and of *intersections* he comes to learn principle Ia, which enables him to state that the intersection of a triangle and lines or parts of lines is 0, 1, or 2

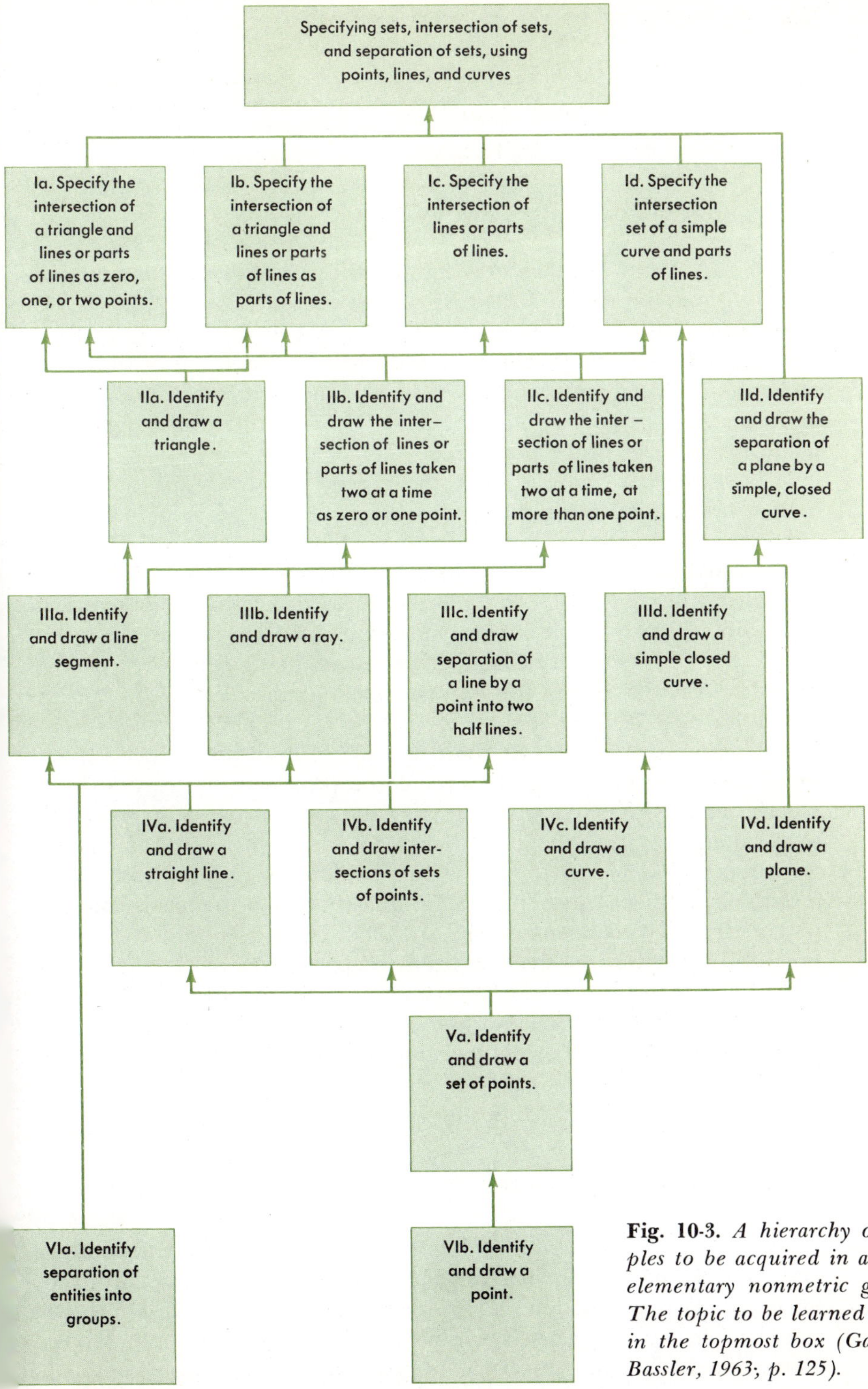

Fig. 10-3. *A hierarchy of principles to be acquired in a topic of elementary nonmetric geometry. The topic to be learned is shown in the topmost box (Gagné and Bassler, 1963; p. 125).*

> points. If he has indeed mastered these principles, one building on the other, he is able at this stage to provide examples of intersections of lines with triangles that form sets of 0, 1, or 2 points, and to justify the drawing he makes.
>
> Such a drawing must not "look" right; the learner will be able at this stage to say why it is right.

Gagné goes on to say that determining the prerequisites for any given principle may be accomplished by asking the question: What does the student have to know in order to be instructed in this principle? Knowing principle IIc, for example, means being able to deal with intersections of sets of points whether these are line segments, rays, half lines, or indefinitely extended lines. Principle IIc is a superordinate principle made up of lower-order principles.

Task analysis reminds us of the necessity of analyzing our subject matter before presenting it to the student. In the case of component concepts, it is necessary to determine which concepts we expect the student to know before we try to teach him the principle. In the case of higher-order principles, it is necessary to determine beforehand the lower-order principles the student must know. Step 2 requires the teacher to ask and answer the question: What does the student have to know in order to be instructed in this principle? Hierarchies of concepts and principles may become research areas for educational psychologists. If such research is successful, it could tell the teacher the proper sequence in which to present the concepts and the principles he teaches. In the absence of this research it is necessary for each of us to do some practical experimentation to find which sequence works best. For example, no sequence has been determined for introducing the principle on the formation of the English plural. Ordinarily this principle is taught as part of the instruction on nouns and noun forms. Should it follow or precede instruction on the formation of possessives or on the singular and plural verb forms? It is very likely that it should precede instruction on these latter principles because it can contribute more to their learning than they can to the learning of our illustrative principle. But we really do not know the best sequence until we experiment with alternative sequences and find out which works best.

Step 3. Assist the Student in the Recall of Component Concepts

In this step you provide contiguity by having the student simultaneously recall the component concepts. In the case of our illustrative principle, this instruction may proceed as follows: You know what singular means. It means one object, person, or place. We can talk about one book, one American, or one country. You also know what plural means. It refers to more than one object, person, or place. We can talk about two books, two Americans, or all the countries in the world. I have listed several words on the board [mother, fathers, teachers, dog, cats, and houses]. Point out which of these words are in the plural form. [Students respond appropriately, and the teacher reinforces correct responses.] You also know what nouns are. I have listed five words on the board [show, boy, girl, run, and fat]. Point out which of these words are nouns [again appropriate response and reinforcement]. You also know the letter *s*. I have several letters on the board [several letters in upper and lower case, including more than one *s*]. Pick out the letter *s*. [Students respond appropriately and obtain reinforcement. Similar instruction is provided for *most*.]

Step 4. Help the Student to Combine the Concepts in the Proper Order

In this step you also provide contiguity of concepts and contiguity for the proper relationship of the concepts. The student's learning requires guidance here. It is not enough to ask him to order the concepts properly. Your questions must guide the ordering. For example, you say this: "Now I want you to tell me how you change most singular nouns into plural nouns." The student should respond, "By adding an *s* to the singular form." You respond (with enthusiasm), "Correct!"

Step 5. Require the Student to Demonstrate the Principle Fully

Here we must refer to step 1 to remind ourselves what performance we selected as our instructional objective. Our objective indicates that it is not enough to give the student a list of positive and negative examples of plural nouns and to ask him to choose the plurals. The objective requires the student to form the plural when given the singular form. Therefore, you say to the student, "Show me how you form the plurals of the list of words I have given to you." Gagné (1966) emphasizes the importance of requiring the student to demonstrate or show the teacher his grasp of the principle. Using the principle of work (work = force × distance), Gagné (p. 86) writes:

> I do not mean to imply by this [demonstration] a single measure of performance such as the question which verbally says to the student "demonstrate work in the following situation" and then describe the situation. Instead, it seems to me that there are a number of different questions that might be asked in order to determine whether a student has learned a principle. One might say, "What is the work done in pushing a body of 1000 grams a horizontal distance of thirty centimeters?" or "Show how to calculate the work done by a force of fifty pounds pushing a trunk along a floor for ten feet." Any of these questions may be considered to reflect what is meant by "demonstrate."

Step 6. Require the Student to Give a Full Statement of the Principle

Again, as in step 4, you can use verbal mediators to elicit the definition. You ask, "How do you form the plural of singular nouns?" The student should respond, "By adding *s* to the singular form."

Step 7. Verify the Student's Learning of the Principle

To be certain that the student has not given a rote definition, you should test further to determine how well he has acquired the new principle. In the case of our example, you present the student with a list of singular nouns and ask him to form their plurals. The student has learned the principle before this step; the verification is primarily an opportunity for the instructor to ascertain how well the new capability has been established.

Step 8. Provide for Practice of the Principle and for Reinforcement of Student Responses

We may well assume, if steps 1 through 7 are properly enacted, that the student knows the principle and that no further practice is necessary. Instructional conditions, however, are not always optimal, and there is usually the practical necessity of providing for review and reinforcement beyond the original learning situation. In the case of plurals, students have the opportunity to identify plurals in their reading and to form them in their writing. Of course, the instructor must monitor the students' practice and reinforce correct responses and point out incorrect ones. Reinforced practice of a principle is particularly crucial when the learning of one principle interferes with the retention of others. Doris Entwisle and W. Huggins (1964) found that beginning engineering students who studied voltage principles first and the corresponding current principles immediately afterward retained less of what they learned than when they studied the voltage principles alone. They also found that learning several principles of electric circuits interfered with retention of each other and caused forgetting. These findings suggest the need for both proper sequencing of the subject matter and reinforced practice of potentially confusing principles.

Summary

We can now list the steps you should take in teaching principles:

Step 1: Describe the performance expected of the student after he has learned the principle.

Step 2: Decide and indicate which concepts or principles the student must recall in learning the new principle.

Step 3: Assist the student in the recall of the component concepts.

Step 4: Help the student combine the concepts in the proper order.

Step 5: Require the student to demonstrate the principle fully.

Step 6: Require the student to give a full statement of the principle.

Step 7: Verify the student's learning of the principle.

Step 8: Provide for practice of the principle and reinforcement of student responses.

You should now return to objectives 21–28 (p. 387) and determine how well you have achieved them.

QUESTION 10-3

In teaching the principle of the formation of plural nouns by adding *s* to the singular form, Mr. Punctilious, at one point in the instruction, gives the students these words: space ships and box cars. He then requests the students to give him the singular forms of these words. Why does Mr. Punctilious do this?

(a) He is describing the expected terminal performance.

(b) He is deciding which concepts the student must recall.

(c) He is assisting the students in the recall of component concepts.

(d) He is helping the students to combine the component concepts in the proper order.

(e) He is requiring the students to demonstrate the principle.

After selecting your answer, give the reasons for your choice and for your rejection of the alternatives.

SUMMARY

The first section of the chapter dealt with the nature and uses of concepts and principles. A concept was defined as a class of stimuli which have common characteristics. Each concept has attributes—distinctive features which vary from concept to concept. Attributes, in turn, have values which describe the particular variations the attributes may undergo. The number of attributes varies from concept to concept. In general, the more attributes the concept has the more difficult it is to learn. The dominance, or obviousness, of attributes also varies. When relevant attributes are not dominant and irrelevant attributes are dominant, the concept becomes more difficult to learn. Attributes combine in three different ways to produce three types of concepts. In a conjunctive concept the appropriate values of several concepts are jointly present. In a disjunctive concept the appropriate values of one attribute or another or both are present. A relational concept has a specifiable relationship between attributes. Conjunctive concepts are easier to learn than disjunctive and relational concepts. A principle is a statement of the relationship of two or more concepts or principles. These statements often take an if-then form. It is necessary to relate the teaching of concepts to the student's level of development and to his preschool learning. Finally, there are many uses of concepts in school learning, ranging from those uses which reduce complexity and the need for constant learning to those misuses of concepts as stereotypes.

I described nine steps for the teaching of concepts: Step 1 requires the description of the student's expected performance after he has learned the concept (the first component of the basic teaching model). Step 2 requires the teacher to reduce the number of attributes to be learned by ignoring some and emphasizing others or by reducing a large number of attributes to a few patterns. Step 2 also requires the teacher to make all relevant attributes dominant. Step 3 requires the teacher to provide the student with useful verbal mediators to prepare him for concept learning. Steps 2 and 3 pertain mainly to the entering behavior of the student.

The remaining steps deal with procedures for teaching concepts when the entering behavior is adequate (component 3 of the basic teaching model). Step 4 requires you to provide positive and negative examples of the concept. You must present enough positive examples to represent the actual range of the concept you are teaching. The presentation of a mixed series of positive and negative examples is more effective than the presentation of a purely positive or a purely negative series. Simplified examples are often more effective than realistic examples, which often present more information than the student can easily handle. Step 5 requires the teacher to provide contiguity by presenting the examples in close succession or simultaneously. Step 6 provides a new positive example of the concept and requires the student to identify it.

The remaining three steps are the teacher's means of verifying, preserving, and extending the original concept learning which occurred in the three preceding steps. For step 7, you verify the student's learning of the concept. For step 8, you require the student to define the concept. For step 9 you provide occasions for reinforced practice beyond the original learning situation. The type and intensity of the reinforcement (feedback) affect concept learning. Shifting the response mode may inhibit concept learning.

Eight steps were described for the teaching of principles. Step 1 requires the teacher to describe the performance expected of the student after he has learned the principle (component 1 of the basic teaching model). Step 2 deals with entering behavior. Here the teacher decides and indicates which concepts or principles the student must recall in learning the new principle. Because there are hierarchies of principles, the learning of a higher-order principle requires the prior learning of a lower-order principle.

The next three steps deal with the third component of the basic teaching model. In step 3 you provide contiguity by assisting the student in the recall of component concepts. In step 4 you help him to combine the concepts in the proper order. In step 5 you require the student to demonstrate the principle fully by more than a single measure of performance.

The remaining steps verify, extend, and preserve the original principle learning. In step 6 you require the student to give a full statement of the principle. Step 7 requires you to verify the student's learning of the principle. Step 8 provides reinforced practice.

SUGGESTED READINGS

These three books of readings deal particularly with the subject matter in this chapter. For the most part these readings report actual research or comprise theoretical discussions upon which the research is based.

Anderson, Richard C., and David P. Ausubel, *Readings in the Psychology of Cognition.* New York: Holt, Rinehart & Winston, Inc., 1965.

De Cecco, John P., *Psychology of Language, Thought, and Instruction: Readings.* New York: Holt, Rinehart & Winston, Inc., 1967.

Harper, Robert J. C., Charles C. Anderson, Clifford M. Christensen, and Steven M. Hunka, *The Cognitive Processes: Readings.* Englewood Cliffs, N.J.: Prentice-Hall, Inc., 1964.

These fairly recent articles and books deal with the various theories and research on concept and principle learning:

Bruner, Jerome S., Jacqueline J. Goodnow, and George A. Austin, *A Study of Thinking.* New York: John Wiley & Sons, Inc., 1956.

Hunt, Earl B., *Concept Learning: An Information Processing Problem.* New York: John Wiley & Sons, Inc., 1962.

Gagné, Robert M., "The Learning of Principles," in *Analyses of Concept Learning,* eds. H. J. Klausmeier and C. W. Harris, pp. 81–96. New York: Academic Press, Inc., 1966.

Kendler, Howard H., "The Concept of the Concept," in *Categories of Human Learning,* ed. A. W. Melton. New York: Academic Press Inc., 1964.

Reitman, Walter R., *Cognition and Thought: An Information Processing Approach.* New York: John Wiley & Sons, Inc., 1965.

No entire volume deals with the teaching of concepts and principles, but these various chapters and articles do:

Gagné, Robert M., *Conditions of Learning.* New York: Holt, Rinehart & Winston, Inc., 1965, Chaps. 5 and 6.

Klausmeier, Herbert J., and Chester W. Harris, eds., *Analyses of Concept Learning.* New York: Academic Press Inc., 1966, Part III (on learning-teaching processes) and Part IV (on concepts in various subject matter fields).

Much of the research on concept and principle teaching and learning is published in the *Journal of Educational Psychology.*

Problem Solving, Creativity, and Discovery Learning

11

In this chapter we consider the methods for teaching the most complex kind of human learning—*problem solving.* We shall view problem solving as a form of principle learning in which lower-order principles are applied in the learning of higher-order principles. In this view, successful problem solving results in the acquisition of new knowledge just as does the successful learning of concepts and principles. Although this chapter emphasizes problem solving as a gain in substantive knowledge, we shall also consider techniques of problem solving which are sometimes called *creative thinking, critical thinking,* and *learning by discovery.* One of the major issues the latter part of the chapter considers is the following: Are there techniques of problem solving independent of particular subject matter and disciplines and, if there are, can you teach them to students?

The chapter has four major sections. The first describes the nature of problem solving. Here we recall our definition of learning and introduce the concepts of habit family hierarchies and transfer of learning. The second section describes and illustrates five steps you can take in teaching problem solving. Later in the chapter you will see that these five steps illustrate learning by guided discovery. The third section describes the nature of creativity and the teaching conditions which foster it. I define creativity as creative abilities, the learning of original responses, and problem solving. The fourth section defines and illustrates a concept of teaching procedures widely discussed currently—learning by discovery. Learning by discovery is compared with expository teaching for its value in achieving various instructional objectives.

Upon reading the first section of this chapter (on the nature of problem solving), you should be able to meet these objectives:

1. Define and illustrate problem solving in terms of the definition of learning given in Chapter 7.

2. Describe and illustrate the differences and similarities in problem solving and principle learning.

3. Define habit family hierarchies in terms of divergent and convergent mechanisms and distinguish between simple and compound hierarchies.

4. Define mediated generalization in terms of increased strength of members of hierarchies and illustrate the process by using an example of verbal mediation in a problem solution.

5. Distinguish between and illustrate a reversal and a nonreversal shift; describe the differences in the ability of younger and older children to make the shifts; and show how these shifts illustrate the effects of verbal mediation.

6. Distinguish between reproductive and productive thinking in terms of habit family hierarchies.

7. Define transfer of learning in terms of two tasks and distinguish between and illustrate the differences between (a) positive, (b) negative, and (c) zero transfer.

8. Define and illustrate problem solving in terms of transfer of learning.

Upon reading the second section of this chapter (on instruction in problem solving), you should be able to describe and illustrate each of the following instructional steps:

9. Step 1: Describe for the students the terminal performance which constitutes the solution of the problem.

10. Step 2: Assess the students' entering behavior for the concepts and principles they will need to solve the problem.

11. Step 3: Invoke the recall of all relevant concepts and principles (including the use of advance organizers).

12. Step 4: Provide verbal direction of the students' thinking, short of giving them the solution to the problem.

13. Step 5: Verify the students' learning by requiring them to give a full demonstration of the problem solution (using other problems of the same class).

Upon reading the third section of this chapter (on instruction for creativity), you should be able to meet these objectives:

14. Define and illustrate creative abilities in terms of flexibility, originality, and fluency.

15. Distinguish (and illustrate the differences) between divergent and convergent thinking.

16. Define tests of creative abilities in terms of response production and indicate the degree of correlation of these tests.

17. Define and illustrate creativity as the learning of new responses.

18. Define and illustrate creativity as problem solving.

19. Distinguish (and illustrate the difference) between presented and discovered problems with known and unknown methods of solution.

20. Define brainstorming in terms of free association and deferred evaluation and list its effects in terms of (a) problem solving, (b) quality of solutions, (c) effects on creative abilities; describe and illustrate its use in invoking recall of concepts and principles in problem solving.

21. Describe and illustrate the use of research skills and creative reading in creative problem solving.

22. Describe and illustrate the ways in which the teacher can reward creative achievement.

Upon reading the fourth section of this chapter (on learning by discovery), you should be able to meet these objectives:

23. Define discovery learning in terms of instructional guidance and in terms of giving or not giving the principle and the problem solution; distinguish (in these terms) between guided and unguided discovery.

24. Define inquiry training in terms of strategies and tactics and describe and illustrate the presentation and practice phases; distinguish (and illustrate the differences) between questions of information and verification and experimental questions.

25. Describe four teaching strategies in terms of three levels of thought (informational, inferential, and predictive).

26. Define expository teaching in terms of instructional guidance and in terms of the teacher's giving or not giving the principle and problem solution and distinguish between expository teaching and discovery learning.

27. List four advantages (Bruner's) for discovery learning in terms of intellectual potency, intrinsic motivation, techniques of discovery, and information storage.

28. Describe the instructional conditions under which, in the studies of Corman and of Gagné and Brown, problem solutions were most successful.

29. Describe four areas in which (according to Wittrock) discovery learning may be helpful.

30. List the advantages of expository teaching by referring to the selecting and organizing of subject matter and the learning of concepts and principles.

31. Describe the mixed method (Johnson and Stratton) by referring to the methods it includes and its effectiveness.

32. Describe and illustrate how programed instruction as represented by the Ruleg system is a form of expository teaching.

33. List unsupportable claims about discovery learning in terms of learning subject matter, developing creative and critical thinking, making the great discovery, and available research.

34. Describe the conditions under which discovery learning should be used by referring to the components of the basic teaching model.

THE NATURE OF PROBLEM SOLVING

Problem Solving as Learning

In Chapter 7, I defined learning as a relatively permanent change in a behavioral tendency which results from reinforced practice. I also described the learning event as consisting of the learner, the stimulus situation, and the response. You will see that both the definition of learning and the description of the learning event apply to problem solving. To understand this point consider the matchstick problems invented by George Katona (1940). The physical stimulus situation consisted of unusual geometric forms made with matches or pencils and paper. Figure 11-1a is an example of one of these geometric forms. The numerical designation beneath the figures indicated that the student had to solve this problem by reducing five squares to four squares and by moving only three matchsticks. The student was also told that the squares were equal in size and that the new figure had to consist of equal squares of the same size as those in the original figure. The student was then given three alterations of the figure which did not constitute solutions. It was not permissible (a) to take away any matchsticks from the table, (b) to form figures which were not squares or to have unused lines, or (c) to have duplication of sides—each square could have only four sides. Figure 11-1b shows each of these unacceptable solutions. In this learning event the stimulus situation consisted of the various physical and verbal stimuli which I have described. To these stimuli the student was to make the acceptable response shown in Fig. 11-1c.

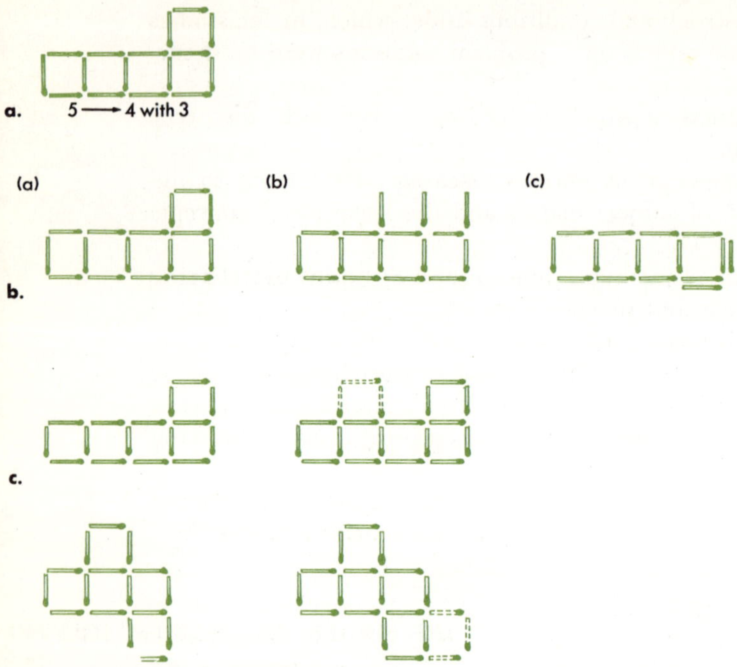

Fig. 11-1 a. *An example of a matchstick problem.* **b.** *Unacceptable solutions to the matchstick problem.* **c.** *Acceptable solutions to the matchstick problem above and to an additional one (after Katona, 1940, pp. 58–60).*

Now we can apply our definition of learning. When the student solves these and similar problems, we can infer a change in behavioral tendency, especially because he could not solve the problems when he was originally presented with them. We also know that the change in behavioral tendency which results from successful problem solving is more permanent than the changes which result from the less complex forms of learning we discussed earlier. With very little practice we can remember how to solve matchstick problems after relatively few trials and long periods of time. When we discuss learning by discovery, you will see however that reinforced practice adds considerably to the long-term retention of problem solutions and to their wide application to new and similar problems. We can, therefore, think of problem solving as a form of learning.

Problem Solving and Principle Learning

Problem solving is closely related to principle learning (Gagné, 1964, 1965c) since it combines two or more previously learned principles into higher-order principle. And, like concept and principle learning, problem solving represents acquisition of substantive knowledge. Gagné (1964) uses this example. A beginning algebra student is given a problem —multiply X^2 and X^3—which he has not seen before. To solve this problem he must have learned two principles: Multiplying a number by n means adding that number n times, and an exponent r represents multiplying the number by itself r times. The combination of these principles produces the solution to the problem and the learning of a higher-order principle: To multiply identical variables with exponents, multiply the variable by itself the number of times represented by the sum of the two exponents. If a student obtains the right answer to this problem, we usually infer that he has learned the higher-order principle without requiring him to state it. We confirm our inference by having him solve other problems of the same class—problems which involve multiplying variables with exponents.

Solution of the matchstick problems also implies the proper application of two principles and the learning of a higher-order principle. One principle refers to the double function of particular sticks—one stick can serve as the side of two squares. The other principle is that the original figure can be loosened by creating holes in it. The higher-order principle is that to make fewer squares with the same number of matchsticks create holes in the original figure and give particular sticks double functions. The student's successful solution of a number of matchstick problems indicates that he has learned the higher-order principle.

This discussion of problem solving as the learning of higher-order principles distinguishes between problem solving as the acquisition of knowledge and problem solving as the learning of some very general techniques which can be applied to a wide variety of problems. As much as we would like to believe in some general problem-solving strategies of wide applicability, the research we have available does not convince us of their existence. We shall discuss some of that research in the latter part of the chapter when we consider the general topics of creativity and discovery learning.

Habit Family Hierarchies

Several theories suggest how problem solving occurs in the individual. Since the theory of Irving Maltzman (1955) is consistent with our view of problem solving as complex learning, I shall give you a simplified version of this theory. A basic principle in it is that of stimulus and response hierarchies. Figure 11-2a shows such a hierarchy. S is a stimulus. R_1, R_2, and R_3 are three responses to this stimulus. The figure indicates that R_1 is stronger (higher in the hierarchy) than R_2, which, in turn, is stronger than R_3. A stronger response is more likely to occur in the presence of the stimulus. For example, if the word *table* represents S, three

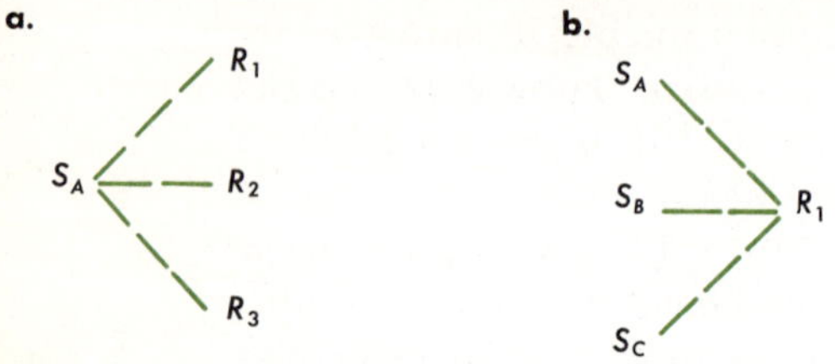

Fig. 11-2 a. *A divergent mechanism. The stimulus has varying tendencies to elicit the alternative responses.* **b.** *A convergent mechanism. The alternative stimuli have varying tendencies to elicit a given response (after Maltzman, 1955, Figs. 1 and 2).*

responses in order of strength might be *chair* (R_1), *legs* (R_2), and *floor* (R_3). *Chair* is a more dominant response than the other two and therefore occupies the highest position in the hierarchy. It is quite possible that in a given situation, however, *floor* is the correct response. Maltzman describes this situation as a *divergent mechanism*—a hierarchy of responses which are made to a given stimulus and in which the correct response is low in the hierarchy. Figure 11-2a depicts a divergent mechanism. A *convergent mechanism,* Fig. 11-2b, is a hierarchy in which various stimuli exhibit varying strengths in eliciting the same response. The words *book* (S_a), *pen* (S_b), and *future* (S_c) can all elicit the same response, *student.* But S_a (*book*) has the strongest tendency to elicit this response, and it therefore occupies the highest position in the hierarchy.

Convergent and divergent mechanisms combine to produce habit family hierarchies, as in Fig. 11-3. S_A (an external stimulus) elicits three responses (in the divergent mechanism) of varying strengths. These responses, in turn, are connected with three stimuli which have varying tendencies to elicit a given response (in the convergent mechanism). R_{GA}

Fig. 11-3. *A habit family hierarchy produced by a divergent and a convergent mechanism (after Maltzman, 1955, Fig. 3).*

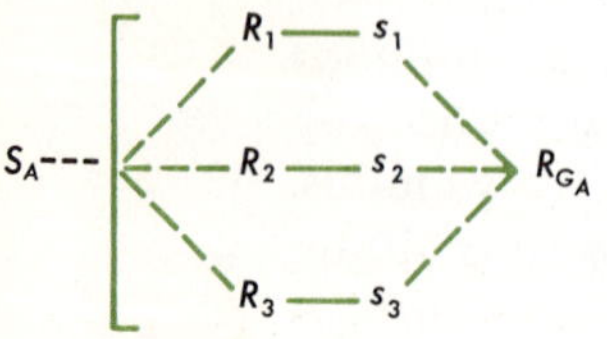

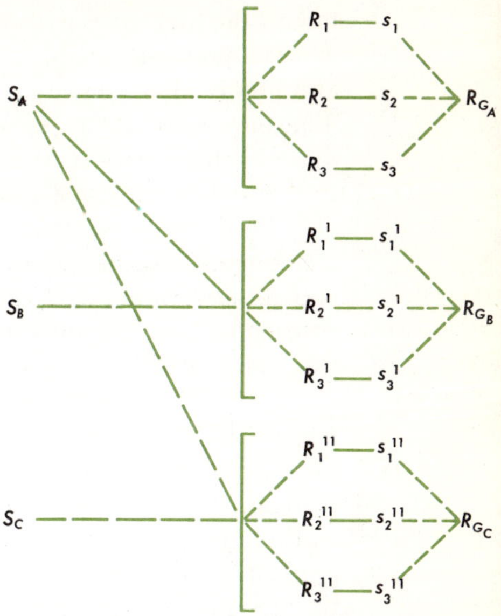

Fig. 11-4. *A compound habit family hierarchy produced by a combination of habit family hierarchies (after Maltzman, 1955, Fig. 4).*

is the problem solution. In Maltzman's theory these habit family hierarchies combine to produce compound habit family hierarchies. In other words habit family hierarchies vary in strength and occupy greater or lesser positions of dominance, just as responses and stimuli vary in dominance. In Fig. 11-4, S_A has the power to arouse its own habit family hierarchy and also the hierarchies of stimuli S_B and S_C. R_1 becomes a member of a convergent mechanism because it can be aroused by S_A, S_B, and S_C. We now have a hierarchy of habit family hierarchies or a class of classes of stimulus-response relationships. Maltzman believes that problem solving may involve the selection of habit family hierarchies as well as the selection of specific response sequences within a hierarchy.

Mediated generalization. In solving a problem, the individual is in this situation. Initially, the correct response is low in a single hierarchy or the correct habit family hierarchy is low in a compound hierarchy. The strength of the correct response or hierarchy must increase for him to solve the problem. According to this theory, the originally dominant but incorrect response or hierarchy will gradually be extinguished as a result of repeated failures to solve the problem. In the meantime, through a process of mediated generalization, the strength of responses low in the hierarchy will increase in strength. In mediated generalization effects upon one member of a hierarchy may influence other members and finally increase the strength of the initially weak but correct member. The effects we refer to are the effects of reinforcement. Through mediated generalization, when one member of a hierarchy is reinforced all individual members of that hierarchy receive added strength.

To illustrate somewhat more clearly what Maltzman means by mediated generalization, I shall describe an experiment by Abe Judson, Cofer, and Sidney Gelfand (1956) in which they used the *two-string* (or two-cord) *problem.* To solve this problem the student must tie together the free ends of two strings suspended from the ceiling to the floor of a corridor. The distance between the two strings is such that the student cannot reach one string if he is holding the other. The solution of the problem requires the student to tie a weight to the end of one string to convert it into a pendulum. By swinging this string, he can catch it while holding the stationary string. He then ties the two strings together and solves the problem.

In this experiment the students were divided into four groups. Three groups memorized lists of words before presentation of the problem, while the fourth (control) group was simply presented with the two-string problem. The lists varied in their relevance to the solution to the problem. Group *A* learned the following list: *rope, swing, pendulum, clock, time.* Group *B* learned only one word from this list, *rope,* and this word was imbedded in the following list: *hemp, tie, twine, package.* Group *C* also learned the word *rope,* but it appeared as the last word in this list: *hemp, twine, tie, package, pendulum.* The learning of these lists, of course, meant that these words, as responses to the problem, were reinforced. But the associations among the words were also reinforced. In the list for group *A,* therefore, the reinforcement of *rope* also meant the reinforcement of the association of *rope* with *swing* and *pendulum.* In the lists for groups *B* and *C,* the word *rope* was primarily associated with words which denoted tying or binding. If each of these lists represented a response hierarchy, the effect of reinforcing one word (or member) would be to reinforce other members (or words) of the hierarchy. This exemplifies what Maltzman means by mediated generalization—the spread of effect from one member to another member of the hierarchy. By reinforcing *rope* in the list for group *A,* we also reinforce *swing* and *pendulum.* The results of of this study showed that students in group *A* produced more solutions to the two-string problem than did students in the other three groups.

A further experiment by Arthur Staats (1957) shows how the status of various responses in the student's habit family hierarchy influences his attempts to solve problems. Staats also used the two-string problem.

Before presentation of the problem the students were asked to list all the different ways in which they could use a screwdriver, balsa wood, and a piece of string. Staats observed which students gave *weight* responses to the word *screwdriver* such as fishing sinker, ballast, and paperweight. Staats found that only seven out of sixty-one students gave verbal weight responses. Consistent with Maltzman's theory however, after solving the problem, which required the student to tie a screwdriver to the end of one string and to swing this string as a pendulum, the students frequently responded to the screwdriver as a weight. The problem-solving experience had increased the strength of the weight response in their response hierarchies. Some evidence in this study also indicated that the stronger the weight response the less time it took the student to solve the problem.

REVERSAL AND NONREVERSAL SHIFTS. In an impressive series of studies on problem solving in children, Howard and Tracy Kendler and their associates (1959, 1960, 1961, 1962) have found that age differences affect the use of mediators. Very young children, under four years of age, do not appear to use verbal mediators. After that age they appear to use mediators with increasing frequency. To test this hypothesis the Kendlers used an ingenious problem which involves reversal and nonreversal shifts. A reversal shift requires the child to respond to the previously relevant attribute (of a concept) but in the opposite way. A nonreversal shift requires the child to respond to the previously irrelevant attribute. Here are two examples. In a reversal shift the child is trained with blocks which differ in size and brightness. Some blocks are large, others are small. Some are white, others are black. In the initial training the child is rewarded for all black blocks he chooses, regardless of size. In the reversal shift, which occurs during the later training, the child is rewarded for all white blocks he chooses, regardless of size. In the nonreversal shift the same child is trained with the same blocks. His initial training is the same; he is rewarded for all the black blocks he chooses, regardless of their size. In the nonreversal shift, which occurs during the later training, the child is rewarded for all the small blocks he chooses, regardless of their brightness (black and white). According to the theory of mediated generalization, verbal mediation is required in the reversal but not in the nonreversal shift. In our example of the reversal shift, if the child states to himself, in the manner of verbal mediation, "Respond to the *opposite* brightness," he will successfully handle the reversal shift, responding now to white, not to black. In the nonreversal shift, however, this verbal mediation does not help because the mediator the child used in the initial training is not useful when he has to respond to a new attribute—size instead of brightness. The interesting discovery that the Kendlers and their associates made is that older children and college students can more easily solve problems involving the reversal than the nonreversal shift. Children four years old or younger have great difficulty with the reversal shift and are relatively more successful with the nonreversal shift. On the surface this finding (for the younger children) is surprising because the nonreversal shift is a more difficult task—you must learn to substitute one response (choosing brightness) for another response (choosing size). According to the Kendlers and the theory of mediated generalization however, the same verbal mediation which enables the older subjects to handle the reversal shift obstructs their handling of the nonreversal shift. The younger children, in their blissful ignorance of verbal mediation, begin to respond to size when the choice of size is rewarded. They do this without trepidation and, apparently, with little worry about the fact that the rules of the game were changed without prior notification.

These three examples of mediated generalization in the solution of problems show that it is a form of verbal mediation. In Chapter 9 you saw how verbal mediators helped students learn lists of paired associates. In Chapter 10 you saw how verbal mediators given to children as part of their pretraining aided them in learning concepts. In still earlier chapters you saw how the absence of verbal mediation, as labeling behavior for example, hindered the learning of the disadvantaged child and how the formation of a verbal plan aided the learning of skills. You can now see how verbal mediation, as mediated generalization, aids in the solution of problems. In all these learning types the verbal mediator acts as a liaison between the presentation of the stimulus and the occurrence of the response. The verbal mediator strengthens the appropriate response tendencies.

PRODUCTIVE AND REPRODUCTIVE THINKING. On the basis of his formulation Maltzman distinguishes between reproductive and productive thinking. In reproductive thinking the student is presented with a succession of problems belonging to the same class. The solution of a series of algebraic problems which require essentially the same operations is an example of reproductive thinking. Another example is the solution of anagrams of the same class. In anagram problems the letters of a word are presented in scrambled form and must be unscrambled to discover the word. If all the anagrams belong to the same category, such as words ending in particular suffixes or beginning with particular prefixes or belonging to the same part of speech, the solution involves reproductive thinking because it elicits various responses of the same habit family hierarchy. This habit family hierarchy becomes dominant in the compound habit family hierarchy because, as we have seen, its response members are reinforced and the responses belonging to different hierarchies are extinguished. The student might still fail to solve a par ticular algebraic problem or anagram however if the particular response within the hierarchy were very low in dominance.

In productive thinking (sometimes called creative thinking), the habit family hierarchy of low dominance must gain strength in the compound hierarchy and the dominant incorrect hierarchies must be extinguished for the solution to be attained. For example, when the student is presented with his first matchstick problem, the tendencies to use matchsticks for only single functions and to create new figures without holes must be extinguished before he can solve the problem. At the same time the initially weak but correct hierarchies (double functions for sticks and loosening the figure by making holes) must gain strength through the reinforcement of their individual response members. Thus productive thinking is more complex and therefore more difficult than reproductive thinking. Reproductive thinking involves primarily the response members of a single hierarchy. Productive thinking involves response competition among several hierarchies. Both types of thinking, however, remain forms of learning.

Later in the chapter, in the discussion of creativity, we shall distinguish between divergent and convergent thinking (Guilford, 1959) by their products—the types of responses made to various test stimuli. In this later formulation, divergent is similar to productive thinking, and convergent to reproductive thinking. The chief distinction between the two formulations is that Maltzman describes a learning process—how these types of thinking occur—while Guilford focuses on the responses—what these types of thinking produce. Also, Guilford, at least in his original formulation of these types of thinking, attributes their origin to variations in personality traits rather than to learning experiences—there seem to be convergent and divergent individuals who exhibit their respective modes of thought.

We have now viewed problem solving as principle learning and in terms of habit family hierarchies. We shall now take another view of this most complex learning.

Transfer of Learning

We can also view problem solving as a form of transfer of learning in which experience in one task influences performance on another task. Ellis (1965, p. 3) uses this example:

> American visitors to England occasionally report that they experience difficulty in driving on the left side of the street because of their established habit of driving on the right. What happens in some instances is the tendency to revert momentarily to driving on

> the right or to vacillate between right and left, even though the rules of diving in England are clearly understood. In a similar vein, a common experience of individuals who begin to drive a car with automatic transmission, after having driven cars with standard transmission, is to attempt to depress a nonexistent clutch pedal. In both these situations we see that earlier learned habits, or modes of responding, can affect performance on some subsequent task that in a general way describes transfer of learning.

Transfer of learning may take three forms: (1) Positive transfer occurs when the previous performance benefits the performance on the subsequent tasks. There is positive transfer from pedaling tricycles to pedaling bicycles and from roller skating to ice skating. (2) Negative transfer occurs when, as in Ellis' two examples above, the previous performance disrupts the performance on the second task. (3) Zero transfer occurs when the previous performance has no effect on the performance of the second task. As far as we know, improving your bowling skills will have no effect on the improvement of your skill in writing novels, except, perhaps, that the time you spend bowling you should spend writing.

Unfortunately we have considerably more research on negative transfer than on positive transfer. An example of negative transfer in human problem solving is the experiment of Herbert Birch and Herbert Rabinowitz (1951). They too used the two-cord (or two-string) problem (see p. 436). In this experiment only two objects could be used as weights—an electrical switch and an electrical relay. To influence the solution of the problem they divided the students into various groups, and gave two of the groups different preproblem experiences. They gave group *A* the task of completing an electrical circuit on a breadboard by using a switch. Group *B* had to complete an identical switch by using a relay, which is simply another type of switch. Group *C* (the control group) consisted of engineering students who had a wide variety of experience in solving circuit problems. The students in the other groups had little or no experience with wiring. After completing the wiring of the circuits, the students were presented with the two-cord problem. The experimenters observed which object—the switch or the relay—the students in the various groups used to make the pendulum. The results were truly impressive. Almost all the students who used the switch in the preproblem experience used the relay to make the pendulum. The reverse was true for the students who first used the relay. The engineering students used the switch and relay with equal frequency.

This experiment demonstrates the effects of negative transfer of prior experience. Later in the chapter you will see how the wise choice of prior experience can aid in the solution of problems through positive transfer. The instructional steps for problem solving described in the

	Task *A*	Task *B*	
Experimental group	*X*	*X*	Reliable difference
Control group		*X*	

Fig. 11-5. *Operations for defining transfer (after Schulz, 1960, Fig. 1).*

following section of this chapter are designed to enhance positive transfer. We can also explain the results of this experiment in terms of habit family hierarchies. The preproblem experiences with relays and switches reduced the dominance of certain hierarchies and increased the dominance of others.

Problem solving as transfer of learning. If we consider the second task in a series of two tasks as a problem, we can view problem solving as transfer of learning. In Fig. 11-5 Rudolph Schulz (1960) depicts the experimental operations which define transfer. In this design, if either the experimental or the control group performs reliably better on task *B* (which represents the problem and problem solution), transfer of learning has occurred. The transfer is positive when the experimental group is superior in performance and negative when the control group is superior. Zero transfer occurs when both groups perform at about the same level. Schulz uses the detour problem to show how his design for transfer of learning can be used in explaining problem-solving behavior. Figure 11-6a diagrams the detour problem. The *O* is the organism or student. The solution of the problem is *G* (goal).

Fig. 11-6 a. *Typical detour problem.* **b.** *The transfer applied to the detour problem (after Schulz, 1960, Figs. 2 and 3).*

a.

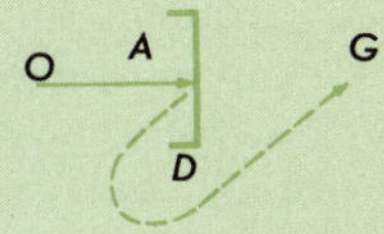

b.

	Stimulus response	
	Task *A*	Task *B*
Experimental group	G—*A*	G—*D*
Control group		G—*D*

The student attempts to solve the problem by using response *A,* a direct approach, but the barrier prevents this response from solving the problem. The solution to the problem lies in making response *D,* the detour approach, which circumvents the barrier.

Figure 11-6b shows the design for transfer of learning as it applies to the detour problem. Task *A* consists of the student's making his customary direct approach to reach the goal (using *A* to reach *G*). Task *B* involves learning to use the detour approach to reach the goal (using *D* to reach *G*). Research on detour problems shows that the student's tendency to make response *A* must be extinguished before he can make the new response *D.* In theory, response *A* initially occupies a higher position in the habit family hierarchy which includes response *D.* Similarly, in the matchstick problems, the student's tendency to create figures without holes must be extinguished before he arrives at the problem solution.

Both Katona (1940) and Gagné (1964) emphasize that a major distinction between problem solving and other learning is that problem solving has high generalizability, or transferability. In problem solving the single solution to the single problem is not important. The correct solution must be an abstraction from the products of responding and not the responses themselves. More simply, we are interested in the student's solving a type of problem rather than in his solving single problems. The measurement of how much learning has occurred in problem solving is the student's ability to solve new problems of the same class. Not the solution of one detour or matchstick problem but the solution of a series of these problems is the test of successful learning. Successful solutions of similar problems is the evidence for positive transfer of learning as well as for successful problem solving. Successful problem solving should result in immediate transferability.

Summary

The first section of this chapter described problem solving as complex learning. Using learning as the basic concept, we have viewed problem solving in three interrelated ways. First, we said that problem solving involved the application of lower-order principles to form higher-order principles. Then we saw that these principles form habit family hierarchies whose response members vary in strength and which can also themselves vary in strength as parts of compound habit family hierarchies. In discussing habit family hierarchies, we considered the influence of verbal mediation (as mediated generalization) on problem solving. Finally we saw that successful problem solving can be described as positive transfer of learning. The principles relevant to the solution of the problem are transferred.

You should now return to objectives 1–8 (p. 429) and determine how well you have achieved them.

QUESTION 11-1

Four educational psychologists were discussing the chief purpose of teaching problem solving in the school and discovered that they had four different viewpoints. Which viewpoint best represents the chief purpose of problem solving described in this chapter? Psychologist *A* believed that the chief purpose was the acquisition of knowledge of wide applicability. Psychologist *B* believed that the chief purpose was learning and using the techniques of problem solution. Psychologist *C* believed that the chief purpose was the learning and transfer of skills, verbal associations, and concepts. Psychologist *D* believed that the chief purpose was the development of the ability to transfer skills acquired through school problem solving to the solution of personal and community problems.

After selecting your answer, give the reasons for your choice and for your rejection of the alternatives.

INSTRUCTION FOR PROBLEM SOLVING

Now that you have developed some basic concepts and principles of problem solving, you are prepared to learn about the steps you must take in providing instruction for problem solving. The five steps described here include all four components of the basic teaching model. I shall describe these steps and the supporting research evidence.

The Pendulum Problem

To make the description of the steps easy to learn I shall use for illustration a problem devised by Norman Maier (1930) in his research on human reasoning, which he began at the University of Berlin. The problem is similar to the two-string problem, but considerably more complex and difficult. Here is Maier's (1930, p. 118) description of it:

> Your problem is to construct two pendulums, one of which will swing over this point [cross indicated on the floor as shown in Fig. 11-7] and one of which will swing over this other point [another cross indicated]. These pendulums should be so constructed that they will have a piece of chalk fastened to them which will make a mark (which can be seen) on the points on the floor just indicated. Naturally you must have something to hang the pendulums to. That is for you to worry about. Otherwise do anything you want to. This

> material is at your disposal [see below]. That chair, however, is not to be a part of your construction; you may use it for a work bench or a place of meditation, or anything you wish so long as it is free when you are through. Ask anything you wish. I'll be glad to assist you in building, only you must tell me what to do.

This was the basic description given to all students in the experiment. Later you will see that some groups of students received additional instruction.

The students were provided with the following materials: two long poles, two shorter poles, one table clamp, two burette clamps, two pieces of wire, and several pieces of chalk. The material was scattered around a table. Figure 11-7 shows these materials properly assembled. The problem solution consisted of placing the long pole against the ceiling and holding it in place by clamping two other poles together in such

Fig. 11-7. *The solution of the pendulum problem (after Maier, 1930, p. 123).*

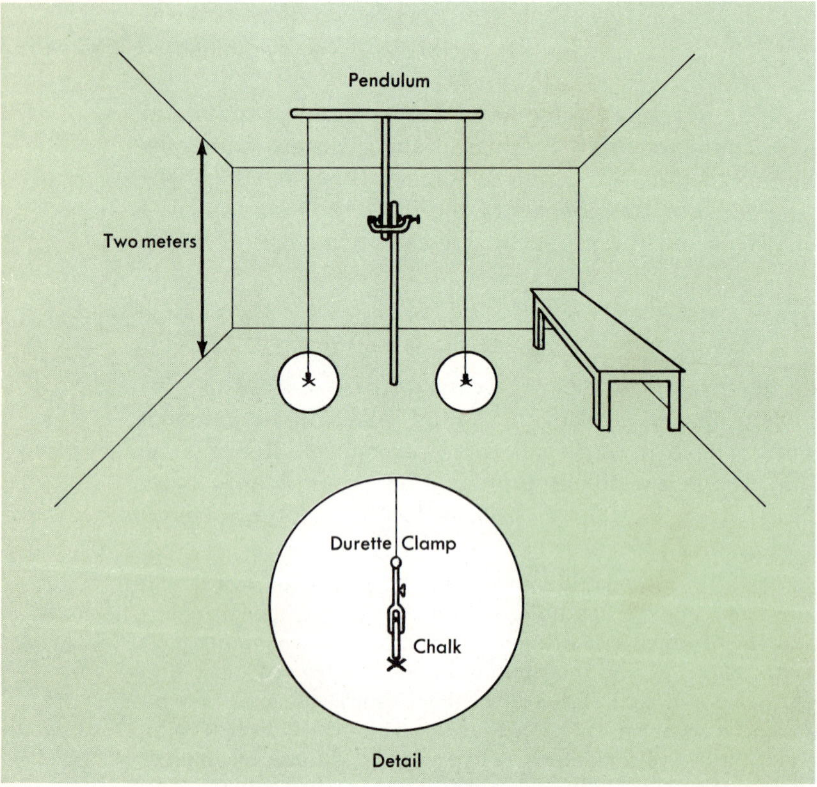

a manner that they were able to reach from floor to ceiling. One pole was wedged against the ceiling and formed a T with the vertical pole. The pendulums could then be hung from both ends of the pole wedged against the ceiling. A piece of chalk fastened to each burette clamp (see detail in Fig. 11-7) formed the pendulum weights. The pendulum was made just long enough to allow the chalk to touch the floor. The structure, Maier tells us, was very simple and stable and required even one less pole than was given.

Although Maier did not observe all the steps for instruction in problem solving, which we are about to describe, he did observe most of them, and, in any case, his problem, as described above, is still useful for illustration.

Step 1. Describe for the Students the Terminal Performance Which Constitutes the Solution of the Problem

This step corresponds to the first component of the basic teaching model. Maier fulfilled this function when he presented the students with the above statement of the problem. In effect, he told the students that they had to create two pendulums which would swing over the designated chalk marks on the floor. This statement, of course, does not tell them how to solve the problem but only what the solution must consist of. Later in the chapter you will see that instruction in problem solving is a form of guided discovery. It stops short of giving the students the problem solution; the students must construct the solution on their own. In one sense then, they discover the solution. The description of the students' terminal performance fulfills two learning conditions: The students' attention is directed to those aspects of the materials which will lead to a particular solution, and they will know when they have solved the problem and thereby generate their own reinforcement for successful moves and for the final solution.

Step 2. Assess the Students' Entering Behavior for the Concepts and Principles They Will Require in the Solution of the Problem

This step fulfills the requirements of the second component of the basic teaching model by requiring the teacher to analyze the problem he presents to his students to determine the lower-order principles the students must know to solve the problem and to find out whether the students know them. The pendulum problem involves the application of three principles: the pendulum principle, which involves making a plumb line with the burette clamp and the piece of chalk; making long poles out of short poles by using the table clamp; and placing one pole against the ceiling and wedging it in place with one or two other poles.

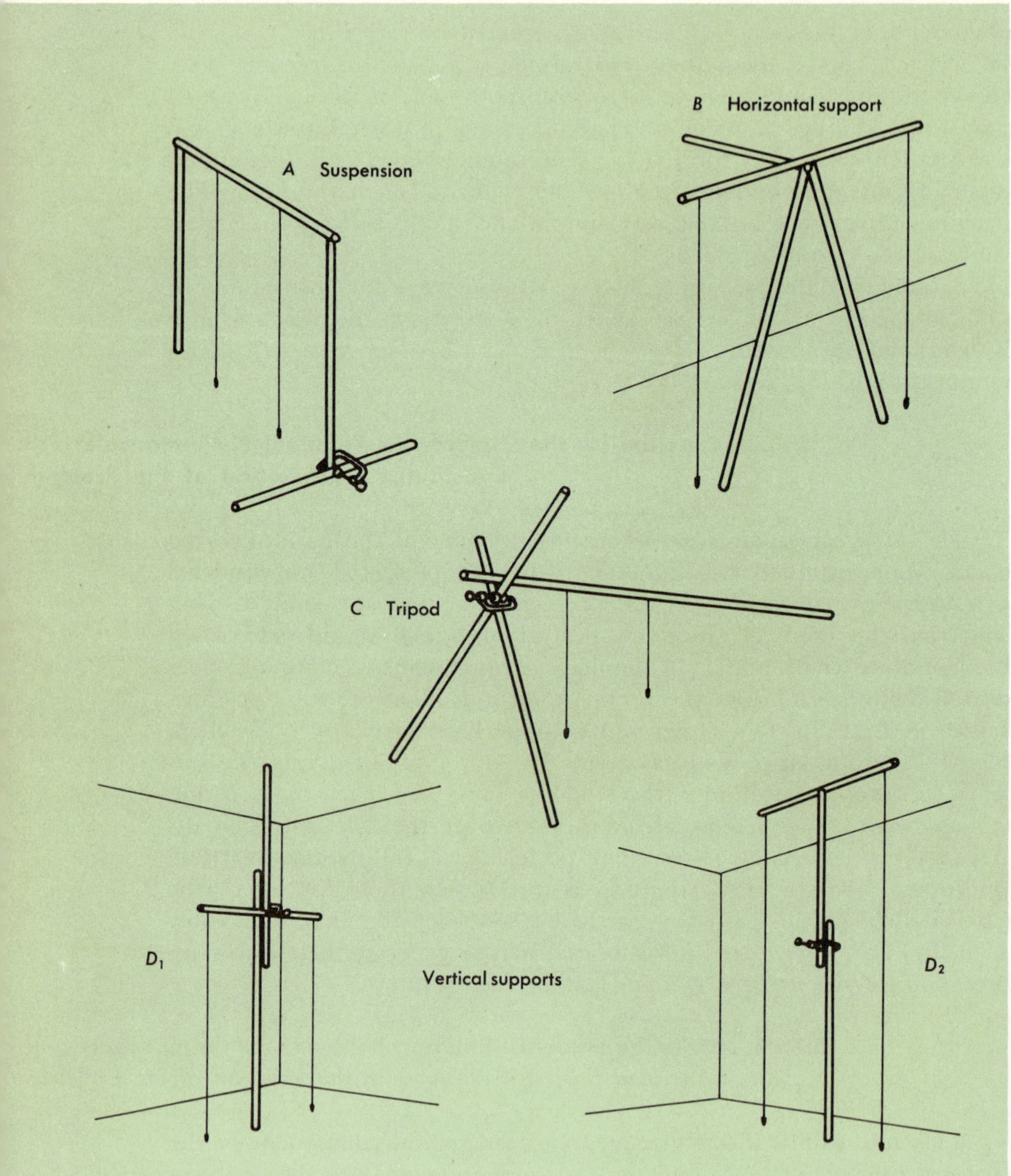

Fig. 11-8. A, B, *and* C *are three incorrect approaches to the solution of the pendulum problem.* D_2 *represents the solution as Maier depicts it in Fig. 11-7.* D_1 *is another possible solution (after Madden and Weaver, 1949, p. 335).*

This is the higher-order principle (or problem solution): In the absence of hammer and nails, two pendulums can be constructed by extending the length of poles by using a clamp and by using the extended poles to wedge another pole against the ceiling. The higher-order principle, as you can see, simply states the relationship of the three component principles. The student whose entering behavior does not include one or more of these principles will fail to solve the problem. Figure 11-8 shows some of the solutions which did not work because collapsible structures were constructed. Although all these unacceptable solutions used the pendulum principle, most of them failed to use the wedging principle.

Step 3. Invoke the Recall of All Relevant Concepts and Principles

This step is our usual provision for contiguity. It is not enough that the students have learned these principles and that they are a part of their entering behavior. They must recall these principles in the presence of the problem and discover the relationship between them (i.e., the higher-order principle) which will result in the problem solution. In a part of the experiment we did not describe, Maier did provide for the recall of the three principles by actually demonstrating each one. He used a burette clamp, pencil, and a piece of wire to make a plumb line; he held a piece of cloth against the wall of a doorway by pressing the side of a flat board against it and kept this in place by wedging another board horizontally between the flat board and the other wall of the doorway; and he used a table clamp to combine two poles to make a longer one. Not all the groups in Maier's experiment witnessed these demonstrations. Even with the demonstrations the problem proved to be very difficult for most students.

Per Saugstad (1957), in replicating Maier's study, found that the demonstration of the principles was not enough because the students failed to see the wide applicability of the principles demonstrated. He points out that even though the students may have known the principle of wedging they still were faced with finding a second flat surface (the ceiling). In fact, Maier did direct the attention of one group to the ceiling, and this group had more problem solutions than the others did. Using a different problem, Saugstad showed that the students who had learned the principles and had them available for application were best able to solve the problem. The problem was to put out a candle placed on one table while standing behind another table. The student had available six hollow glass tubes, a rod, and a lump of putty. The only possible solution was to put the glass tubes end to end around the rod and make the joints airtight with the putty. The student could then kneel down, direct the blowpipe at the candle flame, and by blowing through it, blow out the candle. The solution required the application of three principles: The glass tube had to conduct a stream of air blown through it; the putty had to provide an airtight and possibly a watertight conduit; and the rod had to support objects hung from it when held in a horizontal position. Saugstad administered an availability test to find out which students could recall these functions. In this way he was not only assessing the entering behavior of the students but also determining which students could recall the principles. The availability test consisted of the presentation of the glass tube, the lump of putty, and the rod. The students were required to list all the functions of these objects they could think of. He found that thirteen students listed all the functions necessary for the solution of the candle problem. All thirteen later solved the problem.

Of course, for step 3, the teacher must do more than administer an availability test. By questions and demonstrations he can help the student recall the principles. Although Maier made his demonstrations to invoke recall, the students had not learned two of the principles (extension and wedging) well enough to apply them in the problem solution.

ADVANCE ORGANIZERS. The use of advance organizers may be a convenient means of invoking recall of relevant principles (Ausubel, 1960, 1961, 1963, 1965a). Although Ausubel has developed a unique theoretical framework for the definition and function of advance organizers, in the context of this chapter we may view them as a particular form of verbal mediation. Advance organizers are concepts or principles introduced before the presentation of the main body of instructional material. They are chosen for their usefulness in explaining and organizing that material. In his early study of advance organizers (1960) Ausubel used a specially prepared passage on the metallurgical properties of plain carbon steel. He used two groups in his experiment. The experimental group was given the benefit of the advance organizers in the form of a written passage which they read before they were given the passage on carbon steel. Some of the basic principles (advance organizers) taught prior to the reading of the passage were the major similarities and differences between metals and alloys; their respective advantages and limitations; and the reasons for making and using alloys. The control group received instead an introductory passage of historical material which did not contain these advance organizers. Ausubel found that the experimental group which had the benefit of prior explanation of the relevant principles was more successful in the retention of the material on carbon steel than the control group was.

Using more provocative materials with college seniors, Ausubel and Mohamed Youssef (1963) investigated the effect of advance organizers on learning material on Buddhist and Zen Buddhist doctrines. The experimental group was provided with comparative advance organizers—two short introductory passages which pointed out the chief differences and similarities in Buddhist and Christian doctrines and Buddhist and Zen Buddhist doctrines. Instead of these advance organizers, the control group was given two "nonideational introductory passages of a historical and biographical nature" (p. 333) about Buddhism and Zen Buddhism. Following these introductions, both groups studied the new materials on Buddhism and Zen Buddhism. Both groups then took multiple-choice tests on the oriental doctrines. The results showed that the organizers aided the learning and the retention of the Buddhism but not the Zen Buddhism passage.

Ausubel contends that the procedure of using advance organizers may reverse traditional teaching practice, in which students are required to learn the details of new and unfamiliar material before they have acquired an adequate body of relevant subsumers (concepts and principles). Ausubel reminds us that, if the student lacks the necessary concepts and principles, the teacher should supply them. The student cannot acquire higher-order principles unless he has already learned the component principles.

For his example of the successful use of advance organizers, Ausubel (1963a, p. 80) refers to Boyd's famous *Textbook on Pathology.* Boyd devotes the first half of the book to a discussion of several principles which are used to organize the material in the latter half of the book. For example, he discusses the different categories of pathological processes and their principal causes and characteristics; the various kinds of etiological agents in disease; the interaction between generic and environmental factors in the development of pathological processes; types of humoral and tissue resistance to disease; and the general relationships between pathological lesions and clinical systems. In the second half of the book he discusses the pathology of separate organs. Most textbooks in this subject, according to Ausubel, consider only the major kinds of pathological processes occurring within various organs and organ systems and omit consideration of the more general principles. Ausubel argues for more highly organized instructional material with thorough cross referencing of all related principles. In the context of this chapter, advance organizers are important because of their usefulness in evoking previously learned concepts and principles in the learning of new principles and in problem solving.

Step 4. Provide Verbal Direction of the Students' Thinking, Short of Giving Them the Solution to the Problem

The direction to which I refer is illustrated by the verbal directions Maier (1930, p. 120) gave to two of his experimental groups. This is verbal direction *A*, the direction to use parts:

> I'm going to give you a problem to solve. You will have to construct something. [Problem was then given.] Before you start on the solution I should like to show you three separate things, each of which will involve a principle. If you combine the ideas which I thus give you in the right manner, you will have the best solution to the problem. Try to use them; they are the solution in three separate parts. You do not have to use them, but only by using them will you get the most satisfactory solution. So try to use them.

This is verbal direction *B:*

> I should like to have you appreciate how simple this problem would be if we could just hang the pendulum from a nail in the ceiling. Of course, that is not a possible solution, but I just want you to appreciate how simple the problem would be if that were possible. Now that it is not possible the problem is, as you may find out, quite difficult.

Table 11-1 shows the five groups in Maier's (1930) experiment and the type of instruction they received. Maier discovered that, with the exception of one student, only those students in group V (and only eight of the twenty-two in this group) were able to solve the problem. The demonstration of the three principles, the direction to use them, and the direction about suspending pendulums from the ceiling were all necessary for the problem solution.

Further evidence for the importance of channeling the thinking of students for problem solving is provided in an experiment by Hilgard and his associates (1953). They used Katona's (1940) card tricks to compare methods of instruction for their effects on transfer of learning. One of the card tricks required the use of four red cards and four black

TABLE 11-1

DESCRIPTION OF EXPERIMENTAL GROUPS IN MAIER (1930) STUDY.

	Instruction
Group I (control)	Statement of problem
Group II	Statement of problem and demonstration of three principles
Group III	Statement of problem, demonstration of principles, and verbal direction *A* (to use parts)
Group IV	Statement of problem and verbal direction *B*
Group V	Statement of problem, demonstration of principles, and verbal directions *A* and *B*

TABLE 11-2

NUMBER OF Ss MAKING PERFECT SCORES ON PROBLEM-SOLVING TASKS 4, 5, and 6 (after Hilgard *et al.*, 1953, p. 291).

Group	*N*	Task 4 Three Red, Three Black; Skip One	Task 5 Four Red, Four Black; Skip Two	Task 6 Ten Spades; Skip Two
Memorization	30	3	1	1
Understanding	30	16	7	10
Probability of this difference arising by chance		0.0003	0.03	0.003

cards. The student was shown how to arrange them so that as he played them alternately from the top and from the bottom of the deck, they would appear alternately red and black on the table; that is, they would turn up in this order: *R-B-R-B-R-B-R-B*. This trick was called four red, four black, skip one. The solution required the cards to be arranged in the following order: *R-R-B-R-R-B-B-B*. Two groups of students were taught in different ways. The memorization group was simply given the order of red and black cards (the solution), and they memorized the order. They then arranged the cards in the prescribed order and performed the trick.

The understanding group was presented with the written scheme in Fig. 11-9. The question marks refer to the cards still held in hand. Row 1 contains only question marks because none of the cards has been dealt. The first time through, the alternate cards have to be red and black as in row 2. The four question marks in row 2 indicate that four remaining cards are held in hand and are unknown. The first of the remaining cards has to be red since the last card in row 2 was black.

Fig. 11-9. *Scheme for determining correct order of cards (after Katona, 1940, p. 264).*

1.	?	?	?	?	?	?	?	?
2.	*R*	?	*B*	?	*R*	?	*B*	?
3.		*R*		?		*B*		?
4.				*R*				?
5.								*B*
6.	*R*	*R*	*B*	*R*	*R*	*B*	*B*	*B*

The third card must be black. This information is recorded in row 3. There are still two question marks. In row 4 red is assigned to the first question mark. In row 5 black is assigned to the last question mark. In row 6, these operations are simply summarized, and you have the solution indicated above. After the student was shown how to use this scheme, he was asked to repeat the solution with pencil and paper and then to arrange the cards in the pack and do the trick. Later he was given a similar task to set the stage for the transfer experiments which followed. (The task was eight spades, skip one—solution: A-5-2-7-3-6-4-8.)

The major question was which of the groups would do better when presented with similar but novel problems (transfer of learning). Hilgard found that the understanding groups had the advantage throughout. Table 11-2 shows the highly significant superiority of this group. The significance of this experiment is that it shows the importance of providing that instruction which guides the student toward the solution of problems. You should note however that in this experiment the guidance did not include the solution of the problem except in the first demonstration of the use of the written scheme. Hilgard notes that the understanding method is not an unmixed blessing. Large numbers of errors were made by students in these groups because they grew impatient with the understanding method and adopted the rote method, made careless errors, and were confused because of their partial understanding. He found also that overnight retention was equally good for both groups. Only in transfer was the understanding group definitely superior.

Step 5. Verify the Students' Learning by Requiring Them to Give a Full Demonstration of the Problem Solution (Using Other Problems of the Same Class)

Here you must simply recall our discussion of transfer of learning. We pointed out that the major distinction between problem solving and other learning is that problem solving has high transferability. Once the higher-order principle has been learned, the student should be able immediately to solve new problems to which the principle applies. Both in research on problem solving and in classroom instruction this important step is omitted. However, since it represents the fourth component of the basic teaching model, it is vitally important for assessing the adequacy of the student's learning and the instruction.

Summary

In the second section of this chapter I have described a series of steps you must take in teaching problem solving. The steps, as you have seen, correspond to those of the basic teaching model. You have seen the importance of describing the terminal behavior for the students (step 1). You have also seen the importance of analyzing the problem to find out what the prerequisite concepts and principles are for its solution and to assess the students' entering behavior to see if they know what they must (step 2). The next two steps (3 and 4) deal with the third component of the basic teaching model and are particularly crucial in teaching problem solving. These steps describe the guidance the teacher must provide short of giving the students the solution to the problem. Step 3 requires invoking recall of relevant principles, and step 4 requires that you provide guidance in the combination and application of these principles for the solution of the problem. The last step (5) requires that you assess the performance of the students to see whether they can transfer their learning to new and similar problems.

You should now return to objectives 9–13 (p. 429) and determine how well you have achieved them.

QUESTION 11-2

In aiding the students' solution of the two-string problem (p. 436), Miss Methodical provided these learning conditions: (a) She administered a test which contained questions about the pendulum principle and the dual functions of heavy objects, one of which is to serve as a weight. (b) She demonstrated for the students how the strings could be swung in an arc to reduce the distance between them. (c) She told them how Tarzan could rescue Jane by swinging on a vine over a chasm that separated them. She diagrammed Tarzan's procedure on the board. (d) She asked the students to solve new and unfamiliar problems which involved the application of the weight and pendulum principles. (e) She indicated that the problem would be solved when the student held string *A* in one and string *B* in the other hand.

Arrange these learning conditions in the proper order.

After determining the order, give your reasons for the order you have chosen.

INSTRUCTION FOR CREATIVITY

This section of the chapter considers the nature of creativity and the procedures you can adopt to foster it in your students. Creativity is currently a very popular subject in educational and psychological circles. Considerable research on creativity in the early 1960s resulted in studies of creativity and intelligence (see Chapter 4), of creative artists and scientists, of the creative process as manifested in artistic and scientific achievement, of creative (as well as critical) thinking, and of the relevance of all this to educational practice. Many educators believe that the school should foster creativity in every child. They also feel that the school may unwittingly stultify creative development, as illustrated by the following anecdote told by a dean of a midwestern university (Guilford, 1950, p. 448):

> An old, experienced teacher and scholar said that he tried to encourage originality in his students. In a graduate course, he told the class that the term paper would be graded in terms of the amount of originality shown. One school teacher in the class was especially concerned about getting a high mark in the course. She took verbatim notes, continuously and assiduously, of what the learned professor said in class. Her term paper, the story goes, was essentially a stringing together of her transcribed lecture notes, in which the professor's pet ideas were given prominent place. It is reported that the professor read the term paper himself. When the school teacher's paper was returned, the professor's mark was *A*, with the added comment, "This is one of the most original papers I have ever read."

The anecdote illustrates the pitfall of all subjective judgment, including the teacher's—that we call original or creative those opinions and contributions most congenial to our own.

The Nature of Creativity

So much confusion surrounds the term *creativity* that it is most difficult to discuss and use it. Ausubel (1963a, pp. 99–100) believes that we should use it to refer to "rare and unique talent in a particular field of endeavor." He further states: "Creative achievement . . . reflects a rare capacity for developing insights, sensitivities, and appreciations in a circumscribed content area of intellectual or artistic activity." According to Ausubel, the creative individual who embodies this capacity is, by definition, an uncommon individual, much rarer than the intelligent person.

The following discussion on the nature of creativity will focus on three aspects: creative abilities, the learning or acquisition of these abilities, and their development and use in problem solving. For practical reasons the discussion will consider a low degree of creativity. To some extent everyone has the capacity for creative behavior, but few individuals will make scientific and artistic contributions which will achieve historical distinction.

Creative abilities. These abilities can be defined as the means the individual has for expressing whatever creativity he possesses. Guilford (1950, 1959, 1962) maintains that these abilities are somewhat general and can be applied to a variety of tasks. They are not associated with particular subject matter or disciplines. According to Guilford these abilities together constitute creative thinking. The distinctive aspect of creative thinking is divergent thinking, which is characterized by, among other things, flexibility, originality, and fluency. *Flexibility* is illustrated in Guilford's Unusual Uses Test by the divergent responses made to the word *brick*. The student is given this word and asked to list all the uses he can think of in eight minutes (Guilford, 1959). One student responds: build a house, build a barn, build a school, build a church, build a chimney, build a walk, and build a barbecue. All these responses belong to the same class of uses (i.e., construction) and show little flexibility or divergency. Another student responds: make a door stop, make a paperweight, throw it to a dog, make a bookcase, drown a cat, drive a nail, make a red powder, and use for baseball bases. The latter responses show more flexibility and, therefore, according to Guilford, give evidence of more divergent or creative thinking. *Originality* is illustrated by Guilford's Plot Title Test. A short story is presented, and the student is told to list as many appropriate titles as he can to head the story. One story is about the capture of a missionary by cannibals. The princess of the tribe wins a promise for his release if he will marry her. The choice is clear—death or the princess. The missionary refuses marriage and is boiled alive. One student responds with these titles: Defeat of a Princess, Eaten by Savages, The Princess, The Missionary, and Boiled by Savages. The second student responds: Pot's Plot, Potluck Dinner, Stewed Parson, Goil or Boil, A Mate Worse Than Death, He Left a Dish for a Pot, Chaste in Haste, and a Hot Price for Freedom. Guilford calls the responses of the second student more original (clever) than those of the first student. *Fluency* simply refers to the quantity of output. When asked, for example, to produce a list of items of information of a certain kind, some students produce many more items than others do. The sheer volume of output increases the probability that some responses will be divergent. Guilford contrasts *divergent* and *convergent* thinking. Divergent thinking produces a variety of responses. Convergent thinking produces the single correct answer.

James Gallagher (1964) showed how the questions a teacher asks determine the kind of thinking the student does. In teaching *Hamlet* the teacher may ask, "Explain why Hamlet rejected Ophelia." The student may go through this convergent thinking process in answering this question: Hamlet became disillusioned with all women. Ophelia was a woman. Hamlet rejected Ophelia. The teacher, however, could stimulate divergent thinking by asking these questions: What other ways could Hamlet have used to trap the king? What other courses of action might have been open to Hamlet's mother? Suppose Polonius had not been killed; how would that have modified or changed the eventual outcome of the play?

According to Getzels and Jackson (1962), divergent thinking tends to be stimulus free, while convergent thinking is stimulus bound. To illustrate this point they asked students to respond to a picture of a man reclining in an airplane seat on his return from a business trip or professional conference. The stimulus-bound student constructed this story (p. 39):

> Mr. Smith is on his way home from a successful business trip. He is very happy and he is thinking about his wonderful family and how glad he will be to see them again. He can picture it, about an hour from now, his plane landing at the airport and Mrs. Smith and their children all there welcoming him home again.

The less inhibited, stimulus-free (and presumably more creative) student constructed this story (p. 39):

> This man is flying back from Reno, where he has just won a divorce from his wife. He couldn't stand to live with her anymore, he told the judge, because she wore so much cold cream on her face at night that her head would skid across the pillow and hit him in the head. He is now contemplating a new skidproof face cream.

In both cases the student had four minutes to produce his story. Whereas the first student produced a story of a very conventional family reunion, the second student produced a much more modern story about weird incompatibility and divorce. The latter story shows more divergent thinking than the former story does.

Creativity and learning. The major educational question concerns the possibility of developing whatever creative abilities the student may have. Before we can engage in programs designed to produce this result, we must know whether training (or teaching) can increase creativity. Maltzman and his associates (1958, 1960) carried out a series of experiments based on the assumption that training could increase originality. Maltzman preferred the term *originality* to creativity because he could define originality simply in terms of unusual or uncommon verbal responses without engaging in the debate over whether these responses were creative or only bizarre. In these experiments the learning conditions were arranged to increase the student's output of original responses. In theory, Maltzman tried to raise a response low in the student's response hierarchy to higher positions in the hierarchy. In one experiment he used the five different groups and training conditions summarized in Table 11-3. All the groups began their training with a twenty-five–word list called the *training list*. These words evoked relatively few different responses in a period of free association during which the student had to respond as quickly as possible with the first word which came to mind. At the end of the training all the groups were given a test list of the same length and with the same kind of words to find out if the experimental treatment had increased the originality of the responses. All groups were also given Guilford's Unusual Uses Test.

The types of training for the five groups varied. Group *C* (the control group) received no training. Group C_R was presented with the training list five additional times and asked to give the same responses each time—a treatment obviously designed to inhibit original responses. The three experimental groups were treated as follows: Group *X* was also given the training list five additional times, but it was to give different responses each time. Group X_H was given five new lists of high-frequency (common) words and asked to respond to each word as quickly as possible. Group X_L received five lists of low-frequency (uncommon) words and asked to respond as quickly as possible. Maltzman found that group *X* had the highest originality scores—members of this group gave the greatest number of uncommon responses to the words in the test list. Group X_L did next best. As you might expect, group C_R was the least original. Group *X* also did best on the Unusual Uses Test. On the basis of this research we can conclude that asking students to produce different responses to the same stimulus does increase originalty. To the extent that this procedure is effective, we can say that originality is one form of learned behavior. Through learning, as defined in this experiment, it is possible to increase student originality.

TABLE 11-3

A DESCRIPTION OF THE TRAINING PROCEDURE FOR CONTROL AND EXPERIMENTAL GROUPS IN AN EXPERIMENT ON ORIGINALITY TRAINING (after Maltzman *et al.*, 1960).

	Group	First List Received	Training Procedure	Last List Received
Control	C	Training list	None	Test list
	C_R	Training list	Training list five times and gave same response	Test list
Experimental	X	Training list	Training list five times and gave different response	Test list
	X_H	Training list	Five lists of uncommon words	Test list
	X_L	Training list	Five lists of common words	Test list

CREATIVITY AND PROBLEM SOLVING. Many writers discuss creativity as creative thinking or problem solving. Torrance and his associates (1960), for example, define creative thinking as the process of "sensing gaps or disturbing or missing elements; forming ideas or hypotheses concerning them; testing these hypotheses; and communicating the results, possibly modifying and retesting the hypotheses." Gagné (1965c) also considers creativity to be a form of problem solving which involves intuitive leaps, or a combining of ideas from widely separated fields of knowledge. Gagné (p. 167) gives this example:

> An excellent example of such inventiveness is provided by the kinetic theory of gases. What was known, on the one hand, was a set of principles concerning the behavior of gases, the relations among the variables of temperature, pressure, and volume. On the other hand there were the laws of motion, the effects of force in imparting acceleration to objects of specified mass. The stroke of genius in this case was the hypothesizing that the gas was composed of particles (molecules) that had mass and whose reactions to force could therefore be considered to obey the laws of motion. The solving of this problem resulted in a higher-order principle which had exceptional power to synthesize previously unrelated sets of principles.

The autobiographical sketches in a volume edited by Brewster Ghiselin (1955) provide several examples of these intuitive leaps of genius. In one selection, the French mathematician, Jules Henri Poincaré, describes this experience (p. 36):

> For fifteen days I strove to prove that there could not be any functions like those I have since called Fuchsian functions. I was then very ignorant; every day I seated myself at my work table, stayed an hour or two, tried a great number of combinations and reached no results. One evening, contrary to my custom, I drank black coffee and could not sleep. Ideas rose in crowds; I felt them collide until parts interlocked, so to speak, to make a stable combination. By the next morning I had established the existence of a class of Fuchsian functions, those which come from the hypergeometric series; I had only to write out the results, which took but a few hours.

Unfortunately, in reading these accounts, individuals have emphasized (1) the emotional aspects of the experience—the sudden illumination, the heightened excitement, the esthetic appeal of an idea which has suddenly taken shape, and (2) the accidents of the experience—the drinking of black coffee, the musing under the apple tree, and the simple bathing in a bathtub, as in the case of Archimedes. What is not emphasized often enough are two other factors: These insights which suddenly bridge seemingly unrelated bodies of knowledge can only occur in individuals who have acquired the prerequisite knowledge, and they are often the result of concentrated effort over long periods of time. Creativity, at this level, is advanced problem solving. It is very doubtful that any teacher could deliberately foster such creativity. Although brilliant professors often have brilliant students who carry on for them, whatever the alchemy of these relationships may be, they are not within the grasp of most students and most teachers. When I discuss the fostering of creativity in the next section of the chapter, I am not outlining a program which will create Poincarés or even Hemingways.

Instruction for Creativity

In this section, by *fostering creativity,* I refer only to the development of the creative abilities described earlier. That is, the teacher can provide certain conditions which will increase the flexibility, fluency, and originality of the student's solutions to various problems. I am not referring to ways for developing genuinely new knowledge and new discoveries. In effect, in this section of the chapter, I am viewing creativity as high-order problem solving which may require instructional supports in addition to those already described for the problem solving discussed in the first half of the chapter. The distinction here between the two types of problem solving is not a very clear one, but it may be clear enough to use as a basis for presenting some of the educational research on creativity.

Classify the kind of problems you present to students. Getzels (1964) distinguishes between presented problems and discovered problems. Presented problems are those which are given to the student. Discovered problems are those which exist and must be discovered by the student. Getzels also distinguishes between known and unknown methods of solving problems. Using this classification scheme, he believes that creative thinking begins with situations in which the problem is presented but the method of solution is unknown to the student. From here we can move to the situation in which both the problem and the method of solution are unknown to the student and all of humanity. The less that is known in the problem situation the more the student must create. In the first half of this chapter we limited our consideration to those situations in which the problem is known but the solution is unknown only to the student, not to others. In Getzels' scheme, this would be the lowest level of creativity. It may very well be that the auxiliary problem-solving conditions outlined here apply primarily to those situations in which the student knows neither the problem nor the standard method of solving it. Surely, under such conditions, the student requires considerable assistance from the teacher even though the exact nature of that assistance may not be clear. In any case, you can classify the problems you expect your students to solve using the scheme developed by Getzels.

Provide for the development and use of problem-solving skills. A body of research indicates the usefulness of certain techniques and skills in creative problem solving. The most popular technique is *brainstorming* (Osborne, 1957), which had its first flowering in the business world but has now made its way into the classroom—especially the college classroom. As used in the classroom, after the problem has been presented, the teacher requires the students to list as many solutions as they can think of. Any evaluation of these ideas is deferred until all the solutions are listed. The technique is a form of free association, except that it is often used with groups and it is ideas rather than words that are being freely associated. Both Sidney Parnes and Arnold Meadow (1959, 1960, 1961, 1962) have made the most extensive study of the possible usefulness of brainstorming for problem solving. Their findings can be briefly summarized: (1) Training in brainstorming increases creative problem solving; (2) brainstorming produces more problem solutions than do methods which penalize bad ideas in some way; (3) more good ideas are produced with brainstorming than with conventional techniques; (4) extended effort to produce ideas (the latter part of the brainstorming sessions) leads to an increased number of ideas and proportion of good ideas; and (5) students in creative problem-solving courses (which include brainstorming) obtain higher scores on Guilford's tests of creative abilities than do students who have not had these courses.

Contrary evidence disputes some of these findings. Calvin Taylor and his associates (1958) found that individuals who worked in groups using the brainstorming technique actually produced ideas which were considerably inferior in quantity and quality to the ideas produced by individuals who worked alone. Torrance (1961) found that directions to produce as many ideas as possible without regard to quality resulted in fewer responses than did directions to produce interesting, clever, and unusual ideas.

These somewhat conflicting findings make it difficult to determine under what conditions you should use brainstorming. Although originally devised as a method for producing large numbers of ideas by postponing to a later time the evaluation or criticism of them, brainstorming may be useful in ways which better fit the context of this chapter. It may be a way of assessing the entering behavior of the student since the responses he emits first are probably those which have the greatest strength in his response hierarchy. Persistence in brainstorming, at least theoretically, could ultimately evoke responses of comparatively low hierarchical strength. Brainstorming may also be a way (not necessarily the best way) of invoking recall of concepts and principles necessary for the solution of a problem. It is difficult to understand, however, how this technique can be successful when the students lack the knowledge necessary for the problem solution or when the responses have so little hierarchical strength that they require explicit reinforcement to be successfully applied. Deferring evaluation of the ideas also defers reinforcement. And, by dredging up several ideas when only one or two are useful in solving a given problem, brainstorming may increase the student's difficulty in selecting those ideas which apply to the problem solution. By a combination of proactive and retroactive inhibition the useless ideas interfere with the retention of the useful ideas. Where the teacher finds a great dearth of ideas, however, brainstorming may enable students to pool what little knowledge they have and to proceed together from there.

Teaching certain basic *research skills* may be a second technique for fostering creativity. This technique is consistent with Torrance's definition of creative thinking as forming and testing hypotheses (see p. 458). Torrance and R. E. Myers (1963) taught a course in educational research to gifted sixth grade students. The students learned some basic methods of research in the behavioral sciences, including the formulation and testing of hypotheses. The course took several days. On the first day they played the guessing game "What Is in the Box?" After they arrived at the solution, they outlined the steps of the research process which had led them to it. On ensuing days they participated in three kinds of research projects—historical, descriptive, and experimental. Finally, they carried out an experiment of their own. After these experiences the students were given a test on the basic research principles they had been taught. Although Torrance and Myers report no data, they concluded that the students had a good grasp of basic principles.

Creative reading is another useful problem-solving skill. Torrance and Judson Harmon (1961) have provided some evidence that students can be taught to read creatively with the proper directions and the encouragement to use these directions. In this study, students received these directions (or particular set to read) (p. 208):

> When you read, it is important that you think about the many possible uses of the information which you are reading. It is especially important that you think of various ways in which the information could be used in your personal and professional life. In reading, do not just ask, "What is the author saying?" Also ask, "How can I use what the author is saying?" Do not stop with just one use. Think of as many uses as you can of the important ideas presented. Jot down some of their uses for future reference or action. It may take some practice before you are really successful in assuming this set, or attitude, toward your reading, but do not be discouraged. By the third day, you should find it easy to assume this set.

This study also divided students into two groups and asked them to read research reports. One group was to read the reports critically, the other creatively. The critical group had to think of (1) the defects in the statement of the problem and their importance; (2) the underlying assumptions of the hypotheses studied; (3) the procedures for collecting and analyzing data; (4) the conclusions and interpretations of the findings; and (5) a critical appraisal of the worth of the research. The creative group had to think of (1) new possibilities suggested by the statement of the problem; (2) other possible hypotheses related to the problem and its solution; (3) improvements which could have been made in the collection of the data; (4) other possible conclusions and interpretations of the findings; and (5) an appraisal of the possibilities stemming from the findings. Students in both groups were later required to perform a research project of their own. Those in the creative group were judged to have produced more new and creative ideas of their own than did students in the critical group. No report indicates whether the creative group also produced more bad ideas. The import of these findings and others like them is that teachers should encourage students to suspend their critical functions and to use instead various creative functions. One can well imagine that a student who read the reports both critically and creatively (asking himself both sets of questions) could gain more than students in either group.

The utilization of certain reading sets and research skills may have the distinct advantage of helping the student to identify with the researcher and the writer and to begin to see the many alternatives available in making scientific and literary decisions. The consideration of alternatives, of course, can considerably complicate the learning of any subject matter, and it is often reserved for advanced college classes, gifted students, or the graduate schools. The primary consideration, however, must be the entering behavior of the student. A student who learns what is happening in *Hamlet* (and many students do not) may be in the position to see how it could have all been different and even less tragic. When encouraged to think creatively about the play, a student who has not learned what is happening can only impose his less informed and poetic fantasies upon those which Shakespeare has woven with considerably more consummate skill. No one stands to gain—Shakespeare, the student, or even the teacher, who must hear all over again a version of Shakespeare which is more like *Blondie* than *Hamlet*.

Reward creative achievement. The teacher may not reinforce creative achievement because he fails to recognize it, despises the behavior which accompanies creativity in his students, or is overawed by any classroom manifestation of creativity. Torrance (1960, 1965) lists five ways in which the teacher can encourage and reward creative achievement. You as the teacher, should (1) treat unusual questions which the children ask with respect; (2) treat unusual ideas and solutions with respect; (3) show children that their ideas have value; (4) provide opportunities and give credit for self-initiated learning; and (5) provide chances for children to learn, think, and discover, without threat of immediate evaluation.

Summary

We have now concluded the third section of this chapter. You can see that we have been less explicit about the nature of creativity and instruction for creativity than we have been about the nature of and the instruction for other types of learning. Part of the difficulty is that creativity represents a new area of concern and research in American education and psychology. Few well-defined theortical ideas or terms bind together the little research we presently have. This scientific confusion makes it difficult to apply the findings on creativity to teaching. Added to this difficulty is the ideological fervor with which some people insist that the teachers and the school become more creative—and do it now! Unfortunately, some of the radical adherents of creativity have been led into the position of making rather sweeping attacks on traditional teaching practice, even to the point of accusing so-called *middle-class teachers* of resisting with deep-seated Freudian hostility any attempt of their students to be creative. Sweeping denunciations are easier to make than constructive, practical suggestions. Indeed, the staunch creativity adherents undermine their own position when they substitute almost total criticism for constructive and creative thinking. Whether the teacher implements any of the suggestions for creative teaching which this chapter contains ought to be a decision based on the requirements of the learning situation and not on purely ideological grounds.

You should now return to objectives 14–22 (p. 430) and determine how well you have achieved them.

QUESTION 11-3

Three psychologists are discussing creativity and express three somewhat divergent views. Match the psychologist (and his view) with the alternative below. Psychologist *A:* Divergent and convergent thinking seem to reflect typical and consistent patterns of cognitive behavior found in two different groups of individuals. Psychologist *B:* Creativity manifests itself in sensing gaps and missing elements. Psychologist *C:* By instructing students to think of new and even unique associations for various words, we can increase the number of unfamiliar associations.

(a) Creative abilities
(b) Creativity as learned behavior
(c) Creativity as problem solving

After selecting your answers, give the reasons for each one.

LEARNING BY DISCOVERY

In this final section of the chapter we shall consider some methods of problem solving which involve considerably less guidance than do the procedures I have already described. These methods, which often show remarkable variation, collectively bear the name *learning by discovery*. This section has the following parts: (1) a definition and examples of discovery learning; (2) a definition of expository teaching; (3) the rationale for and research on discovery learning; (4) the rationale for and research on expository teaching; and (5) a critique of discovery learning.

Definition and Examples of Discovery Learning

Unfortunately there has been considerable confusion over whether learning by discovery refers to (1) a method of teaching, (2) a method of learning, or (3) something you learn (Wittrock, 1966). Even when there is agreement that it is something you learn, it is not clear whether this "something" refers to specific principles or problem solutions, the ability to solve many problems by the application of a single principle, a structure of knowledge in a given discipline, the techniques of discovery, or simply interest in the satisfaction of the creative urge (Cronbach, 1965, pp. 88–90). You can take your pick of these and many other outcomes.

For this book to perform some useful pedagogical function with regard to discovery learning, I will adopt a particular definition of it. Discovery learning refers to those teaching situations in which the student achieves the instructional objective with limited or no guidance from the teacher. The chief characteristic is the amount of guidance the teacher provides (Kersh and Wittrock, 1962). Wittrock (1963) developed a useful scheme for classifying the amounts of instructional guidance the teacher may provide in problem solving: (1) The teacher may give the principle and the problem solution—a situation which we later call *expository teaching;* (2) the teacher may give the principle which applies but not give the problem solution; (3) the teacher may not give the principle but give the problem solution; and (4) the teacher may give neither the principle which applies nor the solution to the problem—a situation which we shall describe as *unguided discovery*. Between expository teaching, in which the principle and solution are both given, and unguided discovery, in which neither the principle nor the solution is given, we have an intermediate area often described as *guided discovery*. The procedures which we examined for problem solving fall into this intermediate zone. The teacher assists in the recall and the application of the relevant principles—in this sense he gives the principles but not the solution of the problem. Unfortunately, discussions of discovery teaching often fail to make Wittrock's distinctions and the term is often identified solely with the teaching situation which we described as unguided discovery.

Inquiry training. The examples of discovery learning which have received the most attention are examples of relatively unguided discovery. Richard Suchman (1960, 1962, 1966) devised a teaching method known as *inquiry training.* Since the instructional objectives for Suchman's program are not defined in terms of terminal behavior, it is difficult to know what they are. Suchman (1960) states that he is attempting to teach the strategies and tactics of scientific inquiry. Later (1966, p. 178) he states that "inquiry is the pursuit of meaning" and that "it is motivated by the desire to obtain a new level of relatedness between and among separate aspects of one's consciousness." It would appear that Suchman's major emphasis is the teaching not of substantive knowledge but of the means by which such knowledge, whatever it is, is acquired. His teaching method does not provide either the principles or the problem solution, and, furthermore, it does not view the application of the principles and the discovery of solutions as its major goals.

A description of an inquiry training session indicates the amount and the nature of the instructional guidance provided. The sessions are about one hour in length and are divided into three phases. The first phase is presenting the problem. This is done in a silent film which demonstrates a problem in physics. One of these films, *Ball and Ring,* demonstrates the familiar phenomenon of applying various degrees of heat to a ball and ring to cause their expansion. When the differences in temperature are properly manipulated, the ball will pass through the ring. When both objects are at room temperature, passage is not possible. All the films in Suchman's series deal with such discrepant events. The second phase is the practice session. Here the children ask questions about the film for about thirty minutes. The teacher usually limits his answers to these questions to "yes" or "no." Here is a portion of one practice session (Suchman, 1960, p. 42):

> Pupil: Were the ball and ring at room temperature to begin with?
> Teacher: Yes.
> Pupil: And the ball would go through the ring at first?
> Teacher: Yes.
> Pupil: After the ball was held over the fire it did *not* go through the ring, right?
> Teacher: Yes.
> Pupil: If the ring had been heated instead of the ball, would the results have been the same?
> Teacher: No.
> Pupil: If both had been heated would the ball have gone through then?
> Teacher: That all depends.
> Pupil: If they had both been heated to the same temperature would the ball have gone through?
> Teacher: Yes.
> Pupil: Would the ball be the same size after it was heated as it was before?

Teacher: No.
Pupil: Could the same experiment have been done if the ball and ring were made out of some other metal?
Teacher: Yes.

Suchman believes that the questions must be answered yes or no to discourage the students from transferring control of the inquiry process to the teacher. The above example shows the students asking two kinds of questions: questions of information or verification—"Were the ball and the ring at room temperature to begin with?"—and experimental questions—"If the ring had been heated instead of the ball, would the results have been the same?" If the students' experimental questions are not sufficiently explicit, the teacher is allowed to say "that all depends" and "tell me more." The teacher will not answer some questions because they represent attempts of the students to make the teacher draw the inferences they should draw—"Does the heating of the ring have anything to do with the passage of the ball?" The practice sessions end when the children arrive at the proper explanation of the observed phenomena, can go no further, or have exhausted the time they are allowed. The third and final phase of the training session is the teacher's critique. The teacher reviews and evaluates the strategy and tactics of the group and tries to suggest ways in which they can improve their questions. Sometimes he also plays tape recordings of model inquiry sessions.

Suchman's inquiry training in part resembles the steps we have described for the teaching of concepts, principles, and problem solving. The demonstration film, as later used by the instructor, is a means of invoking recall of relevant concepts and principles, and it is a description of the problem which the students must solve. The students' questions can be viewed as their own attempts to apply various concepts and principles to the solution of the problem. Our procedures for teaching problem solving differ in three ways from inquiry training: The major instructional objective is the acquisition of a higher-order principle as represented in the problem solution rather than the learning of the techniques of inquiry; the teacher gives direct assistance to the student in recalling the component principles and in combining them to arrive at the problem solution; and the student is required to demonstrate fully his new learning in the solution of a new and similar problem. All these differences, presumably, result from the different emphasis placed on instructional objectives, substantive knowledge, and the learning of inquiry methods.

In his major study of the effects of his training method, Suchman (1962) compared groups of children who had inquiry training with those who did not. Here we see that Suchman was interested in both the acquisition of substantive knowledge and inquiry techniques. The two groups were compared for their ability to understand and use inquiry and for their specific knowledge of physics. Several of the test items which were to measure general inquiry skills really measured the students' knowledge of physical principles and the application of these principles to novel problems. It is difficult to see how these items measured strategies and tactics of scientific inquiry apart from knowledge of these principles. Indeed, Suchman found no significant differences between the two groups. On the basis of these findings, as well as others we shall discuss later, there is some room for skepticism about the usefulness of teaching methods which employ relatively unguided discovery.

TEACHING STRATEGIES. Other research programs have attempted to enlarge the teacher's role in discovery learning and even to provide special training for the teacher to enact this role. Taba and her associates (1964b), using a social studies curriculum for the elementary schools, studied the effects of various teaching strategies on thought processes. The curriculum was organized as series of basic ideas the children were to learn and to apply in a variety of contexts. As in the case of Suchman, Taba's major objective was to teach thinking rather than substantive knowledge—although she did not eschew the latter objective. Taba classifies thinking (or thought) as occurring at three levels: The first and lowest level is the grouping and labeling of information; the second level is interpreting information and making inferences; and the third and highest level is predicting consequences. Taba believed that these levels describe specific thought processes the student must master in sequential order. As he introduces new subject matter, the teacher must recycle the student through the three levels of thought.

The teacher employs four teaching strategies in this recycling process: (1) She provides focusing, which establishes both the topic and the particular angle for its treatment. For example, the teacher makes this statement: "If the desert had all the water it needed, what would happen?" In this way the teacher focuses the ensuing discussion. (2) The teacher extends the thought at the same level. He does this by giving or seeking information or by providing elaboration or clarification on already established thought levels. (3) The teacher lifts the thought to a higher level. He may do this, for example, by asking why something occurs—in this case giving information (the first level) is raised to explanation (the second level). (4) Finally, the teacher controls thought by assigning a cognitive task for the student to perform. In effect, this final strategy constitutes an expository rather than a discovery mode of teaching. The teacher is classifying information, making inferences, and predicting consequences.

In Taba's formulation of discovery learning the teacher's role, although still more guiding than directive, does not suffer the same degree of constraint as it does in Suchman's inquiry training. In both programs, however, the emphasis is on the acquisition of techniques of problem solving and not on the acquisition of substantive knowledge. Taba, however, allowed the teacher to perform a variety of functions in response to the student's needs as evidenced in the quality of his verbalized thought. Unfortunately, both Suchman and Taba employed their techniques almost exclusively with groups, so that we do not know how their effectiveness relates to variations in the entering behavior of the students. In any case, you now have two examples of discovery learning. In one example (Suchman) there is very little instructional guidance. In both cases, however, these methods provide less instructional guidance than do the steps for teaching problem solving, as described earlier in this chapter.

Definition of Expository Teaching

Using Wittrock's classification of teaching methods (p. 464), we may define expository teaching as the situation in which the teacher gives both the principles and the problem solutions. In contrast to his role in discovery learning, the teacher presents the student with the entire content of what is to be learned in final form (Ausubel, 1963a); the student is not required to make any independent discoveries. The usual verbal instruction of the lecture hall exemplifies expository teaching. It is sometimes called *deductive teaching* because the teacher often begins with a definition of the concepts or principles, illustrates them, and unfolds their implications. Although expository teaching is a widespread and traditional teaching practice in our schools and colleges, it has attracted very little research (Carroll, 1964). Ausubel (1963a) believes that the reason for the lack of research is that expository teaching has been identified with rote learning. The students, presumably, can only memorize the lectures by constant review and repetition. Indeed, it is possible to present a body of material so poorly that unless the students commit it to rote memory (as in the case of nonsense syllables), they have no way of remembering it. Expository teaching, however, can present a rich body of highly related facts, concepts, and principles which the students can learn and transfer. Textbooks are examples of expository teaching, and as you very well know, they can vary in their methods of teaching subject matter and in their organization of that subject matter.

As in the case of discovery learning, it is probably difficult to find pure examples of expository teaching. In most classes we find a combination of lectures (or teacher explanation) and discussions or lectures and laboratory and field work. In these situations, although most of the instruction is under the direct guidance of the instructor, much of it is the more or less independent effort of the student.

Discovery Learning: Rationale and Research

Perhaps the most eloquent defender of learning by discovery is Bruner. In an early article (1961), "Act of Discovery," Bruner claimed four advantages of discovery learning. First, discovery learning increases intellectual potency. The student acquires information in such a way that it is readily available in problem solving. Second, discovery learning increases intrinsic motivation. It strengthens the student's tendency to carry out his learning activities with the autonomy of self-reward or the reward of discovery itself. Third, discovery learning teaches the student the techniques of discovery. Solving problems through discovery develops a style of problem solving or inquiry that serves for any task—or almost any task—one may encounter. The student improves his technique of inquiry by engaging in inquiry. Finally, discovery learning results in better retention of what is learned because the student has organized his own information and knows where (in his own storage system) to find the information when he needs it. We shall examine some of Bruner's claims below.

Research on discovery learning has provided information on the effects of different types and amounts of instructional guidance. Bernard Corman (1957), using Katona's matchstick problems, studied the effects of various amounts of guidance on the learning, application, and verbalization of the principle and the method required to solve the problems. He used three degrees of guidance: providing no information, some information, and much information about the relevant principle and method. He obtained, in general, the following results: (1) As the amount of information about the principle increased, the successful learning (simple acquisition) of the principle increased; (2) although the amount of information did not affect the verbalization (writing) of the method, students who received information about the principle (either some or much) verbalized the principle better than did students who received no information; (3) giving information was more effective than withholding it as far as application of the principle to new matchstick problems was concerned, although this effect varied with the level of student ability, the difficulty of the problems, and the amount of information (much or some) provided about the principle. Corman concluded that guidance facilitated the learning and application of principles and methods and that withholding guidance could impede problem solutions.

In a study by Gagné and Larry Brown (1961) hints were given about the solution of the problem rather than about the method of solving the problem. The students learned, through programed instruction, two principles involved in the solution of number-series problems. All students received an introductory program which began with the following item (p. 315):

Here is a series of numbers: 1 3 5 7 9 11 13 ______ ______.
What are the next two numbers in this series? ______ ______.

In the introductory program all students learned the prerequisite principles (term value and term number) for the solution of various number-series problems. Then the students were divided into three groups: (1) The rule-and-example group was given the correct formula for the solution of the number-series problems with which they were presented and a number of examples of the rule—a teaching procedure known as the Ruleg system (see below). (2) The discovery group, after a few introductory number-series items, was abruptly asked to state the principle for the solution of these problems. If they needed hints, they were directed to the next cards, which focused their attention on important relationships between the numbers and provided progressively more complete guidance. (3) The guided-discovery group began with the same introductory problems and was taken through a series of steps which helped them state a general principle for the solution of the problems. As measures of terminal performance, a problem-solving test was administered which comprised four new number-series problems for which the students had to find the correct formula. Records were kept of the amount of time needed to solve each problem, the number of hints employed on the test, and the incorrect answers. The best performance scores were obtained by the guided-discovery group, the worst by the rule-and-example group, with the discovery group falling between the other two. Gagné and Brown concluded that what is learned is more important than how it is learned. They state (p. 320):

> Discovery as a method appears to gain its effectiveness from the fact that it requires the individual learner to reinstate (and in this sense, to practice) the concepts he will later use in solving new problems. To the extent that the GD (guided discovery) program was able to identify these concepts, it could then provide systematic practice in their use, and thus lead to a performance superior to that attained otherwise. The practice provided by the R&E [rule-and-example] program, in contrast, did not *require* the use of these essential concepts (although it permitted it). Accordingly, it led to distinctly inferior problem-solving performance.

Other (and most) experiments on discovery learning have stacked the cards against expository teaching (Cronbach, 1966a). Kersh and Wittrock (1962) observe that most of these studies provide opportunities for reinforced practice following the treatment period. With sufficient amounts of reinforced practice, almost any teaching method will work. Cronbach (1966a, p. 90) believes that discovery teaching is seldom superior to expository teaching for putting across single principles. He continues to hope, however, that discovery learning "has special power to make a practicing intellectual out of the student." To confer this benefit, discovery teaching requires a long-term effort with intellectually respectable subject matter. Wittrock (1966) suggests that learning by discovery may prove to be effective in the learning of concepts and subject matter which have been organized into learning structures. It may also be effective in applying concepts to the learning of new concepts, in developing originality, and in teaching the techniques of discovery. He acknowledges, however, that his statements are hypotheses which await experimental verification.

Expository Teaching: Rationale and Research

Ausubel (1963a, p. 19) provides one of our best defenses of expository teaching:

> The art and science of presenting ideas and information meaningfully and effectively—so that clear, stable, and unambiguous meanings emerge and are retained over a long period of time as an organized body of knowledge—is really the principal function of pedagogy. This is a demanding and creative rather than a routine and mechanical task. The job of selecting, organizing, presenting, and translating subject-matter content in a developmentally appropriate manner requires more than the rote listing of facts. If it is done properly it is the work of the master teacher and is hardly a task to be disdained. . . . Beginning in the junior high school period, students acquire most new concepts and learn most new propositions by *directly* grasping higher-order relationships between abstractions. To do so meaningfully, they need no longer depend on current or recently prior concrete-empirical experience, and hence are able to bypass completely the intuitive type of understanding reflective of such dependence. Through proper expository teaching they can proceed directly to a level of abstract understanding that is qualitatively superior to the intuitive level in terms of generality, clarity, precision, and explicitness. At this state of development, therefore, it seems pointless to enhance intuitive understanding by using discovery technics.

To these advantages Carroll (1964) adds others. Expository teaching is more popular in our schools today because it is more efficient and takes less time than discovery learning. When combined with practice, it is very successful in teaching concepts and principles. Expository teaching offers the student the best opportunity to obtain an organized view of the discipline he is studying because the teacher can organize the field much more effectively for learning than the novice student can. In discovery learning the concern to teach the techniques of discovery overrides the concern for learning the unifying principles of a discipline.

We have pointed out that there is little research on expository teaching. We have already noted Ausubel's use of advance organizers expository teaching (p. 448). Donald Johnson and Paul Stratton (196 compared several methods of expository teaching with the usual indu tive method of teaching concepts in three expository programs, one di covery program, and one mixed program set up as follows: (1) Studen were given definitions of terms, similar to those one finds in the dictio ary although each term was related to a higher-order class. Then th students were required to write their own definitions of the terms. (The term was used in sentences which were part of a short story. Aft reading the story, the student was asked to complete a sentence whic required the use of the term. (3) Students were given synonyms for th new term—"alacrity means eagerness" and "altercation means squabble (4) In the classification approach, students were given examples of objec and events and were asked to classify them. The students had to discov the correct categories. (5) A mixed problem was constructed out of m terials in the four preceding approaches. This is an example of instru tion using the mixed method (p. 51):

> To chide someone is to talk to him to get him to correct his mistak Chide means to criticize or reproach. Thus a mother might chide h children for fighting with each other. An example might be a grou of fellows poking fun at a boy with dirty clothes. Now write in yo words what chide means. [This was followed by one block of sy onyms for matching and one block of events for classification, wi correct answers.]

The students who were taught with the mixed method did better tha those in all the other groups. The experimenters (p. 53) concluded th the "superiority of the mixed program supports the common practice teachers and textbooks."

Programed instruction is a form of expository teaching, especial when the Ruleg sequence is used (Glaser, 1966; Chapter 12). In the Rul sequence, the student is presented with an explicit statement of the ru (or principle) followed by one or more carefully chosen examples. He then presented with one or more incomplete examples, which act prompts to reduce the possibility of incorrect responses. The incomple examples also provide the student with the reinforcing activity of direct employing the rule. In comparing the Ruleg system with discovery (inductive) teaching and learning, Glaser (1966, p. 16) states:

> This philosophy leads to the rejection of inductive presentatio With a rule-example sequence, the student can recognize and app a rule with proficiency, and often it seems hazardous and slow approach a rule through induction or through incidental learnin With rule and then example, the student adopts the expert's car

> fully chosen statement of a rule rather than using his own, more fallible induction-derived statement. The limited range of exemplars in most teaching and textbook situations may make it possible for the student to induce what is essentially an incorrect rule but one which happens to fit all the examples presented. This is another possible source of danger in the inductive process.

The rule-example technique is very frequently used in teaching. The teacher provides the student with a general statement of the principle and then offers a series of illustrations. Glaser suggests that this procedure is widely used because it leads to rapid reinforcement for both teacher and student.

Critique of Discovery Learning

An eloquent indictment of learning by discovery has been made by Ausubel (1963a, p. 139):

> Learning by discovery also has its own elaborate mystique. Its legitimate uses and advantages have been unwarrantedly extrapolated to include both educational goals and levels of intellectual maturity, levels of subject-matter sophistication, and levels of cognitive functioning for which it is ill-adapted—and for reasons which derive from sheer dogmatic assertion; from pseudonaturalistic conceptions about the nature and conditions of intellectual development; from outmoded ideas about the relationship between language and thought; from sentimental fantasies about the nature of the child and the aims of education; and from uncritical interpretations of the research evidence.

Ausubel believes that the adherents of discovery learning make several unsupportable claims. Among these are the following: that the discovery method is the best method for transmitting subject matter; that problem solving is the primary goal of education; that there can be training in the techniques of discovery; that every child can become a critical and creative thinker; that expository teaching is authoritarian; and that discovery methods are unique generators of motivation and self-confidence. Ausubel believes that the primary purpose of teaching is to present in some systematic way an organized body of knowledge. The organization should be explicit and given in explicit form to the student. He does not believe that you can teach creative thinking and critical thinking outside the context of a specific discipline. Such thinking, he contends (p. 158), can only be learned by "adopting a precise, logical, analytical, and critical approach to the teaching of a particular discipline, an approach which fosters appreciation of the scientific method in that discipline."

Gagné (1965c) also repudiates the notion that a discovery method of learning if constantly used will finally result in the individual's making the great discovery. He writes (p. 168):

> So far as present evidence is concerned, such a proposition is wishful thinking at best; at worst, it is mere verbal sophistry. The use of discovery as a method of learning principles, as we have seen, may lead to individual capabilities that are highly effective from the standpoint of generalizability, applicability, and retention. In other words, this method of learning may generate a solid basis of *knowledge* in the individual. Furthermore, because it is a method rich in reinforcement value, the solving of problems within structures of knowledge to be learned may create a love of learning, a "thirst for knowledge" in the individual learner. But it is a vastly different thing to suppose that this kind of learning will necessarily predispose the individual to become a "creative" thinker, capable of making a great contribution to science or art.

Cronbach (1966a, p. 91), at the conclusion of his consideration of experiments on discovery learning, addresses remarks to his fellow educational psychologists which can be appropriately heeded also by students of educational psychology and prospective teachers:

> The educational psychologist is torn between two responsibilities. His responsibility as educational specialist is to give schools advice on matters where the evidence is pitifully limited. His responsibility as scientist is to insist on careful substantiation of claims for each educational innovation. In education, unfortunately, there is a great furore about whatever is announced as the latest trend, and the schools seem to careen erratically after each Pied Piper in turn. This giddy chase keeps them almost beyond earshot of the researcher standing on his tiny, laboriously tamped patch of solid ground crying in a pathetic voice, "Wait for me! Wait for me!"

Within the framework of this book and the basic teaching model it is possible to offer this critique of discovery learning. Instrinsic to our concept of teaching is the assumption that the selection of teaching procedures must be based on prior statements of instructional objectives and a description and assessment of the prerequisite entering behavior. The complex interrelationship among objectives, students, and procedures should make all a priori claims about the universal suitability of particular instructional procedures for all objectives and all students immediately questionable.

It seems highly preferable that our selection of teaching procedures be guided by the instructional objectives and the entering behavior of the student. The instructional objectives tell us what is to be learned and the type of learning involved. Descriptions of entering behavior tell us what the students need to know and what in fact they do know as they embark on the instruction which will lead them to achieving the objectives. Once we know the type of learning and the entering behavior, we can select instructional procedures which accommodate the necessary internal and external conditions of learning. Finally, with performance assessment, we have a ready source of feedback on the degree of success of our own and the students' efforts, and we can proceed to make the necessary adjustments among these instructional components. To argue that the teacher should choose his procedures on the basis of current fads and fashions, personal preferences or congeniality, ideological beliefs about what is best for children, or the political question of authoritarian and democratic teaching, is to ignore our present knowledge, no matter how limited, of the psychology of learning and instruction. In practice the teacher may very well discover that purely expository or discovery methods of teaching cannot accommodate or provide all the learning conditions necessary for reaching particular instructional objectives. Indeed, a mixture of the two methods to produce guided-discovery teaching may often be the most suitable instructional method. For the teacher the realistic and scientifically sound question should always be for what purposes and for which students and under what learning conditions should I employ any one method or combination of methods of instruction.

Summary

We have now completed our discussion of discovery learning, the fourth section of this chapter. There we defined learning by discovery and compared it with expository teaching. We presented two examples of relatively unguided discovery teaching. And we looked at the rationales for both expository and discovery teaching and considered some of the available research. The conclusion we arrived at is that a mixture of the two methods (or guided discovery) will often prove to be more practical and effective than strict adherence to one method. The particular mixture we arrive at ought to be determined by the objective requirements of the instructional situation: the instructional objectives, the entering behavior of the student, and the materials and procedures required by the external learning conditions. The step sequences decribed for the teaching of concepts, principles, and problem solving represent a mixture of expository and discovery teaching based on at least one view of the objective requirements of instructional situations.

You should now return to objectives 23–34 (pp. 430–31) and determine how well you have achieved them.

QUESTION 11-4

Which of the following combinations of conditions, concerning instructional objectives and entering behavior, describes the best conditions for the use of discovery learning?

(a) When the instructional objective pertains to basic, skill, or verbal learning and entering behavior shows the prerequisite learning.

(b) When the instructional objective pertains to the learning of techniques of discovery and expository teaching has proved unsuccessful.

(c) When the instructional objective pertains to concept or principle learning or to problem solving and the assessment of entering behavior indicates that the students have the prerequisite entering behavior.

(d) When the instructional objective pertains to the development of originality (or creativity) in problem solving and the assessment of entering behavior indicates deficiencies in knowledge of prerequisite principles.

(e) When there is no explicit instructional objective and assessment of entering behavior indicates that students have little exploratory and manipulatory motivation.

After selecting your answer, give the reasons for your choice and for your rejection of the alternatives.

SUMMARY

The first section of this chapter considered the nature of problem solving. Three interrelated conceptions of problem solving were described. First, as the most complex type of learning we consider in this book, problem solving is the application of lower-order principles to attain higher-order principles. Thus, like the other forms of learning considered in Part 3 of this book, problem solving results in the true acquisition of knowledge. Second, we viewed problem solving in terms of the habit family hierarchy whose response members, in this case, are principles which vary in response strength. Principles can also be hierarchies embedded in compound habit family hierarchies. Finally, we viewed problem solving as positive transfer of learning in which the second in a series of two tasks serves as the problem. The transfer view underscores an important characteristic of this type of learning: Successful problem solving results in learning of high generalizability and transferability—in learning of higher-order principles of wide applicability.

The second section dealt with the steps you should take in teaching problem solving. Like the step for the previous learning, these steps correspond to the components of the basic teaching model. First, you should describe for the students the terminal performance which constitutes the solution to the problem (instructional objective). Second, you must assess their entering behavior for the concepts and principles required in the problem solution. Third, you must invoke recall of all relevant concepts and principles. In this step, which deals with instructional procedures, you can use advance organizers—concepts and principles which mediate the problem solution. Fourth (also a part of procedures), you should provide verbal direction of the students' thinking, short of giving them the solution to the problem. Fifth (as part of performance assessment), you should verify the students' learning by requiring them to give a full demonstration of the problem solution, using other problems of the same class.

The third section dealt with instruction for creativity. In describing the nature of creativity, we examined creative abilities and the tests of these abilities, creativity as learned behavior, and the relationship between creativity and problem solving. In considering instruction for creativity, I provided several guidelines (but not steps): (1) classifying the kind of problems you present to students, (2) providing for the development and use of problem-solving skills, such as brainstorming, research skills, and creative reading, and (3) rewarding creative achievement.

The fourth (and final) section dealt with learning by discovery. Discovery learning was defined as those teaching situations in which the student achieves the instructional objective with little or no help from the teacher. Two examples of discovery learning which provided minimal guidance—inquiry training and teaching strategies—were described. We then considered the rationale and research on discovery learning, and we saw that the results are quite inconclusive although, under certain conditions, it may be an effective means of learning concepts, originality, and discovery techniques. We also considered the rationale of and the research on expository teaching. Earlier, we defined expository teaching as the situation in which the teacher gives both the principles and the problem solutions. Expository teaching, in the opinion of several educational psychologists, has much to recommend it, particularly for the clarity and organization with which subject matter can be presented, the certainty of its results, and the time it saves both teacher and students. Some of the research reported in this chapter (Corman, Gagné and Brown, and Johnson and Stratton) also suggests that discovery teaching and expository teaching can usefully combine to produce a general method of teaching, *guided discovery*. We pointed out that programed instruction (the subject matter of the chapter which follows) is a type of expository teaching. Critiques of discovery learning suggest that it has become a pedagogical mystique (Ausubel), that it will not, as claimed, predispose individuals to become great discoverers (Gagné), and that it is far from being an educational panacea (Cronbach). Rather than reject or accept discovery learning on a priori grounds, you should use a much sounder and more scientific basis for your decision: For what purposes and for which students and under what learning conditions should I employ any one method or combination of methods of instruction?

This chapter also concludes Part 3 of this book. Our concern here has been the design of instructional procedures appropriate for the internal and external learning conditions. The basic learning conditions were described as well as the special conditions required by the types of learning considered in the various chapters: classical conditioning, operant conditioning, skill learning, verbal learning, concept learning, principle learning, and problem solving. In the next part of the book you will find out how recent educational innovations can help you to provide the necessary learning conditions.

SUGGESTED READINGS

These four books of readings contain some of the major theoretical discussions and research on problem solving:

Anderson, Richard C., and David P. Ausubel, *Readings in the Psychology of Cognition*. New York: Holt, Rinehart & Winston, Inc., 1965.

De Cecco, John P., *Human Learning in the School: Readings in Educational Psychology*. New York: Holt, Rinehart & Winston, Inc., 1963.

———, *Psychology of Language, Thought and Instruction: Readings*. New York: Holt, Rinehart & Winston, Inc., 1967.

Harris, Theodore L., and Wilson E. Schwahn, *Selected Readings on the Learning Process*. New York: Oxford University Press, Inc., 1961.

The articles in these collections of particular relevance to the contents of this chapter are the following (the journal citations for these articles are given in the list of references at the end of the book):

Duncan, Carl P. (1959), "Recent Research on Human Problem Solving" (in De Cecco, 1963).

Maier, Norman R. F. (1930), "Reasoning in Humans. I. On Directions" (in Harris and Schwahn).

Maltzman, Irving (1950), "Thinking: From a Behavoristic Point of View" (in Anderson and Ausubel and in De Cecco, 1967).

Schulz, Rudolph W. (1960), "Problems Solving and Transfer" (in Anderson and Ausubel, 1965).

Suchman, J. Richard, "A Model for the Analysis of Inquiry," in *Analyses of Concept Learning*, eds. H. J. Klausmeier and Chester W. Harris. New York: Academic Press Inc., 1966.

These books and articles on problem solving include the material of this chapter but often give a more intensive discussion:

Gagné, Robert M., "Problem Solving," in *Categories of Human Learning*, ed. A. W. Melton, pp. 294–317. New York: Academic Press Inc., 1966.

Katona, George, *Organizing and Memorizing: Studies in the Psychology of Learning and Teaching*. New York: Columbia University Press, 1940.

Wertheimer, Max, *Productive Thinking* (2nd ed.). New York: Harper & Row, Publishers, 1959. This book examines thinking from a view which is much more cognitive than that of this chapter.

This book gives an excellent summary of the theory and research on transfer of learning, with implications for teaching:

Ellis, Henry, *The Transfer of Learning*. New York: The Macmillan Company, 1965 (paper). Also contains several major research articles.

Of the several books and articles on creativity and creative thinking the following may be of particular interest to prospective and active teachers:

Getzels, Jacob W., "Creative Thinking, Problem-Solving, and Instruction," in *Theories of Learning and Instruction*, ed. E. R. Hilgard. The Sixty-third Yearbook of the National Society for the Study of Education. Chicago, 1964.

———, and Philip W. Jackson, *Creativity and Intelligence*. New York: John Wiley & Sons, Inc., 1962.

Maltzman, Irving, "On the Training of Originality," *Psychological Review*, 67 (1960), 229–42 (also in Anderson and Ausubel and in De Cecco, 1963).

Parnes, Sidney J., and Harold F. Haring, eds., *Source Book for Creative Thinking*. New York: Charles Scribner's Sons, 1962.

Taylor, Calvin W., and Frank Barron, *Scientific Creativity: Its Recognition and Development.* New York: John Wiley & Sons, Inc., 1963.

Torrance, E. Paul, *Guiding Creative Talent.* Englewood Cliffs, N.J.: Prentice-Hall, Inc., 1962 (paper).

———, *Education and the Creative Potential.* Minneapolis: University of Minnesota Press, 1963.

———, *Creativity: What Research Says to the Teacher,* Pamphlet No. 28 of the Department of Classroom Teachers and American Research Association (NEA) Washington, D.C., 1963.

These books and articles contain research on and discussions of discovery learning:

Ausubel, David P., *The Psychology of Meaningful Verbal Learning.* New York: Grune & Stratton, Inc., 1963.

Bruner, Jerome S., "The Act of Discovery," *Harvard Educational Review,* 31 (1961), 21–32.

———, Rose R. Oliver, and Patricia M. Greenfield, *et al., Studies in Cognitive Growth,* New York: John Wiley & Sons, Inc., 1966.

Keislar, Evan, and L. M. Shulman, eds., *Learning by Discovery,* Chicago: Rand McNally & Co., 1966.

Kersh, Bert Y., and Merlin C. Wittrock, "Learning by Discovery: An Interpretation of Recent Research," *Journal of Teacher Education,* 53 (1960), 571–75 (also in De Cecco, 1967).

PART FOUR

EDUCATIONAL INNOVATIONS

In Part 1 of this book you learned about the basic teaching model. The organization of the material in the book, Chapter 1 stated, would be a detailed description of that model. Each of the succeeding parts of the book, therefore, has concentrated on particular components of the model. Chapter 2 dealt with the definition of instructional objectives. Part 2 concentrated on the entering behavior of the student. Part 3, using our present knowledge of human learning, described the instructional steps necessary for the teaching of skills, language, concepts, principles, and problem solving.

Part 4 now provides the opportunity to bring together the components of the basic teaching model and to examine how modern educational practices attempt to meet the requirements of each component. I refer to these practices as innovations, although the historian of American education will see the shadow of the past in even the most revolutionary of them. An examination of these innovations should reveal that some provide for the components of the basic teaching model better than others do. Programed instruction, for example, has taken the model more seriously than educational television, especially in the definition of instructional objectives. Computer-assisted instruction more than the new mathematics and the new science has given serious consideration to the careful assessment and use of the entering behavior of students. In evaluating the innovations I am about to describe, you should find the basic teaching model a handy guide.

Part 4 has two chapters. The first (Chapter 12) describes programed instruction and a number of other innovations collectively called educational technology. Chapter 12 describes how you should prepare, write, and revise programed materials. It also describes the instructional uses of films, television, teaching machines, and computers. Finally it describes new efforts to organize instruction, such as flexible scheduling, team teaching, and instructional systems. Chapter 13, the following chapter, describes the new instructional materials and procedures which the physical and life sciences and mathematics have recently developed. Although there is considerable necessary overlapping, Chapter 12 will emphasize the procedures, media, and organization of instruction, and Chapter 13 the new materials or subject matter of instruction.

Programmed Instruction and Educational Technology

12

The development of a modern educational technology, depending on which periodicals and journals you read, has been either heralded as the necessary ingredient of an educational revolution which will lift the schools out of the Dark Ages and into twentieth-century enlightenment or castigated as a movement which can only reduce teachers and students to robots in the manner described by our more pessimistic science fiction. The subject of educational technology is rarely treated by either educators or laymen with the scientific neutrality which would allow them to inquire into what it is and how it might be useful. Perhaps we can expect no better in a cultural milieu which wants to preserve all the advantages of a highly organized, technological society and all the freedom and privacy of the individual who enjoys these advantages. In any case, the debate is on, and we can only hope that the evidence comes in (whatever it may be) before ideologies harden and tempers become unmanageable.

This dispute often fails to distinguish between two meanings of *educational technology* (Lumsdaine, 1964). One meaning refers to the detailed application of the psychology of learning to practical teaching problems. Francis Mechner (1965) uses this analogy: In the same way that an aeronautical engineer believes that he can design an airplane by applying a few basic physical principles and a little art and intuition, the educational technologist believes that he can build in the student a complex repertory of knowledge or behavior by applying a few basic principles of learning psychology in addition to a little art and intuition.

Arthur Melton (1959) observes that an educational technology is based on the assumption that the psychology of learning encompasses all forms of relatively permanent behavioral changes which result from experience, including, of course, the experiences of the child in school. In the first part of this chapter, in which I describe how to program materials, I am applying the psychology of learning to practical teaching problems. In other words, I am describing educational technology in this scientific sense. The programs which such a technology produces are often called the *software* to distinguish them from the machines, or *hardware,* into which the programs are fed. The second meaning of educational technology refers to the application of engineering principles in the development of electromechanical equipment used for instructional purposes. Examples of these devices are motion pictures, tape recorders, teaching machines, and computers—the educational hardware.

The two meanings of educational technology interact in the design and use of equipment to provide control over the learning situation, a rich array of stimulus material (for example, through motion pictures), and interaction between the responses of the learner and the presentation of instructional material (Lumsdaine, 1964). When we organize instruction, as in the case of team teaching, flexible scheduling, and instructional systems, we must combine our application of the psychology of learning with electromechanical engineering to produce the desired results. In fact, H. A. Bern (1967) suggests that the educational psychologist of the future may be a psychologist-engineer.

American entrepreneurial genius, sometimes impersonally called *big business,* has entered the educational scene to hasten the development of educational technology particularly for the purpose of providing the hardware which the future educational markets will demand. In its acquisition of many of the major textbook publishing companies, the business community is also manifesting its interest in educational software. Francis Keppel (1967) observes that the American educator is not accustomed to having business knocking at his door. In fact, according to one popular stereotype of the teacher (and there are many), he has long ago retreated behind his classroom door to protect a hide too sensitive and submissive to have allowed him to function successfully in the more aggressive and remunerative business world. Now, that business world is invading his classroom. In an admittedly overdrawn picture Keppel (p. 187) describes the current fears of the American teacher:

> Knocking at the door of the little red schoolhouse is the giant fis of American business—big business: International Business Ma chines, Xerox, General Learning Corporation (the affiliate of Gen eral Electric and Time, Inc.), Radio Corporation of America Raytheon, merchants of hardware, makers of electronic computers, o

> copying machines that can make a million sheets of paper look exactly like the original, and above all, makers of money. On the other side of the door is the classroom teacher, facing something unknown and frightening, and protecting children huddled in a corner. In seeming competition for the mind of the schoolchild, America's tycoons appear pitted against a lonely, underequipped, underpaid classroom teacher. It is a modern picture of Goliath and David, and it is the result of far more fear than fact.

This chapter deals with educational technology in both its modern meanings. The first section is about programed instruction. Here you will learn how to prepare for program writing, how to write the program, and how to try out and revise the program. The available research is the basis for most of the recommendations made. Here I also describe the various programs and the standards for the selection of commercial programs. Upon completing this section you should have developed some competence in the programing of materials for your major teaching areas. The second and third sections of the chapter are shorter. In the second section you learn about instructional media, particularly the selection and use of films and television programs, and also about computer-assisted instruction and a wide array of audiovisual materials. In the third (and final) section you learn about flexible scheduling. Here we consider the use of modules and modular units in place of the traditional class periods; models of team teaching for content areas, grades, and teaching staffs; and nongraded instruction.

Upon reading the introduction to this chapter (on educational technology), you should be able to meet these objectives:

1. Point out and illustrate the similarities and differences in the two types of educational technology.
2. Describe the source of the influence of educational technology in the schools.

Upon reading the first section of this chapter (on programed instruction), you should be able to meet these objectives:

3. Describe and illustrate each of the following steps in the preparation of a program: (a) select a unit or topic; (b) prepare a content outline; (c) define your objectives in behavioral terms; (d) construct a test of entering behavior; and (e) construct a test of terminal behavior.
4. Describe and illustrate each of the following steps in the writing of a program: (a) present material in the form of frames; (b) require

active student response; (c) provide for confirmation or correction of student response; and (d) provide careful sequencing of the frames.

5. Point out and illustrate the differences and similarities between frames and lesson plans.

6. Describe and illustrate the informational conditions under which overt responding facilitates learning more than covert responding does.

7. Describe and illustrate the differences between prompting and confirmation procedures and indicate the advantages of each.

8. Describe and illustrate the two major purposes of prompts.

9. Describe and illustrate the differences between formal and thematic prompts.

10. Describe and illustrate four formal prompts: partial-response prompts, rhyming prompts, literal prompts, and frame-structure prompts.

11. Describe and illustrate six thematic prompts: pictures, context settings, synonyms and antonyms, analogies, rules, and inductive prompts.

12. Define and illustrate fading in terms of prompts.

13. List the two factors which determine frame sequencing.

14. Describe and illustrate each of the following steps in the tryout and revision of the program: (a) write the original draft; (b) edit the original draft; and (c) try out and revise the draft.

15. Point out and diagrammatically illustrate the similarities and differences in these three types of programs: (a) linear, (b) branching, and (c) adjunct autoinstructional.

16. Describe how you would obtain information to answer each of the following questions in the selection of a program: (a) Is it really programed material? (b) How does the program fit into the curriculum? (c) How well will the program teach in your situation? (d) Can you afford it?

Upon reading the second section of this chapter (on the instructional media) you should be able to meet these objectives:

17. Define the instructional media in terms of electromechanical devices.

18. Point out and illustrate four distinctions between new and traditional media.

19. List three new media.

20. List nine sources from which you obtain information about available media.

21. Define instructional systems design in terms of a comparison of alternatives and of performance criteria.

22. Point out the differences and similarities of the basic teaching model and the instructional system illustrated in Fig. 12-32.

23. Describe and illustrate the conditions under which films and television facilitate learning as much or more than direct instruction.

24. Point out the relationship between the control of realism and the facilitation of student learning.

25. Describe the three machine capabilities of computers for instruction.

26. List three limitations in CAI in the accommodation of individual differences in entering behavior.

Upon reading the third section of this chapter (on flexible scheduling), you should be able to meet these objectives:

27. Define and illustrate course structure in terms of time and students.

28. Define and illustrate phase and section in terms of course structure.

29. Define and illustrate modules and modular units in terms of class size and length of time.

30. Point out the similarities and differences of modular and traditional concepts of course structure.

31. Define team teaching in terms of students, faculty, and aides.

32. List the twelve characteristics of team teaching, referring to functions and personnel.

33. Illustrate team teaching models functioning (a) across grades, (b) across subject matter, (c) across both.

34. Describe the advantages of team teaching for the novice teacher.

35. Define nongraded instruction in terms of grade level and student achievement.

36. Point out the differences between a grade and a phase.

37. Point out the similarities and differences of phases and units.

PROGRAMED INSTRUCTION

A Definition

Figure 12-1 presents three frames, or units, of a program which teaches the use of a symbolic notation for describing and analyzing behavioral contingencies (Mechner, 1961, 1965). If you inspect these frames you will see some of the major characteristics of programed in-

Frame	Answer
1 Your being born <u>was not</u> a response event for you. That is, it <u>was not</u> an action you initiated. Your throwing your rattle out of your crib, however, <u>was</u> an action initiated by you. It <u>was</u> a response event for you. CHECK each sentence below that describes a response event for the person or animal named in the sentence (note that there is no limit to the number of sentences you can check): ☐ a. Clara dyed her hair red. ☐ b. Herman died of old age. ☐ c. The dog has fleas. ☐ d. The cat meowed.	**a** **d**
2 When you hit someone, it (☐ is ☐ is not) your action. It (☐ is ☐ is not) your response event. When the other person hits you back, it (☐ is ☐ is not) your response event. CHECK each sentence below that describes a response event for the person or animal named in the sentence: ☐ a. Philip ran fast. ☐ b. Gregory was run over. ☐ c. Alice cheated on the exam. ☐ d. Mary was reprimanded for cheating. ☐ e. The canary lost all its feathers. ☐ f. The parrot said, "Polly wants a cracker."	**is** **is** **is not** **a** **c** **f**
3 The sentence, "The officer gave Mr. Smith a summons," <u>describes</u> the officer's giving the ticket, but it merely <u>implies</u> Mr. Smith's speeding or going through the red light. Does the sentence describe a response event for Mr. Smith? ☐ yes ☐ no CHECK the statements below that describe, not merely imply, response events for <u>you</u>: ☐ a. You solved a hard math example. ☐ b. Your teacher gave you a good grade in math. ☐ c. You are a doctor. ☐ d. You are studying to be a doctor.	**no** **a** **d**

Fig. 12-1. *Some examples of program frames (after Mechner, 1965, p. 491).*

struction: (1) The material is broken down into small steps (or frames); (2) frequent response is required of the student (for example, the student must make six responses in the second frame); and (3) there is immediate confirmation of right answers or correction of wrong answers for each response the student makes. An additional characteristic, which you cannot observe, is that (4) the content and sequence of the frames were subjected to actual tryout with students and were revised on the basis of the data gathered by the program author. These four factors are the major characteristics of programed instruction and of programed materials. The programed materials, as distinguished from programed instruction, or the actual use of the materials, are simply the educational materials from which the students learn (Jacobs *et al.,* 1966). A *program* accepts the responsibility for the management of the learning situation. According to Arthur Lumsdaine (1964), the program tries to see to it that the student does learn, and it takes the blame for the student's failures. A program can be distinguished from a lesson plan or a book. A book is only a source of materials to which the student exposes himself. There is little or no predetermined interaction between the book and the reader in the form of required responses and feedback. A lesson plan is often a skeletal outline of materials and activities the teacher will use in teaching. The actual instruction is something related to but apart from the lesson outline. A program, however, is the actual instruction. The student's success or failure depends on the program.

The first section of this chapter teaches you how to write and revise a program. Program writing has three major stages: (1) preparation, (2) the actual writing, and (3) tryout and revision.

Preparation

Select a unit or topic. The selection of a topic can be guided by several factors. First, select subject matter with which you are thoroughly familiar. Unfamiliarity will result in misleading and inaccurate materials and will interfere with your learning how to program the materials. Second, restrict yourself to a very small area of subject matter. Robert Filep (1961) suggests that, if you intend to teach English grammar, you should restrict yourself to something as manageable as the agreement between verbs and such pronouns as "each," "either," and "nobody." Third, choose subject matter that is easy to program. Jerome Lysaught and Clarence Williams (1963) suggest that it is easier to write a program on algebra than on the dynamics of political power. The tendency of the beginning programer is to select too wide a topic. The development of a program and the administration of it to the student are usually very time-consuming activities.

PREPARE A CONTENT OUTLINE. This outline should cover all the material you plan to teach (Klaus, 1961). It is frequently the product of a careful examination of a number of textbooks and reference sources. An experienced teacher also has the use of his notes, textbooks, and the assignments he has used in conventional instruction. If you have not taught the material you are about to program, you should consult an experienced teacher who can supply knowledge, specific examples, and interesting illustrations which may be very useful in your program. One of the chief criticisms of programed materials is that they have been published before adequate editing of the manuscript for accuracy and clarity of subject matter and presentation (Soles, 1963). Occasionally an individual with some unpolished programing skills and with little knowledge of the subject matter has accepted the responsibility of writing a program. The results can be and have been disastrous. The chief advantage of the teacher as programer is that he can combine his knowledge of the subject matter with his new knowledge about programed instruction.

DEFINE YOUR OBJECTIVES IN BEHAVIORAL TERMS. I described the importance of and ways for stating these objectives in Chapter 2. The writing of objectives involves both task description and task analysis. Task description, you recall, is the description of the terminal behavior. Task analysis examines the component behaviors the student must acquire in the process of reaching the terminal behavior. Peter Pipe (1966) suggests that you build a pyramid of objectives. Figure 12-2 shows one such pyramid. In the beginning, Pipe advises, it is better to state your objectives in general rather than in behavioral terms. This general statement is an instructional goal. You then analyze this goal by asking yourself what behaviors are needed to attain it. The general statement and the first analysis of it are the top two levels of the pyramid. You proceed to the third level when you determine which component behaviors are necessary in attaining the major behaviors in your program. Pipe suggests that you continue the analysis of behavior (by asking yourself what behaviors are needed to reach the next higher level) until you have reached the probable level of entering behavior. The various levels of the pyramid are the links in the chain between entering and terminal behavior.

CONSTRUCT (AND ADMINISTER) A TEST OF ENTERING BEHAVIOR. The construction of this test requires you to determine the necessary prerequisite behaviors which you will recall but not provide instruction for in your program. The prerequisite behaviors are the bases for writing the items for the test of entering behavior. If you administer such a test to your students early in the development of your program, the test results should indicate at what points your programing must begin. You should write

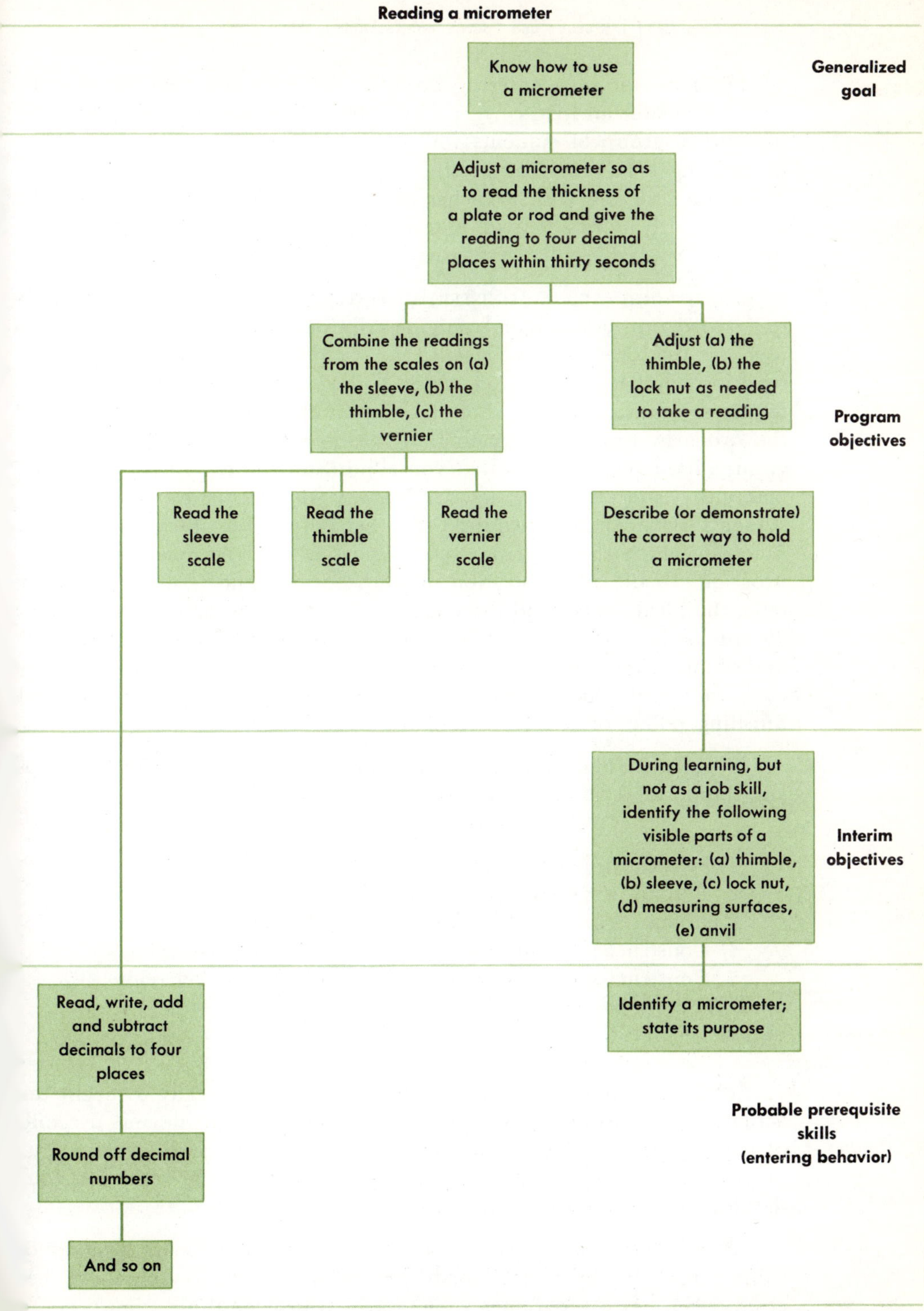

Fig. 12-2. *A pyramid of program objectives (after Pipe, 1966, pp. 24–25).*

several items for each entering behavior to be certain that the student does not answer an item correctly by only making a lucky guess. In dealing with a group of students you may discover considerable variability in entering behavior. One possible way of handling this problem is to develop a program with branches (see p. 520). The program can direct students with more adequate entering behavior than others to skip the introductory frames of the program and to turn to the advanced frames.

CONSTRUCT (AND ADMINISTER) A TEST OF TERMINAL BEHAVIOR. This test, based on your original task description (the third step above), is used for performance assessment, the fourth component of the basic teaching model. You should have at least four test items for each terminal behavior. These should be scrambled and should not follow the order in which the terminal behaviors were acquired in the program. Pipe (1965) suggests that you administer the test to your students before they study the program. In this way you can discover whether any students have already acquired the behaviors your program teaches. Material which the student already knows should be deleted from the program. In the administration of your entering and terminal behavior tests, the ideal result (and therefore the one you can least expect) is that all the students obtain a perfect score on the test of entering behavior and obtain a zero score on the test of terminal behavior. This is, in any case, the result you should aim for in determining the starting and finishing points of your program.

SUMMARY. The preparation of a program consists of the five steps you should take before you begin writing it:

1. Select a unit or topic.
2. Prepare a content outline.
3. Define your objectives in behavioral terms.
4. Construct (and administer) a test of entering behavior.
5. Construct (and administer) a test of terminal behavior.

Program Writing

With the preparatory stage behind you, you are ready to begin the actual construction of your program. Your content outline and pyramic of behavioral objectives, revised in the light of the results of your tests of entering and terminal behavior, should now be the basis for you development of a series of instructional events.

PRESENT THE MATERIAL IN FRAMES. A frame is a small segment o subject matter which calls forth particular student responses (Tabe *et al.,* 1965). As a programer your task is to provide those stimuli neces sary to evoke the student responses which must be acquired as steps toward the terminal behavior. Not only is a frame a unit of subject matter, such as a sentence or paragraph of a chapter, but also it is constructed to call forth particular responses and, eventually, specific terminal behaviors. There are four essential parts of a frame (Klaus, 1961): the stimulus and the stimulus context; the cues or prompts necessary to produce the response reliably; the response(s) the stimulus evokes; and enrichment material which makes the frame more readable or interesting or which recalls previously learned materials to facilitate student response. The frames in Fig. 12-3 illustrate the essential parts. They are part of a high school physics program designed to teach the student to talk intelligently and technically about the emission of light from an incandescent source. In each frame the stimulus and the stimulus context are the words which precede and follow the blank. The blank, of course, provides for the student's response. You should also note that the stimulus context is a familiar one—the flashlight, the flashlight bulb, and the glow of a hot wire. The stimulus material of the frame and the response which the student makes to this material constitute an *S-R* relationship. In programed materials, the new stimulus material is gradually introduced while the cueing (prompting) with familiar material is

1. The important parts of a flashlight are the battery and the bulb. When we "turn on" a flashlight, we close a switch which connects the battery with the ________.

Response: bulb

2. When we turn on a flashlight, an electric current flows through the fine wire in the ________ and causes it to grow hot.

Response: bulb

3. When the hot wire glows brightly, we say that it gives off or sends out heat and ________.

Response: light

Fig. 12-3. *Beginning frames from a physics program (after Skinner, 1958, p. 973).*

29. A nearly "dead" battery may make a flashlight bulb warm to the touch, but the filament may still not be hot enough to emit light—in other words the filament will not be ______ at that temperature.

Response: incandescent

31. When raised to any temperature above 800 degrees Celsius, an object such as an iron bar will emit light. Although the bar may melt or vaporize, its particles will be ______ no matter how hot they get.

Response: incandescent

Fig. 12-4. *Later frames in a physics program (after Skinner, 1958, p. 973).*

gradually withdrawn. In this manner, the student's behavior comes under the control of the new subject matter. Later frames in the physics program illustrate this procedure (Fig. 12-4). In frame 29 you see that the term *filament* now substitutes for the less technical *fine wire*. The additional technical term *incandescent* is evoked in new stimulus contexts to describe in more technical language hot objects which emit light.

You should also note in Figs. 12-3 and 12-4 that each frame presents a relatively small segment of material. As a novice programer your tendency will be to make these segments too large. You should present only enough material to elicit a single response and no other responses. The size of the segment may vary, however, in different parts of the program. Nathan Maccoby and Fred Sheffield (1961) found that (1) short steps are more effective than large steps for initial learning and (2) the progressive lengthening of steps leads to the best performance on the test of terminal behavior. In Fig. 12-5, Scott Parry (1964) shows how a sequence of frames remedies the difficulties of a single frame.

To keep maximum flexibility in the writing and sequencing of your frames, you should use large index cards with the frames on one side and the responses on the other.

Require active student response. An essential part of the frame is the response the student is asked to make. Stuart Margulies (1964) formulated the critical-response rule for the construction of frames: The student can be held responsible only for that portion of the material to

ENGLISH GRAMMAR

In studying **qualifiers** and **modifiers,** this little rule will help you distinguish between **adjectives** and **adverbs:**
Adjectives are words which ______ whereas ______ are words which modify.

Responses: qualify, adverb

Adjectives are words which **describe** (or tell more about) nouns or pronouns.

John has brown **eyes.**

In this sentence, the word ______ describes the noun **eyes.** Therefore, the word **brown** is a(n) ______.[1]

Responses: brown, adjective

[1] Sequence expanding this concept follows.

Now let's meet another part of speech: the adverb. Adverbs tell more about, or ______, verbs, adjectives, or other adverbs.

Response: describe

John runs quickly.
In this sentence, the word **quickly** tells more about the word **runs,** which is a ______. Therefore quickly is a(n) ______.[2]

Responses: verb, adverb

[2] Sequence expanding this concept follows.

As you have seen, adjectives and adverbs are the parts of speech used to ______, or tell more about, other words.

Response: describe

Adjectives are used to describe ______.
Adverbs are used to describe ______.

Responses: nouns and pronouns; verbs, adjectives, adverbs

Fig. 12-5. *A faulty frame (top), which is corrected by a sequence of five frames (after Parry, 1963, p. 4).*

It requires seven days to pack and assemble material after the request is made. It requires three days to label the material for delivery. How long is the time between request and delivery? ______

Response: 10 days

Fig. 12-6. *A program frame (after Margulies, 1964, p. 7).*

which he responds correctly. He cannot be held responsible for learning information which he does not use in making an immediate response. Margulies uses the example in Fig. 12-6. Now the student can be held responsible for learning that delivery takes ten days but not for learning how much time it takes for labeling or for packing and assembling.

It is important that the student be required to make the critical response. Holland (1960) altered the normal version of a program by choosing different response words which had little relationship to the critical content and which could be supplied by observing trivial cues. Figure 12-7 shows a normal and an altered frame. In the posttest, Holland found 18.3 per cent error on the program with normal frames, and 39.4 per cent on the program with altered frames, which was about the same amount of error obtained when the students read complete sentences without responding. Interestingly enough, the students made fewer

If a previously reinforced response is no longer reinforced, it soon occurs (1) ______ frequently. This is called (2) ______.

Responses: (1) less; (2) extinction

If a previously reinforced response is no longer ______, it soon occurs less often. This is called extinction.

Response: reinforced

Fig. 12-7. *A normal frame and an alteration of it (after Holland, 1965a, p. 79).*

errors on the program with the altered frames than on the program with the normal frames. Figure 12-8 shows the results of Holland's study. The absence of errors made during the study of a program can mislead the programer into believing that the students are learning more than they are. By making trivial responses they are learning very little.

Holland (1965b) in another study found that he could obliterate 68 per cent of the words in a program without altering the error rate. In his black-out technique, a black crayon is used to mark out all parts of a frame not needed for answering correctly. Figure 12-9 shows the application of this technique to six frames of a monetary program. The removal of the blacked-out material failed to increase the error rate.

If you analyze the terminal behavior in sufficient detail, you will be able to indicate clearly the critical responses the student should make. The responses in the frames always depend on some important part of the subject matter, such as understanding a new illustration, recognizing important details of the subject matter, or acquiring a new term.

The location of the response blank (if there is one) may also be a

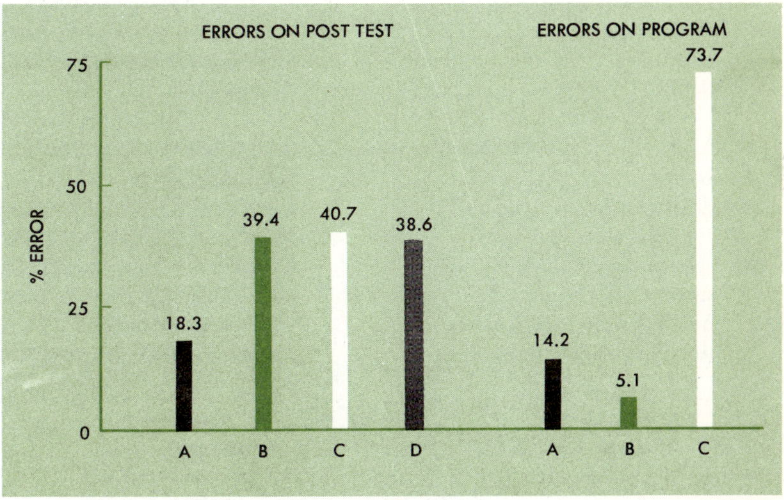

Fig. 12-8. *Percentage of errors on posttest and in the program for four experimental versions. Program* A *is the normal program, with response determined and dependent upon critical content; program* B *has responses determined, but answers relatively unrelated to critical content; program* C *has responses relatively undetermined, but dependent upon critical content; and program* D *has only complete statements with no responses (after Holland, 1965b, p. 3).*

Column I (Normal)	*Column II (Blacked-Out)*
18. To distinguish between domestic trade and international trade the word *draft* (sometimes spelled draught) was created to identify ——— *of exchange* used in domestic trade.	18. [redacted] to identify ——— *of exchange* [redacted]
19. The *bill of e_______* is the forerunner of the modern *check.*	19. [redacted] *bill of e_______* [redacted]
20. A *c___k* is a demand *draft* drawn on a bank.	20. [redacted] *c___k* [redacted]
21. The only difference between a *check* and an ordinary *draft* is that the custodian of the money in case of a *check* must be a b___.	[redacted] the custodian of the money in case of a *check* must be a b___.
22. A *b___ of exchange (draft)* is convenient for the payment of debts.	22. [redacted] *b___ of exchange (draft)* [redacted]
23. The seller of merchandise by sending a *bill of e_______* drawn on the buyer and attaching the shipping documents to a bank for collection can be assured that the merchandise will not be delivered to the buyer until the buyer pays for it.	23. [redacted] *bill of e_______* [redacted]

Fig. 12-9. *Normal and blacked-out items from monetary program. Material covered in blacked-out version can be omitted without influencing the subject's ability to answer correctly. Item 18 can be answered because of previous item (after Holland, 1965a, p. 83).*

source of difficulty. Robert Horn (1963, p. 4) argues that the blank shoul appear as close to the end of the frame as possible because this positio spares the student the awkwardness of flipping his eyes back and fort "skidding around inside frame after frame looking for the relevant m terial." It is often helpful at first to write the frame in question form b cause the question focuses the attention on the form of the require response. It is, of course, entirely permissible that a frame remain in question form. And it is sometimes desirable to use multiple-choice alternatives rather than fill-in blanks.

Whether the responses in programed material should be *overt* or *covert* has been the subject of considerable inquiry. Unfortunately, these terms have shifted in meaning and "one man's overt is frequently another man's covert" (Cummings and Goldstein, 1962). Perhaps the most useful distinction is illustrated in a study by John Krumboltz and Ronald Weisman (1962). Here students who made overt responses wrote down their answers on sheets of paper. Students who made covert responses mentally composed a response to each blank in the frame before turning the page to the correct answer. Although the findings on the relative benefits of overt and covert responding have not always been consistent, Richard Anderson (1967) points to two conclusions which have considerable empirical support: (1) Overt responses facilitate learning when the responses are relevant to the content of the lesson, and (2) overt responses should be required in the learning of unfamiliar and technical terms. A study by Krumboltz and Charles Kiesler (1965) supports the first conclusion. Among other things, it compared the relative effectiveness of asking or not asking a question on the various frames of the program. The subjects were high school students, and the program was on the interpretation of educational test results. They found that the students performed significantly better on the posttest when they were required to answer questions (that is, to make overt responses). Two studies support Anderson's second conclusion. Allana Cummings and Goldstein (1962), using a program designed to teach laboratory technicians to read cardiograms for the diagnosis of myocardial infarction, found that overt responding was better than covert responding when the students were required to make long, intricate, and unfamiliar responses. A later study by Eigen and Margulies (1963) compared overt and covert responding in learning easy and difficult nonsense syllables. They discovered that the overt-responding group learned about twice as many of the difficult syllables as did the covert-responding group. Both groups learned about the same number of the easy (more familiar) nonsense syllables.

The reason overt responding facilitates learning is not clear at present. Ernest Rothkopf (1966) suggests that test questions (and we may include the frames of a program) control what he calls *mathemagenic behaviors*—covert and overt behaviors of the student in the instructional situation which give birth to learning. Mathemagenic behaviors include reading, asking questions, inspecting an object, keeping the face oriented toward the teacher, and mentally reviewing a recently seen motion picture. They also include looking out of the classroom window, yawning, turning the pages of a textbook without reading, writing notes to a student in a neighboring seat, and sleeping either in class or in a library carrel. Some of these behaviors, you can see, are quite unrelated to the achievement of instructional objectives. If it were possible, however, to control mathemagenic behaviors, the control could facilitate learning. Such control, Rothkopf has found, can be obtained through the insertion of questions in reading passages. In one study students were asked to read a very long (thirty-six–page, or about 9,000-word) passage of high factual content. After every three pages, the student was directed to answer two questions and, if he chose, to check the correct answers which were supplied. Students who had the benefit of the questions performed better on a posttest than students who read the passages without the questions. The beneficial effects occurred only when the questions followed the relevant text segment and only when they were inserted fairly frequently. Questions, according to Rothkopf, profoundly affect mathemagenic behaviors which, in turn, affect how much we learn.

In the initial development of your program, overt responding is a practical necessity. The complete written record of your students' responses becomes a major basis for program revision. The program must assume the full responsibility for instruction: It is not the student but the program that fails. A conventional standard used in the revision of a program is the 10 per cent error rate, which requires you to revise a program frame until 10 per cent or less of your students respond incorrectly to it. Parry (1963), however, cautions against an overly stringent application of this rule. He suggests several situations in which the purpose of the frame is best served by an erroneous response by more than 10 per cent of the students: (1) when incorrect or unwanted responses already exist as a result of previous learning; (2) when new learning is best accomplished after the student has responded incorrectly; (3) when the student's appetite is whetted if he is occasionally asked to guess a response; (4) when an occasional slow-down frame forces the student to read more carefully and to avoid the temptation to respond before reading; (5) when the student is asked for an opinion; and (6) when a branching frame determines whether the student requires review before proceeding with the new frame sequences. A study by Robert Goldbeck and Vincent Campbell (1962) found a high percentage of correct test responses for incorrect responses made to frames which were made difficult by reducing the amount of prompting provided by the frame. The evidence thus far does not require the total abolition of student error from our programs.

PROVIDE FOR CONFIRMATION OR CORRECTION OF STUDENT RESPONSES. You have seen in the preceding examples of frames that the correct response to the frame always appears. Providing the correct response, with which the student compares his own response, has been a standard characteristic of programed instruction and, perhaps, its most distinguishing characteristic. When the student discovers that his response is correct, he obtains confirmation; when it is incorrect, he receives correction. The practical necessity or efficiency of immediate confirmation has never been adequately studied. It does appear that early programers, especially those of the Skinnerian persuasion, failed to distinguish between the motivational and informational aspects of immediate knowledge of results. The delay of reinforcement for a hungry rat learning to press a lever to obtain food has consequences far different from those resulting from the delay of informational feedback to a child or an adult attempting to learn a concept. We should also be aware that the correct answer which the program supplies may be quite redundant. Krumboltz and Weisman (1962) found no difference in test performances of students who were supplied the correct answer all the time and of those supplied the correct answer only part of the time. They suggest that supplying the correct response may be more important later than earlier in the program, when most of the prompts for the correct responses are withdrawn. The tight sequencing of program frames, so that one frame interlocks with those which precede and follow it, provides a source of informational feedback apart from that provided by the printed answers. The student finds knowledge of results in more places than the programer may suspect. Although you too may be guilty of redundancy, you should provide feedback for each response and this can be done most conveniently in the usual programing format.

USE PROMPTS TO GUIDE STUDENT RESPONSES. Prompts are cues provided in the program frame to guide the student to the correct response. They are supplementary stimuli in that they are added to a frame to make the frame easier but are not sufficient in themselves to produce the response (Markle, 1964). Figure 12-10 shows two prompted frames (2 and 3) and

Frame 1 The capital of France is ______.

Response: Paris

Frame 2 The capital of France is _ _ _ _ _.

Response: Paris

Frame 3 The capital of France is P______.

Fig. 12-10. *Frames with prompted and unprompted responses (after Markle, 1961, pp. 2–3).*

one unprompted frame (1). In frame 2 the number of dashes serves as a prompt by indicating the number of letters in the correct response. In frame 3, the letter *P* serves as a prompt for the correct response. Alone, these prompts are insufficient to guarantee the correct answer. If the student has never heard of Paris, the prompt is totally ineffective. If he knows the names of other French cities as well as Paris, these prompts eliminate incorrect responses. If the student knows only one French city and this city, fortunately, is Paris, the prompts in frames 2 and 3 at least help evoke this response.

Evidence for the value of prompting is found in studies of response guidance and in studies which compare the effects of prompting and confirmation. The studies of response guidance are similar to those we described under discovery teaching. In one study Kimble and Jepson Wulff (1953) wanted to teach the reading of slide-rule scales. After determining errors the students were likely to make, they made up a series of problems to be used in training and practice. Through the use of filmstrips and workbooks in which slide rules were reproduced, students were trained to find specified values on the scale. The chief variable in the study was prompting. In the prompted group, students received cues which limited the range of possible answers without revealing the correct answer. The other group received no cues at all. In the test following the study, students in the prompted group scored higher on practice items, transfer items, and the most difficult items. These students showed the greatest superiority on those items for which prompts had been provided.

There has been lively debate and considerable research on the relative merits of prompting and confirmation (see Cook, 1963, and Holland, 1964). A simplified statement of the issue is this: Is it better to prompt responses so that errors are avoided in the first place or to correct erroneous responses after they are made? Oliver Cook and his associates (1956, 1958, 1960, 1963) argue in favor of prompting and against needless trial and error. Cook (1963, p. 516) accuses the Skinnerians of superstition in insisting on the use of confirmation:

> There is, in the behavior of devout Skinnerians, as in the behavior of pigeons . . . , a strong element of superstition. In making the transition from training a pigeon in a Skinner box to training a human being with a teaching machine, religious Skinnerians seem to have a certain reluctance to change any detail of the ritual for fear that beneficial results that they enjoyed with the Skinner box might not be forthcoming with the teaching machine.

Cook, of course, refers to the procedure in the Skinner box of rewarding the animal after he responds correctly (a form of confirmation). In one study Cook and Tracy Kendler (1956) used a paired-associate learning task. Students had to learn to pair the letter (the stimulus term) with the

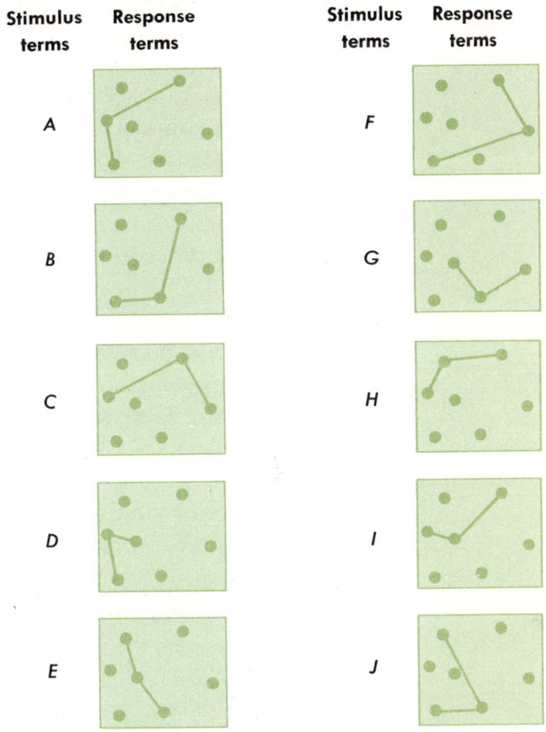

Fig. 12-11. *The paired items used in the study of prompting vs. confirmation procedures (after Cook and Kendler, 1956, p. 92).*

:ode-line drawing (the response term) in Fig. 12-11. The researchers used wo training procedures. In the prompting procedure the student saw the timulus term (the letter) and then saw the response term (the code-line lrawing). He then copied the drawing. In the confirmation procedure he student saw the letter, tried to reproduce the drawing, and then saw he correct drawing. The prompting procedure was like classical condiioning, the confirmation procedure like operant conditioning. They ound that the prompting procedure was superior in both early and late rials. It appears, then, that instructional procedures which furnish the tudent sufficient guidance to avoid mistakes is superior to procedures vhich only correct errors after they are made.

Obviously, there can be too much prompting. The student can turn n an errorless performance on the program frames and fail to answer tems on the test of terminal behavior. To determine the optimal limits f prompting, David Angell and Lumsdaine (1961) used a prompting and a prompting-plus-confirmation procedure to teach the materials in Fig. 12-11. The prompting procedure was identical to that of Cook and Kendler. In the second procedure the students used the prompting procedure for three-quarters of the trials and the confirmation procedure for one-quarter. That is, on every fourth trial the students tried to reproduce the code-line drawing for a particular letter before they saw the drawing. The terminal test for both groups showed only the letters, for which the students were to supply the drawings. The researcher found that the second procedure, which combined confirmation and prompting, was better than the prompting procedure alone. They concluded that there can be too much prompting and that a mixture of prompted and unprompted trials (we could say *frames*) is superior. This finding, you will see, is consistent with the practice of programers of withdrawing prompts from the later program frames.

Prompts have two basic purposes: They guide the student to the correct response without overcontrolling his behavior, and they prevent the student from making unnecessary errors. These purposes suggest that you must avoid both overprompting and underprompting in writing your frames. A common source of overprompting is the *copying frame,* in which the student is asked to make a response given in the frame. Figure 12-12 shows a copying frame. In it the student need only copy the important word to respond correctly. The copying frame is a means for producing the response the first time and is useful as an introductory frame. Since it displays the full response, however, it is not a form of prompting. Julian Taber and his associates (1965) believe that copying frames are overused by many programers. Susan Markle (1964) believes that they can be an insult to students. The chief disadvantage is that the student can make correct verbatim responses which he conceptually does not understand. Margulies (1964) shows how a copying frame can be improved. Frame 1 is the copying frame, and frame 2 is the improved version (Fig. 12-13). The use of copying frames tends to make a program dull and to reduce the amount of student learning. It is not

A *compound* word is made up of *two words.* The word *ballroom* is made of two root words, *ball* and *room,* so ballroom is a ______ word.

Response: compound

Fig. 12-12. *A copying frame (after Taber* et al., *1965, p. 95).*

Frame 1	All Gaul was broken into THREE divisions. Thus Gaul consisted of t- - - - parts.
	Response: T(hree)
Frame 2	Gaul was divided into parts occupied by the Celts, the Belgae, and the Aquitani. Into how many parts was Gaul divided? ________
	Response: Three

Fig. 12-13. *Revision of a copying frame (after Margulies, 1964, p. 7).*

uncommon that students respond correctly to all the frames in a program and still fail to answer correctly questions on the test of terminal behavior. Such a result is usually the result of overprompting and of the liberal use of copying frames.

You are now ready to learn about the two types of prompts which Skinner (1957) distinguishes as *formal* and *thematic.* The formal prompt (Fig. 12-14) provides the student with part of the response. The term *formal* derives from the fact that the prompt supplies some of form of the desired response. Skinner compares the use of this prompt to the function of the theater prompter, who gives the first few words of a forgotten line to the actor. Taber and his associates (1965) distinguish four types of formal prompts, all of which you can use in the construction of your frames: partial-response prompts, rhyming prompts, literal prompts, and frame-structure prompts. Figure 12-14 illustrates a partial-response prompt, in which part of the desired response is given (*rein*). Figure 12-15

To reward an organism with food is to rein____________ it with food.

Response: rein(force)

Fig. 12-14. *Example of a formal prompt (after Taber* et al., *1965, p. 93).*

9 times 7 and just 1 more, is 8 times 8 or ______.

Response: 64

Fig. 12-15. *A rhyming prompt (after Skinner, 1958, p. 972).*

12
12 t w e l v e 12
12

12 twelve 12

12
twelve
12

twelve 12

twelve

Fig. 12-16. *A series of frames showing the gradual withdrawal of literal prompts (after Taber* et al., *1965, p. 98).*

illustrates a rhyming prompt, which provides the student with the wor which rhymes with the correct answer. The literal prompt evokes single response in the presence of several appropriate stimuli. Figur 12-16 shows how the figure 12 is gradually replaced with the wor *twelve* in a program designed to teach children to respond to numbers written words. The number prompt is removed over a series of frames until the child can orally respond to the written word alone. The figure is also a good illustration of the gradual withdrawal of prompts from later program frames. The use of literal prompts is an example of discriminative transfer of learning (Taber and Glaser, 1962). The child learns to distinguish the written form of a number from the written form of other numbers by gradually learning to transfer his identification of the numerical form to the written form.

One final formal prompt is sometimes called *frame-structure prompting* (Taber *et al.,* 1965). These prompts use boldface type, underlining, and dashes to indicate the number of letters missing in a word. Grammatical usage can also be a formal prompt when the article (a, an), plurality, and verb tense cue the correct response. It is also possible to arrange the stimulus materials in the frame in such a way as to prompt the response (as in frame 3 of Fig. 12-17). Figure 12-17 illustrates the use or some frame-structure prompts. Like copying frames, formal prompts must be used with care. They are artificial and tend to distract the student from what he should be learning. Their use often leads to overprompting, which, in turn, leads to correct frame responses and incorrect test responses. Formal prompts are generally most useful early in the program. As the program develops they should be replaced with thematic

Frame 1 Chair factories - - - - - - - - - - - chairs.

Response: manufacture

Frame 2 Greece is a *peninsula* in the Mediterranean Sea.
Florida is a ________ in the Atlantic Ocean.

Response: peninsula

Frame 3
$5 \times 5 = 25$
$5 \times 6 = 30$
$5 \times 7 = 35$
$5 \times \quad = 40$

Response: 8

Fig. 12-17. *Examples of frame-structure prompts (after Taber* et al., *1965, pp. 100–101).*

prompts. Ingenious programers are able to construct programs without the use of formal prompts.

The second type of prompt, the thematic prompt, depends on the student's previous associations of a word or phrase since they derive from the denotations and connotations of the words which compose them. They inform the student about the correct response without revealing the form of that response. Although very little research supports the use of thematic prompts, their use is very similar to the use of mediators in verbal learning. In fact, it may be very helpful to view the use of thematic prompts as the study of the effects of introducing verbal mediators into the instructional process. Figure 12-18 shows the use of a thematic prompt. In this example the thematic prompt is *man's best friend,* a familiar association for most people with *dog.* Markle (1964) and Taber

Canis familiaris is man's best friend. *Canis familiaris* is a technical name for the animal called a ______.

Response: dog

Fig. 12-18. *Example of a thematic prompt (after Markle, 1961, p. 7).*

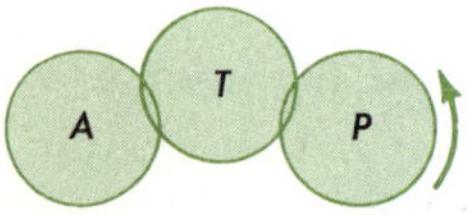

Friction wheel *A* is revolving in a ______________ wise direction.

Response: counterclock(wise)

Fig. 12-19. *A frame with a picture to suggest the correct response (after Taber* et al., *1964, p. 102).*

HEARING

The brain "makes sense" out of the impulses carried from the cochlea by the ______ nerve.

Response: auditory

Fig. 12-20. *A context-setting prompt (after Taber* et al., *1965, p. 102).*

and his associates (1965) have developed a taxonomy, or classification, of thematic prompts. Some of these are (1) pictures, (2) context settings, (3) synonyms and antonyms, (4) analogies, (5) rules, and (6) inductive prompts. Figure 12-19 shows how a picture may suggest the correct answer to a frame. In Fig. 12-20 you see how suggesting the context *hearing* limits the range of possible answers. In Fig. 12-21 you see how antonyms (frame 1) and synonyms (frame 2) are used to prompt the correct responses. In Fig. 12-22 you see how one or more analogies can be presented in a frame and followed by an incomplete analogy to which the student responds. In Fig. 12-23 you see how a rule can serve as a prompt. The rule is the first line of the frame. The next two lines are incomplete examples of the rule which the student completes by correctly applying the rule.

A sophisticated thematic prompt which I shall call the *inductive* prompt requires the stimulus materials to be arranged within the frame in such a way as to lead the student to induce a relationship not explicitly described. Figure 12-24 shows two examples of inductive prompts. In the first frame, the word *also* prompts the correct response (which the student induces). In the second frame, the juxtaposition of the two physical principles provides the student with the basis for inducing their proper relationship.

Thematic prompts add interest and challenge to program frames. Most programers shift from the use of formal to the use of thematic

Frame 1 Learning usually occurs when an individual's response is promptly rewarded or ________.

Response: reinforced

Frame 2 Reinforcement which consists of presenting sought-after stimuli is called positive reinforcement; reinforcement which consists of terminating unpleasant stimuli (e.g., loud noise) is called ________ reinforcement.

Response: negative

Fig. 12-21. *Antonyms and synonyms as prompts (after Holland and Skinner, 1961).*

Frame 1	It is easy to learn about the metric system when one thinks of the money system in relation to it. A dollar has ______ cents (pennies). **Response: 100**
Frame 2	A dollar has 100 cents. A meter has ______ centimeters. **Response: 100**
Frame 3	Thus, a centimeter works somewhat like a cent. Just as 100 cents is 1 dollar, 100 centimeters is ______. **Response: 1 meter**

Fig. 12-22. *Incomplete analogy as a prompt (after Taber* et al., *1965, p. 106).*

$a + b = b + a$
$7 + 2 =$ ______
$3.4 + 8.6 =$ ______

Responses: 9, 12

Fig. 12-23. *A rule as a prompt (after Evans, Glaser, and Homme, 1962, p. 513).*

prompts as they construct the later frames of their programs. Although, as I have noted, little research supports the use of thematic prompts, it has often been reported that programs which skillfully use them enable students to obtain high scores on the tests of terminal behavior. At present we have at least some pragmatic evidence of their usefulness.

The use of prompts to guide student responses requires you to withdraw these prompts so that the student can eventually emit the terminal behavior without supporting cues. The gradual removal of prompts is called *vanishing,* or *fading.* One of the best examples of vanishing is the use of the literal prompt in Fig. 12-16, in which the figure 12 is gradually replaced with the word *twelve.* Figure 12-25 shows how the letter prompts for the word *manufacture* are gradually withdrawn. In this example the these dashes could be replaced with a solid line, thereby vanishing the dashes as formal prompts.

Frame 1	Centigrade and Fahrenheit are both scales of temperature. Kelvin is also a ______. **Response: scale of temperature**
Frame 2	Knowing that most metals expand when heated, and remembering that the period of a pendulum depends on the length of the rod, we would expect that a pendulum clock would ______ time on a cold day. **Response: lose**

Fig. 12-24. *Examples illustrating inductive prompts (after Klaus, 1961, p. 141).*

Fig. 12-25. *Withdrawal of prompts (after Skinner, 1958, p. 972).*

Frame 1	Manufacture means to make or build. Chair factories manufacture chairs. Copy the word here. - - - - - - - - - - - -
Frame 2	Part of the word is like part of the word *factory*. Both parts come from an old word meaning *make* or *build*. m a n u _ _ _ _ u r e
Frame 3	Part of the word is like part of the word *manual*. Both parts come from an old word for *hand*. Many things used to be made by hand. _ _ _ _ f a c t u r e
Frame 4	The same letter goes in both spaces: m _ n u f _ c t u r e
Frame 5	The same letter goes in both spaces: m a n _ f a c t _ r e
Frame 6	Chair factories _ _ _ _ _ _ _ _ _ _ _ _ chairs.

Provide careful sequencing of the frames. The sequence, or order, in which your frames appear depends upon two factors: the description and analysis of the behaviors your program intends to teach and the conditions necessary for the learning required by the various tasks. The sequences described in Part 4 of this book should guide your ordering of the program frames. Figure 12-26 shows how Mechner (1965) developed

Fig. 12-26. *Program frames for reading electrocardiograms and their relationship to the behavioral analysis (after Mechner, 1965, pp. 469–71).*

Questions | Answers

1

The diagram below, taken from the Lead I tracing of a normal subject, shows the standard deflections of the electrocardiogram.

Label the five deflections,
using the conventional letters *P, Q, R, S,* and *T*:
Circle the *QRS* complex.
The *T* wave is ☐ positive ☐ negative

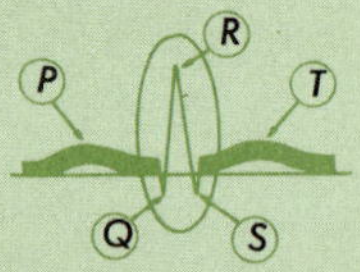

positive

Explanation of the relationship of frame 2 to the behavioral analysis

The *QRS* complex is discriminated from other portions of the tracing.

The *T* wave is discriminated from other portions of the tracing.

The positivity of the *T* wave is discriminated from the possible negativity of the *T* wave.

2

The Q, R, and S waves are defined as follows:
The Q wave is the negative (downward) deflection which initiates the QRS complex.
The R wave is the positive (upward) deflection of the QRS complex.
The S wave is the negative deflection immediately following the R wave.

In each *QRS* complex below, label the Q, R, and S waves if they are present:

(example)

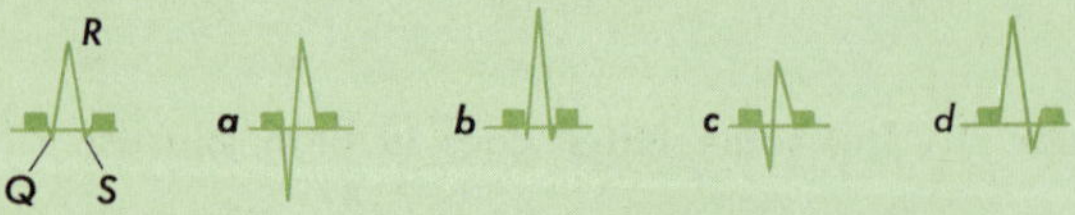

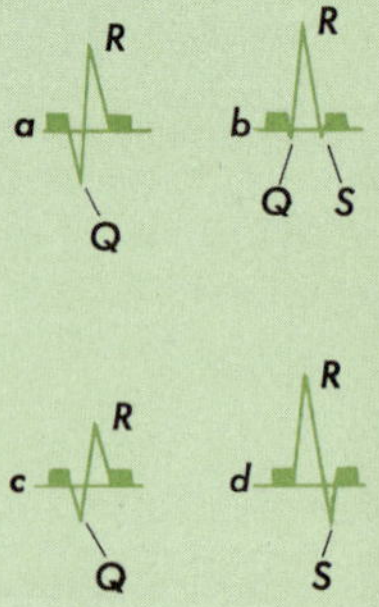

Explanation of the relationship of frame 1 to the behavioral analysis

The student generalizes among different types of Q waves, *R* waves, and *S* waves.

The student discriminates between Q waves, *R* waves, and *S* waves.

Thus, the concepts of the Q wave, the *R* wave, and the *S* wave are formed.

3 *A Q wave wider than one standard division, i.e., longer than 0.04 second in duration, is considered abnormal.*

Under each diagram, indicate whether the Q wave is normal or abnormal:

(a)	(b)	(c)	(d)	(e)
☐ normal	☐ normal	☐ normal	☐ normal	☐ normal
☐ abnormal	☐ abnormal	☐ abnormal	☐ abnormal	☐ abnormal

(a) abnormal
(b) normal
(c) abnormal
(d) abnormal
(e) normal

Explanation of the relationship of frame 3 to the behavioral analysis

Again, the student discriminates the Q wave from other portions of the tracing, thus strengthening his concept of the Q wave.

The student discriminates between Q waves wider than 0.04 second and Q waves narrower than 0.04 second.

Two links of the chain are formed:

"Q wave wider than 0.04 second" ⟶ "abnormal"
"Q wave narrower than 0.04 second" ⟶ "normal"

4 *The S-T segment begins at the end of the QRS complex and ends at the beginning of the T wave. An elevated S-T segment is abnormal.*

For each diagram below, indicate whether the *S-T* segment is normal or abnormal:

(a) *S-T* segment elevated
☐ normal
☐ abnormal

(a)
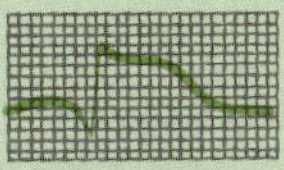

(b) *S-T* segment isoelectric
☐ normal
☐ abnormal

(b)
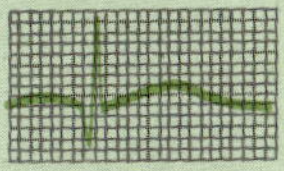

(c) *S-T* segment ☐ elevated ☐ isoelectric
☐ normal
☐ abnormal

(c)
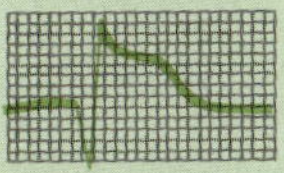

(d) *S-T* segment ☐ elevated ☐ isoelectric
☐ normal
☐ abnormal

(d)
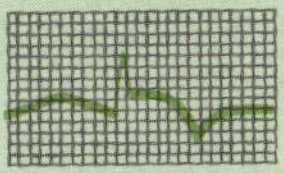

(e) *S-T* segment ☐ elevated ☐ isoelectric
☐ normal
☐ abnormal

(e)
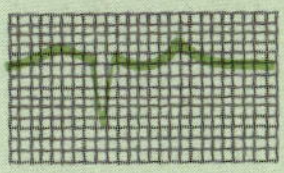

(a) abnormal
(b) normal
(c) elevated
abnormal
(d) elevated
abnormal
(e) isoelectric
normal

Explanation of the relationship of frame 4 to the behavioral analysis

The student discriminates the *S-T* segment from other parts of the tracing.

He generalizes among different kinds of *S-T* segments.

This strengthens the concept of the *S-T* segment.

The student discriminates between elevated and isoelectric *S-T* segments.

He generalizes among different kinds of elevated *S-T* segments.

This strengthens the concept of the elevated *S-T* segment.

Two links in the chain are formed:

"*S-T* segment is elevated" ⟶ "abnormal"
"*S-T* segment is isoelectric" ⟶ "normal"

5

Referring to the diagrams in the panel below, check the correct box:

a. An elevated *S-T* segment suggests .... ☐ ischemia ☐ injury ☐ infarction.

b. A negative *T* wave suggests .... ☐ ischemia ☐ injury ☐ infarction.

c. An abnormally wide Q wave suggests .. ☐ ischemia ☐ injury ☐ infarction.

These diagrams show the ECG changes which, in various combinations, may be observed in myocardial infarction.

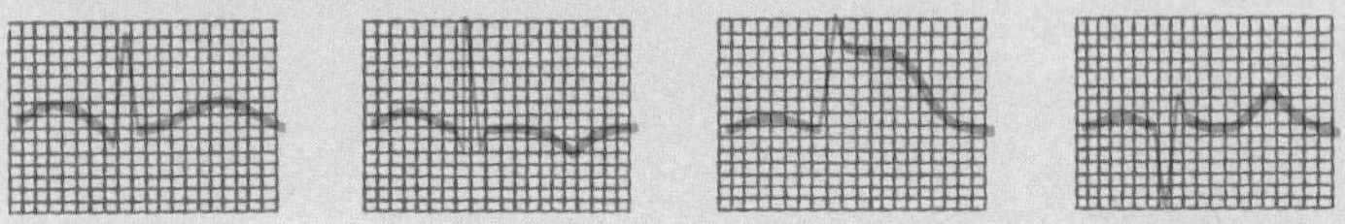

(a) injury
(b) ischemia
(c) infarction

Explanation of the relationship of frame 5 to the behavioral analysis

(a) The student discriminates between an elevated *S-T* segment and the normal *S-T* segment.

The chain link:

"elevated *S-T* segment" ⟶ "injury"

is strengthened, this time with omission of the auxiliary mediating link:

"elevated *S-T* segment" ⟶ "abnormal"

(b) The student discriminates between a negative and a normal *T* wave.

The chain link:

"negative *T* wave" ⟶ "ischemia"

is strengthened.

(c) The student discriminates between an abnormally wide Q wave and a normal Q wave.

The chain link:

"abnormally wide Q wave" ⟶ "infarction"

is strengthened, this time with omission of the auxiliary mediating link:

"abnormally wide Q wave" ⟶ "abnormal"

6 Again referring to the above diagrams, check the correct box:

(a) The difference between the pattern of infarction and the normal pattern is the
☐ negative *T* wave ☐ elevated *S-T* segment ☐ abnormally wide Q wave

(b) The difference between the pattern of injury and the normal pattern is the
☐ negative *T* wave ☐ elevated *S-T* segment ☐ abnormally wide Q wave

(c) The difference between the pattern of ischemia and the normal pattern is the
☐ negative *T* wave ☐ elevated *S-T* segment ☐ abnormally wide Q wave

(a) abnormally wide Q wave
(b) elevated *S-T* segment
(c) negative *T* wave

Explanation of the relationship of frame 6 to the behavioral analysis

The chain links:

"tracing showing an infarction pattern" ⟶ "abnormally wide Q wave"

"tracing showing an injury pattern" ⟶ "negative *T* wave"

and

"tracing showing an ischemia pattern" ⟶ "elevated *S-T* segment"

are formed.

dashes and the letters are formal prompts. The letters are gradually faded until only the number of dashes remains as the formal prompt. Even a sequence of frames for teaching students how to diagnose Lead 1 tracings in an electrocardiogram as ischemia, injury, or infarction. In effect the students were learning three classes of patterns, or tracings, or, we can now say, they were learning three concepts. Figure 12-26 shows not only the program frames but also the relationship of the frames to the prior task analysis which Mechner made and to the learning principles which he selected as the bases for frame construction and sequencing.

It is even possible to develop frames which engage the student in problem solving and discovery learning. The frames which use inductive prompts (see Fig. 12-24 again) are simple illustrations of discovery learning. Kersh (1964, 1965) developed a programed-discovery procedure which prescribed conditions under which the student engaged in searching behavior and which specified occasions for the teacher to give verbal approval to the student for the searching behavior he exhibited as he progressed through the program. Martin Covington (1967) developed a program which fostered originality in visual and other types of problem solving.

All the basic learning conditions—discrimination, generalization, contiguity, practice, and reinforcement—can be embodied in the frame sequences. Frame sequences, of course, can also provide for review and testing whenever these are necessary. One of the major advantages for educational psychologists in studying programed instruction is the freedom allowed in manipulating the basic learning conditions.

Summary. I have described these five steps for the preparation of your program:

1. Present the material in frames.
2. Require active responding.
3. Provide for confirmation or correction of responses.
4. Use prompts to guide student responses.
5. Provide careful sequencing of the frames.

With the first draft of your frames and their arrangement in some sequence you are now ready to proceed to the awesome next phase in the development of your program—tryout and revision.

Tryout and Revision

I have divided the third stage of program development into three steps. The first requires you to develop the first draft of the program while working quite closely with your students. The second step requires you to edit the program on the basis of the original tryout with these students. The third step requires you to revise the program on the basis of terminal-test performance and student responses to the program frames.

WRITE THE ORIGINAL DRAFT. The original frames, I suggested, should be typed on large index cards, with the correct response on the back of the card. At this stage you should not try to produce highly polished frames. After you have written from fifty to one hundred, you should try them out on five to ten students. Thomas Gilbert (1960, p. 480) suggests that you work closely with each student in this stage of program development.

> Take your first crude effort to the student. Remember, he is going to teach you. The student cannot fail. If he doesn't get where you want him to go, you have failed. Try something else. In the absence of anything better, let him be your guide. If you come to a dead end, vary your approach until you have gotten him to where you want him to go. Tape record all sessions. The important thing to remember is to keep varying your behavior until you are successful and to describe what you do. . . . Take your time. Education has been waiting for you since the dawn of history.

In using the index cards, the student should read the frame and turn the card for confirmation or correction. Find out where he makes his mistakes and what you can do about it. According to Gilbert, the mistakes are really yours (or your program's). You have let the student down! Revise the frames or frame sequence until the student learns from them what he is supposed to learn. Gilbert suggests that the first tryouts occur before you have developed the program very far. Once you have invested great time and effort in frame writing, you will have an understandable (but not entirely forgivable) reluctance to make the necessary revisions. At this stage you should try your program on one student at a time and try the revisions you make for one student with the next student.

EDIT THE ORIGINAL DRAFT. Markle (1964) has developed a checklist for the first drafts of the program. This is an abbreviated version: (1) Frames should be written clearly in good English. (2) What is said should be correct. (3) The response required of the student should be relevant to the purpose of the frame. If the student is to learn to do something, you should make him do it rather than talk about doing it. (4) If you use a multiple-choice question, the alternatives should be feasible answers. (5) Frames should contain sufficient context to make clear what is being presented and what is wanted. (6) You should not include more points than the student can respond to in one frame. (7) You should eliminate irrelevant material. (8) In concept teaching, you should provide a representative sample of illustrations and provide for negative examples as well. (8) You should make liberal use of thematic prompts and sparing use of formal prompts. (9) You should make the steps (frames) toward mastery as large as the student can reasonably be expected to make. Let testing tell you when the step is too large. (10) The testing should tell you how much practice and prompting to provide.

TRY OUT AND REVISE. After this editing, you have what Pipe (1966) calls a *fledgling* program to try out. It should be neatly typed and carefully duplicated. You will need about fifteen to forty or more students—but use as many (or as few) as you have. When you administer your program this time, resist any impulse to intervene. The program must now assume the full instructional responsibility. You can supply the students with paper which bears numbered blanks. On these they can check the frames which give them difficulty and give a description of the difficulty. You can also record any questions they ask while studying the program. After finishing the program, the students should take the test of terminal behavior. The students' response records will reveal which frames were missed. From these records you can make a list of common errors. If you group the items of the test by subunits, you can also determine which sections of the program were ineffective. High error rates on particular frames or particular sections indicate a need for revision. The conventional standard has been the 10 per cent error rate. Finally, if you require the students to annotate their copies of the program, their comments can also guide your revision.

SUMMARY. I have described three steps for the tryout-and-revision stage of your program development:

1. Write the original draft.
2. Edit the draft.
3. Try out the edited draft and revise it.

This concludes our description of program writing. Are you now ready to begin the preparation of your own program?

Types of Programs

In this part of the chapter I will distinguish among three types of programs: linear, branching, and adjunct autoinstructional. Each of these has had its eminent creators and followers. Skinner (1958, 1961) not only invented but also eloquently argued for the superiority of the linear program. Norman Crowder (1963a, b) created and stoutly defended the branching program. Sidney Pressey (1963, 1964), who is not sure that either linear or branching programs do anything but make the printed page more difficult to read, has argued for adjunct, or auxiliary, practice materials to accompany conventional texts.

David Klaus (1965) believes that these programs may not be so distinct as their proponents once believed and enunciated. For Klaus, a more useful distinction is between response-centered and stimulus-centered programs. A *response-centered program,* in its purest form, might consist of nothing more than the repetitive opportunities for practicing approximations of the terminal behavior until mastery has been achieved. This is simply trial-and-error learning—that which occurs when the child first begins to draw with crayons and paper. A *stimulus-centered program,* in its purest form, might be limited completely to the presentation of information to the learner. James Holland (1960) succinctly describes the response-centered position when he states, "Behavior is learned only when it is emitted and reinforced." Raymond Hatch (1961, p. 76) expresses the stimulus-centered position when he states, "Learning is presumed to take place at the point of information dissemination, prior to the response." We shall apply the distinction between response-centered and stimulus-centered programs in describing the three types of programs.

LINEAR PROGRAMS. In this program all the students read and respond to the same frames. The program is linear in that there is a single line or path for all students to follow. Figure 12-27 diagrams a linear program. Each circle is a frame, and the student simply proceeds from one frame to the next until he completes the program. Most linear programs use the constructed (or fill-in) response. Most of the frames we used as illustrations in the previous part of this chapter are frames of linear programs. Many new programs, however, use both constructed and multiple-choice responses. The frames in Fig. 12-26 above (Mechner, 1965), for example, use both forms of response. In fact, the appearance of the correct response in the list of alternatives in a multiple-choice question acts as a useful prompt (Markle, 1964). Although most linear programs use shorter frames than those used by the branching programs I describe below, the

Fig. 12-27. *Diagram of a linear program.*

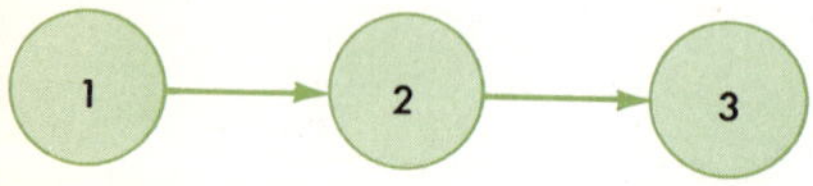

single-sentence or short frame is not an essential characteristic of linear programs. Markle (1964) developed a linear program on programing which contained frames which were paragraphs or longer in length. Even the major characteristic of linear programs—the use of the single path—is no longer rigidly prescribed. Lysaught and Williams (1963) show many ways in which a linear program can be modified into a multipath program. An interesting variation is the linear program with criterion frames. These frames test entering behavior at various points in the program to determine whether the student should go through the sequence of frames which follows. If this procedure is not necessary, the student is directed to a subsequence, which will move him quickly to an advanced point in the program. Figure 12-28 is a diagram of a linear program with a criterion frame and a subsequence.

The linear program is generally response-centered. In each frame only enough material is presented to evoke the correct responses and to permit the reinforcement of each response. However, linear programs which present large segments of material and require the student to re-

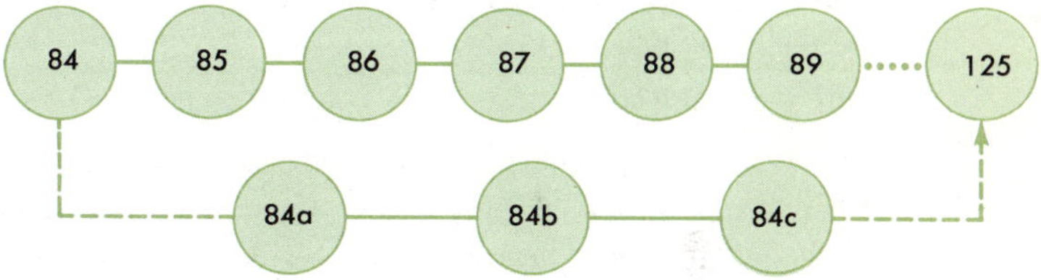

84. Let's see if you have had some experience with the Greek alphabet. Write out the first five letters of that alphabet in proper order—use Greek letters and equivalent English spellings (small letters, not caps).

84. alpha—α
beta—β
gamma—γ
delta—δ
epsilon—ϵ

If right, go on to item 84a. If you made an error, or if you are not sure of Greek letters, go to item 85.

Fig. 12-28. *Diagram of linear program with criterion frame. Frame 84 is the criterion frame (after Lysaught and Williams, 1963, p. 80).*

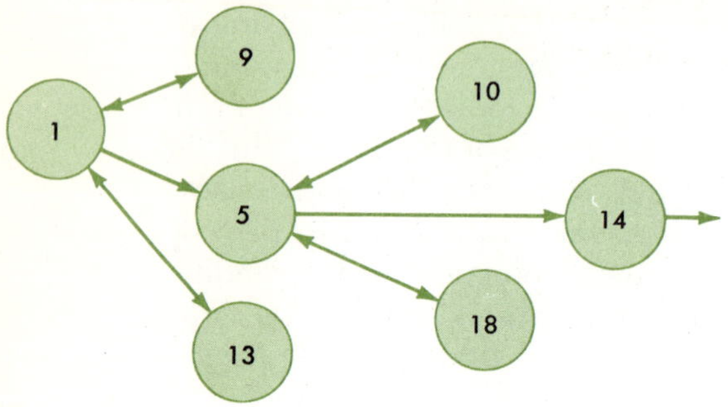

Fig. 12-29. *Diagram of a branching (intrinsic) program (after Lysaught and Williams, 1963, p. 82).*

spond to only part of this material are not response-centered. In such programs the emphasis is on the organized presentation of material rather than on the responses the students make to this material. Branching programs (described below) tend to emphasize the presentation of material rather than the students' detailed responses to this material and are, therefore, generally stimulus-centered programs.

BRANCHING PROGRAMS. In this program the student proceeds to the next frame until he makes an error. The errors branch him to supplementary material designed to give him remedial instruction. The best-known branching technique was developed by Crowder (1960) and is called *intrinsic programing*. It consists of rather long frames which often appear as pages in an ordinary textbook. The student reads the page (or frame) and then responds by selecting the correct alternative in a three-alternative multiple-choice item. Each alternative is associated with a page number which directs the student to another frame. The correct response directs the student to a frame which confirms his response and introduces a segment of new material. Figure 12-29 diagrams an intrinsic program. In this diagram the main sequence (if you make no errors) is frames 1, 5, and 14. Depending on the errors you make in answering the multiple-choice items, you are branched along various paths. Frame 1 has two branches, frames 9 and 13. Frame 5 has two branches, frames 10 and 18. When the frames of a branching program are presented in book form (one frame per page), the book is called a scrambled book. The pages in such a book cannot be read consecutively but only in response to the frames of the program.

COMPARISON OF LINEAR AND BRANCHING PROGRAMS. There has been both considerable argument and research on the relative merits of linear and branching programs. Crowder (1963a) argues that the branching program allows much better adaptation to differences in entering behavior. His intrinsic program, he contends, is an effort to capitalize on these individual differences and to tailor the instruction to them by supplying the student with the remedial materials he needs. The student is spared the necessity of responding to frames which present material he has already mastered and the agony of failing to master new material because of inadequate entering behavior. Adherents of linear programs point out that in actual composition the branching program may have more frames than a parallel linear program does. They claim that in linear programs the student acquires the terminal behavior with fewer errors, with greater interest, and in less time. Most branching programs introduce very limited flexibility into the sequencing of the frames—in actuality they accommodate a very limited range of entering behavior. To provide the required flexibility, it is necessary to use computer-assisted instruction, which can constantly modify the instructional program on the basis of each response of the individual student.

Research has not supported the claims of superiority for either linear or branching programs. Illustrative of these studies is that of Harry Silberman and his associates (1961). They compared the use of linear sequences and branching sequences in teaching high school students logic. The use of a particular sequence was determined by the errors made during the teaching session. In the branching sequences the computer selected items for each student based upon the errors he made in responding. The experiment was designed so that pairs of subjects in both groups received identical sequences of frames. As is typical in experiments which have made this comparison, no significant differences in student achievement were found.

The decision to prepare and use either branching or linear programs should not be based on ideological belief or personal preferences. It must be based on the requirements of the instructional objectives, the entering behavior of the students, and the conditions for particular types of learning. It is quite possible, and indeed increasingly common, that programs include both linear and branching sequences. You saw an example of a mixed program in the diagram in Fig. 12-28. In other words, the programer may decide that at various points in the instruction he should shift from a stimulus-centered to a response-centered presentation of materials or vice versa. Neither linear nor branching programs are pure program types, and only the requirements of the instructional situation should determine whether they be used in isolation or in conjunction.

Adjunct autoinstruction. Pressey, in numerous articles, argues for a less drastic alteration of the learning situation than that produced by programed instruction. This program, adjunct autoinstruction, inserts programed or testing materials into a textbook, laboratory manual, or other materials whenever these supplementary materials are needed. He argues (p. 363) that the textbook writer or the teacher ought to be heard first:

> In a well-organized book, written at a level suitable for its users, elucidative autoinstruction might well be most effective and integrative if placed at the end of each chapter. Or there might be clusters of autoinstructional items at whatever places in the chapter they seem to be needed. Experienced teachers will know fairly well (and informal experimenting and check-up "quizzes" will show more definitely) when and where such material is needed; points where it is needed can be located with greater precision in such subjects as arithmetic and science.

In Pressey's opinion, the conventional instructional materials should carry the main burden of instruction and the programed materials should tackle only that material which is potentially difficult and confusing. His emphasis on the need to organize well the initial presentation of subject matter is consistent with Ausubel's notion of advance organizers, or the presentation of the basic principles of the subject matter followed by its detailed treatment. Pressey objects to the fragmentation of material which occurs when it is broken into frames. In one informal study, Pressey (1964) rewrote all the content material in a 1,100-word program by Holland and Skinner (1961) into a succinct statement of 360 words. This abbreviated statement was read in a median time of one and one-half minutes compared with the twenty-three minutes needed to read the original program. The students who merely read the short statement did as well on an essay test as students who had been through the Holland-Skinner program. There is considerable practical appeal in Pressey's suggestion for adjunct autoinstruction in that it permits the combination of both an expository and a programing style of teaching. To some extent I have adopted adjunct programing in this book by embedding questions within the text at points where they may be most useful for the student. By combining teaching styles, adjunct autoinstruction provides a way for the teacher to shift from stimulus-centered to response-centered instruction.

Summary. You have seen that the three programs—linear, branching, and adjunct—are not pure program types and that they can combine in various ways to meet the requirements of the instructional situation. Although the linear program is more response-centered and the branching program more stimulus-centered, it is fairly easy to shift from one to the other. It is possible, in other words, to add branches to the linear program and to add linear subsequences to the branching program. You have also seen that adjunct autoinstruction provides a way of shifting between expository and programed teaching procedures. At this phase in the development of programed instruction, the overlap in these three programs may be more significant and useful than their lines of demarcation.

The Selection of Programs

Since you cannot write all the programs you may like to use with your students and since more and more published programs are becoming available for school use, you should learn particular criteria to use in the selection of programs. A most helpful booklet for this purpose is *A Guide to Evaluating Self-Instructional Programs* by Paul Jacobs, Milton Maier, and Stolurow (1966). They have developed the following checklist to guide your selection process (p. 28):

A CHECKLIST FOR EVALUATING A SELF-INSTRUCTIONAL PROGRAM

	Yes	No
Is it really programed instructional material?	______	______
How does the program fit into the curriculum?		
A. Does it cover the appropriate topics?	______	______
B. Does it develop the appropriate skills and knowledge?	______	______
C. Is it at the appropriate difficulty level?	______	______
How well would the program teach in your situation?		
A. Are the conditions under which the available data were collected relevant to your situation?	______	______
B. How well does the program meet your objectives?	______	______
Can you afford it?	______	______

IS IT REALLY PROGRAMED MATERIAL? To find the material with which to begin your selection process you should consult *Programed Instruction Materials, 1964–65,* a guide published by the Institute of Educational Technology of Teachers College, Columbia University, and edited by Kenneth Komoski. Figure 12-30 shows the subject matter of the programs for the three periods in which the guide has been published. You can see a significant decrease in the number of programs published from

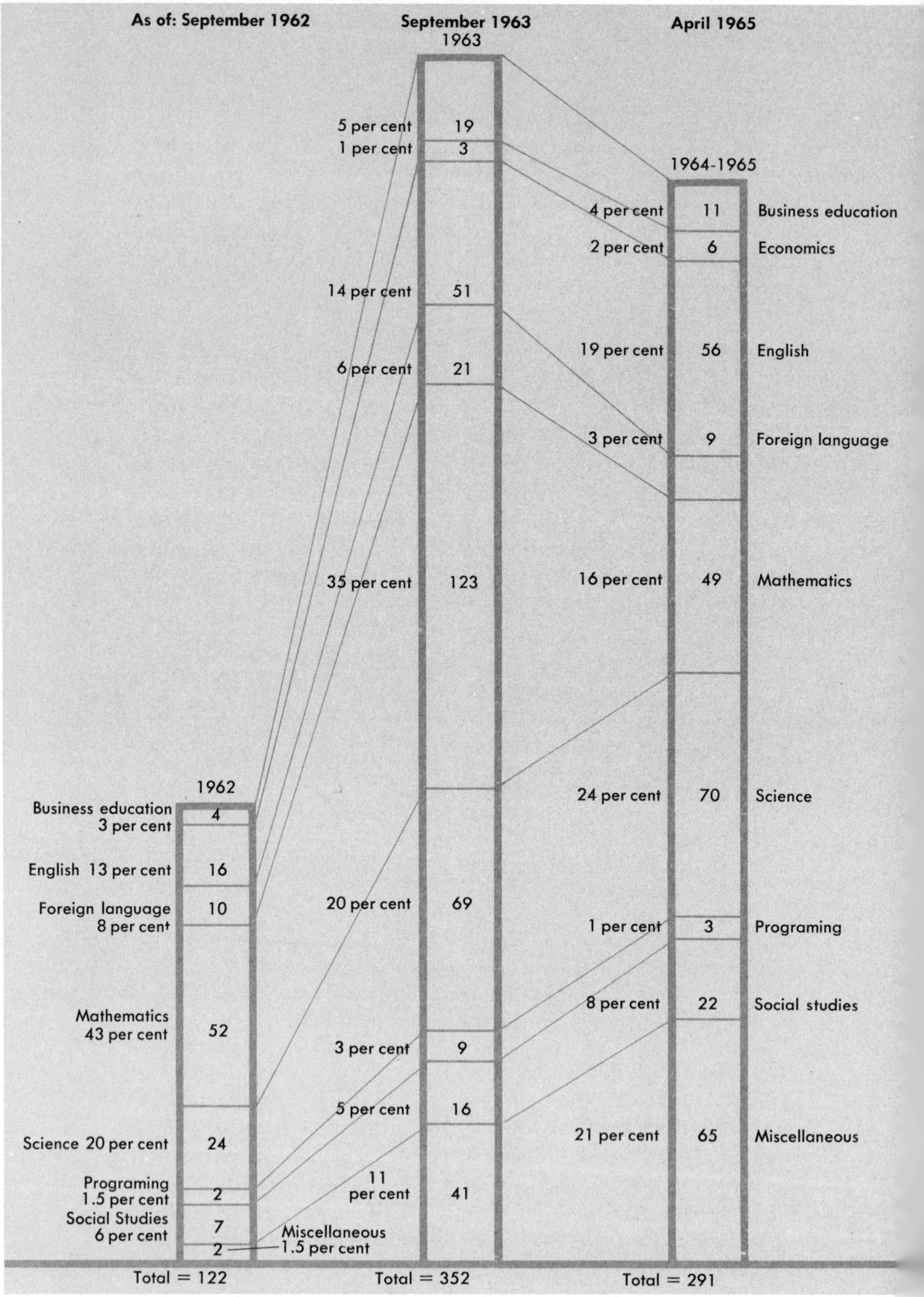

Fig. 12-30. *A comparison of content of programs available for purchase as of: September 1962, September 1963, and April 1965 (after Komoski, 1965, Fig. 1).*

1963 to 1965, except perhaps in the field of the natural and social sciences.

To determine whether the material is really programed, you should apply the definition of programed instruction and materials on p. 487. Essential characteristics are the presentation of material in the form of frames, the provision for student response, and the confirmation or correction of the response. The program should also allow the student to progress through the materials at his own pace.

HOW DOES THE PROGRAM FIT INTO THE CURRICULUM? To answer this question, you must first ask whether the program covers the appropriate topics. It may be based on knowledge which you consider irrelevant, trivial, or outmoded. An inspection of the tables of contents and the sources upon which the program is based provides information on the suitability of the subject matter. The program manual should also provide a detailed summary of the topics the program covers. Second, you must determine whether the program develops the necessary skills and knowledge. A program on fractions, as Jacobs and his associates (1966) point out, could teach students to derive these concepts from formal proof or, more simply, could present them with rules and an opportunity to practice the application of the rules. They suggest that you look at the frames within the program which measure terminal behavior. Sometimes these frames are listed within the program manual. They are, in effect, a statement of the behavioral objectives of the program. Another way to discover the skills and knowledge the program teaches is to examine the items on the achievement test. These items reveal the things the students are expected to know and do after completing the program. Sometimes the publisher may classify the terminal frames and the test items according to skills and knowledge, using taxonomies like those described in Chapter 2. This classification will give you the information you need on the skills and knowledge developed by the program. Third, you must ask whether the program is at the appropriate level of difficulty. You can use three sources of information to answer this question: teachers who have used the program, statements in the manual about age and grade levels, and readability formulas.

HOW WELL WILL THE PROGRAM TEACH IN YOUR SITUATION? This is the third major question on the checklist. The manual which accompanies the program should show that the program has been tried out with typical student groups and should report four kinds of information: changes in student achievement, amount of time to complete the program, percentage of errors for each frame, and student attitudes. The most important information is the amount of change in student achievement. If the manual reports achievement scores for different IQ levels and if you have the IQ scores of your students, you should be able to predict fairly well how much your students will learn from the program. Because some students require varying amounts of time, the manual should indicate how time scores are related to IQ and achievement test scores. As for error rate, the best indication of how much your students will learn is not the error rate for the frames but the results of the test of terminal behavior. Both sources of data, however, can indicate where the program fails to teach and where remedial instruction is required. Finally, the manual should provide information about the students' reactions to the program. Their attitudes after instruction should be compared with their attitudes before. Attitude data should be correlated with IQ and achievement test scores.

As indicated in the checklist, you must now apply this manual information on IQ, achievement, and attitudes to your own students. If, for example, your students are radically different in ability and attitude, the program may be quite unsuitable. The more similar your teaching conditions are to those under which the program was tested and developed, the more confidently you can predict the results of using the program. Finally, you must decide how well the program meets your instructional objectives. Here you must compare the program with alternative instructional materials on the combined basis of achievement, time scores, error rates, and attitudes.

CAN YOU AFFORD IT? Joseph Rigney and Edward Fry (1961) list a number of items which determine the cost of using a program. Among these items are the following: (1) cost per unit (including each program, student, and machine); (2) initial and long-term investment; (3) training time per student; (4) quality of student and instructor required; and (5) logistics (including space, power, maintenance, program reusability, and useful life).

SUMMARY. Using the checklist developed by Jacobs and his associates (1966), I have described several questions you can raise in determining the suitability of published programs for your instructional objectives and for your students. You must determine whether the published material is really programed, how the program fits into your curriculum, how well it will teach in your situation, and how much it will cost. The manual which accompanies the program, if it is complete, should provide the information which will enable you to answer most of these questions. It will still be your responsibility to apply this information to your students and curriculum to determine the degree of fit, or matching, between the conditions under which the program was developed and tested and the conditions under which you will use it.

You should now return to objectives 3–17 (pp. 485–86) and determine how well you have achieved them.

QUESTION 12-1

Inspect the following frames and answer the questions below.*
Frame 1: Pegasus had two _______.
Frame 2: Like a bird, Pegasus had two _______.
Frame 3: Pegasus had two – – – – s.
Place an *X* after each of the following steps which these frames illustrate.

(a) Present the material in the form of frames. _______
(b) Require active student response. _______
(c) Provide for confirmation or correction of student response. _______
(d) Use prompts to guide student response. _______
(e) Provide careful sequencing of the frames. _______

After placing your *X*'s, give reasons for your choices and for your rejection of the alternatives.

* The frames are from Markle, 1964, p. 70.

THE INSTRUCTIONAL MEDIA

In the first section of this chapter the emphasis was on educational technology as the science of instruction. Our concern was with the design of instructional materials rather than with the media or machines into which these materials are fed. To oversimplify the distinction, the first section of the chapter dealt with the software of instruction, while the second section will deal with the hardware. This distinction is useful in organizing the materials of this chapter. In actual practice, however, the design of instructional materials and the design of the media and machines which convey these materials must be a joint enterprise. The materials and the media influence each other and produce an instructional tool recognizably different from their isolated constructions. The interaction of materials and media is a relatively new area of research and will require considerably more inquiry before we can predict and control the effects for our instructional practices.

What Are the Instructional Media?

A medium is a middle condition. Instructional media are the electromechanical devices which act as middle conditions between the student and what he is to learn. An instructional medium is simply a means of transmitting instruction. It is not the substance of that instruction. In an age enamored of technology, it is important to keep in mind that the instructional medium serves as the channel of instruction. What passes through that channel is the substance of instruction.

We can make the distinction between the old, or traditional, media and the more recently developed media (Erickson, 1965). Several traditional media still make important contributions to the instructional process. First, models or mockups are simplified representations of real things. A globe, for example, is a model of the earth. We also have take-apart models of the human torso and the major human organs. Geometric models are increasingly used in the teaching of mathematics. Second, graphic materials are nonpictorial in nature. Examples are maps, graphs, cartoons, diagrams, and charts. Third, the motion picture combines motion, sound, and realism. Increasingly popular is the 8mm single-concept film ready for insertion into its own projector. Fourth, projected still pictures, such as lantern slides and filmstrips, are useful media. Transparencies are used with the overhead projector and are usually made by the teacher. Microscope slides are particularly useful in the teaching of the life sciences. Fifth, the opaque projection materials use a special projector which reflects light from the surface of the picture or object onto a projection screen. Sixth, magnetic tape recordings have become the chief aural instructional medium.

Carlton Erickson also describes the new media: First among these is television. As a medium television has three aspects: It is a composite of auditory and visual presentation; it can reach an audience of unlimited size; and it can transmit program content without delay from the point of origin to the point of reception. Television uses several of the older media. For example, a telecast may consist of a motion picture of a laboratory demonstration which uses slides, models, and transparencies. The second new medium is the teaching machine, which is designed for autoinstruction. The original teaching machines were rather overelaborate page turners for the various pages of programed material. They also provided a way of masking the correct response until the student made his own overt response. The original teaching machines could be described better as metal boxes than as machines. Interest in machine teaching has shifted from these innocuous devices to computer-assisted instruction, which I describe below. Third, Erickson points out the increasing popularity of the instructional kits, which contain a variety of carefully related materials including objects, models, motion pictures, filmstrips, tape recordings, student leaflets, programed materials, apparatus assemblies, and workbooks. Underlying the design and use of these kits are systems analysis and design of instruction.

Selection and Use of the Media

As a teacher your practical problem is to select from this rather formidable array of media those which are most useful in reaching your instructional objectives. Rather than outlining a series of steps you should take in the selection of appropriate media, I shall describe several bases for your selections: information about available media, an analysis and design of an instructional system, and knowledge of the research findings on the use of the media.

Information about the available media. Colleges, universities, and local school systems are developing large educational technology centers, which serve as depositories for the many media of instruction. Unless the media are immediately available, the tendency of the teacher is to use other instructional materials. Erickson (1966) has compiled a list of general references which can be helpful in finding out which media are available:

1. Catalogs of the local school system, school building, and resource center.
2. Magazines such as *Audiovisual Instruction, Educational Screen and Audiovisual Guide,* and journals in particular subject fields.
3. The *Educational Media Index* (McGraw-Hill Book Company), which lists motion pictures, kinescopes, videotapes, filmstrips, records, tapes, models, slides, transparencies, cross-media kits, and programed materials.
4. *Guides to Newer Media* (American Library Association, 50 East Huron, Chicago, Illinois).
5. *Educators Guide to Free Films* and *Educators Guide to Free Slidefilms* (annual publication of Educators Progress Service, Department AVG, Randolph, Wisconsin).
6. Keuffel and Esser Company, Audiovisual Division, Hoboken, New Jersey; Tecnifax Corporation, Holyoke, Massachusetts; and Ozalid Company, Johnson City, New York, for the manufacture of transparencies you desire.
7. Film catalogs of the largest rental film libraries in the nation or in your locality. One of the largest is Pennsylvania State University, University Park.
8. Local audiovisual-education dealers.
9. Catalogs of companies that produce scientific equipment and also of manufacturing promotional agencies such as the Petroleum Institute, the Manufacturing Chemists' Association, and the American Association of Railroads.

From these various sources and others you can find which media are available or can be produced for your use. Much polish has been added to the old and the new instructional media to catch the eye of the potential purchaser. Amidst this mounting market pressure, the teacher must find a sounder basis for selection and use than mere availability, novelty, or visual appeal. The sounder basis lies in systems analysis and research findings.

Systems analysis and design. When you increase the number of objectives you try to reach, the amount of material and the array of media you utilize, and the number of students and teachers involved in a total operation, you usually need comprehensive and detailed planning. Getting the best equipment in the best place for the best people at the best time and at the best price becomes a rather monumental problem. With its emphasis on efficiency and productivity in the competitive market, industry has probably given more serious consideration than any other group has to the systematic planning of complex operations which involve people, machines, materials, and ultimate delivery of a product of precise specifications. The armed services, as well, are often faced with a situation in which men must be trained for the performance of complex tasks in very short periods of time, especially during national emergencies. Here also the systematic planning of instruction is a more critical issue than it is in our schools. In our schools and colleges, however, there is increasing competition for the students' time as we try to crowd the acquisition of increased knowledge and skill into the traditional time limits set on education and as the schools compete for their share of the tax dollar. Because of this additional pressure, we must improve the effectiveness and efficiency of instruction.

Instructional systems design is the application of various methods and tools for the purpose of predicting and comparing the value, effectiveness, and cost of alternative courses of action involving teachers, students, and machines (Meals, 1967). We can inspect each aspect of this definition more closely. First, the systems designer or analyst, as he is called, must select the best alternative. Donald Meals (1967) uses this example. The choice between a language laboratory and conventional instruction involves obtaining information on all the following factors: how rapidly linguistic skill is acquired in the laboratory, the cost and availability of the software, the required amount of teacher training, the amount of maintenance required for the equipment, and so on. One likely outcome of this particular systems analysis is the consideration of those additions to the language-laboratory facilities which would make them useful for other courses. The important point, however, is that the school does not make the decision to install a language laboratory until all the system pieces have been assembled and compared. A second element of the definition deals with performance criteria. On what basis does the systems analyst decide that one alternative is better than another? His criteria are usually effectiveness, efficiency, and cost

Effectiveness depends on how well the students acquire the terminal behaviors. For efficiency, the system can be designed to speed the learning of the student if the time saved can be effectively used in the attainment of other desirable instructional objectives. Cost is determined on the basis of what are called *performance budgets* (Mauch, 1962). Such a budget tells how much it costs to teach students particular subject matter and skills. For example, it might determine that it costs 50 dollars per year per student to teach mathematics. James Mauch observes that the typical school budget is an object (not a performance) budget. It shows us what education buys (books, chairs, the time of the teacher) not what education does (provides instruction in mathematics, science, and history). The performance budget enables the systems designer to make comparisons of and clearer choices among instructional alternatives. Third, the definition implies that systems analysis and design combine knowledge and skill from many disciplines, including mathematics, economics, and industrial and electrical engineering. The systems analyst, according to Mauch, provides a bridge between science and technology, on one side, and education, on the other.

Under the auspices of Michigan State University, a study was made of procedures and costs for the full range of media in instructional systems (see Barson, 1965). This study developed a model for the analysis and design of these systems. Figure 12-31 shows the complex interrelationship of functions, materials, media, and personnel which is possible. It may simplify your understanding of the flow chart if you think of its application to a course you will be teaching. In this case you will be the instructor. In analyzing and designing your course, you will meet with such individuals as a design coordinator, an evaluation specialist, an instructional specialist, an audiovisual specialist, a media specialist, and a technical supervisor. Inspection of Fig. 12-31 quickly reveals that the model is in many respects identical to the basic teaching model and to the procedures for the development of programed materials. Added, of course, are the services of the various specialists who can assist in areas in which the teacher is deficient in knowledge and skill. With enough knowledge, the instructor (that is, you) could carry out alone the entire analysis and design. The various specialists are merely convenient ways of segmenting the general teaching function. In the future, as educational technology (in both senses) grows, it is likely that instructional planning will stretch beyond the single classroom and teacher and include a much wider range of factors and personnel.

Research on the instructional media. Knowledge of research on the media is the third basis you have for the selection of media appropriate to your instructional objectives. Private and Federal grants have brought a considerable increase in research on instructional media.

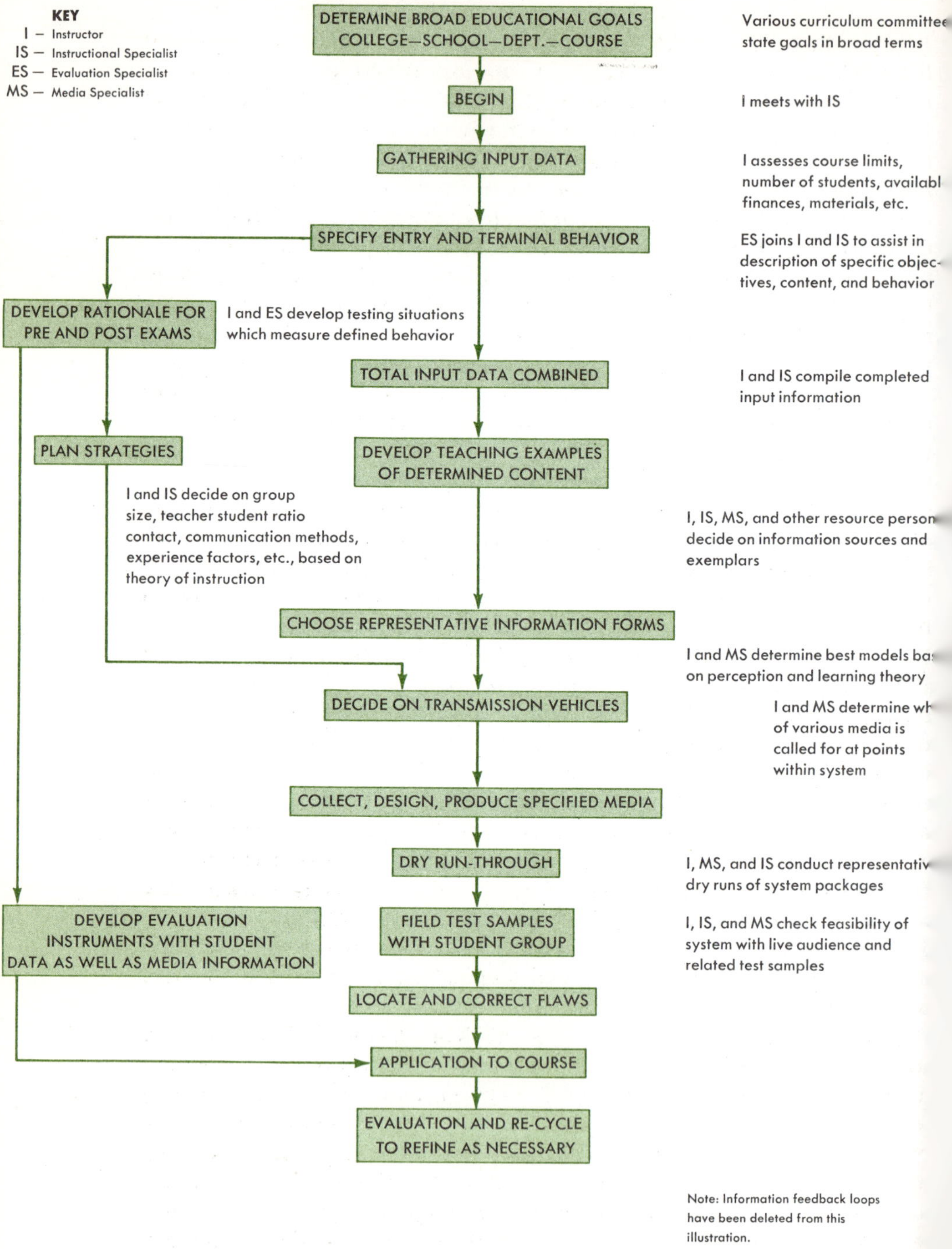

Fig. 12-31. *A flow chart of procedures for analysis and implementation of newer media of communications (after Barson, 1965).*

Between 1918 and 1950 there were over 200 experiments on instructional films (Hoban and Van Ormer, 1950). Almost all the studies on instructional television occurred between 1954 and 1964 (see MacLennan and Reid, 1964). There has been very little research on media other than films and television. The research in this area can be classified as follows (Greenhill, 1964): comparisons of the benefits of and the attitudes toward instructional films and television vs. direct (face-to-face) instruction; studies of other uses of instructional films and television; and research concerned with production variables. I shall review each of these areas, emphasizing instructional television (our major current medium), and then discuss the media in connection with production variables.

Direct instruction vs. films and television. By far the greatest amount of media research has tried to discover the relative benefits of face-to-face and televised instruction. One of the earliest studies (Carpenter and Greenhill, 1955) compared the effectiveness of direct and televised instruction in the teaching of psychology, chemistry, and the psychology of marriage. This study was later extended (1958) to include the teaching of elementary business law, meteorology, music appreciation, and introductory sociology. In both studies the researchers were unable to find significant differences between televised and face-to-face instruction. In one interesting phase of this extensive study, 626 chemistry students alternately experienced both types of instruction. Students with direct instruction were randomly assigned to the front, middle, and rear portions of the lecture hall. After experiencing both treatments, both groups were taught chemistry in the lecture hall. After one week and a half, the students were given the option of remaining in their present lecture seats or moving to the television classrooms. Thirty-two per cent moved to the television classroom. About 50 per cent of those who moved had been assigned seats in the rear of the lecture hall. When asked why they moved, they mentioned close-up views of the television screen, the greater comfort of the rooms, and the lack of distraction. Those remaining in the lecture mentioned the lack of color and the narrow field of view of television as reasons for staying.

A study by Robert Dreher and Walcott Beatty (1958) compared student achievement and attitudes under three conditions: face-to-face instruction, on-campus television instruction, and off-campus (at-home) television instruction. The subjects taught were psychology, economics, basic communication, and creative arts. In general they found no significant differences in achievement for any of the conditions or subject matters. Students with high grade-point averages did significantly better with television than with face-to-face instruction in the psychology course. Students with low grade-point averages did significantly better with televised instruction in both psychology and economics. Students with high IQs in the televised course gained more than did students of comparable ability in face-to-face instruction. Regarding attitude, off-campus students tended to be favorable to television instruction, while on-campus students tended to be disapproving; the face-to-face students were least critical of their courses.

Glenn Macomber and Laurence Sigel (1960) compared the relative effectiveness of televised instruction and instruction in small and large groups. The subject areas were human behavior, air science, animal biology, and American government. Tests which measured the acquisition of subject matter showed no significant differences in the scores of students under the three instructional conditions. In two of the courses, the students were more favorable in attitude toward the face-to-face instruction than toward televised instruction. They also tended to rate the same instructor more favorably in the face-to-face situation than in the televised situation. Generally, high-ability students were less favorable toward instructional television than low-ability students were. In both this study and the one by Clarence Carpenter and Leslie Greenhill, there was a growth of acceptance of instructional television over a period of two or three years. After this time, the students tended to be less concerned with television per se and to react more to the quality than to the medium of instruction. Hence, the researchers found significant course-to-course variation in attitude. The studies by Macomber and Sigel and by Dreher and Beatty both indicated that the professors found instructional television less preferable than face-to-face instruction. They believed that certain intangible educational goals could not be achieved and that both student and instructor were lost in an impersonal electronic world. Shepard Insel and his associates (1963) found that television instruction evoked more other-dependent (than self-dependent) responses in students, as indicated by their description of effective and ineffective teaching incidents in televised and direct instruction.

A wealth of evidence supports the conclusion that there is no significant difference in amount learned from direct and from televised instruction. The decision to use instructional television, therefore, must rest on other bases. One of the advantages of television is its distributive powers. Instruction can be provided in many places at the same time. When instruction is carefully designed and employs a wide range of human talent and instructional media, distinct advantages may result from extending the benefits of this instruction to as many students as may profit by it. Frequently, too, a school must choose between offering the televised course or no course at all in a particular subject or skill. Finally, distinct economic advantages can result from using televised rather than direct instruction.

Other uses of instructional films and television. Greenhill (1964) notes substantial research on the use of television for purposes other than the presentation of subject matter. He describes these additional uses: (1) Television is used for the observation of demonstration teaching. The evidence indicates that trainees gain as much from televised as from direct observation, although they tend to prefer the direct observation. One practical advantage of televised observation is that it permits analysis and discussion of the teaching while it is occurring. The major disadvantage is that classroom conversations are often not adequately picked up by microphones. At Stanford University (see Allen, 1963) videotape records demonstrations by the teacher trainees. When these videotapes are later played back, the teacher, the trainees, and others who can profit from the demonstration analyze and discuss them. (2) Television is used for in-service training and professional training. The research indicates that such training can be effectively provided. (3) Television is used for the teaching of motor skills. For this use of television to be effective the conditions of skill learning which you learned in a previous chapter must be observed.

Production variables. The third research area concerning the use of television and films deals with production variables—variations in the organization and presentation of program content (Greenhill, 1964). Unfortunately, there has been very little research in this area, although the need and the possibilities for it are great. Such research could make important contributions to educational technology as the science of education. Illustrative of studies on production variables is the series of investigations by George Gropper and Lumsdaine (1961) on the use of instructional television in the teaching of high school physics and body chemistry. In one study they taught lessons on heat and on nuclear reaction to junior high school students. Each lesson was presented by conventional television instruction and by a televised programed presentation. In the programed presentation, the television teacher paused long enough to allow students to write down their responses. During the pause, a question mark appeared on the screen. All students took an immediate and a delayed test of terminal behavior. These were the results: (1) The programed presentation resulted in significantly higher achievement than did the conventional television instruction; (2) the high-ability students in the programed course had significantly higher scores than high-ability students in the conventional course did; (3) low-ability students in both groups performed equally well on the immediate posttest, but low-ability students under conventional instruction scored significantly higher on the delayed posttest than the programed students did. For the lesson on nuclear reaction, two of the five comparisons made significantly favored the programed group. A later experiment (1961) in which students were taught how movies work supported these findings on active responding. One group saw a version of the

PLATE I
Oral Presentation:
Group 1

PLATE II
Abstract Linear
Presentation: Group II

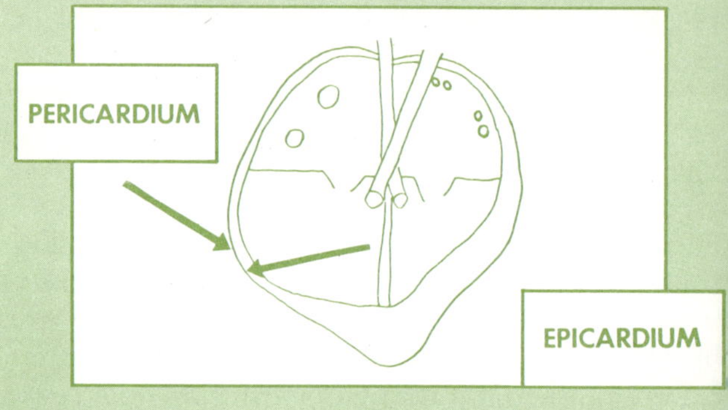

PLATE III
Detailed, Shaded
Drawing Presentation:
Group III

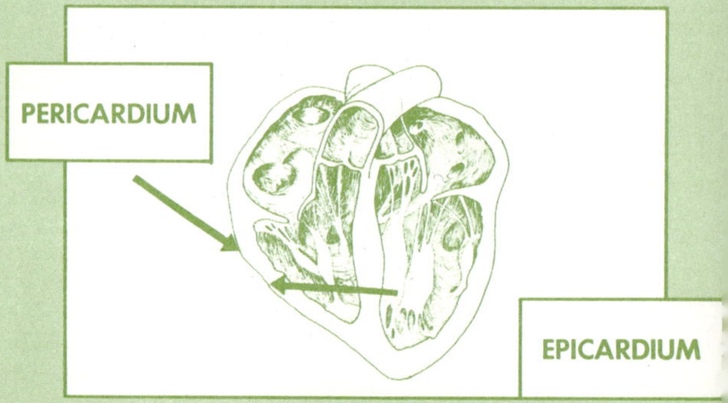

PLATE IV
Realistic Photographic
Presentation: Group IV

Fig. 12-32. *Three types of visual representation varying in degree of detail and realism (after Dwyer, 1967, opposite p. 156).*

televised lesson which required active response; the lecturer supplied the correct answer after the students responded. The second group saw the lesson without active responding. On both the delayed test and the immediate posttest, the active-response group obtained significantly superior scores.

Research on the use of various instructional media indicates that increasing amounts of both audial and visual information do not lead to greater learning. I have already referred to the research of Travers and his associates (1964a) on the amount of realism desirable in teaching the attributes of a concept. On the basis of their findings they conclude that the major purpose of using visual media is "not so much to bring the pupil into close touch with reality, but to help students become more effective in dealing with reality." They point out that the brain can use much less information than our information channels can transmit to it. Most of the stimuli which bombard our senses never really enter into our perception or memory. In emphasizing realism in teaching, the danger is to bombard the student with more information than he can possibly utilize and to distract his attention from the major aspects of the concepts and principles he is learning. A study by Francis Dwyer (1967) with college freshmen compared the relative effectiveness of three types of visual representation which were shown as they were mentioned in an oral presentation: (1) abstract linear representations (see Fig. 12-32, Plate II) of the form and relative locations of the parts of the heart; (2) detailed, shaded drawing (Plate III) representing the parts of the heart; and (3) realistic photographs (Plate IV) of the parts of the heart. A control group received instruction with no accompanying illustrations. To measure student achievement, Dwyer used a heart-model test, a terminology test, a drawing test, and a comprehension test. A total criterion test combined scores on these individual tests. Dwyer found that the abstract linear representations and the detailed shaded drawings were equally effective and that both of these were significantly more effective than the oral presentation alone and the realistic photographic presentation. Interestingly enough, the realistic photographic presentation was no more effective than was the oral presentation alone. Dwyer's findings remind us that instructional visual materials must be designed with experimental knowledge of the effects of various production variables. Rampant color, the existential realism of European motion pictures, and other excesses, whatever their artistic appeal, are not sound bases for the development of visual materials for instruction.

Computer-Assisted Instruction (CAI)

The computer has made its impact on industry and government, and it will, no doubt, make its impact on the school. In handling more and more information about more and more students, the schools need the capabilities of information storage and retrieval which industry and government also require. The first impact of the computer on education will no doubt be in the area of clerical and accounting efficiency.

The computer's impact on instruction will be felt much later because its relationship to teaching and learning requires a great deal of research, some of which must await the fuller development of empirically based theories of teaching. In Chapter 1 I described the computer-based teaching model of Stolurow and Davis (1965). In the absence of a theory of teaching, such models help us launch the necessary research by suggesting the interrelationship of important teaching variables. Use of the computer as a highly adaptive teaching machine weakens the distinction between software and hardware. In computer-assisted instruction there can be no sharp division of functions. According to their definition, a teaching machine must have three capabilities: in a given subject area, it must have at its disposal a number of different programs; when specifying a program for each student, it must make use of the student's entering behavior, general ability, and personality characteristics; and it must be able to change programs during the course of instruction. The computer, of course, is the only machine with these capabilities, and a machine with these capabilities is far different from the metal boxes which industry first marketed as teaching machines.

Ronald Gentile (1967) describes some of the devices used in CAI. In the area of visual communication, (1) typewriters ask a question under computer control and answer a question under student control; (2) film projection devices, on the basis of student responses, select films, present auditory and visual materials, and automatically score student responses; (3) displays superimposed on films highlight certain aspects of the films; (4) with cathode-ray tubes a pen can be used for drawing curves or indicating answers on a screen. These answers can then be evaluated by the computer; and (5) random-access slides and films are available. The area of auditory communication presents many unsolved problems. However, two devices have been developed: In compiled speech, the computer has random access to prerecorded phrases which can be arranged on the basis of student response (e.g., the computer can tell the student a chemical formula); in synthetic speech, the computer uses a set of rules to convert stored speech sounds into meaningful speech patterns.

Considerably more progress has been made with the technical development of CAI than with the problem of writing instructional programs. The chief unsolved technical problem is how to reduce the cost sufficiently to prevent bankruptcy of local school districts. As in the case of the general development and use of the instructional media, the temptation has been to dazzle the student with an array of visual and auditory stimuli which serve more to impress him with the capabilities of the computer than to provide him with the necessary instruction. Although, as Stolurow and Davis point out, CAI promises the best means yet for providing for variation in student entering behavior, Gentile (1967) indicates that several realistic considerations make provision for such individual differences a difficult educational feat. First, how we should provide for individual differences is rarely specified. There are many kinds of differences, and not all of them can be accommodated by allowing the computer to generate sequences on the basis of student response. Second, we need a classification of individual difference variables, especially in terms of learning variables (see Jensen, Chapter 3). Third, the elimination of individual differences by any teaching method is an unrealistic expectation because of prior differences in student verbal abilities and mental sets. Finally, adaptation to individual differences must prove to be superior to teaching which is aimed at the group mean.

At several universities and research facilities there is extensive research on CAI (see "CAI—System and Projects," *Automated Education Letter,* 1 (1966), 3–13). Figures 12-33, 12-34, and 12-35 show two instructional terminals and one computer laboratory. The computer laboratory can operate 200 instructional terminals located in one or more school districts. The older student is seated at a teletypewriter upon which he can compose his answers. The computers in the laboratory type feedback messages and expository material. The younger student can receive auditory, visual, and written materials from the remote computers. He can respond through use of the teletypewriter keyboard or by touching the television screen.

All these facilities and equipment, I must remind you, are much more sophisticated than any theory of teaching we presently have. The temptation in a technological society is to allow our fantastic machines to determine our research problems and our educational practice. It is far more important that we subordinate the machines to the theoretical and practical instructional problems which, undoubtedly, the machines can help us solve.

Summary

You now have an introductory knowledge of the old and the new media of instruction. With an increasingly wide array of media from which to choose, your problem is to find adequate bases for decision. Three bases for the selection and use of the media were suggested: (1) The first basis is availability. Several sources of information on available media were listed along with the names of manufacturers who will

Fig. 12-33. *A computer laboratory which can simultaneously operate 200 instructional terminals located in one or more school districts.*

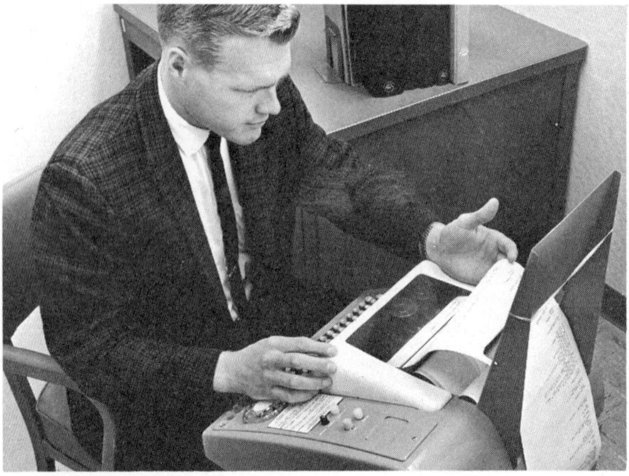

Fig. 12-34. *Student reading feedback from a remote computer to an instructional terminal (photo courtesy of System Development Corporation).*

Fig. 12-35. *Student at an instructional terminal located in a classroom (photo courtesy of RCA Instructional Systems).*

make media that you specially request. (2) The analysis and design of instructional systems show you how to develop a course of instruction with full utilization of a wide range of media and media specialists. (3) Finally, and most importantly, the research on the effectiveness of the media, although much of it is preliminary and inconclusive, now furnishes a fairly solid basis for instructional decisions. Conclusive evidence shows no significant differences in student achievement in televised or face-to-face instruction. The decision to use or not to use televised instruction must clearly rest on other grounds. The need to combine overt responding with viewing and listening to the presentation of lessons has rather convincing research support. However, in our rush to portray all of life on television, in motion pictures, and on slides, we must remember that too much realism impedes student learning. Simplified representations of objects often teach more than the objects themselves. The use of computer-assisted instruction and simulation techniques requires considerably more research. Both activities enable researchers to deal with a complex array of teaching and learning variables. At this time and for the next several years we should view both simulation and computer-assisted instruction as very promising areas of research but not as practical innovations for the school.

You should now return to objectives 17–26 (pp. 486–87) and determine how well you have achieved them.

QUESTION 12-2

As a teacher you want to select the best instructional procedures and materials and those which yield the best performance in terms of achievement, money, and time. Given these standards, which of the following innovations could you adopt to give you the highest probability of meeting them? (a) instructional television (including videotapes); (b) systems analysis and design; (c) computer-assisted instruction; (d) instructional films, with careful control of information input; (e) instructional kits and low-cost items.

After selecting your answer, give the reasons for your choice and for your rejection of the alternatives.

FLEXIBLE SCHEDULING

With the influx of educational technology into the school, with the demand for improved teaching of neglected subjects, such as mathematics and science, and with the public pressure to improve the general quality of American education, it was almost inevitable that some of the oldest traditions of the school are up for review. One of the most venerable traditions made the teacher's classroom his exclusive domain.

Other teachers and even principals entered with trepidation and humility. If the students did not occasionally gossip about their various teachers, colleagues worked in the same building for years in almost virtual ignorance of what was happening (if anything) in their respective classrooms. Another tradition, particularly in the junior and senior high schools, assigned a daily, single, fifty-minute period to each major subject in the student's program. The student had an English period, a history period, a mathematics period, and so on. His schedule varied very little or not at all from day to day. Another tradition, defended with curious zeal, made a class of thirty students, no smaller or larger, the ideal one to teach at one time. Both large-group and individualized instruction were objects of suspicion and protest. Finally, a tradition, which fortunately is also dying out in the medical profession, required each teacher to develop his own lesson plans, teaching materials, teaching tricks, and assignments with little or no consultation with his colleagues or other teachers and specialists. A fair description of these traditions would describe their many advantages, but, in a chapter on educational innovation, we must focus on the rigidity of these practices and the possible alternative ways of organizing the schedule and the teaching personnel of the school.

In this part of the chapter I shall describe alternative ways of organizing schedules and staff and of grouping students for instruction. I shall not argue that the new ways are necessarily better than the old. Such an argument is futile without the supporting evidence, and, unfortunately, in this area of teaching innovation we have much more conjecture, propaganda, and wishful thinking than sound evidence. The alternative ways, however, have certain practical and intuitive appeal to principals, teachers, and students, and even to several educational researchers. This widespread practical appeal is the basis for my describing these innovations here.

As viewed here, flexible scheduling has three aspects: the allocation of time, students, and course units in terms of modules rather than daily periods; the development of teaching teams to replace the individual teacher; and the regrouping of students on the basis of actual achievement rather than on the basis of year or grade.

Robert Bush and Dwight Allen (1964) list several basic assumptions upon which they rest their case for flexible scheduling. Among these are the following: (1) Groups of students in each subject area have needs which are sufficiently distinct to require discrete programs of study. (2) Each subject when taught should include four types of instruction: (a) individual; (b) small group; (c) laboratory; and (d) large group. (3) Adequate instruction in each subject matter requires highly knowledgeable senior teachers and less highly trained assistants. (4) Class size, length of class meetings, and the number and spacing of classes should be determined by the nature of the subject, the type of instruction, and the entering behavior of the students. (5) The use of the computer makes possible the implementation of a large degree of flexibility in the schedule.

Modules and Modular Units

In flexible scheduling, the curriculum is conceived as an area to be scheduled. The subparts of the schedule (or curriculum), the *modular units,* pertain to class size and length of period. Bush and Allen suggest that the modular unit of time (length of period) selected should be the largest amount of time, multiples of which will give the period lengths desired for any instruction. A twenty-minute module is desirable if you want period lengths of 40, 60, and 120 minutes. The modular unit of class size should be the minimum size desired for any instructional purpose. A ten-student module would allow class sizes of ten, twenty, thirty, and so on. In their examples, Bush and Allen use the module of fifteen students meeting for thirty minutes.

To understand their diagrams it is necessary to learn three new terms. *Course structure* describes the overall allocation of time and the various groupings of the students for a period of a week. Figure 12-36 is a diagram of the course structure of an English course. A *phase* is a subdivision of the course structure. In Fig. 12-36 letters *A* through *E* indicate that the English course has five phases. The phases, there-

Fig. 12-36. *Suggested structure for a five-phase English course (after Bush and Allen, 1964, p. 27).*

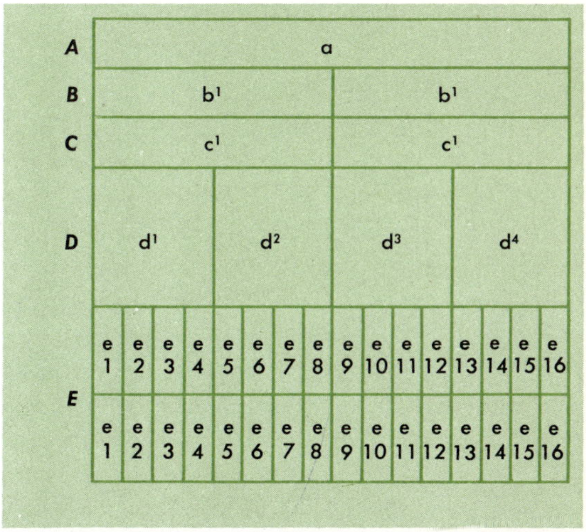

fore, are the rows in the diagram. The phases vary in length of time. If the entire course structure takes five hours each week, phases *A, B,* and *C* are each one-half hour in duration. Phase *D* takes one and one-half hours, and phase *E* is made up of one-hour meetings which occur twice a week. Each *section* is a subdivision of a phase. These are denoted by the lower-case letters. Phase *B,* for example, has two sections (as does Phase *C*). Phase *D* has four sections.

In interpreting Fig. 12-36, remember that the class-size module is fifteen students and the time module is thirty minutes. Also recall that the entire course structure consists of five hours of instruction per week. The distance between the horizontal lines indicates the length of the class period (the time module) and the distance between the vertical lines indicates the class size module. Now that you know all of this you can read the schedule for this course. If the course consists of 240 students, you know that is equal to sixteen class-size modules. Reading the diagram phase by phase, you can see that phase *A* consists of large-group instruction for 240 students for one-half hour. Phase *B* consists of large-group instruction for 120 students, in two sections, for one-half hour. Phase *C* is identical to phase *B*. Phase *D* consists of four sections, sixty students per section, for a period of one and one-half hours. Finally, phase *E* consists of two one-hour class periods (each having two time modules) and sections of fifteen students each (small-group instruction). This course structure, then, shows three types of instruction: large group (phases *A, B,* and *C*), laboratory (phase *D*), and small group (phase *E*). It does not specifically provide for individual instruction.

Team Teaching

A teaching team is a unit which combines three elements (Brownell and Taylor, 1962): a distinct student group, a small faculty group responsible for teaching the student group, and certain persons who assist the teachers and students. This describes the team. The way the team operates is team teaching. Medill Bair and Richard Woodward (1964) list twelve characteristics of team teaching (some of which describe the personnel as well as their functions): (1) A teaching team consists of from three to seven or more teachers jointly responsible for the instruction of 75 to 225 or more students in one or more grade or age levels. (2) Teams may have teachers assigned to different levels of responsibility depending on their ability and experience, with higher salaries and higher status given to the senior teachers and the team leader. (3) Team teaching permits the supervision of the junior members of a team by the senior or leadership personnel. The schedule also permits less experienced personnel to observe the outstanding teacher, adjusting to his program as the teaching-learning situation develops. (4) Team teaching emphasizes the team, rather than the individual teacher, in the planning, teaching, and evaluating cycle. (5) In the classroom situation, however, teaching teams protect the professional autonomy of each teacher and stress the use of his unique abilities in the instruction of children. (6) In many team-teaching programs, each member of the team specializes in a different curriculum area and helps all members of the team plan, teach, and evaluate in the area of his specialty. (7) All team-teaching programs emphasize the effective utilization of the strengths of each member of the staff. (8) As team teaching promotes nongradedness within the school, so does nongradedness promote team teaching. (9) Team-teaching programs emphasize varying class sizes and class lengths based upon instructional objectives, context, techniques, and student needs. (10) Class size and length of period are closely related to the flexible scheduling practices for students and teachers. (11) Many team-teaching programs use aides for nonprofessional tasks. (12) Most team teachers make effective use of the instructional media.

Some of these items are positive assertions of a belief in team teaching more than descriptions of how teams function (see numbers 5 and 7). To balance the picture, John Brownell and Harris Taylor (1962) list some of the common difficulties which teams face under ordinary school conditions: (1) finding teachers who can function harmoniously as a team; (2) finding strong team leaders; (3) scheduling team classes in high schools and organizing flexible groupings in elementary schools; (4) coping with the irritating effects of teams on existing departmental and grade-level organization; (5) creating new and different administrative roles and problems; (6) forcing independent and creative teachers into groups which inhibit their freedom; (7) lowering the morale of nonteam teachers; and (8) locating, training, and supervising teacher aides.

TEAM-TEACHING MODELS: CONTENT AREAS AND GRADES. Teaching teams can function within or across grades and content areas. Brownell and Taylor (1962) give us illustrations of both arrangements. Figure 12-37

Fig. 12-37. *Example of a team organized within a grade and within content areas (after Brownell and Taylor, 1962, p. 152).*

Grade	6					
Classes	A	B	C	D	E	
Language arts	Team					
Science	Team					

Fig. 12-38. *Example of teams organized within content areas and across grades (after Brownell and Taylor, 1962, p. 153).*

is an example of elementary school teams which function within content areas and within a single grade. You can see that all the students are from the sixth grade. All the language arts teachers in the sixth grade are members of the language arts team and all the science teachers in the sixth grade are members of the science team. This model represents a comparatively conservative change in the traditional elementary school schedule. Figure 12-38 is an example of an elementary school team which functions across grades but within content areas. You can see that the students from the first, second, and third grades are brought together for team instruction in the language arts. Students from the fourth, fifth, and sixth grades are combined for team instruction in science. This model represents a major departure in that the usual division of the students into grades is ignored. Later I shall refer to this model as an example of nongraded instruction.

In the high school, teams are often organized across subject matter. Figure 12-39 shows a somewhat radical departure from the traditional schedule. Here teachers from five different content areas join in teaching the same tenth grade students one period each. It is also possible for the teachers from one content area, for one period a day, to form a team and to teach students from several grades.

Fig. 12-39. *Example of a high school team which functions across content areas (after Brownell and Taylor, 1962, p. 154).*

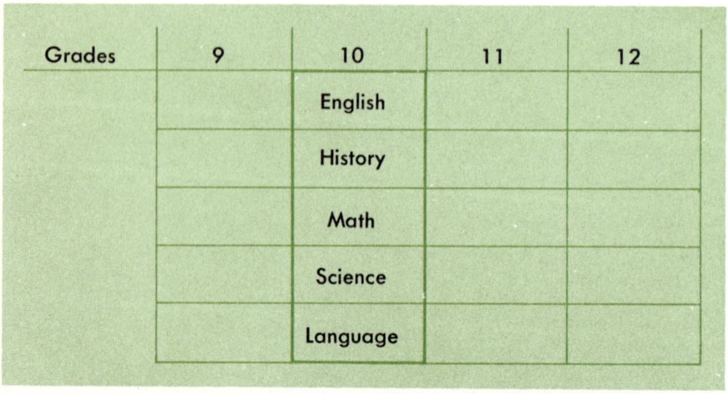

Team-teaching models: the staff. Most proponents of team teaching suggest hierarchical staff organizations similar to those we find in colleges and universities. The two major divisions of the team staff are the professional staff, which is primarily responsible for administration, coordination, and planning; and the supporting staff—teacher trainees, and technical and clerical assistants. Table 12-1 indicates one possible division of functions for the team staff. The instruction assistants, clerks, and general aides constitute the regular supporting staff. The community consultants and staff specialists constitute the part-time supporting staff.

Most descriptions of team teaching differentiate the various teaching functions. Bair and Woodward (1964), for example, distinguish between the team leader, the senior teacher, and the team teacher. In their study the person with the most authority and responsibility is the team leader. His job is to administer, coordinate, and supervise the work and activities of the teachers, students, and aides. He assumes many of the administrative duties once performed by the principal, although the major part of his day is spent teaching. The senior teacher supervises and coordinates activities in his special content area. He helps develop instructional materials, lesson plans, and units. The team teacher teaches most subjects to students, who are put into small and large groups on the basis of their entering behavior. Of all team members, the team teacher has the fewest administrative responsibilities and the most direct contact with students and parents.

Proponents of team teaching believe major advantages are the induction of new teachers and the in-school training of student teachers. The need for realistic training and for the continuing education of the novice teacher have long been recognized (Shaplin, 1961). The difficulty has been finding the appropriate administrative and professional arrangements. Judson Shaplin (1961, pp. 54–55) believes that team teaching is a particularly convenient way to solve this problem:

> Joint planning of instruction becomes possible, as does flexibility in the assignment of teachers to tasks suitable to their capabilities. Instead of being fully responsible from the start, there can be a gradual increase of responsibility under expert guidance. Within the team, teachers see each other at work and join in the evaluation of instruction and learning under natural conditions where the objective is the improvement of instruction and not judgment of their own worth. Teachers with greater technical expertness are responsible for influencing the performance of their less expert colleagues. Talk about teaching becomes legitimate; it is based on common observation and not upon isolated personal experience. The team structure allows the school to identify those teachers who have greater knowledge and skill and to assign them greater responsibility and to reward them for successful performance.

Student teachers are often called *interns* or *intern teachers* (Bush and Allen, 1964). They have the responsibility for some curriculum assistance and some of the teaching. They may also assist in keeping class records. Even without the team organization it is possible to extend the training of the intern in the school. In one study teachers from the regular school staff were designated *intern consultants* (Corman and Ohlmsted, 1964). Each consultant worked with about six interns each year and provided on a systematic basis the guidance and the supervision which in the past had often been fortuitous. In the usual situation, the beginning teacher adopts or is adopted by a buddy teacher, who provides only occasional help—sometimes of an emergency nature.

Although there have been several demonstrations of team teaching throughout the nation, there have been relatively few published assessments of their effectiveness. Assessments made without the use of the proper controls are, of course, uninterpretable. Bair and Woodward (1964) report one comparison of junior high students who came from schools which used and did not use team teaching. Only the team-teaching students in the upper third of the distribution did better than those students who had conventional instruction.

Like other innovations discussed in this chapter, team teaching has some obvious practical appeal in handling many of the problems of scheduling and staffing which beset the modern elementary and high school. Unfortunately, much of the acclamation and much of the derogation of team teaching has had little empirical support. Although obvious research difficulties are involved in investigating something as complex as new organizational patterns for the school, such research is the necessary basis for sound pedagogical and administrative decisions.

Nongraded Instruction

The results of standard achievement tests in almost any grade and in almost any school indicate the wide variation in knowledge and skill of students in the same grade. In the average American public school, students are assigned to grades not on the basis of their entering behavior but on the basis of age. This means that an English teacher in high school may face a class in which some students are reading at a third grade level while others are reading at an advanced college level. So wide a span of reading skill makes uniform instruction and assignments virtually impossible. In aiming his instruction at the class mean, the teacher runs the risk of boring his advanced students and overwhelming those students who cannot understand what is going on. It is a tragic state of affairs so common in our classes that only years of professional practice inures one enough to carry on in some appropriate manner.

TABLE 12-1

IDEAL INSTRUCTIONAL STAFF FOR A HIGH SCHOOL WITH 400 STUDENTS OR FOR EACH 400 STUDENTS IN A LARGER SCHOOL (after Trump, 1959, pp. 20–21).

Type of Staff	Functions and Employment	Training	Number
Professional teachers including teacher specialists and general teachers	Direct learning activities; plan methods and materials of instruction; teach concepts and appreciations; counsel and consult; supervise evaluation; assist with student activities; provide specialized services (employed on full-time basis—also year-around if able and interested)	Masters degree and beyond with specialization as needed	Ten
Instruction assistants	Perform specific aspects of teaching below professional level of teachers and above clerks; read and evaluate some English themes, science reports, etc.; confer with students about their progress and provide teachers with reports; serve as laboratory assistants; supervise specific out-of-school projects; assist with student activities (typically employed ten to twenty hour per week)	Usually college graduate but always trained for specific duties assigned	Two hundred hours service per week
Clerks	Type; duplicate materials; check materials and prepare reports; grade objective tests; keep records; check and distribute supplies; take attendance and perform other routine services (employed on forty-hour per week basis)	High school graduate with business education	One hundred hours service per week
General aides	Control and supervise students on school grounds, in cafeteria, corridors, auditorium, etc., and at extraclass activity functions; work with students in developing maximum self-controls; assist in student activities when competent (typically employed ten to twenty hours per week)	High school graduate with general courses; some college desirable	Fifty hours service per week
Community consultants	Lecture; consult; make tapes, records, kinescopes, slides, films, etc.; typically volunteers, although might be paid (used whenever needed to provide special services)	Unusual competence; selected from file of available persons	Indefinite depending on local circumstances
Staff specialists	Special services in such areas as guidance, research, health, reading, aid to exceptional children, audiovisual materials, and curriculum development; supplement work of teachers (full-time persons who might serve several schools)	Highly trained in area of speciality	Indefinite depending on local circumstances

Any modifications of the school schedule which can assist the teacher in accommodating his instruction to the variations in student entering behavior help fulfill basic instructional requirements. Particular modifications are illustrated in a nongraded high school in Florida (Brown, 1963). When students enter they are sorted on the basis of their scores on standard tests into phases—temporary learning situations from which they can move at any time. One student may remain in a particular phase an indefinite period of time. Another student may progress rapidly through several phases. Frank Brown (1963, p. 207) describes these phases as follows:

> Phase 1—Subjects are centered around remedial work.
> Phase 2—Subjects are concerned with basic skills.
> Phase 3—Subjects are designed for students seeking an average education.
> Phase 4—Subjects are available for students desiring education in considerable depth.
> Phase 5—Subjects are open to students who are willing to assume responsibility for their own learning and plan to go far beyond the boundaries of a single course.
> Phase Q—Students whose creative talents are well developed in special areas should give consideration to this "Quest" phase of the curriculum. This is an important dimension of the phased organization designed to give thrust in the direction of individual fulfillment. In this phase a student may research an area in which he is deeply and broadly curious, either to develop creative powers or in quest of knowledge. A student may spend from one to three hours a day in Quest.
> Phase X—Nonacademic subjects which do not accommodate student mobility; e.g., typing, physical education. These subjects are ungraded but unphased.

All the students are registered for six subjects. But the subjects vary in the level at which they are taught. Here are the various phases in the programs of two students:

STUDENT A	*Phase*	STUDENT B	*Phase*
English	1	English	3
Mathematics	3	Mathematics	2
World history	2	American history	4
Biology	3	Chemistry	3
Physical education	*X*	Band	*X*
Typing	*X*	Art	4

The result of assigning students to classes on the basis of measured achievement has resulted in wide variation in the size of classes. A typing class may have as many as 125 students, while other classes are much smaller.

In another Florida high school, a student progresses through a series of achievement levels called *units* (Kaufman and Bethune, 1964). At the end of each unit the student takes a test, and his score determines whether he moves to the next unit. A student who reports for a certain unit is expected to have a common set of values, skills, and knowledge. A unit requires about one month for the average student. As in the previous school, the student's program is composed of the basic subject matter of the traditional curriculum. The school is equipped with all the instructional media and a data-processing center. A closed-circuit television system permits telecasting throughout the school as well as making videotapes of lessons and lectures for later use. Burt Kaufman and Paul Bethune call it the *space-age school.*

Summary

The introduction of any innovation in our schools must be for the basic purpose of improving the quality of instruction. The primary basis for determining improved quality is student achievement as measured by tests of terminal behavior. In this last section of the chapter we have considered three innovations which, as you saw, are closely related: the planning of the school schedule in terms of modules and modular units; the use of team teaching; and the use of nongraded instruction. None of these practices, as yet, has convincing empirical support. Some have no research support at all. Although all are defended for their flexibility in accommodating variations in student entering behavior, their ability to do so must yet be demonstrated. All have been conceived primarily from an administrative rather than from an instructional point of view. For example, I have been able to find no discussion (to say nothing about research) on how these scheduling innovations improve the provision for essential learning conditions: discrimination, generalization, practice, reinforcement, contiguity, and so on. Until these innovations can be specifically tied to the psychology of learning and instruction, the instructional advantages they may embody remain highly speculative.

As teachers our primary concern is that our students master what we teach them. This responsibility may require a one-to-one relationship with a single student or work with a very small group of students. One of the greatest stumbling blocks in the classroom is our failure to teach the student at his level of entering behavior. The failure, according to Raymond Callahan (1962, p. 264), is not so much the responsibility of the teacher as of the "cult of efficiency" which surrounds the teacher:

> It is true some kinds of teaching and learning can be carried out in large lecture classes or through television but other vital aspects of the education of free man cannot. Until every child has part of his work in small classes or seminars with fine teachers who have a reasonable teaching load, we will not really have given the American high school, or democracy for that matter, a fair trial. To do this, Americans will need to break with its traditional practice, strengthened so much in the age of efficiency, of asking how our schools can be operated most economically and begin asking instead what steps need to be taken to provide an excellent education for our children. We must face the fact that there is no cheap, easy way to educate a human being and that a free society cannot endure without educated men.

It is entirely possible that many or all of the innovations described in this chapter are means of improving the education of American children. Studies of these innovations should reveal the conditions under which they enhance and impede student learning. This theoretical and empirical knowledge rather than fiscal parsimony or blind love of whatever is new and different should guide our future decisions on changing the schools.

You should now return to objectives 27–37 (p. 487) and determine how well you have achieved them.

QUESTION 12-3

To which of the following educational innovations is flexible scheduling related?

(a) The allocation of time, students, and course units in terms of modules.

(b) The development of teaching teams to replace individual teachers.

(c) The regrouping of students on the basis of actual achievement rather than on the basis of year or grade.

(d) All of the above.

(e) None of the above.

After selecting your answer, give the reasons for your choice and for your rejection of the alternatives.

SUMMARY

The introduction to this chapter distinguished between two meanings of educational technology. One meaning refers to the detailed application of the psychology of learning to practical teaching problems. The second meaning refers to the application of engineering principles to the development of electromechanical equipment used for instructional purposes. The two aspects interact in the design and use of instructional equipment, materials, and procedures. A major influence on the schools for the adoption of educational technology is business and industry.

The list section dealt with programed instruction, particularly the preparation, writing, tryout, and revision of programs. Programed instruction includes reducing material to small steps, requiring frequent student response, providing immediate confirmation or correction, and trying out and revising materials. In the preparation of the program there are five steps: selecting a unit or topic, preparing a content outline, defining objectives in behavioral terms, and constructing and administering tests of entering and terminal behavior. In the program writing there are also five steps: presenting the material in the form of frames, requiring active student responses, providing confirmation or correction of student responses, using prompts to guide student responses, and providing careful sequencing of materials. There has been considerable research on the conditions under which overt responding is more facilitating than covert responding. Overt responding may be especially helpful when the learning materials are difficult; when they are easy, overt or covert responding may work equally well. There are also practical program requirements which necessitate overt responding. There are both formal and thematic prompts. Four formal prompts are partial response, rhyming, literal prompts, and frame-structure prompts. Six thematic prompts are pictures, context-setting prompts, synonyms and antonyms, analogies, rules, and inductive prompts. The use of prompts requires vanishing or fading. In the tryout and revision of the program there are three steps: writing the original draft, editing it, and trying it out and revising it. There are three types of programs. The linear program provides a single path for all students to follow. In the branching program, the student branches to supplementary material when he makes an error. Adjunct autoinstruction inserts programed or testing materials into a textbook, laboratory manual, or other materials whenever these supplementary materials are needed. In selecting commercial programs the teacher should ask and answer four questions: Is it really programed material? How does the program fit the curriculum? How well will the program teach in our situation? Can we afford it?

The second section of the chapter dealt with instructional media. Instructional media are the electromechanical devices which act as a middle condition between the student and what he is to learn. The traditional media included mockups, graphic materials, motion pictures, projected stills, and magnetic tape recordings. The new media include television, teaching machines, and instructional kits. Three bases for the selection of media were described: information about available media, an analysis and design of an instructional system, and knowledge of the research findings on the use of the media. In computer-assisted instruction there is no sharp distinction between hardware and software. CAI involves the use of typewriters, film projection, superimposed displays, cathode-ray tubes, and random-access slides.

The third section of this chapter pertained to flexible scheduling, in which the curriculum is conceived as an area to be scheduled. Modular units are the subparts of the schedule. Course structure is the overall allocation of time and students for a period of a week. A teaching team consists of a distinct student group, a small faculty group, and particular persons who assist the teachers and the students. The characteristics of teaching teams can be described in terms of functions and personnel. Teaching-team models can function within or across content areas and grade levels. The teaching staff comprises professional teachers and administrators, nonprofessional assistants, and community consultants. A major advantage of team teaching is the opportunity for further training of novice teachers. Nongraded instruction allows assignment and advancement of the student on the basis of actual school achievement.

The adoption of educational innovations should be based on instructional objectives, student entering behavior, and our knowledge of the psychology of learning and instruction.

SUGGESTED READINGS

Because of the lively current interest in most of these topics, almost a superabundance of literature is available.

In the area of programed instruction and the instructional media, several collections of theoretical discussions and research reports make excellent references for the student who wishes to probe more deeply than this chapter. The most authoritative collections are the following two:

Glaser, Robert, ed., *Teaching Machines and Programed Learning, II: Data and Directions*. Washington, D.C.: Department of Audiovisual Instruction, National Education Association, 1965.

Lumsdaine, Arthur A., and Robert Glaser, eds., *Teaching Machines and Programmed Learning: A Source Book*. Washington, D.C.: Department of Audiovisual Instruction, National Education Association, 1960.

The following less comprehensive collections include major papers and statements of important theoretical issues:

De Cecco, John P., ed., *Educational Technology: Readings in Programmed Instruction*. New York: Holt, Rinehart & Winston, Inc., 1964 (paper).

Ofiesh, Gabriel D. and Wesley C. Meierhenry, eds., *Trends in Programmed Instruction*. Washington, D.C.: Department of Audiovisual Instruction, National Education Association and the National Society for Programmed Instruction, 1964 (paper).

Smith, Wendell I. and J. William Moore, eds., *Programmed Learning*. Princeton, N.J.: D. Van Nostrand Co., Inc., 1962 (paper).

The following books on how to program materials are particularly sound and useful:

Lysaught, Jerome P. and Clarence M. Williams, *A Guide to Programmed Instruction*. New York: John Wiley & Sons, Inc., 1963.

Markle, Susan Meyer, *Good Frames and Bad: A Grammar of Frame Writing*. New York: John Wiley & Sons, Inc., 1964 (paper).

Pipe, Peter, *Practical Programming*. New York: Holt, Rinehart & Winston, Inc., 1966 (paper).

Taber, Julian I., Robert Glaser, and Halmuth H. Schaefer, *Learning and Programmed Instruction*. Reading, Mass.: Addison-Wesley Publishing Co., Inc., 1965.

For excellent summaries and reviews on the research on programed instruction, the instructional media, and related topics see the following articles:

Anderson, Richard C., "Educational Psychology," *Annual Review of Psychology,* 18 (1967), 103–64.

Lumsdaine, Arthur A., "Instruments and Media of Instruction," in *Handbook of Research on Teaching,* ed. N. L. Gage, pp. 583–682. Chicago: Rand McNally & Co., 1963.

——— and M. A. May, "Mass Communication and Educational Media," *Annual Review of Psychology,* 16 (1965), 475–534.

For reading on flexible scheduling, team teaching, and nongraded instruction, see the following books:

Bair, Medill and Richard G. Woodward, *Team Teaching in Action.* Boston: Houghton Mifflin Company, 1964.

Brown, Frank B., *The Nongraded High School.* Englewood Cliffs, N.J.: Prentice-Hall, Inc., 1963.

Bush, Robert N. and Dwight W. Allen, *A New Design for High School Education.* New York: McGraw-Hill Book Company, 1964.

Goodlad, John I., and Robert H. Anderson, *The Nongraded Elementary School.* New York: Harcourt, Brace & World, Inc., 1963.

The New Science and Mathematics

13

This chapter describes curricular reforms of the past decade in the fields of physics, biology, and mathematics. Although these reforms are frequently called the *new science* and the *new mathematics,* the new, or modern, character does not refer to knowledge which is necessarily new to the cognoscenti of the particular fields but rather to the preparation and introduction of new instructional objectives, content, procedures, materials, and tests.

The National Science Foundation sponsors the *Course Content Improvement Programs,* the prime objective of which is to develop improved teaching materials in the sciences and mathematics, with the collaboration of scientists, teachers, and educators. The projects described in this chapter were developed as complete model courses or course sequences, with the use of many learning and teaching aids. Although the original projects were designed for the high schools, several projects are presently underway for the elementary schools and for undergraduate college training. Table 13-1 shows the scope of these programs for the elementary and secondary schools in 1966.

The programs have been prepared by curriculum study groups composed of university and college instructors and researchers, high school and elementary school teachers, as well as educational specialists in supervision, administration, learning, and evaluation. The first group was the Physical Science Study Committee, organized in the fall of 1956. This group was followed by the School Mathematics Study Group, the

Chemical Bond Approach Project, the Biological Sciences Curriculum Study, and the Chemical Education Materials Study. By 1963, commercial versions of course materials were available for general school use. This chapter describes only three complete course models for which work has been underway for about ten years.

The basic teaching model helps organize the material of this chapter. The chapter has three major sections: physics (illustrative of the natural sciences), biology (illustrative of the life sciences), and mathematics. For each chapter section there are six parts: a brief description of the background of the program; a description of the instructional objectives and content; a description of the provisions for entering behavior; a description of instructional procedures, including materials, classroom methods, and, if appropriate, the use of the laboratory and films; a description of the tests used for performance assessment; and, finally, an evaluation of the program, based on the available research.

After reading the first section of this chapter (on modern physics), you should be able to meet these objectives:

1. Describe the background of the Physical Science Study Committee (PSSC) by referring to the types of individuals who prepared the physics program and the method used in revising the program.

2. Distinguish between PSSC and traditional physics course objectives.

3. Describe the content of the course by listing its four major parts and describing the relationship of these parts.

4. Describe the number and kinds of principles which the PSSC course requires as entering behavior.

5. Describe the way in which the reading material is presented in the textbook (*Physics*).

6. Describe the four major parts of the *Teacher's Resource Book and Guide* and the general purpose of the guide.

7. Describe the authorship and intended uses of the Science Studies Series.

8. Describe the three purposes for the films and their relationship to scientists.

9. Describe the intended emphasis of the laboratory and the chief recommendation of the Lab Notes.

10. Describe the chief classroom instructional procedure and its relationship to the home, desk, and lab problems.

11. Describe the materials available for performance assessment.

12. Describe the typical result of comparing the performances of PSSC and non-PSSC students on standard and nonstandard examinations.

TABLE 13-1

PRINCIPAL CURRICULUM STUDY GROUPS FOR ELEMENTARY AND SECONDARY SCHOOLS, SPONSORED BY THE NATIONAL SCIENCE FOUNDATION (*BSCS Newsletter*, No. 28, 1964A, p. 15)

SUBJECT	Study group	GRADES	Code
Mathematics	School Mathematics Study Group (Stanford)	K–12	d-A
		6–12	a-A
	University of Illinois Committee on School Mathematics (University of Illinois)	7–8	c-A
		9	d-B
		10–11	c-A
	Computer-Based Math Education Project (Stanford)	1–2	b-A
		6	b-A
		1–6	D
	Cambridge Conference on School Mathematics (ESI)	K–12	b, d-C
	Madison Project (Webster College)	K–9	c-B
	University of Illinois Arithmetic Project (ESI)	K–9	b-B
Mathematics and Science	Minnesota Mathematics and Science Teaching Project (University of Minnesota): Mathematics	K–3	c-A
		4–5	b-A
		6–9	a-A
	Minnesota Mathematics and Science Teaching Project (University of Minnesota): Science	K–2	c-A
		3–5	b-A
Physics	Physical Science Study Committee (ESI)	12	d-A
	Harvard Project Physics (Harvard)	12	b-A
	Engineering Concepts Curriculum Project (CEE)	12	b-A
Chemistry	Chemical Education Materials Study (University of California)	12	d-A
	Chemical Bond Approach Project (Earlham)	12	d-A
Biol[illegible]	Biological Sciences Curriculum Study (University of Colorado)	10	d-A / c-A
		12	d-A

Area	Project	Grades	Symbol
Social Sciences	High School Geography Project (AAG)	9–10	b, c-A
Social Sciences	Anthropology Curriculum Study Project (AAA)	10–12	c-E
Social Sciences	Sociological Resources for Secondary Schools (ASA)	10–12	b-E
Social Sciences	Social Science Curriculum Program (ESI)	1–6	b-A
Social Sciences	Social Science Curriculum Program (ESI)	10	b-A
Science	Secondary School Science Project (Princeton)	10	c-A
Science	Earth Science Curriculum Project (AGI)	9	c-A
Science	Introductory Physical Science Project (ESI)	9	c-A
Science	Elementary School Science Project (University of Illinois)	5–9	c-E
Science	Science Curriculum Improvement Study (University of California)	3–6	b-A
Science	Science Curriculum Improvement Study (University of California)	K–2	c-A
Science	Elementary School Science Project (University of California)	K–6	b, c-E
Science	Elementary Science Study (ESI)	K–8	b, c-E
Science	Commission on Science Education (AAAS)	K–6	c-A
Science	School Science Curriculum Project (University of Illinois)	K–9	b-E

KEY TO SYMBOLS:

a. Planned or projected
b. Preliminary version
c. Extended trial version
d. Released for general use
A. Text and supplementary materials
B. Teacher training films and course materials
C. Guidelines for curriculum and course development
D. Research in learning
E. Unsequenced units and source materials

CEE Commission on Engineering Education
ESI Educational Services Incorporated
AAG American Association of Geographers
AAA American Anthropological Association
ASA American Sociological Association
AGI American Geological Institute
AAAS American Association for the Advancement of Science

After reading the second section of this chapter (on modern biology), you should be able to meet these objectives:

13. Describe the background of the Biological Sciences Curriculum Study (BSCS) by referring to the types of individuals who prepared the program and the method used in revising the materials.

14. List the major objectives of the BSCS program.

15. Make three distinctions between the BSCS and conventional textbooks.

16. List the unifying themes of the BSCS program.

17. State the underlying purpose of the writers of the program by referring to the level of student ability and the scientific method.

18. List the three versions of the BSCS textbooks and describe the particular emphasis of each version.

19. Describe the entering behavior for which these versions were prepared in terms of grade and ability.

20. Describe the materials which have been prepared for (a) advanced students, (b) low-ability students, and (c) superior students.

21. List six characteristics of the textbooks.

22. Describe the uses of the *Biology Teachers' Handbook*.

23. Describe the purpose and use of the laboratory blocks.

24. Describe the two types of films in terms of their purposes and name three characteristics of the student instructional films.

25. Describe the variations in classroom procedure which Gallagher found in his study.

26. Describe the use of programed instruction in the BSCS course by referring to level of student ability and type of program.

27. Describe the materials available for performance assessment.

28. Describe the use of the *Taxonomy* in the analysis of tests and list the four outcomes identified for the BSCS course.

29. Describe the conclusions drawn from the comparison of BSCS and non-BSCS biology courses in terms of the types of tests used in the studies; in terms of levels of student ability; and in terms of the three versions of the course.

After reading the third section of this chapter (on mathematics), you should be able to meet these objectives:

30. Describe the background of the SMSG program in terms of the types of individuals who prepared it.

31. Describe the objectives of the program in terms of mathematical

skills, the content and structure of mathematics, and the training of students; in terms of research goals; and in terms of acceleration of the curriculum.

32. Describe the content of the program by illustrating the spiraled treatment of two topics; the review of two topics; and the grade placement of algebra, geometry (both solid and analytical), trigonometry, and matrix algebra.

33. Describe three levels of special materials for accommodating above- and below-average entering behavior; the relationship between student acceptance of modern mathematics and their level of ability (high, average, and low); and entering behavior lacking in the average student which the program may require in the elementary school.

34. Describe five parts of the *Commentaries* designed to assist the teacher in presenting the course.

35. Describe four supplementary materials which can be used by students and teachers.

36. Describe the purpose and nature of the SMSG films.

37. Distinguish between tell-and-do and heuristic teaching methods by listing their major characteristics and by providing illustrations of each method.

38. List the similarities between the SMSG and the biology and physics programs; list the differences between these mathematics and science programs.

39. Describe the three provisions made by the program for performance assessment.

40. Describe the results of comparing SMSG and traditional programs by referring to traditional and modern tests of mathematical achievement and level of student ability.

41. List the criticisms made of the discovery teaching of mathematics.

42. Describe the relationship between the teacher's acceptance of modern mathematics and years of teaching experience and his assessment of the difficulty of the material.

43. Describe the bases you can use in selecting and teaching the materials in modern mathematics programs.

44. Describe similarities of the results of and the problems in evaluating the science and mathematics programs.

After reading the chapter summary (pp. 600–601) you should be able to meet this objective:

45. Describe the common characteristics of these programs for each component of the basic teaching model.

PHYSICS

Background

The first curriculum study group sponsored by the National Science Foundation was the Physical Science Study Committee (hereafter called the PSSC). The group combined the knowledge and experience of high school and university physics teachers and specialists in testing, film making, educational administration, and editorial production (Finlay, 1962). The committee began its work in 1956, and the materials which it produced were tried, evaluated, and revised for three years prior to their release in the fall of 1960. By 1965 the course was used by about 6,000 teachers and 640,000 students (see PSSC, 1965a). Some schools were selected for intensive feedback, while questionnaires, periodic reports, and regional meetings supplied the feedback from the remaining schools. There have been continued tryouts with larger numbers of schools and teachers and continued development of materials.

Instructional Objectives and Content

By using the material developed by PSSC and by interviewing several of its members, Leslie Trowbridge (1965, p. 117) compiled the following list of objectives which were unique for the new course.

PSSC OBJECTIVES

A. Broad objectives
   1. To emphasize the continuity and unit of physics

B. Development of student attitudes
   2. To emphasize that physicists are typical people of academic life with typical human aspirations
   3. To develop a view of contemporary physics that is consisten with that of the professional physicist

C. Relatedness to experience (associations, applications)
   4. To emphasize the major concepts and principles of physic from the standpoint of their contributions to physics as a pur science

D. Scope and sequence
   5. To emphasize the study of a few major topics at considerabl depth

E. Teaching aids and techniques (textbooks, tests)
   6. To employ tests as a means of determining the ability of stu dents to reason to logical conclusions when working with u familiar data

F. Teaching aids and techniques (laboratory)

7. To emphasize the use of simple apparatus and inexpensive materials where educationally feasible in the laboratory
8. To emphasize the method of laboratory investigation for learning
9. To emphasize the use of equipment and instruments whose working parts are clearly visible
10. To make the laboratory central in the learning process by designing it as a process of inquiry on natural physical problems

G. Teaching aids and techniques (visual aids)

11. To emphasize an integrated film program for helping to teach the principles of physics

H. Skill and concept development

12. To show the importance of scaling and its role in physics
13. To emphasize development of the ability to organize and display data in useful forms for effective analysis of it
14. To emphasize the understanding and use of physical approximations and models in helping to explain theoretical concepts
15. To emphasize the meter-kilogram-second system of units

I. Content objectives

16. To study electricity predominantly from the standpoint of fundamental charge units, their nature, measurement, and behavior

Trowbridge also listed 39 objectives which were common to both the PSSC and traditional physics courses (pp. 118–9). Trowbridge gathered a list of seventy-two objectives, including seventeen objectives unique to the traditional course which do not appear here. He sent the list (randomly ordered) to samples of one hundred PSSC teachers and one hundred traditional teachers and asked them to respond to each objective in terms of the high school physics course they thought should be taught throughout the nation and to indicate the degree of agreement with and the degree to which they were able to teach the objective. Trowbridge found that about 45 per cent of the objectives elicited significant differences in response with respect to the degree of agreement by the two groups. About 36 per cent of the objectives showed significant differences with respect to the achievement of the objective in practice. The following objectives were favored significantly by PSSC teachers over teachers of traditional courses (p. 121):

1. To emphasize the intellectual, cultural, and liberal education aspects of physics
2. To develop an understanding of the purposes, uses, development, and limitations of scientific "theories" in general

3. To teach some of the important historical and philosophical developments of physics
4. To emphasize that physicists are typical people of academic life with typical human aspirations
5. To emphasize the major concepts and principles of physics from the standpoint of their contributions to physics as a pure science
6. To emphasize the study of a few major topics at considerable depth
7. To emphasize the method of laboratory investigation for learning
8. To emphasize the understanding and use of physical approximations and models in helping to explain theoretical concepts

Traditional teachers were more interested in the practical applications of the knowledge of physics, in fulfilling the formal requirements of the curriculum, and in the simple acquisition of substantive material. For example, they wanted their students to be "intelligent consumers of products of modern technology," they wanted to "cover the requirements of standard state and local syllabi and examinations," and "to use a textbook which helps students learn information. . ." (Trowbridge, 1965, p. 121). The PSSC teachers, on the other hand, were more interested in the relationship of physics to the great body of human knowledge, in physics as a theoretical rather than an applied science, and in the use of the laboratory for conducting scientific investigations. Inspection of the teachers' preferences for physics objectives indicates that PSSC and traditional physics courses do significantly differ.

The content of the PSSC course is best revealed by the parts of the second edition of the text, called *Physics* (see PSSC, 1965a):

Part I: The universe
Part II: Optics and waves
Part III: Mechanics
Part IV: Electricity and atomic structure

The preface to *Physics* describes the content and the relationships of these parts. Part I introduces the student to the basic notions of time, space, and matter—particularly to how they are understood and measured. From here, the student moves on to an understanding of velocity and acceleration, of vectors, and of relative motion. He then studies matter, first in relation to time and space and later in relation to mass, conservation of mass, and atomic structure. Part I, in summary, gives the student an overview of the universe. The remaining parts study these fields in greater detail. Part II deals with light—shadows, mirror reflections, refraction, and, finally, a particle theory or model of light. When the particle theory proves inadequate, the student learns about the wave theory—the properties of waves, their behavior under various conditions, and interference and diffraction. Part III deals with dynamics—the laws of conservation of momentum and energy. Part IV introduces the student to the study of electricity and to the physics of the atom. He learns about the forces between charges, the measurement of very small electric forces, the motion of charged particles, magnetic fields, and, finally, the application of this knowledge to the structure of the atom. This brief résumé of the contents shows a concentration on major ideas and a heavy emphasis on relating the parts to the whole. Other characteristics of the material are described later.

Entering Behavior

The committee attempted to design a course to fit into the current pattern of school curricula. Physics is usually an elective available to students in the eleventh and twelfth grades—usually those in the upper hall of their classes (Finlay, 1964). Since not all these students pursue scientific careers, the committee tried to design a single course for both science and nonscience majors.

Dale Rathe (1965) conducted a study of the principles the student should know before studying the PSSC course. He compiled a list of 223 principles and submitted it to twenty-one PSSC instructors who indictated their degree of agreement. Rathe reached these conclusions: (1) 134 principles were identified as basic and preliminary to PSSC physics; (2) these principles pertained mainly to matter, magnetism, and some aspects of light and energy; (3) principles of relatively low desirability as entering behavior pertained to waves, dynamics, and some aspects of light and energy; (4) the teachers disagreed over the ability of certain scientific terms to convey fairly accurate scientific meaning and over how accurately quantitative relationships should be expressed in preparatory courses.

PSSC is now developing sets of material for students of advanced entering behavior. The tailoring of the present PSSC course to individual students is left to the teacher (see PSSC, 1965b). The teacher, of course, is not expected to use all the available materials which accompany the text and is often free to select those which may best accommodate the entering behavior of particular students. A series of problems, however, called the *home, desk, and lab problems,* are classified in the *Teacher's Resource Book and Guide* as easy, medium, hard, and recommended.

Instructional Procedures

Here we shall consider the instructional materials and equipment, the films, and the procedures (including the laboratory procedures) used in the PSSC program.

MATERIALS. The PSSC materials consist of the following: the textbook (*Physics*), which includes home, desk, and lab problems; the PSSC motion pictures; the *Teacher's Resource Book and Guide* (including the Lab Notes); laboratory apparatus and a laboratory guidebook for students; two sets of tests, each containing ten achievement tests and two comprehensive tests; and the Science Study Series, paperbacks written by expert authors for the student and the lay public. The diversity and scope of these materials indicate the comprehensive nature of the PSSC program.

The core of the materials is the textbook entitled *Physics* (see PSSC, 1965a). It is prepared in such a way that the student moves from the consideration of concrete phenomena to the consideration of abstract concepts (PSSC, 1965b, p. viii). Illustrative of this technique is the opening of the first chapter (PSSC, 1965a, p. 1):

> When a flash of lightning shatters the dark, the radio crackles and your eyes are dazzled for a few seconds. A moment later you hear the roll of thunder, and a loose windowpane rattles. Three states away in a short-location center, a radio locater can pinpoint the lightning stroke; and downtown the weather forecaster, hearing a faraway rumble, nods as if he has been expecting the storm. . . . Take another chain of events. In the test shops of a steel mill you can watch a thin bar of a new alloy pulled at its ends by the powerful jaws of a testing machine as big as a house, which is driven by a fast-whirring electric motor no bigger than a football. The solid bar slowly yields to the pull. It stretches out like a piece of taffy, and breaks a little later with a jangle of sound. How does it all work? . . . Physics enabes us to answer such questions. It gives us the power to predict and to design, to understand and to adventure into the unknown.

The passage begins with the concrete descriptions of a storm and of the reduction of a piece of metal and ends with the abstract notion of scientific inquiry in the field of physics. This technique is similar to the procedures for concept teaching and learning, which require presentation of examples of the concept as the basis for the students' inferring the concept attributes (Chapter 10). The technique is also similar to discovery learning (Chapter 11), except that the text ultimately gives the students the concept or principle which they would otherwise be expected to discover with relative independence.

Teacher's Resource Book and Guide is in four parts, one for each part of the text. The general purpose of the *Guide* is to help teachers translate PSSC materials into classroom and laboratory activities. It consists of (1) Text Notes, which explain the reasons for a particular argument or sequence of ideas and discuss the teaching of the course; (2) suggestions for scheduling the chapter; (3) notes on the use of home, desk, and lab problems, the films, and the books in the Science Study Series; and (4) Lab Notes on the use of laboratory experiments and apparatus. For Chapter 2, for example, the *Guide* makes the following suggestions: an experiment on short-time intervals; films on short-time intervals, long-time intervals, and time and clocks; use of the home, desk, and lab problems which appear in the textbook (with the answers to the problems); and discussions about the purpose, emphasis, and more technical aspects of the material appearing in the textbook. The *Guide* tends to be considerably more detailed and integrated than many conventional course guides.

The Science Studies Series contained in 1965 about forty published books. Written by distinguished authors, the books deal either with the function of physics in modern technology and civilization or with the lives of scientists and their great discoveries. The books are supplementary materials and are not intended as a formal part of the course. The teachers and students can use the books for reference and resource material.

FILMS. The PSSC program developed films to be scheduled at particular points in the program. The films have several purposes: introducing a subject, providing data through an experiment too difficult for the students to perform, and helping to summarize a subject (PSSC, 1965b, p. x). The *Guide* states (p. x):

> Beyond their content the films are intended to show real scientists in action, presenting them not as disembodied intellects, but as normal, active, occasionally fallible human beings, dealing with real problems and deriving satisfaction and at times excitement from their work. In this quietly implicit way the films attempt to show the nature of the scientist and the scientific way of life. Finally, the films are scrupulously honest. Filmed experiments are carefully performed and accurately reported. The films contain no high gloss; they are frankly teaching films.

LABORATORY. I have already described the inductive style of the textbook, which proceeds from descriptions of concrete phonomena to discussions of the related abstract concepts and principles. The intended emphasis is on advancing the "search for understanding rather than just learning the facts" (PSSC, 1965b, p. xiv). The laboratory also emphasizes an inductive, or discovery, approach to learning. And like the films, the laboratory is an integral part of the general instructional procedure. The Lab Notes appear as an appendix in each of the four parts of the *Guide*. These give detailed information on the use of laboratory experiments and apparatus and descriptions of the purposes of and suggestions for the optimal scheduling of the experiments. A Student's Laboratory Guide provides a minimum set of directions and directs attention by asking important questions about an experiment. The Lab Notes recommend that the experiments be done before the topics are taken up in the text so that the students are not told what to expect and so that they learn to enjoy doing experiments for which they do not know the results in advance. The experiments are intended to replace most teacher demonstrations and to reduce the amount of time spent in the classroom on explanations. There have been attempts to integrate the laboratory experimentation with the experimentation depicted by the films.

Classroom procedures. Much of the classroom time is to be used in discussion and analysis of the home, desk, and lab problems. Attempts have been made to order the problems in terms of entering behavior, so that easier and simpler problems precede more difficult and complex problems, even though the order does not follow the conceptual development of the chapter. The *Guide* suggests problems which are best adapted to classroom discussion and matches the problems with the appropriate textbook chapter sections. Although most problems are designed for elucidation and practice of the concepts in the text, some problems are useful for summarizing and relating the various ideas in the chapter. All problems furnish feedback for student and teacher on the degree of mastery of the chapter sections. The heavy emphasis on laboratory experimentation and the discussion and analysis of problems indicate that the PSSC course departs from conventional courses, which lean more heavily on lectures and teacher demonstrations.

Performance Assessment

The PSSC course has two complete sets of achievement tests. Each set contains ten tests, two tests for each part of the course and two finals. There are also two comprehensive examinations, one for the first and one for the second half of the course. The tests are objective and stress the application of knowledge rather than the recall of facts (PSSC, 1965b, p. x). It is also expected that the teacher construct his own quizzes and examinations to supplement these tests. The PSSC tests and examinations; the teacher-made tests and examinations; the home, desk, and lab problems; and the teacher's laboratory and homework assignments are the chief sources of feedback for performance assessment.

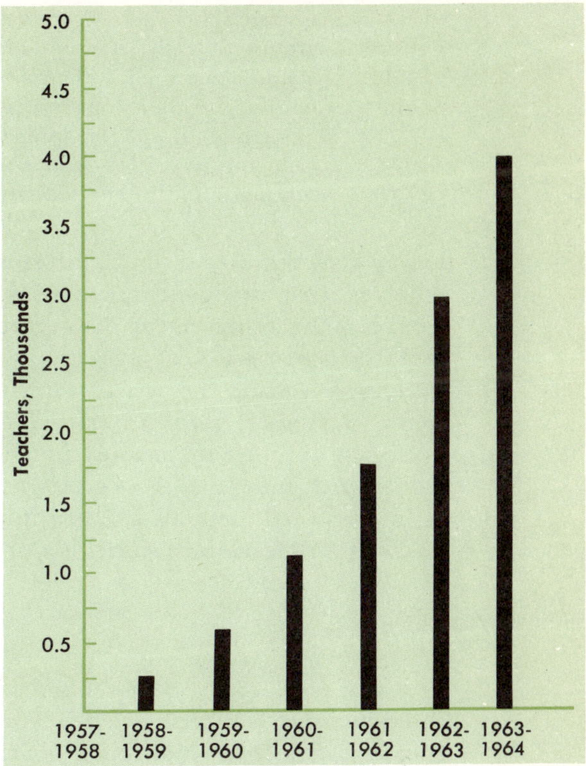

Fig. 13-1. *The growth of the PSSC physics course, 1957–1964, including only those teachers who used the materials as their principal resource, from the* ESI Quarterly *(Winter–Spring 1964), p. 4.*

Evaluation

The major means of evaluation has been the actual tryout of the PSSC course in many schools throughout the nation. Figure 13-1 shows the growth in the use of the course between 1957 and 1964 in terms of number of teachers. Gilbert Finlay (1964) believes that the PSSC course cannot be compared with other courses because it differs in selection of content and in style of development. When standard physics exams have been given to PSSC and non-PSSC physics students, the results indicate that the students have studied different courses. The College Entrance Examination Board, recognizing the uniqueness of the PSSC course, provides separate examinations in physics for PSSC and non-PSSC students. Finlay states (p. 14):

> Certainly it is possible to design an examination on which matched groups of PSSC students and students from other physics courses would achieve equivalent score distributions. This procedure would hardly provide a comparison. It would prove only that such an examination could be prepared. Comparative evaluation requires common objectives—common with reference to fundamentals of substance and intellectual style.

Finlay goes on to state that performance on the PSSC achievement tests indicates that the present course is effective in achieving its own objectives. The achievement tests have been constructed so that average performance consists of answering one-half the questions correctly. A study which made the actual comparison between traditional and PSSC courses (Hipsher, 1961) supported Finlay's contention that a test cannot be an appropriate measure in a course for which it was not designed. Paul Hurd and Mary Rowe (1964) conclude that comparative studies of instructional methods will continue to be premature until we develop teaching and learning theories about the formation of scientific concepts.

Summary

The PSSC course represents the first major curriculum reform sponsored by the National Science Foundation. You have seen how this course differs from traditional courses in objectives, required entering behavior, procedures, and performance assessment. As objectives it emphasizes the continuity and unity of physics, the humane aspects of scientific inquiry, the advanced exploration of basic ideas, and the nature of and satisfaction of engaging in scientific inquiry. The emphasis is on physics as a theoretical rather than as an applied science. The course content is selected and organized so that concepts appearing later in the text build on concepts and skills introduced earlier. The content, that is, tends to be more highly integrated than that in the traditional text. One study of entering behavior indicates that the sudent of the PSSC course must have learned 134 principles which are basic and preliminary to PSSC physics. Regarding instructional procedures, the course has developed a full array of materials: the student textbook (including the home, lab, and desk problems) ; the *Teacher's Resource Book and Guide* (including the Lab Notes); the PSSC films; the Science Study Series; and achievement tests and comprehensive examinations. The textbook uses an inductive style. The *Guide* helps the teacher translate PSSC materials into classroom and laboratory activities. The films introduce subjects, portray difficult experiments, and show scientists at work. The major purpose of the laboratory is to introduce the student to the realities and the satisfactions of scientific inquiry as well as to help him understand the subject matter of the course. The recommended use of the home, desk, and lab problems suggests that the course should emphasize laboratory investigation and classroom discussion and analysis rather than the more traditional lecture and teacher-demonstration procedures. The unit achievement tests and the comprehensive examinations stress application of knowledge rather than recall of facts. Available evidence does not enable us to assay the comparative effectiveness of the traditional and the PSSC physics courses. Internal evaluations produce some evidence that the course does enable students to achieve course objectives. Further evaluation may have to await further development of teaching and learning theory as these pertain to the formation of scientific concepts and principles.

You should now return to objectives 1–12 (p. 557) and determine how well you have achieved them.

QUESTION 13-1

Trowbridge (1965) studied the preferences of physics teachers for various objectives of the physics course. In the list of objectives which follows place an *M* after the objective if it is likely to be favored by teachers of the modern course, a *T* if it is likely to be favored by teachers of the traditional course, and a *J* if it is likely to be a preference of teachers of both types of courses.

(a) To use a textbook which helps students acquire information.

(b) To emphasize the study of a few major topics in considerable depth.

(c) To teach some of the important historical and philosophical developments of physics.

(d) To emphasize the method of laboratory investigation for learning.

(e) To develop intelligent consumers of modern technology.

(f) To prepare students for advanced work in colleges and universities.

(g) To cover as many requirements of state examinations as possible.

After marking each objective with an *M, T,* or *J,* give the reasons for your designations.

BIOLOGY

Background

The Biological Sciences Curriculum Study was sponsored in 1958 by the American Institute of Biological Sciences, the professional organization of biologists in this country. The purpose of the Biological

Sciences Curriculum Study (hereafter called BSCS) was to improve biology education. The fiscal support for BSCS has come from the National Science Foundation and, in the international aspect of the study, from the Rockefeller Foundation. The first writing conference occurred in Boulder, Colorado, in 1960; it consisted chiefly of high school biology teachers and research biologists (*BSCS Newsletter,* No. 7, 1961). The policy committee, however, consisted of high school biology teachers, science supervisors, educational specialists, medical and agricultural educators, and university administrators. Materials were tried and revised by about 1,000 teachers before they were made generally available in 1963 (Mayer, 1966). The BSCS produced three modern biology courses and an abundance of instructional materials. The tryout, revision, and development of new materials continues.

Instructional Objectives and Content

The objectives for the BSCS program were formulated in 1960. The following is one statement of these objectives (BSCS, 1964a, p. 5):

1. An understanding of the diversity of life and the interrelations of all organisms.
2. An understanding of the nature of scientific inquiry: Science is an open-ended intellectual activity, and what is presently "known" or believed is subject to change at any time.
3. An understanding of the limitations of science and of the scientific method: Many problems, some of the greatest importance, cannot be dealt with scientifically.
4. An understanding of the biological basis of problems in medicine, public health, agriculture, and conservation.
5. An appreciation of the beauty, drama, and tragedy of the living world.
6. An understanding of the historical development of the concepts of biology and their dependence on the nature of society and technology of each age.
7. An understanding of what biologists presently know regarding the basic biological problems of evolution, development, and inheritance.
8. An understanding of man's own place in the scheme of nature; that he has much in common with other organisms; and that he interacts with all organisms in the biological system of the earth.

No study compares the objectives of the BSCS course with traditional biology course objectives. The *BSCS Newsletter* (No. 12, 1962), however, makes three distinctions between BSCS biology texts and conventional high school biology texts: The BSCS text is a product of the cooperation of research biologists, high school biology teachers, and educational specialists; it places greater emphasis on laboratory work and on the inquiring processes in science; and it has unifying threads which weave the materials together. These are the threads:

1. Change of living things through time—evolution
2. Diversity of type and unity of pattern of living things
3. Genetic continuity of life
4. Complementarity of organism and environment
5. Biological roots of behavior
6. Complementarity of structure and function
7. Regulation and homeostasis: the maintenance of life in the face of change
8. Science as inquiry
9. Intellectual history of biological concepts.

The *BSCS Newsletter* (No. 17, 1963, p. 7) contains this general statement of the general goals of the BSCS courses.

> The writers' primary purpose was to prepare first high school biology courses, suitable for wide use in the *average* high school, with *average* classes, to give students a basic understanding of science and scientific processes, and in so doing, to build scientific literacy in order to aid in the preparation of the student for later responsible citizenship. The writers aim to teach science as a way of thinking—as a method of seeking answers. To do this, they stress the underlying concepts and understandings. Student work is centered in the laboratory, where real problems are explored; open-ended experiments and other materials are used as the media for conveying an understanding of science. Through emphasis on basic concepts and the illustration of such concepts in many varied ways, the student is given practice in drawing generalizations, in seeking relationships, and in finding answers.

There are three versions of the basic textbook: the blue, the green, and the yellow. These versions differ in emphasis but not in level of difficulty. The major emphasis of the green version is on ecology. The blue version emphasizes physiology and biochemistry. The yellow version emphasizes cell biology, genetics, and evolution. Figure 13-2 shows the various levels of emphasis for these three versions and for conventional texts. The 1963 editions of *BSCS High School Biology* reveal the differences in content and emphases of the three versions. Here are the major headings of the tables of contents for the three versions (*BSCS Newsletter,* No. 17, 1963, p. 9).

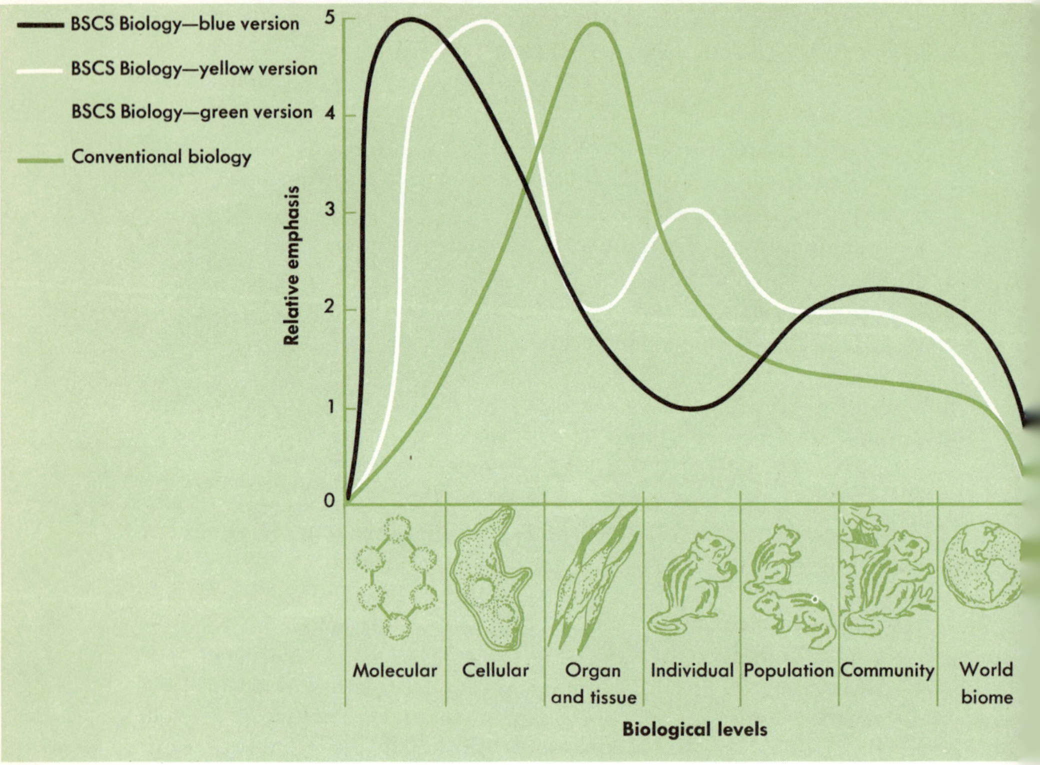

Fig. 13-2. *The differences between the three BSCS course versions and the conventional biology course (*BSCS Newsletter, *No. 17, 1963, p. 8).*

Yellow version: *Biological Science*
- A. Biology of Cells
- B. Microorganisms
- C. Plants
- D. Animals
- E. Genetic Continuity
- F. Change Through Time—Evolution
- G. Organisms and Environment
- H. Synthesis

Blue version: *Biological Science: Molecules to Man*
- Unit One. Biology: the Interaction of Facts and Ideas
- Unit Two. The Evolution of the Cell
- Unit Three. The Evolving Organism
- Unit Four. Multicellular Organisms: New Individuals
- Unit Five. Multicellular Organisms: Genetic Continuity

Unit Six. Multicellular Organisms: Energy Utilization
Unit Seven. Multicellular Organisms: Integrative Systems
Unit Eight. Higher Level of Organization

Green version: *High School Biology*

Section 1. The World of Life: The Biosphere
Section 2. Diversity in the Biosphere
Section 3. Patterns of the Biosphere
Section 4. Within the Individual Organism
Section 5. Patterns of Survival
Section 6. Man and the Biosphere

Entering Behavior

The BSCS textbooks (all three versions) are for tenth grade biology students of average ability (*BSCS Newsletter,* No. 17, 1963). The committee was aware that this group has a wider span of ability than is the case for chemistry and physics students. The materials are not for the "lowest 20 or 30 per cent of the students who take high school biology" (p. 13). Superior ninth grade students are able to use the materials with success. As for previously acquired knowledge, it is desirable but not essential that the student have knowledge of atomic structure and good junior high school courses in physical science and mathematics.

The BSCS second course is for students who are able and who want to continue their study in greater depth. The textbook for the course is *Biological Science: Interaction of Experiments and Ideas* (see BSCS, 1964b). The primary goal of the second course is to provide activities which simulate biological research and which develop in the students an understanding of science from direct experience (Abraham, 1966). Thirty-eight scheduled laboratory investigations and many other related investigations give the teacher breadth in dealing with students of diverse interests and preparation. Accompanying the textbook for the second course is the teacher's edition, which contains photographed pages of the student's edition with annotated comments and appropriate discussions of how the material may be presented.

For students who have difficulty with the three versions, the BSCS Special Materials Committee developed a fourth version. The textbook is *Biological Science: Patterns and Processes* (see BSCS, 1966a); it is accompanied by a *Teacher's Handbook.* This version is best for students who score at the fortieth percentile or lower on the Differential Aptitude Test (Liebherr, 1966). The textbook presents basic biological concepts: ecological relationships, cell-energy processes, reproduction and development, genetic continuity, and organic evolution. The learning situations are more structured than they are in the other versions, and each topic is developed in small steps.

For the gifted student, BSCS has a series of four volumes—*BSCS Research Problems in Biology* (Lanham, 1966). Each volume consists of forty separate investigations, all prepared by active researchers. Student research on these problems could give publishable results. In the early phases of development, the problems were prospectuses dealing with such matters as the nutrition of excised plant tissues and organs, communication by the trail laying of ants, the relationship of water traces to the survival of plant cells, and the detection of the effects of genes carried in heterozygous condition (Schwab, 1963).

Thus, BSCS has a wide range of instructional materials to accommodate differences in student entering behavior. It has concentrated on producing materials for the average student, the slow learner, the gifted student, and the advanced student.

Instructional Procedures

BSCS has produced many instructional materials. I have already referred to the materials produced for the slow learner and for the gifted and the advanced students. Materials have also been prepared for the average student (in addition to the three versions of the textbook), teachers, teacher training, school administrators, and the general public. Figure 13-3 shows the scope and diversity of the BSCS work. We shall first consider the written materials, then the laboratory, the films, and the classroom procedures.

Materials. Among the major instructional materials are the three versions of the BSCS textbook. Using the green version as an example, we see the following characteristics. The textbook is carefully organized so that vocabulary and concepts are sequential and cumulative. Several paragraphs introduce each of the major parts (or sections) of the books by setting the stage, presenting a viewpoint, and relating the section to the whole course. Marginal notes provide pronunciation and meaning of technical terms and call attention to related laboratory exercises. Summaries bring together the major ideas of each chapter, sometimes in new relationships to each other. Guide questions aid in the recall of the chapter material; problems require solving, computation, or even research. Finally there are suggested readings and references to the *Scientific American*.

The teacher can use various guides in presenting the BSCS course. *Biology Teachers' Handbook* (Schwab, 1963) serves as a guide to the content, emphases, themes, and objectives; provides the Invitations to Enquiry; clarifies recent developments in biology; and offers material designed to facilitate the teaching of the course—suggestions for test construction, further reading, and classroom and laboratory activities.

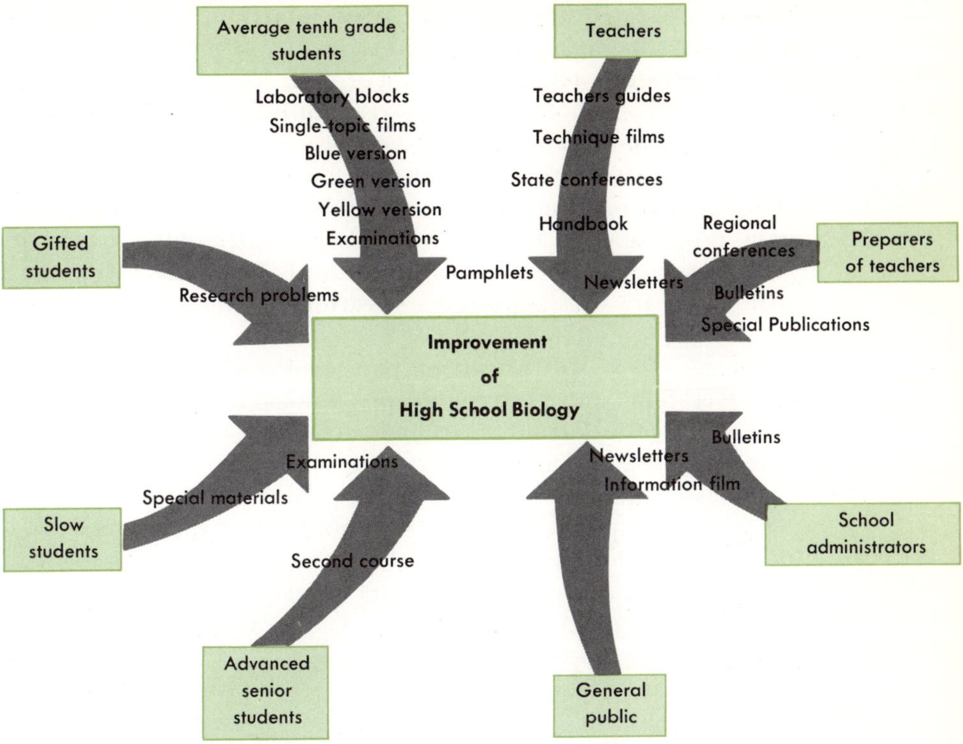

Fig. 13-3. *The materials and activities of the BSCS program and the groups for which they have been provided (*BSCS Newsletter, *No. 27, 1966a, p. 5).*

Each of the versions of the textbook has its own teacher's guide, which contains general considerations for the course and for the particular version of the course and specific suggestions for the use of text and laboratory.

LABORATORY. BSCS has developed many materials for the laboratory. A major contribution is the laboratory blocks, designed to emphasize the laboratory as a place for carrying out investigations in contrast to a place for demonstrations and the practice of routine techniques (Schwab, 1963). They guide the student to his own discoveries and give him the opportunity to carry out investigations in considerable depth. Although questions and problems are posed, no answers are given in advance. Each block takes six weeks, and it is intended that one block be conveniently inserted in the biology course during the school year. The teacher's major task is to fit the block he selects properly into his course. A limited number of topics were selected for block treatment, research biologists prepared materials, and teachers tested the materials in high school laboratories. By 1966, about thirteen laboratory blocks had been prepared. For each laboratory block there is a student and teacher edition. BSCS also published *Innovations in Equipment and Techniques for the Biology Teaching Laboratory* (Barthelemy *et al.*, 1964), a resource book for teachers, which discusses techniques and equipment for the biology teaching laboratory, the culture of microorganisms, laboratory animals and their housing, and so on. In its emphasis on relatively open investigation the BSCS course is like the PSSC course. Both are stressing discovery learning.

FILMS. There are two major parts of the BSCS film program: the techniques films and the single-topic films. The technique films help teachers to master laboratory techniques needed for teaching the course. There have been films on bacteriological techniques, culturing slime-mold plasmodium, genetics techniques, smear and squash techniques, weighing techniques, and so on. The single-topic films are short, silent films which each illustrate a single concept; they are presented in a way which helps students discover and develop the concept that explains the phenomena observed on the screen. The single-topic films are four to five minutes in length. They pose questions, raise problems, and present experimental data. The students are required to form hypotheses to explain the observed phenomena. There is a teacher's guide for each film. Among others, there are films on social behavior in chickens, mimicry, natural selection of the peppered moth, mating behavior in the cockroach, and courtship of the queen butterfly.

CLASSROOM PROCEDURES. James Gallagher (1967) studied the procedures, or styles, used by six biology teachers and their classes of superior-ability students who were using the blue version of the BSCS course. All the teachers were observed introducing the subject of photosynthesis. Observations were classified by a system developed by Mary Jane Aschner, Gallagher, and others (1965) which groups observations by (1) the level of conceptualization and (2) the style of thinking evident in classroom discussion. The level of conceptualization can range from specifics (data) through simple concepts to principles (generalizations). Table 13-2 illustrates the three levels of conceptualization. The instructional procedure can vary from description, expansion, and explanation to evaluation; this procedure is also illustrated for the topic of photosynthesis in Table 13-2.

Gallagher notes that the *Biology Teachers' Handbook* (Schwab, 1963, p. 430) states that discussion is an indispensable instructional procedure in teaching the intellectual arts and skills. Gallagher tallied the number of lines spoken by the teacher and by the students. The percentage of teacher talk varied from 66 to 95 per cent. In the classrooms of

TABLE 13-2

SYSTEM USED TO CLASSIFY BSCS TEACHERS' CLASSROOM PROCEDURES (Gallagher, 1967, p. 11).

		Description	Expansion	Explanation	Evaluation
Level of conceptualization	Generalization	The system of photosynthesis.	What would happen if the system of photosynthesis ceased functioning?	Show how the system of photosynthesis explains the change in the color of leaves from brown to green.	Does this represent an adequate statement for photosynthesis? $CO_2 + H_2O \rightarrow [CH_2O] + O_2$
	Concept	The definition of a heterotroph.	Contrast the autotroph and the heterotroph.	How do we know that the oxygen from photosynthesis comes from water?	Do you believe it was essential that autotrophs developed?
	Data	What colors do you see in the spectroscope?	Compare the black vs. white cloths, their ability to absorb light.	Describe in sequence the experiment by Calvin.	Was our experiment a success?

Xavier and Zorba (fictitious names), the chief procedure seemed to be lecture punctuated by occasional questions. The data for Uriah and Virgil suggest considerable teacher-student interaction and discussion. A further analysis of these data indicated that the teachers generally kept the same proportion of teacher-student talk regardless of the type (or style) of topic being discussed. Gallagher concluded that the teachers did most of the talking in discussion sections, that the amount of student talk allowed varied, and that the amount of talk allowed did not vary with the topic. He further concluded, from an operational standpoint, that there is no such thing as a single BSCS curriculum presentation in the schools. There are instead different teacher interpretations of the curriculum, and the course is taught at different levels of abstraction. The differences often reflect the teachers' special interests and special areas of knowledge.

In *Biological Science: Patterns and Processes,* the text for the slow learners, programed sequences are provided in various places. The linear format is used with frames of about three printed lines in length. Review frames of considerably longer length appear at appropriate places. The materials for average, superior, and advanced students do not have programed sequences.

Performance Assessment

For each version of the major program there are four quarterly achievement tests. Teachers may use two forms of a comprehensive final for all versions. In addition, they may use the Processes of Science Test (POST) as a pretest and a posttest to measure student comprehension of scientific inquiry. Special tests have been or are being constructed for materials used in the special courses.

In the early development of these tests use was made of the *Taxonomy of Educational Objectives* (see Chapter 2). A test grid was developed which listed the major themes of the course (see p. 573) along one axis and the various categories and subcategories of behavior as described in the *Taxonomy* along the other axis (Klinckman, 1963). By applying the test grid to his own test, the instructor could determine how many test items fell within each grid cell (see Chapter 14).

Joseph Schwab (1963) identified four outcomes which the tests are designed to measure: (1) the ability to recall information and to make minor reorganizations of materials learned; (2) the ability to show relations between bodies of knowledge learned at different times or in connection with different topics; (3) the understanding of materials learned as demonstrated by the ability to apply knowledge in new situations; and (4) the ability to use the skills involved in understanding scientific problems and problem solutions.

Evaluation

As in PSSC physics, the major source of feedback for the BSCS course is the actual school tryouts. Also, several studies have attempted to compare student achievement in the BSCS and in conventional or traditional courses. Mary Louise Lance (1964) used the Nelson Biology Test and the Noll What Do You Think? Test to compare achievement in the BSCS and in a conventional course. There were no significant differences in performance on either test. In both courses, however, the boys out-performed the girls, and the ninth graders out-performed the tenth graders. Lorenzo Lisonbee and Bill Fullerton (1964) also found no significant differences in achievement as measured by the Nelson Biology Test. However, using the BSCS comprehensive final to measure achievement, they found that the middle IQ group of the BSCS course did better than the middle IQ group of the traditional course. In a later study which largely confirmed the findings of the previous studies, Olan Moore (1965) found that BSCS students were superior to traditional students in achievement as measured by the BSCS final but that both groups performed equally well on the Nelson Biology Test. The embarrassingly obvious conclusion of these and other studies is that biology students perform best on tests for which their biology courses prepare them. The Nelson Biology Test heavily emphasizes the recall of substantive course content. The BSCS final emphasizes the application of knowledge to new situations and the use of skills to solve scientific problems. It is also very likely that the traditional and the BSCS courses emphasize the same outcomes as those stressed by their respective tests. Comparing the effectiveness of BSCS and traditional courses poses the same problems faced in evaluation of the PSSC course: Courses which do not have the same instructional objectives cannot be compared.

There have also been studies of other aspects of the BSCS program. Marjorie Behringer (1966), using the comprehensive final and the Processes of Science Test, compared the effectiveness of the three levels of the BSCS curricula developed for superior, average, and low-ability students. Each of the modified curricula was compared with the original BSCS course at each level of student ability. She found that there were no significant differences in student achievement between those in the modified and those in the unmodified curricula, that teachers and students liked the modified curricula for the low-ability but not for the superior students, and that achievement was too related to English-language mastery for the low-ability and average student, but not for the superior student. Ralph Cain and Eugene Lee (1963) compared the BSCS and traditional courses for their use of mathematics and found a marked increase in the use of mathematics in the BSCS course. Using the Watson-Glazer Critical Thinking Appraisal, Kenneth George (1965) found that students using the blue version of the course did better than students using the yellow version and that both of these groups did better than students using the green version. Jacob Blankenship (1965), using a personality inventory and a test of personal values, found that teachers with high independence of thought and with three years or less of experience teaching biology reacted more favorably toward the BSCS course than teachers with less independence of thought and with three or more years of experience.

Summary

The BSCS course bears many similarities to the PSSC course. In its educational objectives the BSCS emphasizes the understanding of scientific inquiry, the recurrent basic themes in biological study, and the relationship of biological knowledge to other areas of knowledge and to the social context in which this knowledge emerges. The course content is organized so that concepts learned earlier are utilized later. For superior levels of entering behavior, the two courses have materials which heavily emphasize the research-laboratory function. Regarding instructional procedures, both courses have an impressive array of materials, films, and guides. For performance assessment, both courses have batteries of examinations which attempt to measure research skills as well as the recall of substantive course content. Both courses represent prototypal instructional systems.

The two courses also show some important differences. The original BSCS course had three versions, probably reflecting the greater theoretical diversity in the field of biology as compared with that in physics. Because each version has its own teacher and student manuals, the BSCS course has a greater mass of instructional material. Also, in the case of entering behavior, BSCS has made greater effort to produce modified courses for students of high, average, and low ability. These efforts in part reflect the wider range of ability of tenth grade biology students as compared with that of eleventh and twelfth grade physics students. BSCS also has made a concerted effort to provide a sound and intellectually respectable biology course for all students in the American schools, a goal shared but perhaps not so productively pursued by other NSF programs. BSCS has produced more teacher-training materials—films, pamphlets, and handbooks—than the PSSC course has. Both courses, however, have provided numerous summer workshops for the preparation of teachers.

The evaluation of both courses has proved equally difficult for identical reasons. In both cases the evaluation must rest on theories of teaching and concept learning which are presently lacking. It is also impossible to make comparisons between traditional and new courses when these courses do not share the same objectives, do not teach the same course content, do not use the same films, employ the laboratory in different ways for different purposes, and attract teachers who, like most other human beings, prefer familiar materials and methods, whether new or old, to the unfamiliar and, for them, the untried. However, traditional and new science courses are not mutually exclusive worlds; the teacher's major effort should be to distill from both the best in science teaching.

You should now return to objectives 13–29 (p. 560) and determine how well you have achieved them.

QUESTION 13-2

Below are four test questions for assessing performance in the BSCS course. Using the letter which precedes each question and, if necessary, referring to the *Taxonomy* (p. 580) arrange the questions in the order which reflects the relative emphasis found in the BSCS course on types of objectives. Head the list with the question which reflects the major emphasis and list the remaining questions in order of descending emphasis.

(a) What is the significance of mitosis and cell division to the growth of multicellular organisms? (Schwab, 1963, p. 459.)

(b) In an early chapter of your text Albert Einstein is quoted. He talks about "the face of a watch and the hidden works" to suggest one aspect of the method of science. In the case of Charles Darwin's contribution to biology, what are some of the matters which correspond to the "face of the watch"? To "hidden works"? (Schwab, 1963, pp. 476–77.)

(c) It is believed that complex molecules were formed in the "hot thin soup" of the early seas. These reacted to form large "aggregates," which eventually showed the attributes of life. How would it be possible to determine when the transition from the nonliving to the living clumps of molecules occurred? (Schwab, 1963, p. 459.)

(d) List the names of the stages in mitosis. (Schwab, 1963, p. 458.)

After selecting your answer, give the reason for your choice and for your rejection of the alternatives.

MATHEMATICS

The National Science Foundation has sponsored several curriculum groups in the area of mathematics (see Table 13-1, pp. 558–59). The two projects which have received considerable attention have been the University of Illinois Committee on School Mathematics (UICSM) and the School Mathematics Study Group (SMSG). Because the work of the SMSG has had the broadest scope and cooperation (DeMott, 1962), I have selected it to illustrate the curricular reform in mathematics. It is probably closer to the truth to state that there is not any one new mathematics program, but instead several new programs, most of which share the general characteristics I will describe for SMSG (Spitzer, 1962).

Background

A conference of mathematicians held at the Massachusetts Institute of Technology in February 1958 passed a resolution which directed the presidents of the professional associations of mathematicians and the teachers of mathematics to organize the SMSG, a program eventually supported by the National Science Foundation. Edward G. Begle, a professor of mathematics presently at Stanford University, headed the committee. This committee, in turn, appointed an advisory committee consisting of college and university mathematicians, high school mathematics teachers, professional educators, and representatives from the fields of science and technology (Wooton, 1964a). In this way SMSG was similar to the physics and biology groups in having professional experts, in this case mathematicians, supply the content and in having teachers interpret the work in terms of classroom practice and student capability. As in the physics and biology programs, the textbooks were written by committees of mathematicians, teachers, and supervisors. During the summer of 1959, preliminary versions of the books were produced for grades 7 through 12. They were tried out during the academic year 1959–60 and completely revised at Stanford University during the summer of 1960. During the school year 1961–62, 500,000 volumes of SMSG materials were sold.

Objectives and Content

An early formal statement of SMSG proposed these objectives (Wagner, 1960, pp. 454–5) :

> The world of today demands more mathematical knowledge on the part of more people than the world of yesterday. Our society leans more and more heavily on science and technology. The number of our citizens skilled in mathematics must be greatly increased; an understanding of the role of mathematics in our society is now a prerequisite for intelligent citizenship. Since no one can predict with certainty his future profession, much less foretell which mathematical skills will be required by a given profession, it is important that mathematics be so taught that the students will be able in later

> life to learn the new mathematical skills which the future will surely demand of many of them. To achieve this objective in the teaching of school mathematics, three things are required. First, we need an improved curriculum which will offer students not only the basic mathematical skills but also a deeper understanding of the basic content and structure of mathematics. Second, mathematics programs must attract and train more of those students who are capable of studying mathematics with profit. Finally, all help possible must be provided for teachers who are preparing themselves to teach these challenging and interesting courses.

A statement appearing in the bylaws (*SMSG Newsletter,* No. 11, 1962) states the following purposes:

> The primary purpose of the SMSG is to foster research and development in the teaching of school mathematics. This research will consist, in part, of a continual review of the mathematics curricula in the schools, as an aid in the selection and design of promising experiments. It will also consist in part of an analysis of the results of experimental teaching, as an aid in judging whether the objectives of various programs are being achieved. But the work of the SMSG should consist primarily in the development of courses, teaching materials, and teaching methods.

The earlier statement expresses the concern of SMSG about the original form its materials and courses should take, while the later statement concerns the continued evaluation and development of instructional procedures and materials. As with the physics and biology groups, a central concern was to present to the student a unified view and the basic structure of the particular discipline.

The fact that the SMSG program is to accelerate the teaching of mathematics was reflected in the Cambridge Conference Report of 1963. According to Irving Adler (1966, p. 179) this is the main conclusion of the report:

> A student who has worked through the full thirteen years of mathematics in grades K to 12 should have a level of training comparable to three years of top-level college training today; that is, we shall expect him to have the equivalent of two years of calculus, and one semester each of modern algebra and probability theory. . . . We propose to gain three years through a new organization of the subject matter and the virtually total abandonment of drill for drill's sake, replacing the unmotivated drill of classical arithmetic by probems which illustrate new mathematical concepts.

The SMSG program has produced such a broad scope of materials for all elementary and secondary school grades that it is difficult to outline its content. The skeletal outline (*SMSG Description of Titles,* 1966d) which follows, however, will indicate the major areas of study and the grade placement of these areas.

GRADES K THROUGH 3

Kindergarten: sets; recognizing geometric figures; comparison of sets; subset of a set; joining and removing; comparison of sizes and shapes; ordering; using geometric figures for directions and games; using numbers with sets.

First grade: sets and numbers; numerals and the number line; sets of ten; introduction to addition and subtraction; recognizing geometric figures; place value and numeration; addition and subtraction; arrays and multiplication; partitions and rational numbers; linear measurement.

Second grade: sets and numbers (review); addition and subtraction (review); sets of points; addition and subtraction (further facts and techniques); linear measurement; computing sums and differences; congruence of angles and triangles; arrays and multiplication; division and rational numbers.

Third grade: sets of points; addition and subtraction (review and extension); describing points as numbers; arrays and multiplication; addition and subtraction (shorter forms of computation); length and area; multiplication; quotients and division; rational numbers and division.

An important purpose of these texts is to provide the student the entering behavior he will need for the fourth, fifth, and sixth grade mathematics program. The recurrence (or spiraling) of topics also shows how the SMSG program recycles through the same subject matter when there is a need to recall earlier concepts in teaching new ones. In these early texts students apply the concepts they learn to weight, volume, temperature, and money.

GRADES 4 THROUGH 6

Fourth grade: concepts of sets; numeration; properties and techniques of addition and subtraction—I; properties of multiplication and division; sets of points; properties and techniques of addition and subtraction—II; techniques of multiplication and division; recognition of common geometric figures; linear measurement; and concept of rational numbers.

Fifth grade: extending systems of numeration; factors and primes; extending multiplication and division—I; congruence of common and geometric figures; extending multiplication and division—II; addition and subtraction of rational numbers; measurement of angles, area, and ratio.

Sixth grade: exponents; multiplication of rational numbers; side-angle relationships of triangles; integers; coordinates; division of rational numbers; volume, organizing and describing data; and set and circles.

The fourth grade text repeats earlier material because it was prepared before the earlier texts were ready. The materials for the three grades provide for review and extension of the arithmetic operations which were learned in the preceding grades. There is considerable emphasis on commutative, associative, and distributive properties, numeration systems with different bases, and the inverse operations of addition, subtraction, multiplication, and division. Perhaps the most noteworthy departure from traditional texts is the amount of material on geometry—about one-third of the material for the three grades.

GRADES 7 AND 8

Seventh grade: what is mathematics; numeration; whole numbers; nonmetric geometry; factoring and primes; the rational number system; measurement; area, volume, weight, and time; ratios, per cent and decimals; parallels, parallelograms, triangles, and right prisms; circles; mathematical systems; statistics and graphs; mathematics at work in science.

Eighth grade: rational numbers and coordinates; equations; scientific notation, decimals, and the metric system; drawings and constructions; symmetry, congruence, and the Pythagorean property; real numbers, permutations, and selections; probability; similar triangles and variation; nonmetric geometry; volumes and surface areas; the sphere; and relative error.

Much of this material is a review of the fundamentals of arithmetic and, as such, is not a departure from the traditional courses. The review in the SMSG courses, however, is in a new setting, with emphasis on number systems, which are treated algebraically. Some of the materials in the eighth grade text were planned with the cooperation of the PSSC and the BSCS.

GRADE 9

First Course in Algebra:

sets and the number line; numeral and variables; sentences and properties of operations; open sentences and English phrases; real numbers; properties of addition; properties of multiplication; properties of order; subtraction and division for real numbers; factors and exponents; radicals; polynomial and rational expressions; truth sets of open sentences; graphs of open sentences in two variables; systems of equations and inequalities; quadratic polynomials; and functions.

The ninth grade course covers about the same material as does the traditional algebra text. Some differences, however, may be the careful formulation of definitions and properties and the presentation of the reading material in a way designed to help the student discover ideas.

GRADE 10

Geometry:

common sense and organized knowledge; sets, real numbers, and lines; lines, planes, and separation; angles and triangles; congruences; a closer look at proof; geometric inequalities; perpendicular lines and planes in space; parallel lines in a plane; parallels in space; areas of polygonal regions; similarity; circles and spheres; characterization of sets; construction; areas of circles and sectors; volumes of solids; plane coordinate geometry.

The geometry course differs from the traditional course in three ways: there is no artificial distinction between plane and solid geometry, and a considerable amount of solid geometry is included; the postulate system is a modification of Birkhoff's, and real numbers are used freely throughout the text; and accuracy in the statements and uses of postulates is emphasized. The text is still basically a treatment of Euclidean geometry.

GRADE 11

Intermediate Mathematics:

number systems; an introduction to coordinate geometry in the plane; the function concept and the linear function; quadratic functions and quadratic equations; complex number systems; equations of the first and second degree in two variables; systems of first-degree equations in three variables; logarithms and exponents; introduction to trigonometry; the system of vectors; polar form of complex numbers, sequences, and series; permutations, combinations, and the binomial theorem; and algebraic structures.

The text is similar to conventional texts in that it presents an extension of the basic algebraic skills learned in the preceding course and in that the content is that found in the usual trigonometry course. Also there are many practical applications, illustrative examples and drawings, and an abundant supply of exercises graded in difficulty. The text differs from the traditional text in that it makes greater demands on the student's ability to read, stresses the study of number systems, contains presentations which lead students to predetermined discoveries, develops the function concept spirally throughout the text, introduces early coordinate geometry, and places more emphasis on the understanding of logarithms than on logarithmic computations.

GRADE 12

Elementary functions:

functions; polynomial functions; tangents to graphs of polynomial functions; exponential and logarithmic functions; and circular functions.

Introduction to matrix algebra:

Matrix operations; the algebra of 2×2 matrices; matrices and linear systems; representation of column matrices as geometric vectors; transformations of the plane.

The treatment of the earlier text prepares the student for calculus. The concept of mapping is applied to several functions. The intent of the later text is to put the student close to the frontiers of mathematical thought. It provides concepts useful in many college courses and contains research exercises, which introduce the student to research in mathematics.

In reviewing the list and sequence of topics contained in the SMSG program you can observe three general characteristics (Henderson, 1963): the placement of some topics one or two grades earlier than they were previously placed; the replacement of some obsolescent subject matter; and the use of pervasive concepts to organize the subject matter: number, number line, relation, function, sets, and so on.

This description of the contents of the SMSG course refers only to the major text sequence. Other texts have been developed, some of which are discussed below.

Entering Behavior

At both the elementary and the secondary school levels, SMSG has developed texts for students of below- and above-average entering behavior. For the instruction of the disadvantaged child there are special editions of the teacher's commentary for kindergarten and grade 1 (*SMSG Newsletter,* No. 22, 1966a). At the secondary level there are three texts, each accompanied by an extensive teacher's commentary: *Introduction to Secondary School Mathematics* (two volumes) and *Introduction to Algebra.* To assist the development of the entering behavior of the parent who finds modern mathematics a wholly mysterious phenomenon, there is a booklet called *Very Short Course in Mathematics for Parents.* For the abler and more advanced students there are several texts: *Geometry with Coordinates,* which places more emphasis on analytic geometry than the basic geometry text does, and *Analytic Geometry* and *Calculus.*

A study by Herbert Feldhake (1966) showed how students' acceptance of the SMSG course for the seventh grade was related to their ability and to the difficulty of the course material. In this study the students had learned traditional mathematics the previous year and were learning modern mathematics in the year of the study. Feldhake first determined which chapters in the text the students liked best and least. When he asked the reasons for their preferences and rejections, he found that the chief reason for liking a chapter was that it was easy and the chief reason for not liking a chapter was that it was difficult. He then asked the students whether they preferred the old or the new mathematics. With a statistically significant difference, the upper-ability group had greater preference for the new mathematics than the average-ability group did. When he asked the students to give their reasons for selecting the old or new mathematics, he found that students who chose the new did so because they found it more interesting, whereas students who chose the old did so because they found it easier to understand. He also found that most of the students believed that the new mathematics was more difficult than the old. Feldhake concluded that decreased difficulty in comprehension should be an objective of the new mathematics, especially for the average junior high school student.

Carl Allendoerfer (1965) believes that the SMSG and other new mathematics programs may be designed for the *superelite.* In his opinion, the designers of the new curricula have ignored the problem of what mathematics should be taught to the lower seven-eighths of the ability group, particularly the lower third. In the same vein, Howard Fehr (1966) believes that the introduction of complicated notation, of formal logic, of place systems of numeration, of the distinction between numeral and number, of geometric construction, and of the formal structure and application of arithmetic is out of place in the elementary school. Collections of objects can be called *collections* or *groups* just as well as *sets.* Fundamental additions and computational skill can be developed without using words like *commutative* and *associative laws.* In the teaching of arithmetic operations, Fehr believes that the concept should be developed first, then the facts, then the algorithms, and then there should be sufficient practice to develop skill in computation and problem solving. A most important accommodation of the child's entering behavior is that the textbooks be adapted to his reading level and study ability. His implication is that the textbooks of the modern mathematics programs have become crowded, formal, and difficult.

By developing a mathematics program for the whole sweep of precollege education, SMSG has been able to capitalize on entering behavior acquired early in the program in preparing instruction later in the program. It is too early to learn how well this has been done since there has not been sufficient time for school systems to change over to the new program and for most students to have had all of their instruction in the new mathematics program. Moreover, since there has not been careful study of the learning structures of the important mathematical behaviors we want students to acquire, we cannot be sure that the sequence of topics adopted by SMSG and other modern programs follows the sequence of prerequisite learning sets. Continued basic research of SMSG and other programs may require reordering, substitution, postponement, and even elimination of many topics and concepts which now appear in the programs, at least for students of average entering behavior. There is also a need to examine the new programs in terms of Piaget's concrete and formal operations and to avoid the imposition of an advanced form of thinking on children who have not reached that stage. Careful study of the entering behavior of both elementary and secondary students could greatly strengthen the modern mathematics programs.

Instructional Procedures

We shall now consider the instructional materials, films, and classroom procedures which SMSG provides.

Materials. The major materials are the textbooks provided for students from kindergarten through high school. There are also the special textbooks adapted to variations in entering behavior. Accompanying each of these textbooks is a *Teacher's Commentary.* Illustrative of the *Commentaries* are those for Book 1 (Part 1) of *Mathematics for*

Fig. 13-4. *A teaching page for instruction in set and number (from* SMSG, *1966b, p. 9).*

the Elementary School (SMSG, 1966b) and for Volume 1 (Part 1) of *Introduction to Secondary School Mathematics* (for the college-bound student of undiscovered mathematical talent) (SMSG, 1962). Chapter 1 of the *Commentary* for the elementary text contains a general introduction for the teacher on the concepts of set and number. For each section of the chapter the following materials are provided: a statement of the objective of the section, a list of key vocabulary words, a list of materials, and suggested procedures. Suggested procedures, in turn, are divided into prebook activities, activities which use the pupil's book, and further activities. Teaching pages are included which give pictorial examples of members and nonmembers of a set. Figure 13-5 shows the teaching page for the set of *fruit*.

The *Commentary* for the secondary school text is somewhat less elaborate. For Chapter 1, "What Is Mathematics?" the following materials are provided: (1) some general remarks which explain the chapter purposes and make suggestions for handling the more able and less able students; (2) background material for most of the chapter sections; (3) answers to the section discussion questions and exercises, with explanations; (4) a list of recreational books; and (5) a bibliography for the teacher.

SMSG has also provided for the publication of a series of paperback books called the *New Mathematical Library* (Bold, 1965). The purpose of the *Library* is to disseminate sound mathematics in a way which will awaken the interest of students and present mathematics as a meaningful human activity. About fifteen books had been published by 1965 on such diverse topics as rational and irrational numbers, episodes from the early history of mathematics, groups and their graphs, and Pythagoras and Einstein. In regular courses the teacher may recommend as supplementary reading certain sections of the books relating to course topics which have captured the students' interest. A *Reference Guide* (Bold, 1965) suggests topics in the books for each grade level.

SMSG has published *Supplementary Publications* (*SMSG Newsletter,* No. 17, 1964), a pamphlet series which supplements the regular textbook with new topics or new treatments of old topics and provides enrichment material for the special interests of students. SMSG has also sponsored inexpensive (1 dollar or less) books for supplementary use. Books have been listed for algebra, geometry, probability and statistics, computing machines, and for recreational and general reading. And, supplementary materials in the form of booklets use simple experiments from the physical and biological sciences to introduce and motivate mathematical ideas (*SMSG Newsletter,* No. 22, 1966a). Two series are intended mainly for the teachers: *Studies in Mathematics,* which serve as background reading for the course, and the *Study Guides in Mathematics,* which consist of annotated bibliographies (*SMSG Newsletter,* No. 22, 1966a).

SMSG continues to produce new materials and to influence the production of commercial texts. By the end of 1966 it had prepared units on probability for grades K through 9. These materials for the elementary and intermediate grades include specially designed spinners.

FILMS. SMSG has also made a filmed course for elementary school teachers (*SMSG Newsletter,* No. 22, 1966a); it consists of thirty half-hour films in color intended to provide a foundation in modern mathematics. No mathematical concepts are necessary as entering behavior. The first sixteen films are for teachers of grades K through 3, while the remainder, based on these, are for teachers of grades 4 through 6.

CLASSROOM PROCEDURES. This description of the SMSG materials suggests the heavy emphasis on reading, and the use of precise language, discussion questions, and exercises and homework assignments. The *Teacher's Commentaries* tell the teachers to urge their students to reread difficult textual passages, to use mathematically precise language, to use discussion questions for portions of the text that are particularly difficult, to use the exercises sequentially when concepts are developed in the text in particular sequences, and normally to make assignments only for material which has been discussed in class.

The pervasive issue in the teaching of mathematics has been the relative effectiveness of using one or the other of two types of procedures: tell-and-do or heuristic. Kenneth Henderson (1963) describes the tell-and-do method as consisting of the following steps: (1) stating the item of knowledge to be taught, (2) providing the necessary clarification of the statement used to express the knowledge, (3) defending the truth value or practical usefulness of the item, (4) having student work problems based on what they are taught, and (5) making a bridge to the next item to be taught. If the third step is omitted, the procedure becomes a drill method. If the fourth step is omitted, it becomes a lecture method. The other procedure is called the heuristic (or discovery) method. It can be divided into two subclasses: the inductive method and the deductive method. The inductive method, according to Henderson, involves (1) presenting examples of the item to be taught, which enables the students to form hypotheses; (2) presenting more examples which either confirm or reject various student hypotheses; (3) stating or having the student state the item of knowledge. The inductive procedure is similar to that described in Chapter 10 for the teaching of concepts. The deductive method requires the teacher to present in juxtaposition to the student two or more principles which imply another principle and to infer the student's correct inference of the principle by his appropriate verbal or nonverbal performance. Henderson (p. 1019) uses this example of the deductive method:

> Suppose a student says, "You can't add 2 and $\sqrt{3}$." His statement implies "There exists no real number which is the sum of 2 and $\sqrt{3}$." The teacher might ask, "Is it true that every pair of real numbers has a unique sum?" The student, assuming that he recognizes this as the closure postulate for addition for the field of real numbers, would say "Yes." The teacher would then ask, "Are 2 and $\sqrt{3}$ real numbers?" The student, if we assume that he knew that they are (and if he did not know this, the teacher could use the deductive discovery method to convince him that they are), would again say "Yes." The teacher would then confront him with a pair of contradictory statements which may be paraphrased as "You can't add 2 and $\sqrt{3}$" and "You can add 2 and $\sqrt{3}$." Since the student cannot

> defeat the argument whose conclusion is the latter, he must abandon his claim to the former.

Although SMSG has not endorsed any single instructional method, the use of the inductive discovery method has been emphasized in the UICSM program. Max Beberman (1964, p. 23) writes:

> A . . . major principle which has guided us in developing the UICSM program is that the student comes to understand mathematics if he plays an active part in developing mathematical ideas and procedures. To us this means that after we have selected a body of subject matter to be learned we must design both exposition and exercises in such a way that the student will discover the principle.

Beberman (pp. 25–26) uses this example of the student's devising his own rule for solving equations and inequalities. As part of his entering behavior the student must demonstrate that he can identify an equation and what solving equations requires. He is then presented with the following equations:

$$x \times 3 = 9 \qquad 3x = 15$$

$$2(x + 1) - 5(3 - x) = 29 \qquad \frac{5x + 1}{3} = 17$$

$$x - 3 = 4$$

$$2x + 1 = 7$$

Beberman reports that students are often successful in discovering the rule of *doing the same to both sides* in the process of attempting the solution to the equations above. They learn the formal rule when they encounter equations which cannot be solved by the application of their informal, or common sense, rule. According to Beberman, the deductive discovery method develops an interest in mathematics and skill in mathematical thinking. In addition, because the student does not have to rely on rote rules and routines, it develops versatility in applying mathematics.

As an additional teaching procedure the SMSG program uses programed instruction. The first course in algebra (for the ninth grade) now appears as a programed text (see SMSG, 1966c) drawn from two earlier editions, one based on linear, the other on branching programs. Some frames require constructed responses, while others use a multiple-choice format. After extended tryout of the first editions, several things were added: an index, a review section, more practice sets, and some straight text materials. The text can be used in the classroom or by students who are absent from school. A separate response booklet makes the program reusable.

Performance Assessment

The students' answers to the discussion questions and the exercises provide a major source of feedback on how well they are achieving the instructional objectives. The *SMSG Newsletter* does not offer for sale any achievement tests or comprehensive final examinations. Sample test items are contained in the *Commentaries,* but the teachers are generally expected to constuct their own tests from their own and sample items. In the *Commentary* for Volume 1 (Part 1) of *Introduction to Secondary Mathematics,* sample test items appear at the end of the material for each chapter and in various formats: true-false, completion, and multiple choice. There are also problems for solution.

Evaluation

As in the physics and biology programs, the major source of information on the effectiveness of the SMSG program has been the actual school tryouts. During the academic year 1960–61 the Educational Testing Service undertook a formal evaluation of the SMSG program (Payette, 1961). The evaluation involved seventy-five schools and covered grades 7 through 12 (except grade 8). The fundamental purpose was to compare student achievement in SMSG and non-SMSG courses. The measures of achievement were common tests of traditional mathematics and SMSG mathematics varied for each grade level. On the test of traditional mathematical skills, statistically significant differences favoring the traditional (non-SMSG) program were found for the seventh, ninth, tenth, and twelfth grades. When the comparison was made between experienced SMSG teachers using the SMSG program and teachers using the conventional mathematics, at all the grade levels (except the ninth) the results on the achievement test favored SMSG mathematics. When the original comparison of the study was made using the SMSG-type tests as the measures of achievement, the results showed that students who used the SMSG materials had higher average performances in all grades. Finally, this study determined the relationship between level of student IQ (as measured by SCAT) and achievement on SMSG tests. The considerable overlap between IQ and achievement, particularly in the high school years, indicates that IQ is far from predicting achievement in SMSG, that additional predictors should be used for the upper grades, and that students at all IQ levels can learn considerable segments of SMSG materials. A further study of the relationship between IQ and achievement in the SMSG course (Rosenbloom, 1961) showed that the upper and lower thirds of the students do better on the SMSG course, while the middle third does about equally well in both courses.

In general these findings are consistent with those in the evaluations of the physics and biology courses. Students in the conventional courses do better on the conventional tests than students in the new courses do. Students in the new courses do better on the new tests than students in the conventional courses do. The obviousness of these conclusions is much less an indictment or endorsement of the courses than testimony to the difficulties research faces in making comparison studies which lack theoretical underpinnings (see Chapter 16).

In the *International Study of Achievement in Mathematics* (Husén, 1967, II, p. 298), it is hypothesized that discovery approaches, as contrasted with methods which emphasize drill or rote learning (tell-and-do methods), result in higher mathematics achievement. At the lower age levels this hypothesis was supported. Precollege students, however, showed an inverse relationship between discovery methods and mathematics achievement. These findings remained true even when the level of mathematics instruction and the opportunity to learn items were held constant. Also, a positive relationship between discovery methods and interest in mathematics existed at the thirteen-year-old level. No such relationship existed at the precollege level possibly because of the repercussions of the more conservative methods of instruction and of the examination system.

Bernard Friedlander (1965) argues that the principal difficulty with the SMSG and other modern mathematics programs is their concentration on the selection and articulation of concepts and on the development of conceptual structures and their inadequate attention to how and whether the student learns to use skillfully what he is being taught. Friedlander writes (p. 21):

> At one school I know [of], the SMSG grade 4 curriculum was given an extended trial with bright students and capable teachers. Though the teachers were highly enthusiastic at first about the considerable advances of the SMSG program over traditional approaches to arithmetic, the problem of practice exercises was prominent among a number of serious faults found with Part 1 of the program. Related criticisms were that the SMSG program was often "inhumanly abstract" and bewilderingly remote from the children's experiences, their conceptual abilities, and their skill in performing numerical operations; that it lacked inherent devices to arouse motivation and provide a sense of accomplishment; that it contained insufficient recapitulation of separate topics and transitions between topics. The teachers found it necessary to provide extensive supplementary material to secure adequate illustration and practice.

A study by Alice Huettig and John Newell (1966) explored the relationship between teachers' attitudes toward the introduction of a modern mathematics program and the number of years of teaching experience. Teachers with less experience were significantly less negative to the new program. These findings are confirmed with the evidence that the greater the amount of the training in modern mathematics the more positive is the attitude of the teacher toward it. One item in the questionnaire for which the teachers were to indicate their degree of agreement and disagreement was the following (item 6): The modern mathematics program frequently seems to make the obvious complicated. Regardless of the number of years of experience, all groups agreed on this statement. They also agreed that the new mathematics approaches the same concept from too many angles and that it is often easier to go back to the old methods when the new mathematics makes it difficult to get across a point. The data of this study, according to the authors, indicate the need for extensive training of teachers in the new mathematics—more than that provided in a single workshop.

The somewhat inconsistent and inconclusive findings of the evaluations of the modern mathematics programs, particularly the SMSG program, make difficult the teacher's decisions about the appropriate introduction of the new materials. Undoubtedly more research is necessary which interrelates several factors, such as the entering behavior of the children, methods and materials of instruction, and sequence and level of mathematical instruction (Weaver and Gibb, 1964). Among other things research in mathematics instruction must provide empirical support of theories of learning mathematics, and it must identify factors having significant long-range effects on success in mathematics (Dessart, 1964).

Until the research on the psychology of mathematics learning and instruction provides more refined answers, the teacher can provide the learning conditions required in the teaching of concepts, principles, and problem solving (Chapters 10 and 11). These conditions of learning are internal and external. For internal conditions, the learning of concepts, principles, and problem solving requires the prior acquisition of discriminations and of other concepts and principles. The teacher must determine what specific prior learning (or entering behavior) is necessary for the learning of mathematical concepts and principles, and he should not proceed with new material until he knows that the old prerequisite material is within the easy grasp of the student. External learning conditions pertain to contiguity, reinforcement, and practice. Unless these conditions (and others) are observed the student cannot be expected to acquire the new material. Although the modern mathematics programs offer easy access to an abundance of challenging materials, it may be necessary for the teacher to make several modifications before he puts them to use. He must provide clear statements of instructional objectives, of the determination, assessment, and accommodation of entering behavior, of appropriate instructional procedures, and of careful performance assessment. Depending on the internal and external learning conditions with which he must deal and which he must provide, the teacher may make slight, considerable, and even drastic changes in the packaged materials. Certainly at this stage of the development of the modern curricula, the judgment of the teacher must combine with the utilization of the new materials for the best teaching results.

Summary

You can now see that the new mathematics programs (as represented by the SMSG) have much in common with the new physics and biology programs. The SMSG is similar in background in that it combined the efforts of university teachers and teachers in the schools, was supported by the National Science Foundation, and developed materials which were tried in the schools and subsequently revised. It is similar in objectives and content in stressing the basic content and structure of the field and in the broad scope of materials which have been prepared. It is similar in the accommodation of entering behavior in developing materials for low-ability and advanced students. It is similar in instructional procedures in providing student textbooks, teacher guides, test questions, and supplementary enrichment materials, particularly monographs by prominent scientists in the field. It puts a similar emphasis on the use of discovery methods of teaching. It has also developed films. It is similar in performance assessment in that there are the same major sources of feedback for teacher and student—discussion questions, exercises, and suggested test items. The evaluations of all the programs have had similar results—students tend to do best on the type of examination for which their courses prepared them. Evaluations have been equally inconclusive and, as a basis for science and mathematics instruction, require the teacher to rely on his general knowledge of the psychology of learning and instruction, particularly as this pertains to the teaching of concepts, principles, and problem solving. As yet there is insufficient evidence to warrant the unqualified use or rejection of the materials in the schools. The teacher must adapt the materials to the internal and external conditions of learning with which he must deal.

Compared with the biology and physics programs, SMSG shows some unique characteristics. It is a much larger program because it has developed materials for all the grades, K through 12, rather than for only two or three grades. It has had to deal with relatively abstract subject matter in relatively abstract ways, having the advantage of neither the laboratory nor naturalistic observation. It has had to deal with tightly structured subject matter, with a great interdependence of concepts and principles. The program thus far has not developed the classroom achievement tests and the comprehensive finals of the other programs. It has not developed instructional films for use with the students. Finally, largely because of the program's enormous breadth, more freedom and less guidance is provided the teacher in the actual utilization of the available materials.

You should now return to objectives 30–44 (pp. 560–61) and determine how well you have achieved them.

QUESTION 13-3

Mr. Al Gibra, a seventh grade teacher, must select one of four methods of teaching a major instructional objective in a modern mathematics program. If he were to select the most favored method of those programs, which of the following procedures would he adopt?

(a) He would present examples of a concept he is teaching, then present more examples, and then have the students describe the characteristics of the concept.

(b) He would state the objective, clarify it, describe its practicality, and make a transition to the next objective.

(c) He would present two principles together, and, in the process of getting the student to infer the new principle, would point out contradictory statements.

(d) He would state the objective, clarify it, have students work problems based on what they were taught, and make a transition to the next objective.

After selecting your answer, give the reasons for your choice and for your rejection of the alternatives.

SUMMARY

This chapter has been much more descriptive and less conceptual than those which have preceded it. However, the three courses illustrate some basic characteristics of curriculum design. Using the basic teaching model as our outline, we can review these characteristics here.

Instructional objectives. Each course has expressed as its major purpose the imparting of the basic concepts and principles of the discipline and the teaching of methods of inquiry. Sometimes these basic concepts, principles, and methods are referred to as the *structure of knowledge* (Bruner, 1960).

Entering behavior. The original major effort has been to develop high-quality materials for the student of average ability in these courses, although it has been recognized that physics and advanced mathematics students are frequently above average in IQ. Subsequent development of material, particularly in biology and mathematics, has stressed the accommodation of the entering behavior of the below-average student.

Instructional procedures. (1) Textbook materials are organized around large themes or mathematical and scientific principles to give the courses unity and coherence. Concepts introduced early in the course are expanded and used to explain concepts and principles introduced late in the course. (2) Heuristic, or discovery, methods of learning have been stressed in both the classroom and the laboratory to stimulate inquiry and investigative skills as well as to answer questions. (3) The courses are prototypal instructional systems, using a wide array of academic personnel and educational media (especially films).

Performance assessment. All the courses have developed achievement tests or provide items for the construction of such tests. Two of the courses, physics and biology, have developed comprehensive finals. Tests of scientific thinking have also been constructed. The test items are designed to measure not only the recall of information but also the ability of the student to apply knowledge and to use certain high-level skills, such as drawing inferences from a collection of data and formulating hypotheses.

The teacher has much room for decision in using these materials in the classroom. The necessary learning conditions, both internal and external, for the teaching of concepts, principles, and problem solving were described in preceding chapters. When the arrangement of the packaged materials of these courses fails to provide one or more of these conditions, the teacher must decide which modifications must be made. These modifications can range from the addition of new material (not included in the package) to the substitution, reordering, or elimination of the materials which are made available. None of these courses has reached the level of instructional design at which it can be adopted by a teacher, school, or school system without accommodation to the local conditions of the classroom and to particular students. The courses, however, do offer a rich supply of material of unexcelled intellectual merit which the inventive genius of the classroom teacher, guided by the knowledge of the psychology of learning and instruction, can often find suitable ways of using.

Return to objective 45 (p. 561) and determine how well you have achieved the indicated performance.

SUGGESTED READINGS

For discussions of several modern curricula, including the three we have considered in this chapter, read these books:

Ford, G. W. and Lawrence Pugno, eds., *The Structure of Knowledge and the Curriculum.* Chicago: Rand McNally & Co., 1964 (paper).

Gilcrest, Robert S., ed., *Using Current Curriculum Development,* a report of ASCD's Commission on Current Curriculum Development. Washington, D.C.: Association for Supervision and Curriculum Development, NEA, 1963 (paper).

Goodlad, John I., *School Curriculum Reform in the United States.* New York: The Fund for the Advancement of Education, 1964 (paper).

Heath, Robert W., ed., *New Curricula.* New York: Harper & Row, Publishers, Inc., 1964.

Unruh, Glenys G., ed., *New Curriculum Developments,* a report of ASCD's Commission on Current Curriculum Development. Washington, D.C.: Association for Supervision and Curriculum Development, NEA, 1965 (paper).

In addition to chapters in the books and pamphlets listed above, these chapters, articles, and pamphlets discuss developments in specific disciplines:

BSCS Newsletter, No. 28, 1966. This contains a rather complete description of the materials in the BSCS course.

Finlay, Gilbert C., "The Physical Science Study Committee," *ESI Quarterly Report* (Winter-Spring 1964), 5–16.

Wooton, William, *SMSG: The Making of a Curriculum.* New Haven, Conn.: Yale University Press, 1964.

For research on and evaluation of the new science and mathematics program see the following reviews in *Review of Educational Research,* 34, No. 3 (1964):

Atkin, J. Myron, "Science in the Elementary School," pp. 263–72.

Dessart, Donald J., "Mathematics in the Secondary School," pp. 298–312.

Hurd, Paul DeHart and Mary Budd Howe, "Science in the Secondary School," pp. 286–97.

Weaver, J. Fred and E. Glenadine Gibb, "Mathematics in the Elementary School," pp. 273–85.

For penetrating summary reviews of the research on the teaching of science and mathematics, see the following chapters in the *Handbook of Research on Teaching,* ed. N. L. Gage. Chicago: Rand McNally & Co., 1963.

Henderson, Kenneth B., "Research on Teaching Secondary School Mathematics," pp. 1007–30.

Watson, Fletcher G., "Research on Teaching Science," pp. 1031–59.

Besides the usual psychological and educational journals, articles on the teaching of science and mathematics appear in the following journals:

Arithmetic Teacher (for the elementary school)
Mathematics Teacher (for the secondary school)
School Science and Mathematics
Science Education
Science Teacher

This book gives an evaluation and comparison of mathematics teaching and learning in twelve countries:

Husén, Torsten, ed., *International Study of Achievement in Mathematics.* New York: John Wiley & Sons, Inc., 1967. In two volumes.

PART FIVE

PERFORMANCE ASSESSMENT AND RESEARCH

Part 5 completes our consideration of the basic teaching model and our exploration of the field of educational psychology. The major purpose here is to introduce you to the fine art of performance assessment, the fourth component of the basic teaching model. In the strictest sense performance assessment is the use of classroom and standardized test procedures to measure the terminal performances of your students. Part 5 includes a final chapter on the evaluation of educational research. Many educational psychologists, as you will see in Chapter 16, consider research and theory construction to be the heart of their professional activities and their chief means of ultimately improving educational practice. With so heavy a present-day emphasis on measurement and research, a modern text on educational psychology must give careful consideration to both these topics.

Performance assessment, in the form of classroom and standardized tests and research in educational psychology, is intimately related to all four components of the basic teaching model. You assess those performances described in the instructional objectives—the terminal performances. The closest relationship, therefore, lies between the first and fourth components, instructional objectives and performance assessment. Performance assessment, however, is also a major source of feedback on the adequacy with which we have assessed the variations in student entering behavior and on the appropriateness of our instructional procedures and materials. Similarly, research, in both its basic and applied aspects, pertains to all components of the model. In the previous chapters we considered research on instructional objectives, entering behavior, and instructional procedures. In Part 5 we shall consider research on performance assessment as well as the general research process.

Part 5 has three chapters. The first (Chapter 14) describes absolute and relative standards of assessment, the basic characteristics of good tests, the construction and analysis of classroom tests, and marks and marking systems. The second chapter (Chapter 15) describes the characteristics of standardized, achievement, and creativity tests, interprets standardized test scores, and introduces you to descriptive statistics. The third chapter (Chapter 16) deals with the nature and use of research in educational psychology and the evaluation of research reports and introduces you to the statistical analysis of data.

How to Construct and Use Your Tests

14

This chapter has three sections. The first describes the nature of performance assessment, distinguishing between absolute and relative standards of achievement. We consider four standards which tests of student performance should meet: validity, reliability, objectivity, and efficiency. The second section describes the planning, construction, administration, scoring, and evaluation of your tests. Here we consider procedures and guidelines which, if followed, will help your tests reach the standards described in the previous section. The third section deals with marking and reporting. Here we briefly consider the importance, use, and basis of marking, two marking systems, and the means for reporting marks.

Upon reading the first section of this chapter (on the basic characteristics of performance assessment), you should be able to meet these objectives:

1. Define and illustrate performance assessment in terms of auxiliary and terminal performances.
2. Describe and illustrate the relationship of performance assessment to other components of the basic teaching model.
3. Distinguish and illustrate the differences between absolute and relative standards of performance.
4. Describe and illustrate the disadvantage of using relative standards in performance assessment.

5. Describe and illustrate three important results of using absolute standards.

6. Define and illustrate validity in terms of instructional objectives and test items.

7. Define reliability in terms of consistency.

8. Describe and illustrate three ways in which reliability and validity are related.

9. Define objectivity in terms of scoring and illustrate its use in scoring essay and objective tests.

10. Define efficiency in terms of time and illustrate the comparative efficiency of essay and objective tests.

Upon reading the second section of this chapter (on test construction and revision), you should be able to meet these objectives:

11. Describe the relationship between task analysis and test preparation.

12. List and illustrate four rules for the preparation of tests.

13. Describe and illustrate differences and similarities of essay and objective tests.

14. Describe the appropriate conditions for the use of essay and objective tests.

15. Describe and illustrate types of desirable and undesirable essay questions.

16. Construct two essay questions which follow the guidelines.

17. Score two essay questions by following the guidelines.

18. Distinguish and illustrate differences between free-response and limited-response items.

19. Construct two completion items which follow the guidelines.

20. Define and illustrate distractors, specific determiners, and item stems.

21. Construct five true-false items which follow the guidelines.

22. Construct two matching items which follow the guidelines.

23. Recast a matching item of your own as a multiple-choice item.

24. Construct five multiple-choice items which follow the guidelines.

25. Construct two key-list multiple-choice items which measure principle learning or problem solving.

26. Describe and illustrate the relationship between key-list items and long-term retention.

27. Describe the best arrangement of items for limited and generous time limits.

28. Illustrate properly written directions for a test containing multiple-choice items.

29. Describe three characteristics of efficient test administration.

30. Describe and illustrate how you can prevent or handle three forms of cheating.

31. Describe and illustrate the bad effects of cheating on subsequent student achievement.

32. Describe how you would score a test in terms of a key, assignment of points, and correction for guessing.

33. Describe and illustrate how you would apply the criteria of validity, reliability, objectivity, and efficiency to the evaluation of a test.

34. Define item analysis in terms of discrimination and difficulty indices.

35. Determine the difficulty index and discrimination index for particular test items.

36. Describe and illustrate the use of these indices in the revision of an item.

37. Describe the ways of improving reliability of tests based on relative and on absolute standards of achievement.

Upon reading the last section of this chapter (on marking and reporting), you should be able to meet these objectives:

38. Describe and illustrate (in terms of various official roles) five uses of marks in making decisions.

39. Distinguish and illustrate the differences between marks based on achievement and those based on three nonachievement factors; describe and illustrate the hazards in marking on nonachievement factors.

40. List and illustrate measures of performance other than tests; illustrate how you would assign weights to these measures as well as to the tests.

41. Distinguish between percentage and letter-grade marking systems and describe and illustrate the ambiguity of giving and interpreting percentage grades below 100 per cent.

42. Describe and illustrate the relationship between the assignment of letter grades and marking on the curve.

43. Describe the relationships between marking and the design of instruction.

44. Describe and illustrate reporting in terms of achievement, checklists, and parent-teacher conferences.

BASIC CHARACTERISTICS OF PERFORMANCE ASSESSMENT

The first section of the chapter describes the nature and purposes of performance assessment and of the tests used in this assessment. Here I introduce five basic concepts—absolute and relative standards of assessment, validity, reliability, objectivity, and efficiency—by describing, illustrating, and interrelating them.

Performance Assessment: Definition and Uses

Performance assessment is the process of measuring the student's auxiliary and terminal performances during and at the end of instruction (Glaser, 1962). Auxiliary performances are behaviors which must be acquired at the lower levels of a learning structure before the terminal performances are acquired at the higher levels. In the teaching of a principle, for example, the teacher must determine whether the student has acquired the component concepts, as auxiliary performances, before proceeding with the instruction which arranges these concepts in the proper relationship for the learning of the principle. Terminal performances, you already know, refer to the end products of instruction—usually verbal performances (Chapter 2). The emphasis on the measurement of both auxiliary and terminal performances means that you should not think of performance assessment as occurring only at the end of a unit or a course. The assessment can occur whenever the teacher or the student needs information about the adequacy of the student's present learning for subsequent instruction. In programed instruction, for example, a test, or criterion, frame can occur wherever in the program it is necessary to determine whether the student has acquired essential auxiliary behavior.

Three uses can be made of the information, or feedback, obtained through performance assessment. In Chapter 1 (Fig. 1-2, p. 12) you saw that performance assessment has feedback loops to the other three components of the basic teaching model. These loops describe the three uses of the feedback. First, you use the feedback to determine how well the student has achieved the instructional objective (or terminal performance). If the student has reached the standard of acceptability the instructional objective states, the instruction has been successful and you can proceed to new instruction. Second, you use the feedback to determine the adequacy of entering behavior. This use is appropriate either during the course of instruction, when you are measuring auxiliary behavior, or at the end of instruction, when you are determining why the instruction was unsuccessful. Third, you use the feedback to determine the adequacy of your instructional procedures, particularly when you compare the effectiveness of one with another procedure.

Thus, performance assessment, the fourth component, is an important basis for making appropriate modifications in one or all of the remaining components of the basic teaching model.

Absolute vs. Relative Standards

We can distinguish between two types of tests which measure achievement of the instructional objectives: those which use absolute and those which use relative standards (Glaser, 1962, 1963, 1965). The absolute standard describes the least amount of end-of-unit or end-of-course competence the student is expected to attain. His attainment of that standard determines whether he proceeds to the next unit or course of instruction. A test using the absolute standard provides explicit information about what the student can or cannot do. If, for example, the instructional objective required the student to identify all statements of theories of learning when presented with positive and negative examples of such statements, before you would permit him to proceed to the next unit of instruction (for example, the identification of statements of theories teaching), you would expect him to turn in a perfect performance. If the objective required him to make correct identifications only 90 per cent of the time, then you would hold the student to this standard before allowing him to proceed. The use of the absolute standard in performance assessment requires mastery of the terminal performance at whatever level mastery is specified and is a prerequisite condition for further instruction.

The relative standard compares the performance of one student with that of other students in his group. Tests based on the relative standard tell us that one student is more or less proficient than another but do not tell us how proficient either student is with respect to an absolute standard. For example, a test based on a relative standard indicates that Harriet identified more positive examples of statements of educational philosophy than Elvis did and that Elvis identified more than Daisy did. This information, however, does not tell us whether Harriet correctly identified 100 per cent, 90 per cent, or only 25 per cent of the examples. Similarly, Elvis may have correctly identified 99 per cent of the examples, even though he ranked only second. Furthermore, with the relative standard, the student proceeds to the next unit or course of instruction even though his level of performance falls considerably below an absolute standard of mastery.

The chief shortcoming of performance assessment based on relative standards is that the student proceeds to the next instructional objective and unit of instruction before he has mastered the prerequisite entering behavior. Dorothy Adkins (1958, p. 234) describes some of the practical effects of using the relative standard:

> Consider, if you will, the hundreds of hours devoted to instruction in English by the time a person becomes a college senior. Then ponder his inability to write. Turn to arithmetic . . . and later to algebra and geometry. Then reflect upon the ineptitude of a typical college student in solving the most elementary equation or even adding a column of figures. Recall the idiosyncrasies in spelling which confront you in personal correspondence. Contemplate the current reading hubbub, by no means without foundation. Shudder at the prevalent superstitions and gullibility of the American public.

Adkins believes that what is needed is a curriculum revision which divides each area of subject matter into units arranged according to difficulty, with tests for each unit based on the absolute standard. A particular unit would require each student to achieve a stipulated degree of mastery; after that, he would proceed to the next higher unit. Adkins describes (p. 237) what would happen if we adopted such a practice:

> In 1984, we may be able to say to an employer or to a university that John Doe has mastered mathematics unit 1728, English grammar 642, spelling 1021, physics 303, and so on. The personnel officers will by that time have conducted studies to enable them to predict from such data his relative chances of success as an outer-space radiological isotopist or as a student in a modern household engineering curriculum.

The use of the absolute standard has three important instructional results. First, the standard which the performance of all students must meet is the standard of acceptability specified in the instructional objective. The meeting of this standard is the prerequisite for the introduction of new instructional objectives and materials. Second, all students must meet the standard of acceptability not in a single objective but in all objectives. Presumably you will adopt as instructional objectives only those performances you deem worthy of student achievement. If an objective lacks value, let us say to subsequent learning, then it is highly questionable that you should expend on it your own and your students' time. Once you embark on instruction for a particular objective, the ordinary assumptions are that you expect all students for whom you provide instruction to achieve mastery of the terminal performance and that instruction will continue until all achieve mastery. This, of course, is a most rigorous demand on both teachers and students, but anything less rigorous condemns much instruction to aimless futility. Third, the use of the absolute standard alters some conventional procedures in test construction. When using the relative standard, we construct our tests so that students achieve high, average, and low scores. We are disappointed if everyone receives a perfect or high score because we seek a distribution or spread of scores as a basis for assigning letter grades. To obtain this distribution we include items of high, average, and low difficulty. When using the absolute standard, we construct our tests so that all students who achieve the instructional objective obtain a perfect or near-perfect score. We retain even very difficult and very easy items if they are relevant to the terminal performance. Since each terminal performance becomes entering behavior for subsequent instruction, we continue to provide instruction for those students whose scores indicate that they have not attained a minimum standard of acceptability.

We shall now turn to the consideration of four concepts which deal with the tests used in performance assessment more than with the process itself.

Validity

There are two definitions of a valid test. In the usual definition, a valid test is one which actually measures what it purports to measure. In the context of the basic teaching model, a valid test is one which actually measures the terminal performances described in the instructional objectives. Using a particular instructional objective, Philip Rulon (1946) illustrates the second definition: When presented with one hundred addition problems of the type

$$\begin{array}{ccccccc} 0 & 0 & 1 & 1 & 1 & 2 & 2 \\ +0 & +1 & +0 & +1 & +2 & +1 & +2 \\ \hline \end{array}$$

the student writes the correct answers. A test which presents one hundred addition problems which require vertical addition is a valid test of this objective. Less valid is a test which presents less than one hundred addition problems and also requires horizontal addition (for example, $0 + 1 =$ ________). Still less valid is a test which presents 125 horizontal subtraction problems.

The central problem in constructing a valid test is to engage the student on the test in the same performance the instructional objective requires. Consider this example. This is the instructional objective: When presented with a list of statements of theories of teaching, theories of learning, and philosophies of education, the student will select from the list only the theories of teaching. Is the following item a valid test of this objective?

Write *TT* (for *t*heory of *t*eaching) after each of the following statements which describes a theory of teaching:

**A*. (A short description of Herbart's methodology).
B. (A short description of Combs' and Snygg's theory).
C. (A short description of Dewey's pragmatism).
D. (A short description of Thorndike's learning theory).
**E*. (A short description of Carroll's model for school learning).

This item is valid because it requires the student to engage in exactly that performance described in the instructional objective—to select from a list the appropriate statements (in this case, *A* and *E*). For this same objective compare the validity of the following item:

Match the names of the men below with the theory or philosophy of education they formulated:

Key: *A*. William James
B. John Dewey
C. Arthur Combs
D. Edward Thorndike
E. Lawrence Stolurow
F. John Carroll

1. Theory of teaching (*E, F*)
2. Theory of learning (*D*)
3. Philosophy of education (*B, C*)

This item, besides containing certain intrinsic difficulties, is less valid than the preceding item because it does not require the student to engage in the performance described in the objective—namely, with his knowledge of the characteristics of theories of teaching, to select only those statements which describe such theories. A student with little or no knowledge of these characteristics could answer the second item correctly.

The definition of validity in terms of terminal performances reveals that we are dealing with direct validation (Ebel, 1965, p. 381)—the obvious validity of appropriate items. The former item, which contained statements of theories of teaching, is obviously more valid than the latter item, which contained only the names of the theorists. An item of obvious validity requires the student to perform the very operations on the very materials he has been taught. Surely one of the great advantages of explicit statements of instructional objectives is that the teacher can directly validate his tests by comparing the test items with the instructional objectives. Ebel (1965, p. 384) believes, "The persistent difficulties that plague our efforts to measure some outcomes of education are less attributable to limitations of measurement than to uncertainty about what is to be measured." He further states:

> If one is willing to accept as a definition of what a test is measuring a simple description of the tasks that the test requires the student to perform, then what a test appears to measure and what it really does measure will be practically identical. For example, the question, "What is the sum of 1/5 and 1/6?" appears to measure and really does measure (beyond his ability to read), the student's ability to add two particular common fractions. The tasks in most classroom tests of educational achievement can be described as obviously and sensibly as this one if one is willing to settle for an obvious, common sense description.

The definition of test validity in terms of instructional objectives indicates that it is more closely related to absolute than to relative standards of performance. An explicit statement of an instructional objective, you recall, specifies a minimum standard of acceptable performance. When the student fails to meet this minimum (or absolute) standard, the teacher considers this a failure to achieve the objective. The items on the test and the uses made of test performance must be compatible with an absolute standard. Whether the items are of high, average, or low difficulty is less important than their obvious validity. Having the students all achieve perfect scores is more important than obtaining a distribution of scores. When all or some students receive scores which indicate below-standard performance, the need for further instruction is clear.

Reliability

A reliable test measures terminal performances consistently. On a highly reliable test we expect the student to obtain about the same score on the second administration of the test as he did on the first. We expect, that is, the same consistency of performance for a reliable test as we do for a reliable individual. When tests and individuals are unreliable, we expect erratic, unpredictable, indeed, very inconsistent performance.

At least three factors influence the degree of test reliability (Ebel, 1965, pp. 310–11). First, if the items are too easy, too difficult, or ambiguous they will yield highly unreliable scores. Second, if the students vary considerably in personal behavior—in alertness, energy, emotional balance, and so on—the reliability of the scores will be reduced. Third, if the person who scores the test assigns scores on the basis of momentary considerations rather than on the basis of standards uniformly applied to all test papers, the scores will lack reliability. The first and third factors are discussed at further length in the section on test construction (pp. 618–46).

Reliability and validity are closely related. First, for a test to have validity it must also have reliability. Validity, you recall, pertains to what a test purports to measure. Reliability pertains to how consistently a test measures. If a test fails to measure with consistency, then it cannot purport to measure anything at all. A rubber yardstick which changes its length as you apply different amounts of tension to its ends is neither a reliable nor a valid measure of length or distance. A test of terminal performance which yields different results when administered to the same students a second time, so that we are never clear about their relative levels of achievement, is neither reliable nor valid. Second, the converse of this relationship between reliability and validity is not true: A test may be reliable without being valid. It is entirely possible and not unamusing for a teacher to construct a test which gives about the same scores to the same individuals in successive retests without the teacher's knowing what the test attempts to measure. A teacher who assesses performance of unstated and unknown instructional objectives may some day construct a test of known reliability and unknown validity —a state of instructional affairs no one should emulate. Third, it is possible that by improving the reliability of your test you reduce its validity. Some terminal behaviors are more easily measured than others. Verbal learning, which requires the learning of a list of single or associated terms, is easier to measure than concept and principle learning, which require the student to demonstrate his knowledge. Adequate performance assessment, however, requires you to measure all the learning your instructional objectives embrace and not only those types for which you can easily construct reliable test items.

Objectivity

In an object test the scorer is free of subjective judgments (Gorow, 1966, p. 16). Objectivity is difficult to attain whether the questions are cast in objective or essay form. Responses to questions in the objective form, for example items on multiple-choice and true-false tests, are often the subject of heated debate between instructor and student and even among subject matter experts. It is possible to obtain colleague and expert agreement on particular responses and, in this way, to improve the quality of the test. Responses to essay questions are more subjectively scored because there is no recourse to expert agreement and because each response must be read, interpreted, and scored somewhat in its own terms.

Ebel (1965, p. 296) believes that when experts disagree on the correct answers to objective questions, the fault usually rests with the question. Several factors may reduce the objectivity of various objective items: (1) The question may fail to specify all the conditions and qualifications necessary to make one and only one response correct; (2) the question may pertain to opinions and theories about which there is little agreement; and (3) the question as originally conceived may be satisfactory but its written expression may be faulty. I discuss ways of improving the objectivity of objective and essay tests below.

Objectivity is closely related to reliability. Inconsistency in scoring a test leads to low reliability. This inconsistency occurs most easily in the scoring of essay tests when momentary considerations replace uniform standards of judgment. Inconsistency can also occur in the scoring of objective tests when answers are incorrectly scored, when the response key is altered in the process of scoring the papers, and when the choice of the right answer shifts with the winds of controversy.

Efficiency

An efficient test is one that yields a large number of independent, scorable responses per unit of time (Ebel, 1965, p. 295). An efficient test, therefore, makes the best use of the instructor's and the students' time. Items cast in the objective form, such as multiple-choice items, are time consuming to prepare. They are efficient to use, however, because they can be administered to successive classes and scored very quickly by hand or machine. The essay test is more efficient when a separate examination must be prepared for several classes and when the likelihood of reusing the examination is slight. In terms of the student's time the essay test is less efficient than the objective test because the student must spend most of his time in writing rather than in reading. The typical student can read about ten times as fast as he can write (Ebel, 1965, p. 295). Even objective items which involve interpretation of explanatory materials and problem solutions are less efficient than items involving factual information. Ebel reminds us, however, that these item types are not interchangeable. The instructional objective may dictate the use of the less efficient but more valid item. There must be a balance between validity and efficiency as well as between validity and reliability.

Summary

Performance assessment is the process of measuring the student's auxiliary and terminal performances during and at the end of the course of instruction. Feedback from performance assessment shows how well the student has achieved the instructional objective, the adequacy of his entering behavior, and the effectiveness of the instructional procedures. The measurement of achievement involves the use of absolute or relative standards. The absolute standard describes the minimal level of mastery the student is expected to attain. The relative standard compares the performance of one student with others in his group. Four concepts are basic to test construction and use: Validity is the degree to which a test actually measures terminal performances; reliability is the consistency with which a test measures these performances; objectivity is freedom from subjective judgments in the scoring of the test; and efficiency refers to the number of independent scorable responses per unit of time. The four concepts are related, and the construction of the test requires the teacher to strike a balance among them.

You should now return to objectives 1–10 (pp. 607–8) and determine how well you have achieved them.

QUESTION 14-1

Read the instructional objective and multiple-choice item below and answer the true-false questions which follow.

Instructional objective: When presented with a list of numerical problems requiring various arithmetic operations, the student will select only those problems requiring multiplication.

Item: Circle the letters of those problems which require multiplication.

(a) $34 + 43 + 116 =$
*(b) $782416 \div 42 =$
(c) $7333 - 333 =$
*(d) $823 \times 843 =$
*(e) $(34 + 113) \times 2 =$

Now answer these true-false statements by circling *T* for true and *F* for false.

T F (1) This item is valid for this instructional objective.
T F (2) This item measures a relative standard of achievement.
T F (3) This item is reliable.
T F (4) This item is objective.

After selecting your answers, give the reasons for your choices.

HOW TO CONSTRUCT AND REVISE YOUR TESTS

This section deals with the planning, construction, administration, scoring, and evaluation of essay and objective tests. The guidelines are procedures for incorporating in the body and the use of the test the basic characteristics of performance assessment: validity, reliability, objectivity, and efficiency. First, we shall consider four rules to follow in planning the test. Second, we shall compare the characteristics and uses of objective and essay examinations. Third, we shall consider the construction and scoring of the essay test. Fourth, in the longest portion of this section, we shall deal with the construction of the objective test. Here we consider several types of objective items: completion, short answer, true-false, matching, and multiple choice. Fifth, we consider matters concerned with the use of the test: preparing the test copy, giving the test, scoring the test, and evaluating and revising the test. You are also taught how to do an item analysis as one method of assessing the quality of the objective tests you construct.

Planning the Test

Julian Stanley (1964, pp. 171–84) has formulated four rules which you should follow in planning a test:

1. Adequate provision should be made for evaluating all important outcomes of instruction.
2. The test should reflect the approximate proportion of emphasis of the course.
3. The nature of the test must reflect its purpose.
4. The nature of the test must reflect the conditions under which it will be administered.

We shall now consider each of these rules.

Adequate provision should be made for evaluating all important outcomes of instruction. In the context of the basic teaching model, this means that you must construct items which assess achievement of all the instructional objectives. Since ordinarily there are many objectives, to simplify your task you should use one of the two systems for the classification of behavior described in Chapter 2.

Tables 14-1 and 14-2 show how the use of a chart or grid can simplify the classification of objectives. Table 14-1 employs Gagné's behavior categories. Table 14-2 employs four of the major categories of the *Taxonomy* and also uses course content rather than statements of instructional objectives. The use of such charts increases the likelihood that all important objectives and content are covered in the test.

The test should reflect the approximate proportion of emphasis in the course. In Table 14-2 the figures which appear in the various cells denote the number of items which will be devoted to each topic within a particular behavior class. For example there will be ten items on various aspects of the cell, five in the category of knowledge and five in the category of analysis. The subtotals for each behavior class indicate that the test items have their strongest emphasis on comprehension and their weakest on analysis. These emphases, according to Stanley (p. 183), should reflect the relative amount of emphasis each objective has re-

TABLE 14-1

AN ILLUSTRATION OF A CHART FOR PLANNING OF TESTS, BASED ON GAGNÉ'S CLASSIFICATION OF LEARNING TYPES (Gagné, 1965; see also Chapter 2, pp. 47–50). EMPTY CELLS WILL CONTAIN NUMBERS, INDICATING NUMBER OF ITEMS FOR EACH OBJECTIVE AND LEARNING TYPE.

Instructional Objectives (Chapter 14) / Learning Types (Gagné, 1965c)	Signal Learning	Stimulus-response Learning	Chaining	Verbal Association	Multiple Discrimination	Concept Learning	Principle Learning	Problem Solving
1. Define and illustrate performance assessment in terms of auxiliary and terminal performances.								
2. Describe and illustrate the relationship of performance assessment to other components of the basic teaching model.								
3. Distinguish and illustrate the differences between absolute and relative standards of performance.								
4. Describe and illustrate the disadvantage of using relative standards in performance assessment.								
5. Describe and illustrate three important results of using absolute standards.								
6. Define and illustrate validity in terms of instructional objectives and test items.								
7. Define reliability in terms of consistency.								
8. Define objectivity in terms of scoring and illustrate its use in scoring essay and objective tests.								
9. Describe the relationship between task analysis and test preparation.								
10. Construct two essay questions which follow the guidelines.								

TABLE 14-2

TWO-AXIS CHART OF SPECIFICATIONS FOR A FINAL EXAMINATION IN NATURAL SCIENCE—TERM 1 (after Nelson, 1961, p. 117).

Objectives * / Course Content	Knowledge	Comprehension (Translation, Interpretation, Extrapolation)	Application	Analysis	Total
I. Perception, symbolization, and the methods of science	5	5			10
II. The cell—structure and function; cell principle; spontaneous generation and biogenesis	5			5	10
III. Sexual reproduction in animals and plants; human reproduction and sex hormones	4	6			10
IV. Cellular reproduction; mitosis	4	6			10
V. Meiosis; chromosomes and genes	3	3	4		10
VI. Monohybrid cross		4	6		10
VII. Dihybrid cross		3	3	4	10
VIII. Blood group inheritance; heredity in man		4	6		10
IX. Linkage and crossing-over	3	3	4		10
X. Sex determination and sex linkage	1	1	2	6	10
Total	25	35	25	15	100

* Based on Bloom, 1956.

ceived in the actual teaching of the course. The same course may receive different emphases from two teachers, one teacher stressing the simple acquisition of knowledge and the other stressing the application of knowledge to practical problems. The assignment of test items to the various objectives, topics, and behavior categories must reflect these differences.

Following these two rules will provide the validity of your tests. A test cannot be valid unless the items are relevant to the instructional objectives and materials and to the learning they embody. Unless you take deliberate steps to provide the proper relevance and emphasis, your tests will lack validity.

THE NATURE OF THE TEST MUST REFLECT ITS PURPOSE. Here you must determine whether to employ an absolute or a relative standard of achievement. If your purpose is to determine whether the student has achieved the level of mastery specified in the instructional objective or the prerequisite level of entering behavior (both absolute standards), it is not important to include items which will yield a wide range of scores. Your purpose is to determine the present status of the student's behavior in relation to the specified standard and not in relation to other students in his group. If your purpose is to compare the performance of the student with others in his group (a relative standard), then you must include items which will distribute the scores from high to low. Following this rule provides both validity and reliability. To be valid, a test must purport to measure and actually measure what it was designed to measure. For the relative standard, one of the best ways of improving test reliability is to include items which yield a wide range of scores.

THE NATURE OF THE TEST MUST REFLECT THE CONDITIONS UNDER WHICH IT WILL BE ADMINISTERED. Ebel (1965, pp. 57–83) has identified several conditions about which the teacher must make decisions. First, you must decide how frequently you can test. Ebel believes it is safe to say that few classes are overexposed to good tests. The basic teaching model indicates that performance assessment, or testing, is an integral part of the teaching process and that it should occur during as well as at the conclusion of instruction. Second, you must decide how many questions to include in the test—based on the amount of available time, on the number of instructional objectives, and on the amount of content covered. Although the longer examination often has greater validity and reliability, an examination lasting more than three hours is often impractical. Third, you must decide in which format you will give the test. You should present objective examinations in the form of a printed booklet. You can save space by printing multiple-choice items in double columns rather than across the page. Whether you use objective or essay examinations each student should receive his own copy of the test. Although there have been some recent attempts to administer tests by visual projection, the cost of materials, the tediousness for the teacher, and the sources of distraction for the student discourage its use.

After this initial planning stage, you must decide whether to use an objective or an essay test. The basis for this decision should be your knowledge of the respective characteristics of these tests and the appropriate conditions for their use, the subject matter of our next topic.

Objective and Essay Examinations: Characteristics and Use

Ebel (1965, pp. 84–109) has ably described the following differences and similarities of objective and essay tests:

DIFFERENCES

Objective tests	*Essay tests*
1. Requires student to choose among two or more alternatives.	1. Requires the student to plan his own answer and express it in his own words.
2. Consists of many rather specific questions requiring only brief answers.	2. Consists of relatively few, more general questions which call for extended answers.
3. Students spend most of their time reading and thinking.	3. Students spend most of their time in thinking and writing.
4. Quality is determined by the skill of the test constructor.	4. Quality is determined largely by skill of the grader reading.
5. Is relatively tedious and difficult to prepare, but easy to score.	5. Is easy to prepare, but relatively tedious and difficult to score.
6. Affords much freedom for test constructor to express his knowledge and values.	6. Affords much freedom for the student to express his knowledge and individuality.
7. States student's tasks and the basis for judgment more clearly.	7. States student's tasks and basis for judgment less clearly.
8. Permits and occasionally encourages guessing.	8. Permits and occasionally encourages bluffing.
9. Distribution of scores is determined by the test.	9. Distribution of scores is controlled largely by the grader-reader.

SIMILARITIES

1. Both tests can measure almost any important instructional objective that any written test can measure.
2. Both tests can encourage students to learn concepts, principles, and problem solving.
3. Both tests involve the use of subjective judgment.
4. Both tests yield scores whose value is dependent on objectivity and reliability.

On the basis of these differences and similarities, Ebel (pp. 109–10) describes the conditions for the appropriate use of objective and essay tests. Use essay tests under the following five conditions:

1. The group to be tested is small and the test should not be reused.
2. The instructor wishes to do all possible to encourage and reward the development of student skill in written expression.
3. The instructor is more interested in exploring the student's attitudes than in measuring his achievements. (Whether an instructor should be more interested in attitudes than achievement and whether he should expect an honest expression of attitudes in a test he will evaluate seem open to question.)
4. The instructor is more confident of his proficiency as a critical reader than as an imaginative writer of good objective test items.
5. Time available for test preparation is shorter than time available for test grading.

Use objective tests under these conditions:

1. The group to be tested is large or the test may be reused.
2. Highly reliable test scores must be obtained as efficiently as possible.
3. Impartiality of evaluation, absolute fairness, and freedom from halo effects are essential.
4. The instructor is more confident of his ability to express objective test items clearly than of his ability to judge essay test answers correctly.
5. There is more pressure for speedy reporting of scores than for speedy test preparation.

Use either objective or essay tests for the following purposes:

1. Measure almost any important educational achievement which a written test can measure.
2. Test understanding of ability to apply principles.
3. Test ability to think critically.
4. Test ability to solve novel problems.
5. Test ability to select relevant facts and principles, to integrate them toward the solution of complex problems.
6. Encourage students to study for command of knowledge.

Now that you can describe the similarities and differences in the characteristics and uses of objective and essay tests, we can turn to their construction.

Constructing and Scoring the Essay Test

TYPES OF ESSAY QUESTIONS. C. C. Weidemann (1933, 1941) identified ten types of essay questions, which he arranged in order from simple to complex. These questions begin with (1) *what, who, when, which,* and *where,* (2) *list,* (3) *outline,* (4) *describe,* (5) *contrast,* (6) *compare,* (7) *discuss,* (8) *develop,* (9) *summarize,* and (10) *evaluate.* Ordinarily it is undesirable to start with the words in (1) and (2) because they require simple verbal associations which can be more easily tested with objective items (Thorndike and Hagen, 1961, p. 53). It is also generally undesirable to begin an essay question with *discuss* when the question fails to provide a basis for or the limitations or focus of the discussion. Additional words which adequately introduce essay questions are *give the reasons for, present arguments for and against, give original examples of,* and *explain how or why* (Thorndike and Hagen, p. 53).

It is also undesirable to ask for an expression of opinion when your intent is to measure student learning. Thorndike and Elizabeth Hagen (p. 54) use this example of a poor introduction. The teacher poses this essay question: *Why do you think* the Articles of Confederation provided a poor basis for the formation of our central government? If the teacher wants to determine whether the student knows the basic weaknesses of these Articles, he should recast the question: Why did the Articles of Confederation prove to be unworkable as a framework for our national government? Ordinarily you should avoid introducing essay questions with *what do you think, in your opinion, write all you know about,* and so on. Expressions of opinion or attitude cannot very well be scored, unless you assess only the logic or literary skill with which the student presents and defends his position.

GUIDELINES FOR IMPROVED ESSAY QUESTIONS. Thorndike and Hagen (pp. 53–56) suggest the following guidelines for improving the questions on an essay test. The statement of these guidelines has been slightly altered to fit our terminology. (1) Before writing the question, classify the instructional objective on the basis of its appropriate behavior category, using Gagné's system or the *Taxonomy.* If you are testing principle learning, for example, the question must require the student to demonstrate the principle in a novel situation. (2) Introduce the question with words which require the student to select, organize, and apply his knowledge. (3) Write the question in such a way that the task is clear and unambiguous for the students. This question (p. 54) fails to define a clear and unambiguous task:

> Discuss the factors and influences that led to the writing and adoption of our Constitution.

It does not define what the teacher means by discuss; it fails to indicate which historical event, remote or proximate, the students should begin with; it fails to indicate which historical event they should terminate with; and it fails to define factors and influences. The authors suggest that the question be revised as follows (p. 54):

> Explain how each of the following influenced the provisions written into our Constitution by the delegates to the Constitutional Convention.
>
> *A*. The Magna Carta, the Petition of Right, and the English Bill of Rights.
> *B*. The fear of tyranny or rule by one man or one group.
> *C*. The problems which arose in trying to operate under the provisions of the Articles of Confederation.
> *D*. The fear of small states that they would be controlled by large states.
> *E*. Business rivalries between states.

The revised question indicates the hidden complexity of the original question and provides all students with a common framework for answering it.

Frank Gorow (1966, p. 88) provides another example of improving an ambiguous essay question. The original question was: Discuss the origins of the Cold War. He suggests this modification:

> Assume that Winston Churchill, Nikita Khrushchev, and Harry Truman were invited to speak to our class on "The Origins of the Cold War."
>
> How would each of these men be likely to present the subject?
> What events or ideas might each select as the most significant causal factor?
> On which points, if any, would they probably agree?
> (Support your statements with facts, data, or other evidence.)

In these revised questions you can see that the student's task is clear and that there is a common basis for answering the question.

There are additional guidelines for preparing essay questions. (4) Do not introduce the question with words which require only an expression of student opinion. (5) Do not require the students to answer too many or too lengthy questions for the available time. Thorndike and Hagen estimate that their revised question on the Constitution would take the average student in the eighth grade about forty-five to fifty minutes to answer. The tendency of most teachers is to give too many essay questions for a single class period. Answering an essay question requires the students not only to write but also to recall the appropriate knowledge and to organize it for presentation—processes which take considerable time. (6) Require each student to answer the same questions. Presumably each question determines student achievement of important instructional objectives. Each terminal performance must, therefore, be assessed for each student. Furthermore, if a relative standard is employed, giving a choice of questions does not provide a common base upon which students can be compared. Thorndike and Hagen write (p. 55): "A choice of questions may have a public relations value with the examinees, but it has no justification from the point of view of effective measurement."

SCORING ESSAY TESTS. These authors (p. 56) list five suggestions for scoring essay questions: (1) Before you start to score the questions decide which factors you are assessing. If you are assessing concept and principle learning, you should not score the paper for mechanics of English, spelling, punctuation, and so on. If you are assessing more than one factor, you should score separately for each factor. (2) Before you start to score, also prepare a model answer as a common basis for evaluating each paper. This preliminary model should be checked against a sample of student answers and appropriately revised. At this time you should also determine how many credits you will award for each point in the essay. (3) Read all the answers to one question before going on to the next question. This procedure introduces more objectivity into the scoring, builds a clearer conception of the answer, and avoids the influence of what the student wrote on the previous question. (4) Score the papers as anonymously as possible. Gorow (1966, p. 95) suggests that the students' names be on the back of the sheet or test booklet, preferably at the bottom, where it is most inconspicuous. Your assessment should be in terms of what was written and not who wrote it. (5) If possible, have the questions scored by one or more independent graders, especially if the students' test scores are the basis for important decisions.

Constructing the Objective Test

TYPES OF OBJECTIVE ITEMS. Stanley (1964, p. 204–6) describes two major objective items. (1) Free-response items appear as a direct question, stimulus word or phrase, or an incomplete statement or question. Completion items and short-answer questions are common forms of free-response items. (2) Limited-response items provide all the choices that the student must decide among. True-false, matching, and multiple-choice questions are the common forms of limited-response items. We shall now consider some illustrations of each of these item forms and some rules for their composition.

THE COMPLETION ITEM. In this item the student receives a statement which omits certain key words or phrases. Here is an example of a statement and the completion item based on it (Noll, 1965, p. 140):

> Democracy is that form of government in which the whole people or some numerous portion of them exercise the governing power through deputies periodically elected by themselves.
> Democracy is that form of ——— in which the whole ——— or some numerous portion of them exercise the governing ——— through ——— elected by ———.

Stanley (pp. 211–13) suggests several rules for composing completion items: (1) Avoid indefinite statements; (2) avoid overmutilated statements; (3) omit key words and phrases, rather than trivial details; (4) avoid lifting statements directly from the text; (5) whenever the indefinite article is required before a blank, write it in the form a(n), so that an unnecessary cue does not supply the answer; (6) make the blanks of uniform length; (7) try to choose statements in which there is only one correct response for the blanks; (8) avoid grammatical clues to the correct answer; (9) the required response should be a single word or a brief phrase; (10) arrange the test so that answers are in a column at the right of the sentences; (11) avoid a series of blanks which does not have a unique order; (12) prepare a scoring key which contains all acceptable answers; and (13) allow one point for each correctly filled blank.

Stanley (1964, pp. 211–12) provides several examples of poor completion questions and the revisions which improve them. Which rules do the following two items ignore?

> Item *A:* Abraham Lincoln was born in ———.
> Item *B:* The authors of the first performance test of intelligence were ———.

Item *A* ignores the first and item *B* the eighth rule. There are improved versions of these items:

> Item *A:* Abraham Lincoln was born in the year ———.
> Item *B:* The first performance test of intelligence was prepared by ———.

Because of the vagueness which plagues most completion questions, it is often desirable to combine their use with the multiple-choice form:

> Item: The first performance test of ——— was prepared by Alfred Binet.
> *A.* personality *D.* instruction
> *B.* motivation *E.* perception
> *C.* intelligence

THE SHORT-ANSWER ITEM. This item is a direct question or simple statement which can be answered with a word, short phrase, number, or symbol. Here are some examples:

Item *A:* What is the capital of South Korea?
Item *B:* List the forms of limited-response items.
Item *C:* Elvis has ten marbles. He wins thirty-five from Harriet and then gives twenty-two to Marilyn. How many marbles does he have left?

You can apply most of the rules for composing completion questions to composing short-answer items.

We can now consider the various forms of limited-response items.

SOME BASIC TERMINOLOGY. In discussing limited-response items it is convenient to use particular terms which refer to various aspects of the items: distracters (foils), specific determiners, and stem. Consider the following item (Ebel, 1966, p. 187):

Item: What, if anything, developed in 1955 with respect to relations between Egypt and Soviet Russia?
A. A Russian military force invaded Egypt.
B. Egypt accused members of the Russian embassy of spying and broke off diplomatic relations.
C. Soviet Russia supported Egypt's demand for independence from Britain.
**D.* The Egyptian government arranged to buy arms from the Soviet Union.

Distracters are incorrect alternatives, in this case choices *A, B,* and *C.* *Specific determiners* are unintended clues to the correct answer. In the above statement this clue is the generality of statement *D,* as compared with the specific events named in the alternatives. The *stem* is that part of the item which introduces the alternatives—in the present item it is a direct question.

TRUE-FALSE ITEMS. These items permit only one of two responses. The usual responses are true or false, but they can also be right-wrong, correct-incorrect, yes-no, same-opposite, and a two-choice multiple choice (Stanley, p. 214). Consider the following items, which appear in both the true and false forms (Ebel, p. 144). True form:

Item *A:* The mercantile system requires legislative support.
Item *B:* All eclipses involve shadows.

False form:

Item *A:* The mercantile system requires corporate income taxes.
Item *B:* If light rays could not be bent, eclipses could not occur.

Stanley (pp. 216–19) has gathered several illustrative items in which alternative responses are not true or false. Here are three items from a test on English grammar (Greene, 1939):

Item *A:* Ted is (1. a / 2. an) industrious man.

Item *B:* My father (1. has / 2. hasn't) no money.

Item *C:* I want everyone to help (1. himself / 2. themselves)

Stanley (pp. 219–21) lists fifteen rules for composing true-false items: (1) Avoid specific determiners. Statements are generally false when they contain these words: *all, always, never, nothing, impossible, inevitable,* and so on. Statements are generally true when they contain these words: *some, sometimes, often, frequently, may, generally, as a rule, usually,* and so on. You may use these words, however, if you carefully balance their appearance in the true and the false statements. (2) Make approximately half the statements true and half false and tell the students that you have done this. (3) Avoid the exact wording of the textbook. (4) Avoid trick statements which are false only because of a petty insertion. (5) Limit each statement to a single point. (6) Avoid double negatives. (7) Avoid ambiguous statements which give rise to two or more interpretations, only one of which may be true. (8) Avoid unfamiliar, figurative, or literary language. (9) Avoid sentences with complex structure. (10) Avoid qualitative language whenever possible—words such as *few, many, large, young, old, important,* and so on. *More than* and *most* are permissible because they are parts of quantifiable statements. (11) Avoid using statements of commands, which cannot be true or false. (12) Make the main clause true and the reason true or false if you are testing for the truth or falsity of a reason. (13) Require the simplest method of indicating the response. Stanley suggests that the student write *T* and *F, Y* and *N* rather than *True* and *False, Yes* and *No.* The student can also be directed to circle or underline the correct response or even to use + and −. (14) Indicate by a short line or by ( ) where the response is to be recorded. (15) Arrange the items in groups, possibly of five, to facilitate scoring. Here are three examples (Stanley, pp. 219–21) of undesirable items. Which rules do they ignore?

Item *A:* The gas xenon is generally inert.
Item *B:* As it ages, pure copper turns brown because it oxidizes.
Item *C:* Poe wrote *The Gold Bug* and *The Scarlet Letter.*

Item *A* ignores the first, *B* the twelfth, and *C* the fifth rule. Here are improved versions of these items:

> Item *A:* The gas xenon forms compounds with most elements.
> Item *B:* As it ages, pure copper turns green because it attracts green algae.
> Item *C:* Poe wrote *The Gold Bug.*

MATCHING ITEMS. Another form of limited-response items is the matching item, in which the student must match the elements in one column with those in another. Norman Gronlund (1965, p. 135) lists several examples of column relationships which teachers in several fields considered important.

Column A	Column B
Men	Achievements
Dates	Historical events
Terms	Definitions
Rules	Examples
Symbols	Concepts
Authors	Titles of books
Foreign words	English equivalents
Machines	Uses
Plants or animals	Classification
Principles	Illustrations
Objects	Names of objects
Parts	Functions

Gronlund observes that matching items use visual materials when, for example, the item requires the student to match words with pictures and names of places with map locations.

Here is an example of a matching item (Gronlund, p. 134):

	Column A	Column B
(G)	1. Name of the *answer* in addition problems.	*A.* Difference
(A)	2. Name of the *answer* in subtraction problems.	*B.* Dividend
(D)	3. Name of the *answer* in multiplication problems.	*C.* Multiplicand
(E)	4. Name of the *answer* in division problems.	*D.* Product
		E. Quotient
		F. Subtrahend
		G. Sum

Gronlund (pp. 136–38) describes several rules for composing matching items: (1) Use only homogeneous material in a single matching item. The previous item illustrates homogeneity in two ways: Column *A* concerns only names of answers to problems in arithmetic, and column *B* lists only plausible names for these answers. (2) Include more elements in the second than in the first column and tell the students that they can use each of these elements once, more than once, or not at all. (3) Keep the list of elements to be matched brief and place the shorter elements in column *B*. (4) Arrange words in alphabetical order and numbers in sequence. (5) Indicate in the directions the basis for matching the elements. (6) Place all elements for one matching item on the same page. Gronlund (p. 136) gives this example of a faulty matching item. Which rule does it ignore?

Directions: On the line to the left of each achievement listed in column *A*, write the letter of the man's name in column *B* who is noted for that achievement. Each name in column *B* may be used once, more than once, or not at all.

	Column A	Column B
Item:	(*A*) 1. Invented the telephone	*A*. Alexander Graham Bell
	(*B*) 2. Discovered America	*B*. Christopher Columbus
	(*C*) 3. First United States astronaut to orbit the earth	*C*. John Glenn
		D. Abraham Lincoln
	(*F*) 4. First President of the United States	*E*. Ferdinand Magellan
		F. George Washington
		G. Eli Whitney

This item largely ignores the first rule. The elements are a motley collection of inventors, explorers, and presidents. It is better to have one matching item for each of these categories.

You can also cast the matching item as a multiple-choice item to determine how well the student can relate concepts and principles. Here is an example (Berg, 1965, p. 75):

Key: 1. The entry in column *A* is an example of the opposite entry in column *B*.
2. The entry in column *A* is synonymous with the opposite entry in column *B*.
3. The entry in column *A* and its opposite entry in column *B* are parallel (terms which are subpoints under the same topic).

Column A	Column B	
Item *A:* Villein	Serf	(3)
Item *B:* Baptism	Sacrament	(1)
Item *C:* Middle Ages	Medieval period	(2)

THE MULTIPLE-CHOICE ITEM. Despite the fact that it is the most difficult item to write, test specialists favor the multiple-choice item (Ebel,

p. 60). Practice has shown that a multiple-choice test composed of one-half the number of items on a true-false test has equal reliability. Compared with true-false items, the multiple-choice item tends to distinguish better between high and low achievement, is less subject to ambiguity and misinterpretation, and can be answered correctly by chance less frequently (Ebel, p. 61). The multiple-choice item includes an item stem in the form of a complete or incomplete question or statement and usually four or more alternatives (or options). In the case of four alternatives, three are distractors and one is the correct answer. Here is an example of a multiple-choice item (Ebel, pp. 183–84):

> Item: What is the principal advantage of a battery of lead storage cells over a battery of dry cells for automobile starting and lighting?
> *A*. The storage cell furnishes direct current.
> *B*. The voltage of the storage cell is higher.
> **C*. The current from the storage cell is stronger.
> *D*. The initial cost of the storage cell is less.

Here the distracters are true statements, but only one of these statements (*C*) explains the preference for the storage cell. The stem, of course, is a complete question.

Ebel (pp. 151–70) lists nine suggestions for composing multiple-choice items: (1) Before writing the item make an explicit statement of the idea the item will embody. You can also select key statements, especially those which clearly define concepts and principles, from good instructional materials. (2) Write the item in the way which will allow greater success for those students who have achieved greater mastery of terminal behavior than for those students who have achieved less mastery. (3) Prepare the original draft in such a way as to make revision and assembly convenient. It is best to begin with a pencil draft of each item on a separate sheet of paper. In preparing the alternatives, you should write the correct answer first and then vary randomly the place of the correct answers among the alternatives. (4) Write the stem as a question or incomplete statement which has a concise answer and plausible alternatives. A direct question is usually better than an incomplete statement because it more clearly defines the problem and indicates the teacher's purpose. Here is an example of a concise stem question with concise alternatives (Ebel, p. 158):

> Item: Who were the Huks in the Philippines:
> *A*. A tribe of primitive head hunters.
> **B*. A Communist-supported rebel group.
> *C*. Wealthy Philippine landowners and industrialists.
> *D*. Members of the minority party in the Philippine legislature.

(5) Make the correct answer thoroughly correct, express it clearly, and avoid specific determiners which will betray the answer to the alert but unknowledgable students. Here are two examples of items which fail to avoid specific determiners (Ebel, pp. 162–63):

Item *A:* When used in conjunction with the T-square, the left vertical edge of a triangle is used to draw:
**A.* Vertical lines
B. Slant lines
C. Horizontal lines
D. Inclined lines

Item *B:* How did styles in women's clothing in 1950 differ most from those in 1900?
A. They showed more beauty.
B. They showed more variety.
C. They were easier to clean.
**D.* They were easier to live in, work in, move in, and were generally less restrictive.

The irrelevant cues in both of these items would allow students who knew little or nothing about T-squares and clothing styles in 1950 to select the correct answer. In item *A,* the irrelevant cue is the appearance of *vertical* in both the stem and the correct answer. In item *B,* it is the greater length and detail of the correct answer. (6) Make the distractors thoroughly wrong and yet plausible to the student who knows a little but not enough. Victor Noll (1965, pp. 152–53) illustrates how distracters can vary from being plausible to being absurd:

Item *A.* The capital of the United States is

**A.* Washington	*C.* Chicago
B. New York	*D.* St. Louis
	E. Los Angeles

Item *B.* The capital of the United States is

**A.* Washington	*C.* Reno
B. Atlantic City	*D.* Milwaukee
	E. San Antonio

Item *C.* The capital of the United States is

**A.* Washington	*C.* Tokyo
B. Rome	*D.* Paris
	E. London

Item *D.* The capital of the United States is

**A.* Washington	*C.* China
B. wheat	*D.* air
	E. birds

The plausibility of the alternatives determines the difficulty of the item. If the alternatives are implausible, they serve no useful purpose and consume the students' valuable reading time during the examination. In effect, items *B, C,* and *D* are one-alternative items because their distractors are implausible. One-alternative items hardly function as test items! (7) Write the item as clearly, simply, and correctly as possible. (8) Modify the item, if necessary, so that 50 per cent of the students will answer correctly. (9) Arrange for a colleague to review your original draft. The reviewer should try to answer each question and should check his choices against the answer key.

Multiple-choice items can assess concept learning, principle learning, and problem solving. In the following example (Heenan, 1961, p. 183) the student must be able to identify an example of Epicurean philosophy, an example of Thomistic (Aquinas) philosophy, and a particular attribute of Epicurean philosophy. The item begins with a quotation from a philosophic work.

Quotation: The senses at first let in particular ideas and furnish the yet empty cabinet, and, the mind by degrees growing familiar with some of them, they are lodged in memory, and the names get to them. . . . In this manner the mind comes to be furnished with ideas and the language, the materials about which to exercise its discursive faculty. And the use of reason becomes daily more visible, as these materials giving it employment increase.

Item A: The above quotation reflects the philosophic position of the

A. Empiricists
B. Scholastics
C. Platonists
D. Realists
**E*. Epicureans

Item *B*: Which of the following men would be most inclined to accept this quotation as a true statement?

A. Plato
B. Socrates
C. Descartes
D. Locke
**E*. Aquinas

Item *C*: The school characterized in this paragraph believes that the source of our ideas is

A. divine revelation
B. experience
C. faith
D. study
**E*. unknown

The next item requires the student to demonstrate his knowledge of a principle which involves the relationship between two concepts, mean and standard deviation:

Item: Sam made a score of 70 on an English achievement test which had a mean of 50 and a standard deviation of 10. Helen made a score of 50 on a different English achievement test which had a mean of 40 and a standard deviation of 5. What is your best guess as to the comparative knowledge of English of Sam and Helen?

A. Sam knows more.
B. Helen knows more.
**C.* They both know about the same amount.
D. It depends on which one has the higher IQ.
E. It depends on which one gets the best grades in English.

The following item also requires the student to demonstrate the relationship between concepts he has learned:

Item: *Mean* is to *standard deviation* as *median* is to

**A.* semi-interquartile range
B. mode
C. regression
D. middle score
E. average

The next item requires the student to engage in problem solving, the application of principles (Nelson, 1961, pp. 126–27):

Items 10–16 are concerned with the following series of statements concerning the electrical condenser shown in the diagram [Fig. 14-1]. The outer coating is connected to the earth, as shown, by means of a copper wire. Evaluate each statement (items 10–12) and reason given according to the key below.

Key: 1. The statement given is true and the reason given is accepted as correct and supports the statement.
2. The statement given is true and the reason given is true but it does not support or contradict the statement, i.e., is true but irrelevant.
3. The statement given is true but the reason given is either false or contradicts the statement.
4. The statement is false and the reason is not accepted as correct.
5. The statement is false but the reason is accepted as correct.

Item 10: If the inner coating of the jar is charged negatively, the outer coating becomes charged positively *because* positive charges flow from the earth to the coating along the wire. (3)

Item 11: If the inner coating of the jar is charged positively, the inner coating becomes charged negatively *because* unlike magnetic poles attract. (2)

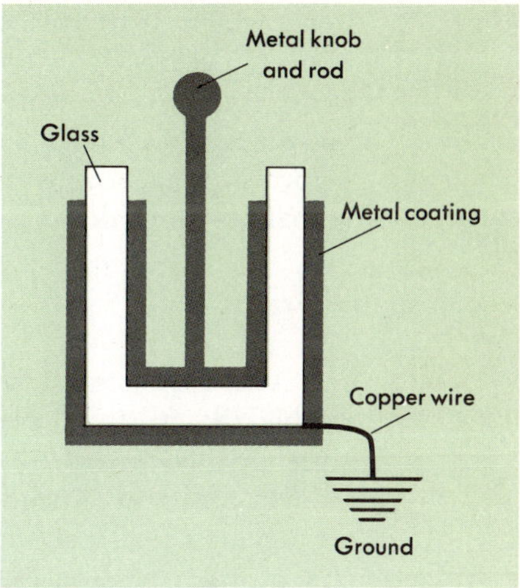

Fig. 14-1. *An electrical condenser (after Nelson, 1961, p. 126).*

Item 12: If the inner coating of the jar is charged negatively, the outer coating becomes charged negatively *because* like charges repel one another. (5)

Such an item is sometimes called a *key-list* multiple-choice item. To the previous suggestions for composing multiple-choice items, Harry Berg (1965, p. 75) adds three more suggestions for key-list items: (1) Avoid basing too many items on a single key—the key must provide appropriate alternatives for each item. (2) Make the alternative in the key broad and significant enough for nearly all students to understand. A student should not miss items only because a part of the key contains highly specialized knowledge. (3) Tell the student that the alternatives in the key can apply to one, more than one, or none of the items.

A study by Morris Weitman (1965) showed that the more a multiple-choice item relied on principle learning and problem solving rather than on verbal association (rote memory), the better the item distinguished between long-term and short-term retention. The measure of long-term retention was the number of items on a final examination in physiology medical students answered correctly at the end of the spring quarter and, several weeks later, at the beginning of the fall quarter. He classified the thirty-one test items on the degree of dependence on rote memory, calling one class items with strong emphasis on rote memory and the other class items with weak emphasis on rote memory. A key-list item, although not used in this examination, is an example of an item with weak emphasis on rote memory. Weitman discovered that the items which distinguished long-term retention (items which the students answered correctly in both the spring and the fall) were those items with weak emphasis on rote memory. This finding is consistent with our knowledge of concept learning, principle learning, and problem solving —forms of learning which suffer fewer of the effects of interference than verbal learning does.

Preparing the Test Copy

After you have constructed your objective test items, you must assemble the fruits of your labor and present them to your students in some printed form. First, you must decide how to arrange the items. Gilbert Sax and Theodore Cromack (1966) studied the effects of four arrangements of test items: easy to hard items (*E*), hard to easy items (*H*), an interspersion of easy and hard items (*M*), and a random arrangement of items (*R*). Using these four conditions one group was given thirty minutes, the other about fifty minutes to complete an examination. Table 14-3 summarizes the results. You can see that the students obtained significantly higher average scores on form *E* (easy to hard) than on the other forms. You can also note that the students in the thirty-minute group obtained the lowest scores on form *H*, in which the hard items preceded the easy items. You can further note that, when the examination time was extended (from thirty to forty-eight minutes), the advantage of form *E* was comparatively less. Finally, mixing easy items with difficult items to produce what is sometimes called a *motivational test* apparently has no advantage over randomly arranging the items. The conclusion of this study is that you should arrange your items in order of ascending difficulty (easy to hard) unless you allow generous amounts of examination time.

Second, you should provide the students with adequate directions and read aloud and explain the directions. If you vary the item form,

TABLE 14-3

EFFECTS OF FOUR ARRANGEMENTS OF TEST ITEMS (after Sax and Cromack, 1966, p. 310).

	Thirty-Minute Group				Forty-Eight–Minute Group			
	E	*H*	*M*	*R*	*E*	*H*	*M*	*R*
Mean	37.83	21.39	27.00	29.12	47.54	45.58	42.65	42.02
S. D.	8.33	8.34	9.40	8.53	10.58	15.47	12.23	13.07
N	72	70	68	66	50	45	49	47

you must provide a new set of directions for each form. For younger students who are unaccustomed to objective tests, it is desirable to follow the directions with a sample item which you answer for them. Here are directions for multiple-choice items which have a separate answer sheet (Thorndike and Hagen, 1961, p. 87):

> Directions:
>
> Read each item and decide which choice *best* completes the statement or answers the question.
>
> Mark your answers on the separate answer sheets. Do *not* mark them on the test booklet. Indicate your answer by blacking out on the answer sheet the letter corresponding to your choice. That is, if you think that choice *B* is the best answer to item 1, black out the *B* in the row after No. 1 on your answer sheet.
>
> Your score will be the number of right answers, so it will be to your advantage to answer every question, even if you are not sure of the right answer.
>
> *Be sure your name is on your answer sheet.*

Third, you must consider the actual format in which the items will appear on the printed page. The format should be one which both teacher (as scorer) and students find clear and convenient. If you do not use a separate answer sheet, you should provide an answer column in the right or left margin of the page. True-false items should appear in groups of five to avoid an overwhelming and confusing solid page of words and letters. To conserve space, multiple-choice items can appear in two columns. The alternatives for these items should not appear in paragraph form; they should be listed, as in the illustrations above.

Administering the Test

Efficient administration of the test should include the following: (1) careful organization and efficient distribution of all the test materials, (2) brief directions and brief answers to questions raised by students, and (3) a record of time on the blackboard to help the students pace their efforts. By following these suggestions, you give the students the maximum time for answering all the test questions. Ebel (p. 208) suggests that the following notation appear on the blackboard:

> No more than ——— minutes remain for you to work on this test.
> If you have not reached item ——— you are working too slowly.

The numbers for completing these statements should be changed about every fifteen minutes. As for the questions about test items which students raise in the course of taking the test, Ebel (p. 208) advises that these interruptions occur as quietly and infrequently as possible and that the teacher give only that help which increases the student's understanding of the task but does not give him an unfair advantage in answering the question.

PREVENTING CHEATING. One of your major responsibilities in administering the test is the prevention of cheating. Ebel (p. 209) lists a number of activities which illustrate cheating:

1. The side-long glance at a fellow student's answers
2. The preparation and use of a crib sheet
3. Collusion between two or more students to exchange information on answers during the test
4. Unauthorized copying of questions or stealing of test booklets in anticipation that they may be used again later on
5. Arranging for a substitute to take an examination
6. Stealing or buying copies of an examination before the test is given or sharing such illicit advanced copies with others.

What can you do to prevent cheating and what should you do when it occurs? Ebel (p. 210) makes the following suggestions: (1) Establish clearly that when cheating occurs it will be punished by a failing grade, loss of course credit, and suspension or dismissal from school; (2) safeguard the security of the test while it is written, duplicated, and stored; (3) use alternate forms of the test when students must sit close together; and (4) take seriously your proctoring duties during the examination period. When the teacher finds a student cheating, his examination materials should be collected and the results of the examination should be voided, made up, or possibly replaced with a failing grade. The use of honor systems, in which one student reports the cheating of other students, is frequently unsuccessful because, as Ebel (p. 211) states, "The honor sought by the honor system thus must be purchased at the price of another kind of honor, that of loyalty to one's close associates. It is not surprising that systems of this kind sometimes break down."

Failure to prevent cheating may have several deleterious effects on student achievement: (1) When cheating occurs with impunity, honest achievement goes unrecognized or punished and reduces student motivation to achieve; (2) there is no way to assess validly or reliably what the student has and has not learned; and (3) ingenuity in devising ways to cheat becomes more important than attainment of the instructional objectives.

Scoring the Test

You should observe three practices in scoring objective tests. First, you should prepare an answer key. The key may be simply an answer sheet which you have filled out or, if you use a commercially made sheet, it may be a cardboard stencil or template which fits over the answer sheets. Second, you should ordinarily assign one point for each correct answer, with no allowance for fractional credit. Giving different weights to different items in a test or to different correct and incorrect alternatives in a particular item usually does not improve the validity or reliability of the test (Ebel, pp. 233–36). Third, you should use a correction for guessing only when some students omit a fairly large number of items (Stanley, p. 196). The correction formula is

$$\text{Score} = R - \frac{W}{n-1}$$

where R = number of correct responses
W = number of incorrect responses
n = number of alternatives for an item

For an item which has only two alternatives, as in the case of true-false items, $n - 1$ becomes $2 - 1$. For an item with four alternatives $n - 1$ becomes 3. For example, if a test contains one hundred multiple-choice items, each with four alternatives, and Elvis answers fifty items correctly and fifty items incorrectly, his corrected score is determined as follows:

$$\text{Score} = 50 - \frac{50}{4-1} = 50 - \frac{50}{3} = 33.34$$

If, however, Elvis answers fifty items correctly and omits fifty items, his corrected score is

$$50 - \frac{0}{3} = 50 - 0 = 50$$

When some students have not omitted a fairly large number of items, the correction for guessing will have little effect: Students will maintain the same relative positions as they had with the uncorrected scores (Ebel, p. 227). Also, students should be encouraged to make rational guesses based on the best knowledge they have.

Evaluating the Test

Criteria. To determine the quality of your test, you must use the four criteria discussed in the first section: validity, reliability, objectivity, and efficiency. Three of these criteria require your own prima facie judgment. The test has validity to the extent that the items assess the terminal performances described in the instructional objectives. The test has objectivity to the extent that a colleague in your discipline would obtain a perfect or almost perfect score. The test has efficiency to the extent that it makes the best use of the students' examination time and of the time you have available for preparing the test and for scoring the test.

ITEM ANALYSIS. You can determine the degree of reliability in a number of ways. In Chapter 15 you will learn how to describe test scores statistically and how to apply reliability formulas. Here we will limit our consideration to a single method for determining reliability, item analysis. Item analysis is a method of determining the level of item discrimination and difficulty. Item discrimination depends on the degree to which an item distinguishes between the high scorers and the low scorers. Item difficulty depends on the percentage of students who answer the item correctly. The formulas and illustrations of item discrimination and difficulty below will be clear once you consider a simple procedure for item analysis.

Before you can determine item discrimination and difficulty, you should take these steps: (1) arrange the tests in order of scores, from high to low; (2) form a group of high scorers by separating the upper 25 per cent or more of the papers; (3) form a group of low scorers by separating the lower 25 per cent or more of the papers; (4) for each group count the number of times they chose each alternative; and (5) record these counts on a copy of the test. Here is an example of this procedure; the upper- and lower-scoring groups each contain one hundred students.

Item: The first premier of Lower Slabovnia was
- *A*. George Washington (hi = 5; lo = 16)
- **B*. Petroff Mehalovich (hi = 27; lo = 18)
- *C*. Sergei Potemkin (hi = 56; lo = 40)
- *D*. Ivan Tito (hi = 12; lo = 26)

The figures appearing after the alternatives are the number of high-scoring (hi) and low-scoring (lo) students choosing each alternative. Originally you should record these numbers as tally marks which you will later sum.

With this information you can now determine discrimination and item difficulty. The formula for item difficulty is

$$\text{Diff.} = \frac{R}{N} \times 100$$

where Diff. = the difficulty index (a percentage)
R = the number of high-scoring and low-scoring students who chose the correct response
N = the total number of students in both groups

For the item above

$$\text{Diff.} = \frac{27 + 18}{200} \times 100 = 22.5 \times 100 = 23 \text{ per cent}$$

We now know that 23 per cent of the sample, comprising 200 papers, chose the correct alternative. The formula for item discrimination is

$$D = \frac{R_{\text{hi}} - R_{\text{lo}}}{0.5N}$$

where $D =$ the discrimination index (a decimal fraction)
$R_{\text{hi}} =$ number of high-scoring students who answered correctly
$R_{\text{lo}} =$ number of low-scoring students who answered correctly
$0.5N =$ one-half the number of papers in the sample (either the upper or lower half)

For the item above

$$D = \frac{27 - 18}{100} = \frac{9}{100} = 0.09$$

Frequently the difficulty and discrimination indices are recorded next to the item number as follows:

23% The first premier of Lower Slabovnia was
0.09

A. George Washington (hi = 5; lo = 16)
**B*. Petroff Mehalovich (hi = 27; lo = 18)
C. Sergei Potemkin (hi = 56; lo = 40)
D. Ivan Tito (hi = 12; lo = 26)

What do these indices tell you about the quality of your test items? Generally speaking, if you are using a relative standard, you can follow these guidelines: (1) The closer the difficulty index is to 50 per cent the better the reliability of the item. You should reject or revise very easy and very difficult items. Very easy items are those which almost all the students answer correctly; very difficult items are those which almost all the students answer incorrectly. (2) The closer the discrimination index is to 0.40 and above the better the reliability of the item. Items between 0.30 and 0.39 probably require minor revisions, those between 0.20 and 0.29 require somewhat more revision, and those below 0.19 require major revision if they are retained at all (Ebel, p. 364).

Item analysis provides the basis for the revision of items. Ebel (p. 368) shows how revision of an item improves its discrimination and reduces its difficulty:

37% What, if any, is the distinction between climate and weather?
0.13

A. There is no important distinction. (1–6)
B. Climate is primarily a matter of temperature and rainfall, while weather includes many other natural phenomena. (33–51)
**C*. Climate pertains to longer periods of time than weather. (43–30)
D. Weather pertains to natural phenomena on a *local* rather than a *national* scale. (23–13)

The item is difficult because considerably less than half (37 per cent) the students answered it correctly. The item discriminates poorly because about the same number of high-scoring (43) and low-scoring (30) students answered it correctly. The following revision improves both item difficulty and discrimination. The revised portions of the item are in italics.

62% What, if any, is the distinction between climate and weather?
0.58

A. There is no important distinction. (2–22)
B. *Climate is primarily a matter of rainfall, while weather is primarily a matter of temperature.* (3–25)
**C*. Climate pertains to longer periods of time than weather. (91–33)
D. *Weather is determined by clouds, while climate is determined by winds.* (4–20)

The revised item is now less difficult. but more discriminating. Although more students chose the correct answer, most of these were high-scoring students (91). The revision of the second alternative reduced its attractiveness for both high-scoring and low-scoring students. With this revision, however, most of the low-scoring students switched to the first and fourth alternatives, while most of the high-scoring students switched to the correct alternative—thus making the item more discriminating.

IMPROVING RELIABILITY. There are several ways to improve the reliability of tests based on relative standards of achievement. First, you can lengthen your tests by adding items of the same average difficulty and discrimination. Second, you can increase the discrimination power of the individual items. Third, you can include items of about 50 per cent difficulty and exclude very difficult or very easy items.

It is more difficult to improve the reliability of tests based on absolute standards of achievement. In such tests all students who have achieved the instructional objectives are expected to answer all items correctly. For each item the difficulty index is 100 per cent and the discrimination index 0.00. In preparing such a test it is necessary that any variation in item difficulty reflect only variations in task difficulty and not irrelevant variations in the items. The quality of these tests is almost entirely a product of how well the instructional objectives have been stated—the specificity of the terminal behaviors, of the conditions under which they must be performed, and of the standards of acceptable performance.

Summary

We have now completed our consideration of the construction and revision of essay and objective tests. In planning the test it is important to make adequate provision for evaluating all instructional objectives if the test is to have the necessary validity. The two major tests are objective and essay. Their characteristics to a large extent determine their appropriate use. Although the essay test is easier to prepare, it is harder to grade with reliability and objectivity. Although the objective test is harder to prepare, it is easier to grade with reliability and objectivity. Both tests can measure almost any important instructional objective that a test can measure. The guidelines for the preparation of essay tests in general suggest a prior determination of the learning you are assessing and a clear and unambiguous delineation of the task the student should perform. The scoring of the test usually requires the preparation of model answers used in grading all the papers. There are several types of objective items: completion, short answer, true-false, matching, and multiple choice. The preparation of these items requires the observance of the particular guidelines described. All these items, particularly multiple-choice items, require you to provide plausible distractors, to avoid specific determiners, and to provide an adequate description of the task in that part of the item which precedes the response. Key-list multiple-choice items can assess the higher types of learning. After the construction of the items particular care must be exercised in the preparation of the test copy, in the test administration, in the prevention of cheating, in the scoring, and in the test evaluation. The scoring of the test should not ordinarily require correction for guessing or differential weighting of items. The evaluation of the test requires an assessment of the test's validity, reliability, objectivity, and efficiency. An easy way to determine test reliability, based on internal test standards, is item analysis. Through item analysis you can determine item difficulty and discrimination and revise items accordingly. By adding items of average difficulty and high discrimination, you can improve the reliability of tests based on relative standards. For tests based on absolute standards, test reliability depends on how adequately you state instructional objectives.

You should now return to objectives 11–37 (pp. 608–9) and determine how well you have achieved them.

QUESTION 14-2

In this multiple-choice item (Ebel, 1965, p. 372), the numbers following the alternatives show the number of high-scoring and low-scoring students who chose each one. Read the item and these data and answer the questions which follow:

Item: A workman lifts planks to the top of a scaffold by pulling down on a rope passed over a single fixed pulley attached to the top of the scaffold. The rope will break under a load of 500 pounds, and the workman weighs 200 pounds. What is the heaviest load the workman can lift with the pulley?

A. 100 pounds (hi = 1, lo = 6)
**B*. 200 pounds (hi = 35, lo = 42)
C. 400 pounds (hi = 32, lo = 23)
D. 500 pounds (hi = 32, lo = 29)

1. Assuming that there are one hundred high-scoring and one hundred low-scoring students in your sample determine (a) the difficulty index and (b) the discrimination index.
2. Is this item easy or difficult?
3. Is this item a good or poor discriminator?
4. How could alternatives *C* and *D* be made less attractive to the high-scoring students?

MARKING AND REPORTING

The tests you construct are a major basis for assigning students their marks. Marks are easily defined as measures of the achievement of instructional objectives. Reports are the means teachers and schools use to convey information about achievement to students and others. In this final section of the chapter I shall briefly deal with the use and the importance of marks and reports, the general and specific bases for their assignment, the differences between absolute and relative marking systems, and two types of reporting—the report card and teacher-parent conferences.

Use and Importance of Marks and Reports

In a society which places increasing emphasis on educational progress, marks and reports have become the bases for crucial decisions about the educational and occupational destiny of the student. Consider how marks are the bases for the following decisions: First, the student uses marks to appraise his own educational accomplishments, to select major and minor areas of study, and to decide whether to terminate or to continue his formal education. Second, teachers and counselors use marks for similar decisions: to assess past accomplishments, to assess present ability, and to help the student make educational and vocational plans for the future. Third, parents use marks to determine which (if not all) of their children they should send to college and to estimate the probability of success any one child might have in advanced study and particular vocations. Fourth, school and college administrators, faced with limited educational facilities, use marks as the basis for admission to advance study and as indications of the student's progress after admission. Finally, employers use marks in selecting the applicant most likely to perform best the service they require. Part of the hue and cry over marks and marking systems stems from the major role marks desirably and undesirably play in the lives of our students.

Marks can also serve as incentives or positive reinforcers. In Chapter 5 you saw how incentives can increase motivation by raising the anticipation of reaching a desired goal. Incentives can yield learned expectancies. A student who has learned to expect good marks for competent performances will approach most educational tasks with more vim and vigor than will the student who has learned to expect poor marks for inadequate performances. Marks, therefore, not only convey information for crucial decisions but also release important motivational influences.

The Bases of Marks

In terms of performance assessment, the basis for the assignment of marks is the student's achievement of the instructional objectives. A valid mark indicates how well the student has achieved the terminal performances described in the instructional objectives. A reliable mark is an accurate measurement of the achievement of terminal performances. A mark can be no more valid or reliable than the measures of achievement upon which it is based.

Unfortunately all teachers do not agree that achievement of instructional objectives should be the exclusive basis for marking. Instead, they use several other bases. First they often base grades on the student's attitude, or citizenship, or desirable attributes of character. A student who shows a cooperative attitude, responsible citizenship, and strength of character receives a higher mark than a student who shows a rebellious attitude, underdeveloped citizenship, and weakness of character. Second, teachers often base marks on the amount of effort the student invests in achieving instructional objectives, whether or not these efforts meet with success. Conceivably, the student who expends more effort and does not succeed may receive a higher mark than does a student who expends less effort and does succeed. Third, teachers base marks on growth or how much the student has learned, even though this amount falls short of that required by the instructional objective.

There are many hazards to not using achievement as the exclusive basis for marking. First, if the mark is no longer a valid and reliable measure of the achievement of instructional objectives, it becomes very ambiguous in meaning and a shaky basis for making important educational decisions. Most of the decisions based on students' marks assume that they are measures of achievement: decisions about academic advancement, concentration of study, vocational career, and termination of formal education. It is indeed possible and not unlikely that the teacher will mark on the basis of nonachievement factors even though others will use the marks as measures of achievement alone. Second, the other bases for marking almost always involve highly subjective judgments or vague goals. It is entirely possible that fostering a cooperative attitude, responsible citizenship, and strong character is a worthwhile instructional objective if it can be explicitly stated and consciously pursued. Unfortunately, however, our estimate of student cooperation, citizenship, and character is highly impressionistic and often reflects little more than the fact that particular students accept or reject in varying degrees our beliefs, values, and classroom control. It is equally difficult to estimate the total amount of effort the student has invested in his work since much of this effort does not occur under our observation; we do not systematically record those observations we can and do make, and so much effort can be superficial busy-work which never accomplishes stated objectives. In lieu of an objective basis for measuring effort, the teacher often resorts to subjective judgment with all the attendant bias I have described. He could, however, with the use of reliable pretests and posttests measure growth or increased knowledge rather than the present attainment of instructional objectives. In one sense the teacher is measuring growth when he measures the student's auxiliary performances (see p. 610). Measures of student progress or growth, however, assume that this development is moving in some identifiable direction, which must be toward one or more instructional objectives. In terms of the basic teaching model it is possible to alter the objectives if the original choices prove unfeasible for the present level of entering behavior and the available instructional procedures. At this point, however, it is incumbent upon the teacher to establish new objectives and not simply to settle for instructional goals vaguely described as progress and growth.

Although achievement of instructional objectives appears to be the only solid basis for marking, the scores which students obtain on your tests should not be the sole means of measuring their achievement. Ebel (1965, p. 435) writes:

> Exclusive reliance on tests, for example, may give an unfair advantage to students who have special test-taking skills and may unfairly handicap students who give the best account of their achievements in discussions, on projects, or in other situations. But irrelevant accomplishments, such as mere glibness, personal charm, or self-assurance, should not be mistaken for solid command of knowledge. Nor should much weight be placed on vague intangibles or subjective impressions that cannot be quantified reliably.

You should require additional demonstrations of terminal behavior: oral reports, classroom discussions, homework, term papers, term projects, laboratory reports, and so on. The use of several measures of achievement raises the question of how much influence, or weight, each measure should have on the final grade. For example, a course in educational psychology may have these measures of student achievement: (1) weekly quizzes, (2) the midterm examination, (3) the final examination, (4) an oral teaching demonstration project, and (5) a written project requiring a detailed design of instruction based on the basic teaching model. You may conclude that some of these measures of achievement—for example, the oral and written projects—are more valid than other measures—for example, the quizzes and examinations. In line with this decision you may assign the following weights:

Weekly quizzes	10 per cent
Midterm examination	15 per cent
Final examination	20 per cent
Oral project	25 per cent
Written project	30 per cent

With these weights the quizzes and examinations will account for less than half of the grade—45 per cent. The use of this weighting requires the teacher to multiply the total points accumulated for each of these measures by the percentage assigned to that measure.

For this weighting to have its intended effect on the grades, you must distinguish between the effective and the possible range of scores for each measure. On a multiple-choice test of one hundred items, the possible range of scores is 100. After scoring the test, however, you may find that about two-thirds of the students scored between 25 and 75, making the effective range only 50. If this test were the final examination, and, as the above weighting scale indicates, you assigned to it a weight of 20 per cent, you should know that 20 per cent of an effective range of 50 will carry less weight than 20 per cent of 100. Similarly, if you assign 100 possible points to the oral and written projects and you score these projects in such a way that you use the full possible range of scores, each project will have twice the weight of a one hundred-item final examination with an effective range of only 50. If to the weight contributed by the greater range of scores you added the weight contributed by the larger percentages, the projects would far outweigh the influence of the final examination on the students' grades. You must remember, therefore, that the weight of each achievement measure is a combination of its percentage weight and its range of attained scores.

Two Marking Systems

Most American schools use two systems in reporting course grades. The less popular system is percentage marking, which assumes that 100 per cent represents perfection and that percentages below 100 are lesser degrees of perfection. Usually a percentage of less than 75 or 60 is considered too imperfect and, therefore, a failing grade. It is sometimes called the *absolute system* because it assumes the possibility of the student's achieving absolute perfection. According to the definition of absolute standards of achievement (see p. 611), 100 per cent could simply mean that the student has attained the standard of acceptable performance specified in the instructional objective. With the absolute standard, it is harder to explain the meaning of any percentage below 100 since the student achieves or does not achieve (all or none) the required standard. A grade of less than 100 per cent could indicate the percentage of the total number of instructional objectives a student has achieved at some point during or at the end of the course. Teachers who use percentage grades rarely adopt this interpretation, and their grades, despite their deceptive arithmetical appearance, convey no clear information about student achievement.

The more popular marking system consists of the assignment of letter grades: *A, B, C, D,* and *F*. *A* denotes superior, *B* good, *C* average, *D* fair, and *F* failing or insufficient achievement. It is sometimes called the *relative system* because the grades are intended to describe the student's achievement relative to that of other students rather than to a standard of perfection or mastery. An ordinary, but by no means universal, assumption of this marking system is that the grading should be on the curve. The curve in question is the normal curve, which Chapter 15 discusses. A teacher who grades on the curve ordinarily expects to give the largest percentage of *C*'s, smaller percentages of *B*'s and *D*'s, and the smallest percentages of *A*'s and *F*'s. It is by now a notorious fallacy that the curve determines the percentages for each grade. The normal curve, you will see, merely describes a particular distribution of scores. Which points in that distribution we assign the letter grades to is a policy decision made by teachers and administrators. A lenient teacher may give considerably more *A*'s than a strict teacher.

A teacher may decide that one class has earned more superior or failing grades than another class which, in turn, has earned more average and good grades. Undoubtedly, if faculties and school districts adopted uniform percentage assignments for each of the five letter grades, they could quiet some of the present criticism directed against the inequities of this marking system.

Despite the rather obvious limitations of validity, reliability, and interpretation, reform of these marking systems has had only temporary appeal. Reforms advocating the elimination of marks have failed because students, teachers, counselors, parents, administrators, and employers believe they enjoy distinct advantages in knowing the student's marks. Many know that marks mislead them, but many believe that some simplified knowledge of the student's achievement is better than no knowledge at all. Reforms advocating either more simplified or more complicated reports of student achievement, such as simple pass or fail or lengthy verbal and arithmetic descriptions, have also failed. The simplified forms do not tell us enough, even though we do not want to be burdened with too much information about the student. The complicated forms break on the rocks of practicality and familiarity.

As viewed here, the marking system is something external to the design of instruction. It has been created largely for use outside the teaching situation. For the careful design of instruction the teacher must have more detailed knowledge of entering behavior and terminal performance than marks usually convey. As a public record marks have obvious utility. As a means of assessing entering behavior and the effectiveness of instructional procedures they have obvious limitations.

Reporting

The most popular method of reporting marks is the report card. Most modern report cards contain grades and checklist items (Stanley, 1964, p. 329). The grades describe the level of achievement, and the checklists describe other areas such as effort, conduct, homework, and social development. Figure 14-2 shows the report card used in the elementary schools of Berkeley, California.

Because the report card does not convey all the information parents sometimes seek and to improve the cooperation between parents and teachers, schools often use parent-teacher conferences. The teacher invites the parents to the school for a short interview. The conferences allow the teacher to provide fuller descriptions of the student's scholastic and social development and allow parents to ask questions, describe the home environment, and plan what they may do to assist their children's educational development. There are inherent weaknesses in the conferences, and ordinarily they should supplement rather than replace the report card (Gronlund, 1965, p. 378).

STORE NO. 1-2133 (Rev. 10/63)

File Copy

BERKELEY UNIFIED SCHOOL DISTRICT

PUPIL PROGRESS REPORT — — **ELEMENTARY LEVEL**

PUPIL'S NAME ______________ (Last) ______________ (First) SCHOOL ______________ GRADE ______________

Checks in the appropriate columns below indicate how well your child has progressed during the particular report period.

	PERIOD I				PERIOD II				PERIOD III			
	EXCELLENT PROGRESS	SATIS-FACTORY PROGRESS	WORKING BELOW CAPACITY	SPECIAL LEARNING PROBLEMS	EXCELLENT PROGRESS	SATIS-FACTORY PROGRESS	WORKING BELOW CAPACITY	SPECIAL LEARNING PROBLEMS	EXCELLENT PROGRESS	SATIS-FACTORY PROGRESS	WORKING BELOW CAPACITY	SPECIAL LEARNING PROBLEMS
LANGUAGE ARTS												
READING	...(Text Level ____________)				(Text Level ____________)				(Text Level ____________)			
COMPREHENSION												
VOCABULARY												
PHONICS & OTHER WORD ATTACK SKILLS												
READING OUTSIDE OF BASIC TEXT												
SPELLING	...(Text Level ____________)				(Text Level ____________)				(Text Level ____________)			
ASSIGNED WORDS												
SPELLING CORRECTLY IN WRITTEN WORK												
ORAL LANGUAGE												
WRITTEN LANGUAGE												
HANDWRITING												
SKILLS OF WRITING												
CONTENT OF WRITTEN WORK												
LISTENING SKILLS												
ARITHMETIC	...(Text Level ____________)				(Text Level ____________)				(Text Level ____________)			
LEARNING & MAINTAINING PROCESSES												
SOLVING PROBLEMS												
SOCIAL STUDIES - Including Geography, History & Civics												
SCIENCE												
HEALTH FACTS & ATTITUDES												
PHYSICAL EDUCATION												
MUSIC												
ART												
BEHAVIOR & ATTITUDES												
BEGINNING & FINISHING WORK PROMPTLY												
FOLLOWING DIRECTIONS												
DOING WORTHWHILE WORK INDEPENDENTLY												
DEVELOPING SELF CONTROL												
OBSERVING CLASS & SCHOOL RULES												
GETTING ALONG WELL WITH OTHERS												
ATTENDANCE	☐ SATISFACTORY		☐ FREQUENTLY ABSENT ☐ FREQUENTLY TARDY		☐ SATISFACTORY		☐ FREQUENTLY ABSENT ☐ FREQUENTLY TARDY		☐ SATISFACTORY		☐ FREQUENTLY ABSENT ☐ FREQUENTLY TARDY	

COMMENTS (Period I) __/__/__ DATE

TEACHER ______________

PARENT ______________

COMMENTS (Period II) __/__/__ DATE

TEACHER ______________

PARENT ______________

COMMENTS (Period III) __/__/__ DATE

TEACHER ______________

PRINCIPAL ______________

GRADE PLACEMENT NEXT YEAR ______________

Fig. 14-2. *Report card used in the elementary schools of Berkeley, California. The first two written reports are presented to parents during fall and spring teacher-parent conferences. The final report is mailed home.*

Summary

Marks are the bases for important decisions made by students, teachers, counselors, parents, school administrators, and employers. They can also serve as incentives for increased motivation. The most solid basis for marking is on the achievement of the instructional objectives. Attempts to base marks on attitudes, effort, and character development lead to subjective judgments and contaminate the meaning of the grades. In determining the student's achievement, you should rarely rely exclusively on tests. The inclusion of other measures of achievement may involve the weighting of each measure. Two marking systems are in current use: grading by percentages and grading by letters. Grading by letters, the more popular practice, is based on a relative standard, which compares the achievement of one student with others in his group. The report card is the conventional method for reporting grades, and the schools sometimes supplement this report with parent-teacher conferences.

You should now return to objectives 38–44 (p. 609) and determine how well you have achieved them.

QUESTION 14-3

Mr. Fairminded decided to weight the various measures of achievement in his biology course as follows:

Laboratory experiments	20 per cent
Collection and classification of specimens	10 per cent
Term project	25 per cent
Class discussion	5 per cent
Three midterm examinations	20 per cent
Final examination	30 per cent

Mr. Fairminded determined the number of points he would allot to experiments, projects, and discussion and used the full range in scoring these activities. The number of points allotted to examinations was simply the number of items on the exams. How would you evaluate his weighting procedure? (Choose one.)

(a) It seems fair enough.

(b) He has failed to consider the effective range of scores on the activities.

(c) He should not allow the exams to determine 50 per cent of the grade.

(d) The exams may account for more or less than 50 per cent of the students' grades.

(e) He would be better off to exclude class discussion as a basis for the grade.

After selecting your answer, give the reasons for your choice and for your rejection of the alternatives.

SUMMARY

This chapter has considered the nature and purposes of performance assessment, the construction and revision of tests, and marking and reporting.

Performance assessment is the fourth component of the basic teaching model. As the process of measuring the student's auxiliary and terminal performances during and at the end of instruction, it is the basic source of feedback on the adequacy of the student's entering behavior and on our instructional procedures. When the instructional objectives specify the minimum level of mastery the student must attain, they employ an absolute standard of achievement. When you compare the performance of one student with others in his group, you are using a relative standard of achievement. All measures of performance should have validity, reliability, objectivity, and efficiency. A valid test actually measures the terminal performances described in the objectives; a reliable test accurately or consistently measures these performances; an objective test is scored with freedom from subjective judgment and according to the consensus of expert opinion; an efficient test makes optimal use of the available time teachers and students can devote to testing.

Test construction and revision are the major content of this chapter. The planning of the test requires careful provision for validity—that is, for the assessment of all stated objectives and for the appropriate emphasis on each objective. The classification of objectives, through either Gagné's or Bloom's system, is one way of assuring adequate coverage of instructional objectives. Objective and essay tests have both differences and similarities. What the objective test gains in reliability and ease in scoring, it loses in difficulty of preparation and in validity. The use of essay questions requires a clear statement of the tasks the student should perform, the provision of adequate time for answering the questions, and scoring practices which assure consistent and unbiased judgment. Objective items are either free-response or limited-response items. I provided guidelines for the preparation of completion items, true-false items, matching items, and multiple-choice items in this chapter. The key-list multiple-choice item offers a convenient way to assess principle learning and problem solving. Suggestions were made for the preparation of the test copy, the administration of the test, and the prevention of cheating. In scoring the test, ordinarily you should allow one point for each correct answer. Correction for guessing is necessary only when some students have omitted a large number of questions. The evaluation of the test involves judgments about its validity, reliability, objectivity, and efficiency. Item analysis is an objective means of determining reliability when the test is based on a relative standard. The results of the item analysis can be the basis for revising items for optimal levels of difficulty and discrimination.

Marks are measures of the achievement of instructional objectives. Teachers and schools use reports, both written and oral, to convey information about achievement to students and others. Marks are important as a basis for crucial decisions about the student's educational and occupational future. They are also sources of increased motivation. Unless the basis of marks is achievement of the instructional objectives, considerable ambiguity is introduced into their use and interpretation. Although achievement of objectives is the most solid basis for marking, test scores should not be the only basis for measuring achievement. The use of additional measures of achievement often involves the weighting of each measure. Of the two marking systems, percentage grades and letter grades, the latter is much more popular. Letter grades are based on a relative standard of achievement. Even if they are based on the curve, the teacher and school must decide as a matter of policy which percentage of students should receive each grade. The report card is the most popular means of reporting grades and other areas of development to parents. The parent-teacher conference can usefully supplement the report card.

SUGGESTED READINGS

Several excellent texts in both hard and soft cover discuss educational tests and measurement. The following hard-cover texts emphasize the psychological theory underlying tests and measurement:

Anastasi, Anne, *Psychological Testing* (2nd ed.). New York: The Macmillan Company, 1961.

Cronbach, Lee J., *Essentials of Psychological Testing* (2nd ed.). New York: Harper & Row, Publishers, Inc., 1960.

Freeman, Frank S., *Theory and Practice of Psychological Testing* (3rd ed.). New York: Holt, Rinehart & Winston, Inc., 1962.

Thorndike, Robert L. and Elizabeth Hagen, *Measurement and Evaluation in Psychology and Education.* New York: John Wiley & Sons, Inc., 1961.

The following hard-cover texts are especially useful for the construction of classroom tests:

Ebel, Robert L., *Measuring Educational Achievement.* Englewood Cliffs, N.J.: Prentice-Hall, Inc., 1965. This book is almost entirely devoted to classroom tests.

Gronlund, Norman E., *Measurement and Evaluation in Teaching.* New York: The Macmillan Company, 1965.

Noll, Victor H., *Educational Measurement* (2nd ed.). Boston: Houghton Mifflin Company, 1965.

Stanley, Julian C., *Measurement in Today's Schools* (4th ed.). Englewood Cliffs, N.J.: Prentice-Hall, Inc., 1964.

Thorndike and Hagen (see above).

The following soft-cover texts are especially useful for the construction of classroom tests:

Gorow, Frank F., *Better Classroom Testing.* San Francisco: Chandler Publishing Co., 1966.

Lindeman, Richard, *Educational Measurement.* Chicago: Scott, Foresman & Company, 1967.

Wood, Dorothy Adkins, *Test Construction.* Columbus, Ohio: Charles E. Merrill Books, Inc., 1960.

How to Interpret Standardized Test Scores

15

The major purpose of this chapter is to introduce you to the nature and use of standardized tests and test scores. The first section deals with the special characteristics of standardized tests—those which pertain to constructing, administering, and scoring the test and establishing the test norms. It then describes several uses of these tests. The second section distinguishes five types of standardized tests—general intelligence, multiple aptitude, special aptitude, achievement, and personality. The discussion here emphasizes achievement and creativity tests since Chapter 4 considered intelligence and multiple-aptitude tests. The third section deals with the interpretation of standardized test scores. Here you are introduced to some basic statistical concepts important in score interpretation: the normal curve, measures of central tendency, measures of variability, derived scores, and measures of correlation. Although this section introduces you to the computation of these statistics, the emphasis is on their use in the interpretation of test scores.

Upon reading the first section of this chapter (on the characteristics and uses of standardized tests), you should be able to meet these objectives:

1. Describe four characteristics of standardized tests and point out an example of each characteristic when given a standardized test and its accompanying manuals.

2. Describe the similarities and the differences of standardized and classroom tests by referring to each of the characteristics in objective 1.

3. Describe and illustrate five uses of standardized tests.

Upon reading the second section of this chapter (on the types of standardized tests), you should be able to meet these objectives:

4. List and illustrate five types of standardized tests.

5. Define a test battery and provide an illustration of your definition, using the ITED.

6. Illustrate the following characteristics of standardized achievement tests by referring to the ITED: (a) relationship of items to test objectives; (b) establishment of test validity; (c) establishment of test norms.

7. Define three factors measured by the Guilford creativity tests, by describing a test for each factor.

8. Define creativity in terms of problems, hypotheses, and testing (Torrance's definition) and, by referring to Torrance's creativity tests, illustrate how they correspond to his definition.

9. Describe the limitation in the use of creativity tests for instructional purposes.

10. List five common personality and interest inventories.

Upon reading the third section of this chapter (on score interpretation), you should be able to meet these objectives:

11. List and illustrate three characteristics of the normal curve.

12. Define central tendency and illustrate three measures of central tendency.

13. Compute the mode, median, and mean of a short series of scores and indicate the appropriate use of each measure.

14. Define variability and illustrate two measures of variability.

15. Compute the range and standard deviation of a short series of scores.

16. Distinguish and illustrate the difference between a raw and a derived score.

17. Define percentile rank in terms of percentage standing and illustrate your definition with specific examples of percentile ranks.

18. Illustrate the relationship of particular percentile ranks to cumulative percentages and to the standard deviations of the normal curve (use Chart 1).

19. Compute the z score from given raw scores and illustrate how it may be used in comparing scores from different tests.

20. Define the T, AGCT, and CEEB scores in terms of the z score.

21. Define deviation IQ scores in terms of the z score and illustrate the importance of knowing standard deviations in using IQ scores.

22. Define and illustrate age-grade scores by using examples of these scores and illustrate one appropriate use and other inappropriate uses.

23. Define correlation and illustrate two measures of correlation.

24. Distinguish among positive, negative, and zero correlations by using coefficients illustrating each one.

25. Compute the product-moment and rank-difference coefficients of correlation for a short series of scores.

CHARACTERISTICS AND USES OF STANDARDIZED TESTS

Standardized tests share the same characteristics of all tests: They must have validity, reliability, objectivity, and efficiency. They also have special characteristics—the procedures they use to enhance these general test qualities: systematic methods of item construction and testing, uniform procedures of test administration and scoring, and the use of test norms in score interpretation. Standardized tests share the same uses with all tests—the assessment of entering behavior and terminal performance. Their special character, however, makes them particularly useful in the evaluation of new instructional programs and procedures, in the assessment of learning over the long haul, in the general assessment of student achievement and ability, and in the diagnosis of entering behavior for classroom purposes. We shall now consider each of these characteristics and uses.

Characteristics of Standardized Tests

The *standardization* of a test is the development of uniform procedures for each administration and scoring of the test. The authors of these tests design procedures which minimize the possibility that variations in scores are due to variations in test procedures. Variations in scores should be the result of the student taking the test and not of the conditions of testing. These tests also employ systematic methods of test construction and interpretation.

CONSTRUCTING THE TESTS. The reliability and validity of the tests are determined by tryout. Objective measurement determines the difficulty level of each item and of the test as a whole. Anastasi (1961, p. 25) describes the method used in the original intelligence scale:

> When Binet and Simon prepared their original, 1905 scale for the measurement of intelligence . . . they arranged the thirty items of the scale in order of increasing difficulty. Such difficulty . . . was determined by trying out the items on fifty normal and a few retarded and feebleminded children. The items correctly solved by the largest proportion of subjects were, *ipso facto,* taken to be the easiest; those passed by a relatively few subjects were regarded as more difficult items. By such a procedure, an empirical order of difficulty was established. This early example typifies the objective measurement of difficulty level in psychological test construction.

Test reliability is determined by observing the consistency of scores obtained by the same individuals when given the same test a second time or an equivalent form of the test. Test validity is determined by the use of external standards of whatever the test is designed to measure. A standardized test of juvenile delinquency would distinguish between two groups of boys, those who have and those who have not been arrested for juvenile offenses. If the test succeeded in distinguishing between these two groups, we could say that it had met its standard of validity or that it was a valid test of juvenile delinquency. Similarly, a standardized test of medical aptitude would distinguish between two groups of students, those who would successfully complete medical training and those who would not. If the test succeeded in distinguishing between these two groups we could say that it was a valid test of medical aptitude. Standardized tests of intelligence, you recall, distinguish with considerable success among students who are above or below average in school achievement and who score above or below average on other intelligence tests. These distinctions (or predictions) are never perfect however because success in school or out is not determined alone by IQ.

Administering the tests. We have observed that the directions for administering the tests are standardized—they are uniform conditions which must be provided whenever the test is used. Directions for administration—usually both general and specific—are contained in the manuals which accompany all standardized tests. The general directions describe the proper physical or classroom conditions and time limits the examiner must provide throughout the test. The specific directions describe what the teacher (or test administrator) must tell the students for particular parts of the test. Directions for the administration of the Stanford Achievement Test (Kelley *et al.,* 1964, p. 7) illustrate general directions:

> 1. Before beginning a test, the examiner should see that the desks are cleared and that each pupil has one or two sharpened, soft-lead pencils. Special electrographic pencils are needed only if

IBM answer sheets are used. . . . PENS SHOULD NOT BE USED. A supply of extra pencils should be at hand. Scratch paper should be provided for use with the arithmetic tests where indicated.

2. When administering the test, the examiner should have a blank copy of the test booklet and of an answer sheet (if an answer sheet is being used) for demonstrating, along with these "Directions of Administering."
3. A natural classroom situation should be maintained as far as possible.
4. Provision should be made to insure quiet and freedom from interruptions of any kind. This may be accomplished best by posting on the door of the room a sign reading, "Testing. Do Not Disturb."

Additional general directions pertain to the kind of assistance the examiner can provide individual students during the course of the examination, adherence to time limits, and the required number of testing sessions.

This test also provides specific directions for particular parts. Here are the specific directions for the test on arithmetic computation (p. 13):

> Before distributing the test materials, SAY: "I shall give you a test booklet again. Do not open it until I tell you to do so."
>
> Pass out the booklets, answer sheets (if they are being used), and scratch paper, making sure that each pupil receives his own booklet and answer sheet.
>
> THEN SAY TO THE CLASS: "Now open your booklet to test 6, Arithmetic Computation, which starts on page 17. Fold the booklet back so that only page 17 is showing." See that the pupils do this.
>
> "Now find the answer spaces for test 6. Then look at the top of the page of your test booklet where it says 'DIRECTIONS.'" Hold up a booklet and point to the proper place.
>
> "The directions say: 'Work the example in each box. Then look at the possible answers at the right side of the box and see if the answer is given. If it is, fill in the space at the right on your answer sheet (if you have one) which has the same letter as the answer you have chosen. If your answer is *not* given, fill in the space which has the same letter as the letter beside the NG (which means "not given"). Use a separate answer sheet for figuring.'" Pause.

Further specific directions pertain to working through a sample item, giving the start signal, recording the starting time, giving the signal to stop, and collecting the test materials.

SCORING THE TESTS. Directions for scoring the tests are also standardized—they are uniformly followed every time the test is scored.

Frequently the test publisher provides special scoring keys or even a centralized scoring service using machine scoring. In the scoring directions for the intermediate battery of the Stanford Achievement Test (Kelley *et al.,* 1964, Form W, Sheet 1a), these are some of the scoring rules provided:

1. Do not attempt to score these tests without using the keys. The keys are provided to make the scoring objective and at the same time quick, convenient, and accurate.
2. The score for each test is the number of correct responses.
3. No part or fractional credit is given for any item. Each item is counted as right, wrong, or omitted.
4. When an answer obviously has been changed by a pupil, the final response is the one which should be scored.
5. Sample items are never scored.
6. The number right will be the number of marks appearing through the holes. The score (number right) should be checked in the *upper* row of the conversion table *at the end of each test.* The number appearing directly under the value checked is the pupil's *grade score* on the test.

Other scoring rules pertain to the use of the scoring key, the time used in scoring, the transfer of grade scores, and checking for accuracy.

Establishing test norms. Standardized tests are based on relative standards of performance. An individual's score has meaning only when compared with the scores others have obtained. A *norm* is the score which indicates average, or normal, performance. For example, if the average child of six can identify correctly ten objects in a picture vocabulary test when he is given a word and asked to select the associated picture (e.g., find the picture of the chair), the six-year-old norm for this test is a score of ten. If the average child of eight can identify fifteen pictures correctly, then the eight-year-old norm is a score of fifteen. By using norms we can determine how close a child's performance is to the performances of children in his own age and grade group.

Establishing norms requires the use of a *standardization sample*—a representative sample of the type of student for whom the test is designed. For example, in developing the Pictorial Test of Intelligence, Joseph French (1964, p. 10) used 1,830 children between the ages of three and eight. In selecting these children, he was careful to represent the various regional areas of the United States (Northeast, North Central, South, and West); communities of various sizes, ranging from over 1 million to under 2,500; and six occupational levels, from the professional and technical to the laboring and service.

Comparison of standardized and classroom tests. The similarities of the two types of tests are easy to identify: (1) They are both means of performance assessment; (2) they both use the same types of test items; and (3) they both require validity, reliability, objectivity, and efficiency. The differences of the two types are only of degree: (1) It is possible that the classroom test may have more direct validity because it is more carefully adapted to your own instructional objectives and subject matter. In an effort to measure the achievement of objectives common to the majority of American schools, standardized tests fail to measure achievement of objectives unique to your course or school or they measure achievement of objectives for which no formal instruction is provided. (2) The quality of the test items on the standardized test is usually superior because they are prepared by test specialists and are revised on the basis of actual tryout and item analysis. These advantages result in tests of high reliability, often between 0.80 and 0.95 (Gronlund, 1965, p. 223). (3) The procedures used in administering and scoring standardized tests are carefully described, and they are standardized (made uniform) for each administration of the test. (4) A very significant difference is the use of norms in the interpretation of the test. The student's score on a standardized test is compared with those of the national sample, whereas his score on classroom tests based on the relative standard compares his performance only with those of other students in the class (a local norm). (5) Finally, publishers of standardized tests prepare test manuals, which report data on test validity and reliability and provide directions for test administration. Such information is usually not available for classroom tests.

Uses of Standardized Tests

Standardized tests assess entering behavior and terminal performance. They also determine the relative effectiveness of various school programs and innovations. Consider the following general uses of standardized tests.

General assessment of student ability. Intelligence tests, which measure general ability, are one type of standardized test. In Chapter 4 we considered several uses of IQ tests: They help us to predict how well the student may do in particular grades and courses, to compare his actual with his potential achievement, and to assign him to various tracks and programs in which instruction is differentiated on the basis of general ability. We also considered the limitations of IQ tests in educational decision making: IQ is an important but not the single factor accounting for successful school achievement; we can make other useful assessments of entering behavior based on the period of intellectual development and on the available detailed descriptions of prerequisite learning sets, abilities, and styles.

General assessment of student achievement. Many standardized achievement tests are batteries which measure achievement in many skill and subject areas. The primary II battery, for grades 2 and 3, of the Stanford Achievement Test includes eight tests: word meaning, paragraph meaning, science and social science concepts, spelling, word-study skills, language, arithmetic computation, and arithmetic concepts. The advanced battery, for grades 7 through 9, also includes eight tests: paragraph meaning, spelling, language, arithmetic computation, arithmetic concepts, arithmetic applications, social studies, and science (Kelley *et al.*, 1964, p. 2). Both batteries provide considerably more breadth of measurement than most classroom tests. The macrocosmic view of student achievement, which the standardized test provides, has several uses: We can compare the student's general level of achievement with his general level of ability (IQ); we can make decisions to promote him to a new grade or to retain him in an old grade on the general level of his achievement; and we can use this general profile of achievement when we counsel him about future courses of study and vocational plans.

Diagnostic assessment in the classroom. The teacher can use the standardized test for detailed assessment of entering behavior. The Gates-MacGintie Reading Tests (1965), for example, measure reading vocabulary, comprehension, and speed and accuracy at various grade levels. By indicating relative strengths and weaknesses in those three areas of reading skill, they tell the teacher which objectives he must emphasize in the reading instruction of particular students. The student who has developed more speed and accuracy than comprehension requires different instruction than the student who has developed comprehension at the price of speed and accuracy. Similarly, with the use of the Stanford Achievement Tests for the intermediate level, we may find that Gus is better in word and paragraph meaning than he is in spelling, language usage, and punctuation. This assessment may indicate that Gus is more skillful in reading than in writing and that the emphasis for him must be on those instructional objectives which stress writing. The use of standardized tests indicates those instructional objectives which the student should most intensively pursue.

Assessment of school programs and instructional procedures. Before we permanently adopt or reject any educational innovation, it is wise to determine the relative success of the new and the old programs and practices. If, for example, you want to determine whether instructional television is more effective than conventional instruction in teaching tenth grade algebra, you must find some common means of measuring achievement for both types of instruction. Possibly you could administer a standardized test of algebra at the beginning and again at the end of the course and determine the relative level of achievement for both types of instruction. Standardized tests are often chosen for these evaluations because of their high reliability and because, in theory at least, of their high validity—their measurement of all important course outcomes. Although this research, as you will see in Chapter 16, has many pitfalls, the difficulty is not in the standardized tests but in the uses to which they are put. In such research the use of standardized tests is warranted only when both types of instruction pursue identical objectives, when the tests are valid measures of these objectives, and when the only variations in entering behavior, instructional procedures, and instructional content are those specifically isolated for study.

Standardized tests are also a means of comparing the general achievement level of various schools, districts, and regions throughout the nation. In Chapter 10 we considered Project Talent and the International Study of Mathematics Achievement, both of which make liberal use of standardized tests. These national and international assessments are a valuable source of knowledge for individuals who want to improve whatever weaknesses may exist in particular school curricula.

Assessment of school learning over the long haul. This assessment is the measurement of cumulative gains in student achievement which result from programs lasting several months or years. For example, what cumulative gains do students make in studying PSSC physics and BSCS biology over a period of one year? Or what are the cumulative gains of students beginning with SMSG mathematics in the first grade and continuing this study through the twelfth grade? Or what are the cumulative gains in language and cultural proficiency in beginning the study of a foreign language in the elementary school and continuing through high school and college? Carroll (1965, p. 249) notes an unfortunate dearth of studies on how student performance improves over a long term:

> Most educational research studies are what we may call "snapshot" studies of school learning: They look at particular aspects of the school learning process for a relatively brief moment. We need also "panoramic" studies that would examine all interrelated aspects of educational growth over a major part of the years spent in school by significant numbers of pupils.

Carroll also points out that the new curricula in science, social science, language, and mathematics emphasize long-term learning. To make an assessment of such learning it will be necessary to develop valid standardized tests; many present standardized tests are valid for conventional courses but do not measure the objectives of the new courses (see Chapter 13).

Summary

Test standardization is the development of uniform procedures for the administration and scoring of the test. In constructing standardized tests, validity, reliability, and difficulty are determined by objective measurement. The uniform conditions provided in the administration and scoring of the test increase the likelihood that variations in scores are the result of variations in student characteristics and performance and not the result of variations in test conditions. The use of standardization samples establishes test norms which provide the basis for the interpretation of individual and group scores. Although standardized and classroom tests share the same major characteristics, it is likely that standardized tests have greater reliability and classroom tests greater validity for local curricula. Standardized tests are useful for general assessment of student ability and achievement, diagnostic classroom assessment, and assessment of school programs and instructional procedures either on a short-term or a long-term basis.

The next section describes particular types of tests and provides illustrations of them.

You should now return to objectives 1–3 (pp. 656–57) and determine how well you have achieved them.

QUESTION 15-1

The Performance Assessment Corporation developed a test to measure knowledge of various drugs and their medical uses and effects. In developing this test the authors were careful to control the difficulty level of the items. They made careful observations of score consistency, prepared and tested procedures for scoring and administering the test, and carefully chose their standardization sample and reported the test norms. In the fuller standardization of this test, which of the following tasks must be done? (a) establishing and reporting test validity; (b) establishing and reporting test reliability; (c) establishing and reporting scores and scoring objectivity; (d) listing which rival tests are superior to the test being marketed; (e) providing more efficient means of test administration.

After selecting your answer, give the reasons for your choice and for your rejection of the alternatives.

TYPES AND EXAMPLES OF STANDARDIZED TESTS

We can distinguish five types of standardized tests: general intelligence tests, multiple-aptitude batteries, special aptitude tests, achievement tests, and personality tests. Chapter 4 dealt with general intelligence tests and multiple-aptitude batteries. Chapter 8 dealt with special aptitude tests of physical skills. In this section we shall consider some examples of achievement, special aptitude, and personality tests.

Types of Tests

Standardized tests are classified on the basis of the aspects of behavior they sample. Anastasi (1961, pp. 32–33) identifies five types: (1) General intelligence tests, described in Chapter 4, measure the general level of intellectual functioning. The Stanford-Binet Intelligence Scale is an example of this type. (2) The multiple-aptitude batteries, also described in Chapter 4, measure the various factors which theoretically constitute intellectual functioning. Thurstone's Primary Abilities Test is an example of this type. (3) Special aptitude tests attempt to measure concrete or practical abilities. The tests of motor and mechanical abilities described in Chapter 8 are examples of this type. Some special aptitude tests measure artistic appreciation and ability, musical ability, and literary appreciation. The creativity tests discussed below are also examples of special aptitude tests. (4) Achievement tests measure the attainment of instructional objectives in various school and training courses. I discuss examples of this type below. (5) Finally, personality tests measure emotional adjustment, social intelligence, character traits, motivation, interest, and attitudes. I shall briefly describe examples of this type.

Achievement Tests

Achievement tests are often survey batteries, series of short tests which cover basic areas of educational achievement. These are among the best-known survey batteries:

California Achievement Tests, grades 1–4
Iowa Tests of Educational Development, grades 9–12
Metropolitan Achievement Tests, grades 1–12
Sequential Tests of Educational Progress (STEP), grades 4–14
SRA Achievement Series, grades 1–9
Stanford Achievement Test, grades 1–12

The successive levels of these batteries often measure the same basic skills at increasing levels of difficulty.

IOWA TESTS OF EDUCATIONAL DEVELOPMENT. The ITED (1963, 8th ed.) illustrates the major characteristics of standardized achievement tests. It is a battery of nine tests with the following titles:

1. Understanding Basic Social Concepts
2. Background in the Natural Sciences
3. Correctness and Appropriateness of Expression
4. Ability to Do Quantitative Thinking
5. Ability to Interpret Reading Materials in the Social Studies
6. Ability to Interpret Reading Materials in the Natural Sciences
7. Ability to Interpret Literary Materials
8. General Vocabulary
9. Uses of Information

The heart of the battery are tests 5 through 7, which deal "not so much with *what* the pupil has learned, in the sense of specific information, but rather [with] how well he can *use* whatever he has learned in acquiring, interpreting, and evaluating new ideas, in relating new ideas to old, in applying broad concepts and generalization to new situations or to the solution of problems" (SRA, 1962, p. 6). These three tests, therefore, measure concept learning, principle learning, and problem solving.

Objectives which the items measure are stated. For example, here are some of the objectives for items in test 7, dealing with literary interpretation (SRA, pp. 27–28):

A. To understand the significance of specific words or phrases in the light of the literary context.
B. To understand the relationships among the ideas and the function of individual ideas in relation to total context.
C. To evaluate the author's purpose, point of view, and attitudes.
D. To become aware of the style and literary techniques used in the development of the passage and appreciate its mood, tone, and emotion.

Table 15-1 contains some of the items which measure these objectives.

The manual clearly describes both general and specific procedures for test administration. A sample item precedes each test, and the answer is marked on the answer sheet in a way which the student can easily follow. The test may be scored manually or by machine. The items are multiple choice in form, there is no correction for guessing, and the score on each test is the number right, with one point for each item. Scores are converted into standard scores, a procedure described below. To facilitate score interpretation, each student's scores are profiled by using the chart in Fig. 15-1. If the student follows the directions in the left margin, he plots his percentile scores defined below.

To establish the validity of the battery, the ITED manual (SRA, 1962) reports, among others, the following correlations:

TABLE 15-1

SAMPLE ITEMS FOR TEST 7 OF THE IOWA TEST OF EDUCATIONAL DEVELOPMENT (after SRA, 1962, pp. 29–30).

It's easy enough to talk of Master Jim, after a good spread, two hundred feet above the sea level, with a box of cigars handy, on a blessed evening of freshness and starlight that would make the best of us forget we are only on sufferance here and got to pick our way in cross lights, watching every irremediable step, trusting we shall manage yet to go out decently in the end—but not so sure of it after all—and with dashed little help to expect from those we touch elbows with right and left. Of course, there are men here and there to whom the whole of life is like an after-dinner hour with a cigar: easy, pleasant, empty, perhaps enlivened by some fable of strife to be forgotten before the end is told—even if there happens to be any end to it.

1. The writer thinks that the lives of most people are
   (1) gay
   (2) uncertain and lonely
   (3) difficult but successful
   (4) easy and empty
2. The phrase "two hundred feet above the sea level," in the first sentence, suggests
   (1) loneliness
   (2) safety
   (3) hardship
   (4) adventure
3. The tone of this passage is
   (1) cheerful
   (2) thoughtful
   (3) angry
   (4) amused
4. The passage is unusual particularly because of
   (1) the thought expressed in it
   (2) its strong emotion
   (3) the way in which the thought is stated
   (4) its purpose
5. What is the writer apparently trying to do?
   (1) defend Jim directly
   (2) complain about life in general
   (3) defend Jim indirectly
   (4) condemn Jim's conduct

Item	*Objective* [see p. 667]
1.	*B*
2.	*A*
3.	*D*
4.	*D*
5.	*C*

Variable X	Variable Y	Correlations
Composite score on ITED	Grade 9 grade-point average	0.73
Composite score on ITED	Cumulative grade-point average through grade 12	0.63
Composite score on ITED	Henmon-Nelson Tests of Mental Ability	0.841
Composite score on ITED at grade 12	College freshmen grades	0.61

HOW TO PROFILE YOUR SCORES

To compare your scores with the scores of the national student group used to develop these tests, use the profile on this sheet in the following way:

1. Place the name and score portions of your *PRESSCORE* in the space provided for each or copy your scores onto the blank space if you are not to use the *PRESSCORE* here.
2. Put a dot on each line opposite the number on the chart corresponding to the one shown in the *shaded* box under each test score. For example, if the number in the box under Test 1 is 65, you should make a dot on the first up-and-down line opposite the number 65. In the same way make a dot for each of the other scores on the lines just below the boxes in which the percentile score numbers appear. Then connect the dots with a solid line. This is your profile.

INTERPRETING YOUR PROFILE

The numbers you have plotted are percentiles. A percentile score tells what percentage of students at your grade level had lower scores than the one corresponding to that position on the chart. For example, a percentile score of 80 means that 80 percent of a very large and typical group of high school students at your grade level received lower scores. The 50 percentile line is printed boldly to indicate the point—called the *national median*—that separates the upper 50 percent of this group from the lower 50 percent.

Your teacher may also want to know how your scores compare with those of other students of your school in your grade. This will require drawing a *dotted line* profile that is based on ten numbers that your teacher will put on the board. Label this profile "school average."

As you look at your profile, it probably does not go straight across the chart. Instead, it has peaks and valleys. It is by noting these high and low positions that you can learn of your strengths and weaknesses in view of (1) your other scores, (2) the national median, and (3) the school average percentiles.

Discuss this report with your teachers and parents. Ask yourself, "Has my educational development been good, fair, or average?" "In what areas am I weakest, and how can I strengthen these areas?" Try to set a fair standard for improving your scores. Your teachers can be of help in this. Remember that a well-educated person is one who has equally high scores on all the *Iowa Tests.*

NAME OF STUDENT

Kramer Carol

GRADE	1-BACKGR'D SOC. STUD.		2-BACKGR'D NAT. SCI.		3-CORR. OF EXPRESSION		4-QUANT'VE THINKING		5-READING SOC. STUD.		6-READING NAT. SCI.		7-READING LIT.		8-GEN'L. VOCAB.		COMPOSITE 1-8		9-USE OF SOURCES	
9	9	34	12	46	13	61	10	48	10	42	9	39	8	28	10	36	10	42	13	61
	STD	%ILE	STD	%ILE	STD	%ILE	STD	%ILE	STD	%ILE	STD	%ILE	STD	%ILE	STD	%ILE	STD	%ILE	STD	%ILE

IOWA TESTS OF EDUCATIONAL DEVELOPMENT—SRA *PRESSCORE*

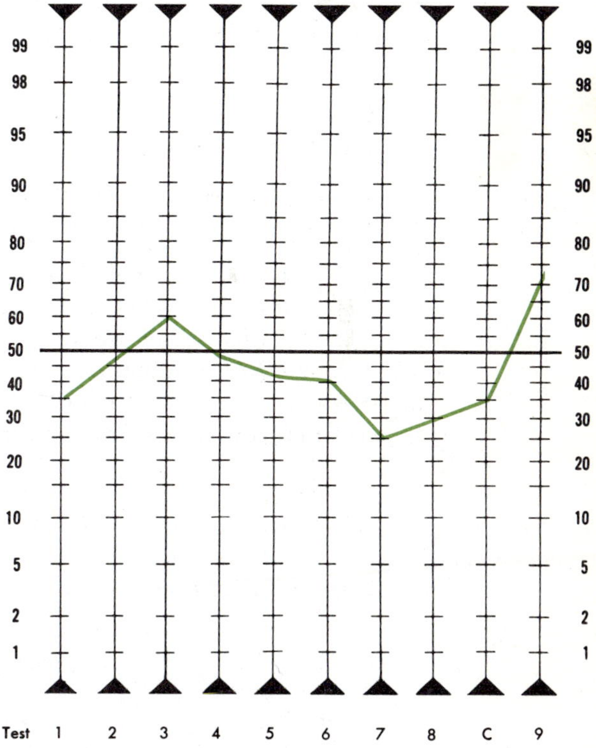

45/2-987

Fig. 15-1. *A sample profile of scores for the Iowa Tests of Educational Development (SRA, 1963, p. 60).*

It appears that the ITED is as good a predictor of success in college, as measured by freshmen grades, as high school grades and IQ are (see Chapter 14). It might even be a *better* predictor of this success than high school grades and IQ are. The correlations for reliability of the various tests are usually very high, between 0.88 and 0.92.

In establishing norms for the ITED, the test authors used 51,098 students in 136 school systems in thirty-nine states. The population to which the norms apply includes all students in grades 9 through 12 in the public high schools of the continental United States. The number of schools in each geographical region used for establishing norms was proportional to the percentage of school population for each region.

According to the test authors (see SRA, 1963, p. 7) the ITED has two purposes: (1) to enable teachers and counselors to keep acquainted with the achievement of each student and to use this knowledge in designing instruction and (2) to provide the school administrator with an objective basis for assessing the total educational offering of the school.

Creativity Tests

One form of special aptitude test is a test of creativity. Chapter 11 discussed creative abilities and thinking and briefly alluded to creativity tests. Here we consider these tests in greater detail.

GUILFORD'S TESTS. According to Guilford (1959), creative thinking is divergent thinking. Whereas convergent thinking produces the single correct answer, divergent thinking produces a variety of responses (see p. 455). Flexibility, originality, and fluency are the three factors which constitute creative, or divergent, thinking. Guilford has developed several tests of creativity to define and investigate these factors. In addition

Fig. 15-2. *Sample items from the Hidden Figures Test. The problem: Which of the simple figures is concealed within each of the two more complex figures? (After Guilford, 1959, p. 475.)*

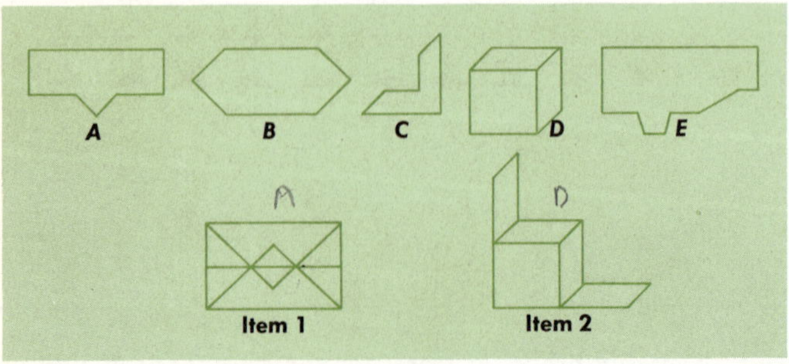

Fig. 15-3. *A sample item from the Match Problem Test. The problem: Take away four matches in A and leave three squares, using all the remaining matches. B is the solution (after Guilford, 1959, p. 474).*

to the Brick Uses Test (p. 455), the Hidden Figures and Match Problem Tests measure flexibility. The Hidden Figures Test requires the examinee to use parts of one figure in new ways to produce parts of another figure. In Fig. 15-2, for example, the student must recognize the simpler figure within the structure of a more complex figure by assigning new functions to particular lines. The Match Problem Test requires the relocation of a specified number of matches to form a specified number of squares, with no matches left over. Figure 15-3 shows one match problem and its solution. If the examinee tries to keep the squares the same size, he will fail to solve the problem. The measure of his flexibility is his ability to produce squares of varying size.

One test of originality is the ability to produce novel titles in the

Fig. 15-4. *The drawing of a student given a high score for creativity (after Getzels and Jackson, 1962, p. 46).*

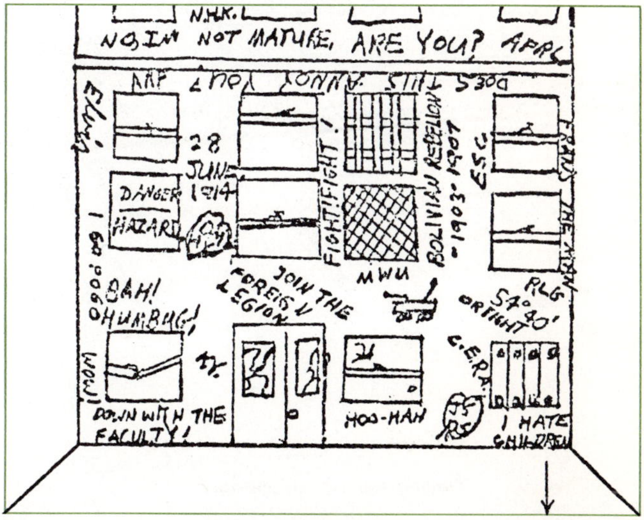

"Playing tag in the school yard" *note: It is ghosts are playing tag.*

Plot Title Test (p. 455). Another is the Symbol Production Test (Guilford, 1959). The examinee produces a pictographic symbol to stand for a noun or verb in a number of short sentences. A third test requires the student to write punch lines for cartoons. In a modification of this test, Getzels and Jackson (1962, p. 43) gave students a sheet of paper with a printed, single-lined border and the title "Playing Tag in the School Yard." The students were to draw any picture they could imagine for this theme. Figure 15-4 is an example of a drawing which was given a high score for creativity, while Fig. 15-5 was given a low score.

There are several tests of fluency. The student may be asked to list as many associations as he can think of for a list of stimulus words (see Maltzman *et al.*, 1960). Or he may be asked to list words which are opposite in meaning to the stimulus words (e.g., *short* for *long*). In another test the student must rapidly form phrases or sentences when given initial letters, as in this example (Guilford, p. 474):

W______ c______ e______ n______.

One subject may write "We can eat nuts," while another subject, with more creativity, may write "Whence came Eve Newton?"

FLANAGAN'S INGENUITY TEST. In this test, part of a large battery, the student must think of "ingenious and effective ways of doing things" (Flanagan, 1957, p. 51). The student is presented with a verbal prob-

Fig. 15-5. *The drawing of a student given a low score for creativity (after Getzels and Jackson, 1962, p. 48).*

"Playing tag in the school yard"

lem, is asked to think of a solution, and then must find his solution among the listed alternatives. Here is a sample problem (p. 51):

> A hostess for a children's party wanted to serve ice cream in an interesting manner, and she decided to make a clown for each child. She placed a ball of ice cream to represent the clown's head on a round cookie which served for a collar, and on top of this she inverted a
>
> *A*. t—— ——e.
> *B*. u—— ——i.
> *C*. r—— ——s.
> *D*. c—— ——e.
> *E*. t—— ——r.

The student selects his answer, as in multiple-choice tests. For this solution the student should think of *cone* since it serves as a hat and can be eaten. Choice *D,* of course, contains the first and last letters of *cone.* In other problem solutions the student must supply the missing letter in two or more words, which in turn complete sentences. Anastasi (1961, p. 419) classifies this test as a test of originality and notes a fairly high degree of correlation between Ingenuity Test scores and ratings for originality in high school art classes.

TORRANCE TESTS OF CREATIVE THINKING. Torrance (1966) has developed a series of verbal and figural tests of creativity. He defines creativity (p. 6) as follows:

> A process of becoming sensitive to problems, deficiencies, gaps in knowledge, missing elements, disharmonies, and so on; identifying the difficulty; searching for solutions, making guesses, or formulating hypotheses about the deficiencies; testing and retesting these hypotheses and possibly modifying and retesting them; and finally communicating the results.

Whereas Guilford's emphasis is on creative aptitudes or traits, Torrance tries to emphasize "creative thinking processes" (p. 9). He uses Guilford's factors, however, to score the problem solutions produced for his tests.

There are the following five verbal tests:

1. Ask-and-guess activities. The student is presented with a drawing in response to which he is to (1) ask all the questions he can think of, (2) list all the possible causes of the action he can think of, and (3) list as many consequences of the action as he can think of.

2. Product improvement. The student is presented with a drawing of a toy and asked to list the most clever, interesting, and unusual ways of changing the toy to make it more fun to play with.

3. Unusual uses. As in the case of Guilford's Brick Uses Test, the student is given the name of an object and asked to list as many interesting and unusual uses as he can think of.

4. Unusual questions. Using the same object, the student must think of unusual questions about particular aspects of the object.

5. Just suppose. The student is presented with an improbable situation to think about, and he must list all the exciting things that might happen if this event occurred.

There are the following three picture tests:

1. Picture construction. The student is presented with a colored curved shape and asked to think of a drawing he could make to incorporate this shape. Then he sticks the shape to a blank sheet of paper and adds pencil or crayon lines to complete the drawing.

2. Picture completion. The student must make interesting objects and pictures out of simple, incomplete nonsense figures and entitle each drawing.

3. Parallel lines. The student must make drawings of objects out of several pairs of straight lines and entitle each drawing.

Reliability and validity. Results of the tests of creative abilities or thinking raise some question about exactly what is being measured and how the scores on the various tests are related. The common characteristic of creativity tests is that the student must produce answers rather than select them from a set of choices presented to him. Also, he is asked to produce multiple responses rather than just one response (e.g., all the uses of a brick he can think of). Since creativity is a pervasive capacity of the individual, we expect that the individual who scores high on one test will score high on all the other tests of creativity. Thorndike (1963) indicates that the correlations among tests of creativity range from near zero to as high as perhaps 0.40. These test data show a modest core running through the various tests which provides the degree of correlation that does exist, but this core appears to play only a minor role as far as success on any given test is concerned. Scores on tests which purportedly measure various factors of intelligence, as you have seen in Chapter 4, correlate more highly than the creativity test scores. If we tried to use the creativity tests to identify children who should receive special instruction to foster the development of extraordinary creative potential, we would face the serious problem of selecting some and excluding other children simply because of the particular tests of creativity we used. There is also the question of the validity of the tests—are they really measuring creativity? Ausubel (1963, p. 100), perhaps somewhat wryly, suggests that "high scores on tests that purportedly measure divergent thinking also reflect the influence of such contaminating factors as verbal fluency and glibness, uninhibited self-expression, and deficient self-critical ability."

Despite these limitations, many of which are recognized by the test authors, there are strong indications that the study of creativity and the development of creativity tests will continue. Anastasi (1961, p. 420) writes:

> One point appears to be fairly clear at this time. . . . Investigations of scientific talent are becoming increasingly concerned with creative abilities. Interest has shifted from the individual who is merely a cautious, accurate, and critical thinker to the one who displays ingenuity, originality, and inventiveness. Thus creativity, long regarded as the prime quality in artistic production, is coming more and more to be recognized as a basis for scientific achievement as well. It is also likely that in the years ahead we shall see many new kinds of tests. The traditional emphasis on understanding and recall that has characterized intelligence and aptitude tests will probably give way to a more comprehensive approach with greater concentration on productive thinking.

Personality Tests

As indicated earlier, personality tests measure a great variety of traits, processes, motives, and interests. Among the most frequently used personality tests and interest inventories are the following:

The *Kuder Preference Record* (Kuder, 1953) is designed to direct the examinee's attention toward occupational areas which appear to be promising in the light of his general preferences. It gives scores in eight areas of general interest: mechanical, computational, scientific, persuasive, artistic, literary, musical, and social service. The manual contains a classification of occupations based on these interest areas.

The *Strong Vocational Interest Blanks* (Strong, 1951) yield scores which direct the examinee's attention to particular occupations or families of occupations. An examinee's pattern of scores is compared with patterns of specific occupational groups. Horace, for example, may show interest patterns which closely resemble those of psychologists, ministers, and vocational counselors, but which are very dissimilar to those of physicists, senior accountants, bankers, and morticians.

The *California Psychological Inventory* (Gough, 1957) measures the personality characteristics of nondisturbed individuals—those characteristics important for social living and interaction. The test has four measures, those which assess (1) poise, ascendancy, and self-assurance; (2) socialization, maturity, and responsibility; (3) achievement potential and intellectual efficiency, and (4) intellectual and interest modes.

The *Study of Values* (Allport, Vernon, Lindzey, 1960) is designed to show the relative strengths of an individual's values in six areas: theoretical, economic, esthetic, social, political, and religious.

The *Minnesota Teacher Attitude Inventory* (Cook, Leeds, and Callis, 1951) measures those attitudes of teachers (or prospective teachers) which indicate how well they will get along with students and how satisfied they are with the teaching vocation. It consists of 150 statements with which the examinee can strongly agree, agree, be undecided or uncertain, disagree, or strongly disagree.

For prospective teachers, the usefulness of personality tests is somewhat dubious. Richard Lindeman (1967) believes that investigation of personality problems lies outside the teacher's province (p. 109):

> There are at least two reasons for this: (1) The teacher usually has his hands full if he is to do a satisfactory job in areas of intellectual development, and (2) investigations into student personality characteristics usually require competence and training distinctly different from those possessed by the classroom teacher. When it appears, on the basis of informal observation, that the source of the pupil's difficulty may lie in this domain, the teacher should seek assistance from the school counselor or psychologist. The use of instruments for assessing personality by persons without proper training may result in real harm to the child.

Ordinarily, in designing the proper conditions for instruction, personality probes and assessments are frequently unnecessary and unfruitful.

Summary

This section described three types of standardized tests: achievement, creativity, and (briefly) personality tests. The Iowa Tests of Educational Development (ITED) show the major characteristics of standardized tests in the construction of the items, the procedures for administration and scoring, the study of their validity and reliability, and the establishment of norms. Tests of creativity are special aptitude tests which frequently measure flexibility, fluency, and originality. Although the tests themselves may be considered measures of creative ability (Guilford), they can also be viewed as measures of creative-thinking processes (Torrance). Personality tests are primarily instruments for clinical diagnosis and treatment. I briefly described some common personality and interest inventories.

You should now return to objectives 4–10 (p. 657) and determine how well you have achieved them.

QUESTION 15-2

> The Performance Assessment Corporation constructed a test to measure the number and quality of different solutions students could produce for a series of social problems presented to them. Most likely this is a test of (a) General intelligence; (b) multiple aptitudes; (c) special aptitude; (d) achievement; (e) personality.
>
> After selecting your answer, give reasons for your choice and for your rejection of the alternatives.

THE INTERPRETATION OF STANDARDIZED TEST SCORES

One of your teaching responsibilities will be the interpretation of standardized test scores. To make this interpretation you must have an elementary knowledge of descriptive statistics. This chapter section, therefore, presents the following statistical concepts: the normal curve, measures of central tendency, measures of variability, derived scores, and measures of correlation. Although this section shows you how to compute these statistics, the emphasis is on their use in the interpretation of test scores.

The Normal Curve

As a distribution of scores, the normal curve has three characteristics: (1) Most of the scores cluster in the middle of the curve; (2) the curve is bell-shaped, combining both concave and convex curves; and (3) it is symmetrical, with 50 per cent of the scores in each half of the curve.

Figure 15-6 is an example of how scores cluster in a normal curve. Each of the squares represents a single score. If you count only the squares completely under the curve, you will see that the two highest columns each contains fifteen squares. Each of the two adjacent columns, to the right and left, contains fourteen squares. The columns become shorter as we move away from the middle until there is one or fewer than one score per column at the extreme ends of the curve. Figures 15-7 and 15-8 are two more examples of normal curves. Figure 15-7, a distribution of IQ scores, shows a normal curve superimposed on the columns of scores. Although the fit is not perfect, the distribution of column scores closely approximates the normal curve. In Fig. 15-8 you see the distribution of scores on a personality test which measures the tendency of college women to dominate or to submit in personal rela-

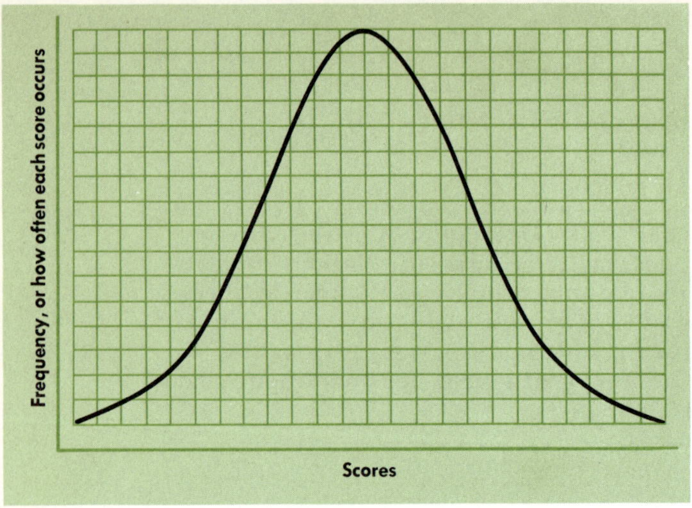

Fig. 15-6. *A normal curve. Consider each square under the curve as the score of one student. Most of the scores, you see, cluster in the middle.*

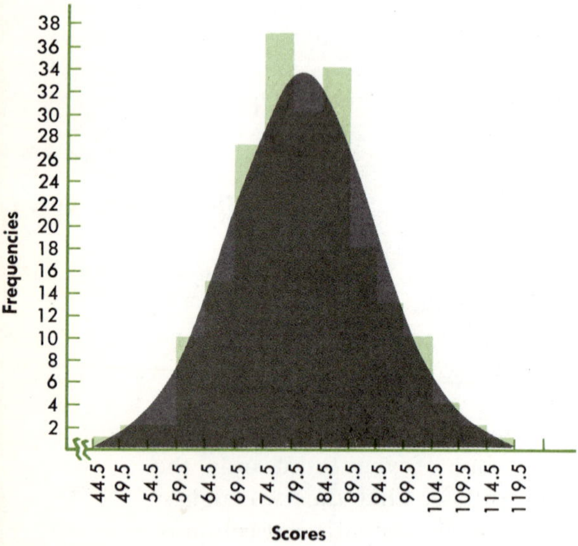

Fig. 15-7. *Distribution of scores on a test of intelligence (after Garrett, 1958, p. 104).*

tionships. The distribution of scores is normal because the scores cluster in the middle and the curve is bell-shaped and symmetrical.

When the distribution of scores is not normal, we say the curve is *skewed.* In Fig. 15-9, for example, the curve is skewed because most of the scores cluster on the right. Figure 15-10 shows another skewed curve, with the majority of scores clustering on the left.

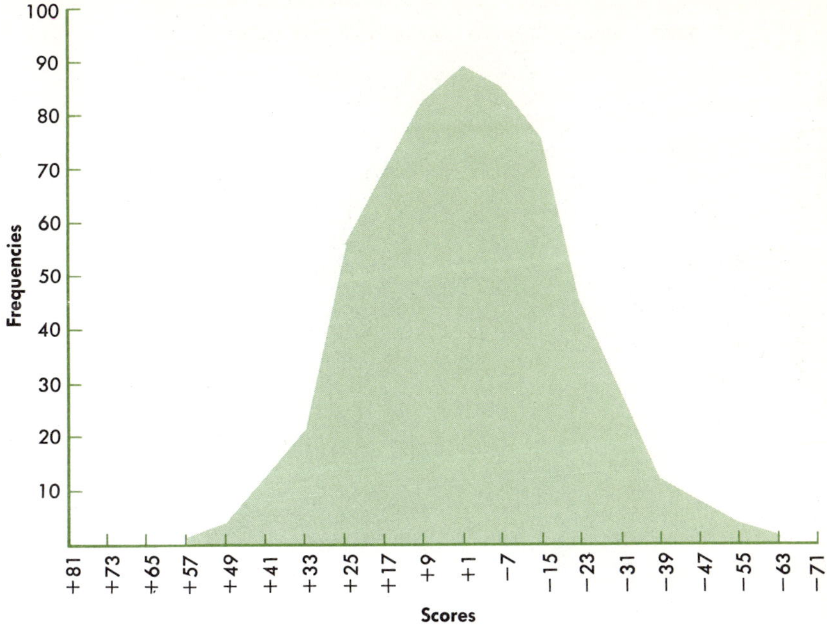

Fig. 15-8. *Distribution of scores on a personality test (after Anastasi, 1958, p. 32).*

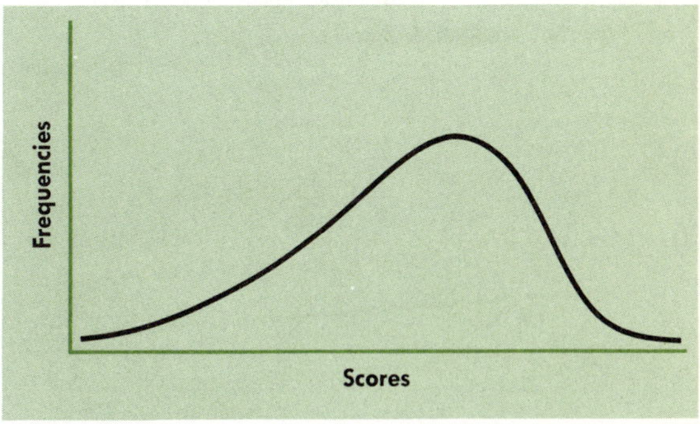

Fig. 15-9. *A skewed curve.*

The scores may also cluster too much or too little in the middle of the curve. Figure 15-11 is an example of a distribution in which the scores spread out too much. In Fig. 15-12 the scores are too peaked in the middle of the curve. Although both these curves show a middle clustering of scores and symmetry, they are not bell-shaped.

In constructing standardized tests, the authors often collect items

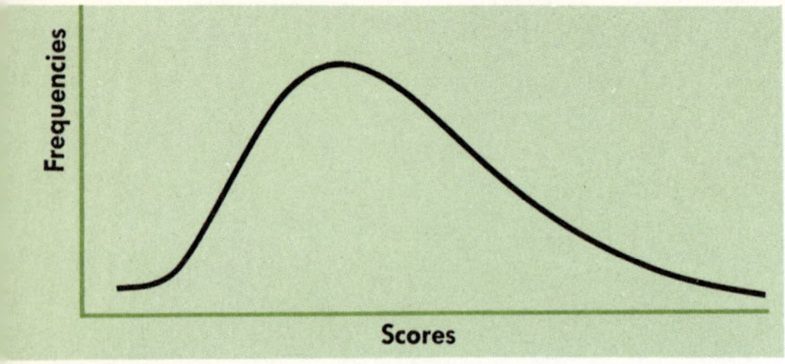

Fig. 15-10. *A skewed curve.*

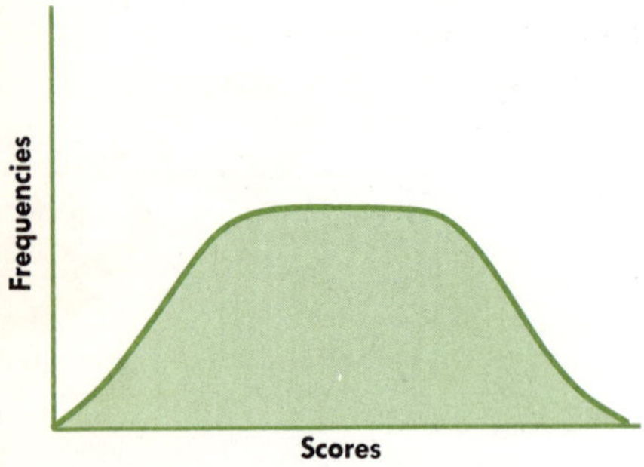

Fig. 15-11. *A curve with too much flatness to be a normal curve.*

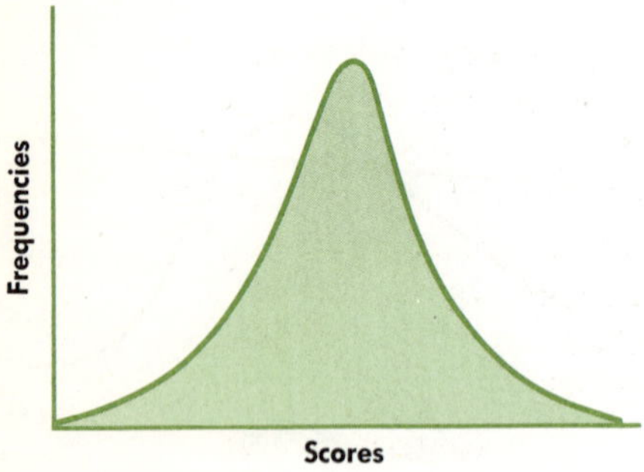

Fig. 15-12. *A curve which is too peaked to be a normal curve.*

that will result in a normal distribution of scores for the population of students for whom the test is designed. If, in the preliminary tryouts of the test, the authors discover too many high or low scores they replace easy with difficult or difficult with easy items.

Measures of Central Tendency

A fourth characteristic of the normal curve is that all measures of central tendency represent the same point on the curve. Central tendency is the inclination of scores to cluster about a point somewhere between the extremes. The *measure* of central tendency is the point around which the scores cluster. These points, in ordinary discourse, are called *averages,* and we can distinguish three types: the mode, the median, and the mean.

MODE. The mode is the score which occurs most frequently in a group of scores. Consider these ten scores: 14, 12, 10, 20, 19, 16, 18, 12, 22. The mode is 12, since 12 is the score which occurs twice, or more frequently than any other score in the group. A group of scores may have one or more modes. Consider the following scores: 14, 12, 10, 12, 16, 14. The distribution is bimodal because it has two modes: 12 and 14.

How useful is the mode? It is convenient to use because it is determined by mere inspection of a series of scores. It is misleading, however, when we use it to represent a typical score, which it may not be. In a group of fifty students, for example, the mode may be 35. If, however, forty-five of the students scored below 35, the mode is a misleading indication of the group's central tendency.

MEDIAN. The median is the midpoint in a distribution of scores. If there are an odd number of scores, it is the middlemost score. If there are an even number of scores, the median is a point between the two middlemost scores. Consider this series of scores: 4, 6, 8, 10, 16. The median is 8, the middlemost score. Table 15-2 shows you how to compute the median for an even and an odd number of scores. When particular scores are obtained by more than one student, the median is more difficult to determine (see Tate, 1965, pp. 47–48).

The median is particularly useful for two reasons: (1) It is easily understood and determined, and (2) it is the measure of central tendency least affected by extremes. Consider the average of these salaries: $50,000, $20,000, $15,000, $13,000, and $12,000. The median salary is $15,000. The arithmetic average salary (obtained by adding the salaries and dividing by five) is $22,000. The median is more representative of this group of salaries because it is less affected than the arithmetic average by the extremely high salary of $50,000.

MEAN. The mean, or arithmetic mean, is the sum of a group of scores divided by the number of scores. Table 15-3 shows you how to compute the mean.

The mean is the most useful measure of central tendency for the following reasons: (1) It can be used in the computation of other statistics, as you will see below; and (2) it tends to give a more accurate

TABLE 15-2

HOW TO COMPUTE THE MEDIAN.

Formula: $\text{Mdn.} = \frac{X_1 + X_2}{2}$

(for an even number of scores)

Mdn. = the median of scores on one test
X_1 = the higher of the two middlemost scores
X_2 = the lower of the two middlemost scores

Problem: Compute the median of the raw scores on the natural science test in Table 15-10 (p. 695).

Step 1: Arrange the scores in ascending order, from low (28) to high (72).

Step 2: Find the two middlemost scores by counting up to the tenth and eleventh scores.
You should obtain $X_1 = 51$; $X_2 = 50$.

Step 3: Substitute the numbers in the formula, as follows:

$$\text{Mdn.} = \frac{51 + 50}{2} = 50.5$$

For an odd number of scores, perform step 1 above, and find the middlemost score by counting from the top or the bottom of the distribution.

TABLE 15-3

HOW TO COMPUTE THE MEAN.

Formula: $M = \frac{\Sigma X}{N}$

M = the mean of scores on one test
Σ = to add these scores (Σ is pronounced "sigma")
X = the raw score
N = the number of students who have scores

Problem: Compute the mean for the raw scores on the natural science test, in Table 15-10 (p. 695).

Step 1: Add the scores to obtain ΣX.
You should obtain 971.

Step 2: Count the number of scores to obtain N.
You should obtain 20.

Step 3: Substitute the numbers in the formula, as follows:

$$M = \frac{971}{20} = 48.55$$

measure of central tendency than the median and the mode do. Ordinarily one should use the mean unless there are good reasons not to.

Measures of Variability

Whereas measures of central tendency describe the clustering of scores, measures of variability describe the spreading out of scores. Consider the following situation, in which knowledge of two measures of central tendency is an insufficient basis for making instructional decisions. Mr. Al Gebra, the geometry teacher, has two classes, each with three students (in a highly enlightened school district). On the basis of average IQ scores for the classes, he wants to determine whether he should use the same instructional procedures and materials in both classes. Here are the IQ scores, means, and medians for both classes:

Class *A*		Class *B*	
Abigail	101	Elvis	150
Clarence	100	Frieda	100
Dexter	99	Patience	50
M =	100	*M* =	100
Mdn. =	100	Mdn. =	100

If Mr. Gebra pays little attention to individual IQ scores and bases his decision on these measures of central tendency, he may decide to teach both classes in the same way. Inspection of the spread of the scores in these two classes quickly indicates, however, the possible disastrous consequences of this decision. The scores in class *B* are much more spread out (variable) than the scores of class *A*. In class *B*, anything Mr. Gebra could add to Patience's knowledge of geometry would bore Elvis and probably Frieda to tears, and he could not significantly add to Elvis' knowledge without hopelessly befuddling Patience and probably Frieda as well. Mr. Al Gebra needs some new measures—ones which describe the variability ("spreadoutness") as well as the clustering of the scores. Two of these measures of variability are the range and the standard deviation.

RANGE. The range is the difference between the highest and the lowest scores. In the preceding illustration, for class *A* the range is 2; for class *B*, the range is 100. The range tells Mr. Al Gebra at once that there is fifty times more variability in class *B* than in class *A*. On the basis of the range alone, he could decide to make different accommodations for entering behavior. The range is a useful statistic because it is easily understood, easily determined, and an accurate estimate of variability when scores are normally distributed. Its chief disadvantage is that it does not tell us about the amount of variability of the intermediate scores, which, as fate has it, constitute about two-thirds of the scores in a normal distribution.

STANDARD DEVIATION. The standard deviation, the most important measure of variability, is defined by the operations used to compute it. Table 15-4 describes these operations. Unlike the range, which is based on only two scores, the standard deviation is based on all the scores in the group. In the table the standard deviation for class *A*, in the ex-

TABLE 15-4

HOW TO COMPUTE THE STANDARD DEVIATION.

Formula: $s = \frac{\sqrt{\Sigma (X - M)^2}}{N}$

s = the standard deviation of one set of scores
Σ = the sum of
X = one raw score
M = the mean of this set of scores
N = the number of students with scores
$\sqrt{\ }$ = the square root of

Problem: Compute the standard deviation of the following three scores: 101, 100, 99.

Step 1: Prepare four columns of figures as follows:

X	M	(X − M)	$(X - M)^2$

Step 2: List the scores under column X, and determine M ($M = 100$).

Step 3: Subtract the mean from each score to obtain figures for column $X - M$, as follows:

X	M	(X − M)	$(X - M)^2$
101	100	1	1
100	100	0	0
99	100	—1	1

Step 4: Square each of the differences in column $X - M$ to obtain the figures in column $(X - M)^2$, as shown above.

Step 5: Add column $(X - M)^2$ to obtain $\Sigma (X - M)^2$. $\Sigma (X - M)^2 = 2$.

Step 6: Divide by the number of students who have scores ($N = 3$).

Step 7: Substitute the numbers in the formula, as follows:

$$s = \sqrt{\frac{2}{3}} = \sqrt{0.66}$$

Step 8: Take the square root of 0.66 to obtain $s = 0.812$.

ample on p. 683, is computed. It is 0.812. The standard deviation for class *B* is about 40. You can see again that the IQ scores in class *B* are fifty times as variable as they are in class *A*. The greater the value of the standard deviation, the more the variability of the scores. Table 15-5 describes a method of estimating the standard deviation.

The relationship of standard deviation to the normal curve is of major importance in the interpretation of test scores. In considering this relationship, make frequent reference to Chart 1, which is on the inside of the back cover of this book. In referring to Chart 1, note the following:

1. About 68 per cent of the scores fall between $-1s$ and $+1s$.
2. About 34 per cent of the scores fall between the mean (the center line in the curve, marked 0) and either $-1s$ or $+1s$ from the mean.
3. About 84 per cent of the scores fall between $-3s$ and $+1s$.
4. The solid vertical lines mark the various standard deviations.
5. Deviations below the mean are preceded by a minus sign, above the mean by a plus sign.

We shall make frequent use of standard deviation in the discussion of the statistics below.

Derived Scores

In the interpretation of standardized test scores you must distinguish between raw and derived scores. The *raw score* is obtained by scoring a test according to the directions in the manual. The *derived score* is a raw score that has been transformed to facilitate interpretation. In this section we shall consider several types of derived scores: percentile rank, standard scores, deviation IQ scores, and age-grade scores.

PERCENTILE RANK. One of the easiest ways of interpreting scores is to rank them from high to low, assigning a rank of 1 to the highest score. The significance of the rank depends on the number of scores in the group: A rank of 1 in a graduating class of three students is not so impressive as a rank of 1 in a class of 300 students. The percentile rank, the most widely used derived score, avoids this limitation. It expresses the student's score in terms of the percentage of his group the student has scored above. If a student has a percentile rank of 45, his score exceeds the scores of 45 per cent of the group. If another student has a percentile rank of 88, his score exceeds the scores of 88 per cent of the group. The percentile, itself, is any one of ninety-nine points which di-

TABLE 15-5

HOW TO ESTIMATE THE STANDARD DEVIATION (A SHORT METHOD).

Step 1: Arrange the scores in ascending order, from low to high.
Step 2: Find the two scores which mark the middle two-thirds of the scores by counting off one-sixth of the scores from the top and one-sixth from the bottom.
Step 3: Find the difference between these two scores and divide by 2. This quotient is the standard deviation.

Problem: Using the short method, estimate the standard deviation of the scores on the reading test in Table 15-10 (p. 695).
Step 1: Arrange the scores in ascending order, from 26 to 80.
Step 2: Find the two scores which mark the middle two-thirds (72 and 38).
Step 3: $s = \frac{72 - 38}{2} = 17.$
(With the formula in Table 15-4, $s = 17.68$.)

vides a set of scores into one hundred groups of equal size. The highest rank is 99 since no individual can score above himself, and the lowest rank is 1 since no individual can score below himself.

Percentile ranks are one of the best ways of interpreting raw scores on standardized tests because their meaning is fairly simple and direct. Many test publishers now provide tables which give the percentile rank for the scores which the students obtain on the test.

Chart 1 (on the inside of the back cover) shows the relationship of percentile rank to the normal curve. Note that percentile ranks are the same as cumulative percentages. A percentile rank of 84, for example, indicates that the student has scored above 84 per cent of the students in his group and that his score lies one standard deviation ($+1s$) above the mean. A percentile rank of 50 means that the student has scored above 50 per cent of his group and that his score lies at the mean.

Given the standard deviation for the student's score, you can estimate his percentile rank. Referring to Chart 1, if you know that a student's IQ score lies halfway between $+1s$ and $+2s$, you can estimate that his percentile rank is about 93. Similarly, if you know that his score falls at $-2s$ on the curve, you can determine that his percentile rank is 2.

Standard scores. The basic standard score is the z score, which is computed in Table 15-6. The z score is very useful in the interpretation of test scores. Referring to Chart 1, you can see that a z score of 0 indicates that the raw score is at the mean. A negative z score means that the raw score is below the mean, a positive z score that it is above the mean. A z score of +3.00 indicates that the score is very high, $+3s$ above the mean.

The use of the z score facilitates the comparison of two or more scores. Consider the situation in which Dexter obtains a raw score of 36 on an English test and 80 on a science test. Let us assume the following means and standard deviations for these tests:

TABLE 15-6

HOW TO COMPUTE THE STANDARD z AND T SCORES.

Formula: $z = \dfrac{X - M}{s}$

z = a standard score
X = one raw score
M = the mean of a set of scores
s = the standard deviation of this set of scores

Problem: Dexter took a test on the interpretation of English literature. He obtained a score of 36. The class mean was 32.3 and the standard deviation 9.2.

Compute Dexter's z score.

Step 1: Find the class mean ($M = 32.3$).
Step 2: Find the standard deviation ($s = 9.2$).
Step 3: Substitute numbers in the formula, as follows:

$$z = \frac{36 - 32.3}{9.2}$$

$$z = 0.40$$

Compute the T score:

Formula: $T = 10z + 50$
Step 1: Find the z score ($z = 0.40$).
Step 2: Multiply the z score by 10.
Step 3: Add 50.

$$T = (0.40 \times 10) + 50$$

$$T = 54$$

	English Test	Science Test
Class mean	32.3	75.3
Standard deviation	9.2	15.4
Dexter's raw scores	36	80

Does the higher score indicate that Dexter is twice as good in science as he is in English? By using the standard deviations, we may be able to answer this question. For the English test, a score of 41.5 lies at $+1s$

(32.3 + 9.2). For the science test a score of 90.7 lies at $+1s$ (75.3 + 15.4). It appears in both cases that Dexter's raw scores lie about midway between the mean and one standard deviation above the mean, indicating that his levels of achievement in science and in English are about the same. By using the z score, however, we obtain a better comparison. Using the formula in Table 15-6, we discover that his z score in English is 0.40, in science 0.30. It now appears that Dexter is slightly better in English than in science. If you want to avoid decimals, you can use the formula for the T score, also in Table 15-6. You discover then that his T score in English is 54, in science 53, indicating the slightly higher level of his English achievement.

Chart 1 also shows other standard scores in common use, the AGCT score and the CEEB score. The AGCT score is obtained on the Army General Classification Test, the CEEB score is obtained on the College Entrance Examination Board tests. Like the T score, they are based on the z score, except for established means and standard deviations, as indicated here:

	Mean	Standard Deviation
T score	50	10
AGCT score	100	20
CEEB	500	100

By referring to Chart 1, you can see the relationships among standard deviations, percentile ranks, and various types of z scores.

DEVIATION IQ SCORES. Both the Stanford-Binet and the Wechsler Intelligence Scales now use means and standard deviations which are constant from age to age. In the Stanford-Binet scale the mean is 100 and the standard deviation is 16. To find a student's IQ you multiply his z score by 16 and then add 100. The Wechsler tests, as shown in Chart 1, use a mean of 100 and a standard deviation of 15. Almost all modern IQ tests use means of 100, but their standard deviations range from 5 to 20. To properly interpret a student's IQ it is not enough to know his IQ score; you must also know the test and the standard deviation of that test. An IQ score of 105, obtained on a test with a standard deviation of 5, equals an IQ score of 115, obtained on a test with a standard deviation of 15. Both scores are one standard deviation above the mean. Similarly, a student with an IQ score of 110, obtained on a test with a standard deviation of 5, has scored above a student with an IQ of 125, obtained on a test with a standard deviation of 15. The former student's score falls two standard deviations above the mean, while the latter student's score falls somewhat short of this point. Most modern IQ tests now provide tables which transform raw scores into derived IQ scores.

Chart 1 also provides one final comparison. Note that the scores on the ITED use a mean of 15 and a standard deviation of 5. This standard score is also used by the National Merit Scholarship Qualifying Examination.

AGE-GRADE SCORES. Standardized achievement tests often use age-grade scores for test interpretation. Table 15-7 is an example of age-grade norms. The norms are based on scores attained by the standardization sample at particular grade and age levels. Note, for example, that a standard score of 123 is equivalent to a grade score of 3.1 and an age score of 8-4. For the grade scores, the school year is divided into nine months. A grade score of 3.1 means the first month of grade 3. A grade score of 5.8 refers to the eighth month of the fifth grade. For the age scores, the calendar year is used. An age score of 8-4 simply refers to the fourth month of the eighth year of age. A score of 18-6 refers to the sixth month of the eighteenth year. Table 15-7 informs us that a standard score of 123 should be the average level of reading comprehension of a child of eight years, four months and in the first month of the third grade.

Age-grade scores have much public appeal because they are based on two ordinary assumptions: (1) that most students of the same ages and grades have about the same amount of knowledge and skill and (2) that students who have achieved above their age and grade levels are equal in achievement to students in advanced grades. Howard Lyman (1963, pp. 125–26) points out the limitations of these assumptions. First, we cannot assume that curricula are uniform throughout the nation. Some students know more or less because they have been taught more or less in general or in particular subject matters and skill areas. This variation in curricula undoubtedly results in considerable variation in achievement and makes the establishment of normal achievement a precarious endeavor. Second, age-grade scores assume that the student learns at a uniform rate throughout the school year and ceases to learn during the summer vacations. The rate of learning, as you saw in Part 3, is influenced by a great many conditions, some of which pertain to the entering behavior and others to the particular type of learning. The student may learn certain arithmetic concepts more rapidly than he improves his reading skills. Third, the age-grade scores of different standardized tests often give conflicting results because they use different standardization samples and give different emphases to the same subject matter. A test which measures achievement of objectives in conventional biology courses is not a valid measure of achievement of the ob-

TABLE 15-7

AGE AND GRADE SCORES FOR COMPREHENSION SUBTEST OF THE IOWA SILENT READING TEST (Greene and Kelley, 1943, p. 15).

Standard Score	Grade Equivalent	Age Equivalent
109		6–5
114	2.0	7–1
118	2.5	7–8
123	3.1	8–4
128	3.8	9–0
132	4.3	9–7
136	4.9	10–1
139	5.3	10–6
140	5.4	10–8
141	5.6	10–10
144	6.0	11–2
148	6.5	11–9
152	7.1	12–4
157	7.9	13–3
162	8.7	14–4
167	9.8	16–3
172	11.1	18–6

jectives in the BSCS course. A standardization sample which includes a higher proportion of urban schools does not produce the same age-grade scores as one which includes a higher proportion of rural or consolidated schools. Fourth, the relative level of the score does not correspond to the relative level of achievement. A high score on one subtest of the same battery may actually be lower (in percentile rank) than a low score on another subtest. Lyman (p. 126) uses this example: A grade score of 8.5 in reading may equal a percentile rank of 60, while a grade score of 8.2 in arithmetic may equal a percentile rank of 98, even though both tests are in the same battery.

Some of these limitations of age-grade scores are overcome if you use them to compare the achievement of your students with their own groups. For example, if Dexter, in the third month of the fifth grade, obtains a reading score equivalent to grade 5.6, we may consider his reading to be above average. If, however, most of Dexter's classmates are reading at grade level 6.6, Dexter's reading is one grade level below the average for his group. Similarly, the average grade score in reading for the seventh grade in an urban school may be 5.1. If Clarence, in the seventh grade of that school, reads at a level equivalent to a grade score

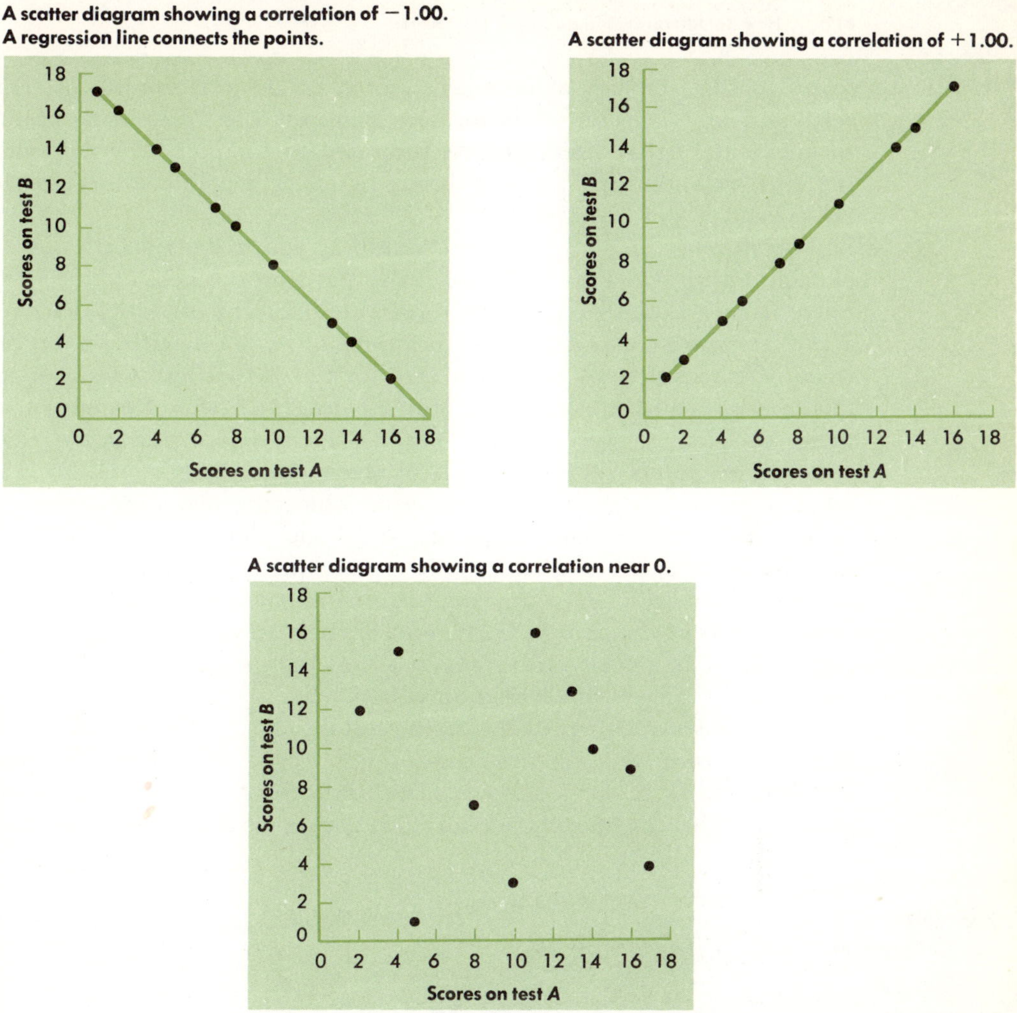

Fig. 15-13. *Three scatter diagrams.*

of 6.3, he is reading above the average for his group. When the curricula and the students of your school differ significantly from the student sample and curricula used in the standardization of the test, comparing the performance of your students with the test norms rather than with the performance of their own group results in misleading interpretations.

Measures of Correlation

Correlation is the relationship of two sets of test scores. For example, you may wish to know the relationship of your students' IQ scores to their biology achievement scores, or the relationship of their reading comprehension scores to their scores on a test measuring ability to interpret English literature. As indicated in Chapter 6 by determining such relationships you can begin to locate possible causes of the performances you observe.

Coefficients of correlation are numbers which describe the degree of relationship which exists between the test scores. These numbers can range from +1.00, through 0, to −1.00. A coefficient of +1.00 describes a perfect *positive* correlation. A coefficient of −1.00 describes a perfect *negative* correlation. A coefficient of 0 (or near 0) indicates little or no relationship between the test scores. Figure 15-13 shows examples of these coefficients of correlation. These figures are known as *scatter diagrams.* The points represent pairs of scores, one score on test *A,* the other score on test *B.* Each point occurs where the two scores coincide. A line is drawn through the points. If all the points fall in a straight line, we have either a perfect positive or a perfect negative coefficient of correlation. In a near 0 correlation, no straight line will pass through or near many of the points. Coefficients of correlation are seldom perfect. Figure 15-14 is a scatter diagram of scores on spelling and arithmetic tests. The coefficient of correlation is 0.73.

The closer the coefficients are to +1.00 and −1.00 the greater is the relationship between the pairs of test scores. The closer the relationships are to 0, the less relationship there is. A coefficient of −0.87 shows a higher degree of relationship than a coefficient of +0.72. A

Fig. 15-14. *A scatter diagram of scores on two tests, showing a correlation of 0.73 (after Tyler, 1963, p. 18).*

Children	Spelling	Arithmetic
Elaine	20	20
Martha	18	25
Bill	15	19
Jim	15	20
Edna	14	19
Harry	14	20
Marie	14	18
Joe	13	19
Lucy	13	18
John	10	16
Grant	8	15

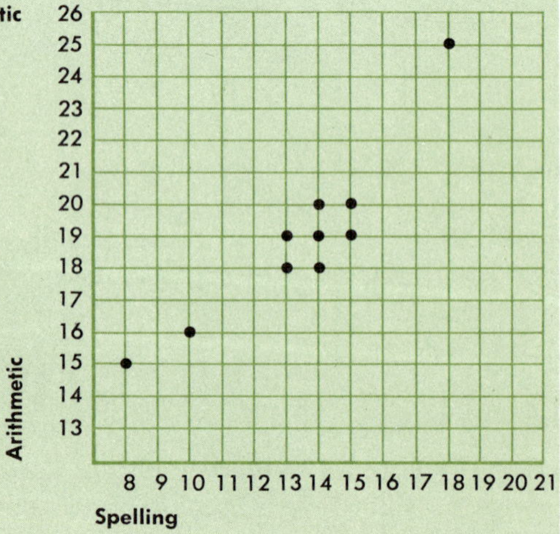

coefficient of +0.32 shows a higher degree of relationship than a coefficient of −0.10. The degree of relationship is shown by the size of the correlation and not by the sign (plus or minus) of the coefficient.

Tables 15-10 and 15-11 show two methods of computing coefficients

TABLE 15-8

HOW TO COMPUTE THE PRODUCT-MOMENT CORRELATION.

Formula: $r = \dfrac{\Sigma (X - M_x)(Y - M_y)}{(N)(s_x)(s_y)}$

r = this coefficient of correlation
Σ = sum of
$X - M_x$ = differences between each score on test x and the mean of that test
$Y - M_y$ = differences between each score on test y and the mean of that test
N = the number of pairs of scores
s_x = the standard deviation of test x
s_y = the standard deviation of test y

Problem: Compute r for these pairs of test scores:

	Test A	Test B
Barney	50	60
Clarence	60	80
Dexter	70	90
Elvis	80	70
Frieda	90	100

Step 1: Prepare four columns of figures for each test, as follows:

	Test A			Test B			
	X	M	$(X - M_x)$	Y	M	$(Y - M_y)$	$(X - M_x)(Y - M_y)$
Barney	50	70	−20	60	80	−20	400
Clarence	60	70	−10	80	80	0	0
Dexter	70	70	0	90	80	10	0
Elvis	80	70	10	70	80	−10	−100
Frieda	90	70	20	100	80	20	400

Step 2: To obtain $\Sigma (X - M_x)(Y - M_y)$ multiply columns $(X - M_x)$ and $(Y - M_y)$ as indicated above; then add these products:
$\Sigma (X - M_x)(Y - M_y) = 700$

Step 3: Determine the standard deviation for each test by using Table 15-4:
$(s_x = 14.14;\ s_y = 14.14)$

Step 4: Substitute the numbers in the formula as follows:

$$r = \frac{700}{(5)(14.14)(14.14)} = 0.70$$

TABLE 15-9

HOW TO COMPUTE THE RANK-DIFFERENCE CORRELATION (RHO).

Formula: $rho = 1 - \frac{6\ (\Sigma D^2)}{N\ (N^2 - 1)}$

rho = this coefficient of correlation

Σ = sum of

D = the difference between the student's rank on test x and that on test y

N = the number of pairs of scores

Problem: Compute *rho* for the five pairs of scores in Table 15-8.

Step 1: Prepare columns of figures for each test as follows:

	X	Rank	Y	Rank	D	D²
Barney	50	5	60	5	0	0
Clarence	60	4	80	3	1	1
Dexter	70	3	90	2	1	1
Elvis	80	2	70	4	–2	4
Frieda	90	1	100	1	0	0

Step 2: Assign rank for each test as indicated above.

Step 3: To obtain D^2, find the difference between the ranks for each student and square the difference, as indicated above. To obtain ΣD^2, add the figures in column D^2. (6)

Step 4: Substitute the figures in the formula as follows:

$$rho = 1 - \frac{6\ (6)}{5(5^2 - 1)} = 1 - \frac{36}{5(24)} = 1 - \frac{36}{120} = 1 - \frac{3}{10} = \frac{7}{10}$$

$$rho = 0.70$$

of correlation. The product-moment coefficient is the more widely used and the better method. It is a more sensitive measure of relationship than the rank-difference coefficient because the ranking of the scores in computing the latter coefficient reduces the effect of the individual score on the resulting coefficient. By preserving the score value, the product-moment coefficient remains sensitive to the amount and direction (positive or negative) of correlation. The rank-difference correlation, as a method of approximation, is useful when you are dealing with a few scores.

The use of correlation coefficients in psychological and educational research and the limited significance of findings based on them are topics considered in the following chapter.

Summary

The normal curve is a bell-shaped, symmetrical curve in which most of the scores cluster in the middle. Curves which are not normal are

TABLE 15-10

RAW SCORES OF TWENTY OF YOUR STUDENTS ON STANDARDIZED SCIENCE AND READING TESTS AND THEIR IQ SCORES.

Name of Student	(Raw Score) Natural Science Test	(Raw Score) Reading Test	IQ
Abigail	52	74	115
Barney	65	52	121
Clarence	22	26	89
Dexter	40	38	98
Elvis	35	41	111
Frieda	72	80	130
Gerhart	51	56	103
Horatio	46	40	93
Isaac	62	69	108
Jarvis	31	45	84
Kate	28	37	95
Lisa	54	64	106
Melanie	50	51	113
Nannette	39	48	90
Opal	61	75	127
Patience	57	61	104
Queenie	59	54	101
Roger	55	46	97
Stella	44	33	99
Timothy	48	57	94

skewed. Central tendency is the inclination of scores to cluster about a point between the extremes. The mean is a more useful measure of central tendency than the median and the mode. Measures of variability describe the spreading out of scores. The standard deviation, based on all scores, is a more sensitive measure of variability than the range, based on only two scores. Raw scores are transformed into derived scores for interpretation. Percentile rank is the most useful derived score because its meaning is fairly simple and direct. There are several standard scores, the most basic of which is the *z* score. Several other standard scores and deviation IQ scores are based on the *z* score. Age-grade scores, although widely used in achievement tests, are usually misleading unless the performances of your students are compared with those of others in their own group. Measures of correlation show the relationship of two sets of test scores. Of the two measures of correlation discussed, the product-moment correlation is more sensitive to the amount and direction of the relationship than the rank-difference correlation which is best used as an approximation.

You should now return to objectives 11–25 (pp. 657–58) and determine how well you have achieved them.

TABLE 15-11

MEANS AND STANDARD DEVIATIONS FOR FICTITIOUS STANDARDIZED TESTS, LISTED FOR EACH GRADE.

Grade	Science Test		Reading Test	
	M	s	M	s
4	30	5	33	4
5	35	7	35	4
6	40	7	38	5
7	45	9	42	7
8	50	10	45	8
9	52	9	49	9
10	54	8	55	10
11	55	9	60	12
12	56	7	65	14

QUESTION 15-3

The following questions are based on Tables 15-10 and 15-11.

How do the means and the medians of your eighth grade class compare with the national means?

Science test: M = 48.55; Mdn. = 50.5. Reading test: M = ______; Mdn. = ______. Science test (using Table 15-11): national M = ______; reading test (using Table 15-11): national M = ______.

Now answer the question above.

QUESTION 15-4

How do the standard deviations of your class compare with the national standard deviations?

Science test: s = ______. Reading test: s = 17.68. Science test (using Table 15-11): national s = ______; reading test (using Table 15-11): national s = ______.

Is your class more variable than the national sample?

QUESTION 15-5

Using Chart 1 and the norms in Table 15-11, find the percentile scores for the following students:

Science test: Dexter ______; Melanie ______; Frieda ______ (approximately); and Elvis ______ (approximately).

Reading test: Barney ______ (approximately); Kate ______; Jarvis ______; and Patience ______.

QUESTION 15-6

Using Table 15-11, determine the grade-level score of these same students:

Science test: Dexter _______; Melanie _______; Frieda _______; Elvis _______.

Reading test: Barney _______; Kate _______; Jarvis _______; Patience _______.

QUESTION 15-7

Do you believe that the percentile or grade-level scores convey more valid information of the achievement of these students? Why?

QUESTION 15-8

How many of your students score at or below the sixth grade mean of the science test? _______; reading test? _______. How many score at or above the tenth grade mean of the science test? _______; reading test? _______.

QUESTION 15-9

Determine the relationship between IQ scores and the test scores, using the designated coefficients.

(a) IQ scores and science scores (use product-moment correlation).

(b) IQ scores and reading scores (use rank-difference correlation).

(c) Which students are achieving below-average scores for their general intelligence level?

(d) Which students are achieving above-average scores for their general intelligence level?

QUESTION 15-10

Jeremiah, a high school senior, has an IQ of 100. He has a choice of two colleges. At Harmony Haven College the freshman class has a mean IQ of 115 and a standard deviation of 7. At Pacifica State College the freshman class has a mean IQ of 115 and a standard deviation of 12.

(a) What percentage of the class will Jeremiah exceed at Harmony Haven? _______; at Pacifica State? _______.

(b) Based on these data, which college should you advise Jeremiah to attend?

SUMMARY

Test standardization is the development of uniform procedures used in each administration and scoring of a test. Such standardization increases the probability that variations in scores are the result of variations in student performance and not the result of test conditions. In the construction of the test, systematic procedures are used for increasing validity and reliability. To establish test norms, a standardization sample, representative of the type of students for whom the test will be used, is carefully selected. In many cases, while classroom tests may have more validity, standardized tests may have more reliability. Teachers may use standardized tests for general assessment of student ability, general assessment of student achievement, diagnostic assessment in the classroom, assessment of school programs and instructional procedures, and assessment of school learning over the long term.

Achievement and creativity tests are among the five types of standardized tests. Achievement tests are often survey batteries or series of short tests covering basic areas of educational achievement. The ITED battery illustrates the major characteristics of standardized tests. Statements of instructional objectives indicate those classes for which the test is valid. The manual describes both specific and general procedures for test administration and for scoring. Norms have been carefully established. The validity of the battery has been checked against scores on other standardized tests and against level of school achievement. The common characteristic of creativity tests is that the student must produce answers. While the Guilford tests emphasize the measurement of the creative attributes of individuals (fluency, flexibility, and originality), the Torrance tests attempt to measure creative-thinking processes. At present the reliability and validity of creativity tests limit their classroom usefulness. Personality tests are primarily instruments for clinical diagnosis and treatment and are ordinarily not useful for classroom purposes.

The interpretation of standardized test scores requires at least an introductory knowledge of statistical concepts. The normal curve is the basis for these scores. The curve describes a series (or distribution) of scores in which most of the scores cluster in the middle. It can be distinguished from skewed, overly peaked, or flat curves. Central tendency is the inclination of scores to cluster at a point somewhere between the extremes. The mean, more than the mode and the median, is the chief measure of central tendency. Measures of variability describe the spreading out of scores. The standard deviation is the chief measure of variability. A derived score is a raw score that has been transformed to facilitate interpretation. The most popular and useful derived score is the percentile rank, a way of expressing a student's score in terms of the percentage of his group he has scored above. The basic standard score is the z score, which is expressed in standard deviation units. The T score, the AGCT score, and the CEEB score are all modifications of the z score. Deviation IQ scores use means and standard deviations which are constant from age to age. To make a proper interpretation of a student's IQ, you must know the standard deviation of the particular test which yielded his score. Age-grade scores, despite their popularity as derived scores, give misleading interpretations of student achievement unless the students are compared with their own groups. Measures of correlation describe the relationship between two sets of test scores. The product-moment correlation is a more sensitive measure of this relationship than the rank-difference correlation is. The significance of measures of correlation for educational research is considered in the chapter which follows.

SUGGESTED READINGS

In addition to the books listed at the end of Chapter 14, the following books are excellent treatments of the material in this chapter:

Lyman, Howard B., *Test Scores and What They Mean*. Englewood Cliffs, N.J.: Prentice-Hall, Inc., 1963. (paper)

Tyler, Leona E., *Tests and Measurement*. Englewood Cliffs, N.J.: Prentice-Hall, Inc., 1963. (paper)

The following programed texts are very useful for descriptive statistics:

Amos, Jimmy, Foster Lloyd Brown, and Oscar G. Mink, *Statistical Concepts: A Basic Program*. New York: Harper & Row, Publishers, Inc., 1965. (125 pp.)

Elzey, Freeman F., *A Programed Introduction to Statistics*. Belmont, California: Wadsworth Publishing Co., Inc., 1965, 1966. (376 pp.)

Gotkin, Lassar G., and Leo S. Goldstein, *Descriptive Statistics: A Programed Textbook,* Vol. 1. New York: John Wiley & Sons, Inc., 1964. (221 pp.)

Several hard-cover texts for descriptive and inferential statistics are listed at the end of Chapter 16.

How to Evaluate Research in Educational Psychology

16

The major purpose of this chapter is to introduce you to the nature, use, and evaluation of research in educational psychology. In dealing with the nature of this research, the first section describes six steps which lead from the most basic to the most applied research on human learning. Summaries of actual investigations illustrate each of these steps. This section also distinguishes among and relates various variables, problems and hypotheses, experimental and control groups, and experimental and correlational studies. The section concludes with the consideration of several uses of research in educational psychology. The second section tells you how to evaluate research reports. It describes six steps, extending from the preliminary reading of the report to the evaluation of its conclusions. It emphasizes the problems of sampling and the sources of sampling bias. The third section deals with the statistical analysis of data. Here I distinguish between research and null hypotheses and discuss levels of statistical significance. I describe the nature, computation, and use of three tests of statistical significance: the t ratio, the F ratio, and the chi square. The section concludes with a brief consideration of nonparametric tests and factor analysis.

Upon reading the first section of this chapter (on the nature and use of educational research), you should be able to meet these objectives:

1. Distinguish between basic and applied research in terms of rigor and relevance.

2. Describe the research continuum in terms of six steps leading from basic to applied research.

3. Identify experimental studies of learning in terms of one or more of these steps.

4. Distinguish between and show the relationship of independent and dependent variables and provide examples of each.

5. Define hypothesis in terms of independent and dependent variables and give two illustrations of hypotheses.

6. Distinguish between and show the relationship of experimental and control groups and provide illustrations of each.

7. List and define five factors (apart from sampling) which require experimental control.

8. Distinguish between and show the relationship of experimental and correlational studies and identify examples of each.

Upon reading the second section of this chapter (on the evaluation of the research report), you should be able to meet these objectives:

9. Identify the four major parts of the research report (statement of problem and hypotheses, description of procedures, results, and conclusions) when given examples of these reports (step 1).

10. Distinguish between adequate and inadequate descriptions for each part (step 2).

11. Evaluate the sampling procedure by indicating uncontrolled sources of sampling bias (step 3).

12. Describe how the standard error of the mean is a measure of sampling error.

13. Evaluate the validity and reliability of the procedures by referring to the original hypotheses and the correct application of procedures and instruments (step 4).

14. Check the analysis of data for adequate and clear reporting of results and the correct choice of significance tests (step 5).

15. Evaluate the conclusions in terms of alternatives which fit the data and in terms of this fit with previous research and ordinary experience (step 6).

Upon reading the third section of this chapter (on the analysis of data), you should be able to meet these objectives:

16. Define and illustrate the null hypothesis and distinguish it from the research hypothesis.

17. Define statistical significance and explain $p = 0.01$, $p = 0.05$, and $p = 0.001$.

18. Define and illustrate the appropriate use of the t ratio and compute the t ratio of two sample means.

19. Define and illustrate the appropriate use of the F ratio and compute the F ratio when given the mean square between groups and the mean square within groups.

20. Define and illustrate the appropriate use of the Chi square test and compute Chi square for three classes of observed frequencies.

21. Distinguish and illustrate the differences between parametric and nonparametric tests.

22. Define and illustrate the use of factor analysis as a means of finding common variables.

THE NATURE AND USE OF RESEARCH IN EDUCATIONAL PSYCHOLOGY

This chapter section introduces you to some of the basic concepts in educational research necessary for your evaluation and use of research reports. The primary theme is the relationship between basic and applied research. In developing this theme we shall consider the following topics: the differences in methodological and theoretical rigor and in the educational relevance of basic and applied research; six steps on the research continuum stretching from the most basic to the most applied research on learning; the distinction between independent and dependent variables; the definition and use of hypotheses; the distinction between and use of experimental and control groups; and the relationship of experimental and correlational studies. We conclude this section with a brief consideration of the uses of research in educational psychology.

Basic and Applied Research

Research in educational psychology is both basic and applied (Cronbach, 1966; Gilbert, 1962; Hilgard, 1964; Melton, 1959; and Wittrock, 1967). Hilgard (1964) makes the following distinctions between them. Basic (or pure-science) research is pursued without regard for the immediate applicability of the results to practical situations. Although the investigator may ultimately be interested in the application of his findings, he does not allow this interest to determine his choice of problem, theory, and research procedures. Basic research is more interested in methodological and theoretical rigor than in practical relevance. Applied research is pursued primarily to develop instructional techniques and products which will have immediate classroom use. Although the early phases of applied research may occur in laboratory classrooms, the research purpose is the engineering of specific products which will be tested (or proved) later under ordinary classroom conditions. Applied research is more interested in educational relevance than in methodological and theoretical rigor.

Although this distinction helps us to separate basic and applied research, it is also useful to think of them as occupying different points on a single continuum. Contrary to popular misconceptions, the psychology of learning is a product of both basic and applied research and often the result of a single research program. In repudiating popular misconceptions, Melton (1959, p. 105) writes:

> These and many other false implications will be avoided if it is remembered that basic and applied research lie on a single continuum, and that the variable involved is the freedom of the investigator in the manipulation of independent variables. Obviously the more constraints one places on the freedom of the investigator to manipulate variables, the more restricted will be the information gained from the research. Much basic research that goes on in our laboratories of psychology in universities suffers constraints, such as the nonavailability of subjects other than college sophomores or the limitation of subject availability to one hour, which act to limit the scientific process and restrict the generality of findings; on the other hand it is not difficult to conceive of a truly basic research effort on concept formation which would be conducted entirely in a school setting.

As an illustration of the laboratory constraints Melton refers to, Gilbert (1960, pp. 484–85) tells this anecdote:

> This friend tells the story of his last venture into the laboratory investigation of human learning when some years ago, as a newly produced experimental psychologist, he set about to study human avoidance conditioning, presumably because there was an old hand-shock grid cluttering the laboratory. He was well equipped in the classical tradition. He had a theory (something about an inscrutable mediating between light and shock). He had a group of male college sophomores, carefully matched for sex and education. He had an experimental design, a properly conservative two-tailed t test. And to complete the Galilean picture, he had a standardized source of uncontrolled variation: a wholly mysterious set of instructions designed to startle the most self-satisfied mediator out of its hypothetical existence. The first of the sixty scheduled sophomores proved too unsophisticated for such a high-level setting. When the experimenter threw the switch which flashed a light and pulsed a shock,

> the subject blandly kept his hand on the grid. Trial after trial the shock intensity increased without a twitch from the indifferent hand when, on the final trial, with the current at a searing maximum, the subject's steady fingers began to smoke. At this point, the experimenter's fine consideration for scientific control gave way to understandable human curiosity, and he asked the subject why he didn't move his hand. The subject's reply provided perhaps the finest opportunity for scientific discovery since Skinner's first automatic food-magazine broke down. The subject simply said, "I thought you were studying how much *guts* I had!" My friend thereupon canceled the schedules of the remaining fifty-nine sophomores, and today he is productively engaged in the investigation of the eating and defecating behavior of hooded rats. Alas, he may have foregone the opportunity to provide us the first systematic and quantitative methodology for the study of human courage.

At the applied end of the continuum, research in educational psychology has often suffered from different constraints: the insistence on developing procedures and products which will immediately revolutionize the modern classroom. In lamenting the serious lack of basic educational research, Cronbach (1966, p. 540) writes:

> But today's proudest educational ideas, as practiced in the shiniest of suburban schools, seem to be little more effective than the stereotyped programs that the majority of American schools have been running off in their sleep for a generation or more. To be sure, the research literature reports that this or that innovation is an improvement; over and over you will find the phrase, "The new method produces greater learning than the old; the difference is statistically significant." This telltale phrase usually means that the difference is not large enough to impress the naked eye, and that statistical analysis had to be invoked to dispel the suspicion that the difference occurred by chance. Educational improvements that really make an impact on the ignorance rate will not grow out of minor variations of teaching content and process. Effective educational designs, worth careful development and field trial, can emerge only from a deep understanding of learning and motivation.

Consistent with Cronbach's position, Wittrock (1967, p. 17) defines educational psychology as the "scientific study of human behavior in educational settings." Such a study, he believes, combines basic and applied research but emphasizes basic research:

> As scientists, we [educational psychologists] should attempt to describe, understand, predict, and control behavior in education. That is, educational psychology should invest most of its resources into its most important activity—basic research aimed at control and under-

standing of the problems and phenomena of instruction in schools. Research explicitly aimed at the production of useful knowledge is an activity defensible in its own right, with its own important *products*—functional relations, generalizations, and theories.

The Research Continuum

Hilgard (1964, pp. 405–10) distinguishes six research steps, which he describes as points on the continuum leading from the most basic to the most applied research on learning. Figure 16-1 shows these steps.

Step 1. Research on learning with no regard for its educational relevance, e.g., animal studies; physiological, biochemical investigations. Learning in the flatworm and learning in the rat with transected spinal cord classify here.

Step 2. Research on learning which is not concerned with educational practices but which is more relevant than that of step 1 because it deals with human subjects and with content that is nearer to that taught in school, e.g., nonsense-syllable memorization and retention. The principles being tested are likely to be theoretical ones, such as the relative importance of proactive and retroactive inhibition.

Step 3. Research on learning that is relevant because the subjects are school-age children and the material is school subject matter or skill, though no attention is paid to the problem of adapting the learning to school practices, e.g. foreign-language vocabulary learned by paired-associate method with various lengths of lists and with various spacing of trials.

Fig. 16-1. *Steps in research on learning—pure research to technological development (after Hilgard, 1964, p. 406).*

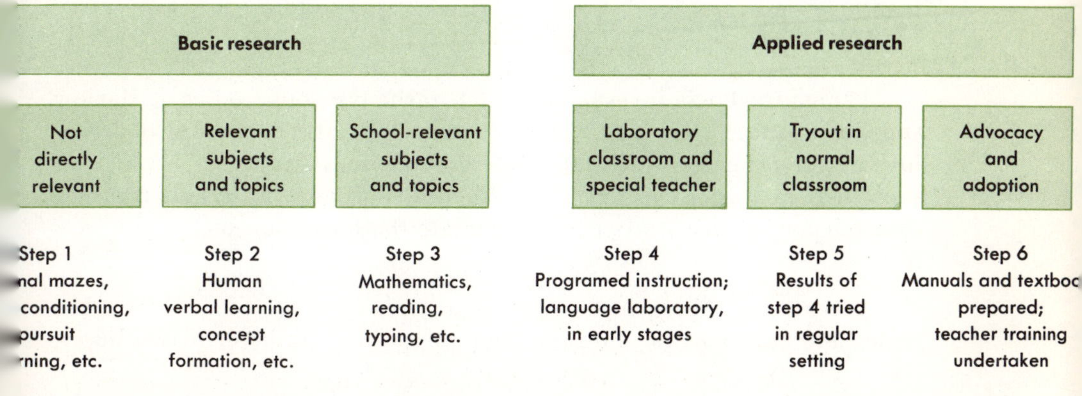

Step 4. Research conducted in special laboratory classrooms, with selected teachers, e.g., bringing a few students into a room to see whether or not instruction in set theory or symbolic logic is feasible, granted a highly skilled teacher.

Step 5. A tryout of the results of prior research in a "normal" classroom with a typical teacher. Whatever is found feasible in step 4 has to be tried out in the more typical classroom which has limited time for the new method and may lack the special motivation on the part of either teacher or pupil.

Step 6. Developmental steps related to advocacy and adoption. Anything found to work in steps 4 and 5 has to be "packaged" for wider use and then go through the processes by which new methods or procedures are adopted by those not party to the experimentation.

Research in educational psychology, according to Hilgard, has been deficient in steps 4 and 5. Educational psychologists have conducted most of their investigations in the area of steps 1 and 2 and then have made inferential jumps to step 6. Research is needed all along the continuum.

Examples of research steps. The following examples of research on learning roughly correspond to the six steps described by Hilgard.

The first study, the formation of learning sets in rats, illustrates step 1. In reading Study I (which you should do at the conclusion of this paragraph) note that the authors are not concerned with the educational relevance of the problem or findings. Note also that the use of animal subjects extends previous animal experimentation and also locates this study at that end of the research continuum farthest from classroom application. Although you know from Chapter 3 that learning sets are useful means of describing entering behavior, this particular study would have to progress several additional steps before classroom application was possible. The next step would be to study learning sets in children (a step that has been taken).

STUDY I. The Formation of Learning Sets in Rats
(Koronakos and Arnold, 1957).

Problem. These investigators refer to the previous studies of Harlow and his associates (see p. 69) which demonstrate the formation of learning sets in primates. They also refer to previous studies of rats which show that at least some rats have the ability to generalize and transfer. The purpose of this study is to investigate the formation of learning sets in rats.

Procedure. The subjects were twenty experimentally naive rats, ten males and ten females. The rats had to learn to push open two doors, one in each of two chambers, to obtain a food reward. The unlocked door in each case was the one door among five which bore a design different from those on the other doors. In one case, for example, the unlocked door bore an *X*, while the four locked doors bore plus signs. The rats also had to select the *X* among a second set of five doors. Each animal had ten trials a day. The correct door never appeared in the same position twice in succession and never was in the same position as the second door. When the rat chose the correct door 80 per cent of the time, it was given the next oddity problem (e.g., four circles, one triangle, choose door with triangle).

RESULTS. Figure 16-2 shows the performance of the only five rats to reach the 80 per cent standard on all seven oddity problems. Each point represents the mean performance on the first ten trials. The figure shows that the rats accelerated their rate of learning; they solved later problems more quickly than earlier ones. By problem 6 they were right about 70 per cent of the time on the first ten trials. Analysis of the performance of individual rats showed great variation in performance but the same general pattern of improvement in the ability of the rats to solve later problems.

Fig. 16-2. *Response curve of the five rats which reached the accepted standard of performance. Note the rise in the curve with successive problems. Each point represents mean performance on the first ten trials for problems 2 to 7 (after Koronakos and Arnold, 1957, p. 12).*

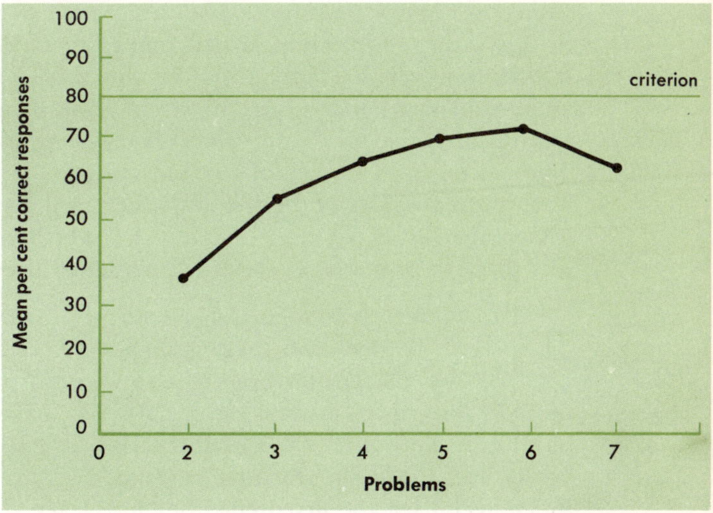

DISCUSSION. The investigators state that the results indicate that rats as well as primates form learning sets. They also state that an alternative explanation of their results is that the problems varied in difficulty and that their presentation in descending order of difficulty yielded these results. Although no objective study was made of problem difficulty, they state that it does not appear reasonable that the results could be entirely explained in this way.

The second study, transfer between paired-associate and serial learning, illustrates step 2. In reading Study II note that the author is not concerned with the educational relevance of the problem and findings. Two characteristics of this study, however, bring it one step nearer to what is taught in the classroom: (1) It deals with human subjects, in this case college students; and (2) it deals with language or verbal learning. Even though the actual learning materials used in the study are not relevant to the classroom, the study could be conducted with verbal materials used in the classroom in teaching particular verbal skills or subject matter.

STUDY II. Transfer Between Paired-Associate and Serial Learning *(Jensen, 1962).*

PROBLEM. Jensen investigates the differences between learning a list of paired associates and learning a serial list (see Chapter 9). He reviews the traditional conception of serial learning, which views it as a form of stimulus-response learning. The stimulus for each successive response, in this theory, is the item which immediately precedes it in the list. Research, however, has not supported this theory because only a negligible amount of transfer has been found in going from a paired-associate (PA) to a serial list, even though the lists are composed of the same elements. The paired-associate list, of course, is acquired through stimulus-response learning. Jensen hypothesizes that there will be more transfer from the PA to the serial list under conditions which make it easy for the subject to carry over his set for PA learning to the serial task.

PROCEDURE. Jensen used 171 college juniors and seniors as subjects. They were divided into three groups: (1) the odd group learned pairs 1-2, 3-4, 5-6, 7-8; (2) the even group learned pairs 2-3, 4-5, 6-7, 8-9; (3) the control group did not learn a PA list. All three groups learned the serial list. Both the PA and the serial lists contained the same items. Jensen facilitated the learning of the odd group by making the first items in the serial list the first items they had learned as paired associates.

RESULTS. Table 16-1 shows that the odd group learned the items of

TABLE 16-1

SUMMARY OF DATA FOR SERIAL LEARNING FOR EXPERIMENTAL AND CONTROL GROUPS (after Jensen, 1962, Fig. 1).

Group	Trial 1 Errors		Trials to Criterion		Per Cent Errors	
	M	S.D.	M	S.D.	M	S.D.
Control	7.83	1.10	24.98	7.73	43.79	7.31
PA (odd)—Serial	5.70	1.49	16.50	6.91	36.69	9.90
PA (even)—Serial	7.02	1.48	22.48	8.40	42.87	9.01

the serial list significantly faster than the even and control groups did. "Trials to criterion" refers to the acceptable standard of performance, in this case three successive trials without error. Using the t ratio (explained below) as the test of significance, he found that the odd group did significantly better than the even group and the control group ($p = 0.001$). The even and control groups did not differ significantly from each other ($p = 1.00$). (The expression p is explained below.)

Discussion. The findings support Jensen's hypotheses that the paired-associate set facilitates serial learning, that, without this set, the subject adopts a strategy peculiar to serial learning; and that serial learning does not occur as a chain of *S-R* connections.

The third study, the role of grapheme-phoneme correspondence in the perception of words, illustrates step 3. In reading Study III note that the authors are concerned with the educational relevance of their research—they are searching for the critical unit of language for reading in English. Three characteristics of this study illustrate step 3: (1) It is the outgrowth of the cooperation of a subject-matter specialist, in this case a linguist (Hockett), and of research psychologists; (2) although the particular subjects in this experiment were not school-age children, the authors could easily replicate the study using these children; and (3) it concerns an important skill taught in the schools—reading. This study remains, however, an example of basic research because the investigators pay no attention to the problem of adapting the learning to classroom conditions.

STUDY III. The Role of Grapheme-Phoneme Correspondence in the Perception of Words

(Gibson, Pick, Osser, and Hammond, 1962).

Problem. The letters in the English alphabet do not always correspond to English phonemes (see Chapter 9). This study investigates the critical unit of language for reading in English. The hypothesis is that this reading unit is comprised of spelling-to-sound correlations. It is not defined by speech alone or by writing alone. By simultaneous exposure to graphic and phonemic stimuli, a child who learns to read well forms useful spelling-to-sound correlations. The hypothesis is based on the work of Charles Hockett in discovering the rules by which pronunciation can be predicted from spelling. The specific hypothesis for this study is: Skilled readers will discriminate pseudowords constructed according to rules of spelling-to-sound correlations better than words that are not constructed according to these rules.

PROCEDURE. The subjects were twenty-one college students in a class on the psychology of language. Two types of pseudowords, using the same letters, were constructed: those observing and those ignoring the spelling-to-sound rules. Examples of the former words are *dink, vuns,* and *glox*. Examples of the latter words (using the same letters), are *nkid, nsuv,* and *xogl*. In random order fifty pseudowords were flashed on a screen, and the students were told to write what they saw.

RESULTS. Figure 9-11 (p. 377) shows that students scored consistently higher on those pseudowords with spelling-to-sound correspondences. Using the Wilcoxon Matched Pairs Signed Ranks Test, the experimenters found that the difference between the two types of words was significant ($p = 0.01$, two-tailed).

DISCUSSION. Results show that a letter group with high spelling-to-sound correlation is reproduced more accurately than an equivalent letter group of low spelling-to-sound correlation. The proper unit for analyzing the reading process is not the alphabet letter but the spelling pattern as it relates to the phonemic pattern. Skilled readers perceive *superforms,* which are compounded from their simultaneous hearing, speaking, and reading of words.

It is more difficult to find illustrations which illustrate the remaining three steps because the conditions of applied research can vary considerably. The following examples are rough approximations of the step characteristics they illustrate.

The fourth study, programed instruction vs. usual classroom procedures in teaching boys to read, roughly illustrates step 4. The study has more classroom relevance than the previous studies because it is directly concerned with the practical problems of reading instruction. In reading Study IV note that the first more than the second phase illustrates step 4. There are three characteristics of the first phase: (1) The instruction occurs in a special laboratory classroom equipped with the necessary instructional media; (2) the use of programed instruction provides highly skilled instruction; and (3) the skill which is taught, certain aspects of reading, is one taught in school. If the study were more typical of step 4, it would use fewer students, live instruction by a highly skilled teacher, and omit the second phase, which more properly illustrates step 5.

STUDY IV. Programed Instruction vs. Usual Classroom Procedures in Teaching Boys to Read

(McNeil, 1964).

PROBLEM. John McNeil refers to previous studies which show that girls are more successful than boys in beginning reading. Since the inferior performance of the boys may be due to the differential treatment they receive from female teachers, McNeil proposes the use of programed instruction as a method of eliminating this treatment. His hypothesis is that boys will do better than girls in beginning reading under programed instruction but will lose this superiority when taught by female teachers.

PROCEDURE. The experiment had two phases, programed reading instruction and live reading instruction using female teachers. McNeil used 130 kindergarten boys and girls in the first phase and followed many of these pupils through the second phase. A pretest measured their knowledge of letter words and their ability to recognize configurations of letters, the content of the programed instruction lessons. Lessons were projected on a large screen in the form of questions. Each child sat in an individual laboratory-type booth equipped with headphones through which he heard a taped commentary. The pupil answered questions by pushing one of three buttons; a green light followed his response if correct, a red light is incorrect. Unlike the situation in the typical reading classroom, the boys and girls had equal opportunity to respond and obtain encouragement. A posttest (covering some of the knowledge and skills of the pretest) followed the first phase. In the second phase, seven female teachers provided live instruction in reading in typical classroom environments. A posttest also followed this phase.

RESULTS. Table 16-2 shows that the boys' achievement was superior to the girls' following programed instruction but inferior to the girls' following live instruction. Also pupils reported that the boys received more disciplinary comments than the girls under live instruction.

DISCUSSION. Boys learn to read better than girls under programed instruction but not under live female instruction. Programed instruction may improve the performance of boys because it reduces peer-group interaction and the number of opportunities to display male aggression.

TABLE 16-2

ACHIEVEMENT ON WORD-RECOGNITION TEST FOR FIRST AND SECOND PHASES (after McNeil, 1964, p. 116).

	Following Programed Instruction		Following Instruction by Female Teacher	
	M	S.D.	M	S.D.
Boys ($N = 49$)	26.4	9.0	31.7	11.0
Girls ($N = 44$)	23.6	8.4	38.3	11.9
	$t = 2.24$		$t = 2.75$	
	$p = 0.05$		$p = 0.01$	

The fifth study, teaching capitalization with a programed text, illustrates step 5. The study has more classroom relevance than the previous studies (with the exception of the second phase of Study IV) because it occurs in typical classrooms. In reading Study V note the following characteristics which illustrate step 5: (1) The experimentation occurs in a regular classroom with regular pupils; (2) we do not know for certain but we may assume that the investigators are using a revised and not the original version of the program even though they indicate that more revision is necessary; and (3) the program is teaching a skill which these pupils must ordinarily learn. If the study were more typical of step 5, we would know more about the original versions of the program, its success and failures in a laboratory classroom, and the effects of substituting carefully designed live instruction for programed instruction. The second phase of Study IV illustrates two characteristics of step 5: moving from the laboratory to the average classroom and using regular rather than expert instruction.

STUDY V. Teaching Capitalization with a Programed Text
(Schutz, Baker, and Gerlach, 1962).

PROBLEM. The purpose of the study is to evaluate the experimental application of a self-instructional program designed to teach elementary students how to capitalize words acceptably. This evaluation should uncover problems programed instruction poses in the typical elementary classroom.

PROCEDURE. The subjects were thirty-six fourth and fifth grade pupils attending summer school. The children varied widely in general level of ability and achievement. After taking a standardized test on capitalization as a pretest, the pupils were taught how to use a program. They were then given the experimental linear program with which they worked from eleven to sixteen days, for a total of about five to eight hours.

RESULTS. Table 16-3 shows the means and the standard deviations for the two grades on the pretest and posttest. The average (mean) gain for the fifth grade pupils is significant ($p = 0.01$) but for the fourth grade pupils it is not. When the investigators inspected individual test scores, they saw that some pupils performed far above and other pupils far below average.

TABLE 16-3

COMPARISON OF PRETEST AND POSTTEST RESULTS FOR THE TWO GRADES (after Schultz *et al.*, 1962, p. 360).

	Grade 4		Grade 5	
	M	S.D.	M	S.D.
Pretest	4.3	1.5	5.9	1.5
Posttest	4.8	1.5	7.2	1.3
Difference	0.5		1.3	

DISCUSSION. The significant effect in the fifth grade can be attributed to particular individuals. The results suggest these inferences for the investigators: (1) The program contains some ambiguous, misleading, and otherwise faulty items; (2) because the program failed to teach capitalization rules well for some students, the revision requires changes which insure that each pupil can state a rule before applying it to a novel situation; and (3) the program does not control for entering behavior, particularly reading vocabulary.

The sixth study, the effect of changes in programed text format and reduction in classroom time, illustrates step 6. The study has complete classroom relevance because this training prepares the students for a job they must soon perform. In reading Study VI, note the characteristics which illustrate step 6: (1) The author is taking steps in developing the program for serious adoption in an industrial training program; (2) the material has been packaged, and it is now being modified to save time and improve learning and attitudes; and (3) previous experimentation shows that the programed material provides at least minimal achievement of instructional objectives. If the study were more typical of step 6, the author of the materials and the original investigator of their use would not be the same individual who tries out the material in this step, and the materials would be used by trainees of other companies.

STUDY VI. Effect of Changes in Programed Text Format and Reduction in Classroom Time on the Achievement and Attitude of Industrial Trainees
(Hughes, 1962).

PROBLEM. In the original program designed to teach the maintenance of a data-processing system, John Hughes found three disadvantages: (1) The student had to turn the page to find the correct answer to a frame; (2) the student wrote answers in the tests, which therefore could not be reused; and (3) frequent repetition of written answers was boring and fatiguing for the student. By introducing certain program modifications, Hughes seeks improvement in (1) learning achievement, (2) trainee attitude, and (3) speed of program completion.

PROCEDURE. Hughes used two groups of subjects, seventy men who used the original program and served as a control group and 129 men, studying at a later period, who used the new program and served as four experimental groups. Both programs were linear and dealt with the names and functions of data processing units—data flow, bit coding, types of computer words, and program steps. The live instructor had only to keep a record of time for program completion. The time for working on the program was reduced from fifteen to eight hours. The treatments of the four experimental groups differed as follows: Group I found the correct frame answers on the next page of the text and wrote all the answers in the text; group II found the correct frame answers on the next page of the text and wrote all the answers on a separate pad; group III found the answers on the back of the page and wrote all the answers on separate answer pads; and group IV found the correct answers on the back of the page and wrote only 17 per cent of the answers on a separate pad (only those answers required by the drawings). All groups received an achievement test and a questionnaire which asked about their reactions.

RESULTS. Table 16-4 shows means and standard deviations for achievement. Hughes found no significant differences among means but he did find significant differences among standard deviations: That for experimental group I was significantly greater than those for the other classes ($p = 0.01$), using Bartlett's test of homogeneity of variance. Also, the standard deviation for experimental group II was significantly greater than that for group III ($p = 0.02$). Using the F test (explained below), Hughes found that reducing the amount of classroom time reduced uniformity of achievement and produced more pronounced individual differences among students. He also found that the reduction in classroom time had a negative effect on the attitudes of the trainees, although in the main they preferred programed to conventional instruction.

DISCUSSION. Variability in achievement is greater with the new than

TABLE 16-4

ACHIEVEMENT TEST SCORES FOR ALL GROUPS (after Hughes, 1962, p. 47).

Experimental Condition	Number of Classes	Number of Students	M	S.D.
Control	6	70	95.1	4.0
I	2	33	93.7	6.8
II	2	28	94.3	4.8
III	3	44	95.0	3.6
IV	2	24	95.3	3.3

with the original program because the reduction in classroom time provides less time to master the subject matter. However, it is possible to reduce presentation time by 47 per cent without affecting mean achievement. Also it is not necessary to write out the answers, and, although the correct frame answers are in plain view and enable the student to cheat, this location of the answer does not reduce achievement.

The last three studies (IV, V, and VI) illustrate that we are dealing with a research continuum rather than discrete types of research. Many research studies you may try to classify may embrace more than one step. You have seen, for example, that Study IV covers steps 4 and 5, Study V covers steps 4 and 5, and Study VI covers steps 5 and 6.

Types of Variables

In designing, communicating, and reading research in educational psychology it is useful to distinguish between independent and dependent variables. There are three characteristics of an *independent variable:* (1) It is the variable manipulated by the experimenter; (2) it is the presumed cause of the experimental effects; and (3) it is the basis for predicting the experimental effects. The previous studies provide many examples of independent variables. Consider these:

	Independent Variables
Study I	Successive trials on oddity problems
Study II	Making the first items in the serial list the first items of the PA list
Study III	Pseudowords which observed and ignored grapheme-phoneme correspondence
Study IV (first phase)	Use of programed instruction to teach reading
Study V	Use of programed instruction to teach capitalization
Study VI	Differences in program format and reduction in classroom time

By comparing the variables in these studies, you can observe that the independent variables of the first three (basic) studies are more precisely defined than the variables of the last three (applied) studies. Programed instruction in the last three studies refers to several independent variables, including the various characteristics of the program and the conditions under which it was used. In all six cases, however, the independent variables are those manipulated by the experimenter, are the presumed cause of the learning, and are the basis for predicting what would probably happen.

A *dependent variable* has two characteristics: (1) It is the presumed effect of manipulating the independent variable, and (2) it is the effect which is predicted. The previous studies provide many examples of dependent variables. Consider these:

	Dependent Variables
Study I	Performance of the rats in solving the oddity problems
Study II	Transfer of learning to the serial list
Study III	Performance of the students in reading two types of pseudowords
Study IV (first phase)	Knowledge of letter words and skill in recognizing letter configurations
Study V	Performance on a standardized test on capitalization
Study VI	Performance on a test of knowledge of computer functions and reactions to a questionnaire on attitudes

Perusal of this list of dependent variables should reveal that they are terminal performances which result from the manipulation of the independent variables in the previous list. In the three applied studies the dependent variables are mostly test performances, while in the three basic studies they are mostly performances the experimenters directly observe.

The dependent variables of one study may be the independent variables of another. In Study IV, for example, we could reverse the position of the independent and dependent variables and study the effect of various levels of reading achievement on the use of programed verbal materials. In this case reading achievement becomes the independent variable and the programed materials the dependent one. Similarly, in Study VI, we could study the effects of trainee attitude on their ability to learn programed materials and thereby reverse the relationship of the two variables.

Hypotheses

A hypothesis is a statement of the probable relationship between independent and dependent variables. Consider these examples of hypotheses:

1. *If* conditions make it easy for the student to carry over his set for PA learning to the serial task, *then* there will be more transfer from the PA to the serial list (Study II).

2. *If* pseudowords constructed according to spelling-to-sound rules are presented to skilled readers, *then* they will recognize them more quickly than words not constructed according to these rules (Study III).

3. *If* boys are taught beginning reading through programed instruction, *then* they will read better than girls (Study IV).

These examples should reveal the following characteristics of hypotheses: (1) They are declarative sentences which specify relations between variables; (2) the independent variables follow the "if," while the dependent variables follow the "then"; and (3) they contain clear implications for objective measurement.

Fred Kerlinger (1965, p. 22) describes three reasons why hypotheses are essential in scientific research. First, they are the working instruments for theory. Because they can be deduced from theory and from other hypotheses, they become the chief means of theory building. Second, they can be tested for their truth and falsity. Acceptance of the relationship the hypothesis expresses must rest on the obtained facts. Third, they are powerful tools for advancing human knowledge because their probable truth or falsity rests outside the experimenters' attitudes and opinions. In summary, we could not have a theoretical and objective science without the use of hypotheses. Kerlinger writes (p. 28): "The scientist cannot tell positive from negative evidence unless he uses hypotheses."

Experimental and Control Groups

Several of the previous studies used experimental and control groups. An experimental group is one in which the independent variable is manipulated. The control group is a comparison group which receives no special treatment or a treatment distinct from that of the experimental group. Consider these examples:

Study	Experimental Groups	Control Groups
II. PA and serial learning	Odd group with PA set and even group without PA set	Group which did not learn PA list
IV. Boys and reading	Boys under programed instruction	Girls under programed instruction; girls and boys under female instruction

VI. Training for computer maintenance	Groups I through IV distinguished by programing format mode of response, amount of learning time	An earlier group who studied the program in the original form and who had more learning time

You can see from these examples that the characteristics of control groups can vary from experiment to experiment. In Study II the two experimental groups each operate with a different set in learning the serial list. The control group is the only one of the three groups which did not learn the PA list. In Study IV, first phase, the boys are the experimental group because the hypothesis tells us that the major relationship investigated is the relationship between the reading achievement of boys and programed instruction. Although the girls receive the same instruction, they serve primarily as a comparison, or control, group. In the second phase, in the comparison of the achievement of the boys under programed and female instruction and in the comparison of their achievement, with the achievement of the girls under these two conditions, the boys in the second phase act as a control for the boys in the first phase, who, indeed, are the same boys. Similarly, in Study V, the pupils act as their own controls when their preprogram capitalization skill is compared with their postprogram skill. In Study VI, the major comparison is between the four groups who use the modified program and have less time and the earlier group who used the original program and had more time. The author calls the original group the control group because they provide the major comparison. The four experimental groups differ in the degree to which their learning conditions are modified. Group I, for example, studies the same program as the control group did but is given less time for study. Group IV, on the other hand, is also given less time but they do not write most of the answers to the frames and can see the correct response when they turn the page.

The primary purpose for using control groups is to eliminate rival hypotheses as alternative explanations of the experimental results. Campbell and Stanley (1963, pp. 175–76) have identified several factors which, left uncontrolled, can effect the dependent variable as much or more than the independent variable. Among these factors are the following:

1. History or the unique events which may occur between a pretest and posttest and affect the results, e.g., an antimachine riot breaking out during an experiment on teaching machines. A repetition of the experiment without these events occurring may produce quite different results.

2. Maturation or the development or changes within the student occurring largely as a result of time. In a reading experiment, for example, some improvement between pretest and posttest may be due to the collateral reading the student does independently of the experiment. Also students grow over time more bored, older, and more tired.
3. Testing or the effect of pretesting on the experimental results. The process of measuring may change what is measured. On intelligence and achievement tests, but particularly on attitude and personality-adjustment tests, students taking the same or alternative form of the test do better the second than the first time.
4. Instrumentation or the decay of the measuring instrument over time. In scoring answers to essay tests, for example, the scorer may shift his standards during different scoring periods or the observer or interviewer may shift their emphases in using their schedules.
5. Reactivity or the increase of the students' sensitivity to the desired experimental outcomes through the use of the pretest. Students ordinarily try to divine the experimenter's intent. The types of roles students assume when they know they are experimental subjects are often unrepresentative of the school situation.

Some other uncontrolled causes of experimental effects described by Campbell and Stanley are considered below under sampling and sampling bias. In examining the design and conclusions of educational research, you should try one or all of these factors as alternative explanations for the experimental results.

Experimental and Correlational Studies

In Chapter 6 (pp. 203–205) we considered the distinction between experimental and correlational studies and their relative usefulness in providing for entering behavior. We can define correlational studies as follows: They investigate the relationship of two or more variables as they exist in nature. Here is a fictitious example (suggested by Campbell and Stanley, p. 235) of a correlational study:

> Dr. I. See decides to study the relationship between the amount of education of school superintendents and the length of their tenure in office. He is also interested in the relationship between the amount of their education and the quality of their schools. He finds these positive correlations: (1) that the greater the amount of education of the superintendents, the higher the quality of the schools, and (2) [that] the longer the tenure of the superintendents, the higher the morale of the schools. Dr. I. See concludes that the edu-

> cation of the superintendents and the stability of their tenure *cause* better schools and higher morale. This study examines the relationship of four variables: amount of education, quality of the schools, length of tenure, and level of morale. It is a correlational study.

Chapter 6 pointed out that correlational studies suggest causes of behavior, while experimental studies isolate causes. The six studies summarized earlier in this chapter are experimental studies; they isolate causes of learning. It is true that Dr. See's study suggests that the education and the stability of superintendents result in better schools and higher morale. It also suggests that better schools with higher morale may attract the better-educated superintendents and hold them longer than the less fortunate schools do, a conclusion which reverses that of Dr. See. This study is useful because it suggests both hypotheses, both of which will require subsequent research. The chief function of correlational studies in educational psychology is to survey several hypotheses to recommend experimental studies of the more promising. Experimental studies are generally more expensive than correlational studies, which can perform the useful function of screening out the less promising independent variables.

Uses of Research in Educational Psychology

The previous quotations of leading educational psychologists suggest several uses of educational research: (1) the development of theories of teaching, (2) improved teaching materials or products, and (3) improved teaching practice in all four components of the basic teaching model.

Concerning the first use, Wittrock (1967, pp. 17, 20) argues strongly for basic research in educational psychology to build an organized body of knowledge:

> I suggest that in our methodology we emphasize the following practices: (1) use as laboratories for research those situations and subjects which sample the phenomena we strive to study; (2) use sophisticated apparatus to control carefully the presentation of stimuli and the recording of responses; (3) use designs and analyses that will evidence interactions among treatments and groups of individuals; (4) in "true experiments," obtain data about treatments which differ from one another conceptually; and (5) test theoretical approaches to instruction.

Kerlinger (1964, p. 12) also believes that the development of theory should be the basic aim of research in education. Theories, he contends, have wider applicability and usefulness than nontheoretical findings do. Kerlinger states:

> Theories, because they are general, apply widely to many phenomena and to many people in many places. A specific relation, of course, is less widely applicable. If, for example, one finds that test anxiety is related to test performance, this finding, though interesting and important, is less widely applicable and less understood than if one first found the relation in a network of interrelated concepts that are parts of a theory.

The next two uses, dealing with improved products and practices, can be outgrowths of the basic research described by Wittrock and Kerlinger or of applied research which has an almost solely practical emphasis. Much of the early research on instructional films and television and on programed instruction and teaching machines focused directly on improved products and practices without considering the theoretical base for such research. Indeed, much more educational research has focused on practice than on theory building. As I mentioned before, Hilgard (1964) believes that there may be too much research in educational psychology at steps 2 and 6 and too little at steps 4 and 5. Indeed, we have very few examples of learning research which progresses from the development of products under laboratory-classroom conditions to their careful tryout and revision under conventional classroom conditions. It may very well be that we need a greater coordination of research efforts all along the research continuum (Gilbert, 1962).

Ebel (1967, p. 81) gives three reasons why basic research will not improve the educational process: Its past record of performance is poor, there are serious basic difficulties which indicate that the future will not improve this poor performance, and the educational process is not a natural phenomenon, such as has rewarded scientific study in fields like physics and biology. In arguing for applied research, Ebel (p. 84) asserts, "Let us also push, and rather more strongly, the kind of survey research that provides data crucial to the decisions we must make. Let us not worship pure science and basic research unrealistically and irrationally."

Hilgard's research continuum is an easy resolution of the two positions, one emphasizing basic research, the other emphasizing applied research. Gilbert (1962, pp. 569–70) emphasizes the coordination of efforts of basic and applied investigators:

> If scientists working in a midwestern university create the basis for developing an efficient means for controlling stuttering, the presence of a similar scientist in an educational development program could

> make the difference in whether the developmental activities began to produce an engineered product now or in ten years . . . the presence of an exploratory [basic] research operation in a developmental setting may be the determining factor in whether or not these scientists work on problems relevant to education.

Gilbert convincingly argues that coordinated efforts keep basic research focused on educational problems and applied research focused on the fruitful use of laboratory findings.

The reading and evaluation of research reports, the major focus of this chapter, also have three practical uses. The reports can (1) suggest further research which must be undertaken before classroom application is possible; (2) indicate which research may be undertaken in a particular school to find out which modifications must be made of practices and products before they can be adopted for local use (step 6 in the research continuum); and (3) suggest changes in procedures and products that can be immediately implemented. In all three cases you, as the consumer of these reports, should keep abreast of the present state of knowledge and know how to proceed in proposing either an extension of the research or the immediate implementation of its findings in your school and classroom.

Summary

Basic research is concerned with theoretical and methodological rigor, while applied research is concerned with practical relevance. They occupy different points on a single continuum, stretching from research on animal learning to the modification of packaged instructional materials for local use. Hilgard has identified six steps on this research continuum from the most basic to the most applied research. I provided an example of a study for each step. Educational psychologists may conduct their research in one or several of these six areas. The variable manipulated by the experimenter is the independent variable. The presumed effect of this manipulation is the dependent variable. The dependent variables of one study may be the independent variables of another. Hypotheses are statements of the probable relationship between independent and dependent variables. In an experimental group, the independent variable is manipulated. The control group is a comparison group which receives no or different treatment. The use of control groups eliminates rival hypotheses as alternative explanations for the experimental results. Correlational studies investigate the relationship of two or more variables. They are useful in suggesting hypotheses for later experimental studies. There are several uses of research in educational psychology, extending from the development of teaching theories to improved teaching practices in the four components of the basic teaching model.

You should now return to objectives 1–8 (pp. 700–701) and determine how well you have achieved them.

QUESTION 16-1

An educational psychologist has assessed under laboratory conditions the effects on student behavior (as indicated by an achievement test) of a film on drug usage; he now intends to assess its effectiveness in public school classrooms. On the basis of this brief description answer the following questions:

(a) At which of Hilgard's six steps does his intended research (in public schools) occur?

(b) What is the independent variable in the intended study?

(c) What is the dependent variable in the study under laboratory conditions?

(d) State the hypothesis in the form of an if-then statement.

EVALUATION OF THE RESEARCH REPORT

Your use of educational research depends largely on your skill in assessing the research reports appearing in educational and psychological journals. This chapter section deals with the four major parts of these reports; it describes their major characteristics and the steps you should take in assessing each part. As the summaries of the six preceding reports indicate, most reports have four major parts: (1) a statement of the problem and hypotheses; (2) a description of the procedures, including the selection and use of subjects and materials; (3) a description of the results, including the analysis of the data; and (4) a statement of the conclusions drawn by the investigator. This section also deals with sampling as it pertains to acceptable research procedure. Sampling is the selection and assignment of subjects to experimental and control groups. I reserve extended consideration of the analysis of data for the following chapter section, which deals with statistical inference and tests of significant differences.

Step 1. Read the Entire Report and Identify the Four Major Parts

Most research reports do not label their major parts as distinctly as the six preceding summaries do. They often provide statements of problems and hypotheses, for example, without using these designations.

The parts may not be clearly distinct; descriptions of hypotheses may appear under procedures, and descriptions of results may include the inferences the investigator draws from the results. To identify the major parts of these reports, you must know their typical characteristics.

THE PROBLEM. Although this first part of the research report shows the greatest amount of variation in the journals, it is possible to identify the following characteristics. First, the description of the problem states the purpose of the study and sets the stage for the reader. The author delimits his study and focuses attention on the particular area of investigation. Second, this section may be very long or very short. In dissertations and lengthy investigations it tends to be long and detailed. In many journals, in which space must be conserved and the authors can assume considerable background knowledge of the reader, it may be very short. Third, this section should ask or at least imply a question about the relationship between variables. In Study II, for example, Jensen asks about the transfer effects of PA learning on subsequent serial learning. In Study VI Hughes asks about the possible effects of changes in programing format and of the reduction of time. Fourth, and most important, this section should contain statements of subproblems or hypotheses. These statements require greater linguistic precision than the general problem statement. Finally, there should be a review of the previous research.

PROCEDURES. There are two parts to this section of the report: a description of the selection and assignment of subjects and a description of the methods of collecting data, including materials, apparatus, tests, and so on. A description of subject selection should include who the subjects are, from what population they are selected, why they are selected, and how they are selected and assigned. The assignment of subjects involves questions about proper sampling and the proper formation of experimental and control groups.

RESULTS. The third part of the report describes the findings of the investigation. This part usually has the following aspects: It summarizes the data as means and standard deviations, and it reduces the data to tables and graphs, as illustrated in the six studies. The summaries of Studies I and III present the data as graphs, while those of the remaining studies present the data as tables. This part has one further characteristic: It provides a statistical analysis of the data to determine the significance of the results.

CONCLUSIONS. In this part the investigator interprets his results. Usually we expect him to provide the following elements: how the data confirm or disconfirm the hypothesis; the limits imposed on his conclusions because of his procedures; alternative conclusions which can be drawn from his data; and the implications his study has for further research and for school use.

Step 2. Inspect the Report for Adequate Descriptions

A report should include adequate descriptions of the hypotheses, previous research, methods of data collection, and selection and assignment of subjects.

Adequately stated hypotheses have these characteristics: The independent variables are described in terms of the procedures used in introducing them; the dependent variables are described in terms of the measuring instruments used to assess terminal performances as experimental effects; and the relationship of the hypotheses to their theoretical base and to previous research is carefully delineated. Because adequate descriptions of hypotheses often require investigators to describe methods of data collection, you may find statements of hypotheses in the procedure section rather than in the problem section of the report. In Studies II and III the statements of hypotheses fulfill all the necessary requirements.

The review of the research should be adequate enough to serve two purposes: to state the theoretical rationale of the problem and to inform the reader of what research there now is and how the investigator plans to extend this knowledge. Jensen, in Study II, carefully explains the theoretical rationale for his hypothesis to show the inadequacies of a stimulus-response explanation of serial learning. Because publishing costs have risen so rapidly, many journals do not provide the authors the space they need for an adequate review of the literature.

The description of methods of data collection must be adequate enough to allow you to evaluate their appropriateness for the problem and the hypothesis and their appropriate application. They should answer most of your questions about how the data were collected and enable you to distinguish between those collection methods and alternative procedures. In the six previous studies you can find detailed descriptions of methods. In Study VI, for example, Hughes describes the exact modifications he made in the program format. In Study III, Gibson and her associates describe the formation and the use of the pseudowords.

Finally, there must be adequate description of the procedures employed in the selection and assignment of subjects. We have already considered what this description must consist of. The previous summaries briefly describe the experimental subjects—rats, college students, elementary school children, and industrial trainees. The five studies using human subjects are not good illustrations of adequate descriptions of sample selection and assignment because, for the most part, they used intact classes.

Step 3. Evaluate the Sampling Procedure

To perform this function you must distinguish between a population and a sample. A *population* is any group of students or scores alike in one or more ways. A *sample* is any group of students or scores less than the total number in that population. Consider the following examples:

Populations	Samples
All college students	Students in Harmony Haven College
All elementary school children	Elementary school children in California
Nannette, Opal, Patience, and Queenie	Nannette, Patience, and Queenie
Populations	**Samples**
Students in Harmony Haven College	Members of the football team at Harmony Haven College
Seniors at Harmony Haven	Seniors majoring in science at Harmony Haven
All achievement test scores	Scores on the mathematics achievement test

In perusing these examples note these characteristics of populations and samples: The sample is always smaller than the population, often representing only a fraction of it; the sample in one example may be the population in another; the population in one example may be the sample in another; and some populations (e.g., all college students, all elementary children) are too large to study in their entirety. In almost all educational research we study samples and not populations.

RANDOM SAMPLING. This method of drawing a sample of a population guarantees that each population member has an equal chance of being selected. Kerlinger (1964, p. 52) states that in random sampling we have a "democracy of selection in which all members are equal before the bar of selection." He uses this example (p. 53):

> Suppose we have a population of one hundred children. The children differ in intelligence. We want to know the mean IQ of the population, but for some reason we can only sample thirty of the one hundred children. If we sample randomly, there are a large number of possible samples of thirty each. These samples have an equal and known probability of being selected. It can be shown that the means of most of these samples of thirty will be relatively close to the mean of the population. A few will not be close. The

> probability of selecting a sample with a mean close to the population mean, then, is greater than the probability of selecting a sample with mean not close to the population mean—if the sampling has not been random. If we do not draw our sample at random, however, some factor or factors unknown to us may predispose us to select a biased sample, in this case perhaps one of the samples with a mean not close to the population mean. If the one hundred children were known to us, we might unconsciously tend to select the more intelligent children. It should be emphasized that it is not so much that we would do so; it is that our method *allows* us to do so. Random methods of selection do not allow our biases or any other systematic selection factors to operate.

Several methods select and assign subjects at random. The best procedure is to use a table of random numbers often found in the appendix of statistics textbooks. These numbers have been machine-generated and have no discernible order. A number is assigned to each subject, and the subject in turn is selected and assigned on the basis of his number alone. A common randomizing procedure, somewhat less reliable than the use of a table of random numbers, involves placing the subjects' names on slips of paper which are tossed into a box and drawn by chance. You can also select and assign subjects by using the roll of dice.

SOURCES OF SAMPLING BIAS. If the investigator uses random sampling, he is likely to avoid sampling bias. If he does not, you, in reading the report, must look for various sources of sampling bias. You can ask the following questions about the soundness of the sampling. First, did the investigator use volunteers? For example, if Hughes in Study VI had used only volunteers for answering the questionnaire on his program and on the amount of class time, he might have obtained many more favorable replies than he did because many disgruntled subjects might have chosen to express no opinion rather than to voice their complaints. Second, have subjects been lost? More technically, the loss of subjects, especially in studies conducted over periods of months and years, is called *subject mortality*. Unfortunately, subjects are not lost on a random basis, and they generally vary from those who remain. In Study IV, for example, if McNeil had lost many of his female and male subjects in the second phase of the experiment, it would be difficult to make his comparison of the effects of programed and live instruction. If, for example, some of the boys who were lost were the poorer readers, then he would find an even greater difference between the effects of the two types of reading instruction. Third, are common sources of school bias avoided? Campbell and Stanley (1963, p. 184) suggest these sources: time of day, day of the week, portion of the semester, nearness to examinations, and choice of investigators. For example, college students who register for an afternoon section of a required course may differ from those who register for a morning section. Also the performance of a student early in the semester may differ remarkably from his performance later on. Fourth, is the sample representative of the population to which the experimental results are applied? If a study of present-day sexual morality of American males and females uses a sample of college men and women, we would indeed question its validity for all American men and women. Fifth, have the subjects been assigned on a random basis? If the investigator wants to discover the effectiveness of programed instruction and assigns to the classes using programed instruction only the brightest students who have already learned well what the program will teach them and assigns to the control classes only the dolts who never seem to learn anything under any conditions, we may suspect a grievous case of sampling bias. The experimenter should not only randomly assign students to experimental and control groups but also randomly assign treatments to these groups. Which groups receive programed instruction should be determined by chance after the groups have been formed. Finally, has the investigator used a large enough sample? A common research rule is to use samples as large as possible. Some sample bias arises from sampling error, which is described next. Within limits, the larger the sample size, the smaller the sampling error. As you will see, the amount of sampling error can be estimated.

SAMPLING ERROR. Sampling error is the variability among the means of many samples drawn from the same population. Consider this situation. You want to determine the level of achievement in physics of all graduating high school seniors. Since you do not have the time, resources, or authority to administer the test to the entire population of graduating seniors, you randomly select 1,000 samples of fifty students each from high schools throughout the nation. After determining the mean scores for each sample of fifty students, you discover that the means and the standard deviations vary. You must decide which mean and standard deviation are the most accurate for the graduating senior population. Unfortunately you have no direct way of finding the population mean and standard deviation, short of administering the test to all graduating seniors, an alternative we need only mention in order to discard. There is a method, however, of estimating the population mean and standard deviation. First you assume that the mean of the sample means is also the population mean. Then you assume that the standard deviation of the sample means is the standard deviation of the population. The resulting statistic is called the *standard error of the mean*. Table 16-5 shows you how this statistic is computed. Later you will see how the standard error of the mean is used in computing the t ratio.

Step 4. Check the Validity and Reliability of the Procedures

The investigator must use those procedures and instruments which yield valid and reliable data. Valid procedures and instruments provide the tests of hypotheses implied in the statement of the problem and of the description of the hypotheses. Using conventional televised and nontelevised lectures as the procedure in determining the effectiveness of programed instruction in mathematics achievement is an example of an invalid procedure. Using personality tests to determine mean IQ is an inappropriate and invalid use of these instruments. To a large extent

TABLE 16-5

HOW TO COMPUTE THE STANDARD ERROR OF THE MEAN.

Formula: $SE_M = \frac{s}{\sqrt{n}}$

SE_M = standard error of the mean
s = standard deviation of the sample means
n = the number of samples

Problem: The investigator draws three samples of IQ scores to estimate the intelligence of children in American cities. He obtains these sample means: 101, 100, and 99. Find the standard error of the mean.

Step 1: Compute the mean of the sample means. ($M = 100$)
Step 2: Compute the standard deviation of the sample means, using Table 15-4. ($s = 0.812$)
Step 3: Substitute the numbers in the formula as follows:

$$SE_M = \frac{s}{\sqrt{n}} = \frac{0.812}{\sqrt{3}} = 0.464$$

the reader can judge the validity of the research procedures in much the same way he judges the validity of classroom tests. If the investigator has developed new instruments and tests, such as interview schedules, questionnaires, and tests of creativity, he must demonstrate their validity independently of the study in which he uses them.

It is also important to collect reliable evidence. This requires the correct application of the procedures and instruments. If, for example, the experimenter does not provide training and care in the use of programed materials and test administration, very good instruments may provide unreliable information. Carelessness in the use of well-designed questionnaires and interview schedules, lack of training in using observation schedules, carelessness in the recording of data, and modifications of procedures after the experiment is underway all result in untrustworthy data. The study should establish and report the reliability of its evidence.

Step 5. Check the Analysis of Data

The report should outline and defend the methods of data analysis. As seen in the previous summaries, it is generally enough to mention the test of statistical significance used if it is a common test. If it is uncommon, the investigator must describe the method in sufficient detail for the competent critic to judge its appropriate and correct application. In the chapter section which follows we will consider several tests of statistical significance.

Step 6. Evaluate the Conclusions of the Report

In his conclusions, the investigator must answer the question of whether the data confirm or do not confirm the hypothesis. He should present his results in statements, tables, and graphs that convey them clearly. He should then provide clear statements of the conclusions, substantiated by the evidence he has collected. He should consider alternative explanations which seem to fit his data. If you, as the reader of the report, can think of suitable alternative conclusions, the investigator has most certainly failed to support his hypothesis. The tone of this section should be scientific and objective rather than partisan and polemic. Most findings of sound research are not shocking violations of common sense. If the report arrives at conclusions which defy ordinary human experience, good judgment, and the findings of earlier related studies, you may suspect and discover serious shortcomings in the design and execution of the investigation.

Summary

I have described six steps in the evaluation of research reports. In the order in which they should be taken they are: (1) Read the entire report and identify the four major parts; (2) inspect the report for adequate descriptions of hypotheses, previous research, methods of data collection, and procedures and instruments; (3) evaluate the sampling procedure; (4) check the validity and reliability of the procedures; (5) check the analysis of data; and (6) evaluate the conclusions of the report.

You should now return to objectives 9–15 (p. 701) and determine how well you have achieved them.

QUESTION 16-2

Mr. I. M. Careful, a research educational psychologist, was conducting a study on curiosity. His hypothesis was that school children subjected for one hour to low-stimulation environments would become more curious than children subjected for one hour to high-stimulation environments. A valid and reliable test of curiosity was his measure of the dependent variable. The children in the school volunteered for the experiment. As they lined up outside and entered his laboratory door he assigned each a number from the table of random numbers and then assigned each to one of three chambers: the high-stimulation chamber, the low-stimulation chamber, or a normal classroom. When the first child entered, for example, he was given a random number and was assigned to chamber 1. When the second child entered, he was also given a random number and was assigned to the second chamber. In this manner and order the other children were assigned to the different experimental conditions.

Which of the following statements is the best evaluation of Mr. Careful's sampling procedure?

(a) It is random in both assignment and selection of subjects.

(b) It is random in assignment but not in selection of subjects.

(c) It is random in selection but not in assignment of subjects.

(d) It is random neither in assignment nor in selection of subjects.

After selecting your answer, give the reasons for your choice.

ANALYSIS OF DATA

This chapter section should help you evaluate the statistical analyses of data which usually appear in the result section of the report. We will consider the testing of the null hypothesis and levels and tests of statistical significance. The significance tests discussed are the t ratio, based on the standard error of the differences between means; the F ratio, based on the analysis of variance; and the Chi square test. This section concludes with a brief consideration of nonparametric tests and factor analysis.

The Null Hypothesis

The null hypothesis states that there is no difference between two populations or samples. Here are some examples of null hypotheses:

1. There will be no significant difference in how quickly children read pseudowords constructed on the basis of grapheme-phoneme correspondence and how quickly they read those not constructed on this basis.

2. Boys will read as well under live female instruction as under programed instruction.

3. Students with the set for PA learning will learn the serial list in the same number of trials as will students without this set.

Although the forms of these statements vary somewhat, each statement asserts that the investigator will find no significant differences between experimental and control groups.

The research hypothesis, unlike the null hypothesis, usually has these characteristics: It asserts that there will be a difference between experimental and control groups, and it is expressed in verbal terms. The null hypothesis, on the other hand, is a statistical hypothesis either stating or clearly implying quantitative measure. Kerlinger (1964, p. 174) writes, "The *null hypothesis* is a statistical proposition which states essentially that there is no relation between the variables (of the problem). The null hypothesis says, 'You're wrong, there is no relation; disprove me if you can.'" In this sense, no matter what the research hypothesis asserts, the experiment must disprove the null hypothesis.

The test of the null hypothesis relates clearly to sampling error and the standard error of the mean. When you test this hypothesis, you try to determine if the difference between the means of the two samples (for example, the experimental group and the control group) is larger than can be expected from sampling error. This is why we say that the difference between the groups must be significant—a small amount of difference may not be enough. If the difference between two samples is larger than that which the investigator can expect from sampling error, he can reject the null hypothesis and assert, with reasonable pride and confidence, that there is a significant difference.

Statistical Significance

For a difference to be statistically significant it must depart from chance expectation. In the previous summaries, note the appearance of these expressions: $p = 0.01$; $p = 0.05$; or $p = 0.10$. The p is the abbreviation for probability. The expression $p = 0.01$ means that the probability of the obtained difference occurring by chance is only one out of one hundred trials. The expression $p = 0.001$ means that the probability of the obtained difference occurring by chance is only one out of 1,000 trials. Although the practice of reporting the value of all *p*'s is becoming widespread, research convention views all *p*'s below 0.05 as not statistically significant—an insufficient basis, that is, for rejecting the null hypothesis. This convention has been frequently challenged because it may result in the rejection of potentially useful hypotheses (Rozeboom, 1960).

How large a difference is significant? Three general guidelines to follow are these: (1) the 0.01 level is about 2*s* from the mean; (2) the 0.05 level is about 2.5*s* from the mean; and (3) the 0.001 level is about 3*s* from the mean. The farther the level is from the hypothetical mean, the less chance there is that the differences are due to chance.

The *t* Ratio

The *t* ratio is the test of statistical significance used when the investigator is dealing with two sample means. In Study II, for example, Jensen used the *t* ratio to determine the possible significant difference in mean learning trials between the odd group (with the PA set) and the even group (without the PA set). McNeil in Study IV used the *t* ratio to determine the possible significant difference between the reading means of the boys and girls following programed instruction. Table 16-6 shows you how to compute the *t* ratio. You see that you must first compute the standard error of the mean and then use a *t*-ratio table to find out whether the *t* ratio is significant.

The F Ratio

When the investigator compares more than two means, he often uses the *F* ratio to determine the possible statistical significance of his results. In Table 16-7, for example, Kerlinger uses the *F* ratio to compare two basic attitudes toward education—progressivism and traditionalism—of three groups of individuals. Kerlinger hypothesized that those individuals outside the university had the highest mean and that the graduate students of education had the lowest mean (i.e., were the least traditional). The independent variable was group membership; the dependent variable was the members' attitudes. The use of the *F* ratio enabled him to reject clearly the null hypothesis since the difference between the means is highly significant. His research hypothesis, therefore, found considerable support.

To compute the *F* ratio, one uses a method of data analysis known as the *analysis of variance*. This method uses variances entirely instead of the standard error of the mean. In essence the investigator compares

TABLE 16-6

HOW TO COMPUTE THE *t* RATIO.

Formula: $$t = \frac{M_a - M_b}{\sqrt{SE_{M_a}{}^2 + SE_{M_b}{}^2}}$$

t = t ratio (also called t test or critical ratio)

M_a = mean of sample a

M_b = mean of sample b

$SE_{M_a}{}^2$ = square of standard error of the mean for sample a

$SE_{M_b}{}^2$ = square of standard error of the mean for sample b

Problem: Mr. Patrick wanted to find out whether students learned programed mathematics better with overt (written) or covert (mentally rehearsed) responses. He selected two samples of one hundred each from the tenth grade population and assigned one group the overt and the other group the covert treatment. Both groups were given a test of mathematics achievement after completing their programs. Mr. Patrick found that the mean score of the overt group was 60, of the covert group 50. The standard deviations of both groups were 10. Using the t ratio, determine whether this difference is significant.

Step 1: Determine the means of samples a (overt) and b (covert). ($M_a = 60$; $M_b = 50$)

Step 2: Compute SE_{M_a} and SE_{M_b} by using Table 16-5. ($SE_{M_a} = 1$; $SE_{M_b} = 1$)

Step 3: Square the results of step 2.

($SE_{M_a}{}^2 = 1$; $SE_{M_b}{}^2 = 1$)

Step 4: Substitute the numbers in the formula and perform the indicated operations:

$$t = \frac{60 - 50}{\sqrt{1+1}} = \frac{10}{1} = 10$$

Using a statistical table, we find $p = 0.001$ (highly significant).

the variance between groups and the variance within groups. In experimental studies the between-group variance is the measure of the dependent variable, the effect produced by the independent variable. The within-group variance is the measure of chance error. Obviously, for the F ratio to reach the level of statistical significance the between-group variance must sufficiently exceed the within-group variance. In Table 16-7 you can see that the within-group variance is far greater than the between-group variance, as indicated by the mean square for each one.

Jimmy Amos and his associates (1965, p. 87), with the use of the

TABLE 16-7

HOW TO COMPUTE THE F RATIO.

Formula: $F = \dfrac{m.s._{\text{bet.}}}{m.s._{\text{with.}}}$

F = F ratio (or F test)

* $m.s._{\text{bet.}}$ = mean square between groups

* $m.s._{\text{with.}}$ = mean square within groups

	Graduate Students	Undergraduates	Persons Outside
n:	157	136	305
M:	3.84	4.43	5.19
S.D.:	0.93	0.84	0.86

Source of Variance	Degrees of Freedom	*s.s.*	*m.s.*	*F*
Between groups	2	197.20	98.60	128.05 (0.001)
Within groups	595	457.85	0.77	
Total	597	655.05		

Data from study of attitudes toward education, based on the Traditionalism attitude scores (Kerlinger, 1964, p. 200).

In computing the F ratio, take these steps:

Step 1: Compute the mean square between groups. ($m.s._{\text{bet.}} = 98.60$)

Step 2: Compute the mean square within groups. ($m.s._{\text{with.}} = 0.77$)

Step 3: Substitute the numbers in the formula and divide.

$$F = \frac{98.60}{0.77} = 128.05$$

Consulting an F ratio table at the indicated degrees of freedom (explained below), you find that this ratio is highly significant ($p = 0.001$).

* For the computation of these statistics, see one of the standard statistics texts listed at the end of this chapter.

Fig. 16-3. *Curves showing the variance of the groups in two experiments. Dr. Smith's groups show greater between-group variance, Dr. Jones's greater within-group variance (after Ames* et al.*, 1965, p. 87).*

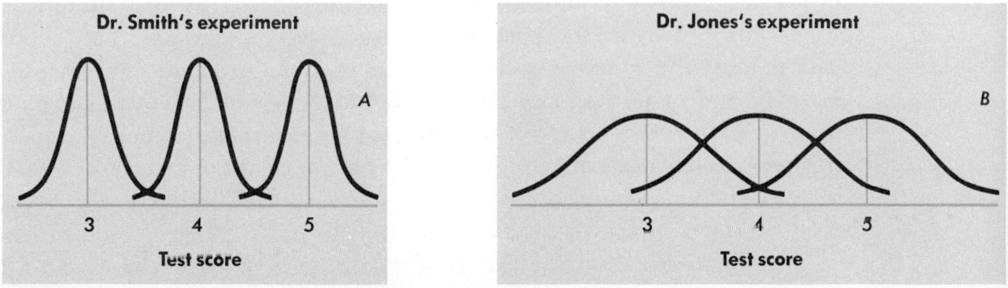

curves in Fig. 16-3, show how three groups of scores compare in two different experiments. In their respective experiments, Drs. Smith and Jones compared three methods of instruction. The curves show the distribution of scores for each method and both experiments. You can see that Dr. Smith's experiment will have a significant F ratio because the variance between groups is greater than the variance within groups (i.e., the scores are less spread out). Dr. Jones's experiment will not have a significant F ratio because there is much more overlap of scores and the variance within the three groups is considerably larger than the variance between the groups (i.e., the scores are spread out too much).

When $F = 1.00$ or less, the difference is always not significant. The size of F in Table 16-7 indicates the high level of significance of this result.

The Chi-square Test

A third test of the null hypothesis is the Chi-square test. Whereas the t ratio and the F ratio deal with the means and the variances of groups, the Chi-square test deals with expected frequencies. Table 16-8 shows the computation of Chi-square as a test of the hypothesis stated there. The particular frequencies are those on an opinion survey of prospective teachers. The observed frequencies are those yielded by the actual survey. The expected frequencies are those hypothesized by the null (no-difference) hypothesis. After obtaining Chi-square (in this case 12.5), you obtain an entry from a Chi-square table according to what are called *degrees of freedom* (*df*). Degrees of freedom are computed with this formula: $df = (r - 1)(c - 1)$, or $(2 - 1)(3 - 1)$, or 2, where r = row and c = column. Unlike the previous significance tests we have considered, the Chi-square test applies to scores which are and are not normally distributed.

Nonparametric Statistical Tests

The investigator uses nonparametric tests when he does not know or ignores the distribution shape and variance of the population scores. Ordinarily (but not always), in using the parametric tests, the t ratio, and the F ratio, we assume that the scores are normally distributed and that variances within the groups are statistically the same. You should recall that in the F test, if the variances within the groups vary widely, the likelihood of finding significant differences between groups is greatly reduced. The F ratio, therefore, may not be significant when there is a significant difference between groups. The use of the t ratio and F ratio

TABLE 16-8

HOW TO COMPUTE CHI-SQUARE.

Formula $\chi^2 = \Sigma \left[\frac{(O - E)^2}{E} \right]$

$\chi^2 =$ Chi-square
$\Sigma =$ sum of
$O =$ observed frequencies
$E =$ expected frequencies

Problem and hypothesis (null): There will be no difference in the number of responses for each of three kinds of responses. Thirty prospective teachers were asked their opinion about the desirability of introducing technological innovations into the classroom. The survey results are below.

Step 1: Record expected and observed frequencies as follows:

	Yes	No	Undecided
O	20	5	10
E	10	10	10
Step 2: $O - E$	10	−5	0
Step 3: $(O - E)^2$	100	25	0
Step 4: $\frac{(O - E)^2}{E}$	10	2.5	0

Step 5: Substitute the numbers in the formula and perform the indicated operations.

$$\chi^2 = 10 + 2.5 + 0 = 12.5$$

Consult Chi-square table, with two degrees of freedom. $p = 0.01$.

also assumes that the measuring instruments are continuous measures with equal intervals. We make this assumption, for example, in using intelligence and achievement tests. When, however, you are merely classifying data, as in the Chi-square test, or ranking scores, as in the rank-order correlation (*rho*), you cannot assume that your measures have equal intervals. In fact, Chi-square and *rho* (Chapter 15) are the two nonparametric tests you have already learned about.

In evaluating research reports, you may well follow Kerlinger's (1964, p. 260) advice: The investigator should be expected to "use parametric statistics, as well as the analysis of variance, routinely, but [to] keep a sharp eye on data for gross departures from normality, homogeneity of variance, and equality of intervals." Since nonparametric tests are often quick and easy to use, Kerlinger also suggests their use as preliminary but not definitive tests. Among the widely used nonparametric tests you will find in research reports are the following ones: the binominal test, the sign test, the median test, the sum of ranks test, the Kruskal-Wallis test, and the Friedman test.*

Factor Analysis

Factor analysis is a method of determining the number of underlying variables among a large number of measures (Kerlinger, 1964, p. 650). These underlying variables are called *factors*. Kerlinger uses this example to illustrate factor analysis. We administer six tests to a large sample of seventh graders and hypothesize that the six tests are not measuring six different variables but a smaller number of variables. These are the names of the six tests and their labels: vocabulary (*V*), reading (*R*), synonyms (*S*), numbers (*N*), arithmetic (*AS*), and a teacher-made arithmetic test (*AT*). We score the tests and compute the coefficients of correlation between each test and every other test. We then make a matrix, or table, of coefficients. Table 16-9 shows the matrix for these six tests. Kerlinger (p. 651) states that we can now ask two questions: (1) How many underlying factors are there? and (2) what are these factors? To answer the first question note the circled coefficients in Table 16-9, cluster I and cluster II. The coefficients for tests *V*, *R*, and

TABLE 16-9

A MATRIX OF CORRELATIONS SHOWING A VERBAL FACTOR (CLUSTER I) AND A NUMERICAL FACTOR (CLUSTER II) (after Kerlinger, 1964, p. 651).

		V	R	S	N	AS	AT
	V		0.72	0.63	0.09	0.09	0.00
Cluster I	*R*	0.72		0.57	0.15	0.16	0.09
	S	0.63	0.57		0.14	0.15	0.09
	N	0.09	0.15	0.14		0.57	0.63
	AS	0.09	0.16	0.15	0.57		0.72
	AT	0.00	0.09	0.09	0.63	0.72	
						Cluster II	

* For a discussion of these and other nonparametric tests see S. Siegel, *Nonparametric Statistics for the Behavioral Sciences*. New York: McGraw-Hill Book Company, 1956.

S in cluster I range between 0.57 and 0.72. Similarly, the coefficients for tests *N, AS,* and *AT* in cluster II range between 0.57 and 0.72. Finally, the tests in cluster I are relatively uncorrelated with those in cluster II, the correlations ranging from 0.00 to 0.16. The two clusters appear to be two underlying factors.

To answer the second question about what the factors are, you must think of names which explain them. It appears that a factor called *verbal ability* is common to cluster I and that a factor called *numerical ability* is common to cluster II. Kerlinger stresses that the name of the factor should describe the common operations in the tests within the cluster. It would be inappropriate, for example, to call the factor in cluster II *arithmetic* since this would omit the operations in test *N*. You should also remember that these names are tentative or hypothetical. If you were to add a seventh test to this six-test battery, you might discover quite different clusters and you would then have to assign new and appropriate names to them.

The mathematical operations involved in factor analysis are beyond the scope of this book. Our illustration uses the cluster method, which depends on inspection and subjective judgment. Centroid methods use more objective factor analyses (see Thurstone, 1947). However, even this brief description of factor analysis should indicate its relationship to multifactor theories of intelligence (see Chapter 4) and to coefficients of correlation (see Chapter 15).

Summary

The evaluation of a research report requires knowledge of the statistical analysis of data. First, you must distinguish between the null hypothesis, which asserts no differences among groups, and the research or nonstatistical hypothesis, which usually asserts that there will be a difference. Second, a statistically significant difference must depart from chance expectation beyond the $p = 0.05$ level. We discussed several tests of statistical significance. In determining the difference between only two means, use the t ratio. When testing the difference between two or more means, use the F ratio, based on the analysis of variance. In determining the differences between frequencies, use the chi-square test. Use nonparametric tests, such as chi square and rho, when scores do not form a normal distribution, when variances are not homogeneous, and when measures do not have equal intervals. Finally, use factor analysis to determine underlying variables among a large number of factors.

You should now return to objectives 16–22 (pp. 701–702) and determine how well you have achieved them.

QUESTION 16-3

> The investigator administered a questionnaire to prospective teachers, asking their degree of agreement or disagreement with the use of team teaching in elementary schools. For each question the respondent could check one of these choices: strongly agree, agree, undecided, disagree, strongly disagree. The investigator wanted to test this hypothesis: There will be no difference among these response choices. Answer these questions:
>
> (a) Which type of hypothesis is he testing?
>
> (b) Which significance test should he use? (1) *t* ratio, (2) *F* ratio, (3) Chi square, (4) rho. Defend your choice.

SUMMARY

This chapter has dealt with the nature, use, and evaluation of research in educational psychology. It has stressed the importance of the relationship of applied and basic research and illustrated points along the research continuum with descriptions of various investigations. The chapter identified many characteristics of formal studies: independent and dependent variables, hypotheses, experimental and control groups, and experimental and correlational studies.

We examined six steps you can take in evaluating research reports: identifying the major parts—the problem and hypothesis, the procedures, the results, and the conclusions; distinguishing between adequate and inadequate descriptions of each part; evaluating the sampling procedures, especially for uncontrolled sources of sampling bias; evaluating the validity and reliability of the procedures and instruments; checking the analysis of data for adequate and clear reporting of results and the correct choice of significance tests; and, finally, evaluating the conclusions by testing alternative explanations.

The most technical aspect of your evaluation is the critique of the statistical analysis of data. To make this part of your evaluation, you must distinguish between the research and the null hypotheses and have familiarity with levels of statistical significance: *t* ratios, *F* ratios, Chi square, nonparametric tests, and factor analysis.

SUGGESTED READINGS

The following excellent texts and handbooks discuss the nature of psychological inquiry and research in education and educational psychology:

Bachrach, Arthur J., *Psychological Research: An Introduction*. New York: Random House, 1962. (paper)

Gage, Nathan L., ed., *Handbook of Research on Teaching*. Chicago: Rand McNally & Co., 1963.

Hyman, Ray, *The Nature of Psychological Inquiry*. Englewood Cliffs, N.J.: Prentice-Hall, Inc., 1964. (paper)

Kerlinger, Fred N., *Foundations of Behavioral Research: Educational and Psychological Inquiry*. New York: Holt, Rinehart & Winston, Inc., 1964.

Travers, Robert M. W., *An Introduction to Educational Research* (2nd ed.). New York: The Macmillan Company, 1964.

The following guides and checklists are useful in the evaluation of research in educational psychology:

Borg, Walter R., "Critical Evaluation of Research," in *Educational Research: An Introduction,* pp. 326–45. New York: David McKay Co., Inc., 1963.

Rummel, J. Francis, "Criteria for Judging Research Reports," in *An Introduction to Research Procedures in Education* (2nd ed.), pp. 267–69. New York: Harper & Row, Publishers, Inc., 1964.

Van Dalen, Deobold B. and William J. Meyer, "Evaluation," in *Understanding Educational Research: An Introduction,* pp. 442–54. New York: McGraw-Hill Book Company, 1966.

Wandt, Edwin, *A Cross-Section of Educational Research.* New York: David McKay Co., Inc., 1965, pp. 7–13. (paper)

The following useful texts deal with statistics in education and psychology:

Amore, Sidney J., *Introduction to Statistical Analysis and Inference for Psychology and Education.* New York: John Wiley & Sons, Inc., 1966.

Blommers, Paul and E. F. Lindquist, *Elementary Statistical Methods.* Boston: Houghton Mifflin Company, 1960.

Popham, W. James, *Educational Statistics: Use and Interpretation.* New York: Harper & Row, Publishers, 1967.

Tate, Merle W., *Statistics in Education and Psychology.* New York: The Macmillan Company, 1965.

The following authoritative texts are for students who want to explore advanced statistical procedures and research design:

McNemar, Quinn, *Psychological Statistics* (3rd ed.). New York: John Wiley & Sons, Inc., 1962.

Winer, J., *Statistical Principles in Experimental Design.* New York: McGraw-Hill Book Company, 1962.

Answers to Questions

1-1

The quotation describes mainly a philosophy of education. It refers to the goals and values which, according to the speaker, an educational system should embrace, such as the development of free minds. The passage is not a theory of teaching, despite the reference to classroom decisions, materials, and procedures. It does not answer the questions which tell how teachers should behave, for what reasons, and with what consequences. The passage is not a theory of learning because it does not describe and explain the conditions under which learning occurs. At best it describes conditions under which learning does not occur.

1-2

The first step of Herbart's method best fits the computer-based model and that part of the model described as the pretutorial phase. Carroll's model is not so strong a choice because it is not explicit enough about the preparation for instruction. The ability to comprehend instruction (in Carroll's model) is more general than the apperceptive mass, but Carroll's notion of aptitude may be similar to that of apperceptive mass. The interaction model is not a good choice because nothing in it is exactly equivalent to the apperceptive mass. Also, while Flanders assumes that learning and teaching should be the emergent products of student and teacher interaction, Herbart assumes that what is to be taught is largely predetermined by the teacher. The purpose of his preparation is to find a common ground between preselected topics and students.

1-3

The Jesuit model is least similar to Smith's. The formalism of the Jesuit school made the flexible interaction implied in Smith's model difficult even though no teaching method entirely rules out the interaction Smith describes. The Socratic method is a poor choice because that method involved the highly skilled interaction of teacher and student, even though Socrates did not have Smith's model to work with. The only respectable defense of this choice is the fact that Socrates may have made a careful assessment of student needs, interest, and so on, although we may also infer, since Socrates was something of a bully, that the student may have carefully tried to perceive and diagnose Socrates' behavior and respond to him. The personal-development model is not a good choice since its basic implication is the accommodation of the needs and interests of the students. The teacher can perceive those needs and interests only through an interaction such as described by Smith. In Smith's model, however, the teacher is probably more of a controlling stimulus than Combs and Snygg would like him to be. In my opinion, the Socratic model is most similar to Smith's model because it comes closest to the balance between student and teacher perceptions which Smith's model describes.

2-1

The best answer is (c). The second objective, you will see, however, fills only one of the requirements of adequate statements of instructional objectives. The two remaining objectives suggest but do not specifically describe observable performance.

2-2

The best answer is (a). The terminal performance is the selection of striated muscles, the standard of performance is 100 per cent mastery, and the condition of performance is the list given to the student. Answer (b) is not acceptable because it does not clearly indicate the acceptable level of performance. Answer (c) lacks a clear description of the conditions under which the student should do the listing. For example, does he have access to charts, reference books? Is he selecting his list from a longer list?

2-3

The best choice is (b). To make the correct identification of fossils the student has to learn the abstract properties of fossils, those properties which characterize all fossils. Such learning involves more than correctly naming a fossil (verbal association) and involves less than the discovery of a higher-order principle (problem solving)—for example, the relationship of fossils to various geological ages.

3-1

The answer is (c). Selecting the proper vowel depends at least on distinguishing between vowels and nonvowels (consonants) and also on the specific recognition of vowels in the trigram context. She did not describe these entering behaviors. Answer (a) is not a good choice because Miss Pegg is not likely to succeed unless through happy coincidence or divine intervention the students know more than she is assuming they know. In the case of (b), terminal performance is adequately defined, but entering behavior is not.

3-2

The answer is (c). By working backward from the instructional objective to discover prerequisite learning, Mr. Chips was using Gagné's method of determining learning sets. The question of ordering examples for the purpose of acquiring concepts (in this case, figures of speech) pertains to selection strategies.

Answer (a) is only partially correct since the statement does not refer to the speed (or conceptual tempo) with which the objective is achieved. Answer (b) is only partially correct since Jensen describes learning abilities as processes within the individual and not as performances (as in the question). Finally, both parts of (d) are incorrect since the question contains no direct references to basic learning sets (learning to learn) or to learning abilities.

3-3

The correct answer is (a). Mr. Wright never prepared a test of entering behavior in the first place. He prepared a pretest or a posttest based on what the students were about to learn (terminal performance) not on what they had already learned (entering behavior). Neither alternative (b) nor (c) is acceptable because Mr. Wright cannot make these decisions until he prepares the proper test and uses it to assess the entering behavior of his students.

4-1

The answer is (c). Such a statement indicates that the child is thinking at the level of concrete operations, which would be typical of a child in the third grade (age 8). Alternatives (a) and (b) are both adequate (if somewhat unsophisticated) statements of the law. They require the child to see a relationship between the plunger's angle of inclination and the ball's angle of reflection after it hits the wall. A child who understands this relationship is thinking at the level of formal operations—a feat we would not expect in the third grade. Answer (c) simply reports an observation which the child can use as an explanation.

4-2

The answer is (b). "Knowing how to find out" crudely identifies what Piaget calls operations and schemata. Answer (a) is a poor choice because the speaker seems to be referring more to actual than to potential capacity. Answers (c) and (d) do not seem very relevant, unless you reasoned that "knowing how to find out" is a single factor (like "reasoning power") or several factors referring to the various ways in which an individual finds information and problem solutions. If you did reason this way, I can still claim that (b) is a better choice because of the reference to development, the major focus of Piaget's theory.

4-3

The answer is (b). This is a test of intelligence designed specifically for college students. It is a group test and requires relatively little time. Choice (a) (the Stanford-Binet) requires individual administration and, with seventy-five advisees, there is hardly enough time. You would not choose (c) if you were convinced by McNemar's findings. The DAT along with other batteries are expensive and time consuming and really make no better predictions than do tests of general intelligence.

4-4

Dr. *A* is the most logical choice. All the information we have indicates that he is the best surgeon, particularly because he would have been graded on his surgical performance during his medical training. We can grant that Dr. *B* is better than Dr. *C*, but what information do we have that he is better than Dr. *A*? Sometimes students choose Drs. *B* and *C* because they believe that these men may combine surgical competence with a warm bedside manner. But to assume that Dr. *A* does not have a warm bedside manner is to be guilty of the stereotyping described previously.

5-1

The best answer is (b). Only this alternative denotes a possible increase in the vigor of the individual's (Horatio's) effort. The alternatives can all be explained in terms of learning or innate ability, and so on. In (a), Hortense's steady progress is simply a measure of her increased learning. In (c), no evidence shows any increase in vigor, and it is suggested that Havelock possesses innate swimming ability. In (d), the reference to Henrietta's habit is also a reference to learning rather than to motivation.

5-2

The best answer is (a), although you may argue. By matching problem difficulty and student ability, Mr. Seiting is dealing with arousal and potential anxiety and frustration. High-anxiety students of superior ability find anxiety facilitating, whereas students of average ability ordinarily find it debilitating—which is why he gives the latter students easier problems. Also by allowing the students to make discoveries, he is heightening interest and arousal. Expectancy (b) may be the next best response in that by providing challenge he is kindling the motive to achieve—but this applies to only some of the students. Expectancies may also be involved in that the students are given problems which they expect to solve. As for incentives (c), no specific incentives are mentioned, unless you consider the successful solution of the problem the incentive—although no success is guaranteed. Finally, as for (d) (punishment), Mr. Seiting does not seem to be using any aversive procedures.

5-3

The best answer is (b). The analogies Miss Litefull drew are incongruous and perhaps even ludicrous (depending on your political and social convictions). There is evidence in her analogies of almost deliberate mismatching. The item contains no reference to levels of student alertness (arousal), learned anticipations (incentives), and rewards and punishment (discipline). Mismatching expectancies, you learned, is a way of generating humor and increasing student motivation.

6-1

The correct answer is (c). If a correlational study suggests a difficulty in some area of entering behavior, the teacher should carefully assess that area when it relates to his instructional objectives. Answer (a) is incorrect because the study was correlational and described no procedure at all. Answer (b) is incorrect because we ordinarily do not avoid teaching subject matter crucial in the learning of all children. It is preferable to raise the level of entering behavior to the prerequisite level for learning the new material. Answer (d) is incorrect because correlational studies do not show single causes; they merely suggest one of a number of causes. In this instance the children may have equal or more difficulty with other parts of speech.

6-2

The correct answer is (a). Since disadvantaged children are often deficient in labeling behavior, their repetition of the label with each presentation of an example of the concept *sailor* should strengthen the use of that label. Answer (b) is less desirable because a yes response is not so effective as a label response in developing labeling behavior. Answer (c) encourages the use of labels with the nonexamples of *sailor* but not with *sailor,* which is the concept Mr. Peabody is teaching. Answer (d), again, may help the children learn the concept but not necessarily the label for the concept.

6-3

The correct answer is (d). Learning sets, when combined into learning structures, are a most effective means of tailoring instruction to entering behavior. Answer (a) is not acceptable because *middle-class values* is an ambiguous concept and is often confused with the need of the school to preserve the order and discipline essential for organized instruction. As for (b), Ausubel believes and the research on curiosity and exploratory behavior shows that arousal of interest often results after the child has some familiarity with and has made some exploration of new materials. Answer (c) is infeasible since we cannot and probably should not reject for instruction children who have not had the necessary educational preparation.

7-1

The brief description illustrates the elements in our definition of learning, answer (a). The change is relatively permanent (it has now lasted one month), practice has been obvious (over a period of two months), and reinforcement has been provided by the successful execution of the skill and by the approval of peers. We must, of course, infer the tendency. As for answer (b), undoubtedly some muscular and neural development is necessary for LeRoy to learn this skill, but this development can well occur without the acquisition of this skill. As for answer (c), tricycle riding is not an instinct; many foreign children never exhibit this behavior. As for answer (d), habituation refers to reduced responsiveness, and, although LeRoy has developed considerable poise he is not less alert to the situation and responses he has mastered.

7-2

The best answer is (b). The children are being taught to discriminate between examples and nonexamples of dogs. They must, in fact, make different responses to two stimuli. To the extent that they pick dogs and ignore the other animals, it may be said that they have learned to discriminate. As for (a), although reinforçement of their responses to the pictures is an important condition of learning, the item made no reference to how the teacher may have provided (if he did so) for this condition. As for (c), in concept learning practice must occur *after* the concept is learned and the indications in this situation are that the children are still engaged in learning the concept. As for (d), generalization is also important in concept learning, but the emphasis in this teaching situation is not on the similarities of the various examples of dogs (making the same response to different stimuli) but on the differences between dogs and other animals.

7-3

The correct answer is (a). The flashing light is the conditioned stimulus, the electric shock the unconditioned stimulus, and the reaction to the shock (and presumably later to the light) the unconditioned and conditioned response. As for (b), in this procedure Mr. Sternski could either reinforce desirable responses, those that conformed to classroom rules, or he could terminate the shock only when the deviant student complied with the rules (negative reinforcement). Since the answer is (a) and not (b), it cannot be (c) or (d).

8-1

The best answer is (b). Relationship among movements refers to coordination of the sequences in which the movements occur. The learning of these movements requires contiguity. As for (a) and (d), although the student will require the different modes and types of feedback for the proper execution of the skill, in this early stage of skill instruction, feedback does not appear to be Mr. Kinetic's major concern. As for (c), practice is a later step in skill instruction, following demonstration. As for (e), if Mr. Kinetic directed the students' attention to particular movement cues or to differences in movements he would be providing discrimination training. Instead, he seems to be providing generalization training.

8-2

The best answer is (d). It is less suitable than the individual tests because these latter tests could better assess the various psychomotor abilities required in different stages of skill learning. As for (a), the test may measure the abilities needed in the initial but not in the later stages of learning tennis. As for (c), the test is related to some but not to all relevant aspects of the entering behavior. As for (b), since the students may perform skills which employ quite different psychomotor abilities than does tennis, even a careful observation would be unrelated.

8-3

The correct answer is (e). He did not provide for one basic learning condition—feedback, or reinforcement. Although practice will provide some of its own feedback (knocking over or not knocking over the bowling balls), students need other forms of feedback in the early stages of learning this skill.

9-1

The correct answer is (c) (*S-V-R* learning). Percival has reached the level at which he can make an internal verbal response (*V*) to an external stimulus (*S*, or Hound Dog) and follow the verbal response with a physical movement (*R*, or touching Hound Dog). Answers (a) and (b) refer to lower levels of verbal development in which the child's responses are still tied to the physical environment rather than to internal verbal responses and stimuli of his own. Answer (d) (*S-V-V-R* learning) is a more advanced level than that which Percival has attained—one in which he will be able to chain one verbal response to another.

9-2

The best answer is (b) (verbal mediation). Each of these words (*finger*, *button*, and *pfug*) is mediating the association between the drawing of the land mass and the name or label attached to it. Answer (a) (meaningfulness) is not so good a choice because pfug is not very meaningful to most students. Answer (c) (instructions to learn) refers to a prior statement of instructional objectives, something Mr. Werdee may or may not have provided. Answer (d) (reinforcement) is not an acceptable choice because we do not know which confirmation procedure Mr. Werdee is using. Since he is not providing the right answers, he is not using a prompting procedure.

9-3

The best answer is (d) (reducing interference). By providing practice on the individual associations, with the possibility of overlearning, she is taking precautions against interference which could arise because of the similarity of the learning materials. Answer (a) does not apply since she does not announce what the students are expected to do (although this is fairly clear because of the nature of the task). Answer (b) does not apply because she does not check these words against word-frequency lists. Answer (c) does not apply because we do not know how confirmation is provided.

9-4

The best answer is (a) since the research of Gibson and her associates furnished the evidence to support this conclusion. Answers (b), (c), and (d) are all contrary to the evidence reported here. The audiolingual method always employs the language laboratory, and yet it is not a superior means of instruction. Berko reported preschool mastery of sophisticated grammatical rules, although the children cannot verbalize these rules. The Initial Teaching Alphabet actually precludes the possibility of the child's forming grapheme-phoneme relationships (as described by Gibson) by making the grapheme conform to the phoneme.

10-1

1. (c) (conjunctive concept); 2. (e) (relational concept); 3. (d) (disjunctive concept); 4. (a) (attributes); 5. (b) (attribute values); 6. (f) (principle). Your reasons ought to be a correct definition of each term.

10-2

The answer is (c). By leaving each card in view after presenting it, Miss D. Voted was performing step 5, which requires the teacher to present positive and negative examples of the concept either in close succession or simultaneously. Either procedure provides contiguity. As for (a), the student should be told the expected performance before instruction is underway. As for (b), the examples themselves are not verbal mediators, although mediators can be used by the student to sort out the examples. As for (d), the verification of concept learning (step 7) occurs after the original examples have been presented and requires the presentation of new examples.

10-3

The answer is (e). By asking the students to form the singular by removing the *s* of the plural form, Mr. Punctilious is performing step 5, which requires the student to demonstrate the principle fully. This demonstration, according to Gagné, should take varied forms, and Mr. Punctilious' procedure is one such variation. There appears to be no statement of objective (a), the decision about component concepts must precede instruction (b), he is providing no help in recalling these component concepts (c), and he is not, at least in the question, helping the students to order the components (d). All the alternatives refer to earlier steps in the instruction.

11-1

The correct answer is psychologist *A*. Problem solving is treated as a form of learning (pp. 431–33), and, since what is learned is higher-order principles, the learning necessarily must have wide application to the solution of many problems within a class of problems. The view of psychologist *B* is not acceptable because I took the position that present evidence does not warrant the assumption that such general techniques, if they exist, are teachable or learnable. Psychologist *C* refers to types of learning of a lower order than problem solving. The view of psychologist *D* is unacceptable because he makes no reference to transfer to out-of-school problems and it is unlikely that complex personal and social problems can be tackled in the same way that we tackle academic problems.

11-2

The correct order is as follows: 1. (e) (instructional objective); 2. (a) (assessment of entering behavior); 3. (c) (invoking relevant principles); 4. (b) (verbal direction of thinking); and 5. (d) (demonstrating ability to solve new problems of the same class).

11-3

The correct matches are as follows: (a) Psychologist *A;* (b) psychologist *C;* and (c) psychologist *B*. As for (a), consistent patterns and types refer to personality traits and abilities. As for (b), psychologist *C* is expressing the view that this form of instruction can result in learning. As for (c), sensing gaps and missing elements describes problem solving (in part).

11-4

The best answer is (c). Wittrock (p. 471) arrived at this conclusion about the type of objectives for which discovery learning may be appropriate. Also adequate provision is made for entering behavior. As for (a), no evidence indicates that discovery learning is useful for these less complex learning types. As for (b), this may be an appropriate objective (according to Wittrock) but expository teaching can prove unsuccessful for several reasons; by providing improved learning conditions, one may eventually make it work. As for (d), this may be an appropriate objective (according to Wittrock) but creativity or creative problem solving is hardly a product of ignorance; intuitive leaps must bridge acquired knowledge. As for (e), an instructional situation without an objective is basically untenable, and there is little or no evidence that students develop this type of motivation in the pursuit of mysterious and unknown goals.

12-1

An *X* should follow (a), (b), and (d). The explanation for (a) is obvious since you are told at the start that there are frames. Active student response (b) is indicated by the blanks which the student must fill in. The frames use both formal and thematic prompts (d). Answer (c) is excluded because the correct response is not indicated. Answer (e) is excluded because the frames appear to be quite independent and because it is poor practice to use formal prompts after using thematic prompts for the same item of information. By doing this you fail to fade or vanish the prompting already introduced.

12-2

The best answer is (b) (systems analysis and design) since the major purposes are the selection of procedures and materials among alternatives and their comparison on the basis of effectiveness and efficiency. Answers (a), (c), and (d) could all be very costly without being comparably more effective and efficient. Although (e) (instructional kits and low-cost items) appear to be more efficient in terms of money, they are less efficient in terms of time and less effective in terms of achievement.

12-3

The answer is (d), all of the above. Although flexible scheduling is most closely related to (c), the regrouping of students on the basis of actual achievement, this regrouping has frequently involved and even required the use of different time units and teaching teams. I am sure no one will have chosen (e).

13-1

This is the key for this question: (a) *T;* (b) *M;* (c) *M;* (d) *M;* (e) *T;* (f) *J;* (g) *T*. These answers are based on Trowbridge's findings. Traditional teachers tended to emphasize formal curricular requirements and practical applications. Modern teachers tended to emphasize concentration on basic ideas, the method as well as the products of scientific investigation, and the place of physics in the spectrum of human knowledge. Both groups, however, appeared to be interested in the students' college preparation and the relationship of physics to society.

13-2

This is the arrangement of the items in order of emphasis:

1. Item (b), which attempts to assess ability to use skills in understanding scientific problems, a major BSCS objective.
2. Item (c), which assesses the ability to apply knowledge to new situations.
3. Item (a), which assesses the ability to show relations between bodies of knowledge.
4. Item (d), which assesses the ability to recall materials learned.

Unfortunately, the length of the alternatives could help you determine the correct answer.

13-3

The correct answer is (c), the deductive discovery method. Answer (a) refers to an *in*ductive discovery method, (b) to the tell-and-do lecture method, and (c) to the tell-and-do drill method. The deductive discovery method is favored by the modern mathematics programs.

14-1

The answers are as follows: (1) *T;* (2) *F;* (3) *T;* (4) *T*. The first statement is true because the items have obvious validity—they can be directly validated. The second statement is false because the instructional objective states an absolute standard, and the item validly assesses achievement of this standard. It is true, however, that such an item can appear on a test using a relative standard of achievement. The third statement is true because the item, as far as we know, is clear and not necessarily too easy or too difficult. The fourth statement is true because it would be fairly easy to arrive at a consensus on the correct answers.

14-2

The difficulty index is 39 per cent or $\frac{35 + 42}{200} \times 100$

The discrimination index is -0.07 or $(35 - 42)/100$. (2) Since an item of average difficulty has an index of 50 per cent, this item is difficult. (3) The item is a poor discriminator. It discriminates negatively, against the high-scoring students. (4) A simple way of making the item easier is to increase the number of pounds in *C* and *D* until they are closer to 1,000 or above.

14-3

The answer is (d) since it appears that he has not considered the effective range of scores on the tests, which may be greater or less than the effective range of scores on the activities. By utilizing the full range of scores for the activities, he has considered effective range for these scores. Although it is hard to reliably measure classroom discussion, this can be done if one can quantify the measure.

15-1

The answer is (a), by elimination. Most of the other things have been done. By observing score consistency they have checked (and presumably reported) test reliability. They have tested their scoring procedures (which also affect reliability). They have tested and presumably perfected the procedures for administering the test. And they are under no obligation to praise their rival test makers.

15-2

The answer is (c), special aptitude. This is a test of creativity, and we discussed creativity tests as special aptitude tests. In the number of problem solutions produced, the test is measuring fluency. In the quality of the solutions, it may be measuring originality.

15-3

Reading test: $M = 52.35$; Mdn. $= 51.5$. Science test: national $M = 50$. Reading test: national $M = 45$. Your class is below average in science, above average in reading. You must remember to use the means for the eighth grade in Table 15-13.

15-4

Science test: $s = 12.73$. If you use the second method for estimating s, $s = 14.5$ for the science test and $s = 17$ for the reading test. The national s for the eighth grade is 10 for the science test and 8 for the reading test. Your class is more variable on both tests than the national sample is.

15-5

The percentile scores are as follows: Science test: Dexter, 16; Melanie, 50; Frieda, 98; and Elvis, 8. Reading test: Barney, 80; Kate, 16; Jarvis, 50; and Patience, 98.

15-6

The grade-level scores are as follows: Science test: Dexter, 6; Melanie, 8; Frieda, off the scale; and Elvis, 5. Reading test: Barney, 9.5; Kate, 5.7; Jarvis, 8; and Patience, 11.2.

15-7

The percentile scores convey more valid information than the grade-level scores do because they compare the students with their own groups.

15-8

With the sixth grade mean, six on the science test and four on the reading test. With the tenth grade mean, eight on the science test and eight on the reading test.

15-9

(a) $r = 0.70$; (b) $rho = 0.70$; (c) Elvis in science; Elvis and Barney in reading; (d) Queenie and Roger in science; Timothy in reading.

15-10

Using Chart 1, (a) he will exceed less than 2 per cent of the freshmen at Harmony Haven, about 12 per cent at Pacifica State; (b) he should attend Pacifica State, where the competition should be less stiff.

16-1

(a) The intended study in the public schools occurs at step 5, in which previously tested materials (the film) are now tested under typical classroom conditions. The previous study under laboratory conditions illustrates step 4. (b) The independent variable in the intended (as well as in the previous) study is the film. (c) The dependent variables in the laboratory (as well as in the classroom) study are student scores on the achievement test. (d) Possible statement of hypothesis: If the students see the film on drug usage, then they will significantly improve their scores on the drug achievement test.

16-2

The best answer is (d). It is not random in selection because the children were volunteers and may have differed especially in degree of curiosity, from children who did not volunteer. It is not random in assignment because he assigned the children to the various experimental conditions in the order in which they entered his laboratory. It is not unlikely that some more curious children may have hurried to the laboratory before the others, and others may have been distracted en route. Although he assigned the children random numbers, he did not use these numbers for assigning them to groups.

16-3

He is testing the null hypothesis. He should use Chi-square because he is dealing with frequencies rather than means and variances. Furthermore, we do not know whether the questionnaire scores form a normal distribution, and the five response choices do not form an equal-interval scale.

Bibliography

Adams, Thurston (1939), *Motion Pictures in Physical Education.* New York: Teachers College Press, Columbia University.

Adkins, Dorothy C. (1958), "Measurement in Relation to the Educational Process," *Educational and Psychological Measurement,* 18, 221–40.†

Adler, Irving (1966), "The Cambridge Conference Report: Blueprint or Fantasy?" *The Arithmetic Teacher,* 13, 179–86.

Allen, Dwight (1963), Demonstration of the Use of the Videotape Recorder in Teacher Training. Stanford, Calif.: Stanford University.

Allendoerfer, Carl B. (1965), "The Second Revolution in Mathematics," *The Mathematics Teacher,* 58, 690–95.

Allport, Gordon W., Philip E. Vernon, and Gardner Lindzey (1960), *Study of Values Test Booklet* (3rd ed.). Boston: Houghton Mifflin Company.

Alpert, R., and Ralph N. Haber (1960), "Anxiety in Academic Achievement Situations," *Journal of Abnormal and Social Psychology,* 61, 207–15.

Amidon, Edmund J., and Ned A. Flanders (1963), *The Role of the Teacher in the Classroom: A Manual for Understanding and Improving Teachers' Classroom Behavior.* Minneapolis: Amidon & Associates.

Ammons, Robert B. (1954), "Knowledge of Performance: Survey of Literature, Some Possible Applications, and Suggested Experimentation," *USAF WADC Technical Report No. 54-114.* Wright-Patterson Air Force Base, Ohio.

Amos, Jimmy R., Foster L. Brown, and Oscar G. Mink (1965), *Statistical Concepts: A Basic Program.* New York: Harper & Row, Publishers.

* This list contains the full description of references made in the text. It omits items appearing only in the lists of suggested readings.

† In periodical entries the first number is a volume number.

Anastasi, Anne (1958), *Differential Psychology* (3rd ed.). New York: The Macmillan Company.

——— (1961), *Psychological Testing* (2nd ed.). New York: The Macmillan Company.

Anderson, Richard C. (1967), "Educational Psychology," *Annual Review of Psychology,* 18, 129–64.

Angell, David, and Arthur A. Lumsdaine (1961), "Prompted Versus Unprompted Trials Versus Prompted Trials Only in Paired-Associate Learning," in *Student Response in Programmed Instruction,* ed. A. A. Lumsdaine, pp. 389–98. Washington, D.C.: National Academy of Sciences—National Research Council.

Annet, John (1964), *The Role of Knowledge of Results in Learning: A Survey.* Port Washington, N.Y.: U.S. Naval Training Device Center.

Archer, James E. (1962), "Concept Identification as a Function of Obviousness of Relevant and Irrelevant Information," *Journal of Experimental Psychology,* 63, 616–20.

——— (1966), "The Psychological Nature of Concepts," in *Analyses of Concept Learning,* eds. H. J. Klausmeier and C. W. Harris, pp. 37–49. New York: Academic Press Inc.

Arlitt, Ada H. (1921), "On the Need for Caution in Establishing Race Norms," *Journal of Applied Psychology,* 5, 179–83.

Aschner, Mary Jane, James J. Gallagher, Joyce Perry, Sybil Afsar, W. C. Jenne, and Helen Farr (1965), *A System for Classifying Thought Processes in the Context of the Classroom Verbal Interaction.* Urbana, Ill.: University of Illinois, Institute for Research on Exceptional Children.

Atkin, Myron J. (1964), "Science in the Elementary School," *Review of Educational Research,* 34, 263–72.

Atkinson, John W. (1958), ed., *Motives in Fantasy, Action, and Society.* Princeton, N.J.: D. Van Nostrand Co., Inc.

Ausubel, David P. (1959), "Viewpoints From Related Disciplines: Human Growth and Development," *Teachers College Record,* 60, 245–54.

——— (1960), "Use of Advance Organizers in the Learning and Retention of Meaningful Verbal Material," *Journal of Educational Psychology,* 51, 267–72.

——— (1963a), *The Psychology of Meaningful Verbal Learning: An Introduction to School Learning.* New York: Grune & Stratton, Inc.

——— (1963b), "A Teaching Strategy for Culturally Deprived Pupils: Cognitive and Motivational Considerations," *The School Review* (Winter), pp. 454–63.

——— (1965a), "A Cognitive Structure View of Word and Concept Meaning," in *Readings in the Psychology of Cognition,* eds. R. C. Anderson and D. P. Ausubel, pp. 58–75. New York: Holt, Rinehart & Winston, Inc.

——— (1965b), "The Effects of Cultural Deprivation on Learning Patterns," *Audiovisual Instruction,* 10, 10–12.

Ausubel, David P., and Pearl Ausubel (1963), "Ego Development Among Segregated Negro Children," in *Education in Depressed Areas,* ed. A. H. Passow, pp. 109–41. New York: Teachers College Press, Columbia University.

Ausubel, David P., and Donald Fitzgerald (1961), "The Role of Discriminability in Meaningful Verbal Learning and Retention," *Journal of Educational Psychology,* 52, 266–74.

Ausubel, David P., S. H. Schpoont, and L. Cukier (1957), "The Influence of Intention on the Retention of School Materials," *Journal of Educational Psychology,* 48, 334–43.

Ausubel, David P., and Mohamed Youseff (1963), "The Role of Discriminability in Meaningful Parallel Learning," *Journal of Educational Psychology,* 54, 331–36.

Bachman, Jerald G. (1964), "Motivation in a Task Situation as a Function of Ability and Control Over Task," *Journal of Abnormal and Social Psychology,* 69, 272–81.

Bair, Medill, and Richard G. Woodward (1964), *Team Teaching in Action.* Boston: Houghton Mifflin Company.

Baldwin, Alfred L. (1967), *Theories of Child Development.* New York: John Wiley & Sons, Inc.

Bandura, Albert (1962), "The Influence of Rewarding and Punishing Models on the Acquisition and Performance of Imitative Responses," an unpublished manuscript. Stanford University.

Bandura, Albert, and Richard H. Walters (1963), *Social Learning and Personality Development.* New York: Holt, Rinehart & Winston, Inc.

Barnes, Jean M., and Benton J. Underwood (1959), "Fate of First-List Associations in Transfer Theory," *Journal of Experimental Psychology,* 58, 97–105.

Barson, John (1965), *A Procedural and Cost Analysis Study of Media in Instructional Systems Development.* Final Report, Grant No. OE-3-16-030.

Barthelemy, Richard E., James R. Dawson, and Addison H. Lee (1964), *Innovations in Equipment and Techniques for the Biology Teaching Laboratory.* Austin, Tex.: University of Texas Press.

Bayley, Nancy (1966), "Learning in Adulthood: The Role of Intelligence," in *Analyses of Concept Learning,* eds. H. J. Klausmeier and C. W. Chester, pp. 117–38. New York: Academic Press Inc.

Beach, Frank A. (1956), "Characteristics of Masculine Sex Drive," in *Nebraska Symposium on Motivation,* ed. M. R. Jones, pp. 1–32. Lincoln, Neb.: University of Nebraska Press.

Beach, Frank A., M. W. Conowitz, F. Steinberg, and A. C. Goldstein (1956), "Experimental Inhibition and Restoration of Mating Behavior in Male Rats," *Journal of Genetic Psychology,* 89, 165–81.

Beberman, Max (1964), "An Emerging Program of Secondary School Mathematics," in *New Curricula,* ed. R. W. Heath, pp. 9–34. New York: Harper & Row, Publishers.

Becker, Howard S. (1952), "Social Class Variations in the Teacher-Pupil Relationship," *Journal of Educational Sociology,* 25, 451–65.

Behringer, Marjorie P. (1966), "The Development of Differentiated Curricula for Ability Grouped Biology Classes, Including Teacher Training and Program Evaluation," *BSCS Newsletter, No. 30,* p. 23.

Berg, Harry D. (1965), "The Objective Test Item," in *Evaluation in Social Studies,* ed. H. D. Berg, 35th Yrbk. of the National Council for the Social Studies, pp. 47–76. Washington, D.C.: National Education Association.

Berko, Jean (1958), "The Child's Learning of English Morphology," *Word,* 14, 150–77.

Berlyne, David E. (1957a), "Conflict and Information-Theory Variables as Determinants of Human Perceptual Curiosity," *Journal of Experimental Psychology,* 53, 399–404.

——— (1957b), "Recent Developments in Piaget's Work," *British Journal of Educational Psychology,* 27, 1–12.

——— (1960), *Conflict, Arousal, and Curiosity.* New York: McGraw-Hill Book Company.

Bern, Henry A. (1967), "Wanted: Educational Engineers," *Phi Delta Kappan,* 48, 230–36.

Bernstein, Basil (1961), "Social Structure, Language and Learning," *Educational Research,* 3, 163–76.

Bexton, William H., Woodburn Heron, and T. H. Scott (1954), "Effects of Decreased Variation in the Sensory Environment," *Canadian Journal of Psychology,* 8, 70–76.

Bilodeau, Edward A., and Ina M. Bilodeau (1961), "Motor-Skills Learning," *Annual Review of Psychology,* 12, 243–80.

Birch, Herbert G., and Herbert S. Rabinowitz (1951), "The Negative Effects of Previous Experience on Productive Thinking," *Journal of Experimental Psychology,* 41, 121–25.

Blackman, Leonard S., and Paul Heintz (1966), "The Mentally Retarded," *Review of Educational Research,* 36, 5–36.

Blankenship, Jacob W. (1965), "Biology Teachers and Their Attitudes Concerning BSCS," *Journal of Research in Science Teaching,* 3, 54–60.

Bloom, Benjamin S. (1964), *Stability and Change in Human Characteristics.* New York: John Wiley & Sons, Inc.

Bloom, Benjamin S., *et al.* (1956), eds., *Taxonomy of Educational Objectives: Handbook I: Cognitive Domain.* New York: David McKay Co., Inc.

Bold, B. (1965), "Reference Guide to the *New Mathematical Library,*" *SMSG Newsletter No. 21.* Stanford, Calif.: SMSG Publications.

Book, William F. (1908), *The Psychology of Skill.* University of Montana Publications in Psychology, No. 53.

Borg, Walter R. (1963), *Educational Research: An Introduction.* New York: David McKay Co., Inc.

Brackbill, Yvonne, John E. Wagner, and Dorothy Wilson (1964), "Feedback Delay and the Teaching Machine," *Psychology in the Schools,* 1, 148–56.

Braley, Loy (1963), "Strategy Selection and Negative Instances in Concept Learning," *Journal of Educational Psychology,* 54, 154–59.

Brim, Orville G. (1965), "American Attitudes Toward Intelligence Tests," *American Psychologist,* 20, 125–30.

Bronfenbrenner, Urie (1961), "The Changing American Child," *Journal of Social Issues,* 17, 6–117.

Broudy, Harry S. (1963), "Historic Exemplars of Teaching Method," in *Handbook of Research on Teaching,* ed. N. L. Gage, pp. 1–43. Chicago: Rand McNally & Co.

Broudy, Harry S., and John R. Palmer (1965), *Exemplars of Teaching Method.* Chicago: Rand McNally & Co.

Brown, Frank B. (1963), "The Non-Graded High School," *Phi Delta Kappan,* 44, 206–9.

Brown, Roger W. (1957), "Linguistic Determinism and the Part of Speech," *Journal of Abnormal and Social Psychology,* 55, 1–5.

——— (1965), *Social Psychology*. New York: Free Press of Glencoe, Inc.

Brownell, John A., and Harris A. Taylor (1962), "Theoretical Perspectives for Teaching Teams," *Phi Delta Kappan*, 43, 150–57.

Bruner, Jerome S. (1960), *The Process of Education*. Cambridge, Mass.: Harvard University Press.

——— (1961a), "The Act of Discovery," *Harvard Educational Review*, 31, 21–32.

——— (1961b), "The Cognitive Consequences of Early Sensory Deprivation," in *Sensory Deprivation*, ed. Philip Solomon. Cambridge, Mass.: Harvard University Press.

Bruner, Jerome S., Jacqueline J. Goodnow, and George A. Austin (1956), *A Study of Thinking*. New York: John Wiley & Sons, Inc.

Bruner, Jerome S., Rose R. Olver, Patricia M. Greenfield, *et al.* (1966), *Studies in Cognitive Development*. New York: John Wiley & Sons, Inc.

Bryan, W. L., and N. Harter (1897), "Studies in the Physiology and Psychology of the Telegraphic Language," *Psychological Review*, 4, 27–53.

——— (1899), "Studies on the Telegraphic Language: The Acquisition of a Hierarchy of Habits," *Psychological Review*, 6, 345–75.

BSCS (Biological Sciences Curriculum Study) (1961), *BSCS Newsletter No. 7*. Boulder, Colo.: American Institute of Biological Sciences.

——— (1962), *BSCS Newsletter No. 12*. Boulder, Colo.: American Institute of Biological Sciences.

——— (1963), *BSCS Newsletter No. 17*. Boulder, Colo.: American Institute of Biological Sciences.

——— (1964a), *Teacher's Guide*, Green Version. Boulder, Colo.: American Institute of Biological Sciences.

——— (1964b), *Biological Science: Interaction of Experiment and Ideas*. Englewood Cliffs, N.J.: Prentice-Hall, Inc.

——— (1965a), *BSCS Newsletter No. 24*. Boulder, Colo.: American Institute of Biological Sciences.

——— (1965b), *BSCS Newsletter No. 27*. Boulder, Colo.: American Institute of Biological Sciences.

——— (1966a), *BSCS Newsletter No. 28*. Boulder, Colo.: American Institute of Biological Sciences.

——— (1966b), *Biological Science: Patterns and Processes*. New York: Holt, Rinehart & Winston, Inc.

Bush, Robert N., and Dwight W. Allen (1964), *A New Design for High School Education*. New York: McGraw-Hill Book Company.

Buss, Arnold H. (1950), "A Study of Concept Formation as a Function of Reinforcement and Stimulus Generalization," *Journal of Experimental Psychology*, 40, 494–503.

"CAI—System and Projects" (1966), *Automated Education Letter*, 1, 3–13.

Cain, Ralph W., and Eugene C. Lee (1963), "An Analysis of the Relationship Between Science and Mathematics at the Secondary School Level," *School Science and Mathematics*, 43, 705–13.

Callahan, Raymond E. (1962), *Education and the Cult of Efficiency: A Study of the Social Forces That Have Shaped the Administration of the Public Schools*. Chicago: University of Chicago Press.

Campbell, Donald T., and Julian C. Stanley (1963), "Experimental and Quasi-Experimental Designs for Research on Teaching," in *Handbook of Research on Teaching,* ed. N. L. Gage, pp. 171–246. Chicago: Rand McNally & Co.

Carpenter, Clarence R., and Leslie P. Greenhill (1955), *Instructional Television Research Project No. One: An Investigation of Closed-Circuit Television for Teaching University Courses.* University Park, Pa.: The Pennsylvania State University.

Carpenter, F. (1954), "Conceptualization as a Function of Differential Reinforcement," *Science Education,* 38, 284–94.

Carroll, John B. (1960), "Wanted: A Research Basis for Educational Policy on Foreign Language Teaching," *Harvard Educational Review,* 30, 128–40.

Pittsburgh: University of Pittsburgh Press.

——— (1962), "The Prediction of Success in Intensive Foreign Language Training," in *Training Research and Education,* ed. R. Glaser, pp. 87–136.

——— (1963), "A Model of School Learning," *Teachers College Record,* 64, 723–33.

——— (1964a), "Words, Meanings, and Concepts," *Harvard Educational Review,* 34, 178–202.

——— (1964b), *Language and Thought.* Englewood Cliffs, N.J.: Prentice-Hall, Inc.

——— (1965), "School Learning Over the Long Haul," in *Learning and the Educational Process,* ed. J. D. Krumboltz, pp. 249–69. Chicago: Rand McNally & Co.

Carson, Arnold S., and A. I. Rabin (1960), "Verbal Comprehension and Communication in Negro and White Children," *Journal of Educational Psychology,* 51, 47–51.

Chapanis, Alphonse (1964), "Knowledge of Performance as an Incentive in Repetitive and Monotonous Tasks," *Journal of Applied Psychology,* 48, 263–67.

Charters, W. W. (1963), "The Social Background of Teaching," in *Handbook of Research on Teaching,* ed. N. L. Gage, pp. 715–813. Chicago: Rand McNally & Co.

Chomsky, Noam (1957), *Syntactic Structures.* The Hague: Mouton & Co.

Clark, L. Verdelle (1960), "Effect of Mental Practice on the Development of a Certain Motor Skill," *Research Quarterly,* 31, 560–69.

Cloward, Richard A., and James A. Jones (1963), "Social Class: Educational Attitudes and Participation," in *Education in Depressed Areas,* ed. Harry Passow, pp. 19–126. New York: Teachers College Press, Columbia University.

Cofer, Charles N., and Mortimer H. Appley (1964), *Motivation: Theory and Research.* New York: John Wiley & Sons, Inc.

Coleman, James S. (1961), *The Adolescent Subculture.* New York: Free Press of Glencoe, Inc.

Combs, Arthur W., and Donald Snygg (1959), *Individual Behavior: A Perceptual Approach to Behavior.* New York: Harper & Row, Publishers.

Committee for the White House Conference on Education (1956), *A Report to the President.* Washington, D.C.: Government Printing Office.

Conners, Keith C. (1964), "Visual and Verbal Approach Motives as a Function of Discrepancy from Expectancy Level," *Perceptual and Motor Skills,* 18, 457–64.

Cook, John O. (1958), "Supplementary Report: Processes Underlying Learning a Single Paired-Associate Item," *Journal of Experimental Psychology,* 56, 455.

——— (1963), "Superstition in the Skinnerian," *American Psychologist,* 18, 516–18.

Cook, John O., and Tracy S. Kendler (1956), "A Theoretical Model to Explain Some Paired-Associate Learning Data," in *Symposium on Air Force Human Engineering, Personnel and Training Research,* Publication No. 455, eds. G. Finch and F. Cameron, pp. 90–98. Washington, D.C.: National Academy of Sciences—National Research Council.

Cook, John O., and M. E. Spitzer (1960), "Supplementary Report: Prompting Versus Confirmation in Pair-Associate Learning," *Journal of Experimental Psychology,* 59, 275–76.

Cook, Walter W., Carroll H. Leeds, and Robert Callis (1951), *Minnesota Teacher Attitude Inventory Manual.* New York: Psychological Corp.

Corman, Bernard R. (1957), "The Effect of Varying Amounts and Kinds of Information as Guidance in Problem Solving," *Psychology Monographs,* 71, No. 2 (Whole No. 431).

Corman, Bernard R., and Ann G. Olmsted (1964), *The Internship in the Preparation of Elementary School Teachers: A Description and Analysis of a Program.* East Lansing, Mich.: College of Education, Michigan State University.

Coulson, John E. (1962), "A Computer-Based Laboratory for Research and Development in Education," in *Programmed Learning and Computer-Based Instruction,* ed. J. E. Coulson, pp. 191–204. New York: John Wiley & Sons, Inc.

Covington, Martin V. (1967), "Fostering Originality in Visual Problem Solving of Programmed Instructional Techniques." Paper read at the Western Psychological Association Meeting, San Francisco.

Cox, John A., and Lynn M. Boren (1965), "A Study of Backward Chaining," *Journal of Educational Psychology,* 56, 270–74.

Cremin, Lawrence A. (1964), *The Transformation of the School: Progressivism in American Education.* New York: Vintage Books.

——— (1965), *The Genius of American Education.* New York: Vintage Books.

Cromwell, Rue L. (1956), "Factors in the Serial Recall of Names of Acquaintances," *Journal of Abnormal and Social Psychology,* 53, 63–67.

Cronbach, Lee J. (1960), *Essentials of Psychological Testing* (2nd ed.). New York: Harper & Row, Publishers.

——— (1963), *Educational Psychology* (2nd ed.). New York: Harcourt, Brace & World, Inc.

——— (1966a), "The Logic of Experiments on Discovery," in *Learning by Discovery,* eds. L. S. Shulman and E. R. Keislar, pp. 77–92. Chicago: Rand McNally & Co.

——— (1966b), "The Role of the University in Improving Education," *Phi Delta Kappan,* 47, 539–45.

Crossman, E. R. F. W. (1959), "A Theory of the Acquisition of Speed-Skill," *Ergonomics,* 2, 153–66.

Crowder, Norman A. (1963a), "On the Differences Between Linear and Intrinsic Programming," *Phi Delta Kappan,* 44, 250–54.

——— (1963b), "The Rationale of Intrinsic Programming," in *Human Learning in the School,* ed. J. P. De Cecco, pp. 183–89. New York: Holt, Rinehart & Winston, Inc.

Cummings, Allana, and Leo S. Goldstein (1962), "The Effect of Overt and Covert Responding on Two Kinds of Learning Tasks," in *Technical Report 620919.* New York: Center for Programmed Instruction.

Dave, R. H. (1963), "The Identification and Measurement of Environmental Process Variables That Are Related to Educational Achievement." Doctoral dissertation, University of Chicago.

Davids, Anthony (1966), "Psychological Characteristics of High School Male and Female Potential Scientists in Comparison with Academic Achievers," *Psychology in the Schools,* 3, 79–87.

Davies, Dorothy R. (1945), "The Effect of Tuition upon the Process of Learning a Complex Motor Skill," *Journal of Educational Psychology,* 36, 352–65.

Davis, Allison (1948), *Social-Class Influence upon Learning.* Cambridge, Mass.: Harvard University Press.

Davis, Allison, and Kenneth Eells (1953), *Davis-Eells Games.* New York: Harcourt, Brace & World, Inc.

Deese, James (1958), *The Psychology of Learning* (2nd ed.). New York: McGraw-Hill Book Company.

Deese, James, and Stewart H. Hulse (1967), *The Psychology of Learning* (3rd ed.). New York: McGraw-Hill Book Company.

DeMott, Benjamin (1962), *Hells and Benefits.* New York: Basic Books, Inc.

Dessart, Donald J. (1964), "Mathematics in the Secondary School," *Review of Educational Research,* 34, 286–97.

Deutsch, Cynthia (1964), "Auditory Discrimination and Learning: Social Factors," *Merrill-Palmer Quarterly,* 10, 277–96.

Deutsch, Martin (1963a), "The Disadvantaged Child and the Learning Process," in *Education in Depressed Areas,* ed. A. Harry Passow, pp. 163–79. New York: Teachers College Press, Columbia University.

——— (1963b), "Nursery Education: The Influence of Social Programming on Early Development," *Journal of Nursery Education* (April), pp. 191–97.

——— (1964), "Facilitating Development in the Pre-School Child: Social and Psychological Perspectives," *Merrill-Palmer Quarterly,* 10, 249–63.

Deutsch, Martin, and Bert Brown (1964), "Social Influences in Negro-White Intelligence Differences," *Journal of Social Issues,* 20, 24–35.

Deutsch, Morton (1960), "The Effects of Cooperation and Competition on Group Process," in *Group Dynamics: Research and Theory,* eds. D. Cartwright and A. Zander, pp. 414–48. Evanston, Ill.: Row and Peterson.

Dollard, J., L. W. Doob, N. E. Miller, O. H. Mowrer, R. R. Sears, C. S. Ford, C. I. Hovland, and R. T. Sollenberger (1939), *Frustration and Aggression.* New Haven, Conn.: Yale University Press.

Dollard, John, and Neale Miller (1950), *Personality and Psychotherapy.* New York: The Macmillan Company.

Dominowski, R. L. (1965), "Role of Memory in Concept Learning," *Psychological Bulletin,* 63, 271–80.

Doré, L. R., and Ernest R. Hilgard (1938), "Spaced Practice as a Test of Snoddy's Two Processes in Mental Growth," *Journal of Experimental Psychology,* 23, 359–74.

Downing, John (1964), "Teaching Reading with i.t.a. in Britain," *Phi Delta Kappan,* 45, No. 7, 322–29.

Dreher, Robert E., and Walcott H. Beatty (1958), *Instructional Television Research Project Number One: An Experimental Study of College Instruction Using Broadcast Television.* San Francisco: San Francisco State College.

Duncan, Carl P. (1951), "The Effect of Unequal Amounts of Practice on Motor Learning Before and After Practice," *Journal of Experimental Psychology,* 42, 257–64.

——— (1959), "Recent Research on Human Problem Solving," *Psychological Bulletin,* 56, 397–429.

Dwyer, Francis M., Jr. (1967), "Adapting Visual Illustrations for Effective Learning," *Harvard Educational Review,* 37, 250–63.

Ebbinghaus, Hermann (1885), *Ueber das Gedächtnis.* Translated by Henry A. Ruger and Clara Bussenius as *Memory,* Educational Reprint No. 3. New York: Teachers College Press, Columbia University, 1913.

Ebel, Robert L. (1963), "The Relation of Testing Programs to Educational Goals," in *The Impact and Improvement of School Testing Programs,* Part 2 of the 62nd Yrbk. of the National Society for the Study of Education, pp. 28–44. Chicago: University of Chicago Press.

——— (1965), *Measuring Educational Achievement.* Englewood Cliffs, N.J.: Prentice-Hall, Inc.

——— (1967), "Some Limitations of Basic Research in Education," *Phi Delta Kappan,* 49, 81–84.

Educational Policies Commission (1961), *The Central Purposes of American Education.* Washington, D.C.: Educational Policies Commission of the National Education Association.

Eigen, Lewis D., and John Feldhusen (1964), "Interrelationships Among Attitude, Achievement, Reading, Intelligence, and Transfer Variables in Programmed Instruction," in *Educational Technology,* ed. J. P. De Cecco, pp. 376–86. New York: Holt, Rinehart & Winston, Inc.

Eigen, Lewis D., and Stuart Margulies (1963), "Response Characteristics as a Function of Information Level," *Journal of Programed Instruction,* 2, 45–54.

Ellis, Henry (1965), *The Transfer of Learning.* New York: The Macmillan Company.

Elwell, J. L., and G. C. Grindley (1938), "The Effect of Knowledge of Results on Learning and Performance. I: A Coordinated Movement of the Two Hands," *British Journal of Psychology,* 29, 39–53.

Elzey, Freeman F. (1965), *A Programed Introduction to Statistics.* Belmont, Calif.: Wadsworth Publishing Co., Inc.

Entwisle, Doris R., and W. H. Huggins (1964), "Interference in Meaningful Learning," *Journal of Educational Psychology,* 55, 75–78.

Erickson, Carlton W. (1965), *Fundamentals of Teaching with Audiovisual Technology.* New York: The Macmillan Company.

Ervin-Tripp, Susan (1961), "Changes with Age on the Verbal Determinants of Word Association," *American Journal of Psychology,* 74, 361–72.

——— (1964), "Language and Thought," in *Horizons of Anthropology,* ed. Sol Tax. Chicago: Aldine Publishing Co.

ESI Quarterly Report (1964) (Winter-Spring), p. 4.

Espenschade, Anna S. (1963), *What Research Says to the Teacher: Physical Education in the Elementary Schools.* Washington, D.C.: National Education Association.

Evans, James L., Robert Glaser, and Lloyd E. Homme (1962), "The Ruleg System for the Construction of Programmed Verbal Learning Sequences," *Journal of Educational Research,* 55, 513–18.

Fehr, Howard F. (1966), "Sense and Nonsense in a Modern School Mathematics Program," *The Arithmetic Teacher,* 13, 83–91.

Feldhake, Herbert J. (1966), "Student Acceptance of the New Mathematics Program," *The Arithmetic Teacher,* 13, 14–19.

Feldhusen, John F., and Herbert J. Klausmeier (1962), "Anxiety, Intelligence, and Achievement in Children of Low, Average, and High Intelligence," *Child Development,* 33, 403–9.

Ferris, Frederick L., Jr. (1960), "Testing for Physics Achievement," *The American Journal of Physics,* 28, 269–78.

Ferster, Charles B., and B. F. Skinner (1957), *Schedules of Reinforcement.* New York: Appleton-Century-Crofts.

Filep, Robert T. (1961), "Programming for Your Classroom," *Programed Instruction,* 1, No. 1, 3–4.

Finlay, Gilbert C. (1962), "The Physical Science Study Committee," *The School Review,* 7, 70.

——— (1964), "The Physical Science Study Committee," *ESI Quarterly Report* (Winter-Spring), pp. 5–16.

Fitts, Paul (1951), "Engineering Psychology and Equipment Design," in *Handbook of Experimental Psychology,* ed. S. S. Stevens, pp. 1237–40. New York: John Wiley & Sons, Inc.

——— (1962), "Factors in Complex Skill Training," in *Training Research and Education,* ed. R. Glaser, pp. 177–97. Pittsburgh: University of Pittsburgh Press.

——— (1964), "Perceptual-Motor Skill Learning," in *Categories of Human Learning,* ed. A. W. Melton, pp. 243–85. New York: Academic Press, Inc.

Fitzpatrick, E. A. (1963), *Ignatius and the Ratio Studiorum.* New York: McGraw-Hill Book Company.

Flanagan, John C. (1957), *Flanagan Aptitude Classification Tests.* Chicago: Science Research Associates, Inc.

Flanagan, John C., *et al.* (1964), *Project Talent: The Identification, Development, and Utilization of Human Talents Final Report.* Pittsburgh: Project Talent Office, University of Pittsburgh.

Flanders, Ned A. (1951), "Personal-Social Anxiety as a Factor in Experimental Learning Situations," *Journal of Educational Research,* 45, 100–110.

——— (1960), *Teacher Influence, Pupil Attitudes, and Achievement.* Minneapolis: University of Minnesota.

——— (1964), "Some Relationships Among Teacher Influence, Pupil Attitudes, and Achievement," in *Contemporary Research on Teacher Effectiveness,* eds. B. J. Biddle and W. J. Ellena, pp. 196–231. New York: Holt, Rinehart & Winston, Inc.

——— (1966), "Interaction Analysis and In-Service Training," *California Journal for Instructional Improvement,* 9, 14–31.

Flavell, John H. (1963), *The Developmental Psychology of Jean Piaget.* Princeton, N.J.: D. Van Nostrand Co., Inc.

Fleishman, Edwin A. (1962), "The Description and Prediction of Perceptual-

Motor Skill Learning," in *Training Research Education,* ed. R. Glaser, pp. 137–75. Pittsburgh: University of Pittsburgh Press.

——— (1964), *The Structure and Measurement of Physical Fitness.* Englewood Cliffs, N.J.: Prentice-Hall, Inc.

Fleishman, Edwin A., and Walter E. Hempel, Jr. (1954), "Changes in Factor Structure of a Complex Psychomotor Test as a Function of Practice," *Psychometrika,* 19, 239–52.

——— (1955), "The Relation Between Abilities and Improvement with Practice in a Visual Discrimination Reaction Task," *Journal of Experimental Psychology,* 49, 301–10.

Flexman, Ralph E., William G. Matheny, and E. L. Brown (1950), "Evaluation of the School Link and Special Methods of Instruction." *University of Illinois Bulletin,* 47, No. 80.

Ford, G. W., and Lawrence Pugno (1964), *The Structure of Knowledge and the Curriculum.* Chicago: Rand McNally & Co.

Fowler, Harry (1965), *Curiosity and Exploratory Behavior.* New York: The Macmillan Company.

Fowler, William (1962), "Cognitive Learning in Infancy and Early Childhood," *Psychological Bulletin,* 59, 116–52.

Freeman, Frank S. (1962), *Theory and Practice of Psychological Testing.* New York: Holt, Rinehart & Winston, Inc.

Fremont, Herbert (1964), "Some Thoughts on Teaching Mathematics to Disadvantaged Groups," *Arithmetic Teacher,* 11, 319–22.

French, Joseph L. (1964), *Pictorial Test of Intelligence Manual.* Boston: Houghton Mifflin Company.

French, Will, *et al.* (1957), *Behavioral Goals of General Education in the High School.* New York: Russell Sage Foundation.

Friedlander, Bernard Z. (1965), "A Psychologist's Second Thoughts on Concepts, Curiosity, and Discovery in Teaching and Learning," *Harvard Educational Review,* 35, 18–38.

Fries, Charles C. (1963), *Linguistics and Reading.* New York: Holt, Rinehart & Winston, Inc.

Frost, Joe L., and Glenn R. Hawkes (1966), eds., *The Disadvantaged Child: Issues and Innovations.* Boston: Houghton Mifflin Company.

Gage, Nathan L. (1963), "Paradigms for Research on Teaching," in *Handbook of Research on Teaching,* ed. N. L. Gage, pp. 94–141. Chicago: Rand McNally & Co.

——— (1964), "The Theories of Teaching," in *Handbook of Research on Teaching,* ed. N. L. Gage, pp. 268–85. Chicago: Rand McNally & Co.

Gagné, Robert M. (1962a), "The Acquisition of Knowledge," *Psychological Review,* 69, 355–65.

——— (1962b), "Military Training and Principles of Learning," *American Psychologist,* 17, 83–91.

——— (1964), "Problem Solving," in *Categories of Human Learning,* ed. A. W. Melton, pp. 294–317. New York: Academic Press Inc.

——— (1965a), "Educational Objectives and Human Performance," in *Learning and the Educational Process,* ed. J. D. Krumboltz, pp. 1–24. Chicago: Rand McNally & Co.

——— (1965b), "The Analysis of Instructional Objectives for the Design of Instruction," in *Teaching Machines and Programmed Learning II: Data and Directions,* ed. R. Glaser, pp. 21–65. Washington, D.C.: Department of Audiovisual Instruction, National Education Association.

——— (1965c), *Conditions of Learning.* New York: Holt, Rinehart & Winston, Inc.

——— (1966), "The Learning of Principles," in *Analyses of Concept Learning,* eds. H. J. Klausmeier and C. W. Harris, pp. 81–96. New York: Academic Press Inc.

Gagné, Robert M., and Otto C. Bassler (1963), "Study of Retention of Some Topics of Elementary Nonmetric Geometry," *Journal of Educational Psychology,* 54, 123–31.

Gagné, Robert M., and Larry T. Brown (1961), "Some Factors in the Programming of Conceptual Learning," *Journal of Experimental Psychology,* 62, 313–21.

Gagné, Robert M., and Edwin A. Fleishman (1959), *Psychology and Human Performance.* New York: Holt, Rinehart & Winston, Inc.

Gagné, Robert M., J. R. Mayor, H. L. Garstens, and N. E. Paradise (1962), "Factors in Acquiring Knowledge of a Mathematical Task," *Psychological Monographs,* 76, No. 7 (Whole No. 526).

Gagné, Robert M., and N. E. Paradise (1961), "Abilities and Learning Sets in Knowledge Acquisition," *Psychological Monographs,* 75, No. 14 (Whole No. 518).

Gallagher, James J. (1964), *Teaching the Gifted Child.* Boston: Allyn and Bacon, Inc.

——— (1967), "Teacher Variation in Concept Presentation in the BSCS Curriculum Program," *BSCS Newsletter No. 30,* pp. 8–18.

Garrett, Henry E. (1958), *Statistics in Psychology and Education.* New York: David McKay Co., Inc.

"Gates-MacGintie Reading Tests" (1965), *Teacher's Manual Survey E.* New York: Teachers College Press, Columbia University.

Geis, George L., William C. Stebbins, and Robert W. Lundin (1965), *Reflex and Operant Conditioning.* New York: Basic Systems, Inc.

Gentile, J. Robert (1967), "The First Generation of Computer-Assisted Instructional Systems: An Evaluative Review," *AV Communication Review,* 15, 23–53.

George, Kenneth D. (1965), "The Effect of BSCS and Conventional Biology on Critical Thinking," *Journal of Research in Science Teaching,* 3, 293–99.

Getzels, Jacob W. (1964), "Creative Thinking, Problem Solving, and Instruction," in *Theories of Learning and Instruction,* ed. E. R. Hilgard, Part 1 of the 63rd Yrbk. of the National Society for the Study of Education, pp. 240–67. Chicago: University of Chicago Press.

Getzels, Jacob W., and Philip W. Jackson (1962), *Creativity and Intelligence: Explorations with Gifted Students.* New York: John Wiley & Sons, Inc.

Gewirtz, Hava B. (1959), "Generalization of Children's Preferences as a Function of Reinforcement and Task Similarity," *Journal of Abnormal and Social Psychology,* 58, 111–18.

Ghiselin, Brewster (1952), ed., *The Creative Process.* Berkeley, Calif.: University of California Press.

Gibson, Eleanor J., Anne Pick, Harry Osser, and Marcia Hammond (1962), "The

Role of Grapheme-Phoneme Correspondence in the Perception of Words," *American Journal of Psychology,* 75, 554–70.

Gibson, O. O. (1941), "A Critical Review of the Concept of Set in Contemporary Experimental Psychology," *Psychological Bulletin,* 38, 781–817.

Gilbert, Thomas F. (1960), "On the Relevance of Laboratory Investigation of Learning to Self-Instructional Programs," in *Teaching Machines and Programmed Learning: A Source Book,* eds. A. Lumsdaine and R. Glaser, pp. 475–85. Washington, D.C.: Department of Audiovisual Instruction, National Education Association.

——— (1962a), "Mathetics: The Technology of Education," *Journal of Mathetics,* 1, 7–73.

——— (1962b), "A Structure for a Coordinated Research and Development Laboratory," in *Training Research and Education,* ed. R. Glaser, pp. 559–78. Pittsburgh: University of Pittsburgh Press.

Gilcrest, Robert S. (1963), ed., *Using Current Curriculum Development, a Report of ASCD's Commission on Current Curriculum Development.* Washington, D.C.: Association for Supervision and Curriculum Development, National Education Association.

Glaser, Robert (1962), "Psychology and Instructional Technology," in *Training Research and Education,* ed. R. Glaser, pp. 1–30. Pittsburgh: University of Pittsburgh Press.

——— (1963), "Instructional Technology and the Measurement of Learning Outcomes," *American Psychologist,* 18, 519–21.

——— (1965), "Toward a Behavioral Science Base for Instructional Design," in *Teaching Machines and Programmed Learning II: Data and Directions,* ed. R. Glaser, pp. 771–809. Washington, D.C.: Department of Audiovisual Instruction, National Education Association.

——— (1966), "Variables in Discovery Learning," in *Learning by Discovery,* eds. L. S. Shulman and E. R. Keislar, pp. 13–26. Chicago: Rand McNally & Co.

Glaser, Robert, and James H. Reynolds (1966), "Instructional Objectives and Programmed Instruction: A Case Study," in *Defining Educational Objectives,* ed. C. M. Lindvall. Pittsburgh: University of Pittsburgh Press.

Glaze, J. A. (1928), "The Association Value of Nonsense Syllables," *Journal of Genetic Psychology,* 35, 255–67.

Gleason, H. A., Jr. (1955), *Introduction to Descriptive Linguistics.* New York: Holt, Rinehart & Winston, Inc.

——— (1965), *Linguistics and English Grammar.* New York: Holt, Rinehart & Winston, Inc.

Gnagey, William J. (1965), *Controlling Classroom Misbehavior.* Washington, D.C.: Department of Classroom Teachers, American Educational Research Association, National Education Association.

Goldbeck, Robert A., and Vincent N. Campbell (1962), "The Effects of Response Mode and Response Difficulty on Programmed Learning," *Journal of Educational Psychology,* 53, 110–18.

Goldberg, Lewis (1965), "Grades as Motivants," *Psychology in the Schools,* 2, 17–23.

Goldberg, Miriam L. (1964), "Adapting Teacher-Style to Pupil Differences: Teachers for Disadvantaged Children," *Merrill-Palmer Quarterly,* 10, 161–78.

Goodlad, John I. (1964), *School Curriculum Reform in the United States*. New York: The Fund for the Advancement of Education.

Goodlad, John I., and Robert H. Anderson (1963), *The Nongraded Elementary School*. New York: Harcourt, Brace & World, Inc.

Gorow, Frank F. (1966), *Better Classroom Testing*. San Francisco: Chandler Publishing Co.

Gotkin, Lassar G., and Leo S. Goldstein (1964), *Descriptive Statistics*, Vol. 1. New York: John Wiley & Sons, Inc.

Gottlieb, David (1964), "Teaching and Students: The Views of Negro and White Teachers," *Sociology of Education*, 37, 345–53

Gough, Harrison G. (1957), *California Psychological Inventory Manual*. Palo Alto, Calif.: Consulting Psychologists Press.

Grambs, Jean D., and William J. Iverson (1952), *Modern Methods in Secondary Education*. New York: Dryden Press.

Green, Donald Ross (1964), *Educational Psychology*. Englewood Cliffs, N.J.: Prentice-Hall, Inc.

Green, Robert L., and William W. Farquhar (1965), "Negro Academic Motivation and Scholastic Achievement," *Journal of Educational Psychology*, 56, 241–43.

Greene, H. A. (1939), *The Iowa Every-Pupil Tests in Basic Skills*. Iowa City, Iowa: Extension Division, State University of Iowa.

Greene, H. A., and V. H. Kelley (1943), *Iowa Silent Reading Tests*. (Elementary Tests: Manual of Directions for Forms Am (revised) and Bm (revised), Cm and Dm.) Chicago: World Book Encyclopedia, Inc.

Greenhill, Leslie P. (1964), "A Review of Some Trends in Research on Instructional Films and Instructional Television," in *Abstracts of Research on Instructional Television and Film: An Annotated Bibliography*, eds. D. W. MacLennand and J. C. Reid, pp. 1–32. Stanford, Calif.: Institute for Communication Research, Stanford University.

Greenspoon, Joel, and Sally Foreman (1956), "Effect of Delay of Knowledge of Results on Learning a Motor Task," *Journal of Experimental Psychology*, 51, 226–28.

Groff, Patrick J. (1964), "Culturally Deprived Children: Opinions of Teachers and Views of Riessman," *Exceptional Children* (October), pp. 61–65.

Gronlund, Norman E. (1965), *Measurement and Evaluation in Teaching*. New York: The Macmillan Company.

Gropper, George L., and Arthur A. Lumsdaine (1961), "An Experimental Comparison of a Conventional TV Lesson with a Programmed TV Lesson Requiring Active Student Response. Studies in Televised Instruction, Reports No. 2, 3, USOE Project No. 336," *AV Communication Review*, 9, A-50–51.

Gross, M. M. (1946), "The Effect of Certain Types of Motivation on the Honesty of Children," *Journal of Educational Research*, 40, 133–40.

Gross, N. (1953), "Social Class Identification in the Urban Community," *American Sociological Review*, 18, 398–403.

Guilford, Joy P. (1950), "Creativity," *American Psychologist*, 5, 444–54.

——— (1952), *General Psychology* (2nd ed.). Princeton, N.J.: D. Van Nostrand Co., Inc.

——— (1959), "Three Faces of Intellect," *American Psychologist*, 14, 469–79.

——— (1962), "Factors That Aid and Hinder Creativity," *Teachers College Record*, 63, 380–92.

Guilford, Joy P., and J. I. Lacey (1947), *Printed Classification Tests*. Washington, D.C.: Government Printing Office.

Guthrie, Edwin R. (1952), *The Psychology of Learning*. New York: Harper & Row, Publishers.

Guttman, Norman, and Harry I. Kalish (1963), "A Generalization Gradient Obtained from Pigeons," in *Principles of Psychology* (2nd ed.), eds. G. A. Kimble and N. Garmezy, p. 145. New York: The Ronald Press Company.

Haggard, Ernest (1954), "Social Status and Intelligence: An Experimental Study of Certain Cultural Determinants of Measured Intelligence," *Genetic Psychological Monographs,* 49, 141–86.

Hamp, Eric P. (1967), "Language in a Few Words: With Notes on a Rereading, 1966," in *Language, Thought, and Instruction,* ed. J. P. De Cecco, pp. 5–23. New York: Holt, Rinehart & Winston, Inc.

Harlow, Harry F. (1949), "The Formation of Learning Sets," *The Psychological Review,* 56, 51–65.

Harlow, Harry F., Margaret K. Harlow, and Donald R. Meyer (1950), "Learning Motivated by a Manipulation Drive," *Journal of Experimental Psychology,* 40, 228–34.

Harrison, Maurice (1964), *Instant Reading. The Story of the Initial Teaching Alphabet.* London: Sir Isaac Pitman & Sons, Ltd.

Hatch, Raymond S. (1961), "More on the Response Mode Controversy," *AID,* 1, 76–77.

Haubrich, Vernon F. (1963), "The Culturally Different: New Context for Teacher Education," *Journal of Teacher Education,* 14, 163–67.

Havighurst, Robert J. (1964), "Who Are the Socially Disadvantaged?" *Journal of Negro Education,* 33, pp. 210–17.

Havighurst, Robert J., and Hilda Taba (1949), *Adolescent Character and Personality*. New York: John Wiley & Sons, Inc.

Hawker, James R. (1964), "The Influence of Training Procedure and Other Task Variables in Paired-Associate Learning," *Journal of Verbal Learning and Verbal Behavior,* 3, 70–76.

Heald, James (1964), "In Defense of Middle-Class Values," *Phi Delta Kappan,* 46, 81–83.

Hebb, Donald O. (1949), *Organization of Behavior*. New York: John Wiley & Sons, Inc.

——— (1955), "Drives and C.N.S. (Conceptual Nervous System)," *Psychological Review,* 62, 243–54.

——— (1966), *A Textbook of Psychology*. Philadelphia: W. B. Saunders Co.

Heenan, David K. (1961), "Evaluation in the Humanities," in *Evaluation in Higher Education,* eds. Paul L. Dressel *et al.,* pp. 157–91. Boston: Houghton Mifflin Company.

Hempel, Walter E., Jr., and Edwin A. Fleishman (1955), "A Factor Analysis of Physical Proficiency and Manipulative Skill," *Journal of Applied Psychology,* 39, 12–16.

Henderson, Kenneth B. (1963), "Research on Teaching Secondary School Mathematics," in *Handbook of Research on Teaching,* ed. N. L. Gage, pp. 1007–30. Chicago: Rand McNally & Co.

Henry, Jules (1965), "White People's Time, and Colored People's Time," *Trans-Action* (March-April), pp. 31–34.

Herbart, Johann F. (1883), *The Science of Education*. Translated by H. M. Felkin and Emmie Felkin. Boston: D. C. Heath & Company.

Hieronymus, Albert N. (1951), "A Study of Social Class Motivation: Relationships Between Anxiety for Education and Certain Socio-Economic and Intellectual Variables," *Journal of Educational Psychology,* 42, 193–205.

Hilgard, Ernest R. (1964), "A Perspective on the Relationship Between Learning Theory and Educational Practices," in *Theories of Learning and Instruction,* ed. E. R. Hilgard, Part 1 of the 63rd Yrbk. of the National Society for the Study of Education, pp. 402–15. Chicago: University of Chicago Press.

Hilgard, Ernest R., and Gordon H. Bower (1966), *Theories of Learning* (3rd ed.). New York: Appleton-Century-Crofts.

Hilgard, Ernest R., R. P. Irvine, and J. E. Whipple (1953), "Rote Memorization, Understanding and Transfer: An Extension of Katona's Card-Trick Experiments," *Journal of Experimental Psychology,* 46, 288–92.

Hill, Winfred F. (1963), *Learning: A Survey of Psychological Interpretations.* San Francisco: Chandler Publishing Co.

Hillson, Henry T., and Florence C. Myers (1963), *The Demonstration Guidance Project: 1957–1962.* New York: Board of Education of the City of New York.

Hipsher, Warren L. (1961), "Study of High School Physics Achievement," *Science Teacher,* 28, 36–37.

Hoban, C. F., and E. B. VanOrmer (1950), "Instructional Film Research, 1918–1950," *Technical Report No. SDC 269-7-19.* Port Washington, N.Y.: U.S. Naval Training Devices Center.

Holland, James G. (1960), "Design and Use of a Teaching-Machine Program." Paper read at the American Psychological Association Convention, Chicago.

——— (1964), "J. O. Cook's Tour de Farce," *American Psychologist,* 19, 683–84.

——— (1965a), "Research on Programming Variables," in *Teaching Machines and Programmed Learning II: Data and Directions,* ed. R. Glaser, pp. 66–117. Washington, D.C.: National Education Association.

——— (1965b), "Response Contingencies in Teaching Machine Programs," *The Journal of Programmed Instruction,* 3, 1–8.

Holland, James G., and B. F. Skinner (1961), *The Analysis of Behavior.* New York: McGraw-Hill Book Company.

Hollingshead, A. B. (1949), *Elmtown's Youth.* New York: John Wiley & Sons, Inc.

Horn, Robert E. (1963), "The Rhetoric of Programming," *Programed Instruction,* 2, No. 6, 4–5.

Horton, Carrell P., and Perry E. Crump (1962), "Growth and Development: XI. Descriptive Analysis of the Backgrounds of 76 Negro Children Whose Scores Are Above or Below Average on the Merrill-Palmer Scale of Mental Tests at Three Years of Age," *Journal of Genetic Psychology,* 100, 255–65.

Hovland, Carl I. (1938), "Experimental Studies in Rote-Learning Theory: II. Reminiscence with Varying Speeds of Syllable Presentation," *Journal of Experimental Psychology,* 27, 271–84.

Hovland, Carl I., and Walter Weiss (1953), "Transmission Information Concerning Concepts Through Positive and Negative Instances," *Journal of Experimental Psychology,* 45, 175–82.

Huettig, Alice, and John M. Newell (1966), "Attitudes Toward Introduction of Modern Mathematics Program by Teachers with Large and Small Number of Years' Experience," *The Arithmetic Teacher,* 13, 125–30.

Hughes, John L. (1962), "Effect of Changes in Programed Text Format and

Reduction in Classroom Time on the Achievement and Attitude of Industrial Trainees," *Journal of Programed Instruction*, 1, 43–54.

Hull, Clark L. (1952), *A Behavior System: An Introduction to Behavior Theory Concerning the Individual Organism*. New Haven, Conn.: Yale University Press.

Hunsicker, Paul (1963), *What Research Says to the Teacher: Physical Fitness*. Washington, D.C.: American Educational Research Association, National Education Association.

Hunt, Earl B. (1962), *Concept Learning: An Information Processing Problem*. New York: John Wiley & Sons, Inc.

Hunt, J. McVicker (1964), "The Psychological Basis for Using Pre-School Enrichment as an Antidote for Cultural Deprivation," *Merrill-Palmer Quarterly*, 10, 209–48.

Hurd, Paul deHart, and Mary B. Rowe (1964), "Science in the Secondary School," *Review of Educational Research*, 34, 286–97.

Hurlock, Elizabeth B. (1924), "The Value of Praise and Reproof as Incentives for Children," in *Arch. Psychology*, 11, No. 71.

——— (1925), "An Evaluation of Incentives Used in School Work," *Journal of Educational Psychology*, 16, 145–59.

Husén, Torsten (1967), ed., *International Study of Achievement in Mathematics: A Comparison of Twelve Countries*. New York: John Wiley & Sons, Inc. In two volumes.

Huttenlocher, Janellen (1962), "Some Effects of Negative Instances on the Formation of Simple Concepts," *Psychological Reports*, 11, 35–42.

Inhelder, Bärbel, and Jean Piaget (1958), *The Growth of Logical Thinking from Childhood to Adolescence*. New York: Basic Books, Inc.

Insel, Shepard A., Kurt Schlesinger, and Winifred Desrosiers (1963), "Dependency Responses to Televised Instruction," *Journal of Applied Psychology*, 47, 328–31.

Irion, Arthur L. (1966), "A Brief History of Research on the Acquisition of Skill," in *Acquisition of Skill*, ed. E. A. Bidoleau, pp. 1–46. New York: Academic Press Inc.

Itard, J. M. G. (1932), *The Wild Boy of Aveyron*. Translated by G. Humphrey and M. Humphrey. New York: Appleton-Century-Crofts.

Jacobs, Paul I., Milton H. Maier, and Lawrence M. Stolurow (1966), *A Guide to Evaluating Self-Instructional Programs*. New York: Holt, Rinehart & Winston, Inc.

James, William (1892), *Talks to Teachers on Psychology and to Students on Some of Life's Ideals*. New York: W. W. Norton & Company, Inc., 1958.

Jenkins, J. G., and Karl M. Dallenback (1924), "Oblivescence During Sleep and Waking," *American Journal of Psychology*, 35, 605–12.

Jensen, Arthur R. (1960), "Programmed Instruction and Individual Differences," *Automated Teaching Bulletin*, 1, 12–17.

——— (1962a), "Spelling Errors and Serial-Position Effect," *Journal of Educational Psychology*, 53, 105–9.

——— (1962b), "Transfer Between Paired-Associate and Serial Learning," *Journal of Verbal Learning and Verbal Behavior*, 1, 269–80.

——— (1963), "Learning Ability in Retarded, Average, and Gifted Children," *Merrill-Palmer Quarterly*, 9, 124–40.

——— (1965), "Individual Differences in Learning: Interference Factor," *U.S.*

Office of Education Cooperative Research Project No. 1867. Berkeley, Calif.: University of California.

——— (1966a), "Individual Differences in Concept Learning," in *Analyses of Concept Learning,* eds. H. J. Klausmeier and W. Harris, pp. 139–54. New York: Academic Press Inc.

——— (1966b), "Verbal Mediation and Educational Potential," *Psychology in the Schools,* 3, 99–109.

——— (1968), "Social Class and Verbal Learning," in *Social Class, Race, and Psychological Development,* eds. M. Deutsch, A. R. Jensen, and Irwin Katz. New York: Holt, Rinchart & Winston, Inc.

John, Vera P., and Leo S. Goldstein (1964), "The Social Context of Language Acquisition," *Merrill-Palmer Quarterly,* 10, 265–75.

Johnsen, Kathryn P., and Gerald R. Leslie (1965), "Notes on Research in Child-rearing and Social Class," *Merrill-Palmer Quarterly,* 11, 345–58.

Johnson, Donald M., and Charlene A. O'Reilly (1964), "Concept Attainment in Children: Classifying and Defining," *Journal of Educational Psychology,* 55, 71–74.

Johnson, Donald M., and R. Paul Stratton (1966), "Evaluation of Five Methods of Teaching Concepts," *Journal of Educational Psychology,* 57, 48–53.

Johnson, Joan (1966), "The Effects of Verbalization upon the Learning of Selected Motor Skills." Unpublished study.

Johnston, Raymond, Robert Davis, Nicholas Fiel, and Horace Hartsell (1966), *Preparatory Laboratory for Physiology 501.* Laboratory 3, East Lansing, Mich.: Michigan State University.

Jokl, Ernest (1966), "The Acquisition of Skills," *Quest,* Monograph VI, pp. 11–28.

Jones, John Gerald (1965), "Motor Learning Without Demonstration under Two Conditions of Mental Practice," *Research Quarterly,* 36, 270–81.

Jordan, James F. (1963), "Socratic Teaching," *Harvard Educational Review,* 33, 96–104.

Judson, Abe, Charles Cofer, and Sidney Gelfand (1956), "Reasoning as an Associative Process: II. Direction in Problem Solving as a Function of Prior Reinforcement," *Psychological Reports,* 2, 501–7.

Kagan, Jerome (1965), "Impulsive and Reflective Children: Significance of Conceptual Tempo," in *Learning and the Educational Process,* ed. J. D. Krumboltz, pp. 133–61. Chicago: Rand McNally & Co.

Kagan, Jerome, Leslie Pearson, and Lois Welch (1966), "Modifiability of an Impulsive Tempo," *Journal of Educational Psychology,* 359–65.

Kagan, Jerome, Bernice L. Rosman, Deborah Day, J. Albert, and W. Phillips (1964), "Information Processing in the Child: Significance of Analytic and Reflective Attitudes," *Psychological Monographs,* 78, No. 1 (Whole No. 578).

Kates, Solis L., and Lee Yudin (1964), "Concept Attainment and Memory," *Journal of Educational Psychology,* 55, 103–9.

Katona, George (1940), *Organizing and Memorizing: Studies in the Psychology of Learning and Teaching.* New York: Columbia University Press.

Kaufman, Burt, and Paul Bethune (1964), "Nova High: Space Age School," *Phi Delta Kappan,* 46, 9–11.

Kearney, Nolan C. (1953), ed., *Elementary School Objectives.* New York: Russell Sage Foundation.

Keller, Fred S. (1954), *Learning: Reinforcement Theory*. New York: Random House.

Kelley, Truman L., Richard Madden, Eric F. Gardner, and Herbert C. Rudman (1964), *Stanford Achievement Test Directions for Administering. Intermediate I Battery*. New York: Harcourt, Brace & World, Inc.

Kelley, Truman L., Richard Madden, Eric F. Gardner, Lewis Terman, and Giles M. Ruch (1953), *Stanford Achievement Test Directions for Administering*. New York: Harcourt, Brace & World, Inc.

Kendler, Howard H. (1964), "The Concept of the Concept," in *Categories of Human Learning*, ed. A. W. Melton, pp. 211–36. New York: Academic Press Inc.

Kendler, Howard H., and Robert Vineberg (1954), "The Acquisition of Compound Concepts as a Function of Previous Training," *Journal of Experimental Psychology*, 48, 252–58.

Kendler, Tracy S., and Howard H. Kendler (1959), "Reversal and Nonreversal Shifts in Kindergarten Children," *Journal of Experimental Psychology*, 58, 56–60.

——— (1961), "Inferential Behavior in Children: II. The Influence of Order of Presentation," *Journal of Experimental Psychology*, 61, 442–48.

Kendler, Tracy S., Howard H. Kendler, and B. Learnard (1962), "Mediated Responses to Size and Brightness as a Function of Age," *American Journal Of Psychology*, 75, 571–86.

Kendler, Tracy S., Howard H. Kendler, and D. Wells (1960), "Reversal and Nonreversal Shifts in Nursery School Children," *Journal of Comparative and Physiological Psychology*, 53, 80–87.

Kennedy, Wallace A., and Herman C. Willcutt (1964), "Praise and Blame as Incentives," *Psychological Bulletin*, 62, 323–53.

Keppel, Francis (1967), "The Business Interest in Education," *Phi Delta Kappan*, 48, 186–90.

Keppel, Geoffrey, and Leo Postman (1966), "Studies of Learning to Learn: III. Conditions of Improvement in Successive Transfer Tasks," *Journal of Verbal Learning and Verbal Behavior*, 5, 260–67.

Kerlinger, Fred N. (1964), *Foundations of Behavioral Research*. New York: Holt, Rinehart & Winston, Inc.

Kersh, Bert Y. (1963), "The Motivating Effect of Learning by Discovery," *Journal of Educational Psychology*, 53, 65–71.

——— (1964), *Directed Discovery Versus Programmed Instruction: A Test of a Theoretical Position Involving Educational Technology*. Monmouth, Oregon: Oregon State System of Higher Education.

——— (1965), "Programming Classroom Instruction," in *Teaching Machines and Programmed Learning. II: Data and Directions*, ed. R. Glaser, pp. 321–68. Washington, D.C.: Department of Audiovisual Instruction, National Education Association.

Kersh, Bert Y., and Merlin C. Wittrock (1962), "Learning by Discovery: An Interpretation of Recent Research," *Journal of Teacher Education*, 13, 461–68.

Kientzle, Mary J. (1946), "Properties of Learning Curves Under Varied Distribution of Practice," *Journal of Experimental Psychology*, 36, 187–211.

Kight, Howard R., and Julius M. Sassenrath (1966), "Relation of Achievement Motivation and Test Anxiety to Performance in Programmed Instruction," *Journal of Educational Psychology*, 57, 14–17.

Kimble, Gregory A. (1961), *Hilgard and Marquis' Conditioning and Learning.* New York: Appleton-Century-Crofts.

——— (1964), "Categories of Learning and the Problem of Definition," in *Categories of Human Learning,* ed. Arthur W. Melton, pp. 32–45. New York: Academic Press Inc.

Kimble, Gregory A., and Edward A. Bilodeau (1949), "Work and Rest as Variables in Cyclical Motor Learning," *Journal of Experimental Psychology,* 39, 150–57.

Kimble, Gregory A., and Norman Garmezy (1963), *Principles of General Psychology* (2nd ed.). New York: The Ronald Press Company.

Kimble, Gregory A., and J. Jepson Wulff (1953), "The Effect of Response Guidance on the Value of Audience Participation in Training Film Instruction," in *HFORL Report No. 34,* TMPL abstract, pp. 646–47. Washington, D.C.: U.S. Air Force Human Factors Operations Research Laboratories.

Klaus, David J. (1961), "The Art of Auto-Instructional Programming," *Audio-visual Communication Review,* 9, 130–42.

——— (1965), "An Analysis of Programming Techniques," in *Teaching Machines and Programmed Learning. II: Data and Directions,* ed. R. Glaser, pp. 118–61. Washington, D.C.: Department of Audiovisual Instruction, National Education Association.

Klausmeier, Herbert J., and William Goodwin (1966), *Learning and Human Abilities: Educational Psychology* (2nd ed.). New York: Harper & Row, Publishers.

Klinckmann, Evelyn (1963), "The BSCS Grid for Test Analysis," *BSCS Newsletter No. 19,* 2–21.

Klineberg, Otto (1950), "Tensions Affecting International Understanding: A Survey of Research," in *SSRC Bulletin 62.* New York: Social Science Research Council.

Knapp, Clyde G., and W. Robert Dixon (1952), "Learning to Juggle: II. A Study of Whole and Part Methods," *Research Quarterly,* 23, 398–401.

Kohn, Melvin L. (1959), "Social Class and Parental Values," *American Journal of Sociology,* 64, 4.

Komoski, Kenneth P. (1965), ed., *Programed Instruction Materials, 1964–65: A Guide to Programed Instruction Materials for Use in Elementary and Secondary Schools as of April, 1965.* New York: Institute of Educational Technology, Teachers College, Columbia University.

Koronakos, Chris, and Arnold J. William (1957), "The Formation of Learning Sets in Rats," *Journal of Comparative and Physiological Psychology,* 50, 11–14.

Kounin, Jacob S., and Paul V. Gump (1958), "The Ripple Effect in Discipline," *Elementary School Journal,* 59, 158–62.

Kounin, Jacob S., and James Ryan (1961), "Explorations in Classroom Management," *Journal of Teacher Education,* 12, 235–46.

Krathwohl, David R., *et al.* (1964), eds., *Taxonomy of Educational Objectives: Handbook II: Affective Domain.* New York: David McKay Co., Inc.

Krech, David, Mark R. Rosenzweig, and Edward L. Bennett (1962), "Relations Between Brain Chemistry and Problem Solving Among Rats Raised in Enriched and Impoverished Environments," *Journal of Comparative and Physiological Psychology,* 55, 801–7.

Kreuger, W. C. F. (1929), "The Effect of Over-Learning on Retention," *Journal of Experimental Psychology,* 12, 71–78.

Krumboltz, John D., and Charles A. Kiesler (1965), "The Partial Reinforcement Paradigm and Programed Instruction," *Journal of Programed Instruction,* 3, 9–14.

Krumboltz, John D., and Ronald G. Weisman (1962), "The Effect of Intermittent Confirmation in Programmed Instruction," *Journal of Educational Psychology,* 53, 250–53.

Kuder, Frederic G. (1953), *Kuder Preference Record. Examiner Manual for Vocational Form—C.* Chicago: Science Research Associates, Inc.

Lackey, Melvin W. (n.d.), *An Example of Programmed Instruction.* Bethesda, Maryland: U.S. Naval Dental School. (Mimeo.)

Lado, Robert (1964), *Language Teaching: A Scientific Approach.* New York: McGraw-Hill Book Company.

Lance, Mary Louise (1964), "A Comparison of Gains in Achievement Made by Students of BSCS High School Biology and Students of a Conventional Course in Biology." Doctoral dissertation, University of Georgia.

Lanham, Url (1966), "BSCS Research Problems in Biology Investigations for Students," *BSCS Newsletter No. 28,* p. 13.

Lavin, David E. (1965), *The Prediction of Academic Performance.* New York: Russell Sage Foundation.

Lawson, Reed (1965), *Frustration: The Development of a Scientific Concept.* New York: The Macmillan Company.

Lawther, John D. (1966), "Directing Motor Skill Learning," *Quest,* Monography VI, pp. 68–76.

Lazarus, Richard S. (1963), *Personality and Adjustment.* Englewood Cliffs, N.J.: Prentice-Hall, Inc.

Leshan, Lawrence L. (1952), "Time Orientation and Social Class," *Journal of Abnormal and Social Psychology,* 48, 589–92.

Liebherr, Harold (1966), "Special Materials," *BSCS Newsletter No. 28,* p. 12.

Lindahl, Lawrence G. (1945), "Movement Analysis as an Industrial Training Method," *Journal of Applied Psychology,* 29, 420–36.

Lindeman, Richard (1967), *Educational Measurement.* Chicago: Scott, Foresman & Company.

Lipsit, Lewis (1961), "Simultaneous and Successive Discrimination Learning in Children," *Child Development,* 32, 337–47.

Lisonbee, Lorenzo, and Bill J. Fullerton (1964), "The Comparative Effect of BSCS and Traditional Biology on Student Achievement," *School Science and Mathematics,* 44, 594–98.

Lockhart, Aileene (1966), "Communicating with the Learner," *Quest,* Monograph VI, pp. 57–67.

Lorenz, K. (1937), "The Companion in the Bird's World," in *Auk,* 54, 245–73.

Lorge, Irving (1930), *Influence of Regularly Interpolated Time Intervals upon Subsequent Learning,* Teachers College Contributions to Education, No. 438. New York: Teachers College Press, Columbia University.

Lorge, Irving, and Edward L. Thorndike (1935), "The Influence of Delay in the After-Effect of a Connection," *Journal of Experimental Psychology,* 18, 186–94.

Lovell, K. (1959), "A Follow-Up Study of Some Aspects of the Work of Piaget and Inhelder on the Child's Conception of Space," *British Journal of Educational Psychology,* 29, 104–17.

Luh, C. (1922), "The Conditions of Retention," *Psychological Monographs,* 31, No. 142.

Lumsdaine, Arthur A. (1963), "Instruments and Media of Instruction," in *Handbook of Research on Teaching,* ed. N. L. Gage, pp. 583–682. Chicago: Rand McNally & Co.

——— (1964), "Educational Technology, Programed Learning, and Instructional Science," in *Theories of Learning and Instruction,* ed. E. R. Hilgard, Part 1 of the 63rd Yrbk. of the National Society for the Study of Education, pp. 371–401. Chicago: University of Chicago Press.

Lumsdaine, Arthur A., and M. A. May (1965), "Mass Communication and Educational Media," *Annual Review of Psychology,* 16, 475–534.

Lyman, Howard (1963), *Test Scores and What They Mean.* Englewood Cliffs, N.J.: Prentice-Hall, Inc.

Lysaught, Jerome P., and Clarence M. Williams (1963), *A Guide to Programmed Instruction.* New York: John Wiley & Sons, Inc.

McClelland, David O. (1955), ed., *Studies in Motivation.* New York: Appleton-Century-Crofts.

——— (1961), *The Achieving Society.* Princeton, N.J.: D. Van Nostrand Co., Inc.

——— (1965), "Toward a Theory of Motive Acquisition," *American Psychologist,* 20, 321–33.

McClelland, David O., John W. Atkinson, Russell A. Clark, and Edgar L. Lowell (1953), *The Achievement Motive.* New York: Appleton-Century-Crofts.

Maccoby, Nathan, and Fred D. Sheffield (1961), "Combining Practice with Demonstration in Teaching Complex Sequences: Summary and Interpretation," in *Student Response in Programmed Instruction,* ed. A. R. Lumsdaine, pp. 77–85. Washington, D.C.: National Academy of Sciences—National Research Council.

McDonald, Frederick J. (1965), *Educational Psychology* (2nd ed.). Belmont, Calif.: Wadsworth Publishing Co., Inc.

Mace, Lawrence L. (1966), "Sequence of Vocal Response-Differentiation Training and Auditory Stimulus-Discrimination Training in Beginning French," *Journal of Educational Psychology,* 57, 102–8.

Mace, Lawrence L., and Evan R. Keislar (1965), "Reversibility of Stimulus and Response Terms Following Discrimination Learning of French Phonemes," *Journal of Educational Psychology,* 56, 46–49.

McGeoch, John A. (1942), *The Psychology of Human Learning.* New York: David McKay Co., Inc.

McGraw, Myrtle, B. (1940), "Neural Maturation As Exemplified in Achievement of Bladder Control," *Journal of Pediatrics,* 16, 580–90.

McGuigan, F. J., and Eugene F. MacCaslin (1955), "Whole and Part Methods in Learning a Perceptual Motor Skill," *American Journal of Psychology,* 68, 658–61.

McKee, John P., and Florence B. Leader (1955), "The Relationship of Socio-Economic Status and Aggression to the Competitive Behavior of Preschool Children," *Child Development,* 26, 135–42.

McLaughlin, Barry (1965), "Intention and Incidental Learning in Human Subjects: The Role of Instructions to Learn and Motivation," *Psychological Bulletin,* 63, 359–76.

MacLennan, Donald W., and J. Christopher Reid (1964), eds., *Abstracts of Research on Instructional Television and Film: An Annotated Bibliography.* Stanford, Calif.: Institute for Communication Research, Stanford University.

McNeil, John D. (1964), "Programed Instruction Versus Usual Classroom Procedures in Teaching Boys to Read," *American Educational Research Journal,* 1, 113–19.

McNemar, Quinn (1964), "Lost: Our Intelligence? Why?" *The American Psychologist,* 19, 874–79.

Macomber, Glenn F., and Laurence Sigel (1960), *Final Report of the Experimental Study in Instructional Procedures.* Oxford, Ohio: Miami University.

McPhee, John (1965), *The New Yorker* (January 23), p. 42.

Mager, Robert F. (1962), *Preparing Objectives for Programmed Instruction.* Palo Alto, Calif.: Fearon Publishers, Inc.

Mager, Robert F., and J. McCann (1961), *Learner-Controlled Instruction.* Palo Alto, Calif.: Varian Associates.

Maier, Norman R. F. (1930), "Reasoning in Humans. I. On Direction," *Journal of Comparative Psychology,* 10, 115–43.

Maltzman, Irving (1955), "Thinking: From a Behaviorist Point of View," *Psychological Review,* 62, 275–86.

——— (1960), "On the Training of Originality," *Psychological Review,* 67, 229–42.

Maltzman, Irving, W. Bogartz, and L. Breger (1958), "A Procedure for Increasing Word Association Originality and Its Transfer Effects," *Journal of Experimental Psychology,* 56, 392–98.

Maltzman, Irving, L. O. Brooks, and S. S. Summers (1958), "The Facilitation of Problem Solving by the Prior Exposure to Uncommon Responses," *Journal of Experimental Psychology,* 56, 399–406.

Maltzman, Irving, Seymore Simon, David Raskin, and Lenard Licht (1960), "Experimental Studies in the Training of Originality," *Psychological Monographs,* No. 493, pp. 1–23.

Mandler, George (1967), "Verbal Learning," in *New Directions in Psychology,* Vol. III, pp. 1–50. New York: Holt, Rinehart & Winston, Inc.

Margulies, Stuart (1964), "Some General Rules of Frame Construction," *Programed Instruction,* 4, No. 1, 6–8.

Markle, Susan Meyer (1961), *A Programed Primer on Programing,* Vols. 1 and 2. New York: Center for Programed Instruction.

——— (1964), *Good Frames and Bad: A Grammar of Frame Writing.* New York: John Wiley & Sons, Inc.

Marks, Melvin R., and Charles K. Ramond (1951), "A New Technique for Observing Concept Evocation," *Journal of Experimental Psychology,* 42, 424–29.

Marquart, Dorothy I. (1955), "Group Problem Solving," *Journal of Social Psychology,* 41, 103–13.

Martin, Barclay (1963), "Reward and Punishment Associated with the Same

Goal Response: A Factor in the Learning of Motives," *Psychological Bulletin,* 60, 441–51.

Martin, William E., and Celia B. Stendler (1959), *Child Behavior and Development.* New York: Harcourt, Brace & World, Inc.

Maslow, Albert H. (1954), *Motivation and Personality.* New York: Harper & Row, Publishers.

Masserman, Jules M. (1943), *Behavior and Neurosis.* Chicago: University of Chicago Press.

Mauch, James (1962), "A Systems Analysis Approach to Education," *Phi Delta Kappan,* 43, 158–62.

May, Mark A. (1946), "The Psychology of Learning from Demonstration Films," *Journal of Educational Psychology,* 37, 1–12.

Mayer, William V. (1966), "The Long Hot Summer," *BSCS Newsletter No. 29,* pp. 1–2.

Meals, Donald W. (1967), "Heuristic Models for Systems Planning," *Phi Delta Kappan,* 48, 199–203.

Mechner, Francis (1961), *Programming for Automated Instruction,* Vol. 3. New York: Basic Systems, Inc.

——— (1965), "Science Education and Behavioral Technology," in *Teaching Machines and Programed Learning. II: Data and Directions,* pp. 441–507. Washington, D.C.: National Education Association.

Mehler, Jacques (1963), "Some Effects of Grammatical Transformations on the Recall of English Sentences," *Journal of Verbal Learning and Verbal Behavior,* 2, 346–51.

Melton, Arthur W. (1959), "The Science of Learning and the Technology of Educational Methods," *Harvard Educational Review,* 29, 96–106.

Miller, George A. (1956), "The Magical Number Seven, Plus or Minus Two: Some Limits on Our Capacity for Processing Information," *Psychological Review,* 53, 81–97.

——— (1962), "Some Psychological Studies of Grammar," *American Psychologist,* 17, 748–62.

——— (1965), "Some Preliminaries to Psycholinguistics," *American Psychologist,* 20, 15–20.

Miller, George A., Eugene Galanter, and Karl L. Pribam (1960), *Plans and the Structure of Behavior.* New York: Holt, Rinehart & Winston, Inc.

Miller, N. E. (1935), "The Influence of Past Experience upon the Transfer of Subsequent Training." Doctoral dissertation, Yale University.

Miller, Robert B. (1962a), "Task Description and Analysis," in *Psychological Principles in System Development,* ed. R. M. Gagné, pp. 187–230. New York: Holt, Rinehart & Winston, Inc.

——— (1962b), "Analysis and Specification of Behavior for Training," in *Training Research and Education,* ed. R. Glaser, pp. 31–62. Pittsburgh: University of Pittsburgh Press.

Mintz, Natalie, and Herbert Fremont (1965), "Some Practical Ideas for Teaching Mathematics to Disadvantaged Children," *Arithmetic Teacher* (April), pp. 258–60.

Montague, David (1964), "Arithmetic Concepts of Kindergarten Children in Contrasting Socio-Economic Areas," *Elementary School Journal,* 64, 393–97.

Montessori, Maria (1964), *The Montessori Method.* New York: Schocken Books, Inc.

Montgomery, K. C. (1954), "The Role of Exploratory Drive in Learning," *Journal of Comparative and Physiological Psychology,* 47, 60–64.

Moore, Olan C. (1965), "An Evaluation of the Effectiveness of the BSCS Approach to Teaching Biology to High Ability Students in the Ninth Grade." Doctoral dissertation, Arizona State University.

Murray, Edward J. (1964), *Motivation and Emotion.* Englewood Cliffs, N.J.: Prentice-Hall, Inc.

Naylor, James C. (1962), "Parameters Affecting the Efficiency of Part and Whole Training Methods: A Review of the Literature," in *NAVTRADEVCEN Technical Report,* N. 950-1. Port Washington, N.Y.: United States Training Devices Center.

Nelson, Clarence H. (1961), "Evaluation in the Natural Sciences," in *Evaluation in Higher Education,* eds. Paul L. Dressel *et al.,* pp. 113–56. Boston: Houghton Mifflin Company.

Nelson, Dale O. (1957), "Effects of Slow Motion Loop Films on the Learning of Golf," *Research Quarterly,* 27, 364–73.

Newton, Eunice S. (1960), "Verbal Destitution: The Pivotal Barrier to Learning," *Journal of Negro Education* (Fall), pp. 111–13.

Nisbet, Robert (1959), "The Decline and Fall of Social Class," *Pacific Sociological Review,* 2, 11–17.

Nissen, H. W. (1953), "Instinct As Seen by a Psychologist," *Psychological Review,* 60, 291–94.

Noble, Clyde E. (1952), "An Analysis of Meaning," *Psychological Review,* 59, 421–30.

Noll, Victor H. (1965), *Introduction to Educational Measurement* (2nd ed.). Boston: Houghton Mifflin Company.

Olson, James L., and Richard G. Larson (1965), "An Experimental Curriculum for Culturally Deprived Kindergarten Children," *Educational Leadership* (May), pp. 553–58, 618.

Olson, LeRoy A. (1963), "Concept Attainment of High School Sophomores," *Journal of Educational Psychology,* 54, 213–16.

Osborne, Alex (1957), *Applied Imagination.* New York: Charles Scribner's Sons.

Ozolin, N. G. (1958), "Motor Concepts in Teaching Sports Technique," *Theory and Practice of Physical Culture,* 21, 6. Translated from the Russian by Michael Yessis.

Packard, Vance (1957), *The Hidden Persuaders.* New York: David McKay Co., Inc.

Page, Ellis B. (1958), "Teacher Comments and Student Performance," *Journal of Educational Psychology,* 49, 173–81.

Parnes, Sidney J. (1961), "Effects of Extended Effort in Creative Problem Solving," *Journal of Educational Psychology,* 52, 148–52.

Parnes, Sidney J., and Harold F. Haring (1962), eds., *Source Book for Creative Thinking.* New York: Charles Scribner's Sons.

Parnes, Sidney J., and Arnold Meadow (1959), "Effects of Brainstorming Instructions on Creative Problem-Solving by Trained and Untrained Subjects," *Journal of Educational Psychology,* 50, 171–76.

——— (1960), "Evaluation of Persistence of Effects Produced by a Creative Problem-Solving Course," *Journal of Educational Psychology,* 7, 357–61.

Parry, Scott B. (1963), "Faulty Frames: Some Problems of Internal and External Evaluation of Programmes," *Programed Instruction,* 3, No. 2, 4–5, 7.

Pavlov, I. P. (1927), *Conditioned Reflexes: An Investigation of the Physiological Activity of the Cerebral Cortex.* Translated and edited by G. V. Anrep. London: Oxford University Press, 1927.

Payette, Roland F. (1961), "Summary Report of the School Mathematics Study Group Curriculum Evaluation," *SMSG Newsletter No. 10,* pp. 5–11. Stanford, Calif.: SMSG Publications.

Peel, E. A. (1959), "Experimental Examination of Some of Piaget's Schemata Concerning Children's Perception and Thinking, and a Discussion of Their Educational Significance," *British Journal of Educational Psychology,* 29, 89–103.

Piaget, Jean (1932), *The Moral Judgment of the Child.* London: Routledge & Kegan Paul, Ltd.

——— (1952), *The Origins of Intelligence in Children.* New York: International Universities Press, Inc.

Pipe, Peter (1966), *Practical Programming.* New York: Holt, Rinehart & Winston, Inc.

Postal, Paul M. (1964), "Underlying and Superficial Linguistics Structures," *Harvard Educational Review,* 34, 246–66.

Postman, Leo (1947), "The History and Present Status of the Law of Effect," *Psychological Bulletin,* 44, 489–563.

——— (1964), "Short-Term Memory and Incidental Learning," in *Categories of Human Learning,* ed. Arthur W. Melton, pp. 146–201. New York: Academic Press Inc.

Postman, Leo, and Virginia L. Senders (1946), "Incidental Learning and Generality of Set," *Journal of Experimental Psychology,* 36, 153–65.

Pressey, Sidney L. (1963), "Teaching Machine and Learning Theory Crisis," *Journal of Applied Psychology,* 47, 1–6.

——— (1964), "Autoinstruction: Perspectives, Problems, Potentials," in *Theories of Learning and Instruction,* ed. E. R. Hilgard, Part 1 of the 63rd Yrbk. of the National Society for the Study of Education, pp. 354–70. Chicago: University of Chicago Press.

Priebe, Roy E., and William H. Burton (1939), "The Slow Motion Picture as a Coaching Device," *School Review,* 47, 192–98.

PSSC (Physical Science Study Committee) (1965a), *Physics* (2nd ed.). Boston: D. C. Heath & Company.

——— (1965b), *Teacher's Resource Book and Guide,* Part 1 (2nd ed.). Boston: D. C. Heath & Company.

Ragsdale, C. E. (1950), "How Children Learn the Motor Type of Activity," in *Learning and Instruction,* Part 1 of the 49th Yrbk. of the National Society for the Study of Education, pp. 69–91. Chicago: University of Chicago Press.

Ramsay, Ogden, and Eckhard H. Hess (1954), "A Laboratory Approach to the Study of Imprinting," *Wilson Bulletin,* 66, 196–206.

Rathe, Dale (1965), "Certain Physics Generalizations Desirable for Students to

Attain Before Taking the Physical Science Study Committee's High School Physics Course," *Science Education,* 49, 127–37.

Rhine, R. J., and B. A. Silun (1958), "Acquisition and Change of a Concept Attitude as a Function of Consistency of Reinforcement," *Journal of Experimental Psychology,* 55, 524–29.

Riessman, Frank (1962), *The Culturally Deprived Child.* New York: Harper & Row, Publishers, Inc.

Rigney, Joseph W., and Edward B. Fry (1961), "Current Teaching-Machine Programs and Programming Techniques," *Audiovisual Communication Review,* 9, Supplement 3.

Robb, Margaret (1966), "Feedback," *Quest,* Monograph VI, pp. 38–43.

Rosenbloom, Paul (1961), "Minnesota National Laboratory Evaluation of SMSG, Grades 7–12," *SMSG Newsletter No. 10,* pp. 12–26. Stanford, Calif.: SMSG Publications.

Rothkopf, Ernest Z. (1966), "The Instructional Process." Paper presented at a symposium entitled Research Approaches to the Learning of School Subjects. Berkeley, Calif., 1966.

Rozeboom, William W. (1960), "The Fallacy of the Null-Hypothesis Significance Test," *Psychological Bulletin,* 57, 416–28.

Ruffa, Edward J. (1936), "An Experimental Study of Motion Pictures as Used in the Teaching of Certain Athletic Skills." Master's thesis, Stanford University.

Rulon, Philip J. (1946), "On the Validity of Educational Tests," *Harvard Educational Review,* 16, 290–96.

Rummel, Francis J. (1964), *An Introduction to Research Procedures in Education.* New York: Harper & Row, Publishers.

Russell, Wallace A., and Lowell H. Storms (1955), "Implicit Verbal Chaining in Paired-Associate Learning," *Journal of Experimental Psychology,* 49, 287–93.

Sarason, Seymour B., and George Mandler (1952), "Some Correlates of Test Anxiety," *Journal of Abnormal and Social Psychology,* 47, 810–17.

Saugstad, Per (1957), "An Analysis of Maier's Pendulum Problem," *Journal oj Experimental Psychology,* 54, 168–79.

Sax, G. (1960), "Concept Acquisition as a Function of Differing Schedules and Delays of Reinforcement," *Journal of Educational Psychology,* 51, 32–36.

Sax, G., and Theodore R. Cromack (1966), "The Effects of Various Forms of Item Arrangements on Test Performance," *Journal of Educational Measurement,* 3, 309–11.

Scherer, George A. C., and Michael Wertheimer (1964), *A Psycholinguistic Experiment in Foreign Language Teaching.* New York: McGraw-Hill Book Company.

Schiller, Belle (1934), "Verbal, Numerical, and Spatial Abilities in Young Children," *Archives of Psychology,* No. 161.

Schoer, Lowell (1963), "Effect of Intralist Item Similarity on Paired-Associate Learning by Learners of High and Low Ability," *Journal of Educational Psychology,* 54, 249–52.

Schulz, Rudolph W. (1960), "Problem Solving Behavior and Transfer," *Harvard Educational Review,* 30, 61–77.

Schutz, Robert E., Robert L. Baker, and Vernon S. Gerlach (1962), "Teaching Capitalization with a Programmed Text," *AV Communication Review,* 10, 359–62.

Schwab, Joseph J. (1963) (supervisor), *Biology Teachers' Handbook.* New York: John Wiley & Sons, Inc.

Science Research Associates (SRA, 1962), *ITED: The Iowa Tests of Educational Development. Examiner's Manual.* Chicago: Science Research Associates, Inc.

——— (1963), *ITED: The Iowa Tests of Educational Development. How to Use the Test Results: A Manual for Teachers and Counselors.* Chicago: Science Research Associates, Inc.

Scottish Council for Research in Education (1953), *Social Implications of the 1947 Scottish Mental Survey.* London: University of London Press.

Sears, Pauline S. (1940), "Levels of Aspiration in Academically Successful and Unsuccessful Children," *Journal of Abnormal and Social Psychology,* 35, 498–536.

Sears, Pauline S., and Ernest R. Hilgard (1964), "The Teacher's Role in the Motivation of the Learner," in *Theories of Learning and Instruction,* ed. E. R. Hilgard, Part 1 of the 63rd Yrbk. of the National Society for the Study of Education, pp. 182–209. Chicago: University of Chicago Press.

Sechrest, Lee, and Judith Schmerling Kaas (1965), "Concept Difficulty as a Function of Stimulus Similarity," *Journal of Educational Psychology,* 56, 327–33.

Sechrest, Lee, and John Wallace (1962), "Assimilation and Utilization of Information in Concept Attainment Under Varying Conditions of Information Presentation," *Journal of Educational Psychology,* 53, 157–64.

Semler, Ira J., and Ira Iscoe (1963), "Comparative and Developmental Study of the Learning Abilities of Negro and White Children Under Four Conditions," *Journal of Educational Psychology,* 54, 38–44.

——— (1966), "Structure of Intelligence in Negro and White Children," *Journal of Educational Psychology,* 57, 326–36.

Shaplin, Judson T. (1961), "Practice in Teaching," *Harvard Educational Review,* 31, 33–59.

Siegel, S. (1956), *Nonparametric Statistics for the Behavioral Sciences.* New York: McGraw-Hill Book Company.

Silberman, Harry R., Ralph J. Melaragno, John E. Coulson, and Donald Estavan (1961), "Fixed Sequence Versus Branching Autoinstructional Methods," *Journal of Educational Psychology,* 52, 166–72.

Siller, Jerome (1957), "Socio-Economic Status and Conceptual Thinking," *Journal of Abnormal and Social Psychology,* 55, 365–71.

Skinner, B. F. (1938), *Behavior of Organisms.* New York: Appleton-Century-Crofts.

——— (1948), *Walden Two.* New York: The Macmillan Company.

——— (1953), *Science and Human Behavior.* New York: The Macmillan Company.

——— (1957), *Verbal Behavior.* New York: Appleton-Century-Crofts.

——— (1958), "Teaching Machines," *Science,* 128, 969–77.

——— (1961), "Why We Need Teaching Machines," *Harvard Educational Review,* 31, 377–98.

Smedslund, Jan (1961a), "The Acquisition of Conservation of Substance and

Weight in Children. I. Introduction," *Scandanavian Journal of Psychology,* 2, 11–20.

——— (1961b), "The Acquisition of Conservation of Substance and Weight in Children. II. External Reinforcement of Conservation of Weight and of the Operations of Addition and Subtraction," *Scandanavian Journal of Psychology,* 2, 71–84.

Smith, B. Othanel (1960), "A Concept of Teaching," *Teachers College Record,* 61, 229–41.

Smith, Frank, and George A. Miller (1966), eds., *The Genesis of Language.* Cambridge, Mass.: M.I.T. Press.

Smode, A., and Paul Fitts (1957). Unpublished study made at Ohio State University on physical education instructors' opinions on training (see Fitts, 1962, p. 185).

Smoke, Kenneth L. (1933), "Negative Instances in Concept Learning," *Journal of Experimental Psychology,* 16, 583–88.

SMSG (School Mathematics Study Group) (1962), *Introduction to Secondary School Mathematics.* New Haven, Conn.: Yale University Press.

——— (1964), *SMSG Newsletter No. 17.* Stanford, Calif.: SMSG Publications.

——— (1966a), *SMSG Newsletter No. 22.* Stanford, Calif.: SMSG Publications.

——— (1966b), *Teacher's Commentary for "Mathematics for the Elementary School."* New Haven, Conn.: Yale University Press.

——— (1966c), *Programmed First Course in Algebra.* New Haven, Conn.: Yale University Press.

——— (1966d), *Description of SMSG Titles.* New Haven, Conn.: Yale University Press (a catalog).

Snygg, Donald, and Arthur W. Combs (1949), *Individual Behavior: A New Frame of Reference for Psychology.* New York: Harper & Row, Publishers.

Soles, Stanley (1963), "Educational Quackery External to Our Schools: What Is a Professional Response?" *Phi Delta Kappan,* 44, 299–302.

Solley, William H. (1952), "The Effects of Verbal Instructions of Speed and Accuracy upon the Learning of a Motor Skill," *Research Quarterly,* 23, 231–40.

Solomon, Richard L. (1964), "Punishment," *American Psychologist,* 19, 239–53.

Spearman, Charles (1927), *The Abilities of Man.* New York: The Macmillan Company.

Spence, Kenneth W. (1956), *Behavior Theory and Conditioning.* New Haven, Conn.: Yale University Press.

Spielberger, Charles D. (1966a), "Theory and Research on Anxiety," in *Anxiety and Behavior,* ed. C. D. Spielberger, pp. 3–20. New York: Academic Press Inc.

——— (1966b), "The Effects of Anxiety on Complex Learning and Academic Achievement," in *Anxiety and Behavior,* ed. C. D. Spielberger, pp. 361–98. New York: Academic Press Inc.

Spiker, Charles C. (1963), "Verbal Factors in the Discrimination Learning of Children," *Monograph of the Society for Research in Child Development,* 28 (Whole No. 86), 53–69.

Spitzer, Herbert F. (1962), *What Research Says to the Teacher: Teaching Arithmetic.* Washington, D.C.: Department of Classroom Teachers and the American Educational Research Association, National Education Association.

Staats, Arthur W. (1957), "Verbal and Instrumental Response-Hierarchies and Their Relationship to Problem-Solving," *American Journal of Psychology,* 70, 442–46.

Staats, Arthur W., and Carolyn K. Staats (1963), *Complex Human Behavior.* New York: Holt, Rinehart & Winston, Inc.

Stanley, Julian C. (1964), *Measurement in Today's Schools* (4th ed.). Englewood Cliffs, N.J.: Prentice-Hall, Inc.

Stern, Carolyn (1965), "Labeling and Variety in Concept Identification with Young Children," *Journal of Educational Psychology,* 56, 235–40.

Stewart, Naomi (1947), "A.G.C.T. Scores of Army Personnel Grouped by Occupation," *Occupations,* 26, 5–41.

Stolurow, Lawrence M. (1964), "Social Impact of Programmed Instruction: Aptitudes and Abilities Revisited," *Educational Technology,* ed. J. P. De Cecco, pp. 348–55. New York: Holt, Rinehart & Winston, Inc.

Stolurow, Lawrence M., and Daniel Davis (1965), *Teaching Machines and Computer-Based Systems. Teaching Machines and Programed Learning II: Data and Directions,* ed. R. Glaser, pp. 162–212. Washington, D.C.: Department of Audiovisual Education, National Education Association.

Strong, Edward K. (1951), *Strong Vocational Interest Blank for Women.* Palo Alto, Calif.: Consulting Psychologists Press.

Suchman, J. Richard (1960), "Inquiry Training in the Elementary School," *Science Teacher,* 27, 42–47.

——— (1962), "The Elementary School Training Program," in *Scientific Inquiry.* Urbana, Ill.: University of Illinois Press.

——— (1966), "A Model for the Analysis of Inquiry," in *Analyses of Concept Learning,* eds. H. J. Klausmeier and Chester W. Harris. New York: Academic Press Inc.

Suppes, Patrick (1964), "Modern Learning Theory and the Elementary-School Curriculum," *American Educational Research Journal,* 1, 79–93.

Taba, Hilda (1964a), "Cultural Deprivation as a Factor in School Learning," *Merrill-Palmer Quarterly,* 10, 147–48.

Taba, Hilda, and Freeman F. Elzey (1964b), "Teaching Strategies and Thought Processes," *Teachers College Record,* 65, 524–34.

Taber, Julian I., and Robert Glaser (1962), "An Exploratory Evaluation of a Discriminative Transfer Learning Program Using Literal Prompts," *Journal of Educational Research,* 55, 508–12.

Taber, Julian I., Robert Glaser, and Halmuth H. Schaeffer (1965), *Learning and Programmed Instruction.* Reading, Mass.: Addison-Wesley Publishing Co., Inc.

Tate, Merle W. (1965), *Statistics in Education and Psychology.* New York: The Macmillan Company.

Taylor, Calvin, and Frank Barron (1963), *Scientific Creativity: Its Recognition and Development.* New York: John Wiley & Sons, Inc.

Taylor, D. W., P. C. Berry, and C. H. Block (1958), "Does Group Participation When Using Brainstorming Facilitate or Inhibit Creative Thinking?" *Administrative Science Quarterly,* 3, 23–47.

Terman, Lewis M., and Maud A. Merrill (1937), *Measuring Intelligence.* Boston: Houghton Mifflin Company.

——— (1960), *Stanford-Binet Intelligence Scale: Manual for the Third Revision.* Boston: Houghton Mifflin Company.

Terman, Lewis M., and Melita H. Ogden (1950), *The Gifted Child Grows Up.* Stanford, Calif.: Stanford University Press.

Terrel, Glenn, Kathryn Durkin, and Melvin Wiesley (1959), "Social Class and the Nature of the Incentive in Discrimination Learning," *Journal of Abnormal and Social Psychology,* 59, 270–72.

Thompson, W. R., and Woodburn Heron (1954), "The Effects of Restraining Early Experience on the Problem-Solving Capacity of Dogs," *Canadian Journal of Psychology,* 8, 17–31.

Thorndike, Edward L. (1911), *Animal Intelligence.* New York: The Macmillan Company.

——— (1913), *The Psychology of Learning.* New York: Teachers College Press, Columbia University.

Thorndike, Edward L., and Irving Lorge (1944), *The Teacher's Work Book of 30,000 Words.* New York: Teachers College Press, Columbia University.

Thorndike, Robert L. (1963), "The Measurement of Creativity," *Teachers College Record,* 64, 422–24.

Thorndike, Robert L., and Elizabeth Hagen (1961), *Measurement and Evaluation in Psychology and Education.* New York: John Wiley & Sons, Inc.

Thurstone, L. L. (1938), "Primary Mental Abilities," in *Psychometric Monograph No. 1.* Chicago: University of Chicago Press.

——— (1941), "Factorial Studies of Intelligence," in *Psychometric Monograph No. 2.* Chicago: University of Chicago Press.

——— (1947), *Multiple Factor Analysis.* Chicago: University of Chicago Press.

Torrance, E. Paul (1960), "Creative Thinking Through the Language Arts," *Educational Leadership,* 18, 13–18.

——— (1961), "Priming Creative Thinking in the Primary Grades," *Elementary School Journal,* 42, 34–41.

——— (1962), *Guiding Creative Talent.* Englewood Cliffs, N.J.: Prentice-Hall, Inc.

——— (1963a), *Creativity: What Research Says to the Teacher.* Washington, D.C.: Department of Classroom Teachers and American Educational Research Association, National Education Association.

——— (1963b), *Education and the Creative Potential.* Minneapolis: University of Minnesota Press.

——— (1965), *Gifted Children in the Classroom.* New York: The Macmillan Company.

——— (1966), *Torrance Tests of Creative Thinking. Norms Technical Manual.* Princeton, N.J.: Personnel Press.

Torrance, E. Paul, and J. A. Harmon (1961), "Effects of Memory, Evaluative, and Creative Reading Sets on Test Performance," *Journal of Educational Psychology,* 52, 207–14.

Torrance, E. Paul, and R. E. Myers (1963), "Teaching Gifted Elementary Pupils Research Concepts and Skills," *Gifted Child Quarterly,* 6, 1–6.

Torrance, E. Paul, K. Yamamoto, K. Schenetzki, N. Palamutlu, and B. Luther (1960), *Assessing the Creative Thinking Abilities of Children.* Minneapolis: Bureau of Educational Research, University of Minnesota.

Travers, John F. (1965), *Learning: Analysis and Application.* New York: David McKay Co., Inc.

Travers, Robert M. W. (1964), "Transmission of Information to Human Receivers," *Educational Psychologist,* 2, 1–5.

——— (1963), *Essentials of Learning.* New York: The Macmillan Company.

Travers, Robert M. W., Mary C. McCormick, A. P. Mondfrans, and F. E. Williams (1964), *Research and Theory Related to Audiovisual Information Transmission.* U.S. Office of Education Cooperative Research Project N. 3-20-003. Salt Lake City: Bureau of Educational Research, University of Utah.

Travers, Robert M. W., R. Keith Van Wagenen, Danielle H. Haygood, and Mary McCormick (1964), "Learning as a Consequence of the Learner's Task Involvement Under Different Conditions of Feedback," *Journal of Educational Psychology,* 55, 167–73.

Trowbridge, Leslie W. (1965), "A Comparison of the Objectives and Instructional Materials in the Two Types of High School Physics Courses," *Science Education,* 49, 112–22.

Trump, J. Lloyd (1959), *Images of the Future: A New Approach to the Secondary School.* Washington, D.C.: National Education Association.

Tuddenham, Read D. (1948), "Soldier Intelligence in World Wars I and II," *American Psychologist,* 3, 54–56.

Twining, Wilbur E. (1949), "Mental Practice and Physical Practice in Learning a Motor Skill," *Research Quarterly,* 20, 432–35.

Tyler, Fred T. (1964), "Issues Related to Readiness to Learn," in *Theories of Learning and Instruction,* ed. E. R. Hilgard, Part 1 of the 63rd Yrbk. of the National Society for the Study of Education, pp. 210–39. Chicago: University of Chicago Press.

Tyler, Leona E. (1963), *Tests and Measurements.* Englewood Cliffs, N.J.: Prentice-Hall, Inc.

——— (1965), *The Psychology of Human Differences.* New York: Appleton-Century-Crofts.

Tyler, Ralph W. (1934), "Some Findings From Studies in the Field of College Biology," *Science,* 18, 133–42.

——— (1949), "Achievement Testing and Curriculum Construction," in *Trends in Student Personnel Work,* ed. G. Williamson. Minneapolis: University of Minnesota Press.

——— (1950), "The Functions of Measurement in Improving Instruction," in *Educational Measurement,* ed. E. F. Lindquist. Washington, D.C.: American Council on Education.

——— (1964), "Some Persistent Questions on the Defining of Objectives," in *Defining Educational Objectives,* ed. C.M. Lindvall. Pittsburgh: University of Pittsburgh Press.

Underwood, Benton J. (1949), *Experimental Psychology: An Introduction.* New York: Appleton-Century-Crofts.

——— (1957), "Interference and Forgetting," in *Psychological Review,* 64, 49–60.

——— (1959), "Verbal Learning in the Educative Process," *Harvard Educational Review,* 29, 107–17.

——— (1961), "Ten Years of Massed Practice on Distributed Practice," *Psychological Review,* 68, 229–47.

——— (1964a), "The Representativeness of Rote Verbal Learning," in *Categories of Human Learning,* ed. Arthur W. Melton, pp. 48–78. New York: Academic Press Inc.

——— (1964b), "Laboratory Studies of Verbal Learning," in *Theories of Learning and Instruction,* ed. E. R. Hilgard, Part 1 of the 63rd Yrbk. of the National Society for the Study of Education, pp. 133–52. Chicago: University of Chicago Press.

——— (1966), "Some Relationships Between Concept Learning and Verbal Learning," in *Analyses of Concept Learning,* eds. H. J. Klausmeier and C. W. Harris. New York: Academic Press Inc.

Underwood, Benton J., and Jack Richardson (1957), "Studies of Distributed Practice: XVII. Interlist Interference and the Retention of Paired Consonant Syllables," *Journal of Experimental Psychology,* 54, 274–79.

Underwood, Benton J., and Rudolph W. Schultz (1960), *Meaningfulness and Verbal Learning.* Philadelphia: J. B. Lippincott Co.

Van der Riet, Hani (1963), "The Effects of Praise and Reproof on Paired-Associate Learning in Educationally Retarded Children," *Dissertation Abstracts,* 24, 1250.

Van Wagenen, R. Keith, and Robert M. W. Travers (1963), "Learning Under Conditions of Direct and Vicarious Reinforcement," *Journal of Educational Psychology,* 54, 356–62.

Verducci, Frank (1967), personal communication, April 6.

Vernon, Philip E. (1958), "Education and the Psychology of Individual Differences," *Harvard Educational Review,* 28, 91–104.

Verplanck, William S. (1955), "The Control of the Content of Conversation: Reinforcement of Statements of Opinion," *Journal of Abnormal and Social Psychology,* 51, 668–76.

Vince, M. A. (1953), "The Part Played by Intellectual Processes in a Sensory-Motor Performance," *Quarterly Journal of Experimental Psychology,* 5, 75–86.

Vroom, Victor H. (1964), *Work and Motivation.* New York: John Wiley & Sons, Inc.

Wagner, John (1960), "The Objectives and Activities of the School Mathematics Study Group," *The Mathematics Teacher,* 53, 454–59.

Wallace, John (1964), "Concept Dominance, Type of Feedback, and Intensity of Feedback as Related to Concept Attainment," *Journal of Educational Psychology,* 55, 159–66.

Wallen, Norman E., and Robert M. W. Travers (1963), "Analysis and Investigation of Teaching Methods," in *Handbook of Research on Teaching,* ed. N. L. Gage, pp. 448–505. Chicago: Rand McNally & Co.

Wandt, Edwin (1965), *A Cross-Section of Educational Research.* David McKay Co., Inc.

Ward, J. N. (1956), "Group Versus Lecture-Demonstration Method in Physical Science Instruction for General Education College Students," *Journal of Experimental Education,* 24, 197–210.

Ward, Lewis B. (1937), "Reminiscence and Rote Learning," *Psychological Monographs,* 49, No. 4 (Whole No. 220).

Warner, W. Lloyd, Marcia Meeker, and Kenneth Eells (1949), *Social Class in America.* Chicago: Science Research Associates, Inc.

Waterhouse, Ian K., and Irvin Child (1953), "Frustration and the Quality of Performance," *Journal of Personality,* 21, 298–311.

Waugh, Nancy C. (1961), "Free Recall Versus Serial Recall," *Journal of Experimental Psychology,* 62, 496–502.

Weaver, H. E., and E. H. Madden (1949), "Direction in Problem Solving," *The Journal of Psychology,* 27, 331–45.

Weaver, J. Fred, and E. Glenadine Gibb (1964), "Mathematics in the Elementary School," *Review of Educational Research,* 34, 273–85.

Weber, Max (1904), *The Protestant Ethic and the Spirit of Capitalism.* Translated by T. Parsons. New York: Charles Scribner's Sons, 1930.

Webster, Staten W. (1966), "The Teacher as an Alien: Some Theoretical Considerations Regarding Teachers for Disadvantaged Schools," *Educating the Disadvantaged Learner,* Part III of the *Disadvantaged Learner,* ed. S. W. Webster, pp. 454–64. Chicago: Science Research Associates, Inc.

Wechsler, David (1949), *Wechsler Intelligence Scale for Children: Manual.* New York: Psychological Corp.

——— (1955), *Wechsler Adult Intelligence Scale Manual.* New York: Psychological Corp.

Weidemann, C. C. (1933), "Written Examination Procedures," *Phi Delta Kappan,* 16, 78–83.

——— (1941), "Review of Essay Test Studies," *Journal of Higher Education,* 12, 41–44.

Weikart, David P., Constance K. Kamii, and Norma L. Radin (1964), *Perry Preschool Project: Progress Report.* Ypsilanti, Mich.: The Public Schools.

Weitman, Morris (1965), "Item Characteristics and Long-Term Retention," *Journal of Educational Measurement,* 2, 37–47.

Welford, A. T. (1962), "Research on Skills," in *Discovery,* pp. 27–33. London: Professional and Industrial Publishing.

Wertheimer, Max (1959), *Productive Thinking.* New York: Harper & Row, Publishers.

Wheeler, Lester R. (1942), "A Comparative Study of the Intelligence of East Tennessee Mountain Children," *Journal of Educational Psychology,* 33, 321–34.

White, Robert W. (1959), "Motivation Reconsidered: The Concept of Competence," *Psychological Review,* 66, 297–333.

Whiteman, Martin (1964), "Intelligence and Learning," *Merrill-Palmer Quarterly,* 10, 297–309.

Whiting, J. W. M., and O. H. Mowrer (1943), "Habit Progression and Regression—a Laboratory Study of Some Factors Relevant to Human Socialization," *Journal of Comparative Psychology,* 36, 229–53.

Wilder, Nancy, and Donald Ross Green (1963), "Expressions of Concepts Through Writing and Drawing and Effects of Shifting Medium," *Journal of Experimental Psychology,* 54, 202–7.

Wilkerson, Doxey A. (1965), "Programs and Practices in Compensatory Education for the Disadvantaged Children," *Review of Educational Research,* 35, 426–40.

Williams, A. C., and Ralph E. Flexman (1949), "Evaluation of the School Link as an Aid in Primary Flight Instruction," *University of Illinois Bulletin,* 46, No. 71.

Wilson, Alan B. (1963), "Social Stratification and Academic Achievement," in *Education in Depressed Areas,* ed. A. Harry Passow, pp. 217–36. New York: Teachers College Press, Columbia University.

Witkin, H. A., *et al.* (1954), *Personality Through Perception.* New York: Harper & Row, Publishers.

Witmer, Helen L. (1964), "Children and Poverty," *Children* (November-December), pp. 207–13.

Wittrock, Merlin C. (1962), "Set Applied to Student Teaching," *Journal of Educational Psychology,* 53, 175–80.

——— (1963), "Verbal Stimuli in Concept Formation: Learning by Discovery," *Journal of Educational Psychology,* 64, 183–90.

——— (1966), "The Learning by Discovery Hypothesis," in *Learning by Discovery,* eds. L. S. Shulman and E. R. Keislar, pp. 33–76. Chicago: Rand McNally & Co.

——— (1967), "Focus on Educational Psychology," *Educational Psychologist,* 4, No. 2, 17, 20.

Wittrock, Merlin C., and Evan Keislar (1965), "Verbal Cues in the Transfer of Concepts," *Journal of Educational Psychology,* 56, 16–21.

Wittrock, Merlin C., Evan Keislar, and Carolyn Stern (1964), "Verbal Cues in Concept Identification," *Journal of Educational Psychology,* 55, 195–200.

Wolf, Eleanor, and Leo Wolf (1962), "Sociological Perspective on the Education of Culturally Deprived Children," *School Review,* 70, 873–87.

Wolfe, J. B., and M. D. Kaplon (1941), "Effect of Amount of Reward and Consummative Activity on Learning in Chickens," *Journal of Comparative Psychology,* 31, 353–61.

Wooton, William (1964a), "The History and Status of the School Mathematics Study Group," in *New Curricula,* ed. Robert Heath, pp. 35–53. New York: Harper & Row, Publishers.

——— (1964b), *SMSG: The Making of a Curriculum.* New Haven, Conn.: Yale University Press.

Wrightstone, J. Wayne, *et al.* (1964), "Evaluation of the Higher Horizons Program for Underprivileged Children," in *Cooperative Research Project No. 1124.* New York: Bureau of Educational Research, Board of Education of the City of New York.

Yamamoto, K. (1964), "Role of Creative Thinking and Intelligence in High School Achievement," *Psychological Record,* 14, 783–89.

Yudin, Lee, and Solis L. Kates (1963), "Concept Attainment and Adolescent Development," *Journal of Educational Psychology,* 54, 177–82.

Index

A

B

D

K

L

M

S

62